The Hidden

THE TIBETAN BOOK OF THE DEAD

The Hidden History of
The Tibetan Book of the Dead

Bryan J. Cuevas

OXFORD
UNIVERSITY PRESS

2003

OXFORD

UNIVERSITY PRESS

Oxford New York
Auckland Bangkok Buenos Aires Cape Town Chennai
Dar es Salaam Delhi Hong Kong Istanbul Karachi Kolkata
Kuala Lumpur Madrid Melbourne Mexico City Mumbai Nairobi
São Paulo Shanghai Taipei Tokyo Toronto

Published by Oxford University Press, Inc.
198 Madison Avenue, New York, New York 10016

www.oup.com

Oxford is a registered trademark of Oxford University Press

Library of Congress Cataloging-in-Publication Data
Cuevas, Bryan J., 1967–
The hidden history of the Tibetan book of the dead / Bryan J. Cuevas.
p. maps cm.
Includes bibliographical references.
ISBN 0-19-515413-4
1. Karma-gliṅ-pa, 14th cent. Bar do thos grol—Criticism, Textual. 2. Intermediate
state—Buddhism. 3. Death—Religious aspects—Buddhism. 4. Funeral rites and
ceremonies, Buddhist—China—Tibet. I. Title.
BQ4490.K373 C83 2002
294.3'423—dc21 2002027400

2 4 6 8 9 7 5 3 1

Printed in the United States of America
on acid-free paper

For Laura Elizabeth Christian Mosley

Preface

The Tibetan Book of the Dead was first translated and published in English in 1927, has since gone through numerous reprints and translations into most major European languages, and continues to inspire many new translations from the original Tibetan texts. The book has truly become one of the foremost spiritual classics in world history. The aim of this study is to investigate the Tibetan history of this celebrated book. Recognizing that western scholarship has been too apt to view *The Tibetan Book of the Dead* as an abstraction outside of real time and space, I set out in this book to explore the origin and transmission of this literature in Tibet within its own complex religious and social arenas. As a carefully contextualized study of religious texts and their history, this book is an exploration not only of certain religious ideas and practices embedded in historicized texts but also of the texts themselves. It is my hope that the detailed focus of this study may help to provide a clear vantage point from which to survey more general aspects of the transmission of religious ideas, the production and distribution of religious literature, and the influence of institutions on religious practice within Tibet and neighboring areas.

Much of the research for this book was originally conducted for my doctoral dissertation submitted to the Department of Religion at the University of Virginia. I owe, therefore, a special debt of gratitude to my supervisors, Jeffrey Hopkins and David Germano, and to my readers, Paul Groner and Daniel Ehnbom. I am especially grateful for their thoughtful criticisms and suggestions for improvement. My research benefited also from the inspiration and charitable assistance offered to me by many scholars around the world. I should like to express my sincerest gratitude to E. Gene Smith, executive director of the Tibetan Buddhist Resource Center (TBRC), whose vast knowledge of Tibetan bibliography, history, and lineage is second to none. I have gained so much from his wisdom and patient generosity. I thank Henk Blezer for the many spirited and insightful discussions of our shared interest in this literature and related topics. I am thankful as well to Toni Huber for his unfailing support and friendly encouragement. Without the good-natured library assistance of Nawang Thokmey, bibliographer of the Tibetan Collection at the University of Virginia, much of the primary research for this book would surely never have been completed. My thanks to Burkhard Quessel, curator of the Tibetan Collections of the British Library, for providing invaluable bibliographical information and generous access to electronic images of rare Tibetan manuscripts. Thanks are also due to Tsering Wangyal Shawa, geographic information systems librarian at Princeton University, who prepared the fine Tibetan maps reproduced in the book.

I wish also to thank the following individuals and institutions that generously provided all types of assistance, reference materials, and answers to my endless queries over the long course of research for this book: the American Institute of Indian Studies (New Delhi), John Ardussi, the Central Institute of Higher Tibetan Studies (Sarnath), Lawrence Epstein, Karma Phuntsho, Karma Rikdzin, Khenpo Dorje Tsering, Khenpo Namdrol Tsering, Khenpo Nyima Dondup, Khenpo Sangye Tenzin Jongdong, Kunzang Lama, Lobpon Tenzin Norgyay, Dan Martin, Menri Bonpo Monastery (Dolanji Village), Menri Ponlob Trinley Nyima Rinpoche, Namdroling Nyingma Monastery (Bylakuppe), Neema Phenthok, Nyichang Rinpoche Thuptan Chodak Gyatso, Trent Pomplun, Ramon Prats, Françoise Pommaret, Andrew Quintman, Sangak Tenzin Zangpo, Kurtis Schaeffer, the Shelley and Donald Rubin Foundation, Tandin Situ, Phil Stanley, Thinley Tenzin, the Tibetan and Himalayan Digital Library, Jeff Watt, and David White.

Finally, closest to home, my most profound gratitude must go to my parents, Janice and John, for a lifetime of inspiration and unconditional support. My thanks also to Kathy and Jim Morgan, who have given me fortitude in so many ways. And to my wife, Amanda, for just about everything.

Contents

A Note on Tibetan Words

It is now common for scholarly books on Tibet to begin with a note on how difficult and exasperating it can be for nonspecialist readers to pronounce or much less make sense of Tibetan words rendered in their proper spelling according to the standard academic system of transcription. This book is no exception. Tibetan words in their correct written form are not read phonetically. For example, the name *Nam-mkha'-rdo-rje* is actually pronounced *Namkha Dorje*. For ease of reading, therefore, I have employed throughout the main body of the text a phonetic system based generally on the pronunciation of Tibetan words in the common Lhasa dialect of Central Tibet. In this regard, I should highlight a few basic rules. The syllable "th" is never pronounced like English "think" but always hard with strong aspiration, like in "ho*th*ouse." Likewise, "ph" is never soft like the English "f" but aspirated as in "to*p-h*at." The hanging letter "e" is never silent and should be pronounced like the French *é* in *résumé*, or English "ay" as in "play." For example, read "Dorjay" for Dorje, "Rinpochay" for Rinpoche, and so on.

Proper Tibetan spellings are given according to the Wylie transcription (Wylie 1959) in the notes, after each phonetic equivalent in the Tibetan word list at the end of the book, and also in the main body of the text italicized in parentheses for technical terms and the first mention of Tibetan titles. Specialists should note that in my transcriptions I capitalize initial letters only, not "foundation letters" (*ming-gzhi*), and follow standard English rules for the capitalization of titles, proper names, and so forth. In so doing, I have generally followed the methods outlined in Martin (1997).

The Hidden History of
THE TIBETAN BOOK OF THE DEAD

Introduction: The Saga of
The Tibetan Book of the Dead

No one scribe could have been its author and no one generation its
creator; its history as a book, if completely known, could only be the
history of its compilation and recording.
          —Walter Y. Evans-Wentz, *The Tibetan Book of the Dead*

Sometime in early 1919, a British political officer and dilettante Tibetan scholar, Major W. L. Campbell, purchased a collection of Tibetan blockprints while visiting the town of Gyantse in southwestern Tibet (see fig. 1.1). Upon returning to his station in Sikkim, he presented these books to the American-born, Oxford-educated anthropologist Walter Yeeling Evans-Wentz,[1] who was himself traveling the region in search of exotic books and had recently purchased an illuminated Tibetan manuscript in Darjeeling.[2] At the end of that year, Evans-Wentz met Kazi Dawa Samdup, a respected translator and teacher of a host of previous foreign travelers and the headmaster of the Maharaja's Bhutia Boy's School in Gangtok.[3] Evans-Wentz commissioned Dawa Samdup to prepare English translations of his Darjeeling manuscript and the books he had acquired from Major Campbell. Included among these books was a small set of texts gathered under the title *Great Liberation upon Hearing in the Bardo* [*Bar-do thos-grol chen-mo*], the same title of the Darjeeling manuscript. This specific collection of texts, which is derived from a much larger body of literature called *Self-Liberated Wisdom of the Peaceful and Wrathful Deities* [*Zhi-khro dgongs-pa rang-grol*], was apparently of singular interest to both men. For the next two months, Dawa Samdup worked through the texts of the *Great Liberation upon Hearing in the Bardo*, with Evans-Wentz close at his side, and together they produced a draft of what would later become *The*

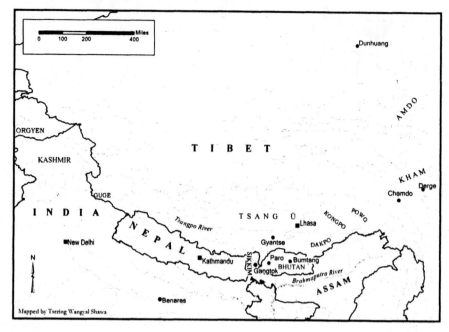

FIGURE I.I. Tibet and surrounding countries.

Tibetan Book of the Dead; arguably the most famous and widely read work of Tibetan literature in America and Europe.

It has been almost a century since its first publication in 1927, and popular enthusiasm for *The Tibetan Book of the Dead* seems to have grown increasingly strong, such that we now have at least eight major translations from Tibetan, with the promise of more in the making.[4] The book has also inspired a handful of traditional studies and scholarly commentaries,[5] as well as a video series,[6] an adapted script for a dramatic play,[7] and even a libretto for a musical opera.[8] This proliferation of multiple voices commenting on the text (in translation) has created a singular phenomenon that was never known in Tibet. The remarkable fame of this book in the west is markedly disproportionate to how the original Tibetan texts were perceived in their own country.[9] In fact, as Donald Lopez recently observed, *The Tibetan Book of the Dead* "has been made to serve wide-ranging agendas in various fields of use, agendas that have far more to do with the twentieth-century cultural fashions of Europe and America than with how the text has been used over the centuries of its history in Tibet."[10] But what is its history in Tibet? There have been many in the west who have claimed to speak for the text, to explain its ideas, and to expose its hidden meanings, but none of them has uttered a word about its history.

This study is a response to this important but neglected topic. In the chapters that follow, I will attempt to piece together the unwritten history of this intriguing set of texts, highlighting in particular how the original Tibetan collection, the *Great Liberation upon Hearing in the Bardo*, was compiled and in the process telling the story of the lives of those who preserved and transmitted it. For the sake of clarity, throughout the book I will refer to the actual Tibetan texts by their proper title, *Great Liberation upon Hearing in the Bardo* (henceforth abbreviated as *Liberation upon Hearing*). I will use the contrived English title, *Tibetan Book of the Dead*, to refer only to the western-language editions of the Tibetan collection.[11] In the end, I hope to demonstrate that *The Tibetan Book of the Dead* in the form we know it today, and the *Liberation upon Hearing* on which it is based, was actually derived from a single Tibetan textual lineage, represented both in Evans-Wentz's Darjeeling manuscript and in Major Campbell's Gyantse blockprint collection. This single textual tradition, which reached back to the late fourteenth century, was eventually standardized at the end of the seventeenth century by a controversial sorcerer from eastern Tibet named Rikzin Nyima Drakpa (1647–1710). Nyima Drakpa's standard arrangement of the *Liberation upon Hearing* became the *editio princeps* of subsequent Tibetan-language editions and served as the basis for the first western-language translation by Kazi Dawa Samdup and Walter Evans-Wentz. In this chapter, I will examine briefly the celebrity of *The Tibetan Book of the Dead* in the west, introduce the basic elements of its history in Tibet, and offer a few general comments about the methods employed in the task of writing this history. I begin by considering a few of those "wide-ranging agendas" that this text has been made to serve.

Western Fantasies, Scholarly Pursuits

At the beginning of his lengthy introduction to *The Tibetan Book of the Dead*, Evans-Wentz informs us that its translator was cautious to avoid "misinterpretation and consequent misuse" of his translated Tibetan text and thus had requested that his explanatory notes be included with the translation.[12] Tragically, Dawa Samdup had died in 1922, just a few years before Evans-Wentz had begun to collate the materials for publication. Evans-Wentz thus took it upon himself to "correlate and systematize and sometimes to expand the notes thus dictated." Over the course of several years, he reworked, edited, and composed a mass of notes to the surviving translation. His extensive published commentary was drawn less from traditional Tibetan Buddhist interpretations, with which he was really only vaguely familiar, and more from his own spiritualist leanings and early twentieth-century intellectual prejudices. With his truly idiosyncratic interpretations of Dawa Samdup's text pervading every part of its published version, Evans-Wentz both inaugurated and authorized in one fell swoop a distinctive style and method of commentarial tradition that would mark *The Tibetan Book of the Dead* throughout its many lives in western popular culture. Even academic specialists in Tibetan studies have found it difficult to escape the intoxicating power of Evans-Wentz's romance.[13]

How was he able to do this? Why was his book (and the later versions that it inspired) so appealing? Why does *The Tibetan Book of the Dead* continue to attract the attention of both popular and scholarly audiences? I believe the answers lie, in part, in how the book has been presented to the west, and the remarkable ways in which its meaning and significance have been shifted to accommodate the interests and concerns of each new generation. But we should bear in mind that the translated *Book of the Dead* is in many ways unique and quite a different book from the Tibetan one on which it is based, the *Liberation upon Hearing*. To be sure, each new and creative presentation of this text has been, in spite of Dawa Samdup's early warning, "peculiarly liable to misinterpretation and consequent misuse." This tendency for misinterpretation has been sustained for the most part by a misunderstanding, or perhaps even willful ignorance, of the actual context of the Tibetan texts themselves. As Per Kvaerne has correctly noted, the "ritual use of the text is well-known; yet in the West it has too often been presented as a *literary* text, even as a kind of psychological document. This it no doubt may be; yet it must be clearly understood that outside of the ritual context the text has no function at all in Tibetan religion."[14] Western appropriations, or misappropriations as the case may be, of the *Liberation upon Hearing* are not the focus of my study, although I do feel it necessary to highlight at the beginning some of the key facets of the translated book's peculiar legacy over the past seventy-two years, particularly in America. My aim in this effort is simply to demonstrate that in most incarnations of *The Tibetan Book of the Dead*, no matter how unique, each of its compositors has shared uncritically the presumption that the book communicates an ancient and universal truth.[15] With few exceptions, this presupposition, whether ultimately accurate or not, has led problematically to a homogenized understanding of the Tibetan literature that has been typically universalist and ahistorical. It is my hope that by the end of this brief discussion the reasons become more obvious, though no less regrettable, why a sufficient history of these Tibetan texts has not appeared in the secondary literature.

We can begin to understand the appeal of *The Tibetan Book of the Dead* if we first recognize that the book has been presented consistently, to borrow one of Peter Bishop's phrases, as "a powerful symbol of highly organized spiritual attainments, an affirmation of a pure spiritual science."[16] This "spiritual science" is believed to have ancient roots in Tibet. Through proper initiation into its mysteries, it is thought to provide access to a persistent and universal wisdom. Each new author/translator of *The Tibetan Book of the Dead* has claimed the authority to introduce us to this hidden truth concealed behind the words of the text. Each has generally resorted to what Lopez has termed "the trope of the esoteric meaning," in which at least two layers of meaning are assumed: one that is literal, the "exoteric," and another that is symbolic, the "esoteric."[17] It is the latter, of course, that is considered correct by those who really know the truth. Here I should make clear that Lopez's distinction evokes a traditional and longstanding Buddhist trope, in which religious scriptures are divided between texts that require interpretation (*neyārtha, drang-don*) and texts that are to be taken literally (*nithārtha, nges-don*).[18] Truth in both cases is contingent, however, upon the goals and impressions of its beholder. In my mind, there have been three basic "truths," or more accurately orientations to truth, that have compelled specialists and nonspecialists alike to comment on the "real" meaning of *The Tibetan Book of the Dead* and that in turn have attracted legions of devoted readers. These three approaches can be identified in the most basic terms as the scientific, the psychological, and the humanistic. Generally speaking, the first approach seeks a rational and empirically verifiable foundation; the second insists on a symbolic and archetypal reality; and the third pursues the promise of the individual's capacity for self-transformation. Principal examples of each of these three are considered in what follows.

The first approach, the scientific perspective, was initially formulated by Evans-Wentz in his introduction to *The Tibetan Book of the Dead*. It can be best summed up in the following statement: "The *Bardo Thödol* [*Liberation upon Hearing in the Bardo*] seems to be based upon verifiable data of human physiological and psychological experiences; and it views the problem of the after-death state as being purely a psycho-physical problem; and is, therefore, in the main, scientific."[19] Once uttered, this idea that the *Book of the Dead* offered a verifiable "science of death" was forged permanently into something on the order of a fundamental proposition, an underlying presupposition that was never again called into question. From that point on, subsequent generations of commentators would hold firm to this proposition, in one form or another, but it was Evans-Wentz who was the most vigorously extreme in his attempts to substantiate the position. Nowhere is this more clear than in his discussion of reincarnation.

Inspired by the spiritualist ideas of Madame Blavatsky, founder of the Theosophical Society, Evans-Wentz interprets the doctrine of rebirth—which he declares to be the fundamental principle of the *Book of the Dead*—in light of a semi-Darwinist theory of genetic and biological evolution. In this period, any explanatory model founded on Darwin's evolutionary premises was for the most part openly supported as self-evidently correct.[20] Under the spell of this breed of scientific rationalism, Evans-Wentz argues against Buddhist doctrine and claims vehemently that humans can only be reincarnated as humans, animals as animals, and so forth. This, he proclaims, is the true, or "esoteric," interpretation of the traditional "exoteric" Buddhist doctrine.[21] He asserts further that since it is only the esoteric teaching that communicates a universal truth, the exoteric viewpoint should be dismissed as irrational, as nothing more than popular misunderstanding.[22] Central to this standpoint is the notion of the corrupt text:

> Similarly, as the popular interpretation appears to have fundamentally shaped the *Jātaka* [stories of the previous lives of the Buddha] so it may have also affected the compilation of the *Bardo Thödol*; for like all treatises which have had at least a germ-origin in very ancient times and then grown up by the ordinary process of amalgamating congenial material, the *Bardo Thödol*, as a Doctrine of Death and Rebirth, seems to have existed at first unrecorded, like almost all sacred books now recorded in Pali, Sanskrit, or Tibetan, and was a growth of unknown centuries. Then by the time it had fully developed and been

set down in writing no doubt it had lost something of its primitive purity. By its very nature and religious usage, the *Bardo Thödol* would have been very susceptible to the influence of the popular or exoteric view; and in our own opinion it did fall under it, in such manner as to attempt the impossible, namely, the harmonizing of the two interpretations. Nevertheless, its original esotericism is still discernible and predominant.[23]

The principle that we see Evans-Wentz arguing for in this statement implies acceptance of a broad theory of cultural corruption, popular among intellectuals of the nineteenth century. Such a theory assumes a pure pristine origin of religious truth that over the course of time becomes gradually polluted by popular and misguided beliefs, more often termed superstitions.[24] Here, Evans-Wentz asserts that the first step in this process of degeneration occurs when "truth" is set down in writing and that subsequent transmissions of the written word only serve to produce layers on layers of corrupted truth, obscuring the "primitive purity" of the original. He sees as his primary task, therefore, the revelation of the hidden truth, the esoteric meaning conveyed within the texts. In exposing this truth, he deliberately ignores, and many times condemns, the actual character and function of the texts themselves. His efforts are thus divorced from any historical interest whatsoever. Needless to say, the pursuit of universals has almost always superseded concern for particulars. It is not difficult to imagine, then, just how truly insignificant any consideration of the Tibetan context of the *Liberation upon Hearing* would have been for Evans-Wentz.[25]

A more recent example of a variation of the scientific approach to the *Book of the Dead* is found in the translation-study published by Robert Thurman.[26] Thurman's orientation actually represents a hybrid of two approaches, the scientific and the humanistic.

> It is important to understand the inner scientific dimension of the *Book of Natural Liberation Through Understanding in the Between* [*Bar-do thos-grol*], in order to approach it practically and use it effectively. The original is useful to Tibetans in two main ways. First, it is considered a scientific handbook on the realities and experiences of death. . . . Second, it is considered a guidebook for spiritual practice on two levels: It helps the yogi and yogini develop the abilities they need to traverse the death crisis with skill and confidence; and it gives those who feel unable to prepare fully for death, and are not confident of their abilities, a religious sense of how to seek help from enlightened divine and angelic beings.[27]

Unlike Evans-Wentz, who was satisfied merely to uncover the pure scientific truth of the text, Thurman is interested also in its practical uses. For Thurman, the appeal of the book's "science of death" lies in its promise of empirically verifiable techniques for cultivating the "art of dying."[28] He holds firm to his faith in the text's status as both a "scientific handbook" and a "guidebook for spiritual practice." As such, the Tibetan text, he believes, provides not only access to a universal wisdom, but also a systematic technology that can be utilized by any seeker of spiritual truth.[29] Thurman's fervent acceptance of this book as a pure and boundless document of Tibet's ancient "mind science" sustains the generalist perspectives of his predecessors. His overt nostalgia for a perennial wisdom exposes a not-so-latent new-age orientalism that often forces him to make oversimplified statements on the order of a "we-they" duality and tends to hamper recognition of the complexity of social forces that helped to construct the Tibetan texts translated.

The first commentator to approach the *Book of the Dead* in purely psychological terms was the famous Swiss psychologist Carl Jung. His "Psychological Commentary" appeared in English for the first time in the third edition of Evans-Wentz's *Tibetan Book of the Dead* (1957).[30] Jung's insightful essay not only attracted the attention of the intellectual community but also generated considerable interest in nonacademic circles. His psychological approach would come to have an enormous impact on all future interpretations of the Tibetan texts, such as those offered by Lama Anagarika Govinda (1898–1985), Chögyam Trungpa (1939–1987), and Detlef Ingo Lauf. Here, Jung boldly announces: "The *Bardo Thödol* is in the highest degree psychological in its outlook".[31] From there he proceeds to describe in some detail the great psychological truths conveyed in the text and succeeds in pressing some of the Tibetan concepts into his service, thereby appearing to authorize or substantiate his own psychological theories.[32] Thus, for instance, in these pages we learn less about the implicit truths of karma or of the Tibetan post-mortem states (*bardo*) and more about Jung's notions of psychic heredity, archetypes, delusions of consciousness, and the collective unconscious. For Jung, the *Book of the Dead* provides access to the universal structures of the human psyche and is significant only inasmuch as it validates his own psychological propositions. We can hardly be surprised, then, that Jung's descriptive approach takes neither time nor history into account nor even the specific contexts to which the Tibetan texts belong. To his credit, however, Jung does recognize that his unique interpretation of the *Book of the Dead* does not fully mesh with traditional Tibetan perspectives on it.

> The reversal of the order of the chapters, which I have suggested here as an aid to understanding, in no way accords with the original intention of the *Bardo Thödol*. Nor is the psychological use we make of it but a secondary intention, though one that is possibly sanctioned by *lāmaist* custom. The real purpose of this singular book is the attempt, which must seem very strange to the educated European of the twentieth century, to enlighten the dead on their journey through the regions of the *Bardo*.[33]

This praiseworthy sentiment seems to have been lost on Lama Govinda, who also follows a psychological orientation in his "Introductory Forward," included in the 1957 Evans-Wentz edition. Here Govinda rehearses the themes that would form the basis of his own *Foundations of Tibetan Mysticism*, a popular study of the symbolic, acoustic, and geometric systems of Tibetan tantra.[34] In his commentary on the *Book of the Dead*, he declares that the book is "a key to the innermost recesses of the human mind, and a guide for initiates, and for those who are seeking the spiritual path of liberation."[35] Govinda seems to espouse a viewpoint similar to the one cultivated decades later by Thurman. But unlike Thurman, Govinda is critical of traditional interpreters, namely Tibetans, who seem not to have recognized the true meaning of the Tibetan texts. With remarkable conceit he argues, against well-established Tibetan custom, that the *Liberation upon Hearing* is not actually addressed to the dead and dying and that the expression "liberation upon hearing" (*thos-grol*) in the Tibetan title does not really mean what it says. These mistaken ideas, he asserts, arise from ignorance of an ancient universal code of initiation; a code, we might add, that appears to have been known only by a few privileged intellectuals of the nineteenth century.[36] It is really quite astounding just how far Govinda tries to push his orientalist agenda. In his hands the *Liberation upon Hearing* loses its very identity as a Tibetan work. The fact that this German-born bohemian did not know the Tibetan language and was thus forced to base his ideas solely on secondary western-language sources might help to explain his radically decontextualized perspective.

The 1975 translation-study of the *Book of the Dead* by Francesca Fremantle and Chögyam Trungpa represents another distinctive example of a psychological approach to the text. Based on lectures presented at Trungpa's own Buddhist institute in Vermont, this edition of the translated texts bears the distinctive imprint of its author's peculiar blend of American counterculture individualism and Tibetan Buddhist orthodox conservatism. It is clear that Trungpa's commentary owes a large debt to Carl Jung. Trungpa argues that the postmortem experiences described in the *Liberation upon Hearing* should be understood as part of the individual's basic psychological makeup, as defined not so much in traditional Buddhist categories but more strictly within the Euro-American discipline of psychotherapy.[37] Thus Trungpa proposes that the concepts of the text are best described using terms borrowed from modern psychoanalysis, such as *ego, neurosis, projection, paranoia*, and so forth: "In other words, the whole thing is based on another way of looking at the psychological picture of ourselves."[38] The study's greatest virtue is its ability to convey a psychoanalytic vision of the *Book of the Dead* in a familiar and compelling style unburdened by the cumbersome and quasi-biblical language of the earlier Evans-Wentz edition. However, what Trungpa's text makes up for in accessibility it loses in critical integrity. Trungpa makes no attempt to step outside the network of ideas at play in the idiosyncratic language of the translation itself. Consequently, the book does little to illuminate the specific contexts, either cultural or historical, from which such ideas emerge.[39]

In the same year that Trungpa and Fremantle's translation appeared, readers were treated also to a second study of the *Book of the Dead*. This was a German study by Detlef Ingo Lauf entitled *Geheimlehren tibetischer Totenbücher*, subsequently translated into English in 1977 as *Secret Doctrines of the Tibetan Books of the Dead*. On the surface, Lauf's book appears to mirror the work of Lama Govinda in that he similarly attempts to elaborate the complex symbol systems operating within the whole of Tibetan tantra. Moreover, Lauf draws upon a similar psychological vocabulary. But his study, on closer reading, proves itself a more rigorous and insightful work, no doubt in part the result of the author's ability to read the actual language of the texts. Lauf begins his study with a refreshing survey of the various textual traditions of the Tibetan "Books of the Dead." He then devotes much of the remaining sections to a detailed analysis of the basic conceptual components at work in those books, including a valuable overview of their attendant rituals. From there he offers a comparative analysis and attempts to establish shared conceptual patterns between the Tibetan traditions and those of the ancient civilizations of India, Egypt, Persia, Greece, and Rome. This section, his most problematic, seems to echo the prior concerns of Evans-Wentz, who had suggested earlier in his own work the possibility of common origins for all these diverse traditions.[40] Such an approach is by nature generalist and ahistorical and is almost always subject to some dubious maneuver that seeks to explain similarities between ideas as the result of derivation from a common source. Nevertheless, Lauf's study remains a noteworthy introduction to many of the key ideas and symbols found in the Tibetan traditions associated with the *Liberation upon Hearing*.

I now consider a third approach to the *Book of the Dead*, the humanistic orientation. Typical humanistic approaches to these Tibetan traditions have pursued the promise of an individual's capacity for self-transformation. Such a position, therefore, centers on the interests of the human individual, usually with an additional emphasis on a nontheistic spirituality. In this instance, the term "spirituality" refers very specifically to a relatively modern phenomenon. Donald Lopez provides a basic definition:

> "Spiritual" no longer refers to contact and communication with the spirits of the dead. Instead it evokes an ethos beyond the confines of the merely religious, pointing back to that which was the original life blood of religious traditions but was ultimately free from them, confined as they were by institution and by history. The spiritual was instead at once both universal and personal, accessible not only through the experiences of the mystics of the great "world religions" but also, perhaps in a more pristine form, through Asian traditions or through shamanism, nature worship, or the cult of the goddess, what was once regarded as primitive.[41]

As we can see here, the "spirituality" perspective tends to stress several key principles that are reminiscent of views held, for example, by Evans-Wentz and other similar intellectuals of the nineteenth and early twentieth century. This basic viewpoint attempts to establish connections between notions of an original, pure, and universal religious essence, uncontaminated by culture and history and the privitized experiences of the individual. It is in such light that this perspective can be properly described as humanistic. Needless to say, the driving ambition of those who adopt such a view is rarely ever to achieve a higher awareness of the particulars of historical context. Far from it. The primary objective is personal awareness and the discovery of techniques for self-transformation. Indeed, as Govinda notes, "it is the spiritual point of view that makes [*The Tibetan Book of the Dead*] so important for the majority of its readers."[42] Humanistic interpretations of this book are distinguished clearly by the purposes expressed by their authors. In every case, the aim has been to produce ever more accessible versions of the text for those who wish to benefit from the trials and errors of "ancient" tradition. In terms of form and content, these versions have tended to avoid academic styles that are generally perceived as unnecessarily obscurantist, say, for example, scholarly footnotes. In addition, the translations of the Tibetan texts have often been accompanied by the oral commentaries of contemporary Tibetan lamas. The whole point, it appears, has been to present, in the clearest possible terms, an easy-to-read and tradition-authorized "guidebook for spiritual practice."

Several of the studies already discussed might be better suited for this humanistic category, for example the translations of Trungpa and Thurman, but other examples not considered might also be included, such as Timothy Leary, Ralph Metzner, and Richard Alpert, *The Psychedelic Experience: A Manual Based on the Tibetan Book of the Dead*;[43] Eva K. Dargyay, *Das tibetische Buch der Toten*;[44] John Myrdhin Reynolds, *Self-Liberation Through Seeing with Naked Awareness*;[45] Ramon Prats, *El libro de los muertos tibetano*;[46] B. Allan Wallace, *Natural Liberation: Padmasambhava's Teachings on the Six Bardos*;[47] and Stephen Hodge and Martin Boord, *The Illustrated Tibetan Book of the Dead*. Although each of these studies is distinctive in its own right, they all share a common conviction, which is perhaps best expressed in the old words of Lama Govinda: "Under the guise of the science of death, the *Bardo Thödol* reveals the secret of life; and therein lies its spiritual value and its universal appeal."[48]

As I see it, the main problem with the humanistic approach, and equally with that of the scientific and psychological, is that its followers have been too apt to neglect the actual Tibetan texts on which their studies have been based. The truth is that these texts were produced, and continue to be produced, within very specific contexts, which is to say that these textual traditions have had "a place within the mess, confusions and power struggles of social life."[49] More to the point, these texts have a history, and that history, with only slight exception, has not been sufficiently documented in the secondary literature. I think one of the main reasons it has taken so long for a history of the *Liberation upon Hearing* to be written should be clear by now. Proponents of the three positions just outlined have been primarily doctrine oriented and have typically adopted a methodological stance that is by nature generalist and universalizing. At the risk of sounding overly dramatic the three standpoints, though insightful and illuminating in some respects, have had a somewhat negative effect on the study of the history of the Tibetan texts themselves.

It is interesting to note, however, that there have been a few exceptional cases, such as the Italian translation-study of Giuseppe Tucci, *Il libro tibetano dei morti—Bardo Tödöl*;[50] the philological studies of Dieter Michael Back, *Eine buddhistische jenseitsreise*[51] and *Rig pa ńo sprod gcer mthoń rań grol: Die Erkenntnislehre des Bar do thos grol*;[52] and the recent conceptual history of Henk Blezer, *Kar gliń Źi khro: A Tantric Buddhist Concept*.[53] A few brief comments about these works are in order.

First, we have Giuseppe Tucci, one of the century's foremost Tibetologists. Tucci was the first to recognize the importance of establishing the textual history of the *Liberation upon Hearing*. It is indeed remarkable that at such an early date he was already quite aware of some of the potential problems confronting the would-be textual historian. For example, in his introduction, he rightly observes that the history of the compilation of this Tibetan collection is a rather complicated affair. As he notes, the texts were compiled gradually from a mix of locally determined materials of uncertain origin, all reflecting the varied interests of individual schools and monasteries. It would be the task of future scholars to work out the chronology of these textual layers.[54]

In fact, one of those future scholars was Dieter Michael Back, whose research on the *Liberation upon Hearing* and associated texts has been to date unsurpassed. His two philological studies of some of the central texts of the cycle are noteworthy both for their extensive documentation and for their critical reflections on many of the text-historical complexities of the variety of collections themselves. Almost as if responding directly to Tucci's earlier call, Back makes a noble attempt at establishing the basic structure (*grundstruktur*) of the original *Liberation upon Hearing*.[55] His analysis, however, loses ground somewhat in his failure to clarify the actual historical circumstances involved in the compilation and transmission of the texts that make up the collection. Unfortunately, what little historical data Back does examine he perceives through the lens of philology, which tends to flatten his perspective and to force him to make comparisons between historically unrelated ideas.

Henk Blezer's *Kar gliṅ Źi khro* is the published version of his doctoral thesis defended at the Rijksuniversiteit te Leiden. Blezer's meticulous study of the conceptual structures evident in the texts of the *Liberation upon Hearing* and related literature stands as a truly impressive contribution to our knowledge of these materials. The general focus of the book is on the conceptual and historical relations that exist between the Buddhist doctrine of postmortem transition (*antarābhava, bar-do*) and the Indo-Tibetan notion of a structured vision, or *mandala*, of peaceful and wrathful deities (*zhi-ba dang khrobo'i lha-tshogs*). Blezer theorizes that the relatively late conflation of these two concepts resulted in the creation of one of the two most prominent texts of the *Liberation upon Hearing*, the *Reminder of the Bardo of Reality-Itself* [*Chos-nyid bar-do gsal-'debs*].[56] To support this thesis, Blezer marshals a formidable array of primary source materials (in Pali, Sanskrit, and Tibetan) and, with the precision of a well-seasoned philologist, sets about analyzing and comparing the basic terminology of the texts in question. Blezer's method has been appropriately described as "a historicism framed along etymological lines and based in a careful chronological ordering of texts."[57] But, despite an apparent concern for history, Blezer seems to stumble over the same problem we observe in Dieter Back's work—that is, a difficulty in fixing the proper chronology of the textual sources resulting from a tendency to overlook the cultural contexts in which those texts developed.

We see, then, that even in these exceptional cases, in which the commentators profess a certain historical focus, lack of attention to the essential details of historical context persists. At the risk of oversimplification, it is my opinion that this inattentiveness to context has been a consistent and fundamental weakness in every study of the *Liberation upon Hearing*, including the impressive studies of Tucci, Back, and Blezer. In saying this, my criticism is not directed at what has been said about the ideas conveyed by the texts, or even about the potential spiritual and psychological benefits such ideas might offer to sympathetic modern western audiences, but rather what has *not* been said about the texts themselves and the contexts in which they emerged. As the noted textual scholar G. Thomas Tanselle has remarked: "Critical sophistication in the extracting of meaning from words on a page can—and frequently does—coexist with the most uncritical attitude toward the document itself and the trustworthiness of its texts."[58] The point here is that the nature of the document, the artifact as it were of the text itself, including, more importantly, the contexts to which it belongs, should be a principal, if not crucial, concern of those whose goal it is to comment on its meanings. Is it not true, in fact, that it is the physical text that provides the basis on which critical interpretations are initially founded?

In the final analysis we see that in every case the *Great Liberation upon Hearing in the Bardo* has been approached from the sole perspective of its conceptual content; the typical assumption being that its content communicates some generalized and universal wisdom. This doctrine-oriented view has tended toward an implicit denial of the relevance of the text's history. We must recognize, however, that the history of a given text has as much bearing on understanding its significance as does the wisdom of its words. This study is thus intended as a response to historical indifference. It is my hope that such a shift in focus may help to bring a more contextualized and thus comprehensive approach to studies of the *Liberation upon Hearing*, and Tibetan religious literature in general. With this in mind, let us now turn our attention to the actual Tibetan collection itself.

The Treasures of Gampodar Mountain

Tradition attributes authorship of the *Liberation upon Hearing* to the eighth-century exorcist Padmasambhava, the Lotus Guru, who hailed from the western region of Orgyen (Uḍḍiyāna) (see fig. 1.2).[59] This mysterious figure, according to legend, was invited to Tibet in the late eighth century by the emperor Trhi Songdetsen (742–c. 797) in order to subdue the indigenous spirits who had been obstructing the efforts to bring Buddhism into the country. While in Tibet, Padmasambhava is believed to have concealed a vast array of religious "treasures" (*gter-ma*) in unusual and remote locations so that they could later be revealed at an appropriate time. Those who subsequently discovered these treasures were known as "treasure revealers" (*gter-ston*). Among the many famous excavators of Padmasambhava's hidden treasures was an obscure fourteenth-century mystic named Karma Lingpa (see fig. 1.3).

FIGURE 1.2. Padmasambhava, the Lotus Guru. Thanka painting, nineteenth century. (Courtesy of The Shelley and Donald Rubin Foundation, no. 188)

FIGURE 1.3. A rare image of Karma Lingpa, revealer of the hidden treasures of Gampodar Mountain and "author" of the original *Tibetan Book of the Dead*. Detail from Karling picture cards (*tsa-ka-li*), fifteenth century. (Courtesy of The Shelley and Donald Rubin Foundation, no. 289)

Karma Lingpa was from the southeastern region of Dakpo, an area renowned for its dense forests and fertile meadowlands. This had been the birthplace of the eponymous Dakpo Kagyu tradition founded by Gampopa (1079–1153). The monastery that Gampopa established in 1121, on the jagged ridges of the ancient Daklha Gampo mountain range,[60] became the principal center for the religious practice of the Great Seal, or Mahāmudrā (*phyag-rgya-chen-po*)—a tradition that was actively maintained at this site by the successive generations of Gampopa's family and lineal descendants until the early eighteenth century. Legend proclaims that it was within this very same mountain environment, on a small peak known as Gampodar, that the treasure revealer Karma Lingpa unearthed a cache of scriptural treasures believed to have been concealed there six centuries earlier by Padmasambhava.[61] This treasure contained esoteric yoga teachings focused on a mandala of one hundred peaceful and wrathful deities (*zhi-khro*) and included detailed instructions on religious practices to be employed at the moment of death, during a perilous and prolonged postmortem phase called *bardo*, and during the confused journey into a new existence. Its various combination of pieces originated in the separate Buddhist communities of India from roughly the fifth through tenth centuries and in the Buddhist and non-Buddhist indigenous groups of Tibet over the span of several hundred years, from the late tenth through fourteenth centuries. These were Karma Lingpa's textual revelations, commonly referred to collectively as the *Karling Peaceful and Wrathful* [*Kar-gling zhi-khro*]: a large literary cycle entitled *Self-Liberated Wisdom of the Peaceful and Wrathful Deities* (henceforth abbreviated as *Peaceful and Wrathful Deities*) and a smaller set of funerary texts called *Great Liberation upon Hearing in the Bardo*. We must be careful to make a clear distinction between these two collections since each of their respective transmission histories in Tibet is unique. I will show that unlike the multistratified lineal tradition of the *Peaceful and Wrathful Deities* there was apparently only a single teaching-line (*brgyud*) for the *Liberation upon Hearing*.

We know with some certainty that in the late fourteenth century the Karling (abbreviation of Karma Lingpa) treasure tradition originated in Dakpo and, for a relatively short period after its compilation, remained and was fostered in that general vicinity. The area of its earliest diffusion flowed slightly beyond Dakpo to the north and east, in Longpo and Kongpo, respectively. The ritual significance of Kongpo, in particular, is indicated in the myths and legends of the origins of the Tibetan empire that ruled from the seventh through the mid–ninth century. The first Tibetan emperors (*btsan-po*) were said to have descended from heaven by a special cord (*dmu-thag*) and, at death, to have returned to heaven by the same cord, leaving behind no physical remains. It was only with the death of the eighth emperor, Drigum Tsenpo, that imperial corpses began to be left behind on earth.[62] After Drigum, the Tibetan kings were memorialized according to a newly prescribed funeral rite and subsequently buried in tombs.[63] Erik Haarh has interpreted the Drigum legend as a myth that preserved the memory of a monumental conflict between two indigenous Tibetan clans, the Jatrhi settled in Yarlung and the Nyatrhi from Kongpo. Presumably, the former empire was defeated by the Kongpo tribes and eventually collapsed after the death of the last member of its imperial line.[64] The myth of Emperor Drigum's death points symbolically to this great political and cultural transition, the founding of the Tibetan empire, which had culminated with the introduction of an entirely new ritualized perspective on death and the dead. Although we must acknowledge that Haarh's historical reconstruction is highly speculative and based on fragmentary evidence, the link with Kongpo is important. It is appropriate that the ancient cult of the dead in Tibet is believed to have hailed originally from the vicinity of

Kongpo, since we now know that it was also from within this area that the famous funeral liturgy of Karma Lingpa's *Peaceful and Wrathful Deities* tradition first blossomed. It was only after the institutionalization of its rituals in the same region, sometime in the late fifteenth century, that Karma Lingpa's treasure revelations then found their way to other parts of Tibet.

Generally speaking, in the periods leading up to the fifteenth century, the transmission of religious teachings in Tibet was dominated by direct oral exchange between teachers and their students, as well as quite often larger groups made up of pious laity. Since the religious education of the masses was generally quite elementary, the essential content of the teachings was rarely communicated to these audiences in writing or through public or private reading.[65] The book in Tibet, when available, served a variety of ennobling purposes, the least of which was reading. The devotion of the majority of Tibetans in this age was primarily expressed in the recitation of prayers and in performance of rituals, and books were themselves fundamental components of these rites as physical embodiments of sacred power that, among other benefits, could protect against evil influences. For those wealthy enough to absorb the costs, moreover, the act of commissioning the copying of sacred books was itself a ritual designed to accrue merit and ensure for its donor a positive future in this and the next life.[66] A select and comparatively limited group of Tibetan literati (*phyag-dpe-ba*) did utilize books for memorization, recitation, and study. Nevertheless, we must bear in mind that at every level the dominant form of the "book" in this period was the manuscript written by hand, hence the physical text was a rather scarce and precious item. I think it is too easy and precarious a trap to approach the transmission of religious teaching in Tibet with a modern postindustrial impression of a relatively high rate of literacy and of the widespread access of printed matter. The manuscript age in Tibetan history predominated until at least the year 1410, when the first xylograph or woodblock print of the Tibetan Kanjur was produced in Beijing.[67]

Some scholars have suggested that xylography, or the engraving of texts on woodblocks, did not become a practical alternative to writing in Tibet until the first half of the eighteenth century.[68] In light of this, I should emphasize that the manuscript was the primary, but certainly not the sole, means of transmission of religious content in Tibet prior to the eighteenth century and that only after this period did Tibetans yield gradually to the printed book. One of the more frustrating aspects of textual scholarship in Tibetan studies is that precious little of pre-xylographic-age Tibetan literature has survived or is readily accessible. Save for the manuscript fragments recovered from Dunhuang[69] and the valuable private and public manuscript collections housed in Europe and Asia,[70] the vast majority of Tibetan literature has come down to us in the form of xylographic prints and reproductions from blocks carved only in the last two centuries.[71] Tibetanists must become more fully conscious of the fact that the nature of the textual artifact, the form in which the book itself is codified and distributed, influences critically the outcome of any historical claims about scriptural transmission in Tibet and the diffusion of specific religious ideas.

In this context, this matter is entirely relevant when one pauses to consider that the fourteenth-century cycle of revealed scriptures attributed to the treasure revealer Karma Lingpa may not have been fully redacted and made widely available in printed form until the eighteenth century, when possibly for the first time woodblocks made from manuscript copies were prepared and a xylograph edition was produced. In one case in particular, the result was the production of a small set of Tibetan blocks that would later form the basis of most known xylograph redactions of the *Liberation upon Hearing*. In the centuries prior to the printing of the Karling treasure anthologies, the individual texts were circulated in manuscript form and scattered about in various temple libraries and in the personal collections of individual lamas, each reflecting the particular lineage affiliations and local customs of the surrounding community. By the eighteenth century, in the age of xylograph printing, it became easier and more economically feasible for the newly formed large monastic institutions to gather these local manuscripts and assemble them into printed volumes which then served to represent the authoritative collection of a given textual lineage. This is in fact how the multiple editions of the cycle of the *Peaceful and Wrathful Deities* came to be produced. The widespread diffusion of these texts could not have been possible before the first half of the eighteenth century, when the technology of printing in Tibet reached a greater level of practicality and accessibility such that books could be produced, and stored, in sufficiently large quantities with a relatively constant supply of materials. Centralized institutions that could provide the necessary space and funds for the large-scale production of books, including the labor and materials involved in papermaking, copying, carving, and so forth, did not exist in Tibet before the middle years of the fifteenth century, and in many localities (primarily to the east) not even until the seventeenth.

We should be clear that the transmission of religious knowledge, whether in the form of texts or direct oral instruction, was actually a rather fluid process in Tibet throughout much of its early history. Given the complexity of the interrelationships between families and clans, local alliances, religious orders, and so forth, contacts and exchanges between teachers and students were often quite open. In other words, despite a popular misconception, religious ideas and practices in Tibet were frequently passed along lines moving in multiple directions, rather than strictly along a vertical axis defined by a particular sectarian affiliation. It is this fluid dynamic that explains the diversity of the Karling tradition, which from its inception had gathered followers from both the Nyingmapa and Kagyupa orders, especially the Zurmang, Zhamarpa, and Pawo subsects. The connection particularly with the Karma Kagyu groups is not unusual, given that historically the regions surrounding Dakpo and Kongpo were strongholds of that sect up until at least the seventeenth century.[72]

Some of the fundamental texts of the cycle of the *Peaceful and Wrathful Deities* appear to have taken shape at two relatively obscure monasteries in southeastern Tibet, namely Tsele in Dakpo and Thangdrok in Kongpo. These institutions shared close alliances with leaders of the Zhamarpa and Pawo subsects of the Karma Kagyu and sheltered religious followers—lay and celibate—of both the Kagyu and Nyingma orders. I will show that the written texts of the *Liberation upon Hearing*, in particular, were perhaps initially formulated exclusively at Tsele and Thangdrok monasteries. This famous collection of death texts, in rough form, was probably derived from preexisting materials composed or compiled by Karma Lingpa himself and later revised by his immediate successors, including, most important his father Nyida Sangye, his son Nyida Chöje, and the nebulous lamas Nyida Özer (b. 1409 or 1421) of Longpo and Gönpo Dorje of Kongpo. Both Gönpo Dorje and Nyida Özer were the first subsidiary links in the spread of the *Liberation upon Hearing* transmissions later received at Tsele and Thangdrok, and I should also add at Zurmang monastery in eastern Tibet.

The abbot from Menmo monastery in Kongpo named Gyarawa Namka Chökyi Gyatso (b. 1430) played the first active role in the institutionalization of the *Peaceful and Wrathful Deities*. He transformed the earlier nonclerical tradition by creating a coherent liturgical program that could be easily disseminated. This was all made possible by the status and security of his monastic position. In Tibet, it was primarily the monasteries that controlled the rites for the dead, and thus the success of such liturgy depended on ecclesiastical support, as well as the support of pious laity in the form of patronage. The significance of the monastic center in the propagation of the Karling rituals cannot be overstated, although we must be careful to recognize the precise factors involved in that process. As knowledge of the *Peaceful and Wrathful Deities*, including the *Liberation upon Hearing*, spread throughout Tibet, it gradually became established within certain Nyingmapa and Kagyupa communities as a primary source for the performance of the Buddhist funeral rites. But, despite its eventual popularity and widespread distribution in those communities, the liturgy was never established as a dominant religious system identified exclusively with a single monastic tradition, as for example we find in the case of the Nyingmapa monastery of Dorje Drak with its Jang Ter (*byang-gter*), or Northern Treasures, system, believed to have been revealed by Rikzin Gödemjen (1337–1409).[73] The relative success or failure of any given treasure tradition depended as much on the influence of external social and political forces as on the internal strength of its perceived religious efficacy. Although a few monasteries are known to have been established by early holders of Karma Lingpa's transmissions, these never seemed to have developed into politically powerful institutions. Without a strong political foundation, the Karling tradition, dispersed as it was, could never support the organization of a proper sect in its own right. In later centuries, this treasure tradition would be reduced to a relatively anonymous liturgical tradition represented only by a loosely bound and widely varied set of popular ritual texts with no distinctive institutional identity.

Although at present we lack sufficient comparative evidence to argue definitively that the rituals accompanying the *Peaceful and Wrathful Deities* and *Liberation upon Hearing* were just one of several competing ritual forms in Tibet and surrounding regions, it does stand to reason that the Karling liturgy was not the only ritual program for death and dying available in Tibet. As is clear in Turrell Wylie's study of Tibetan funerary customs at Sakya, for example, the early death practices of the Sakyapa tradition prior to the eighteenth century involved mainly recitation of passages from the *Hevajra* and *Vajrayoginī Tantras* and not a single reading from the *Liberation upon Hearing*.[74] In addition to these tantric prayers, Tibetan specialists from various periods turned also to the cycle of rituals associated with the *Tantra on the Elimination of All Evil Rebirths* [*Sarvadurgatiparisodhana-tantra*], one of the earliest tantras translated in Tibet during the first propagation of Buddhism in that country.[75] As I will show, the prayers and ritual acts inscribed in this particular tantra emphasized the purification of sins and provided a framework of ritual action regarded as necessary to eliminate obstacles that might hinder an auspicious destiny for the recently deceased. The Buddhist tantras, such as the *Elimination of All Evil Rebirths* and the *Hevajra*, helped to shape a variety of ritual responses to death that developed in Tibet long before the institutionalization of the Karling liturgy in the fifteenth century. Indeed, the older ritual programs were preserved and must have continued to circulate alongside the newer and perhaps even competitive models prescribed in later ritual and literary collections such as the *Peaceful and Wrathful Deities* and *Liberation upon Hearing*.

The various texts and rituals of the Karling tradition were passed between separate teaching-lineages and maintained alongside other similar systems, like those of Ratna Lingpa (1403–1479) and Pema Lingpa (1450–1521), at many different monasteries often completely independent of one another. Each of these institutions possessed its own version of Karma Lingpa's treasure collection, comprising texts from widely diverse periods and provenances. The individual works of these anthologies were produced in accordance with a particular lineage of transmission, and in them were preserved the local ritual customs of the affiliated religious community. To understand the history of Karma Lingpa's tradition within and beyond the borders of Tibet, we must first have a clear knowledge of the lineages that preserved and actively promoted its liturgy. For this purpose, therefore, I offer this study.

Approaching the Sources

This is the first historical study of the formation and transmission in Tibet of the *Book of the Dead*. More precisely, it is a history of the treasure revelations of Karma Lingpa, the *Self-Liberated Wisdom of the Peaceful and Wrathful Deities* and the *Great Liberation upon Hearing in the Bardo*. At one level, it is a detailed narrative account of the transmission of a particular set of texts, of a distinctive collection of literature comprising specific rites and prayers for the dead and dying. At another level, it is an examination of the historical process that produced the variations in the manuscripts and blockprints of that textual tradition. Its sources are thus literary (biographies, monastic chronicles, and so forth) and liturgical (lineage prayers, ritual manuals, etc.).

Because I have derived my research from sources that are for the most part historical and archival, my focus has been on the social and institutional histories of the texts and of their traditions rather than on questions of their religious meaning. Since the history of this literature on the whole has not been addressed in contemporary scholarship, it is my hope that by expanding the focus of investigation this study may highlight important information that has gone previously unnoticed. Finally, in the interests of those specialists pursuing topics in Tibetan historiography and religious history, I hope that I have been somewhat successful in demonstrating the fruitful qualities of certain types of primary source materials—too long neglected—for constructing history, and especially bibliographical history and textual transmission in Tibet. Toward this aim, a few specific words are in order on the methods and materials used in writing this particular history.

This study is based first of all on a reading of Gyarawa Namkha Chökyi Gyatso's *Garland of Jewels: An Abridged History of the Transmission Lineage* [*Brgyud-pa'i lo-rgyus mdor-bsdus nor-bu'i phreng-ba*].[76] This work, composed in 1499, provides the earliest known account of the Karling transmissions. It is, therefore, of great historical significance. Save for a few brief references in the work of Dieter M. Back, the text has remained relatively unknown. I have consulted it primarily for information on the lives of Karma Lingpa and his immediate successors, including, most important, Gyarawa himself. To begin to construct a coherent picture of the tradition's development, I compared the details of Gyarawa's text with the relevant accounts found in various other religious histories (*chos-'byung*), as well as important "treasure histories" (*gter-'byung*).[77] I found that some of the materials offered conflicting information, and so I had to make decisions of probability based on a close examination of all the evidence gathered before me. My first step was to order the sources chronologically so that I could analyze changes over time and prevent myself as much as possible from making anachronistic conclusions. This allowed me to see more clearly points of agreement and divergence in the various narratives and to better determine what material might have been added by later generations. From this data I was able to piece together a basic story. This story is the main topic of part II. I realized, however, that the full history of this tradition required much more rigorous comparative analysis, so I then concentrated my efforts on additional biographical evidence from alternative sources.

It has often been remarked that Tibetans have tended toward a certain preoccupation with history. Such emphasis appears for the most part to be based on concern about legitimizing claims to authenticity. One way this was accomplished was through appeal to lines of authority leading backward unbroken in time. Records of lineal succession (*brgyud-rim*) and prayers to past masters (*brgyud-pa'i gsol-'debs*) abound in Tibetan religious literature. All the various anthologies of the *Peaceful and Wrathful Deities* include texts of this genre. In the most basic terms, such works comprise lists upon lists of names, usually arranged in chronological order, that belong to a particular doctrinal or ritual lineage. These short texts are significant in that they often provide the names of identifiable personalities. For my study, I was intent on gathering this type of information in order, first to establish the number of separate transmission lineages that existed throughout the history of the Karling tradition, and second to trace relationships between individual members of those lineages.

With this task in mind, I also turned my attention to another type of archival document known as "records of (teachings) heard" (*gsan-yig*)—or, as the case may be, of "(teachings) obtained" (*thob-yig*), properly understood as registries of a particular individual's religious and scholastic education. Typically autobiographical, these records contain meticulous lists of the titles of written texts, verbal instructions, and ritual initiations received throughout the author's life, and include the names of the teachers from whom such materials were obtained. Many of the more extensive documents, much like lineage prayers, record the complete history of the transmission series for each received item. These archival documents are thus extremely valuable for the light they shed on Tibetan intellectual and bibliographical history. To date, however, few scholars have paid close attention to them.[78] For my own research, I have relied on several works of this genre, most notably the voluminous seventeenth-century records of both the fifth Dalai Lama (1617–1682) and Terdak Lingpa (1646–1714).[79] From these documents, and from the aforementioned lineage supplications, I was able to establish the widest possible range of textual lineages involved in the transmission of the *Peaceful and Wrathful Deities* and *Liberation upon Hearing* in Tibet. Also, importantly, I was able to begin to uncover the institutional affiliations of the individuals in those lineages.

One of my methods of using all of these documents was to read them side by side with the relevant abbatial records (*gdan-rabs*) of the specific monasteries that I had identified as possible centers for the practice of the Karling rituals.[80] In reading through these monastic histories, I first looked for proper names that were familiar from the lists of teaching-lineages. I then read the appropriate sections carefully and took extensive notes, paying close attention to the fine points of the person's life and religious training. I discovered that many of these passages contained information similar to that found in the archival records, such as the names of teachers and of texts received. However, the added value of the monastic records was that they provided dates of people and events. They also described the founding of the monastery and details about both its internal affairs and external contacts. This proved incredibly valuable for determining the nature of the relations between various institutions and for elucidating some of the social and political contexts in which the textual traditions developed. To this material I then added information taken from the hagiographies (*rnam-thar*) and autobiographies (*rang-rnam*)[81] of a few prominent monastic leaders, notably Tsele Natsok Rangdröl (1608–1680),[82] Terdak Lingpa,[83] and Rikzin Nyima Drakpa.[84] In part III I discuss the biographical details of the various transmission lineages and of the institutions with which they were associated.

The materials I used for the study of the Karling texts themselves included the previously mentioned teaching records, as well as various catalogues (*dkar-chag*)[85] and printing indexes (*par-tho*)[86]—in both Tibetan and western languages—and the colophons (*mjug-byang*)[87] of selected works. My aim was to identify, organize, and compare the multiple editions, in all extant forms, so that I might better understand some aspects of the historical content and physical history of these books. The analytical evidence I derived from this intensive investigation, corroborated with western bibliographical records and other secondary evidence, revealed a complex history of localized variation, annotation, and emendation.

Readers may note that the meanings and symbolic content of the ideas and rituals of the Karling tradition are not so central in this study as they could be, or perhaps should be. This is because I saw that the history of the transmission of the texts themselves was the most pressing scholarly task. Some may object that I have not tackled so thoroughly questions of the sociopolitical contexts of these rituals in Tibet. Again I felt that the origin, structure, and circulation of the texts required a more comprehensive examination before such broader questions could be adequately addressed. The social and political history of this literature is a subject I now hope scholars will pursue more rigorously. Finally, readers should be aware that the *terminus ante quem* of this study is the middle of the eighteenth century. By that period, at which time xylograph production was more or less in the mainstream, although the Karling tradition in general continued to develop in localized settings, its basic structural and practical components appear to have been in place. The block-printing of the Karling texts almost certainly assured the widespread transmission of the tradition, in a somewhat standardized form, to later generations within and beyond the borders of Tibet.

I

DEATH AND THE DEAD

Beginnings: Funeral Ritual in Ancient Tibet

Tibetan Buddhism has for centuries maintained that crucial moments of transition are charged with great transformative potential, particulary the intervening moments between death and rebirth. The Tibetan expression for this postmortem interval is "bardo."[1] This Tibetan word and the concept to which it refers are by now quite familiar to western readers. In Tibetan the term has come to refer to any state of suspended reality in which a being-in-transition confronts the nature of "reality-as-such" (chos-nyid). In the specific case of passage after death, it is proclaimed that the dead are presented with a series of opportunities for recognizing the actual "truth" (de-bzhin-nyid) of that moment. Accordingly, in some circles it is held that if the deceased at certain times is capable of perceiving correctly the confusing and often terrifying bardo visions as simply mental projections reflective of the previous life's thoughts and deeds, then it is said that buddhahood will be attained. Failure to recognize these visions, however, leads eventually to rebirth and further suffering in the cycle of existence (saṃsāra). Traditionally, to help the deceased travelers (re)gain insight into their ambiguous situation, a monk or skilled layperson will recite guiding instructions and inspirational prayers from special funeral texts, the so-called Tibetan Books of the Dead.

This rather general and uncomplicated description of the bardo is reflective of a popular understanding of the Tibetan concept. But, despite the simplicity of this basic presentation, the Buddhist theory of postmortem transition and its development in Tibet is quite a complex and convoluted matter, and one that has not been well documented or seriously examined. In this and the chapters that follow, I will explore the changing perceptions of death and afterlife among the Tibetans before and after the arrival of Buddhism and attempt to chart the course of development of the bardo concept from its origins in India, its

introduction to Tibet, and the various subsequent phases of its reformulation leading up to the fourteenth-century treasure revelations of Karma
Lingpa and the spread of the cycles of the *Peaceful and Wrathful Deities*
and the *Liberation upon Hearing*. I begin by surveying the ancient concepts
of death and afterlife in imperial Tibet during the age of the so-called Yarlung
dynasty.

The King Who Fell to Earth

Before the introduction of Buddhism to Tibet, which according to later legend began sometime in the late seventh century, court-sanctioned Tibetan
religious practice was focused largely on the person of the king (*btsan-po*).
Since it was held that the welfare of the kingdom depended on the welfare of
its ruler, special rituals were performed to protect and prolong the king's life
and, when he was dead, to guarantee his safe passage to the heavens above
(*dgung du gshegs*). According to some of the early historical records discovered at Dunhuang (the earliest dating possibly to the late eighth century or
early ninth century),[2] the priests that performed such rituals were identified
by the name *bonpo* and their beliefs by the term *bon*.[3] Although it is commonly claimed that this ancient pre-Buddhist class of Tibetan priests became
the Bon religion of modern times,[4] historical evidence indicates that Bon
developed into an organized and distinctive religious tradition only in deliberate opposition to Buddhism no earlier than the late tenth century. More than
probably, an instituted Bon religion never fully existed in pre-Buddhist Tibet.
In other words, the developments of Buddhism and Bon were separate but
simultaneous processes in the later history of Tibetan religious culture.[5] Over
the centuries the mixture of indigenous Tibetan beliefs and practices with those
of Buddhism and Bon has succeeded in almost completely obscuring any
distinctions between them. What appears to be certain is that imperial Tibetan
religion revolved essentially around ideas about the creative and destructive
powers of nature, particularly those of the earth, and the constitution and
persistence of the "soul" (*bla*).[6] Certain elements of these ideas have survived
and can be discerned in Bonpo and also, as the case may be, in Buddhist literature, but such ideas themselves are fundamentally different from the basic
doctrines of the Bon religion that we know had been instituted originally only
after the arrival of Buddhism to Tibet. Scholars have suspected that some of
the literature and liturgy of the Bonpos, and also particularly of the oldest
sects of Buddhism in Tibet, contain deep within their layers a constellation
of Tibetan ideas on death and the hereafter that have more or less survived
from ancient times.[7]

Evidence contained in the Dunhuang manuscripts suggests that a highly
sophisticated funerary tradition with no connection whatsoever to Buddhism
was in place and active very early on in Tibet. However, we still know precious little about the ancient Tibetan concepts of life and death, living and
dead, despite the availability of a considerable amount of early and poten-

tially fruitful material. Regrettably, few Tibetologists have ventured to reach beyond the earlier studies of Marcelle Lalou, Erik Haarh, and Rolf A. Stein "to explore, even superficially, this blank spot on the map of ancient Tibetan culture and history."[8] The paucity of research on the subject indicates perhaps some lack of interest or motivation on the part of scholars to take up Haarh's call to future researchers: "The fact that the autochthonous, Tibetan religious history has until recently remained a virgin soil, that considerable material for its exploration is available and has been for more than a century, ought to be an inspiration and instigation to further studies in this field."[9] Sadly, Haarh's statement, published thirty years ago, still stands even today as an accurate portrayal of our current and fledgling state of research.

In this chapter I will review some of the relevant materials dealing with ancient Tibetan funeral custom and attempt to draw out the basic concepts of death and afterlife prevalent during the imperial period through the mid–ninth century. In the chapters that follow I hope to argue for the continuity of many of these ideas in the Tibetan Buddhist and Bonpo traditions and to trace their influence on later and better-documented concepts such as the notion of a prolonged postmortem intermediate period or bardo (antarābhava).

I have noted that in Tibet prior to the influx of Buddhist influences there already existed a broad range of accepted beliefs and approaches to the problems generated by death and the dead. Perhaps the most detailed, well-documented, and persuasive reconstruction of the early history of such ideas remains Erik Haarh's book *The Yar-luṅ Dynasty*, a study inspired in part by the earlier speculations of Giuseppe Tucci.[10] This vast and impressive work purports to be a study of ancient Tibetan history derived to a large extent from a variety of myths and legends from later Tibetan Buddhist historiographical sources. Haarh organizes his book around three established Tibetan traditions concerning the origin and nature of the first Tibetan king, Nyatrhi Tsenpo (also Nyaktrhi Tsenpo, Öde Purgyel).[11] In chronological sequence, the three mythic traditions are referred to as: (1) Ultra Secret Tradition of the Spirits of the Dead called *The'urang* (yang-gsang the'u-rang-lugs), (2) Tradition of Renowned Bon (grags-pa bon-lugs), and (3) Secret Tradition of Buddhism (gsang-ba chos-lugs).[12] The first tradition describes the progenitor king as a descendant of a *the'urang* spirit from the land of the dead,[13] while the Bon tradition maintains his descent from the celestial (gnam) *lha* deities with close connections to the *tsen* (btsan) forces of the earth (sa) and the aquatic *lu* (klu) and ancestral *tshün* (mtshun) spirits of the underworld (sa-'og).[14] The Buddhist tradition proclaims an Indo-Buddhist identity and describes the progenitor as an exiled Indian prince. As Gibson has noted, this third tradition is almost certainly a "transparent attempt at legitimation by connection with the sacred land of Buddhism."[15] This is not the place to provide an overview of Haarh's elaborate discussion of these three traditions. It will suffice to evaluate certain pertinent conceptual features of the origin myths presented, especially those of the so-called Renowned Bon, for these traditions provide significant clues as to how death might have been conceived and dealt with during this early period.

Haarh argues extensively that each of the origin myths reflects important political transitions and religious transformations.[16] The first and most radical shift is preserved in the myth of the eighth king of the Tibetan dynasty, Drigum Tsenpo, and his son and successor Jatrhi (or Shakyhi), otherwise known as Pude Gungyel.[17] Versions of the myth are extant in a number of variant sources,[18] the earliest of which is found as a section of the Dunhuang manuscript Pelliot Tibetain (PT) 1287, the famous *Old Tibetan Chronicle* dating possibly to the late eighth or early ninth century.[19] It is the later Buddhist account, however, from the fourteenth-century *Mirror Illuminating the Royal Genealogies* [*Rgyal-rabs gsal-ba'i me-long*] that has prevailed as the version most commonly endorsed.[20] In that account, Drigum Tsenpo challenges his minister Longam Tazi[21] to a battle in which the king's "*mu*-cord" (*dmu-thag*) is severed and he himself is killed.[22] According to the cosmology of the Renowned Bon tradition, Tibetan kings prior to Drigum were said to have descended from heaven by this special rope. At death, they returned to heaven by the same means and left no physical remains. With the death of Drigum Tsenpo, however, this crucial link connecting the ruler to heaven was broken, and a corpse now remained on earth. This required the establishment (or importation) of a ritual technique for dealing with corpses, and thus Drigum and the following kings were memorialized according to a newly prescribed funeral rite and subsequently buried in monumental tombs. According to the myth's narrative, just after Drigum's death his three sons, Shatrhi, Nyatrhi, and Jatrhi, flee to the three districts of Kongpo, Nyangpo, and Powo, respectively. In a dream Drigum's queen has a vision of the mountain-god Yarlha Shampo (of Nyang) and later gives birth to a miraculous son, Dzangibu Rulakye. This son avenges his father's death by first murdering Longam Tazi and then recovering Drigum's corpse, which had been deposed in the river Nyangchu Kyamo. Rulakye is said also to have built a tomb for the king at Darthang in Chingyul[23] and brought the prince Jatrhi back from Powo. Jatrhi was later enthroned as the ninth Tibetan emperor Pude Gungyel.

The earlier Dunhuang version of the myth from the *Old Tibetan Chronicle* gives a different account of Drigum Tsenpo's death at the hands of Longam Tazi. Here the battle between Drigum and Longam ends with the king being led into the sky by a deity called Dela Gungyel, a name that appears to represent the ruler's "soul" (*bla*) or more specifically his "embodied soul" (*sku-bla*).[24] By some obscure means Longam Tazi causes Dela Gungyel to be cast into the womb (*rum*) of the Mount Tise (Kailash) glacier where, as a result, both Dela Gungyel and Drigum finally die.[25] As in the Buddhist version, Drigum's corpse is recovered by a son of unusual pedigree, in this case he is named Pükyibu Ngarlekye. This boy finds that the king's body has been deposited in the stomach of a serpent deity (*klu*),[26] and together the two strike a deal. In return for the corpse, Pükyibu Ngarlekye must give the serpent a human ransom with very specific features such as eyes that open from below like those of a bird. The boy finds an appropriate substitute in the person of a young girl. As recompense, the girl's mother asks that in the future certain burial rituals be performed for the corpses of dead kings. After pledging to fulfill this request, Pükyibu Ngarlekye takes the daughter and leaves her in the stomach of the serpent as a ransom for the release of Drigum's corpse, which is later ritually buried by the king's two sons, Nyakyhi and Shakyhi (Jatrhi in the Buddhist account). The former son became ruler of Kongpo while the latter settled in Chingwa and became known as Pude Gungyel, the ninth Tibetan king. Haarh argues that this particular version of the story functions as a unique and unprecedented etiological explanation of the origin of the rites performed in the preparation of the corpse for burial.[27] Likewise, the myth also seems to provide justification for the ritual offering of ransoms (*glud*) in the form of sacrifice.[28] In this regard, it is noteworthy that ransom rituals, in benign form, continue to play an active and fundamental role in Tibetan funeral liturgy.[29]

The myth of Drigum's death, in all of its variants, points very clearly to changes in religious and cultural traditions. The emperor Drigum Tsenpo, as Tucci noted, "personifies the memory of a transition of great significance in the history of Tibetan culture."[30] The myth is symbolic of a transition not only between two very different concepts of ruler but also between an older cosmology and that of an entirely new religious worldview, or more precisely between two distinct conceptions of the living and the dead. Haarh writes:

> Tucci describes Gri-gum-bstan-po [Drigum Tsenpo] as "a symbol of a fracture in the current of ideas", and in a wider sense we may imply that the time symbolized by the two kings [Drigum and his son Pude Gungyel] indicates a crisis, political and religious, and a transition between two ages of culture symbolized by father and son. We have seen, moreover, that the essential difference between these two ages is to be found in the change of religious ideology or, more concretely, in the fundamentally different concepts of Man's position towards the world of the defunct. Having previously been haunted by fear of the dead, defenseless towards the powers of the earth, Man now received means to master and subdue the chthonic powers. We have postulated that this change of the concept of the mutual relation between Living and Dead presented the spiritual background for the rise of the Dynasty.[31]

This crucial shift in religious paradigms was fundamentally a change in funeral custom—a change personified in the mythic form of Drigum's son and successor, Jatrhi/Shakyhi, or Pude Gungyel. What distinguishes the two paradigms is the presence in the latter of a new sense of the meaning of death and of the place of the dead vis-à-vis the living. In this way, the myth is viewed as a symbolic narrative of the introduction of a new and perhaps foreign constellation of concepts concerning the recently and distantly deceased. These concepts expressed a particular understanding of the dead and of the ritual treatment of corpses.

> The idea of a second world of existence prevailed, a world of the Dead which in its entity was antagonistic towards that of the Living, the fundamental difference between the Living and the Dead Being was contingent upon the presence or absence of bLa, life-power. Death meant no end, but the transition of Man to a new form of existence in which he, the Dead, conscious of his loss of life-power, became inimical towards the Living, and noxious or mischievous,

gdug pa can, to him in his desire to recover his own life-power or destroy that of the Living. To the Tibetans these ideas were the cause of a constant fear of the dead relatives, the ancestors, or the realm of the dead as a whole, from which the ancestral cult or the cult of the dead of their imagined manifestations took its origin.[32]

Such notions were introduced into Tibet, or more precisely into the Yarlung valley, via the introduction of a new and somewhat obscure ritual tradition perhaps hailing originally from the vicinity of Kongpo.[33] This new ritual tradition would later be identified retroactively with the Bonpo funeral cult known as "cemetery Bon" (dur-bon).[34] Since it was believed that the dead, the ancestral spirits (mtshun), continued to manifest a hostile power over the living, the primary and predominant function of this new cult was therefore to contain the aggressive menace of the dead by closing them off in tombs. A type of ritual expert or funeral priest (dur-gshen)[35] served this purpose by a special ritual treatment of the corpse and by a variety of mortuary rites in general.[36] The same belief in the effective relationship between the living and the dead has endured throughout Tibet's religious history and is still prevalent in the Buddhist funeral rites associated with, for example, the *Peaceful and Wrathful Deities* and the *Liberation upon Hearing*, where we find explicit the idea that surviving relatives can positively effect the condition of their dead by performing various rituals aimed at purifying the sins of the deceased.

Since it was also accepted in this ancient period that in life the soul (bla) was capable of wandering ('khyams-pa) away from the body, or worse yet that it might be seduced and taken away by demons or other evil manifestations of the dead,[37] a further object of these ritual specialists was to shepherd the soul (bla-'gugs), or recapture it by means of a ransom (bla-glud), to summon its return (bla-'bod), and to guarantee its safe passage (lam-bstan). This rather ancient Tibetan belief in the vulnerability of the soul seems to have instilled a profound and longstanding sense of fear and anxiety in the face of crises brought on by illness and death. Evidence for this has survived in the later ritual literature of the Buddhists and Bonpos that describe techniques for ransoming the soul (bla-bslu), for calling the life (tshe-'gugs),[38] and for safely guiding ('dren-pa) the deceased through the perilous pathways of the bardo (bar-do 'phrang). In this light, we can be confident that a real continuity exists between the ritual beliefs of ancient Tibet and those preserved by the later ritual traditions.[39] As I will show, for instance, the Tibetan notion of the soul (bla) and its attendant rituals, rather than dissolving into the collective memory of an archaic past, seems instead to have been adopted into and only superficially masked by certain Indo-Buddhist concepts, most explicitly the theory of a postmortem intermediate state and of a consciousness that sheds the physical body at death and wanders ('khyams-pa) in search of its next birth.

Clearly, the conflation of both indigenous and imported concepts contributed to the formation in Tibet of an entirely unique liturgical program that can be appropriately termed "bardo ritual" (bar-do cho-ga).[40] This specific ritual program, however, does not appear to have been systematically formulated before the thirteenth or fourteenth centuries, although there is evidence that some features of the practice might have been established as early as the eleventh. Some of the developments of this liturgical program may be hidden from us, but enough traces have been left behind to indicate that even in its earliest stages the Tibetan bardo ritual emphasized the purification of sins through ritual actions and prayers devised for the dead that would follow the deceased through the extended process of purification in the bardo and incorporation into a new existence. A distinctive feature of the bardo ritual was the evocation of the journey after death during which the deceased's destiny might still be altered.

The Path of Wandering Souls

Further examples of ancient Tibetan ideas concerning death, including some Buddhist adaptations of indigenous beliefs relating to the dead, are known from several other manuscripts found at Dunhuang. The most notable work is probably manuscript PT 239, parts I–II,[41] which was studied first by Marcelle Lalou (part 1), followed then by Rolf Stein (part 2), and later discussed at some length by Ariane Macdonald.[42] The manuscript consists of eighteen folios containing two smaller texts (I–II), the first appearing on the front side and the second on the back. To the end of the eighteenth side of the first text an additional folio is attached that has been catalogued PT 733, from a comparative reading of another version of the same work (contained in PT 37).[43] A possible title of the first part of PT 239/I is found on the recto of PT 733, where is written "teaching of the path to the god realm" (*lha-yul du lam bstan-pa*).[44] The very first sentence of the text, however, "teaching of the path of the dead" or "showing the path of the dead" (*gshin-lam bstan-pa*),[45] seems to provide a more fitting title, given the general subject of the narrative. Therefore, for lack of an official designated title, I shall call this short text *Showing the Path of the Dead*. Since the text obviously begins as if it were already in progress, Macdonald has remarked that the dangling first sentence may indicate that PT 239/I, *Showing the Path of the Dead*, comprises only part of a more complete funerary ritual that was perhaps similar to that described in PT 37.[46]

A central theme of these Dunhuang texts is that of the various paths by which the dead travel. In the particular example of the two-part manuscript PT 239/I–II, the influence of Buddhist ideas becomes quite explicit. In this dual text we find that the indigenous Tibetan notion of the deceased's path connecting the two opposing regions of gods (*lha-yul*) and ghosts (*gshin-yul*) has now been adapted to the Buddhist notion of rebirth in the round of existence (*saṃsāra*).[47] Following this view, Yoshiro Imaeda suggests that the text might be situated on the brink of a new beginning in Tibetan religious history, the first stage in the transformation of pre-Buddhist rites into Buddhist practices.[48] Per Kvaerne, on the other hand, adopts a more contentious perspective:

> When combating the ancient death rituals, Buddhist strategy was to retain at least part of the ancient terminology while systematically identifying it with Buddhist ideas, thus emptying it of its original content. This strategy was in

the end so successful that by the 10th or 11th century the ancient beliefs outlined above had apparently been more or less forgotten by the Tibetans, although as we shall see, certain elements, now with a completely new significance, were preserved.[49]

Unfortunately, Kvaerne gives no examples of this ancient terminology erased
by Buddhist strategy, but his comments do echo Haarh's statement regarding
Buddhism's combative encounter with certain indigenous concepts of the
dead:

> When Buddhism began to spread in Tibet, its representatives recognized on a
> broad basis the existing traditions, gradually modifying them in conformance
> to the ideology of the Doctrine. Only where the concept of the Dead and the
> funeral and ancestral cult were concerned does Buddhism seem to have dis-
> played radical efforts at suppression, so that the literature presents only ves-
> tiges of these features of Tibetan culture before Buddhism.[50]

Some insight into what may have been behind these alleged Buddhist efforts
at suppression of preexisting non-Buddhist ritual may be drawn from one of
the earliest known Tibetan historical records of the imperial period, the influential *Testament of Ba* [*Dba'/Sba'-bzhed*].[51] This work offers an account
of the Tibetan adoption of Buddhism during the reign of Trhi Songdetsen
(742–c. 797) at the end of the eighth century and narrates the agonistic events
leading up to the establishment of Samye, the first court-sanctioned Buddhist
temple in Tibet. The work exists in a number of variant versions, the original
apparently is lost to history. Recently, however, an old manuscript version
was discovered in Lhasa, the central core of which appears to date to the eleventh century.[52] If that dating is correct this would be the oldest edition of the
Testament of Ba currently available.

For my present purposes, this newly discovered *Testament of Ba* is of
particular interest for the possibly even older section appended to the end of
the narrative proper, titled "History of the Ritual Food Offering" [*Zad-gtad
lo-rgyus*].[53] This short appendix details a court controversy, following the
death of Trhi Songdetsen, between Bonpos and Buddhists over the appropriate imperial rites to be performed and the ultimate triumph of the Buddhist
funeral liturgy.[54] This particular debate must be viewed within the context of
a persisting antagonism between the two groups that, according to the *Testament of Ba*, had culminated only a generation before with the suppression of
the Buddhist funerary rites following the death of Trhi Songdetsen's father,
the emperor Trhi Detsuktsen (705–755).[55] These rites, called *tshe* (probably
for a type of food offering or ritual fast to assist the dead),[56] had been introduced earlier by the Chinese princess Jincheng Gongzhu (d. 739), the wife of
Trhi Detsuktsen.[57] The Buddhist *tshe* rites were eventually reintroduced in
secrecy after the sudden deaths of the two children of the minister Ba Selnang,
one of the central protagonists of the *Testament of Ba*.[58]

The "History of the Ritual Food Offering" opens after Trhi Songdetsen has
already passed away and when his son and successor, Munetsenpo, is still in
his minority. The royal ministers in charge of official decisions in the inter-

regnum declare that the imperial funeral rites for Trhi Songdetsen must be performed according to Bon custom. When several hundred Bonpo priests arrive for this purpose, the young Munetsenpo relays a dream he has had the night before in which he has seen his father in the company of the Buddhas Vairocana and Vajrapāṇi and the Bodhisattva Mañjuśrī. All of them were reciting sutras and other Buddhist doctrinal texts in the Pure Land of Akaniṣṭa. Munetsenpo interprets the dream as an omen indicating that his father's funeral rites cannot be performed by the Bonpos but must be performed according to Buddhist custom. With that the court ministers, the Bonpo priests, and a group of Buddhist monk-scholars assemble to formally discuss the matter. The lead minister speaks first and briefly recounts the history of the Tibetan imperial funeral rites, emphasizing how in the past great fortune and prosperity had been secured for Tibet through the practice of these traditional rites. He concludes with a warning that should the Bon funeral be abandoned in favor of the Buddhist ritual, Tibet's political authority would certainly deteriorate. The Buddhists are then given an opportunity to respond, their spokesman is the famous monk Vairocana of the Pagor clan.

Vairocana begins by describing the basic principles of Buddhist cosmology, the conception of existence in the mundane world as an endless round of rebirth governed by karma, and holds out the promise of a completely pure and joyous realm of buddhas that transcends the suffering domain of birth and death. He proceeds to address the specific problems inherent in the views and practices of the Bonpos by first establishing the powerlessness of their mighty deities in the face of the great divine protectors of Buddhism. Then, he goes on to demonstrate the ineffectiveness of Bon funerals and the inevitable misfortunes that result from their performance by underscoring the miserable fate of the neighboring kingdoms that had patronized Bon and worshiped its deities—the history of the conquest and fall of these once mighty kingdoms offered as proof of the ruinous nature of Bon rituals.[59] Vairocana concludes by appealing to the lawlike operation of karma, stressing the moral authority of Buddhism and highlighting the fruits that can be obtained through virtuous action, namely, the rewards of a higher rebirth. In the end, Vairocanca's arguments succeed in persuading the young emperor Munetsenpo to decide in favor of the Buddhists, and the funeral is performed according to Buddhist custom.

Although this story sheds some light on how later Tibetan tradition views the rationale behind the imperial adoption of Buddhist ritual to replace existing pre-Buddhist practices—and in this light, the goal of the text might best be understood as legitimizing the importation of foreign death rites—the text offers very little specific detail about either set of rituals. Indeed, we learn almost nothing of the content of the Bon funerals and only a few fine points about the Buddhist liturgy, though descriptions of the purported subject of the text, the so-called ritual food offering (zas-gtad), are nowhere to be found. Interestingly, in the context of later custom, the elements of the Buddhist rite that are briefly mentioned in the text include the setting up of mandalas (the Vajradhātu), the recitation of mantra, and the reading of scripture such as the

Prajñāpāramitā-sūtra (Sutra on the Perfection of Wisdom). The text ends by identifying the main text and mandala allegedly used in all funerals from the time of Munetsenpo onward, these being the *Tantra on the Elimination of All Evil Rebirths* [*Sarvadurgatipariśodhana-tantra, Ngan-song thams-cad yong-su sbyong rgyud*][60] and the mandala of Kunrik (Sarvavidyā), a deity associated with the Buddha Vairocana.[61] I will have reason to return to these important subjects later.

Here, I am particularly concerned with the specific components of Bon funerals—the pre-Buddhist rites, in other words—that so troubled the Buddhists. A brief reference in the "History of the Ritual Food Offering" text suggests that the compassionless killing of animals may have been a major point of contention with the early Buddhists in Tibet.[62] The predominance of animal and possibly human sacrifice[63] in the funerary rituals of the early court priests ran counter to the fundamental moral principles of Buddhism, although Samuel has suggested that Tibetan emphasis on this point probably had more to do historically with the marking of "Tibetan Buddhist dominance over local pre-Buddhist deity cults" than with traditional Buddhist prohibitions against taking life.[64] The disavowal and self-righteous condemnation of ritual sacrifice among Buddhists in Tibet is preserved, for example, in a passage from a central text included in the *Liberation upon Hearing*, wherein the deceased (and living audience) is warned that sacrifices performed by the surviving relatives may lead to rebirth in hell:

> When visions of the higher realms arise, should your relatives [*gson-po*] near the place you left behind sacrifice many sentient beings dedicated for the benefit of the dead, you will have impure visions and become extremely angry. This will cause you to be reborn in hell. So whatever [your relatives] do in the place you left behind, do not grow angry, but cultivate love.[65]

At the same time of the Buddhist attacks on indigenous practices, the early Buddhists of Tibet, as Imaeda has observed, "attempted on the one hand to find in the terminology of the pre-Buddhist religion a meaning that conformed to Buddhist doctrine, and on the other hand, to transpose the indigenous notions onto those Buddhist ideas more or less related."[66] Clearly, these ancient concepts were never wholly suppressed, and, indeed, some were fully assimilated with only minor variation into the Buddhist worldview that very quickly came to dominate the culture of Tibet. The old concepts of the wandering soul (*bla-'khyams-pa*), of its ritual ransom (*glud*), and of its guidance (*lam-bstan*) are just a few examples of ideas that have survived and flourished in Buddhist Tibet.

Thus far the particular ancient materials introduced here have offered only vague and inexplicit ideas concerning the hereafter. The emphasis in those sources is on ritual to guarantee a safe passage for the dead and protection against their certain hostility. Returning to Dunhuang manuscript PT 239/I, *Showing the Path of the Dead*, it is apparent that a dominant Buddhist orientation prevails and the afterdeath state is described in very clear terms.[67] Here the deceased's journey may follow one of three negative paths (*ngan-song*):

one leading into hell (na-rag), another into the realm of the hungry ghosts (yi-dwags), and a third into the realm of animals (dud-'gro). Each of the three lower realms is associated with a specific bodhisattva—Avalokiteśvara, Gaganagañja, and Durgatipariśodhana, respectively—whose mantra the deceased (tshe-'das-pa) is called on to invoke in order to escape that particular evil destiny. A fourth and final path is indicated that leads upward to the northern summit of Mount Meru, called Ālaka, divine residence of Buddha Vajrapāṇi. This is the sacred realm of the gods, a place of peace and perfect happiness.[68] Ultimately, the deceased must endeavor to reach this higher realm. The apparent purpose of the text was thus to ensure a safe and successful journey upward. This goal was accomplished in part by calling the dead by name (ming-nas smos-nas or ming-nas brjod-nas), offering descriptions of the specific topography of the lower worlds, and reminding ('dren-pa) the deceased of the proper mantras to be recited.

Given its principal objective and the prominent role played by the mantra of the bodhisattva Durgatipariśodhana,[69] it is almost certain that the text Showing the Path of the Dead was connected intimately to the ritual cycle of the Tantra on the Elimination of All Evil Rebirths.[70] This important tantra was among the earliest Buddhist Sanskrit works translated into Tibetan.[71] As I have noted, the text offers a distinctive funeral litany centered around the cult of Kunrik (Sarvavidyā) and associated with the Buddha Vairocana.[72] It includes a host of liturgical instructions on confession rites (bshags), ransom certificates (byang-bu), fire offerings (sbyin-sreg), "dredging the depths of hell" practices (na-rak dong-sprug), wrathful deity meditations (khro-bo'i lha sgom-pa), and cremation rites (ro-sreg).[73] In this respect, the ritual appears clearly to have been somewhat akin to the practices later developed more fully in the bardo rituals of the fourteenth and fifteenth centuries. Indeed, it is likely that the death rituals belonging to the cycle of the Elimination of All Evil Rebirths might have served a similar function in the ritual life of Tibetans in the centuries leading up to the systematization of Tibetan Buddhist liturgies like those prescribed in the Liberation upon Hearing. The Dunhuang manuscript Showing the Path of the Dead may represent an early and very much simplified prototype of this larger program.

The prevalence of both sacrificial rites and the purification practices of the Elimination of All Evil Rebirths in Tibetan funerary custom is indicated in the later texts accompanying the rituals of the Liberation upon Hearing. In the Direct Introduction to the Bardo of Becoming [Srid-pa bar-do'i ngo-sprod], a core text from that cycle, we find reference to various rituals performed for the dead, including the sacrifice of animals and the purification of sins.[74] This is noteworthy because certain components of Tibetan death practice are identified here that must have coexisted alongside the liturgy of the Liberation upon Hearing, and most likely predated it.

Again, when the kangkani ritual of the dead is recited for your benefit and the Elimination of Evil Rebirths and so forth are performed for your sake, you will see with subtle clairvoyance impurities and the performers being distracted and so forth, breaking their vows and commitments, and acting carelessly. In this way, you will be aware of their lack of faith and disbelief, fear and sinful actions, and inaccuracies [*ma-dag-pa*] in the liturgy and rites, and so you will think "Alas! They are deceiving me, certainly they are deceiving me!" Thinking this you will become very saddened and depressed, and losing your respect and devotion, you will disbelieve and lose faith, and so you will certainly go to the lower realms.[75]

Here we see two rituals mentioned explicitly by name, the so-called *kangkani* ritual of the dead and the *Elimination of Evil Rebirths*. I have as yet been able to identify precisely the *kangkani* rite, although Evans-Wentz remarks that it involved the recitation of mantra believed to transmute sacrificial food into acceptable offerings for the dead.[76] In like manner, Thurman translates *kangkani* as "exorcistic food-offering rites."[77] The Tibetan term *kangka* refers to a type of bird, a crane or heron, with a black head and white back that feeds on corpses (synonyms include *kang-bya* and *dur-bya*). As a ritual *kangkani*, therefore, might refer to the common Tibetan practice of "sky burial" or vulture-disposal (lit., "bird-toss", *bya-gtor*).[78] However, according to Matthew Kapstein, it is more likely that the term *kangkani* refers to the *dhāraṇi* of the buddha Akṣobhya, who is frequently invoked in connection with funeral rites.[79] The second ritual mentioned in the text is clearly a reference to the practices associated with the *Tantra on the Elimination of All Evil Rebirths*, which supports my claim that the older rites affiliated with this tantra had survived and persisted in the face of newer and perhaps more competitive ritual developments represented in texts such as the *Liberation upon Hearing*.

A striking feature of the passage quoted here is its explicit criticism of those who perform the rites improperly and with poor attitude. Could it be that this might also imply some questioning of the true effectiveness of the older rituals over and against the instructions of the *Liberation upon Hearing* itself? In the earlier rites, such as those in the *Tantra on the Elimination of All Evil Rebirths*, prayers and ritual actions emphasized the purification of the dead, and particularly of the corpse, over that of the soul. In Dunhuang manuscript PT 239/I, *Showing the Path of the Dead*, we encounter a slight shift of emphasis away from the body, with the goal of the ritual becoming more about leading the deceased safely along the path that leads to the heavens above. Later, in the so-called bardo rituals, such as those accompanying the texts of the *Peaceful and Wrathful Deities* and the *Liberation upon Hearing*, we still find the notion of the varied paths of the dead, but now we see more of an emphasis on the consciousness of the deceased with particular stress placed on the importance of guiding the consciousness through a long process of purification in the bardo and eventual incorporation into a new existence. The concept of an extended transitional period between death and rebirth has a rich history in Tibet and is thus a subject that requires further discussion. We will examine this concept in the next chapter.

3 🍃 ─────────────────────

Transitions: The Buddhist
Intermediate State

Although we can cite evidence of a pervasive Buddhist orientation in the old
Tibetan documents from Dunhuang on the subject of death and the afterlife,
very little is known about the status of the Buddhist intermediate state
(*antarābhava*) doctrine during Tibet's imperial age (seventh through mid–
ninth century). We do know, however, that in Tibet the idea surfaces as a
distinctive doctrine sometime during the early decades of the eleventh century among certain tantric groups. It seems that when the Indo-Buddhist intermediate state theory entered the Tibetan religious arena from India, it had
already been reconfigured and embellished as a distinctively tantric idea and,
in Tibet, was initially absorbed into the indigenous socioreligious patterns
that had survived the influx of Buddhism, only later to emerge as a thoroughly
Tibetanized concept.

As we might expect, the earliest Tibetan notion of a postmortem transitional
state or bardo was developed from a non-Tibetan prototype based on the Indo-
Buddhist model expounded in the Abhidharma literature, particularly that of
the Sarvāstivāda school. In that model, following closely the patterns set forth
by Vasubandhu (400–480), four stages in the life-cycle of a sentient being were
recognized: (1) birth (*upapattibhava*), (2) the period from birth to the moment
of dying (*pūrvakālabhava*), (3) death itself (*maranabhava*), and (4) the period
between death and the next birth (*antarābhava*).[1] Over time changes in the
interpretation of this scheme were brought on by a synthesis of the orthodox
Abhidharma perspective and particular esoteric tantric strategies. The merger
inspired further innovations in both theory and practice.

In this chapter, I will review some of the principal Indian Buddhist texts
that put forth the intermediate-state theory and offer a few historical observations on the development of some of the more significant Tibetan changes

and points of divergence from the earlier Indian concepts. I will conclude by examining the major sources that exerted a profound influence on the creation in Tibet of a coherent liturgical system constructed around the bardo theory. This system, the so-called bardo ritual (*bar-do cho-ga*), is best exemplified by the fifteenth-century ritual program of the *Great Liberation upon Hearing in the Bardo*, which belongs to the large treasure cycle of Karma Lingpa, the *Self-Liberated Wisdom of the Peaceful and Wrathful Deities*.

The Indian Concept

In an earlier study I attempted to establish a thematic link between the Buddhist intermediate state and the Vedic and post-Brāhmaṇic realm of paternal ancestors (*pitṛloka*).[2] My goal was to set up certain questions regarding the conceptual origins of the intermediate state in Buddhist discourse. In particular, I was interested in the specific factors that might have led to the early Buddhist appropriation of the Vedic *gandharva* in discussions of the postmortem intermediate state. I do not intend to repeat my earlier arguments here, since my conclusions were based for the most part on rather impressionistic grounds. The main questions I raised, however, still remain to be addressed by specialists in the field, although it would appear that some answers may soon be forthcoming. In this regard, the recent work of Robert Kritzer deserves explicit mention. In a series of concise and well-documented articles based on primary Sanskrit, Chinese, and Japanese sources (most of which are not available in western languages), Kritzer offers important preliminary materials for a detailed textual history of the intermediate state.[3] The following summary of the Indian Buddhist literature on this subject is based fundamentally on the contributions of Kritzer and a few scholars before him.

Among the early schools of Buddhism in India, the status of the intermediate state, of literally existence (*bhava*) in an interval (*antarā*), inspired considerable controversy. Not all of the sects accepted the theory, most notably the Theravāda.[4] The problem it seems, as formulated for example in the *Kathāvatthu* (Points of Controversy) of Moggaliputta Tissa (second century B.C.E.),[5] centered around divergent interpretations of the sutra expression "completed existence within the interval" (*antarābhavūpagaṃ*).[6] One view was that this phrase supported claims for the existence of an intermediate period of a week or more before rebirth. The counterposition based itself on the fact that such an intermediate period was never taught explicitly by the Buddha. Citing references to the Buddha's statement that there are only three realms of existence—desire (*kāma-dhātu*), form (*rūpa-dhātu*), and the formless (*arūpa-dhātu*)—the opponents (i.e., Theravādins) argued that an intervening realm could not be included in those three cateogories and thus does not exist. To complicate matters even more, the schools that did proclaim the intermediate state, such as the Sarvāstivāda and Sautrāntika, were not always in agreement as to how that term should best be understood. It was to this purpose that Vasubandhu in his monumental *Abhidharmakośa-bhāṣya* (Com-

mentary on the Treasury of Abhidharma) codified the theories of the intermediate state and compiled all the arguments in favor of its existence. In later
centuries, the views expressed in the *Abhidharmakośa*, representing essentially the position of the Mūlasarvāstivāda, became subsequently the standard
presentation of postmortem transition adopted by the Tibetans in the earliest
phases of the introduction of Buddhism to Tibet.[7]

The third chapter of Vasubandhu's *Abhidharmakośa-bhāṣya*, entitled "Exposition of the World" [*Lokanirdeśa*], contains a number of descriptive epi-
thets for the intermediate state aimed at proving its reality. Bear in mind that in
this context the term "intermediate state" is employed interchangeably to refer
to both the postmortem state of transition and to the subtle entity that abides in
that state. In the relevant sections, Vasubandhu attempts to establish through
scholastic reasoning the existence and essential characteristics of the liminal
being. His presentation can be summarized in five basic points.[8] First, the
intermediate-state passenger is defined as "that being which arises between the
existence at death and the existence at rebirth between (these) two locations in
order to gain rebirth."[9] Second, the intermediate state must exist because (I) it
is called by that name in the relevant scriptures; (2) it is a *gandharva*;[10] (3) it is
named among the five "nonreturners" (*anāgāmin*)—individuals who, having
left this world, are born in a Pure Land where they will be set to achieve eventual buddhahood;[11] and (4) it is substantiated in the *Saptasatpuruṣagati-sūtra*
(Sutra on the Seven Destinies for Good Persons).[12] Third, the shape and form
of the intermediate-state being resembles that of the beings in the realm where
it is to be reborn. Fourth, the intermediate-state being can be seen by the beings of its own class and by those with the pure divine eyes.[13] Moreover, its
organs are complete, no one can resist it, and it cannot be turned away. Because the intermediate state being eats fragrance it is called *gandharva*, literally "that which eats [*arvati*] odors [*gandham*]."[14] The *gandharva*, in turn, is
the access (*sagamana*) through which the intermediate-state being, emerging from its previous existence (*pūrvakālabhava*), reaches its new existential
course (*gati*).[15] This leads us to point five, that rebirth occurs when the mind
(*mati*), troubled by intense oedipal desire on the sight of its future parents
having sex, is propelled into a new existence.[16] The *gandharva* enters the
womb and becomes male if it is attracted to its future mother and repulsed by
its father, or female if attracted to its future father and repulsed by its mother.
The disruptive thoughts of desire and hatred cause the mind to cohere to the
semen and blood found in the womb. At that point the aggregates (*skandhas*)
coagulate, the intermediate state being perishes, and the embryo is conceived.[17]

These descriptions found in Vasubandhu's *Abhidharmakośa-bhāṣya* were
not actually the earliest or even most detailed doctrinal exposition of the intermediate state in India.[18] That particular qualification is reserved for the
enormous compilation *Mahāvibhāṣā* (Great Commentary),[19] a second-century
Abhidharma commentary on the Sarvāstivādin *Jñānaprasthāna-śāstra* (Treatise on the Establishment of Knowledge).[20] The former work is extant only
in Chinese translation, and its chapter on the intermediate state has yet to be
critically examined in western-language sources. In the *Mahāvibhāṣā* we find

an elaborate description of the intermediate state that is strikingly similar to Vasubhandu's explanation.[21] The text offers several elaborate proofs for the existence of the intermediate state, with citations from various sutra passages adduced as evidence. Many of the topics discussed are already familiar from Vasubandhu's own account, including the three conditions necessary for conception (i.e., the mother must be healthy, the parents must be engaged in sexual intercourse, and a *gandharva* must be present), the five types of "nonreturner" (*anāgāmin*) and individuals who obtain nirvāṇa in the intermediate state (*antarāparinirvāyin*), the mechanism of rebirth, and the special characteristics of the liminal being.[22] Points of divergence between the *Mahāvibhāṣā* and the *Abhidharmakośa* are also evident. Kritzer suggests that a study of these differences may help scholars "understand the extent to which the great philosopher Vasubandhu deviates from Sarvāstivāda."[23] At any rate, we can conclude that the Sarvāstivādins and related schools, including the Sautrāntikas and Mahāyāna Yogācārins, posited and firmly supported the existence of a postmortem intermediate state and that this basic concept had been formalized by at least the fifth century.

In India the intermediate state was known also in several sutras, notably the *Garbhāvakrāntinirdeśa-sūtra* (Sutra on Entering the Womb)[24] and the *Saddharmasmṛtyupastāna-sūtra* (Sutra on Stability in Contemplation of the True Dharma).[25] Both scriptures at some point during their evolution appear to have been influenced by Abhidharma interpretations.[26] The *Garbhāvakrāntinirdeśa-sūtra* is extant in four versions, apparently the earliest being a Chinese translation.[27] This Chinese recension does not include many of the details found in the later versions from the *Mūlasarvāstivāda-vinaya* (Monastic Rules of the Mūlasarvāstivāda). These omitted elements are typically glossed in the Abhidharma texts, which suggests that the *Garbhāvakrāntinirdeśa* may have been influenced by that tradition later in its development.[28] Briefly, the *Mūlasarvāstivāda-vinaya* versions detail the progression of the intermediate-state being from the final moment of death to conception in the future mother's womb, and subsequently through each week of fetal development. The *Garbhāvakrāntinirdeśa* was unique on several levels. First, the text appears to have been the primary source for the elaborate descriptions of postmortem transition in the *Yogācārabhūmi* (Yogācāra Level).[29] Second, in Tibet the text came to represent one of the most significant canonical sources for Tibetan medical literature on the science of human reproduction and growth.[30] Third, it provided a standard source for later Tibetan presentations on death, transition, and rebirth. In particular, we find that the sutra was cited often in the relevant Tibetan literature of those schools that relied most heavily on the Indian canonical sources.[31]

The *Saddharmasmṛtyupastāna-sūtra*, an influential resource for descriptions of Buddhist cosmology, includes elaborate discussion of as many as seventeen individual intermediate states.[32] Some features of this exposition accord with certain Abhidharma interpretations and resemble later tantric descriptions that we encounter in the Tibetan literature. As an illustration, consider the following passage translated from the Chinese version of this sutra.

When a human being dies and is going to be reincarnated as a human being
... when the time of his death is approaching he sees these signs: he sees a
great rocky mountain lowering above him like a shadow. He thinks to himself, "The mountain might fall down on top of me," and he makes a gesture
with his hand as though to ward off this mountain. His brothers and kinsmen
and neighbours see him do this; but to them it seems that he is simply pushing
out his hand into space. Presently the mountain seems to be made of white cloth
and he clambers up this cloth. Then it seems to be made of red cloth. Finally,
as the time of his death approaches he sees a bright light, and being unaccus-
tomed to it as the time of his death he is perplexed and confused. He sees all
sorts of things such as are seen in dreams, because his mind is confused. He
sees his (future) father and mother making love, and seeing them a thought
crosses his mind, a perversity (viparyāsa) arises in him. If he is going to be
reborn as a man he sees himself making love with his mother and being hindered by his father; or if he is going to be reborn as a woman, he sees himself
making love with his father and being hindered by his mother. It is at that
moment that the Intermediate Existence is destroyed and life and consciousness arise and causality begins once more to work. It is like the imprint made
by a die; the die is then destroyed but the pattern has been imprinted.[33]

The cryptic references in this passage to the crumbling mountain, white and
red colors, and the bright light are all reminiscent of standard Tibetan tantric
descriptions of the process of dying and of the concurrent dissolution of the
psychophysical constituents. The image of the falling mountain, for example,
is usually found as the first of four so-called fearsome enemies (*'jigs-pa'i dgra-
bzhi*) experienced during the collapse of the elements earth, water, fire, and
wind.[34] The white and red colors are descriptive of the experience of dissolution of the subtle levels of consciousness. White refers to the white appearance (*snang-ba dkar*) envisioned after the disintegration of the eighty ordinary conceptions (*rang-bzhin brgyad-cu'i kun-rtog*), while red is the red
increase (*mched-pa dmar*) that arises after the previous mind of white appearance (*snang-ba dkar lam-pa'i sems*) disappears.[35] The bright light is quite
obviously a reference to the clear light of death (*'chi-ba'i 'od-gsal*), the most
fundamental level of "reality-itself."

The conflation of a Buddhist tantric model on the orthodox sutric concept
of intermediate states inspired much innovation. Certainly by the fifth century
the Abhidharmic descriptions of the transitional state had been solidified, following a standardized model first established in works such as the *Mahāvibhāṣā*.
Subsequent transformations and amendments to this scheme would not be widespread until tantrism began its sweep across northern India in the seventh and
eighth centuries. The Buddhist tantric siddha cults of this period and beyond
co-opted, reinterpreted, and embellished the earlier intermediate-state theory
in the context of specific metaphysical and soteriological projects that were in
part defined and codified in the esoteric and highly controversial scriptures called
tantras. These tantric siddha traditions were introduced into Tibet through diverse and complicated channels beginning in the eleventh century.

A paucity of sufficient historical material has for the most part prevented
scholars from solving many of the problems relating to the introduction and

establishment of the siddha traditions in Tibet. Despite a multitude of informative biographies of the most renowned Indian and Tibetan tantrikas, an exhaustive and thorough history of the Tibetan siddha movement has not yet appeared.[36] This fact makes it difficult for us to explore the Tibetan developments of a tantric concept of the intermediate state within well-documented contexts. Nevertheless, we can scrutinize and reevaluate the existing Tibetan sources, many of which are biographical in nature, and begin to trace various conceptual developments and patterns of dissemination. In this regard, a chronological focus on the classification schemes of the concept of bardo and the attention to details pertaining to lineal relations should give us some indication of the movement of this idea in Tibet. The development of specifically tantric theories of the intermediate state on Tibetan soil will be the focus of the remaining sections of this chapter.

Tantric Developments and the Siddha Transmissions in Tibet

One of the most striking developments of the tantric reinterpretation of the intermediate state was the expansion of the term's meaning to include a plurality of diverse intermediate states. It seems that this broadening of the semantic horizon may have already been prepared for by the doctrine of the four "existences" (*bhava*) and by some earlier conflation of the Abhidharma intermediate-state theory with the doctrine of a buddha's three bodies (*trikāya, sku-gsum*)—reality body (*dharmakāya, chos-sku*), enjoyment body (*saṃbhogakāya, longs-sku*), and emanation body (*nirmāṇakāya, sprul-sku*). The triune arrangement of a buddha's body in combination with aspects of the intermediate-state concept was then grafted onto the elaborate twofold yogic system of what the Tibetans were later to classify as Supreme Yoga Tantra (*anuttarayoga-tantra*), in which were described the successive stages referred to as the generation phase (*utpannakrama, bskyed-rim*) and the completion phase (*saṃpannakrama, rdzogs-rim*). Various teaching-lineages (*parampara, brgyud*) of this tantric program were introduced into Tibet as early as the eleventh century.

Briefly, according to standard Tibetan exegesis of the Supreme Yoga program, the generation phase involves a series of contemplative techniques designed to transform the practitioner's awareness of mundane forms, sounds, and thoughts and to enhance recognition of these as expressions of specific deities, mantras, and pristine wisdom (*ye-shes*). During this phase the meditator gradually constructs a mandala and imagines that he or she and the central deity are one and the same entity. This self-visualization process is said to function similarly to the practice called "bringing the three bodies to the path" (*sku-gsum lam-'khyer*). Here, "path" refers to the generation-phase meditation itself, and the three bodies are linked conceptually to a threefold scheme related in various degrees to death (*'chi-ba*), intermediate state (*bar-do*), and rebirth (*srid-pa*), depending on the particular system employed.[37]

The completion phase of tantric practice, on the other hand, consists of a series of advanced yogic techniques involving the radical manipulation of the
psychophysical energies—the winds (*lung*) and seminal fluids (*thig-le*)—
within the channels (*rtsa*) of the subtle body (*phra-ba'i lus*) to bring about
transformative nonordinary states of consciousness, in many cases said to be
identical with the experience of dying. The overall purpose is to develop direct experience of the pristine wisdom (*ye-shes*) induced by the four types of
bliss (*dga'-ba bzhi*). It is during this phase that there is an actual mixing or
blending (*bsres-ba*) of the three bodies on the path, by which the successful
practitioner is said to overcome ordinary death, intermediate state, and rebirth
and to attain the trinity of buddhahood. The history of the bardo in Tibet is
essentially the history of conceptual developments within the framework of this
twofold system of tantric practice. A variety of distinctive reformulations of
the bardo concept occurred as a consequence of the proliferation of instructional lineages adhering to the diverse teachings of particular yogis, which seems
to have begun in Tibet by at least the eleventh century and possibly much earlier.

Tibetan tantric interpretations and descriptions of the intermediate state
are largely contained in a genre of literature known as instructional advice
(*gdams-ngag*).[38] This category of literature comprises teachings on a multitude of yogic and contemplative techniques believed to have been inspired
from the hands-on experience of advanced tantrikas. All the major and minor
Tibetan traditions possess such a literature.[39] As Matthew Kapstein has noted,
the genre of instructional advice "has come to form the basis for an important set of distinctions among Tibetan Buddhist traditions, corresponding in
general to distinctions of lineage, while crosscutting distinctions of sect."[40]
The preeminence of lineage and sect in this context cannot be overstated. In
Tibet, as it was in India, the transmission of esoteric religious instruction was
dominated in most cases by direct oral exchange between teachers and disciples. Over time these individual teaching-lineages crystallized and were
arranged into distinct systems of practice associated with particular sects and
groups of tantric texts. The vast majority of these lineages or religious
"schools" emerged in Tibet during the Buddhist renaissance of the eleventh
century, at the beginning of the period of the so-called later propagation of
the doctrine (*bstan-pa phyi-dar*).[41] Around this time, those groups that held
firm to the tantric scriptural traditions established during the period of the
former propagation of the doctrine (*bstan-pa snga-dar*)—or at the very least
to traditions claiming to be from that early period—came to be known as the
"ancient ones" or Nyingmapa (*rnying-ma-pa*), in contradistinction to the "new
ones," or Sarmapa (*gsar-ma-pa*), those groups following the more current
scriptural traditions derived from new translations of Sanskrit works imported
directly from India.

By the thirteenth century the numerous traditions of instructional advice
circulating throughout Tibet had been classified into an eightfold scheme.[42]
This is not the place for a discussion of all eight categories, since only two of
them are of interest here: namely, the instructional precepts of the Nyingmapa
and, among the Sarma traditions, the instructional precepts of the Kagyupa.

The former set of instructions were derived primarily from the teachings of Padmasambhava and Vimilamitra. The instructional precepts affiliated with the various Kagyu lineages were derived essentially from the teachings of the Indian siddhas Tilopa (988–1069), Nāropa (1016–1100), and Maitrīpa and transmitted to a few notable Tibetans such as Marpa Chökyi Lodrö (1012–1097) and Khyungpo Neljor (d. c. 1135). Much of the instructional advice literature of both the Kagyu and Nyingma traditions provide details and commentary on tantric methods for manipulating and purifying the ordinary dying experience and subsequent bardo period of transition. Consequently, the texts of these teaching-lineages provides crucial materials for reconstructing the history of the bardo in Tibet. In this section I will explore some of the earliest developments of the Tibetan intermediate-state theory by considering several of the most distinctive and influential formulations of the instructional advice traditions of the Kagyupa from the eleventh to thirteenth centuries. An examination of the instructional precept tradition of the Nyingmapa will follow at the conclusion of the chapter.

I mentioned the proliferation of teaching-lineages affiliated with specific tantric masters. Although it is certain that there were many early lineages that transmitted distinctive intermediate-state doctrines, these have not been clearly identified or demarcated in western academic studies. Fortunately, the same cannot be said of the Tibetan sources. To my knowledge one of the earliest explicit references to the variety of bardo lineages prevalent in Tibet can be found in a thirteenth-century work by Yangönpa (alias Lhadongpa, 1213–1287), a follower of the Dö subsect of the Drukpa Kagyu tradition. In his text entitled *Responses to the Questions of Tseringma, History of "Deliverance from the Perilous Straits of the Bardo"* [*Bar-do 'phrang-sgrol-gyi lo-rgyus tshe-rings-ma'i zhus-len*]—a commentary on one of Milarepa's famous "Songs of Realization" (*Rnam-mgur*)—Yangönpa says that he knows of at least fifteen separate traditions of instructional advice on the bardo.[43] From among this group he provides the names of eight distinct teaching-lineages, many of which can be easily identified. Rearranged in roughly chronological order, they are:

1. Bardo Instructions of Ngadak Nyang Relpajen[44]
2. Three Distinct Bardo Systems of the Six Doctrines[45]
3. Father Lineage of Paṇḍita Ngönshejen[46]
4. Bardo Instructions of Tsünmojen[47]
5. Tradition of Jomo Lhajema [i.e., Machik Zhama][48]
   a. Oral Bardo Lineage
   b. Ḍākinī Bardo
   c. Direct Perception Bardo
6. Bardo Instructions of Shangpo Riwoche[49]
7. Essential Bardo Explanations of Zhang Rinpoche[50]
8. Bardo of Yardön Umapa, Nectar Vehicle Dispelling Illness[51]

Since Yangönpa's list appears to be one of the earliest Tibetan classifications of bardo traditions in Tibet, I will take this scheme as paradigmatic and frame my discussion accordingly. All but the first of these eight teaching-lineages can be linked to the so-called Sarma traditions that began to emerge in Tibet during the Buddhist renaissance of the eleventh century. Undoubtedly, the most significant of these newer sects in terms of bardo speculation and innovation was the Kagyupa, although a few exceptions can be noted.[52] My primary focus, therefore, in the section that follows will be on the Kagyu bardo transmissions.

The most influential siddha teachings on bardo in Tibetan history can be traced without much difficulty to the Indian Mahāsiddhas Tilopa and Nāropa (corresponding to lineage number 2 in the preceding list). The latter codified a diverse system of yogic instruction that would come to be widely known in Tibet as the Six Doctrines of Nāro (nā-ro chos-drug). The set of tantric instructions received through Tilopa, Nāropa's mentor, provided the fundamental source for this sixfold teaching. According to Tilopa's biographies, he is said to have received bardo transmissions from several teachers, namely Lavapa (Kambala), Lalitavajra, and Subhaginī.[53] The latter figure, a female yoginī, can be identified also as Sumati Samantabhadrī and the Sukhasiddhī mentioned in Tilopa's Instructional Advice on the Six Doctrines [Ṣaḍdharmopadeśa]. She is believed to have been a contemporary of Nāropa's consort Niguma.[54] Each of these teachers bestowed on Tilopa teachings drawn from specific tantras. Subhaginī transmitted bardo instructions from the Mātṛ-tantras (Mother Tantras).[55] The teachings of Lavapa and Lalitavajra were taken from the Hevajra-tantra. Arguably, Tilopa's distinctive contribution to the tradition was his success in bringing these diverse instructions together and organizing them into a coherent system. He later transmitted the teachings in that form to his disciple Nāropa. This transmission provided the fundamental source for Nāropa's famous Six Doctrines program.

Tilopa's particular understanding of bardo is known from his brief Instructional Advice on the Six Doctrines, which is included in some recensions of the Tibetan Tenjur.[56] Here we find a simple explanation of bardo in relation to the practice of generation-phase tantric meditation:

> The yogin at the time of death,
> brings the sense-powers and the elements together,
> gathering the winds of the sun and moon at the heart,
> giving rise to a variety of yogic concentrations [samādhi].
> When consciousness is directed to external objects,
> they appear like objects in a dream.
> The visions of death appear for seven [or] seven-times-seven days,
> then surely there will be rebirth.
> At that time, cultivate deity yoga,
> or, remain in the state of suchness.
> Afterwards, when it is time to be reborn,
> by the master's deity yoga,
> cultivate deity yoga with all that appears and exists.
> By that [method] the bardo will be blocked.
> this is the instructional advice of Sukhasiddhī.[57]

The practice of deity yoga (lha-yi rnal-'byor) is recommended for those intent on stopping the bardo experience, which is likened to the vision of dreams.

As I will show, the matching of the bardo to the dream state had definite and far-reaching consequences. In Tilopa's verse, moreover, the phrase "obstructing the bardo" (*bar-do khegs-par 'gyur*) is similar to the idea of closing the womb door (*mngal-sgo 'gag-pa*) later expounded by disciples of subsequent generations, beginning with Milarepa and Gampopa. To close the womb door is essentially to block the liminal being from entering a new birth. This specialized technique, accomplished through various tantric yogas, appears to have been one of the hallmarks of the esoteric reinterpretation of earlier intermediate-state formulations.

In the hands of Nāropa, Tilopa's chief disciple, the intermediate-state concept seems to have achieved an unprecedented complexity. Indeed he appears to have been the innovator of the threefold system that became standard in most subsequent Tibetan works affiliated with the Six Doctrines tradition. The basic pattern involved a conflation of some aspects of the doctrine of the four "existences" (*bhava*), the three bodies theory, and both the generation and completion phases of the Supreme Yoga. The result was a precise yogic system that emphasized the contemplative "blending" (*bsres-ba*) of these triune components in a practice commonly referred to as "bringing the three bodies to the path" (*sku-gsum lam-'khyer*). Nāropa's exposition of this program is found in the *Vajra Verses on the Oral Tradition* [*Karṇatantravajrapada*] included in the *Tenjur*:

> The teaching of the thoroughly profound meaning of the direct introduction
>   to the bardo
> cuts off the bardos of [1] birth-to-death, [2] of dreams, and [3] of becoming.
> Without correspondence there are signs,
> without seeing there is supreme seeing.
> This is natural awareness, radiant, empty, non-conceptual, free from all
>   obscurations,
> great bliss, the sphere of reality, utterly pure pristine wisdom,
> by its own nature indivisible and naturally manifest as the three bodies.
>   Behold!
> In the three types of bardo, unrealized embodied beings should blend
> the generation stage, illusory body, and clear light as the reality body
>   [*dharmakāya*].
> The elements—earth, water, fire, and air—dissolve gradually.
> After the eighty [conceptual minds] have ceased, three visions pass.
> White, red, and mind are combined within the lotus.
> Recognize the clear light and mix inseparably mother and child.[58]

We find here reference to several sets of three—three bardo states, three buddha bodies, three levels of practitioner, and three visions during the dying process. All these categories are conceptually interlinked in some fundamental way, and the goal of this so-called bardo yoga (*bar-do rnal-'byor*) is to effect their union at specific points during the meditation session or at the actual moment of death.

To my knowledge, Nāropa's threefold bardo system and the yoga of blending each of its elements was a pioneering development in the history of the bardo concept. It is certainly possible, and indeed likely, that such a program had already been developing among the siddha cults in northern India and that Nāropa was simply inheriting the insights and techniques of these earlier groups, perhaps mainly through Lavapa and his teacher Tilopa. Whatever its provenance, we can see in the system associated with him the introduction of certain key innovations in how the intermediate state would later be conceived in Tibet. First and foremost, the concept of a single transitional period was expanded to include three separate intermediate states—the bardo of birth-to-death (skye-shi bar-do), the bardo of dreams (rmi-lam bar-do), and the bardo of becoming (srid-pa bar-do). In these individual states were incorporated conceptual features of the earlier Abhidharma doctrine of three of the four "existences" (i.e., pūrvakālabhava, maraṇabhava, and antarābhava) in combination with aspects of a more mundane transition state between sleeping and waking (i.e., the dream state), and all of this within the broad context of the two-stage meditative tantric program of the Supreme Yoga.

I can summarize how the three bardo states were defined in Nāropa's scheme: the deceptively long period between birth and death was identified as the first bardo state, called bardo of birth-to-death; the ethereal interval between sleep and waking consciousness was appropriately termed the bardo of dreams;[59] and the transitional period between death and rebirth, the original and familiar intermediate state proper, was given the name bardo of becoming. All three intermediate phases were said to provide an opportunity for yogic practice, the goal of which was to bring the three divine embodiments of buddhahood into each of these transitional moments. In later generations this threefold categorization of the intermediate state inspired even further enumerations and elaborations; the possibilities seemed endless. There were, however, some who remained true to Nāropa's basic triune system, such as Khyungpo Neljor and Zhang Rinpoche (1123–1193)—corresponding, respectively, to lineages 6 and 7 in the foregoing list.[60] Both figures propounded meditative programs constructed around a set of three bardo states similar to that outlined in Nāropa's teachings.[61]

We find alternative and contemporaneous threefold bardo categorizations in works by Gampopa[62] and his disciple Phakmo Drüpa Dorje Gyelpo (1110–1170).[63] It is possible that Phakmo Drüpa's work in particular may be representive of the oral lineage of Jomo Lhajema mentioned in Yangönpa's list (corresponding to lineage 5) since she is cited as one of Phakmo Drüpa's (and also Gampopa's) teachers.[64] Jomo Lhajema (alias Machik Zhama, 1062–1150) was a sexually promiscuous disciple and consort of Ma Lotsawa (1044–1089) and an early preserver of the "path and fruit" (lam-'bras) instructions affiliated with the Sakyapas.[65] Since her teacher was a student of Khyungpo Neljor, it is also likely that her bardo system was similar, if not identical, to that of Niguma, Nāropa's consort.

In the bardo text of Phakmo Drüpa, and similarly in Gampopa's Advice on the Practical Instructions on Bardo [Bar-do'i dmar-khrid-kyi zhal-gdams], the transitional state is again divided into three phases, but the names and descriptions diverge somewhat from Nāropa's model. Here a threefold system is developed around specific techniques employed during the completion stage of tantric yoga rather than during meditation at the three levels of subtle consciousness—waking, sleeping, and intermediate state—as found in Nāropa's scheme. Hence, for Phakmo Drüpa and Gampopa, the first bardo (*bar-do dang-po*) is correlated with apprehending the clear light (*'od-gsal la ngos-bzung-ba*), the second with apprehending the illusory body (*gnyis-pa sgyu-lus ngos-bzung-ba*), and the third with closing the womb door (*gsum-pa mngal-gyi sgo-dgag-pa*).

Not surprisingly, we find similar bardo presentations expounded in later works by authors affiliated with the Gandenpa or Gelukpa tradition, such as its founder Tsongkhapa (1357–1419)[66] and the eighteenth-century monk-scholar Yangjen Gawe Lodrö (alias Akya Yongzin, 1740–1827).[67] It is well known that Gampopa was a respected Kadampa monk and the first Kagyu scholar to combine the special mental purification (*blo-sbyong*) teachings of Atīśa (982–1055)[68] with what would later be referred to as the Great Seal or Mahāmudrā (*phyag-rgya-chen-po*) instructions of Tilopa, Nāropa, and Maitrīpa. The convergence of these two diverse teaching-lineages (referred to as "the convergence of the two rivers, bka' and phyag," *bka'-phyag chu-bo gnyis-dres*) became the hallmark of the Dakpo Kagyu tradition, which is the source of the four major and eight minor subschools of the Kagyu lineages. The chief disciple of Gampopa's student Phakmo Drüpa was Jikten Gönpo (1143–1217), founder of the Drigung Kagyu.[69] It was through this tradition, via the Sakyapas of Zhalu, that Tsongkhapa received the transmission of Nāropa's Six Doctrines.[70] Consequently, Tsongkhapa and the subsequent generations of his Gelukpa followers maintained a syncretic bardo system derived from both the Phakmo Drü and Drigung traditions.

Previously I noted the importance of individual tantras, and particularly those of the Supreme Yoga class, as the root of the various Tibetan siddha teachings on bardo. Among the earliest and most celebrated of these esoteric scriptures was the *Guhyasamāja-tantra* (Tantra of Secret Union) considered one of the most authoritative tantric texts among the Sarmapa or "new" Tibetan religious sects that had begun to appear in the eleventh century.[71] We know from later historical records that Nāropa had received a *Guhyasamāja* transmission from Tilopa, who had received it earlier from Nāgabodhi.[72] This transmission, however, does not appear to have been the main *Guhyasamāja* lineage that reached Tibet. According to the Gelukpa scholar Panchen Sönam Drakpa (1478–1554), that main lineage came from a tradition received through two of Nāropa's contemporaries, the Bengali scholar Ngönshejen (Abhijñā) and the Zahor scholar Tsünmojen (Zahor Yoṣa).[73] It was this transmission that was eventually passed to Marpa Chökyi Lodrö, who then brought it to Tibet. The particular instructional advice on bardo associated with this *Guhyasamāja* lineage is identified in the foregoing list as lineages 3 and 4, respectively. Of the two major tantric scriptural categories, mother (*ma-rgyud*) and father (*pha-rgyud*), the set of bardo instructions of Ngönshejen and Tsünmojen are said to belong to the father lineage, as that is the category typified by the *Guhyasamāja-tantra*. Later Tibetan doxographers, like Panchen

Sönam Drakpa, distinguish between father and mother tantras mainly on points of emphasis. These distinctions can be quite complicated, but it is generally held that the father tantras place stress on methods for attaining the illusory body (sgyu-lus) whereas the mother tantras emphasize techniques for apprehending the clear light ('od-gsal).[74] Because of its formal resemblance to the dream state, the bardo is frequently regarded in this context as a component of the illusory body yoga and hence affiliated most closely with the father tantras.

Regrettably, it has not been possible to trace the specific bardo instructions of Ngönshejen and Tsünmojen in the available Tibetan sources. Presumably their teaching-lineages would have been preserved by Marpa, a student of both masters (though more famous as the chief student of Nāropa), but no specific bardo instructions linked directly to Marpa have surfaced for us to investigate. Nevertheless, some ideas may be recovered from the works of his disciples. It is possible that the presentations of Ngönshejen and Tsünmojen might have resembled the basic bardo exposition of Nāropa, though apparently not derived explicitly from his lineage. Thus, this so-called father lineage of instructional advice on bardo would probably have consisted of instructions on the three blendings (bsres-ba) and the practice of bringing the three bodies to the path. By Marpa's time this threefold scheme of the bardo yoga seems definitely to have been the preferred format.

I have already mentioned that Nāropa's chief Tibetan disciple was the translator Marpa Chökyi Lodrö. Our knowledge of the specific features of Marpa's bardo doctrine is incomplete. From some of the recorded teachings of his primary students, namely Tshurdön Wange (alias Wangi Dorje)[75] and Milarepa, we can gather that Marpa's system must have been referred to as the practice of "cutting off the bardo with the mind" (bar-do blos-chod-pa or bar-do blo-nas gcod-pa).[76] The idea expressed in this label is reminiscent of Tilopa's "obstructing the bardo" (bar-do khegs-pa) practice, whereby the womb door leading to a new existence is blocked or closed through various yogic techniques, the most effective of which is deity yoga, a generation-phase visualization. In the work entitled Oral Precepts on Cutting Off the Bardo with the Mind [Bar-do blos-chod-kyi man-ngag], indicated as one of the special instructions of Marpa (referred to in this text by the name Jetsün Lhodrakpa) and possibly authored by Tshurdön himself but certainly representing his tradition,[77] the bardo is described as threefold based on the triune doxographical scheme of basis (gzhi), path (lam), and fruit ('bras-bu). Here, basis refers to the correct view (lta-ba) of "suchness" (de-bzhin-nyid), path to the method for cultivating (sgom-pa) that view, and fruit to the attainment of the goal of practice.[78] Curiously, there is also reference in this text to alternative traditions that speak of four, five, and even six individual bardo states, although these are not elucidated.[79] Such reference to various sets of bardo enumerations suggests to me that the text may actually have been composed sometime after Tshurdön Wange, following the early decades of the twelfth century when we begin to see clear evidence of a proliferation of bardo categories.

In the text's first presentation, the "bardo of the basis, ascertaining the view" (*lta-ba gtan-la 'beb-pa gzhi'i bar-do*), emphasis is placed on the importance of connecting (*sbrel*) at the moment of death with the lama's instructions about natural awareness (*rang-gi rig-pa*) and reality-itself (*chos-nyid*). It is assumed that such instruction had been previously obtained through direct personal introduction (*ngo-sprod*) to the essence of the teaching while the student practitioner was alive and well. The second topic, the "bardo of the path, practicing meditation" (*sgom-pa nyams-su len-pa lam-gyi bar-do*), is divided according to the capacity of each individual practitioner, whether a superior subitist (*rab cig-car-ba*), meaning one who is enlightened instantanously, or average gradualist (*'bring rim-gyis-pa*). Note that a below average (*tha-ma*) category of practitioner is not mentioned. For the superior yogi—that is, one who has successfully recognized the clear light at the moment of death—the visions of the bardo simply do not arise. The average meditator on the other hand must rely on either emptiness meditation without signs (*mtshan-med stong-nyid bsgom-pa*) or deity meditation with signs (*mtshan-bcas lha-sgom-pa*) in order to achieve in place of the bardo the illusory body that will eventually transform into a buddha's divine form.[80] The final topic, the "bardo of the fruit, manifesting the goal" (*don mngon-tu gyur-pa 'bras-bu'i bar-do*) is subdivided into three parts: (1) persons with direct apprehension (*gang-zag dngos-su bzung-ba*), (2) ways in which the three bardos manifest (*bar-do gsum-gyi 'char-lugs*), and (3) ways to call to mind the instructional advice (*gdams-ngag gdab-lugs*). What is most relevant for my purposes is the second section on how the three bardos manifest, where we find that the first bardo is identified as the clear light of reality-itself (*chos-nyid 'od-gsal*); the second as the bardo in which one emerges in a mental body (*yid-kyi-lus*); and the third as the bardo in which appear the distorted visions (*'khrul-snang*) of cyclic existence. Without much difficulty these three bardo states can be correlated to Nāropa's threefold scheme, with one very important variation. The first bardo comes at the final moment of the dying process when the nature of reality-itself suddenly dawns. We will see that this bardo, which is reminiscent of the Abhidharma *maraṇabhava* (dying state), is later referred to particularly in Nyingmapa presentations as the bardo of dying (*'chi-kha'i bar-do*). Could this bardo category have been developed by Marpa and his immediate followers? We can only speculate, but it is noteworthy that Nāropa's bardo of birth-to-death (corresponding conceptually to the *pūrvakālabhava* in Abhidharma sources) does not seem to be represented in this presentation, while his bardo of dreams and bardo of becoming do correspond closely to the second and third bardo states described here in this scheme.

With Milarepa we find an explosion of multiple bardo phases derived essentially from the instructional lineage of Nāropa received through Marpa. In a text representing instructions granted by Milarepa to his student Rechung Dorje Drak (1083–1161), entitled *Profound Instructional Advice on the Direct Introduction to the Bardo, Cutting Off the Path with the Mind* [*Lam blo-nas gcod-pa bar-do ngo-sprod-kyi gdams-ngag zab-mo*], three overarching bardo states are elucidated: (1) the basic bardo of embodied beings (*lus-ldan gzhi'i bar-do*); (2) the bardo of the signs of definite knowledge (*nges-shes rtags-kyi bar-do*); and (3) the bardo of the fruit of direct encounter (*ngo-sprod 'bras-bu'i bar-do*).[81]

This is not the place to discuss the complex structure and technical details of the numerous subdivisions of the bardo described in this important text. I should note, however, that this elaborate presentation seems to be rather unprecedented in the Tibetan bardo traditions of this period. It appears then that by the first half of the twelfth century there had already been such a remarkable proliferation of ideas inspired by the generic notion of a period of transition between two states of consciousness that for Milarepa's generation seemingly every significant experience or phase of existence (*bhava, sridpa*) could be divided into a graded series of intermediate states.

Henk Blezer has made a similar observation but from a slightly different angle. In attempting to point out the continuity of the traditional Abhidharma scheme in the tantric programs of Milarepa, Blezer argues that early in its history the Tibetan term *bar-(ma-)do* had come to refer to a rather generic notion of any such intermediate existence and thus became the semantic equivalent of the Sanskrit *bhava* (existence) as understood in the Abhidharma context.[82] Indeed, the early Tibetan translators did at times employ the term "being" (*srid*, equivalent to the Sanskrit *bhava*) as translation for the general term *antarābhava*.[83] The point that should be emphasized is that this generalizing of the meaning of the Tibetan term *bardo* as equivalent to the concept *bhava* may have provided the initial spark for the creative formulation of multiple intermediate states following roughly the traditional scheme of the four "existences" (*bhavas*). Consequently, in some of the subsequent Tibetan models, the *upapattibhava* (birth state) became, for example, the bardo of birth (*skye-gnas bar-do*), the *pūrvakālabhava* (life state) the bardo of birth-to-death (*skye-shi bar-do*), and the *maraṇabhava* (dying state) became the bardo of dying (*'chi-kha'i bar-do*), while the *antarābhava* (the intermediate state proper) remained constant as the bardo of existence or, more precisely, the bardo of becoming (*srid-pa bar-do*). It is not certain whether the Indian intermediate state was understood in the same way, although clearly the application of certain components of the four-*bhava* theory to a general concept of transition states was evident in the early system developed outside Tibet by Nāropa in his Six Doctrines program.

In any event, the earlier classifications were never abandoned, they were simply incorporated into this burgeoning scheme. For example, in Milarepa's *Cutting Off the Path with the Mind*, Nāropa's original triune arrangement appears with slight variation of terminology as the subdivisions of category 1, the "basic bardo of embodied beings" and is enumerated in the following terms: the bardo of appearance from birth-to-death (*snang-ba skye-shi'i bar-do*), the bardo of karmic latencies and dreams (*bag-chags rmi-lam-gyi bar-do*), and the bardo of the dark visions of becoming (*snang-mun srid-pa'i bar-do*).[84] Furthermore, the central doctrine of the path of blending (*bsre-ba lam*) in conjunction with the three-body principle is found in category 3, the "bardo of the fruit of direct encounter."[85]

We possess another source for Milarepa's instructions on bardo. This is the *Song of the Symbolic Meaning of the Questions and Responses on the Essential Bardo, Deliverance from the Perilous Straits entitled "The Golden Rosary"* [*'Phrang-sgrol gnad-kyi bar-do la dris-pa lan dang bcas-pa'i brda-don glur-blangs-pa mgur chu-gser-gyi phreng-ba*], or simply *Song of the Golden Rosary*, contained in the famous fifteenth-century *Songs of Milarepa* [*Mi-la'i mgur-'bum*] of Tsangnyön Heruka (1452–1507).[86] In most cases it would be problematic to make historical claims on concepts believed to have existed in the eleventh century based solely on written evidence known to have been composed or compiled four hundered years later, and indeed the bulk of the *Songs of Milarepa* (composed between 1488 and 1495) is certainly no exception to this rule, but the *Song of the Golden Rosary* appears to be somewhat peculiar.

This short work on deliverance from the dangers of the bardo is one of four chapters presented as instructional songs to the five Tseringma Ḍākiṇīs. From the colophon we learn that the song was compiled by Milarepa's disciples Guru Bodhirāja (alias Ngamdzong Repa) and Ökyi Thajen (alias Neljorpa Zhiwa Ö).[87] The four Tseringma chapters are the only songs from Tsangnyön Heruka's anthology where compilers' names are indicated. Charles D. van Tuyl has argued convincingly, based on textual analysis, that these five chapters, including the *Song of the Golden Rosary*, represent an independent literary unit embedded within the larger narrative of the *Songs of Milarepa*. In addition, this unified set of devotional songs appears to be quite older than the rest of the collection, perhaps even dating back to the early twelfth century and actually linked to Bodhirāja and Zhiwa Ö, as is claimed in the individual colophons. In this regard, we should emphasize that the *Song of the Golden Rosary* is quoted almost verbatim in Yangönpa's thirteenth-century commentary, the *Responses to the Questions of Tseringma, History of "Deliverance from the Perilous Straits of the Bardo."* Hence there is very little doubt that at least this small piece on bardo predated the *Songs of Milarepa* by several centuries. Indeed, the descriptions of the bardo states found in the *Song of the Golden Rosary* must have been quite ancient and perhaps roughly contemporaneous with Milarepa himself.

Chapter 30 of the *Song of the Golden Rosary* relates the story of Tashi Tseringma, the leader of the five Tseringma sisters, who had been burned by fires started by local shepherds. Critically injured and angry, the Ḍākiṇī requests Milarepa to cure her life-threatening ailment and also to drive out the demons of disease that had subsequently swept through the area. Milarepa consents and performs a cleansing ritual (*khrus-chog*) that restores Tashi Tseringma's health. The five sisters show their gratitude to the yogi by pledging loyalty to Buddhism and by offering themselves as his spiritual consorts. Moved by their sincerity, Milarepa sings the *Song of the Golden Rosary* as religious instruction to avoid the sufferings of death and the dangers of the bardo. In this song we find references to the familiar three-bodies doctrine, the three blendings, and a multiple of individual intermediate states derived from variations on conceptual themes from Nāropa's original triunal system.[88]

Each of the various transitional states described by Milarepa are associated with a particular yogic practice by which the meditator can be successfully delivered from the perilous straits of the bardo (bar-do 'phrang-sgrol).

This particular Tibetan expression, "deliverance from the perilous straits of the bardo" (perhaps to be identified originally with Milarepa himself), is found in later sources as an alternative name for the general tradition of Nāropa's Six Doctrines.[89] The phrase appears also with some frequency in the liturgical literature attributed to the treasure revealers Karma Lingpa[90] and Ratna Lingpa,[91] as well as in some of the Bonpo treasures of Dampa Rangdröl Yeshe Gyeltsen (1149–1206)[92] and in the works of Jatang Namkha Lhündrup.[93] In the Gelukpa tradition, we even find the expression as the centerpiece of a devotional work by the first Panchen Lama Lozang Chökyi Gyeltsen (1567–1662) and in its eighteenth-century commentary by Yangjen Gawe Lodrö.[94] In a less formal scholastic setting, we find reference to the difficult passage of dead souls through the window of the Tsi'u Marjok Ukhang, a protector-temple of the wrathful guardian Tsi'u Marpo at Samye, Tibet's first Buddhist monastery. The gruesome description of the passage of souls through this window bears repeating:

> According to popular belief this chamber is supposed to be the place where Tsi'u dmar po [Tsi'u Marpo] sits in judgement of the souls of men, an activity assigned otherwise by orthodox traditions to Yama, the ruler of the hells. The chamber is said to have only one extremely narrow window, and legends claim that through this fissure the souls of the dead have to squeeze through at night-time, in order to appear before Tsi'u dmar po. As some of them find it rather difficult to pass, one is able—as the legend tells—to see around this window numerous scratches which these unfortunate spirits had caused by their nails. Some people even allege that a strong smell of blood comes out of this window, as inside the chamber, after the judgement had been pronounced, the souls are cut to pieces by the acolytes of Tsi'u dmar po.[95]

The image of perilous passage between narrow pathways ('phrang-lam) was and continues to be associated in Tibet not only with the postmortem journey but also with topological features at sacred pilgrimage sites known to be particularly dangerous. Safe passage through these narrow straits is akin to moving successfully through the bardo after death.[96] We see then that the concept of deliverance from the perilous straits of the bardo (bar-do 'phrang-sgrol) has a long and varied history in Tibetan religious culture. It also seems to have become in later years a rather common but evocative expression for the distinctive qualities of the transitional experience and techniques for liberating oneself from its dangers. In this idea we see a clear continuity between the ritual beliefs of ancient Tibet concerning death and the vulnerable passage of souls and those ideas preserved by the later Tibetan Buddhist tradition of a prolonged and dangerous postmortem transition.

Milarepa's Song of the Golden Rosary provides the central reference point for a thirteenth-century exposition of the bardo doctrine and its attendant practices composed by Yangönpa, whose work I have referred to throughout this section.[97] In a series of six short commentarial works, Yangönpa frames his discussions around the theme of deliverance from the perilous straits (*'phrang-sgrol*). In keeping with the tradition established by Milarepa, he makes reference throughout these texts to a variety of bardo states and describes many of them in some detail. There does appear nevertheless to be a standard enumerated list from which Yangönpa derives his interpretations. Six individual bardo states are delineated in his *Instructions on the Text "Deliverance from the Perilous Straits of the Bardo"* [*Bar-do 'phrang-sgrol-gyi gzhung-gdam-pa*]: (1) bardo of the natural state,[98] (2) bardo of ripening from birth-to-death,[99] (3) bardo of meditative stabilization,[100] (4) bardo of karmic latencies and dreams,[101] (5) bardo of dying, in reverse order,[102] and (6) bardo of becoming, in progressive order.[103]

The directional expressions "reverse" and "progressive" in the last two categories refer to a cosmological notion, common in Tibetan Supreme Yoga Tantra, of the microcosmic process of death and rebirth in which the psychophysical elements either disintegrate inwardly in reverse order (as in dying) or reintegrate progressively outward (as in gestation). These six bardo states are notably different from the six presented in Milarepa's song. In that song, as I have shown, the categories represent variations on three basic themes that revolve around the transitional states of ordinary life, dreams, and death. Yangönpa, on the other hand, adds to these categories a meditation bardo (reminiscent of Tshurdön's "bardo of the path, practicing meditation") and makes a more refined distinction between the bardo states of life, death, and rebirth.

The fact that Yangönpa's list diverges so much from the *Song of the Golden Rosary* suggests that he probably relied on alternative interpretations prevalent among his contemporaries. We know, for instance, that he was born into a Nyingmapa family of the Dong clan and studied with numerous teachers of various religious sects. For example, in 1223 from the Nyingmapa lama Sangye Mikyö Dorje he received Great Perfection or Dzokchen (*rdzogs-chen*) teachings and the treasures of Nyangrel (1124–c. 1192). From Kodrakpa Sönam Gyeltsen (1181–1261) of the Sakya tradition he received the path and fruit (*lam-'bras*) instructions of Jomo Lhajema, and presumably also her bardo transmissions.[104] Yangönpa's writings on bardo might then be viewed as a synthesis of diverse traditions.

His Nyingmapa connections are particularly intriguing. As I will soon show, the Dzokchen scriptures of the Nyingma tradition frequently contain descriptions of bardo that are at least nominally similar to Yangönpa's sixfold enumeration. This similarity is perhaps most readily apparent in the Dzokchen-styled *Great Compassionate One, Instructions on the Lamp which Dispels the Darkness of the Bardo* [*Thugs-rje chen-po bar-do mun-sel-gyi sgron-me'i gdams-pa*] from the text cycle *Disclosure of the Hidden* [*Gab-pa mngon-byung/phyung*] belonging to the eclectic *Maṇi Kambum* [*Ma-ṇi bka'-'bum*] tradition.[105] This interesting work presents a sixfold division of the bardo that is almost identical to Yangönpa's arrangement, although the meanings of the terms are quite distinct.[106] As we might expect, the bardo exposition in this *Maṇi Kambum* work is structured on a metaphysics tied to the deity Thukje

Chenpo, the Great Compassionate One (Mahākarūṇika), another name for the cardinal bodhisattva Avalokiteśvara; this we do not find in the texts composed by Yangönpa. I tend to think, however, that both presentations are roughly contemporaneous and are representative of the state of bardo speculation then prevalent in Tibet.[107] This might mean that by the middle of the thirteenth century a sixfold structure of the intermediate state may have become the preferred format among followers of the Nyingmapa and Kagyupa lineages, although we cannot be certain as to what exactly the six states may have been at any given time. We can say without hesitation that four of the six bardos described in Yangönpa, and in varying terms in the *Disclosure of the Hidden*, remained relatively stable throughout the next several centuries leading up to Karma Lingpa's *Great Liberation upon Hearing in the Bardo*; these four being (1) the bardo of meditative stabilization, (2) the bardo of dreams, (3) the bardo of dying, and (4) the bardo of becoming. On the other hand, the bardo of the natural state and the bardo of birth-to-death were somewhat indeterminate, each apparently interchangeable. Also during this period, the peculiar bardo of reality-itself (*chos-nyid bar-do*), so familiar in the Dzokchen literature, also began to appear in lists containing multiple bardo states, although we do not know precisely when this may have first occurred. This intriguing topic is the focus of the next section.

Dzokchen Innovations

Beginning in 842 with the assassination of emperor Lang Darma (Trhi Dudumtsen, b. c. 803), Buddhism was officially stripped of its rank as the state religion in Tibet. This was the end of the period referred to in Tibetan records as the "former diffusion of the doctrine" (*bstan-pa snga-dar*). Buddhism, however, did not entirely disappear from the Tibetan religious arena. Despite the lack of state support, the religion continued to survive in areas outside the tumultuous and fractured region of central Tibet. In this loose environment, Buddhism was cultivated in a variety of forms and developed without centralized control. These diverse religious movements were largely diffused throughout the region by the efforts of wandering yogis and self-styled religious savants, many of whom claimed lineal descent from "authentic" Indian, Chinese, and Central Asian Buddhist masters. Scholars have speculated that it was during this so-called Dark Age (mid–ninth to late tenth century) that some of these religious groups—later to be identified by the names Nyingmapa and Bonpo—formulated systems of thought and elaborated on earlier traditions established during the height of Tibet's dynastic period in the eighth and early ninth century.[108] In truth, we possess very little historical evidence to date securely any of these alleged Dark Age movements and their affiliated religious systems before the eleventh century.

During the Tibetan Buddhist renaissance era when new competing sects had begun to appear (in part the result of a revival of an institutionally based Buddhism), both the Nyingmapa and Bonpo were set apart and explicitly identified as distinct from these newer groups, the Sarmapa. Although their differences were largely described in terms of doctrinal divergence, the influence of political and economic factors should not be ignored. In particular, the independent kingdoms of western Tibet were in an exceptionally strong position to attract teachers from India and Kashmir and to encourage concentrated scholarly activity, which included the mass importation and translation of significant Indian Buddhist scriptures. These kingdoms were also quite capable of providing the support needed for building temples and monasteries. Many of the new traditions that developed in this environment rejected the validity of the religious systems that had previously flourished without institutional sponsorship. They argued that the texts of these "old school" groups were not authentic and were simply Tibetan fabrications, since it could not be proven that the older texts had been translated from Sanskrit originals. Consequently, the controversial scriptures were later excluded from the "official" Tibetan Buddhist canon of the Sarmapa but were alternatively preserved by their enthusiasts in a Nyingmapa canon and collection known as the *One Hundred Thousand Tantras of the Ancients* [*Rnying-ma'i rgyud-'bum*]. This group of tantras and associated exegetical materials was distinctive primarily in terms of the philosophical system on which the majority of its teachings were founded, namely the religious doctrine known as Dzokchen (*rdzogs-chen*), the Great Perfection. It is not necessary to delve into the long and complicated history of this unique system in Tibet, since several scholars have discussed the development in some detail.[109] Instead, a brief examination of its basic conceptual framework in an effort to contextualize the bardo elaborations specific to the Nyingmapa (and Bonpo) traditions will suffice. Here emphasis will be on an entirely unique intermediate state concept called "bardo of reality-itself" (*chos-nyid bar-do*). As I will show, this concept is derived essentially from the combination of specific Dzokchen ideas with a mandala of one hundred peaceful and wrathful deities (*zhi-khro rigs-brgya*) borrowed from the Mahāyoga (*rnal-'byor chen-po*) tradition. This discussion will provide a good foundation to begin exploring the history of Karma Lingpa's Dzokchen-derived treasure revelations, the *Self-Liberated Wisdom of the Peaceful and Wrathful Deities* and the *Great Liberation upon Hearing in the Bardo*.

We encounter some of the important tantric innovations that may have developed prior to but possibly during Tibet's Dark Age in the pivotal scripture *All-Creating King* [*Kun-byed rgyal-po*], the fundamental text of Dzokchen, alleged to have been translated from Sanskrit and redacted by the Indian scholar Śrī Siṃha and the monk Vairocana sometime in the eighth century.[110] The text's origins, however, are not entirely clear—an ambiguity that sparked a long history of controversy in Tibet.[111] We do know at least that the work was extant by the early eleventh century, not long after the emergence of the Buddhist renaissance in Tibet and the development of sectarian groups. It was also during this period that the Nyingthik (*snying-thig*), or Heart-essence, tradition of Dzokchen is thought to have begun taking shape.[112]

The doctrinal position formulated in the *All-Creating King*—later embellished by the emerging Nyingthik system in the eleventh century—offered a complete cosmogony centered around the concept of a primordial ground (*gdod-ma'i gzhi*) as the fundamental basis that underlies the universe and that activates its varied manifestations. In this view, the primordial ground is a "pure source potential" (*'char-gzhi*), a dynamic and unified openness from which arises all that will exist. Utterly devoid of categorical distinctions, the primordial ground is "original purity" (*ka-dag*), and its intrinsic dynamism or "spontaneous presence" (*lhun-grub*) serves as the source potential of all that comes to exist. Furthermore, the primordial ground's potentiality, its openness, is imbued with a "primordial intelligence" (*ye-shes*). This ground is described in terms of a triunal identity—essence (*ngo-bo*), nature (*rang-bzhin*), and compassion (*thugs-rje*)—and correlated to the traditional and by now familiar principle of a buddha's three bodies: the reality body (*chos-sku*), whose essence is empty, the enjoyment body (*longs-sku*), whose nature is radiant luminosity, and the emanation body (*sprul-sku*), which is manifest and compassionately active in the world. The cosmos in its primordial condition is thus shown to be always already harmonious with the thoroughly awakened embodiment of buddhahood.

We should take a brief moment here to introduce the basic framework of Dzokchen cosmogony as developed by later Dzokchen Nyingthik thinkers such as the famous Longchenpa (1308–1363). The description that follows is typical of late thirteenth- and fourteenth-century Dzokchen formulations of the sort that would have served as a prime conceptual basis for Karma Lingpa's ritual and literary tradition only a century later. Begging the indulgence of my readers, I offer in what follows an admittedly narrativized overview of Dzokchen cosmogony, freely appropriating the language and tone of the tradition's own formulations. My reason for doing this is to capture some of the evocative flourish of Dzokchen's kaleidoscopic worldview while introducing the technical details of its conceptual system.[113]

The triune identity of the primordial ground remains in its primeval dimension as a self-contained and interiorized potentiality, and as such it is understood metaphorically as a "youthful body in a vase" (*gzhon-nu bum-pa sku*). In this metaphorical image, the youthful body refers to the ground's dynamic luminosity, its spontaneous presence as yet unrealized. Freshly vibrant and free from the corruptions of exteriorized actuality, this body of pure potentiality, brimming with the vigor of youth, is concealed from view, encased within its own vessel of original purity. At some obscure point and for reasons unknown the encasing seal of this "vase" is opened up by a stirring of a primordial gnostic wind (*ye-shes-kyi rlung*). The energy of this wind causes awareness (*rig-pa*) to be elevated from the primordial ground and a cosmos begins to spiral outward from the singular interiority of the ground's pure potential. This cosmos, consisting of numerous galaxies of manifest luminosity, emerges in a hierarchically arranged triunal pattern described as the exteriorization of the forms of awakened energy, the ground's natural appearance or "self-presencing" (*rang-snang*). Envisioned in the context of the three-body principle, the reality body (*dharmakāya*) manifests above like a cloudless sky, while directly in front the Pure Lands of the enjoyment body (*saṃbhogakāya*) pervade the vast expanse of the sky. Just below them are the manifestations of the emanation body (*nirmāṇakāya*) and further down, the sixfold world system (*rigs-drug*). This unfolding process, described technically as the ground's transition from internal radiance (*nang-gsal*) to external radiance (*phyir-gsal*), opens up at least two paths: a pure gateway leading to enlightenment (*nirvāṇa*) and an impure gateway leading into cyclic existence (*saṃsāra*). At this point, the potential trajectory of the evolutionary process is entirely dependent on the capacity for self-awareness deriving from the ground's compassionate energy (*thugs-rje*).

In the crucial moment of the ground's spontaneous exteriorization, that which manifests is instantly confronted by a panoramic spiraling of five different rainbow-colored lights; its capacity for awareness, emerging from the playful shining forth of the ground, provides an opportunity for recognition of these lights as its own self-presencing, an awakening to its own enlightened reality (*rig-pa*). But if the lights are not recognized as such, there is nonawareness (*ma-rig-pa*) and "straying" ('*khrul-pa*) into dualistic conditioned reality. The first being to recognize itself and the five-colored lights is Samantabhadra or Kuntu Zangpo (All Good), the very instant of primordial enlightenment personified (Ādibuddha). In this first moment of recognition, the empty essence is expansively (*rgyas*) awakened (*sangs*) within the ground into a buddha's (*sangs-rgyas*) manifest enlightenment. Kuntu Zangpo's instantaneous realization climaxes into full self-awareness, stimulating a reversal of the evolutionary process in eight phases, each corresponding to the individual modes of the ground's initial manifestation. In this process of cosmic dissolution, a return to the ground's pure source potential, the ground retains its self-awareness and a buddha is actualized. In the Dzokchen scripture *All-Creating King*, this buddha is described as the creator (*byed-pa-po*) of the universe, or more literally, as the title indicates, the "king who creates everything" (*kun-byed rgyal-po*).

The first moment of nonrecognition, on the other hand, triggers a movement into cyclic existence. At that instant, when failing to recognize its own nature it strays ('*khrul-pa*) into dualistic experience, distinct subjects and objects are apprehended. From within this dualistic experience of otherness, the five afflictive emotions (ignorance, desire, hatred, pride, and jealousy) arise in their latent form, and awareness grasps at the five corresponding sensual objects (visible forms, sounds, scents, tastes, and mental phenomena). An individual sentient being materializes just at the very moment that the primordial ground's initial radiance is obscured by this emergent distorted subjectivity. The ground's luminosity, previously manifesting as the five rainbow-colored lights, now begins to congeal into solidified objective matter, resulting in the emergence of the five material elements that constitute the physical universe (earth, water, fire, wind, and space). With the psychophysical components of distorted existence now in place, the impure gateway leading to birth is rent asunder and the gradual process of corporeal and neurotic development is set in motion. At this point the voluted descent into one of six possible realms of existence cannot be avoided.

From this characteristically Dzokchen perspective, birth and death are understood as being analogous to the cosmological drama. In this way, the ordinary dying and rebirth process is described explicitly in terms of the ebb and flow of the cosmos itself. The primordial ground's exteriorization and its capacity for self-recognition are repeated at the samsaric level of straying during the transitional event (bardo) following a sentient being's death, when the coarse psychophysical components begin to dissolve back into the ground's originally pure radiance. As in the cosmogonic process just outlined, failure to recognize the pure luminosity of reality-itself (*chos-nyid 'od-gsal*) sparks the impure movement into a new material existence, while recognition leads into the expansively awakened condition of Kuntu Zangpo, the primordial Buddha. We see then that the dying process is directly correlated to the involutive process of the return of the manifest cosmos to its primordial condition of original purity. The capacity for self-recognition at this moment proves crucial to one's release from the cycle of conditioned existence and the attainment of buddhahood.

If there is no awareness then there is rebirth in cyclic existence (*saṃsāra*). Implicit in this view is the idea that the round of rebirth and its sufferings are a function of an epistemological dualism, the bifurcation of consciousness into subject and object, out of which the world of a sentient being's experience is constructed. Dzokchen soteriology, therefore, entails the recovery of a primordial state of realization (*ye-shes*) before such bifurcation takes place. To continue employing the language of this tradition, because the process by which suffering comes about is predicated on an awareness that is obscured (*ma-rig-pa*), it is possible to reverse (*zlog-pa*) the process by successively dispelling the darkness (*mun-sel*) and experiencing the awareness (*rig-pa*) that is always already awakened to the intrinsic purity of reality (*chos-nyid*), thereby freeing oneself from the bondage of conditioned existence (*saṃsāra*). Freedom (*grol-ba*) can be achieved in this life by means of dependence on specific Dzokchen techniques, for example, the practices of "breakthrough" (*khregs-chod*) and "direct transcendence" (*thod-rgal*), or it may be realized during the experiences of dying and postmortem transition or bardo, when the entire deevolutive cosmic cycle is repeated naturally. It is this particular model of death and bardo that is expounded most distinctively in the Dzokchen Nyingthik texts of the *Seventeen Tantras of the Ancients* [*Rnying-ma'i rgyud bcu-bdun*], which the tradition claims was revealed in India to the mystic Garap Dorje, believed to be the first human teacher of Dzokchen. The fact that an identical conceptual pattern is reflected in Karma Lingpa's *Peaceful and Wrathful Deities*, and especially in the texts that the *Liberation upon Hearing* comprises, indicates clearly that the Karling literary and ritual tradition was operating from within a similar cosmological framework established earlier in the scriptures that the Dzokchen Nyingthik corpus comprises.

The *Seventeen Tantras* is the canonical core of the Dzokchen Nyingthik tradition and is usually included in the larger Nyingmapa anthology of scriptures known as the *One Hundred Thousand Tantras of the Ancients*. The seventeen interrelated Dzokchen Nyingthik scriptures are accepted by tradition as divine revelation received by the aforementioned mystic Garap Dorje.[114] The *Seventeen Tantras* nevertheless betrays signs of being compiled over a long period of time by multiple hands. The precise identity of these unknown redactors is a riddle that I hope may soon be solved. Whatever the case, we must accept that the collection in the form it is known to us today is comprised of several layers of history reflecting diverse influences. David Germano argues that the texts of the *Seventeen Tantras* "were almost certainly Tibetan compositions originating in the eleventh century."[115] Recall that this was also the era of the great siddhas Nāropa, Marpa, and so forth, who were especially championed by the various Sarmapa groups. With paradigmatic texts such as those found in the *Seventeen Tantras of the Ancients* and the *All-Creating King*, it is clear that tantric innovation was not exclusive to the Sarmapa. Tibetan reformulations of the earlier Indian intermediate-state theory were expounded also by followers of the Nyingmapa (and Bonpo) lineages. Like the instructional advice traditions of the Kagyu siddhas, the Nyingmapa developed systems of multiple bardo states. Many examples can be cited from the large tantric anthology *One Hundred Thousand Tantras of the Ancients*, where we find traditions of speaking of one, three, four, five, and even six separate bardo phases.[116] But it is with the *Seventeen Tantras* that we encounter perhaps the first systematic presentation of a distinctively Dzokchen reformulation of the bardo concept that had emerged in Tibet after the mysterious Dark Age.[117]

Among these seventeen texts, the most significant in terms of bardo speculation is undoubtedly the *Tantra of the Secret Union of Sun and Moon* [*Nyima dang zla-ba kha-sbyor-ba chen-po gsang-ba'i rgyud*].[118] The basic plot of the tantra is structured around a dialogue between the Buddha Vajradhāra and a bodhisattva named Mitok Thupa, who asks a series of questions concerning the methods that sentient beings may employ to achieve liberation. Vajradhāra responds by describing systematically the experiences an individual undergoes during the various transitional bardo periods, and in due course teaches Mitok Thupa how to resolve the oral instructions of his teacher. Four bardo states are enumerated: (1) bardo of the natural state,[119] (2) bardo of dying,[120] (3) bardo of reality-itself,[121] and (4) bardo of becoming.[122]

The subtext of the narrative is pragmatic. Release (*grol-ba*) can be achieved during these four periods of transition by making the proper offerings, following the necessary meditative instructions, and recognizing the truth taught by former masters. It is the text's metanarrative that suggests the *Secret Union of Sun and Moon* may have been more than just a literary document of the bardo journey. The text offers a varied program for an array of performance styles, involving death prognostication (*'chi-brtags*),[123] ritual exorcism (*'chi-ba blu-ba'i cho-ga*),[124] and long-life practices (*tshe-thabs*).[125] A fluid relationship, then, appears to have existed between the narrative of the text and, for lack of a better term, its liturgy. Just as I will show more explicitly in the case of Karma Lingpa's *Peaceful and Wrathful Deities*, the *Secret Union of*

Sun and Moon integrated components of both doctrine and ritual to operate almost as a complete liturgical system designed to ensure an auspicious destiny for the dead and the living. That being said, however, the text does not offer a ritual directive that could be viewed as comprehensive, as for example we find in the later texts of the *Liberation upon Hearing*. The codification of fully structured Dzokchen death liturgies among the Nyingmapa did not occur before the fourteenth century, although such rites were certainly based on much earlier models. The *Secret Union of Sun and Moon* is a case in point.

In this context we could argue that one of the distinctive innovations of the Dzokchen Nyingthik was the development of a unique bardo concept that combined the Dzokchen cosmogonic theory of the process of cosmic emanation and dissolution (a dynamic also operative at the microcosmic level of the human being) with the notion of transitional phases between multiple states of consciousness. This new bardo concept, given the name "bardo of reality-itself" (*chos-nyid bar-do*) and corresponding to the third bardo enumerated in the *Secret Union of Sun and Moon* referred to earlier, was the result of elaborations and embellishments of the earlier and more far-ranging tantric concept of luminosity or the clear light ('*od-gsal*) said to be experienced briefly by all human beings at the moment of death, by advanced yogic practitioners in the highest levels of the completion phase meditation, and unceasingly by all buddhas. Interestingly, this very subtle radiance is believed also to be experienced, though rarely noticed, in more mundane moments such as fainting, sneezing, and orgasm, as well as in the first instant before and after dreaming.[126] In the *Secret Union of Sun and Moon*, and other Nyingthik scriptures, the brief moment of the clear light encounter was extended so that it came to span an entirely new conceptual space. This amplified experience of luminosity was described in terms of a separate transitional period distinct from the other bardo states commonly expounded in the Kagyu instructional advice traditions that I examined in the preceding section.

With the Dzokchen concept of the bardo of reality-itself, emphasis was on the clear light as equivalent to the primordial ground's original pure radiance. The ensuing postmortem drama mirrored the cosmogonic process of the ground's exteriorization and of Kuntu Zangpo's initial enlightenment. The capacity for self-recognition at this moment determined the direction and path of the deceased's future destiny. Awareness (*rig-pa*) was said to lead immediately to buddhahood, wheras nonawareness (*ma-rig-pa*) sparked the next sequential bardo phase, the bardo of becoming (*srid-pa bar-do*), culminating in rebirth as a sentient being in one of the six realms of existence. The decidedly Dzokchen flavor of this interpretation allows us to see just how distinctive the Nyingma theory of bardo was in contrast to the ideas expounded by the Sarmapa traditions, in which the bardo concept lacked a thoroughly cosmic or rather cosmogonic dimension.

One of the most prominent features of the Dzokchen bardo of reality-itself that sets it apart from all other bardo states of both the Sarma and certain Nyingma traditions is the doctrine of peaceful and wrathful deities (*zhi-khro*). In its earliest conceptual form, the idea of spontaneous visions of peaceful and wrathful deities during the bardo of reality-itself cannot be traced, although there is ample textual evidence of the inclusion in this context of the appearance of five Buddhas or teachers (*ston-pa lnga*) familiar from standard Mahāyāna exegesis.[127] Consider for example the following passage from the reality bardo section of the *Secret Union of Sun and Moon*.

> Again, these visions [of light] self-manifest as pure bodies. These bodies are neither large nor small, but well-proportioned with ornaments, colors, postures, thrones, and gestures. These pure bodies are present as five forms, each one encircled by light. Possessing the implements of father and mother, the male and female bodhisattvas and all [five] mandalas abide all at once.[128]

It is not altogether clear when precisely a mandala of one hundred or more peaceful and wrathful deites was first assimilated into this model (see fig. 3.1). The topic has been the subject of a few preliminary investigations by Henk Blezer, but his findings so far have not been conclusive.[129] Whatever the precise historical details, it is certain that by the fourteenth century this specific set of deities had been inserted into the Dzokchen doctrine of the bardo of reality-itself and, once incorporated, became a quintessential feature of that concept.

The mandala system of peaceful and wrathful deities appears to have been derived originally from teachings found in the eighth-century *Web of Magical Emanation* [Tib., *Sgyu-'phrul drwa-ba*, Skt., *Māyājāla*], and specifically its central scripture the *Great Tantra of the Secret Nucleus* [*Gsang-ba'i snying-po*].[130] This tantra is representative of the first of three distinctively Nyingmapa textual classifications of the so-called inner tantras (*nang-rgyud*)—Mahāyoga, Anuyoga, and Atiyoga or Dzokchen. There are claims that the Mahāyoga tantras were translated from Indian originals in the eighth to ninth century by both Indian and Tibetan scholars and comprise certain doctrines and practices prevalent in India during that time, but little evidence exists to support such statements. Nevertheless, we can speak confidently about the content of these tantras. The soteriological thrust of the Mahāyoga texts is centered on particular generation-phase tantric techniques, such as deity yoga, designed to bring about a union with what is called the "nondual superior truth" (*lhag-pa'i gnyis-med bden-pa*). Among the eighty-two chapters of the long recension of the text, the first twenty-eight concern the emergence of the peaceful deities while the remaining fifty-four detail the wrathful mandala.[131] This set of peaceful and wrathful deities represents a uniquely Mahāyoga interpretation of the standard set of five Buddha families (*rigs-lnga*) common to all tantric Buddhist systems. Essentially, these five Buddhas are viewed as the enlightened emanations of a corresponding fivefold set of primordial wisdom (*ye-shes*)[132] and of both cosmological and psychological relationships that are all brought together in the five psychophysical components of a sentient being. The *Secret Nucleus* amplifies and inflates the basic fivefold set of Buddhas into the array of peaceful and wrathful deities, and maps out in meticulous detail all their intricacies. The text is structured around an elaborate exegesis of the involved processes of consecration, emanation, and absorption of this

FIGURE 3.1. Mandala of the peaceful and wrathful deities. Thanka painting, eighteenth century. (Courtesy of The Shelley and Donald Rubin Collection, no. 505)

divine entourage. With some notable variation, the *Secret Nucleus* mandala is essentially the same mandala that would be later sanctified in the treasure revelations of Orgyen Lingpa (1323–c.1360),[133] Karma Lingpa,[134] Sherap Özer (1518–1584),[135] and Jatsön Nyingpo (1585–1656).[136]

The assimilation of elements of the Mahāyoga system into the full spectrum of Dzokchen, including several other tantric features of the Supreme Yoga and Great Seal traditions, resulted in the expansion of this latter tradition to include an entirely new series of complex innovations, best encapsulated in the Nyingthik movement that began to emerge around the eleventh century. The vast literature of this tradition was systematically codified in the fourteenth century by the religious savant Longchenpa, to whom I have referred earlier. His influential writings on the Dzokchen Nyingthik, as Germano argues, represented

> its first systematic exposition attributed explicitly to an indigenous Tibetan author. Not only did he put this tradition in its classical form, he also managed to integrate its doctrines and practices into the increasingly normative modernist (Sarmapa) discourses that had taken shape from the contemporary Indian Buddhist logico-epistemological circles, Madhyamaka, Yogācāra, and tantric traditions of the late tenth to thirteenth centuries.[137]

Longchenpa's exposition of the complete system of the Nyingthik, contained principally in the voluminous *Four Branches of the Heart-essence* [*Snying-thig ya-bzhi*] and in his own *Seven Treasuries* [*Mdzod-bdun*], has practically become canonical in its importance and influence among the Nyingmapa. In particular, his various interpretations of the bardo doctrine unique to this tradition have served collectively as an authoritative standard and one of the main sources on which most subsequent commentary on the subject has been based.[138]

This having been said, I should point out that Longchenpa and his writings are never referred to explicitly in any of the core literary works of Karma Lingpa's treasure cycle or in the works of subsequent holders of his teaching-lineage, even though this characteristically Nyingthik ritual and literary tradition was unmistakably influenced by Longchenpa's efforts in systematizing the Dzokchen tradition. The *Secret Union of Sun and Moon* and other works of the *Seventeen Tantras* collection, on the other hand, are quoted extensively and almost exclusively in the Karling literature. Perhaps Longchenpa's writings were really not that well known before their rediscovery in the eighteenth century.[139]

The distinctive Nyingthik tradition that originated with Longchenpa passed in two lineal streams through a number of important Tibetan teachers, including Longchenpa's own son, Tülku Drakpa Özer (b. 1356). Not suprisingly, both teaching-lineages included figures that also played prominent and active roles in the transmission of the Karling teachings, providing yet another clue of that tradition's doctrinal orientation. One lineage was received through Ösel Longyang, disciple and son of Namkha Dorje.[140] This transmission eventually reached Dzokchen Sönam Wangpo (1550–1625) and Ngawang Yeshe Drupa. The former became the teacher of Tsele Natsok Rangdröl, while the

latter acted as mentor to Zurchen Chöying Rangdröl (1604–1669), the principal Nyingma tutor of the fifth Dalai Lama. A second transmission, which
passed directly through Drakpa Özer, was received by Kunga Gyeltsen
Pelzangpo (alias Gyama Mingyurwa, 1497–1568).[141] It was this transmission
that reached Tülku Natsok Rangdröl (1494–1570), founder of the monastery
of Dargye Chöling, the ancestral seat of Mindroling and the principal center
of Dzokchen activity in central and southern Tibet during the mid–sixteenth
to late seventeenth centuries. The successors of Tülku Natsok Rangdröl's
tradition included the Sungtrül incarnations of Pema Lingpa, situated at
Lhalung monastery in Lhodrak, and the patrilineage of the great Terdak Lingpa
The point I want to highlight here is that these individuals were not only the
principal curators of Longchenpa's Dzokchen Nyingthik tradition but were
also directly responsible for maintaining and distributing the Nyingthik-styled
teachings of Karma Lingpa. I will explore the history of these various lines
of transmission further in chapters 9–11.

In concluding this broad discussion of the history of Tibetan ideas and practices surrounding death and the dead, let me summarize my view of the general
direction the postmortem intermediate-state doctrine took after its standard
formulation in the literature of the Sarvāstivāda, with special reference to its
succeeding history in Tibet. By the fifth century the Abhidharma descriptions
of the intermediate state had solidified following a standardized model first
established in the representative works, for example, the *Mahāvibhāṣā* and
Vasubandhu's *Abhidharmakośa-bhāṣya*. The Buddhist siddha cults of the
eighth and ninth century first adopted this orthodox theory in the context of a
distinctively tantric soteriology and expanded the term's meaning to include
a plurality of intermediate-state phases. This multistratified tantric model was
derived initially from aspects of the Abhidharma doctrine of the four *bhavas*
and the conflation of the original intermediate-state idea with the three bodies
doctrine. When introduced into Tibet this model inspired further innovations.
The development of exclusively tantric conceptions of the intermediate state
on Tibetan soil, galvanized by the ancient ritual and cosmological beliefs of
the pre-Buddhist tradition, culminated in the eleventh century with the
codification of various siddha transmissions—some of which came to be known
collectively as the "Six Doctrines of Nāropa." Eventually traditions arose that
spoke of not only three but four, five, and even six separate bardo states.

Simultaneously, we find evidence of an alternative development of the
bardo doctrine among certain older Tibetan Buddhist lineages, the Nyingmapa
(and Bonpo). By the fourteenth century an entirely unique intermediate state,
the bardo of reality-itself (*chos-nyid bar-do*), had emerged from within these
traditions that combined the cosmogonic models of the Dzokchen Nyingthik
system with a mandala of one hundred peaceful and wrathful deities borrowed
from the Mahāyoga tantras and derived particularly from the *Great Tantra of
the Secret Nucleus*.

Between the fourteenth and fifteenth centuries, the earlier conceptual innovations of the various Nyingma and Sarma teaching-lineages began to be

systematized into complete liturgical programs designed for the most part to guide the deceased through the perils of the bardo. In these rituals we find a layering of old and new conceptions. We see in them not only a creative re-invention of the original Indo-Buddhist intermediate state and the assimilation of the popular Tibetan notion of perilous passage between narrow pathways (*'phrang-lam*) but also the preservation of the ritual beliefs of the ancient indigenous tradition. In the following centuries, most of the subsequent doctrinal and liturgical contributions were more or less derivative of these previous developments, which by the late fifteenth century had already achieved in Tibet a certain standardized authority. It was in that period that the funeral liturgies of the *Peaceful and Wrathful Deities* and the *Liberation upon Hearing* were first instituted. Soon thereafter this liturgy became the most complete and widely distributed form of the bardo ritual within Tibet and surrounding areas. The eventual popularity of the Karling tradition must surely have been a consequence of the success of its rituals in giving a balanced and compelling expression to many of the cultural attitudes toward death and dying that had for centuries flowed throughout the Tibetan region. The next chapter provides a general overview of this ritual program for the dead and dying.

4

From Death to Disposal

The rituals of the *Peaceful and Wrathful Deities* and the *Liberation upon Hearing* are built around a coherent set of actions and a fully developed ritual sequence that recognize the value of confession (*bshags-pa*) and expiation (*bskang-ba*) in the purification of sins (*sdig-pa*) and the efficacy of prayer and ritual performance for guiding the deceased through the perilous pathways of the bardo and into the next life. This brief chapter examines the general structure of the Tibetan bardo liturgy, relying on both textual and ethnographic data. The textual material will be drawn from the Karling literature itself, while the ethnographic details will be based primarily on several important anthropological studies, as well as information gleaned from a modern Tibetan pamphlet by Thupten Sangay entitled *Tibetan Ceremonies for the Dead* [*Bod-mi'i 'das-mchod*].[1] Although there are variations in each of these sources, certain features can be found in common. These shared elements will provide the basis for my account of the generalized pattern of the bardo rites.

In matters of burial practice, Tibetans have traditionally disposed of their dead in one of five ways: interment or earth burial (*sa-sbas gtong-ba*), cremation (*ro-sreg*), water burial (*chu-bskyur*), mummification (*pur phung-bzos*), and vulture disposal (*bya-rgod 'don*).[2] As I noted in chapter 2, the practice of burying the corpse in the earth was the prevalent custom of the early Tibetan kings before the court-sanctioned arrival of Buddhism. Burial rites during this ancient period consisted largely of offerings of food and various objects such as clothes, jewelry, and so forth, as well as the blood sacrifice of animals. The remains of the Tibetan kings were buried in large funerary mounds.[3] In modern times, interment is reserved exclusively for those who have died as a result of certain epidemic diseases, such as smallpox, leprosy, or tuberculosis.[4] Wylie has suggested that the custom of burning the corpse, or cremation, emerged as a popular alternative to burial sometime after the eleventh century, especially among populations where wood for such fires was easily available.[5] As to why cremation became a widely favored method in Tibet, the historical record offers few clues. Whatever the reason, it seems that nowadays cremation is practiced widely among the Tibetan refugee communities primarily in keeping with the customs of India.[6] Disposal in water appears to have been a method rarely practiced, although in exceptional cases it was performed for the corpses of pregnant or barren women, lepers, and those who have met a violent death.[7] Mummification was generally reserved for high-ranking religious leaders or incarnate lamas.[8] The most common method of disposal in premodern Tibet, however, was that of offering the corpse to vultures.[9] Consequently, my discussion will focus exclusively on this particular mode of ritual disposal.

In the first part of the funeral, during the first two or three days after death, attention is focused largely on the corpse. When death has been determined, word is sent immediately to close family and friends. The body is left in the position in which it last rested and is not touched or handled by anyone. The belief is that if the corpse is touched, the deceased's consciousness may exit prematurely from the point of first contact, which is generally thought to have rather unfortunate consequences. An attempt is made by a local lama or lay ritual specialist to draw the consciousness out of the body through the crown of the head—this is the orifice that is believed best to lead to a favorable rebirth in a buddha's pure realm. This specialized technique of transference ('pho-ba) is usually performed at the house where the person has died. In Mumford's opinion, the transference rite is more or less symbolic, for the rest of the funeral proceeds under the assumption that the ritual had not been successful.[10] Soon other monks are assembled to perform the necessary rites and blessings (mgyogs-bsngo) and to prepare for the casting of the death horoscope (gshin-rtsis). Throughout all of this, offering-rites are performed to keep demons (bdud-gdon) away from the corpse. The threat of demonic possession is particularly great once the consciousness has left the body. It is feared that evil spirits may enter the corpse and reanimate it, in which case the body may be transformed into a zombie (ro-langs).[11] To guard against such attacks, the corpse is watched (snye-srung) continuously throughout the day and night. During the day, the monks chant prayers and perform purification rites. Among other matters, the presence of demonic forces is determined by reading the death horoscope.

The astrologer (rtsis-pa) is given the deceased's year of birth and the date and time of death. From this information he is able to determine the best day for disposal of the corpse and whether any special rituals should be performed to protect the deceased's family against demonic attacks.[12] Mumford offers the following explanation.

> The death horoscope (rtsis) answers a number of questions. First, it tells whether or not the death was timely. Second, it specifies the type and direction of demonic attack, and warns of subsequent attacks that threaten the living. Third, it tells whether the birth horoscopes of members of the community are incompatible with that of the deceased, to indicate who may prepare, carry, or cre-

mate the body. Fourth, it reveals the previous life of the deceased and predicts future possible lives, so that the best among these can be promoted by funerary remedies.[13]

The reading of the death horoscope is thus essential for organizing the rest of the funeral ceremony. In other words, every subsequent ritual action is based on the conclusions reached by the astrologer. Among the most significant of these calculations are the immediate cause of death, the prediction of future destiny, and the handling, timing, and direction of corpse removal. It is predicted frequently that the deceased will spend a short period of time in hell (*dmyal-ba, na-rak*) as a result of the fruition of sins accumulated in previous lives. The lama assures the family that the deceased will eventually achieve a favorable rebirth, but only if certain conditions are met, and these tend to be determined by whether or not the family has enough wealth to commission the lama to perform various merit-generating rituals,[14] such as "dredging the depths of hell" (*na-rak dong-sprugs*) or the rites of confession and expiation (*bskang-bshags*).

The corpse is kept inside the house until the day and time determined by the astrological calculations. To prevent the corpse from smelling, it is washed by monks in an iron, copper, or wooden tub containing water scented with camphor, saffron, or other fine fragrances.[15] The bodily orifices are blocked with butter or tied with wool or cotton to prevent any discharge of fluids, and the body is then bound with rope into a crouching position, as described by Ramble, "with the feet together and the knees drawn up. The arms are secured around the thighs with the hand tied between the legs, and the back is broken by pulling the head up and jerking it forward. The head is then pushed down between the knees and the corpse is left to stiffen in that position."[16] Sangay has suggested that breaking the back of the corpse and bundling it in such a way not only prevents it from becoming a zombie but also relieves some of the financial burden of having to hire more than one person to carry the corpse to the cemetery.[17]

The corpse is taken from the house at the specified time. Prior to its removal, however, the bundled body is first wrapped in a white shawl and placed on a platform (*ro bcug-sa*). A framework of four short upright poles is erected around the corpse, with a fifth bound horizontally across the shoulders (representing the arms), and the entire frame is covered in clothing appropriate to the deceased's gender.[18] This construction is designed to serve as an effigy or surrogate body (*sob*) of the deceased. Its head and face are represented by a large ball of wool covered with a white cloth and a sheet of paper on which is sketched the rough features of the deceased's countenance. With incense burning near the doorway to purify the threshold, the platform is turned in the auspicious direction indicated by the astrologer and then carried on the shoulders of several men, each chosen in accordance with the horoscope reading. The procession is led by a lama carrying incense, who is followed by other lamas playing various instruments. Another lama follows behind, holding in his left hand a long white scarf that drags along the ground. This scarf is intended to indicate (*bstan*) to the deceased the path (*lam*) to the cemetery.[19] The symbolic gesture is reminiscent of the ancient Tibetan practice of "showing the path of the dead" (*gshin-lam bstan-pa*) discussed in chapter 2.

When the procession reaches the cemetery (*dur-khrod*), the body is removed from the platform and placed face down on a large flat rock. The framework effigy is dismantled. As a preliminary, the ritual specialist responsible for dismembering and disposing of the body, the so-called corpse-cutter (*phung gtor-pa*, but often *gcod-pa*), burns a heap of purifying incense and slashes the corpse several times with a knife.[20] He then secures the body by tying its neck to a stone and begins to cut it into parts. The scavenging birds (*dur-bya*) that have gathered in the sky are then allowed to consume the body. After the flesh is completely devoured, the brain matter (*klad*) is removed from the skull with a flat stone and placed under a heavy rock while the bones are pulverized into a powder. If the skull has been requested by a lama or by a member of the family, it is set aside, otherwise the skull is also pounded along with the bones. The brain is then taken from underneath the rock and mixed with the powdered remains.[21] The bone and brain mixture are worked into a dough, which is often pressed into the shape of miniature stupas or images of deities (*tsha-tsha*) to be distributed in various pure locations, such as caves, streams, and the branches of trees.[22]

When the procession returns to the house, each person is purified with sacred water and the smoke of burning juniper branches. In this way the entire group is cleansed of the pollution of death. Until the funeral rites are completed, it is believed that the family and home continue to be infected by the impurity of death. Constant fumigation with incense and water are thus necessary. The dangerous presence of spiritual contagion is marked by various ritual taboos that cannot be lifted before the final rites have been performed. Family members wear their hair loose without braids or ribbons and do not wash their faces, wear jewelry, or put on bright-colored clothing.[23] For forty-nine days (believed to be the longest possible duration of the bardo experience) singing and dancing are prohibited, and the family undergoes the prescribed period of mourning.

Throughout the period of mourning, exorcisms are performed. Exorcisms are essentially rites of purification.[24] It is assumed that the demon who ultimately caused the death (*gshed-ma*) may continue to linger near the home, and thus exorcism is performed in order to prevent this evil spirit from seizing another family member. Demons represent the presence of afflictive agents and stand as harbingers of destruction. Generally, demonic attack is explained in terms of principal Buddhist doctrines. It is presumed that demon possession is caused ultimately by the fruition of negative karma and that the only means available for eliminating these past stains and for destroying the afflictive demon is to commission the powers of a lama or lay ritual specialist. In order to perform the exorcism rites, a small ransom effigy (*glud*) is constructed. A figure is carefully crafted by the presiding lama and painted with dyes. This substitute is embellished symbolically in such a way that the demon will be tricked into entering it rather than seizing the life of a family member. A process of deceiving the demon begins with recitation from an exorcism text. As the lama chants verses from the text, he highlights the specific karmic cause of the demon possession. By seizing on this crisis point and linking it to an ethical causal sequence, the lama is able to frame and render intelligible an experience that might otherwise appear as an arbitrary evil. The implicit value of the exorcism lies, therefore, in the lama's power to place potentially incoherent suffering within an acceptable and familiar framework; namely, the ethical sphere of karmic retribution and responsibility.

Through various tantric techniques of visualization and recitation, the lama positions himself deliberately "betwixt and between" the two realms inhabited on one side by the human sponsors and on the other by the afflictive demon. By manipulating his liminal position and luring the demon into the effigy, the lama is able to reenact the critical moment in which the deceased was seized by the death demon. In ritually repeating the first moment of attack, the lama reverses its effect by diverting the evil spirit away from the surviving relatives and into the lifeless substitute, where it is then trapped and rendered powerless. All of this requires an extraordinary spiritual prowess. Tibetan exorcists are thus often perceived as possessing special divine powers and capable of great magical feats. For this reason, they are usually approached with an ambivalence of fear and respect. I will have a chance to return to this subject when I examine the controversial life of Rikzin Nyima Drakpa in chapter 11.

After the rites of disposal, purification, and exorcism are complete, attention turns to the deceased. Since it is believed that in most cases the dead cannot help themselves while traveling along the perilous path of the bardo, they must require the assistance (*rogs-ram*) of their surviving relatives. As I have already begun to show, this assistance is mediated usually by the monastery through a series of rituals prescribed in texts such as those included in the *Peaceful and Wrathful Deities* and *Liberation upon Hearing*. This relationship implies a contractual agreement between lama and patron and rests on faith in the efficacy of the monastery's prayers and rites for the dead. Most participants, monks and laity alike, believe that the deceased can be aided and even liberated by these ritual activities. A passage from a core text of the *Liberation upon Hearing*, the *Direct Introduction to the Bardo of Becoming*, provides a set of reasons for conviction in the lama's guiding power and the benefits of the funeral rites:

> It is impossible that any person of superior, average, or below average capacities not be liberated by these [prayers and ritual actions]. If asked why this is so, it is because [1] consciousness in the bardo possesses mundane clairvoyance and thus it can hear whatever I [the lama] say; [2] even though it is deaf and blind, now its sense faculties are complete, and so it can understand whatever I say; [3] constantly pursued by fear and terror, it thinks with undistracted concentration "What should I do," and thus it always listens to whatever I say; [4] since the consciousness has no support [i.e., body], it immediately goes to whatever is placed before it, and so it is easy to guide; [5] mindfulness is nine times more lucid, so even though it may be stupid, the intellect at this point

has become so clear by the power of karma that it is capable of meditating on everything that is taught. These qualities are the reason it is beneficial to perform the rituals for the dead. It is extremely important, therefore, to persevere in reading this *Great Liberation upon Hearing in the Bardo* for up to forty-nine days.[25]

In basic terms, the bardo ritual is a plea for the purification of the sins of the departed, for release from the perilous pathways of the bardo, and for auspicious rebirth among one of the three higher destinies (human, demigod, or god). The prescribed texts that accompany these rites, such as those included in the *Peaceful and Wrathful Deities* and the *Liberation upon Hearing*, ritually recreate the circumstances of the deceased's journey through the bardo after death and invoke the image of buddhas and bodhisattvas coming down to lead the departed along the path:

> When the time has come to go alone and without friends, may the compassionate ones [i.e., buddhas and bodhisattvas] provide refuge to so-and-so [name of the deceased] who has no refuge. Protect her, defend her, be a refuge from the great darkness of the bardo, turn her away from the great storms of karma, provide comfort from the great fear and terror of the Lord of Death, deliver her from the long and perilous pathway of the bardo.[26]

Some of the Tibetan death texts (usually the ones most familiar in the west) describe the psychophysical process of dying and the separation of consciousness from the body, while others paint images of the harrowing experiences of transition and rebirth. The vast majority of death texts, however, provide ritual directions and prayers for assisting the dead and dying.

On the third or fourth day after death, the lamas gather in the village monastery for the beginning ceremony of the bardo liturgy. This is also the time believed to be the first day of the deceased's journey in the bardo. Prayers are recited and preparations are made for the important guidance rite (*gnas-'dren cho-ga*). A large earthenware jar is suspended from a roof beam in the deceased's home, usually over the site where the corpse had been laid.[27] The jar is dressed in a manner resembling the platform effigy and adorned with various ornaments. Burnt offerings (*sbyin-sreg*) are provided by the family every morning and evening. It is understood that the fragrance from these smoke offerings draws the consciousness of the departed to the house and into the earthen jar. Clearly, this ritual mechanism is founded on the old Indo-Buddhist conception of the bardo consciousness existing in the form of a *gandharva* (*dri-za*), or one "that eats [*arvati, za*] odors [*gandham, dri-ma*]."

Seven days later, the first series of the "seven-day juncture" rites (*bdun-tshigs cho-ga*) are performed. The principle behind this weekly sequence of ritual is the old idea reaching back to the *Abhidharmakośa* that the intermediate state is divided up into seven short phases, each lasting a week, for a total of up to forty-nine days. The ceremony is conducted by the monks at the deceased's home. At the start of the ritual the monks prepare offering cakes (*gtor-ma*) for the performance of a ripening initiation (*smin-byed dbang-grub*), which is believed to purify the sins and enhance the virtues of the departed.

Offerings are placed on an altar or the household shrine, which has been furnished with pictures and objects necessary for the guidance ritual. The images consist usually of various buddhas and bodhisattvas, symbols of ritual offerings, and paintings of the one hundred peaceful and wrathful deities.[28] These pictures (*tsa-ka-li*) are used throughout the guidance ceremony as a means of properly identifying the deities encountered by the deceased along the bardo path (see fig. 4.1).

Prayers and instructions are then read from the texts of the *Peaceful and Wrathful Deities* or the *Liberation upon Hearing*. At best, the reading of these texts occurs throughout each of the seven-day junctures until the forty-ninth day has been reached. It is not uncommon, however, for the full seven-week sequence to be abbreviated.[29] In fact, Martin Brauen has related that in Tibet there actually existed three types of funeral ceremony, each defined in terms of the duration of its performance: "[1] a long ceremony lasting at least one week, but which, when performed in full, could even last seven weeks; [2] a medium-length ceremony lasting two or three days; [3] a short rite lasting two or three hours."[30]

FIGURE 4.1. Picture cards (*tsa-ka-li*) used in the Karling funeral rites, fifteenth century. (Courtesy of The Shelley and Donald Rubin Foundation, no. 289)

The length and frequency of recitation and ritual performance is dependent largely on the wealth of the family.[31] The complete bardo liturgy can be extremely expensive and time-consuming. In my experience among Tibetans in India, rites were observed for several weeks only and rarely exceeded the third juncture of twenty-one days. In all cases, the reasons for the shortened ceremony were both the lack of money and the unavailability of specific high-ranking lamas who were most favored by the sponsors. In spite of the fact that the full forty-nine-day ceremony is not very common, I have chosen to focus here on the complete sequence of the bardo ritual since it best represents the ideal structure inscribed in the ritual texts.

In the third or fourth week, a merit-making ceremony is performed on an astrologically appropriate day.[32] All the monks gather again in the village monastery to perform various purification rites. The effigy is reassembled and placed in front of the main altar along with a printed image (*byang-bu*) of the deceased, which is stamped with his or her name and gender.[33] This name card (*mtshan-byang*) is attached to a stick, placed on a lotus molded from clay or dough, and set in front of a burning candle on the altar so that it faces the larger effigy. The consciousness is then tranferred from the earthenware jar (previously brought from the home) into the printed picture. The leader of the liturgy recites prayers and guiding instructions directly to the printed card. The essential elements of this rite are described by Lauf:

> The sByang-bu [printed image] of the dead person occupies the central position in the ritual, and is addressed during the ceremony, admonished, guided, and imbued with spiritual powers by various abhiṣeka-consecrations, just as if it were an active participant. It is a question of the ability of the awareness-principle to find its way, spontaneously and with the guidance of the lamas, to liberation beyond the places of rebirth. The sByang-bu receives the place of honor in the view of the lama directing the ceremonies and is invited by him to take part in the ritual activity. The dead person's image represents him, and during the death ritual it travels in a symbolically ordered sequence on a specially prepared surface through all the various realms of incarnation that are possible places of rebirth. This surface as a cosmic plan of the six worlds or existence (T. 'Gro-ba'i khams drug) is placed on a rectangular wooden board or on a kind of maṇḍala of the worlds. In the middle row of the rectangular field are six squares representing the six worlds. This row is bordered on either side by another row of six squares. Small bowls of sacrificial rice are placed on the squares of one row for the six Buddhas, and on the other row bowls with small cakes of dough (T. gTor-ma) are placed, which are offered to the inhabitants of the six worlds in the name of the dead person. These gTor-ma offerings are gifts for the evil and demonic spirits of the lower worlds which strive to harm the departed soul.[34]

As the lama describes each of the six realms of rebirth, he places the printed card on the appropriate square, offering a small bowl of rice to the realm's attendant buddha and ritual cakes (*gtor-ma*) to its inhabitants. For each offering made by the lama it is believed that the deceased experiences the corresponding realm. As each move is completed, the gate to that world is symbolically closed and rebirth in that particular location prevented. Here, we should not forget the specialized technique of closing the womb door (*mngal-sgo 'gag-pa*) expounded early on by such figures as Milarepa. We might recall that the notion of obstructing the bardo (*bar-do khegs-par 'gyur*) was one of the hallmarks of the tantric reinterpretation of the exoteric intermediate-state doctrine. That being said, when all gates of rebirth have been shut, the rectangular board is taken away and the lama holds the printed image over the flame of the burning candle. As the fire consumes the paper, the lama pronounces that the sins of the departed have been reconciled and the deceased has found his or her destiny.[35]

The burning of the printed name card marks the end of the standard bardo ritual performed for the average adult.[36] The ashes of the printed card are spared and mixed into the powdered bone and clay mixture retrieved from the cemetery, and all this is formed into small cones or miniature replicas of stupas, buddhas, and bodhisattvas (*tsha-tsha*). For the family on that day the long period of mourning is over and they are permitted to bathe, comb their hair, and so forth.[37] These refreshing and cleansing activities signal the symbolic return of the family to the community of the living and correspond directly to the rites that introduce the deceased into a new world.

The remaining chapters of this study explore the historical process in Tibet that produced the specific set of funerary texts known collectively as the *Self-Liberated Wisdom of the Peaceful and Wrathful Deities* and the *Great Liberation upon Hearing in the Bardo*. Inscribed in these texts are some of Tibet's most popular rites and prayers in preparation for dying, litanies for the aid of the departed, and directives to accompany the general funeral services. In the process of this examination, I will also investigate at some depth the lives of those who created, preserved, and transmitted these texts, and in the end offer a few conclusions about the standardization of the *Liberation upon Hearing* itself with an eye toward the details of its printed history. The next series of chapters addresses the topic of origins, the content and structural unity of Karma Lingpa's treasure revelations, and the earliest propagation of the Karling textual lineages.

II

PROPHECY, CONCEALMENT, REVELATION

5 🍃

Prophecies of the Lotus Guru

This chapter and the next three chapters examine the Tibetan biographies of Karma Lingpa and of his principal disciples, exploring the early history of the transmission of the *Self-Liberated Wisdom of the Peaceful and Wrathful Deities* and the *Great Liberation upon Hearing in the Bardo*, considering the problems encountered in the various narrative accounts of this history with a speculative attempt at resolution, and concluding with the argument that the institutionalization of the liturgy of the *Peaceful and Wrathful Deities* was largely the responsibility of a fifteenth-century monk from southeastern Tibet named Gyarawa Namkha Chökyi Gyatso (b. 1430), the fourth lineage-holder of the Karling transmissions and grand-disciple of Karma Lingpa's son Nyida Chöje. It was this obscure monastic leader and holder of the abbatial throne of Menmo Tashi Gön who composed the largest number of commentaries and instruction manuals on the performance of the Karling rituals, as well as the earliest known history of the tradition.

Since the historical evidence is scattered and difficult to interpret, our knowledge of the origins of the *Peaceful and Wrathful Deities* and of the main figures involved in its discovery and distribution is fragmented and incomplete. What little we do know is based on a small number of Tibetan sources from different historical periods. The most detailed, and hence most important, accounts of the early period can be found in Gyarawa's own *Garland of Jewels: An Abridged History of the Transmission Lineage [Brgyud-pa'i lo-rgyus mdor-bsdus nor-bu'i phreng-ba]*[1], in the brief work of his student Chöje Gedün Gyeltsen (b. 1446),[2] entitled *Precious One from Orgyan's Prophecy of the Treasure Revealer and the Series of the Authentic Lineage Teachers [O-rgyan rin-po-che'i gter-ston lung-bstan dang khung-btsun-pa bla-ma brgyud-pa'i rim-pa rnams]*,[3] and in the *Religious History* of Guru Tashi (eighteenth century).[4] An anonymous seventeenth-century work, the *History of the Treasures*, has also proved quite helpful.[5] The additional histories of Karma

81

Migyur Wangyel (seventeenth century),[6] Kunzang Ngedön Longyang (b. 1814),[7] Jamgön Kongtrül (1813–1899),[8] and Dujom Rinpoche (1904–1987)[9] are generally repetitive but nevertheless useful, and occasionally provide details not found in our four principal texts.

The details concerning the prophecies (*lung-bstan*) of Padmasambhava on the future revelation of the *Peaceful and Wrathful Deities* are drawn almost exclusively from an incomplete cursive manuscript extant in only one recension of the Karling cycle. This is a work entitled *Revelation Prophecy and Authorizing Order of "The Profound Doctrine of the Self-Liberated Wisdom of the Peaceful and Wrathful Deities" and "Great Compassionate One, the Peaceful and Wrathful Lotus"* [*Zab-chos zhi-khro dgongs-pa rang-grol dang thugs-rje chen-po padma zhi-khro las lung-bstan bka'-rgya*].[10] The manuscript is unfortunately missing its concluding folios, so we have no access to its colophon. But since the prophecy was an integral component of treasure revelations in Tibet, we can only assume that the *Revelation Prophecy and Authorizing Order* was included among the earliest works attributed to Karma Lingpa. It is certainly possible that Karma Lingpa wrote the text himself to authenticate and explain the existence of his discoveries. The question of scriptural authenticity was never far from the minds of those Tibetans who came into contact with the so-called treasure revealers (*gter-ston*) and their treasures (*gter-ma*). Often suspected of fraud and deceit, these scriptural visionaries were compelled to demonstrate a living connection to authoritative events and personalities in the significant past.[11] In particular, as I will show later, the treasure cults in the age of Karma Lingpa usually looked to the extraordinary figure of Padmasambhava, a legendary eighth-century exorcist from Orgyen, who, according to some late Tibetan Buddhist narratives, had been invited to Tibet by the emperor Trhi Songdetsen to subdue the malevolent spirits indigenous to that country.

In Part II, I will draw from the sources just introduced to construct a purely descriptive narrative of the prophecies, early personalities, and events surrounding the treasure revelations of Karma Lingpa. Derived as it is from scriptural sources that are more or less "carefully contrived ideal paradigms," the picture presented may not be properly historical in the usual sense of the term.[12] This, however, should not detract from the overall purpose of these chapters. Here my primary concern has been to piece together from fragmented and often conflicting details the founding story of the Karling transmissions as the proponents of the tradition themselves appear to imagine it. This story offers a glimpse of how some Tibetan historians have envisioned the nature of certain religious texts and the power of scriptural revelation. I shall now proceed to narrate their vision.

Concealed Treasures

The collection of texts that make up the *Peaceful and Wrathful Deities*, including the *Liberation upon Hearing*, are claimed to have been originally composed in the eighth century by Padmasambhava. This obscure yogi, who was later to be retroactively identified as the founding father of Tibetan Buddhism and of its most ancient tradition, the Nyingmapa, is believed to have concealed a vast array of texts and religious objects in unusual and remote locations so that they would later be discovered at the appropriate time by some treasure hunter who had been especially mandated as the appointed excavator. These prophesied individuals were known as treasure revealers (gter-ston). Among the many famous discoverers of these hidden treasures was Karma Lingpa.

As a genre, the treasure (gter-ma) constitutes an unquestionably Tibetan class of heterogenous literature that began to appear in Tibet around the eleventh century.[13] Typically understood as concealed apocrypha, the treasure texts came to be accepted primarily by the Nyingmapa as authentic relics from the golden age of the Tibetan emperors.[14] In addition to creating and sustaining a paradisaic mythology of Tibetan dynastic history—which incidentally could be utilized as a tool for furthering political agendas—many of the treasure texts introduced new and innovative interpretations of older religious ideas and techniques, or simply popularized in the form of prayer and liturgy what had previously existed only in the clandestine and rarefied atmosphere of elite yogis and scholarly monks. The Nyingthik tradition of Dzokchen, for example, extended its renown in part by circulating its esoteric theories in the form of scriptures claiming to have been excavated from buried sources. These apocryphal statements of doctrine were authenticated by the religious experience of the revealer, whose revelation re-called into being the original intention of Padmasambhava, or some other buddhalike figure in Tibet's glorified past. The treasure text itself granted direct access to that earlier period when Tibet was powerful and Buddhism was at its zenith. In this way, the treasure tradition provided a means for producing legitimate scripture outside the limits of the canonical hegemony, in most cases believed to have direct links to India.[15] Indeed, of most relevance in the present context, it is among these hidden treasures that much of Tibet's conceptual and liturgical innovations surrounding death and afterlife can be located. Hence it appears that treasure was the prime mechanism by which the distinctive systems found in the ritual and literary works of the Peaceful and Wrathful Deities were first articulated.

Generally speaking, in the Tibetan treasure traditions the first moments in the creation and subsequent transmission of the actual treasure doctrine (gter-chos) is said to take place in three successive phases: (1) the wisdom-mind transmission of the victorious buddhas (rgyal-ba'i dgongs-brgyud); (2) the symbolic transmission of the awareness-holders (rig-'dzin brda'i-brgyud); (3) the authentic oral transmission of human beings (gang-zag snyan-khung-du brgyud-pa).[16] Since these three modes are used to frame the narrative presented in Gyarawa's Garland of Jewels, I will employ this scheme as a way to organize my discussion hereafter. Briefly, in Gyarawa's descriptions of the first and second phases in the transmission of the Peaceful and Wrathful Deities, he does not recount the entire myth but rather summarizes the key features of the standard narrative, beginning with the silent but profound exchanges between the dharmakāya buddha Samantabhadra and the buddhas Vajradhāra and Vajrasattva.[17] The second period of the symbolic transmission commences with the blessings of Vajrasattva on the siddha Garap Dorje. The story of this enigmatic figure is narrated along conventional lines, from his immaculate conception to his meditative exploits at the great charnel ground Cool Grove (Tib., *Bsil-ba'i-tshal*, Skt., *Sītavana*).[18] It is at this famous cemetery that we are also introduced to the ascetic Śrī Siṃha.[19] Using secret signs, Garap Dorje bestows on Śrī Siṃha the essential meaning of the six million four hundred thousand Dzokchen tantras. Sometime later, at the charnel ground Sosaling (Skt., *Sosadvīpa*), Padmasambhava, together with the Paṇḍit Vimalamitra and king Jñānasūtra, come to sit respectfully at the feet of Śrī Siṃha to receive his blessings. In a burst of pulsating light issuing from a stupa in the center of the charnel ground, the three humble disciples awaken to all the essential points of Dzokchen doctrine.[20] With this last spectacular event, Gyarawa's account of the first two transmissions comes to a close. The last phase, the authentic oral transmission of human teachers, is the focus of the greater part of the *Garland of Jewels*.

The treasure of Karma Lingpa, like most literature of this kind, is described as having its literary roots in Tibet's dynastic past. In Janet Gyatso's recent analysis of the treasure of Jikme Lingpa (1730–1798), she identifies a distinctive but apparently universal feature of the treasure myth, noting that the "origin myth is part of the larger narrative cycle that relates the introduction of Buddhism to Tibet."[21] Indeed, the treasure records frequently contain stories of the emperors Songtsen Gampo (c. 609–649) and Trhi Songdetsen, of the Indian monk-scholar Śāntarakṣita, of the great debates between the Indian "gradualist" Kamalaśīla and the Chinese "subitist" Heshang Moheyan or, most important, of the timely arrival of Padmasambhava to clear a space in Tibet's wild domain for the adoption of Buddhism. The profoundly emotional significance of Padmasambhava in the "national memory of Tibetan Buddhists" is beyond dispute, for

> he is given credit for making possible the conversion of the country to Buddhism, a fundamental component of Tibetan identity certainly by the eleventh century. An integral part of that accomplishment, at least according to the Treasure lineages, was the compassion that the Precious Guru directed toward the Tibetans of the future when he concealed special texts and other Treasures for their benefit.[22]

Padmasambhava's concern for the happiness and well-being of future generations is thus identified as the motivating force behind his creation and subsequent concealment of the *Self-Liberated Wisdom of the Peaceful and Wrathful Deities*, and especially the teachings that would later be known as the *Great Liberation upon Hearing in the Bardo*. As is typical of the treasure-founding narratives, this story, which is drawn mainly from the *Revelation Prophecy and Authorizing Order*, begins at the court of the Tibetan emperor Trhi Songdetsen.

Prophecies

The construction of Samye, the first Buddhist monastery in Tibet, was completed in the late eighth century (probably around 779). To celebrate its successful establishment, according to the *Revelation Prophecy and Authorizing Order*, the emperor Trhi Songdetsen is said to have invited his queen Tshepong, Padmasambhava and his consort Yeshe Tshogyel, the translator Choro Lu'i Gyeltsen, and the royal ministers to the Maitreya temple Jambaling at the newly erected monastery. The text recounts that while this group is discussing the extent of the emperor's dominion, the divinity of Tibet, and the fortunes of her people, who had now begun practicing the ten Buddhist virtues,[23] Padmasambhava speaks out in a cautionary tone:

> Alas! Now that the emperor's intentions have been fulfilled, Tibet has become a happy and joyous place, blessed by supreme translators, teachers, and people practicing the ten virtues. But one day, all of these things will fall victim to impermanence and disappear. Generally speaking, all compounded things are impermanent and before long fall apart, especially the divine joys and pleasures of Tibet, which are as transient and fleeting as a colorful rainbow in the sky. Consequently, you should think now about what will happen in the future and examine [your thoughts] very closely.[24]

After Padmasambhava speaks, the group grows anxious. Respectfully bowing down before the teacher, they offer him gifts and plead: "O, Buddha of the three times who has prophetic knowledge of the future, we ask that you give us a prophecy in order to dispel our doubts." Padmasambhava smiles benevolently and from his smile a beam of light radiates out and strikes their hearts. The bliss-energy of this magnificent light causes their bodies to tremble and their minds become focused one-pointedly.[25] Padmasambhava then establishes himself in deep meditative concentration. From within this state, he says:

> Listen, supreme translators, teachers, royal ministers, and the people of Tibet! Religious laws are impermanent. All leaders will perish [eventually]. As a prophetic sign that the imperial rule is disintegrating, the Tibetan people will no longer heed the emperor, his lawless ministers will disobey him, and no one will be skilled in applying the Buddha's teaching for the welfare of living beings. Who then will gain the merit resulting from the fruition of past enlightened activities? Lhasa, Trhadruk,[26] and Samye will be weakened. Manure, meat, and liqour will be stored up in the monasteries, and the Three Jewels will be thrown out like corpses. In particular, loving mothers and fathers will be beaten like criminals. All the religious centers established by the emperor will fall to ruins, and the people who live nearby will suffer. One day there will be no religion at all in Tibet. Also, for many years to come there will be neither lords nor subjects. Tibetans will fear the Hor [i.e., Mongolians] and there will be little joy. Tibet's riches will be depleted. O! The Buddha's true teaching [will be handed over to] demons who will pervert the vows. Gradually, fear will arise.[27]

Padmasambhava warns relentlessly of the horrors that await Tibet and her people. His focus then turns to the inevitable collapse of the monastic institution and the subsequent distortion of Buddhist doctrine:

As an early omen of the breakdown of monastic discipline, a demonic emanation of the serpent-goddess (*klu-mo*) Gangzang Bumo Özer will possess the
hearts of Tibetan women, and male renunciants will become deeply entwined
in the five passions [desire, hatred, delusion, pride, and envy]. Women will
devour malicious gossip like a delicious meal, and sleep around behind their
husbands' backs [*smad-tshong*]. They will bathe themselves clean and then
speak [alluringly] and make flirtatious gestures. Even though Buddhist doctrine warns that lust is to be avoided, these [enticing] women will appear very
attractive to the monks and will satisfy [their desires]. [After becoming pregnant, the women] will nurture their babies. This sort of "religious practitioner" will accumulate sins, and the Tibetan people will lose faith in Buddhism.
Out of pride, people will seek initiation into the religious life in pursuit of fame
and fortune. They will have little compassion and will refuse to obey the rules.
Behaving poorly, they will engage in violent and destructive activities. As a
result, the dark demonic forces will rejoice and the light divine forces will be
defeated, followed by the destruction of the doctrine.[28]

By this point in the story Padmasambhava's audience seems to have grown
despondent, for he is said to have exhorted them to seek refuge in the Three
Jewels—Buddha, dharma, and sangha. Acknowledging the difficulty of dis-
ciplined practice, he emphasizes the importance of the teacher and then gives
them the instructions and initiations for the worship of the lama.[29]

Gyarawa's account of these prophecies in his *Garland of Jewels* differs
slightly from that of the presumably earlier *Revelation Prophecy and Authorizing Order*, suggesting perhaps that the unique elements are of Gyarawa's own
invention or creative interpretations. In the *Garland of Jewels*, Gyarawa relates
that the emperor Trhi Songdetsen, the translator Lu'i Gyeltsen, and the others
in the royal entourage offer Padmasambhava a gold and turquoise mandala and
in despair ask him to give them a secret teaching that will liberate them in one
single lifetime without any effort whatsoever.[30] Padmasambhava responds by
offering them a teaching said to be so powerful that it requires no practical effort:
"By simply being heard, this teaching will close the gates leading to rebirth in
the lower realms; by simply understanding it, you will depart to the realm of
Great Bliss [Sukhāvati]; and by pondering its meaning, you will reach the level
of nonregression."[31]

Padmasambhava then warns them about Tibet's dark future, adding that
his own doctrines are destined to be misunderstood and slandered by foolish
people. Padmasambhava then condenses all the Dzokchen teachings into a
single abridged scripture, gives it the title *Self-Liberated Wisdom of the Peaceful and Wrathful Deities*, and conceals it as a treasure on Gampodar mountain in Dakpo. In connection with this momentous event, Padmasambhava
offers a prophecy forecasting the future discovery of the treasure.

Padmasambhava's treasure prophecy is found, in somewhat varied form,
both in the *Revelation Prophecy and Authorizing Order* and in the anonymous *History of the Treasures*. In the former version, the prophecy is made
in reference not to the *Self-Liberated Wisdom of the Peaceful and Wrathful
Deities,* as we might expect, but rather to the other treasure cycle attributed
to Karma Lingpa, the obscure *Great Compassionate One, the Peaceful and*

Wrathful Lotus. The significance of this attribution is not clear, but it is note-worthy that evidence exists in the literature suggesting that these two trea-sure collections may have been conflated with one another very early in the history of the tradition. Perhaps the confusion may have been the result of the similarity in content of the two cycles.

In the later version contained in the *History of the Treasures*, Padma-sambhava's treasure prophecy is written as follows.

> In order to preserve and maintain for [future] dissemination this profound teach-ing called *Self-Liberated Wisdom of the Peaceful and Wrathful Deities*, I have hidden it as a precious treasure. Alas! O noble children! The fortunate one who is destined to uncover this teaching will come endowed with a beautiful silver body, outspoken [*smra-'don*], and in wrathful form. At times he will be as ill-tempered as a brute and at other times appear in the form of an aimless child.[32] O! This noble son will be surrounded by divine mothers and ḍākinīs. With great power of faith, insight, and sharp intelligence he will appear in a dragon or snake year with a glorious name in the form of an independently-minded hero [*mi-sems mi-'dzin dpa'-po*]. This very being [will be the incarnation of] the translator Lu'i Gyeltsen. By connecting up with this [fortunate one] my doctrine will become priceless. By being both seen and heard, this teaching will put an end to the cycle of existence. The revealer of the treasure will come to have ten disciples gathered around him.[33]

In the *Revelation Prophecy and Authorizing Order*, a troubling future is forecast for this revealer of the treasure:

> [He will be] white in color, sweet-smelling, with beautiful eyes, and a longish nose. Smiling, he will be like the long and slow movements of the Khyung bird's wings.[34] In the year of the mouse he will serve as protector for all living beings. He will be handsome and, as a sign of his enlightened mind, will have a mole on his right thigh. This good person will have a glorious name and will either come from Nyang, Kongpo, or Kham. Not before the teaching of a thou-sand Buddhas is complete will the teaching of this leader of beings named "Karma" be exhausted. [All who] venerate him will be born in the realm of Great Bliss [Sukhāvati], and [all who] have a spontaneous visionary under-standing of only a portion of his teaching will certainly purify their karmic obscurations within seven rebirths. His enlightened mind will be an emana-tion of Avalokiteśvara's and his liberation is certain. As lord he will surely serve as protector of his Tibetan followers. Wherever they happen to be, that place will be full of luxury. [But] some disruptive demon will create a sudden danger. Perilous obstructions will originate from within this fortunate one's own circle. [In the year of] the iron pig, beware of the violator of the samaya vows, the defilement of the black one![35]

In Gyarawa's *Garland of Jewels*, Padmasambhava simply offers a prayer to the appointed revealer of the concealed teachings. The prophecy of betrayal is not mentioned:

> Alas! The pinnacle of all the teachings [is this *Self-Liberated Wisdom of the Peaceful and Wrathful Deities*],
> it is the supreme essence of all unexcelled secrets,
> The method that liberates into great bliss those who suffer.

It is the spontaneous attainment of manifest buddhahood right now,
it is the meaningful essence of the wisdom of the victorious buddhas of the
    three times.
This condensed elixir is like the refined essence of butter.
It was concealed by Padmasambhava of Orgyen,
as a precious treasure to be written, but not disseminated, for the benefit of
    future generations.
At the end of the [degenerate] age when the lifespan is only fifty years,
all those who do not possess instructions such as these,
will without doubt go to the lower realms.
For the benefit of sentient beings living in degenerate times,
I put this teaching in writing and concealed it at Gampo mountain.
At some point during the degenerate age, my supreme and worthy heart-son
    will come.
His father will be a siddha named Nyida.
He, who will be called Karma Lingpa, will have religious courage.
As a sign of his revelatory pristine wisdom, his right thigh will be marked
    with a mole.
[He will be born] in a dragon or snake year into a heroic lineage possessed
    of good karma. May this teaching connect up with this fortunate being.[36]

In Gedün Gyeltsen's *Series of the Authentic Lineage Teachers*, Padmasambhava speaks of the transmission of the treasure itself, his transmission
prophecy. According to this source, the treasure had in fact been divided into
two separate collections, the *Self-Liberated Wisdom of the Peaceful and
Wrathful Deities* and the *Great Compassionate One, the Peaceful and Wrathful
Lotus*. We are told that the first collection was not to be revealed to others,
"not even to the wind itself," for at least three generations. Padmasambhava
warns of serious complications if the doctrines are disclosed before the appropriate time.[37] The second collection, the *Peaceful and Wrathful Lotus*, is
to be immediately distributed to the treasure revealer's most qualified students, who are also asked to keep it secret until the time of the third-generation
disciple. Once the third-generation disciple has received the transmission, the
texts are again to remain secret for a specified number of years.[38] Only after
seven years, for example, can the seal be broken on the *Liberation upon
Hearing in the Bardo*, which presumably was drawn from both collections,
the *Peaceful and Wrathful Deities* and the *Peaceful and Wrathful Lotus*. On
the other hand, the entire *Peaceful and Wrathful Deities* is to be propagated
only after a period of nine years, but then not all at once.[39] Several traditional
reasons are offered as explanation for this peculiar fixation on secrecy and
the almost obsessive preoccupation with the precise year in which the treasure is to be transmitted,[40] but I agree with Janet Gyatso's suggestion that all
this secrecy seems "to reflect an anxiety within the tradition about a proliferation of Treasures and an attempt to regulate their formulation."[41] It is as if
these texts were threatened from every angle, and such precautionary mea-
sures were of paramount importance for their continued survival. Perhaps this
was the guarded response of a perceived antagonism, real or imagined, di-

rected against those groups that openly accepted the authority of the ideas and practices contained in these treasures.

The treasure regulations recorded in Gedün Gyeltsen's *Series of the Authentic Lineage Teachers* differs from the ones in Gyarawa's *Garland of Jewels*. Statements styled as eighth-century divine prophecy in the former text appear in the latter to have been simply the human injunctions of Karma Lingpa's son, Nyida Chöje, to the lama Nyida Özer (often referred to by the Sanskrit form of his name, Guru Sūryacandraraśmi). In Gedün Gyeltsen's version of events, Nyida Chöje, rather than Padmasambhava, enjoins that the *Self-Liberated Wisdom of the Peaceful and Wrathful Deities* is to be kept secret for six years (rather than seven) and that a smaller text cycle entitled *Great Bliss of the Lower Orifice* is to be silently practiced for ten.[42] No mention is made of either the *Peaceful and Wrathful Lotus* or the *Liberation upon Hearing in the Bardo*.

Gedün Gyeltsen continues by noting a rather specific transmission prophecy that in a future degenerate age the treasure, identified here as the "transmitted precepts of Daklha Gampo," will first appear in the southeastern regions of Dakpo and lower Kongpo, and then its practice will become concentrated in areas such as Longpo, Drakpo, and upper Kongpo.[43] It is then related that because of certain negative forces very few Tibetans will understand the treasure doctrines, and so people will slander them with all sorts of false claims and distorted interpretations. This is offered as one compelling reason for secrecy. A small group of clandestine yogins will nevertheless succeed in perfecting the treasure's practice. They will be abused and persecuted by demons, but to no avail. The guardian spirits (*srung-ma*) charged by Padmasambhava to protect the treasure will ensure that they are entrusted to the proper beneficiary. Finally, Padmasambhava proclaims that from this fortunate individual the treasure will spread in a succession of single one-to-one transmissions (*gcig-brgyud*) from teacher to student.[44]

The detail provided here by Gedün Gyeltsen is noteworthy, particularly his identification (in the prophetic voice of Padmasambhava) of the specific regions of Tibet where the treasure of the *Peaceful and Wrathful Deities* would be most active. In Gyarawa's *Garland of Jewels*, we read that Padmasambhava simply prophesied a spread of the treasure "throughout the northern region." The actual names of Tibetan districts in this general area are absent.[45] So then why do place names appear in Gedün Gyeltsen's version of the transmission prophecy? The answer may be historical. By the time Gedün Gyeltsen had begun to compose his short history of the Karling transmission, its practices had already begun to be spread from his teacher's home region of lower Kongpo. The convenient fact that Padmasambhava was said to have previously predicted that this movement would take place simply reflects the author's conviction in the treasure's validity and provides a rationale for its continued transmission. Indeed, we do know that the area of the earliest diffusion of the *Peaceful and Wrathful Deities* were those parts of Tibet indicated in this text; namely, Dakpo, Longpo, and Kongpo. It is certain that the treasure of Karma Lingpa originated in Dakpo and, for a relatively long period after its discovery, remained and was fostered in the general vicinity of Longpo and Kongpo. It was only after Gyarawa's institutionalization of its practices sometime in the late fifteenth century that the *Peaceful and Wrathful Deities* and the *Liberation upon Hearing* found their way to other regions of Tibet.

The preceding descriptions of the various prophecies proclaimed at the court of the emperor Trhi Songdetsen, have established a general context for investigations into the history of Karma Lingpa's textual tradition. The next chapter continues the story by introducing the biographies of the early players in this history.

6 🍃

A Tale of Fathers and Sons

Planting the Stalk at Black Mandala Lake

According to the *Religious History* of Guru Tashi, in Padmasambhava's pronouncements before the royal court of Trhi Songdetsen he not only spoke of a discoverer named Karma but also introduced the prophecy of the coming of one who would be known as Nyida Sangye (Sun-Moon Buddha), elsewhere known as Ngödrup (Accomplished Adept).[1] The anonymous author of the *History of the Treasures* interprets the following prophetic statement as a reference to this figure:

> In the year of the sheep, there will come one bearing the name Ngödrup,
> with big eyes and a prominent forehead,
> intelligent, hardworking, faithful, and courageous.
> As a sign of his [good] karma, he will be handsome with a mole on his
>   belly.
> By virtue of these [qualities] he will nurture and protect the lama's complete
>   liberation.[2]

This Ngödrup, also known as Nyida Sangye, was born in Dakpo as the rebirth of Trhi Songdetsen's royal minister Nyima. According to a legend described briefly in Guru Tashi's *Religious History*, the minister Nyima had mysteriously set fire to his own house, killing a number of people and destroying the family's herd of livestock.[3] As a result, he accumulated a mass of negative karma and was afflicted by great suffering. Speaking on his behalf, the emperor asked Padmasambhava for a religious practice that would purify the minister's sins. Instantly, Padmasambhava traveled magically to Sukhāvati (Blissful Realm) and met personally with the buddha Amitābha, who gave him teachings called *Profound Instructions on the Rainbow Body Transference* [*Gdams-zab 'pho-ba 'ja'-gzugs-ma*], also known as

Planting the Stalk [*'Jag-zug-ma*].[4] Padmasambhava drew blood from the middle finger of his left hand and copied down Amitābha's instructions on a palm leaf. Afterward he placed the parchment leaves sequentially in five caskets (*sgrom*) made of gold, silver, turquoise, crystal, and iron and concealed them in a mandala-shaped lake behind Gampo mountain in Dakpo.[5] As a boon, the royal minister Nyima offered Padmasambhava the "golden sun and silver moon," meaning he heaped upon him a mass of precious gifts. Pleased that the circumstances surrounding this offering were genuinely auspicious, Padmasambhava prophesied that Amitābha's treasure would be discovered in the future by one named Nyida (Sun Moon).[6] The expression "sun-moon" (*nyi-zla*) occurs prominently in the names of the first three lineage-holders of Karma Lingpa's treasure tradition.

Sometime in the late thirteenth or early fourteenth century, a treasure revealer by the name of Nyida Sangye extracted from the Black Mandala Lake (*mtsho maṇḍala nag-po*) in Dakpo a hidden cycle of instructions on consciousness transference (*'pho-ba*)[7] and offered them as a gift to the serpent-king Tsukna Rinchen.[8] So powerful was this treasure, we are told, that all the spirits and creatures living in the lake were said to be able to attain buddhahood simply by practicing its techniques. Nyida Sangye also discovered a marvelous statue of the eleven-faced Avalokiteśvara in the Turquoise Lake (*g.yu-mtsho*) at Tsari.[9] According to Guru Tashi, this statue could still be seen in his day in the southern region of Nyel.[10]

We know relatively little about the life of Nyida Sangye. He appears to have been a student of the second Zhamarpa Khachö Wangpo (1350–1405),[11] which would place him in the late fourteenth century.[12] This lineal connection to the Karma Kagyu tradition may explain why Nyida Sangye's son was named Karma Lingpa. The generic prefix "Karma" has traditionally been the ordination name for followers of the Karma Kagyu order. In addition, as I will show in part III, this early Kagyu affiliation may also help to explain the fact that several other important Zhamarpa hierarchs played active roles as teachers of some of the key holders of Karma Lingpa's treasure transmissions. Moreover, the important monasteries that maintained the Karling rituals shared close alliances with the Karmapa tradition, for example, the monasteries of Dakpo Tsele and Kongpo Thangdrok. This is not surprising, since in this period the regions surrounding Dakpo and Kongpo were strongholds of the Karma Kagyu school, particularly of the Zhamarpa and Pawo subsects.

Nyida Sangye is claimed to have assisted his son in uncovering concealed treasure from Gampodar Mountain in Dakpo.[13] Nyida Sangye's involvement in the discovery of his son's treasure apparently led to a minor confusion surrounding the proper identity of the revealer of both the *Great Compassionate One, the Peaceful and Wrathful Lotus* and a teaching entitled the *Three-Bodied Teacher* [*Bla-ma sku-gsum*], which is perhaps an abbreviated title for Karma Lingpa's *Yoga of the Three-Bodied-Teacher* [*Sku-gsum bla-ma'i rnal-'byor*].[14] According to the story, Nyida Sangye seemed one day to disappear into thin air but had actually traveled magically to the celestial Copper-colored Mountain to meet personally with Padmasambhava. At this

splendid site he received teachings on the special practice of consciousness
transference ('*pho-ba*).[15] It was this teaching on consciousness transference
in the form of a hidden treasure that some identified as Karma Lingpa's *Peaceful and Wrathful Lotus*. Guru Tashi argues against this identification, claiming that the *Peaceful and Wrathful Lotus* could not have been discovered by
Nyida Sangye because the historical sources say it was found by his son Karma
Lingpa.[16] It is still possible, however, that Nyida Sangye may have helped
his son recover and distribute this teaching, and in fact Guru Tashi notes that
the doctrinal lineage (*chos-brgyud*) of the *Peaceful and Wrathful Lotus* appears to have been spread more by Karma Lingpa's father than by Karma
Lingpa himself.[17] In the unfortunate absence of the texts in question the issue
remains a mystery. Nevertheless, the suggestion that Nyida Sangye was the
main distributor of the *Peaceful and Wrathful Lotus* is compelling. He is said
to have long outlived his son by several decades.[18]

The Strange Case of the Poisoned Visionary

The eighth-century translator Choro Lu'i Gyeltsen, in accordance with the
prophetic declarations of Padmasambhava, is claimed to have been reborn as
the treasure revealer Karma Lingpa in the fourteenth century in a town called
Khyerdrup in eastern Dakpo.[19] Karma Lingpa was the eldest son of the treasure-hunting siddha Nyida Sangye. At fifteen, we are told, Padmasambhava's
prophecy and the auspicious connections (*rten-'brel*) converged, and Karma
Lingpa excavated a series of treasures from Gampodar Mountain deep within
the jagged heights of Daklha Gampo (see fig. 6.1). These Gampodar treasures
comprised two major literary collections, the *Self-Liberated Wisdom of the
Peaceful and Wrathful Deities* and the *Great Compassionate One, the Peaceful
and Wrathful Lotus*. In some of the later histories a third work was also said
to be included, the *Eight Classes of Protectors* [*Mgon-po sde-brgyad*].[20]

Karma Lingpa presented the *Peaceful and Wrathful Lotus* to fourteen of
his most qualified students, while at the same time severely restricting the
circulation of the *Peaceful and Wrathful Deities*.[21] The teachings and initiations specific to the latter collection were given only to one person as a
single transmission.[22] In doing this Karma Lingpa was merely following the
mandates set by Padmasambhava in the prophecies discussed in the last chapter
concerning the proper transmission of the treasure. Evidently, he did choose to
distribute more freely a special set of bardo instructions drawn from both cycles;
this was the *Guiding Instructions on the Six Bardos* [*Bar-do drug-khrid*].

These instructions form the work known to us as *Completion Stage Guidebook to the Six Bardos* [*Rdzogs-rim bar-do drug-gi khrid-yig*], or simply *Self-Liberated Wisdom-Mind: The Experiential Instructions* [*Nyams-khrid dgongspa rang-grol*], which is extant in only one recension of the Karling collection.[23]
This significant set of short yogic manuals draws heavily on the Nyingthik
techniques of the Dzokchen system. Although its colophon indicates that the
collection was one of Karma Lingpa's original revealed works,[24] I am of the

FIGURE 6.1. The jagged peaks of the Daklha Gampo mountain range in Dakpo. (Photograph by Andrew Quintman)

opinion that the texts may actually have been written in the mid-fifteenth century by Nyida Özer, student of Karma Lingpa's son Nyida Chöje. As I will show briefly later, the fact that Nyida Özer is the only disciple explicitly named as recipient of this transmission leads me to believe he must have had a major hand in the production of the texts themselves, either as author, editor, or compiler. If this is true, then it is likely that Nyida Özer was working from Karma Lingpa's original instructions, transmitted to him, in some form or another, by the treasure revealer's son. In this regard, Nyida Özer may have been preserving for the first time in writing the oral lineage leading back directly to Karma Lingpa himself.[25]

The fact that some of the most significant of Karma Lingpa's bardo instructions were found in both the *Peaceful and Wrathful Deities* and the *Peaceful and Wrathful Lotus* collections is noteworthy, since it suggests that the latter cycle was also an important source for teachings on death and dying. In this context, recall that the *Peaceful and Wrathful Lotus* had been mistakenly conflated with the instructions on consciousness transference (*'pho-ba*) transmitted in a vision from Padmasambhava to Karma Lingpa's father, Nyida Sangye. The one text we do have that identifies itself as belonging to this elusive corpus is devoted entirely to the postmortem drama of the bardo of becoming (*srid-pa bar-do*). This text, entitled *Self-Liberation of the Bardo of Becoming: Instructions on "The Presentation of the Natural Form of Virtue and Vice in the Bardo of Becoming"* [*Srid-pa bar-do'i dge-sdig rang-gzugs bstan-pa'i gdams-pa srid-pa bar-do rang-grol*] describes the final period of the deceased's wandering in the bardo and presents an account of judgement before the Lord of the Dead, Shinje Chökyi Gyelpo.[26] It has been suggested that this text, representing a sort of morality play, lies at the center of a popular Bhutanese dance of the judgement of the dead, called Dance of Many Rakṣa (rakṣa-mang-'chams), as well as Dance of the Rakṣa from Below (rakṣa-mar-'chams). This is performed during the religious festival known as Tshechu (tshes-bcu).[27] Françoise Pommaret writes about the sources of this famous danse macabre:

> In Bhutan, this dance is extremely popular and the tradition attibutes the origin to Karma-gling-pa, the famous gter-ston [treasure revealer]. . . . One may recall in particular that this gter-ston had exerted a determining influence on the accounts of the 'das-log [i.e., people who have died and returned to life] thanks to his text the Bar-do thos-grol [Liberation upon Hearing in the Bardo]. However, just as one finds in both the Bar-do thos-grol and the 'das-log accounts a section that deals with some judgement of the dead, i.e. of the retribution of actions after death, the dance which has been inspired by the writings of Karma-gling-pa is also devoted to this theme.[28]

The drama is also performed regularly in Tibet, at all of the monasteries and nunneries that still foster liturgies of the Karling tradition, for example, the Zhotö Tidro nunnery near Drigung.[29] It is not suprising that this nunnery has continued to maintain an active Karling tradition, given its earlier connection to the treasures of Rinchen Phüntshok (1509–1557). As I will soon show, this important Drigungpa figure, together with his student Karma Guru (1550–1602), had played an important role in the distribution of the teachings of both Karma Lingpa and his father Nyida Sangye.

Although it appears that the two Peaceful and Wrathful cycles discovered by Karma Lingpa each included teachings on the bardo, the actual organized set of such teachings called Great Liberation upon Hearing in the Bardo seem to have been derived solely from the Self-Liberated Wisdom of the Peaceful and Wrathful Deities. There is reason to believe, however, that the Peaceful and Wrathful Lotus also contained its own Liberation upon Hearing. In the opening lines of the Presentation of the Natural Form of Virtue and Vice in the Bardo of Becoming mentioned earlier, we find the expression, "[this text is included] in the Liberation upon Hearing in the Bardo of the Peaceful and Wrathful Lotus" (padma zhi khro'i bar do thos grol las).[30] It is unclear whether this particular Liberation upon Hearing was the same as that found in the Peaceful and Wrathful Deities. If the two are in fact related, then the Liberation upon Hearing as we know it would probably have represented a mixture of materials from both cycles. In time, the particular Liberation upon Hearing that belonged to the Peaceful and Wrathful Lotus must have been eclipsed by the apparently alternative version included in the Peaceful and Wrathful Deities. For now, unfortunately, the actual historical relationships between these texts must remain a mystery.

Questions concerning the historical identity of the popular Liberation upon Hearing collection introduce some rather complicated problems. Likewise, the legends surrounding the transmission of these textual treasures are also complex. The tale is not sweet; it is a bizarre blend of distorted connections, woeful inexperience, and murder. Although there are a number of different versions of the narrative, all of them end in tragedy. Unlike the usual Tibetan hagiography, the life of Karma Lingpa is far from perfect. The circumstances in which he found himself were dark and sinister, full of paranoia, misfortune, and betrayal. The inauspicious events of his life are encapsulated in three short episodes. I begin with the tale of mistaken auspices.

Generally it is held that the successful discovery of a hidden treasure requires the fulfillment of the completion phase (rdzogs-rim) of tantric practice, in which special meditative techniques are employed that usually involve the manipulation of sexual energies. In these types of practices, the treasure revealer is expected to engage in certain sexual activities with a female consort. His union with this consort is designed to generate and reawaken in his mind the radiant light of bliss-emptiness (bde-stong-gi 'od-gsal)—the medium in which Padmasambhava had originally concealed the treasure in the mind of the discoverer's past incarnation.[31] By generating this radiant bliss-emptiness, the treasure revealer recreates his previous state of mind when Padmasambhava had first initiated him into the teaching.[32] This process opens the door to Padmasambhava's secret hiding place and permits the discoverer to find the treasure hidden there. The successful fulfillment of this practice, however, is not as straightforward as this description would lead us to believe. The treasure revealer cannot get involved with just any female acquaintance; she must be the right woman, that is, the specific woman chosen by Padmasambhava, or by his consort Yeshe Tshogyel, to be the exclusive partner of the appointed discoverer. If for some reason the proper consort cannot be found, or cannot provide the necessary support, the discovery might become complicated or altogether impossible, or even worse, the life of the treasure revealer himself may be threatened.[33] Such was the unfortunate circumstance for Karma Lingpa.

By one account Karma Lingpa's female partner, who had been indicated in the treasure prophecy, was supposed to be a beautiful young brahmin's daughter from India with a glorious birthmark. She was to serve as his spiritual consort (phyag-rgya, mudrā).[34] For reasons not made clear, however, the auspicious connection linking these two together had been fouled up ('phyugs-pa).[35] As a result, Karma Lingpa was forced to choose another woman, who it so happens bore him a son. The relationship is said to have aroused gossip and malicious rumor, presumably among the villagers in and around Dakpo.[36] Perhaps the clamor had more to do with a spurned family connection than it did to Karma Lingpa's inability to unite with the right woman.[37] Whatever the real story, this whole affair sealed Karma Lingpa's fate. His mistaken auspices and unfulfilled prophecy directly caused a disruption in his life, guaranteeing an untimely demise.[38] Oddly enough, it seems these misfortunes had little adverse effect on his ability to decode the treasure and later transmit its teachings.

In the life of a treasure revealer, the climatic moment of discovery occurs precisely when the essence of the treasure itself appears or is revealed in some symbolically encoded form. The medium on which this coded teaching is carried is usually called the yellow paper (shog-ser), or paper scroll (shog-dril). As Gyatso has argued, this scroll "is the manuscript, written by Padmasambhava or a disciple, that is physically buried; it is the treasure substance itself. It is also one of the few material traces whose existence is sometimes cited as actual evidence of a treasure discovery."[39] According to tradition, when Padmasambhava's teachings were copied down on this yellow paper prior to their being concealed, they were first encrypted in a special Ḍākinī script. This script could be deciphered only by the individual prophesied as the treasure's revealer. In this way it was ensured that the teachings would be safely preserved over time and that their secrets would not fall into the wrong hands. Although the texts do not seem to warn explicitly against the appointed discoverer showing this yellow scroll to others, we can assume that at least in the case of Karma Lingpa's treasure it is certain that such actions were believed to garner severe consequences.

The mistaken auspices between Karma Lingpa and his appointed consort was not the only cause of his shortened life.[40] We are told also that he suffered because he showed one of his yellow pages to someone before the appropriate time.[41] In only one source is a reason given for this odd turn of events. In his Series of the Authentic Lineage Teachers, Gedün Gyeltsen explains that just prior to his death Karma Lingpa asked one of his trustworthy students to watch over his young son, who was not yet mature enough to receive instruction.[42] To this student he entrusted the yellow scroll: "Take good care of my little boy until he grows up enough to think for himself. Then later deliver [this yellow paper] to him and [tell him] that he should entrust it to his own student, the one named Nyida, the third-generation [successor of my lineage]."[43]

Nowhere does Gedün Gyeltsen suggest explicitly that this event might justify Karma Lingpa's showing prematurely the yellow scroll to someone else, but it seems plausible that the author may have provided this sensible detail in response to the failure of previous lineage historians to give a proper explanation of the circumstances involved. Gedün Gyeltsen is also the only historian of the tradition who describes Nyida Chöje as still a child when his father is dying. Most of the other sources are silent on this point, and yet they all unanimously claim that Nyida Chöje received the Peaceful and Wrathful Deities directly from Karma Lingpa. The discrepancies are worth noting, for they help to pinpoint the elements that demand further investigation, the cracks in the seemingly uncomplicated narratives. These fissures often indicate where the story really lies.

The sources claim that Karma Lingpa was keenly aware of his impending death caused both by his failure to connect with the proper consort and by his imprudent display of the secret yellow document. He is said to have given numerous prophecies and made several clairvoyant statements about his own spiritual prowess, boasting that after his death many auspicious designs and marks would appear miraculously on his own corpse.[44] Such signs would be proof that he was a truly advanced and enlightened being. In some accounts we also learn that a year or so later, on the verge of dying, Karma Lingpa gave his son the initiations and readings (lung) of the Peaceful and Wrathful

Deities and told him to keep it secret until he met a holy man named Nyida, on whom he was then to bestow the treasure.[45] Shortly thereafter, Karma Lingpa died. But the story is not yet finished. There is in fact a third version of Karma Lingpa's death that is much less pristine and that should alert us to the possible cover-up of some private scandal.

We may recall that in one of his prophecies, Padmasambhava warned of a sudden danger caused by someone from within Karma Lingpa's own circle of associates: "Beware of the violator of the samaya vows, the defilement of the black one!"[46] Indeed, in what appears to be the fulfillment of the prophecy, this seditious and traitorous demon did appear, but he was not alone. The bizarre tale of the murder of Karma Lingpa by his close attendant (*nye-gnas*) and his mistress (*jo-mo*) first appears in the seventeenth century, in the anonymous *History of the Treasures*.[47] All subsequent retellings of this story seem to have been inspired by this leading work, which itself may have been based on an earlier account no longer extant.[48] Curiously, the story is nowhere to be found in Gyarawa's *Garland of Jewels*, the earliest known history of the Karling transmisions. In the *History of the Treasures* account, Karma Lingpa's student and mistress, his consort referred to earlier, run away together and plot to murder their teacher. Pretending to have an important question to ask, they approach the treasure revealer, prostrate respectfully before him, and make the requisite offerings. After the two leave, Karma Lingpa suddenly becomes very sick. We learn that the offerings of food had been tainted with poison. Here the story connects on certain points with the previous legend, for it is related that on the verge of dying Karma Lingpa transmits the *Peaceful and Wrathful Deities* to his son, Nyida Chöje.[49] In other versions, Karma Lingpa transmits his treasure before he is poisoned—one says that he offered only his father, Nyida Sangye, the complete precepts (*gdam-ngags*),[50] while another relates that he appointed both his father and son as sole "masters of the teaching" (*chos-bdag*) before his life was threatened.[51] The whole matter is complicated even further if we acknowledge Karma Migyur Wangyel's odd interpretation that the traitorous attendant was actually Karma Lingpa's son, Nyida Chöje![52] If this were true, then a number of puzzling questions would need to be answered. For instance, would Karma Lingpa's own son run off with his mother (or step-mother)? Or why would Karma Lingpa, aware that he had been poisoned, still insist on transmitting his secret treasures to his own murderer? Clearly, the problem must lie with Karma Migyur Wangyel's understanding of the story, which apparerently led him to mistakenly conflate Karma Lingpa's attendant with his son.[53] From all other accounts, the two are completely separate individuals.

At any rate, on the verge of dying Karma Lingpa is said to have offered a final testament to his father: "No ordinary medicine in the world can cure this illness of mine, so in order to perform the [yoga of] entering a corpse [*grong-'jug*] I must fetch the death-curing elixir from the northern slope of Mount Meru. After doing so, I will return in three days. During that time, father, I ask that you bind and protect my corpse."[54] Shortly after this testament Karma Lingpa expired, but not before he was able to transfer his consciousness into the body of a dead bird. On the morning of the third day, against the father's protests, the nefarious couple begin cremating Karma Lingpa's corpse. Suddenly a beautiful multicolored bird appears above them in the sky, carrying in its beak a purple fruit of a magical tree from the slopes of Meru. The awesome bird swoops down and lands on the mouth of the burning corpse. Just when this bird, possessed by the mind of Karma Lingpa, begins to concentrate on dissolving its consciousness into the dead body, the evil attendant beats the bird away with a stick. Tragically, the magical fruit is lost in the fire, Karma Lingpa's efforts to revive his body through transference yoga are thwarted, and the only chance to save his own life is brutally taken away from him by his corrupt disciple. In the end, Karma Lingpa is forced to depart to a buddha's pure land. From that point on we learn nothing more about either the attendant or the mistress, other than the fact that the lineage transmitted through the student never flourished in Tibet because it had been irreparably defiled by the stain of broken vows.[55]

The couple's betrayal may have been socially and economically motivated. Their act of poisoning was not incidental. In Tibet there is widespread and longstanding belief in the magical efficacy of poison. As Michael Aris has argued, if a person "succeeds in poisoning someone rich and successful, it is held that the fortune and glory of the victim is magically transferred to the poisoner".[56] Once the attendant had received the proper initiations from Karma Lingpa, he may have thought he could then acquire it all by stealing his teacher's good fortune (g.yang), his life-force (srog), and even his own consort. Interestingly, the territory in Tibet where these tragic events are said to have taken place and where the earliest lineage-holders of Karma Lingpa's tradition were first active—that is, Dakpo and Kongpo—have long been renowned as risky and dangerous.[57] The people of these areas are often thought to be ruthless poisoners intent on seizing the essence and vitality of their victims, usually religious personalities or innocent travelers.[58] Consequently, the region has developed a sinister reputation, and its people suffer from stereotypes that portray them as witches and horned demons.[59] Indeed, it seems quite appropriate that this was the territory that spawned a young visionary who was later poisoned after recovering a buried set of ancient and arcane books about death and the dead.

The sources record that after Karma Lingpa's death both Nyida Sangye and Nyida Chöje divided up his possessions, including a number of manuscripts from the *Great Liberation upon Hearing in the Bardo*. I will assume that Karma Lingpa had been working on a set of bardo texts just before his death. These would have probably included the *Triad of Bardo Prayers* [*Bar-do'i smon-lam rnam-gsum*],[60] the *Religious Liturgy of the Self-Liberation of Karmic Latencies* [*Chos-spyod bag-chags rang-grol*], and a variety of teachings on the bardo that would later be more formally arranged as distinct texts, such as the *Reminder of the Bardo of Reality-Itself* [*Chos-nyid bar-do'i ngo-sprod gsal-'debs*], the *Direct Introduction to the Bardo of Becoming* [*Srid-pa bar-do'i ngo-sprod*] and the *Completion Stage Guidebook to the Six Bardos*. Perhaps Karma Lingpa's father and son found these old manuscripts and rewrote or elaborated them. It should be emphasized that the Karling texts appear to have been controlled by their original author for only a brief while. In a very short time after Karma Lingpa had recovered these texts, it would appear that they were being reordered and revised by others close to him. The suggestion here is that both Nyida Sangye and Nyida Chöje helped to create the *Liberation upon Hearing* and were actually the ones responsible for transmitting some of Karma Lingpa's most distinctive work. Indeed, the elusive *Four Initiations: Self-Liberation of Whatever Is Encountered* [*Dbang-bzhi 'phrad-tshad rang-grol*][61] is even said to have been transmitted directly from Nyida Sangye to his grandson Nyida Chöje, bypassing Karma Lingpa altogether.[62] The exchange between grandfather and grandson is also indicated in the teaching-lineages listed in several prominent *Transmission Records* [*Gsan-yig*], as well as in a few transmission lists reproduced in some of the printed editions of the *Liberation upon Hearing*.[63] The fifth Dalai Lama explains:

> Nowadays, almost all of the transmission lists say that Karma Lingpa gave the teachings to his son. But, since Karma Lingpa did not live very long he did not have time to give it to his son directly. His father [on the other hand] lived for one hundred and twenty years, so he was the one who gave it [to Karma Lingpa's son]. There are some who argue that Karma Lingpa died [early] because of a stain of broken vows and that there is no lineage of transmission from him.[64]

The mysterious and seemingly unorthodox lineage that leads from Nyida Sangye to Nyida Chöje continued through the obscure lama Gönpo Dorje of Kongpo. Generations later, we find listed in this transmission line the name of a controversial treasure revealer from Kham, Rikzin Nyima Drakpa (1647–1710). Nyima Drakpa was expressly linked to the tradition of Karma Lingpa's *Peaceful and Wrathful Deities* and appears particularly to have had an enduring influence on the *Liberation upon Hearing* transmission. I will have more to say about this colorful figure and the Karling lineage associated with him in chapter 11.

Other than father and son, the only mention of Karma Lingpa's actual family is a curious statement that appears first in the *History of the Treasures* and is then repeated by Karma Migyur Wangyel. Here, it is said that Karma Lingpa's lineage of disciples (*slob-brgyud*) flourished throughout Ü, Tsang, and Kham but that his family descendants, his "bone lineage" (*gdung-rgyud*), though they may still reside in Tibet, had failed to produce any great benefits.[65] The implication here is that Karma Lingpa's ancestry had not spawned any significant religious personages or in a more unlikely scenario, that his family never generated any materially significant benefit such as that gained in large donations to influential monasteries or in the patronage of charismatic religious figures. One has to wonder what tone is intended by this comment. Is this a criticism or just simply a social point of fact? At any rate, the short and tragic tale of Karma Lingpa has come to a close. The focus now turns to the content of his treasure cache discovered on Gampodar Mountain.

7

The Gampodar Treasures

As noted in the previous chapter, in the second half of the fourteenth century the treasure revealer Karma Lingpa is said to have excavated treasures from a location on Gampodar Mountain in the southeastern region of Dakpo. These discoveries comprised two major textual collections, the *Self-Liberated Wisdom of the Peaceful and Wrathful Deities* and the *Great Compassionate One, the Peaceful and Wrathful Lotus.*[1] The latter work has not yet been traced, and so its precise content is unknown. Nevertheless, both collections supposedly included instructions for practice on the six types of bardo (*bar-do rnams-drug*).[2] The specific set of texts that we know as the *Great Liberation upon Hearing in the Bardo*, however, seems to have been derived solely from the *Self-Liberated Wisdom of the Peaceful and Wrathful Deities*, with a few possible exceptions.[3] After Karma Lingpa's untimely death, we are told that his father and son divided up his possessions, including various books and shrine images. Among these items were found a number of complete and incomplete manuscripts detailing the cycle of initiation rites of the *Liberation upon Hearing.*[4] The implication is that Karma Lingpa had already written out a small selection of manuscripts on bardo and related topics and had been working on additional materials just before his death. It is possible that Karma Lingpa's father and son found these old manuscripts, used them as a basis, and then rewrote or extended the originals. As the historical record indicates, both father and son were more than just Karma Lingpa's first disciples, they were also the first and most effective transmitters of the Karling revelations. I will return to this story, but for now it is important to note that the texts inspired by Karma Lingpa's discoveries were perhaps only for a brief moment controlled by a single hand. In a very short time after Karma Lingpa had recovered the texts, they were being copied, reordered, and revised by others close to him, but not by him. This tells us much about the nature of the text collection believed to have come from the treasure trove of Gampodar and to have been unearthed by the revealer Karma Lingpa in the fourteenth century.

Despite the widespread popularity in later centuries of the cycle of the *Peaceful and Wrathful Deities*, including the *Liberation upon Hearing*, and its clear associations with a figure named Karma Lingpa, the extent to which the contents of the present recensions of the collection actually reach back in time to Karma Lingpa's original revelations is unknown; neither a list of contents nor the traditional certificate of prophecy (*kha-byang*) have been preserved in the surviving literature.[5] Our knowledge of the texts included in these collections is derived almost entirely from the available reprint editions and from a few notable but rather late *Transmission Records*. In cases such as this, where an original or relatively early list of contents cannot be located, the correct identification of the core set of texts is extremely difficult. The composite and cumulative nature of Tibetan treasure literature creates certain problems for the textual historian. First of all, most of the available recensions of the *Peaceful and Wrathful Deities* and the *Liberation upon Hearing* come to us in the form of xylographic prints and facsimile reproductions from blocks carved only in the last two centuries. This means that we have little choice but to compare texts from invariably late stages of the literary tradition. Barring the obvious obstacles that this introduces, there is also the problem that these relatively recent collections all comprise a locally determined blend of supplemental material from different historical periods. This material reflects the persistence of local variations on what appears to be a unifed tradition whose boundaries are inexactly defined. To complicate matters even further, the works contained in these editions are in many cases authored anonymously, with attributions to specific compositors occurring only sporadically. These fluid textual boundaries have over time kept space open for the inclusion of new material as well as for the alteration, adaptation, and expansion of older works and ritual programs. Although such revision certainly reflects the changing values and interests of newer generations of religious practitioner, and provides important insights into the history of the cycle's transmission, these intriguing layers of history obscure the foundational structure, or core unity, of the literary tradition. By "core" I mean those texts that are either historically speaking the earliest documents of the tradition, or practically speaking the central works around which the supplemental literature has been orchestrated. With an eye toward locating this fundamental core, I provide here a typology and cursory overview of the main categories of literature found in Karma Lingpa's treasure collection, with identification of some of the more significant works in each category.

An Inventory of the Treasure

In the *Transmission Record* of the fifth Dalai Lama the texts of Karma Lingpa's *Peaceful and Wrathful Deities* are organized into five categories based on the main subjects addressed. These topics include: (1) prophecies and lineal history (*lung-bstan, rgyud-pa'i lo-rgyus*), (2) generation stage initiations and sādhanas (*dbang-sgrub bskyed-rim*), (3) completion-stage hearing and wearing liberation texts (*grol-byed thos-pa, btags-pas grol-ba'i rdzogs-rim*), (4) completion-stage path-of-means practices (*thabs-lam la brten-pa'i rdzogs-rim*), and (5) teachings on the assembly of dharma protectors (*bka'-srung skor*).[6] With only slight variation, these rubrics are repeated in the *Transmission Records* of Terdak Lingpa, of Zhapdrung Sungtrül I Chokle Namgyel (1708–1736), and of Dujom Rinpoche.[7] From these lists a standard classification scheme can be formulated as a useful tool for arranging the individual texts of the treasure cycle and, more important, to introduce some order to this rather large and unwieldy treasure collection. The resulting scheme thus comprises seven categories:

1. History (*lo-rgyus*)
2. Liturgy (*sgrub-dbang, dbang-sgrub*)
3. Liberation upon hearing (*thos-grol*)
4. Liberation upon wearing (*btags-grol*)
5. Path of means (*thabs-lam*)
6. Religious protectors (*bstan-srung*)
7. Catalogue (*dkar-chag*)

On the basis of close inspection of the content of the texts themselves and following the classification of rituals employed in the catalogue (*dkar-chag*) of the monumental and authoritative *Precious Anthology of Treasures* [*Rinchen gter-mdzod*], the second category, on liturgy, can be further subdivided into eight rubrics:[8]

2a. Sādhana (*sgrub-thabs*)
2b. Initiation (*dbang*)
2c. Prayer and recitation (*smon-lam, bsnyen-sgrub*)
2d. Expiation and confession (*bskang-bshags*)
2e. Ritual cake offerings (*gtor-ma*)
2f. Guidance rituals for the dead (*gnas-'dren, gnas-lung*)
2g. Burnt offerings (*sbyin-sreg*)
2h. Cremation ritual (*ro-sreg*)

It is not possible in the present context to explore fully the depths of these Tibetan typologies, including all their associated texts; many of the topics have been sufficiently addressed in the existing scholarship.[9] An overview of some of the basic features of each genre, with representative bibliographical citations, must suffice.

History

The texts from within the treasure cycle itself that serve as our best source for a critical history of the literary tradition consist primarily of the prophecies (*lung-bstan*) of Padmasambhava, the fulfillment certificate (*them-byang*), biographical sketches, records of lineal succession (*brgyud-rim*), and supplications to the lineage teachers (*brgyud-pa'i gsol-'debs*). We must approach with some caution, however, those texts that we presume to be "historical" documents. Still, it is fairly clear that the most valuable works of the historical genre in the Karling collection include the text composed by Gyarawa Namkha Chökyi Gyatso, the *Garland of Jewels* (1499), and the brief work written by his student Gedün Gyeltsen, the *Series of the Authentic Lineage Teachers* (1503 or 1515). We are indeed fortunate that Gyarawa's work is still extant, for at the moment it is the earliest source for our knowledge of his life and the life of his teacher Nyida Özer. Given the considerable importance of the *Garland of Jewels* for understanding the early history of the tradition, it is peculiar that there have been almost no references to it in western academic studies.[10]

The second most valuable historical document is Gedün Gyeltsen's *Series of the Authentic Lineage Teachers*. As noted in chapter 5, this text consists primarily of a series of quotes extracted from the prophecies of Padmasambhava concerning the future discovery and subsequent diffusion of the *Liberation upon Hearing* instructions. Although there are a few very brief biographical references to Karma Lingpa and his immediate disciples, the value of Gedün Gyeltsen's work lies in the fact that it preserves passages from the cycle's prophetic literature that are no longer independently extant.[11] The prophecies provide potentially significant historical clues, some of them at least derived from older sources.

In addition to the transmission records and prophecy statements, the Karling treasure collection also contains a number of distinctive lineage supplications (*brgyud-pa'i gsol-'debs*). These works are simply devotional petitions addressed to particular members of a teaching lineage, the names of which are often listed in chronological order. Although typical petitions address each figure with only four lines of verse, the prayers are significant in that they provide the names of identifiable personalities. Equipped with this information it is then possible to trace relationships not only between members of the lineage but also between individual texts, and from there to begin to distinguish the possible institutions and groups responsible for maintaining and disseminating the tradition as a whole.

Liturgy

From early in its development, the Tibetan treasure tradition consolidated a large collective of technical works elucidating an array of religious doctrine, prayers, and practical directives outlining the requisite activities for ritual performance. It is among these revelatory materials that much of the evidence concerning rites for the dead and dying in Tibet can be located. The preeminence of the ritual context of death-related treasure and of Tibetan religious literature in general has remained widely ignored by scholars in the field. On this point, Yael Bentor's recent remark about the role of ritual in Tibet deserves to be highlighted and repeated:

> Ritual texts constitute a significant part of nearly every Tibetan library. Furthermore, in the majority of Tibetan monasteries the performance of rituals is the principal undertaking of most monks. Even in monastic educational insti-

tutions monks devote part of their time to rituals. It should be emphasized that almost all forms of Tibetan meditation are highly ritualized and therefore fall within this category as well. Western scholarship, however, has not yet adequately reflected this Tibetan preoccupation with ritual.[12]

The cycle of the *Peaceful and Wrathful Deities* offers an extensive variety of ritual literature presented largely within the context of a generation phase (*bskyed-rim*) tantric system that conjoins the distinctive Dzokchen theory of the bardo with a visualized mandala inhabited by a group of one hundred peaceful and wrathful deities (*zhi-ba dang khro-bo'i lha-tshogs*). As noted previously in chapter 3, this peaceful and wrathful mandala was probably derived from the central Mahāyoga scripture, *Great Tantra of the Secret Nucleus*. The stages in the cultivation of the mandala are detailed in the liturgical texts known by the Sanskrit term *sādhana*, or "methods for accomplishment" (*sgrub-thabs*) (2a). Among the sādhanas of the Karling treasure there are three that are repeatedly mentioned in the colophons and commentarial literature as preeminent; their importance is reflected also in the great frequency with which they appear in the various printed editions. They are:

1. *Religious Liturgy of the Self-Liberation of Karmic Latencies* [*Chos-spyod bag-chags rang-grol*][13]
2. *Threefold Self-Liberation of Feeling: Practice Manual of the Peaceful and Wrathful Deities* [*Zhi-khro'i las-byang tshor-ba rang-grol gsum*][14]
3. *Self-Liberation of Speech: Confession to the Expanse of the Peaceful and Wrathful Deities* [*Zhi-khro'i klong-bshags brjod-pa rang-grol*][15]

Although rarely acknowledged, the peaceful and wrathful sādhana, as represented in these three ritual works, lies at the very heart of the Karling liturgical tradition. In this specialized ritual context, where a distinctively Dzokchen conception of bardo provides the principal frame of reference, the sādhana guides the efforts of the deceased to visualize the mandala of one hundred deities and to recall the appropriate mantras (ritualized speech) and mudrās (ritualized gestures) during the transition between lives. In more elaborate presentations, the peaceful and wrathful sādhana serves as the foundation of a program designed explicitly to reorient the dead and to assist them in the recollection of previous religious instruction, all aimed at protecting against fear (*'jigs-skyobs*) and liberating from the dangerous pathways of the bardo (*bar-do 'phrang-sgrol*). As I shall demonstrate later, the sādhana that is the basis of the Karling ritual, and thus of greatest practical importance to the tradition as a whole, is without doubt the *Religious Liturgy of the Self-Liberation of Karmic Latencies*. The other two works just listed are in many respects simply supplements to this principal text. Although a few studies have carried passing references to the *Self-Liberation of Karmic Latencies*, it has yet to attract the attention it deserves.[16]

Curiously enough, the fifth Dalai Lama in his categorization of the various Karling sādhanas includes two titles that we might not expect to find listed in this category. These are the *Reminder of the Direct Introduction to the Bardo of Reality-Itself* [*Chos-nyid bar-do'i ngo-sprod gsal-'debs*] and the *Reminder* of the *Direct Introduction to the Bardo of Becoming* [*Srid-pa bar-do'i ngo-sprod gsal-'debs*].[17] For obvious reasons, we might instead look for these titles under a more appropriate heading, such as "liberation upon hearing" (*thos-grol*). They are, after all, the Tibetan texts most familiar to western audiences as "liberation upon hearing" works, since together in translation they constitute the main body of what has become celebrated as the *Tibetan Book of the Dead*. Although there is a possibility that the texts familiar to the fifth Dalai Lama are not the same texts that we have today, we can be fairly certain that these titles refer to two earlier texts widely accepted as constituting the quintessence of the *Great Liberation upon Hearing in the Bardo*. But in no other source do we find these texts identified as sādhana, so why does the fifth Dalai Lama categorize them as such? And if indeed they are sādhanas, then what sort of text can we call "liberation upon hearing"? The answer to the first question is straightforward. The *Reminder of the Bardo of Reality-Itself* and the *Direct Introduction to the Bardo of Becoming* were viewed by the fifth Dalai Lama as nothing more or less than texts that provided a "means for achieving" (*sgrub-thabs*) visualization of a prescribed mandala during the interval between this and the next life. In other words, the two texts were taken to be sādhanas. This answer, no doubt, would further confirm my statement that the peaceful and wrathful sādhana is the very backbone of the Karling liturgy. As for the second question, I will return to answer it in my discussion hereafter.

The vast majority of Karling texts remaining in the category of liturgy are devoted to the standard generation-phase practices involving the bestowal of initiations (*dbang-bskur*), recitation of mantra ('*dzab-bzlas, bsnyen*), offerings of ritual cakes (*gtor-'bul*), rites of confession and the expiation of broken vows (*bskang-bshags nyams-chag*), and burnt offerings (*sbyin-sreg*). One category, however, stands out as being especially significant with respect to the funeral rites accompanying the Karling literature; namely, the ceremony for guiding the deceased to a favorable destiny (*tshe-'das gnas-'dren*). In chapter 2 I showed that the concept of soul guidance was a familiar component of the Tibetan worldview prior to the influx of Buddhism and persisted in Tibetan Buddhist rites for the dead. Rituals to "show the way" (*lam-bstan*) were thus derived from very ancient beliefs. But these indigenous ideas were not the only source of the later rites. Equivalent concepts can also be found in the early Buddhist literature. Recall, for example, Dunhuang manuscript PT 239/I, *Showing the Path of the Dead*, where we found evidence of a ritual for the dead designed to guarantee safe passage upward to the divine residence of the buddha Vajrapāṇi. Here it was apparent that this early text drew its inspiration from the purification rituals of the *Tantra on the Elimination of All Evil Rebirths*. Similarly, the later guidance texts of the *Peaceful and Wrathful* cycle, identified in the literature as auxiliaries (*cha-lag*) of the expiation and confession rites,[18] seem also to have been derived from the very same source.[19] In the Karling collections, the exemplary work of this type would have to be the elusive *Self-Liberation of the Six Classes of Beings*,

Guiding the Deceased to a Higher State [*Tshe-'das gnas-'dren 'gro-drug rang-grol*]. I say elusive because although a number of supplements to this work exist in the collection—the majority of which were composed by Karma Chakme in the seventeenth century—the actual text has not been located.[20]

I emphasized at the end of chapter 4 that the guidance ritual (*gnas-'dren cho-ga*) is also aimed at purifying the sins (*sdig-sgrib*) of the departed in order to clear a path for him/her in the bardo after death. This is accomplished through the rite of confession (*bshags-pa*) and reconciliation (*bskang-ba*) (2d). Such ritual activity draws on common Buddhist themes of karmic cleansing as extensions of life practices that are in general directed toward purification of the deceased and preparation for the afterlife. These practices carry with them the sense that every sin has its antidote, and evils not atoned for in life will have to be expiated after death. The prototype is represented by the ritual of cremating the corpse (*ro-sreg-gi cho-ga*) outlined in the *Tantra on the Elimination of All Evil Rebirths*. There the officiant is required to generate through visualization a mandala inhabited by wrathful deities. By means of a series of consecrations (*dbang-bskur*) he is expected to transform the corpse into the exalted body of the central deity. Through recitation of the specified mantras and the gestures of the appropriate mudrās, all past sins and transgressions are gradually burned off, and the deceased is ultimately delivered to the higher realm of the gods.[21] A similar program is at work in the confession texts of the Karling tradition, only in this context emphasis is largely on the purification of the deceased's consciousness, rather than on the corpse. The deceased is purified through initiation into the complete peaceful and wrathful mandala and through respectful homage (*gus-pas phyag-'tshal-ba*) to each of its inhabitants. The two most exemplary confession texts of the cycle of the *Peaceful and Wrathful Deities* are:

1. *Self-Liberation of Broken Vows through Expiation and Confession* [*Bskang-bshags nyams-chags rang-grol*]
2. *One Hundred Prostrations: The Self-Liberation of Sin and Defilement* [*Brgya-phyag sdig-sgrib rang-grol*][22]

The first work, the *Self-Liberation of Broken Vows through Expiation and Confession*, does not exist as an independent text in any of the existing recensions of the Karling collection, although there are a number of supplemental materials related to it.[23] From the colophons of the second exemplary work, the *One Hundred Prostrations: The Self-Liberation of Sin and Defilement*—perhaps the only surviving work from Karma Lingpa's *Peaceful and Wrathful Lotus*—we learn that this text is considered an auxiliary (*cha-lag*) of the *Liberation upon Hearing*, a facilitating tool (*cha-rkyen*) of the *(Avoiding) Hell through Expiation and Confession* [*Na-rag bskang-bshags*], and the epitome (*don-'dus*) of the *Threefold Practice Manual of the Peaceful and Wrathful Deities* [*Zhi-khro las-byang gsum*].[24] Altogether the expiation and confession texts are a fundamental component of the Karling ritual program.

Liberation upon Hearing

As I discussed in chapter 5, one of the prophecies reported in Gyarawa's *Garland of Jewels* relates that Padmasambhava was asked by several prominent individuals, including the likes of the emperor Trhi Songdetsen and the translator Choro Lu'i Gyeltsen, for secret instructions on a swift and powerful method for liberating oneself in a single lifetime without any effort whatsoever. Padmasambhava responded by offering a teaching which he claimed was so effective that it could shut the gates to the lower realms simply by being heard (*thos-pa tsam-gyis ngan-song-gi skye-sgo gcod-pa*).[25] This is alluded to in a passage from the *Direct Introduction to the Bardo of Becoming*:

> This great liberation upon hearing (*thos-grol chen-mo*) is a teaching that awakens expansively (*sangs-rgyas*) without meditation, a teaching that liberates just by being heard, a teaching that guides great sinners along the secret path, a profound teaching that differentiates (*bye-brag phyed-pa*) and thoroughly enlightens in an instant, such that those sentient beings whom it reaches cannot possibly go to the lower realms.[26]

This instruction that liberates upon being heard became the treasure concealed in writing by Padmasambhava and uncovered six centuries later on Gampodar Mountain by the treasure revealer Karma Lingpa. We know, and have known for some time, that these ancient instructions, guaranteed to liberate upon hearing (*thos-grol*), came to encapsulate the very essence of the Karling discoveries. The specific texts that our Tibetan sources have uniformly categorized as exemplary of the liberation-upon-hearing genre, however, do not always offer as easy a method as that promised by Padmasambhava. On the contrary, the vast majority of the identified liberation-upon-hearing works are drawn from a highly refined category of advanced religious instruction called the direct personal introduction (*ngo-sprod*). Typically the texts of this genre contain advanced instruction imparted by a tantric master to a qualifed student meant to serve as an unmediated introduction to the expert techniques of a given doctrinal or liturgical tradition. "Hearing" (*thos-pa*) in this case refers more to a disciple's recognition through actively "listening" to the instructions of the teacher (and in this sense the term comes to mean "to study" or "to learn") than through passively "hearing" the words of a text. This evokes the standard trio of study (*thos-pa*), reflection (*bsam-pa*), and meditation (*sgom-pa*), which in Buddhism are the three activities required for mastery of any religious instruction. Two distinct categories of liberation-upon-hearing literature exist. The first is this esoteric brand of yogic instruction, the direct personal introduction. The second is a more mundane and hence more easily accessible form of practice, the devotional prayer (*smon-lam*).

The exemplary work of the first type is the *Completion Stage Guidebook to the Six Bardos*,[27] which actually comprises six smaller instruction manuals, or guidebooks (*khrid-yig*), each devoted to one of the six bardos. This intriguing set of yogic teachings draws heavily on the Nyingthik of the

Dzokchen tradition and presupposes a knowledge of "breakthrough" (*khregs-chod*) and "direct transcendence" (*thod-rgal*) practice.[28] Although the *Guiding Instructions on the Six Bardos* is accepted as an original revealed work of Karma Lingpa, its colophon might lead us to believe otherwise: "The siddha Karma Lingpa excavated [this treasure] from Gampodar Mountain. A single lineage was established and Nyida Özer received the authorization to be the master of this profound teaching."[29]

The fact that the fifteenth-century lama Nyida Özer is the only disciple explicitly named as recipient of the text's authorized transmission leading back through a singular and unbroken stream suggests that the anthology as we know it today may actually have been compiled by this third holder of Karma Lingpa's lineage. Before him we would have expected at least to have seen first one of the names of either the father Nyida Sangye or the son Nyida Chöje, since they are usually listed in that order, but this is not the case here. It would appear then that we have two choices for interpretation: either the later tradition viewed Nyida Özer as carrying a special connection to the *Guidebook* text and thus only listed his name as the first holder of its transmission; or Nyida Özer was himself responsible for the text's redaction. It may be relevant to mention also that Nyida Özer is the known author of a detailed outline, the only one of its kind, for this specific set of *Guidebook* texts, the *Self-Liberated Key: A Topical Outline [Sa-bcad lde-mig rang-grol]*.[30] I will have more to say about Nyida Özer and his role in the dissemination of Karma Lingpa's treasure in the next chapter.

Among other possibly significant examples of the direct personal introduction variety of liberation-upon-hearing teachings, we should mention again the two texts *Reminder of the Bardo of Reality-Itself* and the *Direct Introduction to the Bardo of Becoming*. As noted, these texts were not identified by the fifth Dalai Lama as belonging to the classification "liberation upon hearing", or direct personal introduction, despite being labeled as such in their titles. They were, instead, identified as "liturgy" (*dbang-sgrub*). This classification, I argued earlier, was not entirely inappropriate. Until we can locate and consult the actual texts available to the fifth Dalai Lama, his rationale may be forever lost to history. It is certainly noteworthy that in the *Transmission Record* of Terdak Lingpa the *Reminder of the Bardo of Reality-Itself* and the *Direct Introduction to the Bardo of Becoming* are categorized as direct personal introduction.[31] Were the texts known to the fifth Dalai Lama really all that categorically different from those familiar to his contemporaries, or did he have some alternative understanding of the structure and purpose of these works? Whatever the case, the later indices of Chokle Namgyel and Dujom Rinpoche corroborate Terdak Lingpa's classification.[32] The texts as we know them today, although based on sādhana, can be easily viewed as "direct personal introduction" to crucial doctrines described therein. The authoritative and self-conscious voice of the narrative takes the place of the absent teacher, and like a teacher it conveys important religious instruction to the frightened student who wanders aimlessly in the bardo.

O son of good family, if you do not know how to meditate in this way, then be mindful of the Buddha, the Dharma, the Sangha, and the Lord of Great Compassion, and pray to them. Meditate on all frightening and terrifying visions as the Lord of Great Compassion, or as your own personal deity [*yi-dam*]. Remember your lamas and whatever initiation names you received in the human world, and do not fear the Dharmarāja, Lord of the Dead.[33]

In addition to the direct personal introduction manuals there is the second classification of liberation-upon-hearing literature, the customary aspiration prayers (*smon-lam*), which have come to form a type of appendix to the standard collection of the *Liberation upon Hearing* and to the various editions of the *Tibetan Book of the Dead*. This category is best exemplied by the *Triad of Bardo Prayers* mentioned previously; these being the *Root Verses on the Six Bardos*, the *Prayer for Deliverance from the Perilous Straits of the Bardo*, and the *Bardo Prayer that Protects from Fear*. With the addition of the *Prayer Requesting the Buddhas and Bodhisattvas for Assistance*[*Sangs-rgyas dang byang-chub sems-dpa' rnams-la ra-mda' sbran-pa'i smon-lam*],[34] these short devotional works represent a cohesive set of prayers that have been uniformly grouped together and incorporated into almost every manuscript and facsimile edition of the Karling cycle. In addition, many of the verses are found deeply embedded in the body of some of the larger works, such as the *Religious Liturgy of the Self-Liberation of Karmic Latencies* and the *Reminder of the Bardo of Reality-Itself*, indicating the persistence of possibly older layers of ritual expression in newer liturgical books. I strongly suspect that the prayers actually constitute the nucleus of the liberation-upon-hearing teachings and that the more expansive bardo texts of the *Peaceful and Wrathful Deities* and the *Liberation upon Hearing* were in fact derived from them. More than likely, the *Liberation upon Hearing* as we know it today represents the culmination of a gradual process of extension and elaboration on an earlier and basic stock of prayers intended for practical use in some preexisting funeral liturgy, such as that outlined in the *Tantra on the Elimination of All Evil Rebirths* or as backdrop to texts such as Dunhuang manuscript PT 239/I, *Showing the Path of the Dead*. The collective aim of these prayers was, and still is, straightforward and uncomplicated: to provide comfort and assistance to the deceased believed to be suffering from confusion, fear, and anxiety during the chaos of the transition between lives.

Liberation upon Wearing

The texts of the category "liberation upon wearing" (*btags-grol*) are expressive of the longstanding Tibetan faith in the book as a physical embodiment of sacred power that, among many other advantages, can protect against death and evil influence. In the Karling treasure literature, the liberation-upon-wearing genre predominantly consists of mantras designed to be carried in one form or another on the body. The mantras can be printed on small pieces of paper, folded, and placed in an amulet (*ga'u*) or sewn into cloth and worn around the neck. Alternatively, the text can also be attached to the corpse prior to cremation. If it is placed over the heart, it is believed that when the text is consumed with the body in the funeral pyre, the deceased's sins are burned away and the frightening appearances of the bardo do not arise.[35] The exemplary text of this type is the *Self-Liberation of the Body: Liberation upon Wearing* [*Btags-grol phung-po rang-grol*].[36]

Path of Means

"Path of means" (*thabs-lam*) refers to a distinct type of practical method corresponding to the completion phase (*rdzogs-rim*) of tantric practice, in which special yogic techniques are employed that require the manipulation of sexual energies. In the specific context of the Karling treasure teachings, this path is pursued by those superior practitioners intent on closing the entrance to the womb (*mngal-sgo 'gag-pa*) via the four joys (*dga'-ba bzhi*).[37] As noted in chapter 3, the concept of closing the womb entrance was one of the hallmarks of the tantric reinterpretation of earlier intermediate-state formulations, as for example we witness in the *Sutra on Entering the Womb*. The specialized form of this technique, involving the generation of the four joys, is usually accomplished through employing the services of a qualifed female consort. According to the *Guidebook to the Bardo of Becoming* [*Srid-pa bar-do'i khrid-yig*], the principal goal of such practice is to develop direct experience of the pristine wisdom (*ye-shes*) of the four types of bliss (*bde-ba bzhi*), so that at the moment when the consciousness descending toward a new birth perceives the future mother and father in passionate embrace, the true wisdom nature of the parents' sexual excitement will be recognized and rebirth will be avoided.

> If you do not apprehend [the pristine wisdom-bliss] there [in the bardo of reality-itself], then in the bardo of becoming, upon seeing a male and female having sex, you will apprehend the wisdom of unconditioned coemergent joy, the pristine wisdom of the bliss [associated with] the third initiation.[38] Then, the entrance to the womb will be closed and you will surely be liberated in the bardo.[39]

The scenario of the oedipal descent into a womb alluded to here is essentially identical to that described in Vasubandhu's *Commentary on the Treasury of Abhidharma*, with one fundamental difference. In this tantric scenario there is an advanced mechanism at work that makes it possible for the descending consciousness to stop its momentum and essentially to reverse the rebirth process. That technique, generally referred to as "path of means," was not a method available to the early followers of the Abhidharma. Among the texts of this category in the Karling treasure cycle, the most important appear to be two works authored by the lama Nyida Özer; namely, the *Self-Liberation of Desire: Experiential Guiding Instructions on the Great Bliss of the Lower Orifice* [*'Og-sgo bde-chen 'dod-chags rang-grol-gyis nyams-khrid*][40] and its supplement, the *Self-Liberation of Bliss* [*Bde-ba rang-grol*].[41]

Religious Protectors

The texts concerned with the protectors of religious teachings (*bstan-srung*), or "dharma protectors" (*chos-skyong*), provide generally the requisite details

for the performance of a type of invocation liturgy belonging to a class of
generation-phase sādhana practices. The general purpose of the ceremony is
to invoke the power of specific deities who have been bound by oath (*dam-can*) to guard a particular set of religious teachings against evil influence.[42]
The history of these defenders of religion is the epic tale of the conversion
through subjugation of Tibet's indigenous demonic forces to the divine laws
of Buddhism.[43] In many cases we also find evidence of the iconographic assimilation of Indian divinities. According to Tibetan legend, these special
guardians had once been the wild and unruly spirits of the earth that were
given form perhaps in the cosmologies of the ancient Ultra Secret *The'urang*
(*yang-gsang the'u-rang*) and Renowned Bon (*grags-pa bon*) traditions.[44] When
Buddhism began to spread in Tibet, these local deities (*yul-lha, gzhi-bdag*)
fought viciously against the new religion. We may recall that it was for the
purpose of taming these hostile spirits that the Indian exorcist Padmasambhava
was invited to Tibet.

In the context of the great treasure traditions, these subjugated spirits,
known subsequently as treasure defenders (*gter-srung*) are contacted in ritual
and bound to its service. In the Karling tradition, in particular, there are a
number of liturgical texts devoted to these powerful protectors, the earliest
and most important text being Gyarawa's redaction of the *Self-Liberation of
Poisons: Requests for Expiation to the Assembly of All the Dharma Protectors of the Seven Classes of Oath-Bound Defenders* [*Bka'-srung dam-can sde-
bdun chos-skyong kun-'dus-kyi bskang gdug-pa rang-grol*].[45] This work
ennumerates seven groups of religious protector:

1. The father class of glorious hermaphrodite protectors and masters of the
   treasure (*gter-bdag dpal mgon-ma-ning pho-rgyud*)
2. The mother class of female protectors of mantra, including Ekajāti and the
   deep purple mother goddesses of pristine wisdom (*sngags srung-mo rgyud,
   smug-nag ye-shes ma-mo*)[46]
3. The mother goddesses of karma led by Rematī (*lha-mo ma-mo, las-kyi ma-
   mo*)[47]
4. The life-force-attaining butchers, including the four classes of murderers
   (*srog-sgrub bshan-pa, srog-gcod sde-bzhi*)[48]
5. The eight classes of planetary demons, including Rāhula and the eight
   classes of planet-faced constellation envoys (*gza'-bdud sde-brgyad, gza'-
   gdong sde-brgyad rgyu-skar pho-nya*)[49]
6. Dorje Lekpa and the bewitching *tsen* demons, including the servants of the
   tsen and the *tenma* goddesses (*rdor-legs btsan-'gong, btsan dang brtan-
   ma'i g.yog*)[50]
7. The red butcher harmful demons, including the four classes of murderous
   butchers (*bshan-dmar gnod-sbyin, bshan-pa srog-gcod tshogs sde-bzhi*)[51]

In addition to this colorful collection of demons and deities, other sources
refer to the famed brotherhood of warrior gods (*dgra-lha-mched*).[52] The
mythology surrounding the Tibetan protective divinities is extremely complex, and a thorough study of their role in Tibetan religion is much needed. It
is strikingly evident even in the oldest texts accompanying the rites of the

Karling tradition that these powerful and ambivalent forces played active and profound roles in the liturgy of the *Peaceful and Wrathful Deities*. I will pause here to consider a few questions relating to the identity of these oldest texts and to the core works of Karma Lingpa's treasure.

Seeking the Treasure's Core

It is perhaps saying the obvious to claim that the nature of the textual artifact, the form in which a text itself is codified and distributed, influences critically any historical investigation into the process of that text's transmission and the diffusion of its particular religious content. Nonetheless, in this context this is a crucial issue, since Karma Lingpa's textual revelations may not have been widely available in printed form until the eighteenth century. Before that period, each of the individual textual collections were circulated in manuscript form and preserved in various monastic libraries, each reflecting particular lineage affiliations and local customs. During the late seventeenth century, it became more economically feasible for the larger ecclesiastical institutions to assemble these local manuscripts and to print them as books. This is in fact how divergent multiple editions of the *Self-Liberated Wisdom of the Peaceful and Wrathful Deities* and the *Great Liberation upon Hearing in the Bardo* came to be produced. Although this may seem clear enough, the history of the process involved in the production and circulation of these texts has not been the subject of critical study. An account of the broader history of the Karling treasure literature can only begin with an understanding of the collections themselves, and so in order to provide a basis for their study I will briefly explore here the structure of this treasure cycle.

An analysis of the contents of the various recensions of Karma Lingpa's *Self-Liberated Wisdom of the Peaceful and Wrathful Deities* reveals, in the words of Janet Gyatso,

> that successive textual layers exist, amongst which we can often recognize a text or texts that seem to be intended to represent the revelatory teaching as such. We may consider these texts as the "visionary core" of the cycle. They are similar to the *mūla* or *kārikā* genres of Indic literature in that they are the referents of the commentaries and subsidiary rituals in the visionary system.[53]

Here, according to Gyatso's definition, the core text can be viewed as a sort of "primary visionary document," meaning that it can be thought of as "a kind of transcription of the actual revelation."[54] In this regard, the core text is believed to contain the original and fundamental teachings of the concealed treasure. Gyatso continues:

> Such visionary core texts are almost always anonymous. The core text may be labeled in a variety of ways. Often versified, it is in some cases a separate text, in others an embedded passage. In the Discovered Treasure literature, the visionary core will be a separate item called the Treasure Book (*gter gzhung*). This is usually a short aphoristic or laconic text which lays out the spiritual

authority for the Discovered Treasure of which it is a part, and outlines a particular philosophy or meditative system.[55]

From among the texts of the *Peaceful and Wrathful Deities*, the work that best approximates the type of treasure book described by Gyatso may be the terse *Direct Introduction to Awareness: Self-Liberation through Naked Vision* [*Rig-pa ngo-sprod gcer-mthong rang-grol*], which has been the subject of several western-language studies.[56] In the modern facsimile editions it is generally included among the texts of the famed *Liberation upon Hearing*, and scholars have tended to treat it as the theoretical basis of the concepts contained in that cycle.[57] The *Direct Introduction to Awareness* is attributed explicitly to Padmasambhava, who is said to have concealed it in the standard fashion for the benefit of future generations. The text offers in nine-syllable verse a rather brief poetic description of the view (*lta-ba*) of the Dzokchen philosophical tradition. As I have noted, it is from this specialized tradition that the treasure of Karma Lingpa derives its conceptual focus. Still, although it may be true that the *Direct Introduction to Awareness* epitomizes the doctrinal foundation of the *Liberation upon Hearing*, and in turn also of the larger text cycle of the *Peaceful and Wrathful Deities*—and so, in this light, can be suitably viewed as the "root" text per se—the text does not appear to be the most fundamental in terms of being the historically earliest document, or even in practical terms the central text around which the later supplemental literature revolves. Whatever the case may be, at least on the issue of chronology, the absence of verifiable data means that any speculation here must necessarily remain tentative and may have to be modified, or even rejected, as possible further evidence is introduced. The important point is that we should attempt to make a finer distinction between what "core" might mean in the present context.

I wish to make clear that for my purposes the label "core text" (*gzhung-rtsa*) is descriptive of two categories of literature. The first type is best expressed by what Gyatso has termed "ancient writing" (*yig-rnying*) and covers "a range of literary genres which can function as core texts, including *sādhana-s* and liturgies, and indicates simply that the text may be *the first written form of a tradition*."[58] In this sense, the root texts of the Karling treasure are only those that can be traced back to Karma Lingpa himself, or to one of his immediate disciples, such as Nyida Sangye or Nyida Chöje. From this perspective, the core texts can be understood as the earliest artifacts of the literary tradition. It would appear likely that such truly archaeological treasures could provide a relatively stable marker by which the cycle's movement could be traced through time and place. However, these primary documents are not so easily determined because of the composite and cumulative nature of the collection as a whole. Furthermore, given the unusual character of the treasure's origin and mode of transfer—that is, the direct transmission of texts believed to have been prepared in the eighth century but only later "discovered" and distributed from the late fourteenth century—the question of authorship becomes problematic. In other words, the manner in which the

original texts were first set down in writing poses a dilemma not easily resolved. The nature of author, text codification, and historical authenticity,
therefore, become crucial issues in understanding the formation of the *Peaceful
and Wrathful Deities* and its subsequent transmission in Tibet. The task of
sifting out primary documents is not made easier even when the most famous
and widely distributed set of texts drawn from this large treasury are considered; namely, the elusive *Liberation upon Hearing*. The question of whether
an authoritative collection known by that title can actually be identified, not
to mention which of the many texts said to belong to the discoveries of Karma
Lingpa are to be included in this enigmatic corpus, has yet to be satisfacto-
rily resolved, and may not be until more diverse arrangements of the *Liberation upon Hearing* come to light and are made available in print.[59]

So, in the final analysis it becomes evident that accurate determination of
the earliest documents of the Karling treasure tradition is extremely difficult,
to say the least. For those works that do not carry reference to identifiable
authors, we cannot generally rely on what the texts claim for themselves. A
great number of the anonymous works are marked at their conclusion by the
generic and unremarkable label "a treasure of Karma Lingpa" (*karma-gling-
pa'i gter-ma'o*). Furthermore, we certainly cannot base our calculations on
the presence or absence of specific conceptual premises, since it has been
demonstrated that this literature is largely derivative of a complex network
of preexisting ideas already well formulated and prevalent by the fourteenth
century. A meticulous and thorough text-critical investigation of all relevant
works would perhaps be the only viable method for possibly exposing the
various layers of history. However, in the absence of witnesses dating back
before the seventeenth century, this method could not possibly uncover an
"original" layer but could only provide us with information relative to the
earliest of available documents. This does not mean that such data would be
insignificant, for we could learn much about the provenance of the existing
texts, but just that from text analysis alone we cannot know anything definite
about the actual content of the oldest books. The original manuscripts of
Karma Lingpa and of his immediate disciples, the very first documents of the
tradition, are essentially lost to us forever.

The label "core text" might then be used more profitably to refer to something different. In this alternative sense, the descriptive category of "core text"
covers those principal texts that have been historically treated as the most
important works of the literary and ritual tradition. These are the central texts
of the cycle, the ones invariably referred to in the commentaries and subsidiary rituals. We could speculate that these historically significant core texts
are also historically prior to most of the auxiliary literature, and in this way
we could combine the two meanings of "core" just outlined. If we do this,
though, we have to keep in mind that the central texts will not necessarily be
the earliest texts, or even the significantly older ones. In fact, the most important texts of a given collection are often younger than the other works
contained therein, as for example in the case of texts recently authored by
prominent leaders of a particular teaching-lineage that come to serve as pre-

eminent works in an older collection affiliated with that specific lineal tradition. The seventeenth-century Karling texts of Rāgasya Karma Chakme (associated with the Nedo and Payul lineages) or those of the nineteenth-century Jamgön Kongtrül (representing the Nedo and Rime lineages) are examples that immediately come to mind.[60] Admitting that the central and authoritative texts of a cycle may not in every case reflect "ancient writing" but are nonetheless almost always the primary works, we should now consider what texts might constitute the core structure of Karma Lingpa's *Self-Liberated Wisdom of the Peaceful and Wrathful Deities*.

In speaking of the central texts of this collection, I would like to return to the sevenfold typology of contents introduced in the previous section and offer the following argument. I will assume that all the fundamental teachings of this treasure cycle are to be found within these seven classifications. Based on internal evidence drawn from the opening and closing sections of the texts themselves, and on comparative data derived from analysis of the titles referenced by the other works, as well as the frequency with which each text appears in the various printed arrangements of the cycle, I would argue that the core structure of Karma Lingpa's *Peaceful and Wrathful Deities* consists of five texts, or rather a fivefold network of texts, as follows.

1. *Self-Liberation of Broken Vows through Expiation and Confession*
   1a. *One Hundred Prostrations: The Self-Liberation of Sin and Defilement*
   1b. *Self-Liberation of Speech: Confession to the Expanse of the Peaceful and Wrathful Deities*
2. *Self-Liberation of Feeling: Practice Manual of the Peaceful and Wrathful Deities*
3. *Religious Liturgy of the Self-Liberation of Karmic Latencies*
4. *Self-Liberation of the Body: Liberation upon Wearing*
5. *Great Liberation upon Hearing in the Bardo*
   5a. *Reminder of the Bardo of Reality-Itself*
       5a.1. *Manifestation of the Bardo of Wrathful Deities* [61]
   5b. *Direct Introduction to the Bardo of Becoming*
   5c. *Prayer Requesting the Buddhas and Bodhisattvas for Assistance*
   5d. *Triad of Bardo Prayers*
       5d1. *Root Verses of the Six Bardos*
       5d2. *Prayer for Deliverance from the Perilous Straits of the Bardo*
       5d3. *Bardo Prayer That Protects from Fear*

Several of these titles are associated with a rather extensive collection of supplementary literature, some of which is shared by more than one text. The *Self-Liberation of Broken Vows through Expiation and Confession*, for example, is complemented by as many as twelve associated works,[62] and editions of the *Liberation upon Hearing* frequently contain not only the *One Hundred Prostrations: The Self-Liberation of Sin and Defilement* but also the *Religious Liturgy of the Self-Liberation of Karmic Latencies*. For this reason, it is necessary to view the five works in relation to one another as a constellation of liturgical texts that derives, in part, from a few basic ritual components; namely, rites of expiation and purification (text 1), generation-stage sādhanas (texts 2 and 3), and wearing and hearing liberation teachings (texts 4 and 5). The main characteristics of each of these subjects have been discussed earlier. We are now in a position to determine which text from among these core works is actually the most fundamental to the Karling tradition as a whole. Here we want to find the core of the core, as it were, and from there to make a few tentative historical claims about the status of this root text in relation to a so-called Tibetan Book of the Dead (*bod-kyi gshin-yig*).

I should begin by refining my definition of "core" in this context to mean, in the most practical terms, the main text recited in the Karling ritual. Since the *Peaceful and Wrathful Deities* is generally identified first and foremost as a funeral treasure, it stands to reason that the core text of the collection would be the principal liturgical text recited during the accompanying funerary rites. The ritual essence of the *Peaceful and Wrathful Deities* can be condensed into the first three core texts listed earlier, the *Self-Liberation of Broken Vows through Expiation and Confession*, the *Self-Liberation of Feeling: Practice Manual of the Peaceful and Wrathful Deities*, and the *Religious Liturgy of the Self-Liberation of Karmic Latencies*.[63] I contend, furthermore, that the *Self-Liberation of Karmic Latencies* is the most central of this triad. The practical importance of this text had already been recognized by Evans-Wentz as an effective ritual digest of the more elaborate *Liberation upon Hearing*:

> Chös-spyod-bag-chags-rang-grol (pron. *Chö-chod-bag-chah-rang-dol*), the title of a metrical version, in brief form, of the *Bardo Thödol*, which, being easy to memorize and thereafter recite as a matter of habit, is referred to as liberating because of such acquired habit or propensity on the part of the deceased, it being supposed that the deceased knows the ritual by heart and that its reading will remind him of it and thereby bring about his liberation.[64]

The *Religious Liturgy of the Self-Liberation of Karmic Latencies* is a basic Mahāyoga sādhana employing a mandala of forty-two peaceful and fifty-eight wrathful deities, the divine entourage of the *Peaceful and Wrathful Deities*. The body of the text is constructed around the verses of two of three primary bardo prayers mentioned in the foregoing list, the *Prayer for Deliverance from the Perilous Straits of the Bardo* and the *Bardo Prayer That Protects from Fear*. Nowadays, according to the Nyingmapa liturgical programs followed at the Payul monastery in Bylakuppe, South India, and at the Dzokchen monastery in Tokyo, the *Self-Liberation of Karmic Latencies* is the principal text recited in the Karling funeral ritual as a means of conveying practical instruction to the deceased wandering in the bardo.[65] In contrast, the *Reminder of the Bardo of Reality-Itself* and the *Direct Introduction to the Bardo of Becoming*—the two works that are almost always accepted without question to be synonymous with the *Liberation upon Hearing* itself, hence the popular *Tibetan Book of the Dead*—are identified as special meditation texts (*ngo-sprod*) to be utilized by advanced Dzokchen practitioners, rather than ritual manuals to be recited in the *Peaceful and Wrathful* liturgy. The interpretation of these two texts as advanced meditation manuals is borne out in the classification schemes from the various *Transmission Records*. Recall that in those sources these two bardo texts were in most cases categorized as direct personal introductions (*ngo-sprod*) and liberation-upon-hearing (*thos-grol*) texts rather than works of liturgy (*sgrub-dbang*). This is important because the prevailing and evidently mistaken opinion in both academic and popular circles is that the *Reminder of the Bardo of Reality-Itself* and the *Direct Introduction to the Bardo of Becoming* are the main ritual texts used in Tibetan funeral liturgy. The primary reason that this unquestioned opinion has become so widespread is probably the result of the pride of place given to these texts in the English language editions of the *Tibetan Book of the Dead* going back to 1927. From these popular books a distorted perception of the importance of these two texts has come to dominate and in many ways restrict our understanding of the Tibetan materials. The most compelling evidence against this view lies in the texts themselves.

In the colophons of its many printed versions, the *Religious Liturgy of the Self-Liberation of Karmic Latencies* is uniquely and uniformly identified as an extremely lucid religious practice for gathering the peaceful and wrathful deities (*zhi-khro 'dus-pa'i chos-spyod rab-gsal*); the practical application (*nyams-len*) of the *Liberation upon Hearing*; the essential heart (*snying-po*) of the *Self-Liberation of Feeling: Practice Manual of the Peaceful and Wrathful Deities*; the facilitating practice (*cha-rkyen*) of an unknown work entitled *Self-Liberated Awareness: The Secret Bardo Initiation* (*Rig-pa rang-grol bardo gsang-dbang*);[66] and the main body (*dngos-gzhi*) of the *Self-Liberation of Broken Vows through Expiation and Confession*. Given these distinguished qualities, and considering that the *Religious Liturgy of the Self-Liberation of Karmic Latencies* is included in no less than twenty of the twenty-one extant editions of the Karling treasure cycle, and has even been published by itself in a separate volume[67]—an unprecedented occurrence, for no other text, barring the *Self-Liberation of Speech: Confession to the Expanse of the Peaceful and Wrathful Deities* (included in eighteen editions), has been incorporated into so many different printed versions—it is certain that the *Self-Liberation of Karmic Latencies* is the core text of the *Self-Liberated Wisdom of the Peaceful and Wrathful Deities* and lies also at the very heart of the *Great Liberation upon Hearing in the Bardo*.

Questions remain concerning the extent to which Karma Lingpa participated in, altered, and/or redirected the structure and meanings of the rites and doctrines inscribed in the core treasure texts associated with him. What was precisely the accomplishment of this obscure visionary whom tradition depicts as a discoverer of some previously hidden treasures? As my discussion in chapter 6 made clear, the historical record offers only vague and fragmented evidence. Nevertheless, what does seem clear is that after Karma Lingpa the remarkable and indeterminate series of texts that would be identified collectively as the *Liberation upon Hearing* took its earliest shape at two monasteries in southeastern Tibet. This literary tradition was later transmitted to the treasure revealer Rikzin Nyima Drakpa, who would come to standardize it in the late seventeenth century.

At this point I want to introduce a basic sketch of the development of the Karling tradition that I will embellish in later chapters. Around the end of the fourteenth century, Karma Lingpa and those immediately close to him, including, most important, his father Nyida Sangye and his son Nyida Chöje, brought together a variety of liturgical materials drawn primarily from earlier Dzokchen sources put into circulation during the previous few centuries and synthesized these into a coherent and practical ritual complex. With alterations and additions by various figures such as the lama Nyida Özer, this ritual complex was then given an institutional foundation in the late fifteenth century at the hands of Gyarawa Namkha Chökyi Gyatso. Gyarawa's program subsequently became the basic ritual response to death and dying among most of the major Nyingmapa monastic orders, and in a few instances among certain followers of the Kagyu tradition, for long afterward. The topic of the later propagation and transformation of the various teaching-lineages of the Gampodar treasures will be considered further in part III. For the moment I will return to the story of the earliest transmission of treasure revelations immediately following Karma Lingpa's death.

8

The Third Generation

The Sun-Moon Disciples

A confusion seems to have existed concerning the identity of Karma Lingpa's most immediate disciple(s). As we noted previously in chapter 6, several of the histories claim that Karma Lingpa appointed his father, Nyida Sangye, and his son, Nyida Chöje, as the sole masters of the doctrine (*chos-bdag*). After the treasure revealer himself, the doctrine-master, also known as treasure-master (*gter-bdag*), is the most significant individual in the lineage, for it is he who preserves the tradition and insures that it is properly transmitted in the future.[1] There are two types of doctrine-master depending on how the "mind-mandate transmission," the actual entrustment (*gtad-rgya*) of the teaching, had been received from Padmasambhava. The primary doctrine-master is the one who, together with the treasure revealer, originally received the mandate in person; the secondary or minor master is the one who received it through some intermediary.[2] The sources do not make it clear where in this scheme Nyida Sangye and Nyida Chöje actually fit. Some would argue for the primacy of Nyida Sangye, since he is believed to have assisted Karma Lingpa in uncovering the Gampodar treasures and to have later received from him their complete oral precepts. This argument, I believe, reflects the fifth Dalai Lama's point of view. Others might claim Nyida Chöje as the chief doctrine-master, for it is through him that the main lineage, by most accounts, is said to have passed. In any event, it is certain that both Karma Lingpa's father and son were his first significant disciples and the most effective early transmitters of the Karling revelations. Nyida Sangye, I have shown, was a successful treasure revealer himself who discovered, among other religious objects, a potent set of teachings concerned with the yoga of transference at the moment of death (*'pho-ba*). His life is shrouded in mystery. We know just as little about his grandson, Nyida Chöje.

Nyida Chöje, referred to also as Namkha Sangye,[3] may have been Karma Lingpa's only son. In keeping with hagiographic convention, he is said to have been a religious prodigy, capable of high intellectual achievement and gifted insight. He was a well-loved, compassionate teacher. Early on he had become expert in all five special sciences[4] and had especially mastered the essential teachings of Dzokchen.[5] By the time he was seventeen he had begun giving religious instruction and was skilled in bestowing initiations.[6] He had become an able teacher and ritual specialist and is claimed to have served as an inspiration to all his students. For reasons that are not made clear, Nyida Chöje left his home region of Dakpo and traveled east to Longpo,[7] where he first encountered a lama by the name of Nyida Özer (referred to also as Sūryacandraraśmi, the Sanskrit form of his name). This lama had earlier appeared to him in his dreams, signaling that the connections linking them together were auspicious and in proper alignment.[8] Nyida Chöje immediately recognized Nyida Özer as the third appointed disciple forecast in the prophecy of Padmasambhava.[9] He thus presented Nyida Özer with the complete cycle of the *Self-Liberated Wisdom of the Peaceful and Wrathful Deities*:

> You have been prophesied as the third lineage-holder [of my father's treasure]. I've never given this teaching [to anyone else], not even to the wind. [In the prophecy] it is declared: *For up to three generations it is crucial that [this treasure] be transmitted to only one individual [at a time]. After the third generation there will arise immeasurable benefits for all living beings.*
>
> Do not show [these instructions to anyone] for at least six years. Put them into practice. Then, after six years, give them to another. Great benefit will come for all living beings. [Again, the prophecy says] *Karma Lingpa's beneficial [treasure] will spread to the north.* This statement forecasts that the teaching will be disseminated and flourish in the northern districts.[10]

We read elsewhere that Nyida Chöje also made an injunction to Nyida Özer regarding another cycle of teachings from Karma Lingpa's treasure: "Do not teach for at least ten years the cycle of the *Great Bliss of the Lower Orifice*, which is included within this profound treasure. After that time, this teaching will be free from obstacles."[11] With this brief description of the first extrafamilial transmission of Karma Lingpa's treasure, we not only move geographically along the Tsangpo River (upper Brahmaputra) northeast to the region of Longpo and lower Kongpo but we also move into a more clearly articulated historical space. Here the mythic overlays familiar to us in the legends of Karma Lingpa, his father, and his son fade slightly into the more historically concrete, albeit romantic, accounts of the lama Nyida Özer and his student from Kongpo, Gyarawa Namkha Chökyi Gyatso. Unlike their predecessors, both figures can be dated with some certainty and their clans and family lineages identified. Moreover, both can be located and tied to known Tibetan institutions. Nevertheless, the picture of their lives remains hazy and incomplete. In this chapter I will examine as closely as possible the life and contributions of these two lineage-holders. We begin with Nyida Chöje's entrusted student and Gyarawa's teacher, the lama Nyida Özer.

The few details we are given about Nyida Özer are sketchy at best. The earliest reference to him appears in Gyarawa's *Garland of Jewels*, which served as the main source for the later version in Guru Tashi's *Religious History*. The early sixteenth-century description by Gyarawa's student Gedün Gyeltsen, in his *Series of the Authentic Lineage Teachers*, is remarkably specific though quite brief. This latter account contains information that bears little resemblance to that found in the other two works, which suggests that at least one of these authors had mistakenly conflated Nyida Özer with some other Tibetan lama. Given that Gyarawa was closest in time to Nyida Özer, his presentation is probably the more reliable. Nevertheless, in constructing the story of Nyida Özer I think it is fruitful to examine the various accounts together in order to decide what facts are the most probable in light of the evidence presented.

Nyida Özer was born in Longpo Tsikar in the female ox year 1409 or 1421 into the lineage descending from Langchen Pelgyi Senge.[12] He is said to have been the incarnation of an obscure Indian revealer of medical treasure named Vajramati (mid-thirteenth or early fourteenth century), although several of the sources are not so clear on this point.[13] His father was a doctor named Yangyel and his mother was named Yungdrung Gyen.[14] He was the second oldest of four brothers and, as would be expected, was quickly recognized as a child prodigy. At the age of four he had already learned how to read and write. By the time he was six he had mastered the art of painting and sculpture. When he was eight he began composing religious treatises.[15] When he was still quite young, he ran off to practice meditation in solitude and so gained an early reputation for being an extremely devout and advance meditator. His numerous teachers, such as one Jetsün Drakpa Rinpoche,[16] helped him to become learned in scholastic exegesis, debate, and composition.[17] Nyida Özer was supposedly the author of many volumes of philosophical writings collectively entitled *Cycle of the Ninefold Ocean of Treatises* [*Bstan-bcos rgya-mtsho dgu-skor*].[18] Unfortunately, it appears this literary cycle is no longer extant, although a number of Nyida Özer's other works are available in some of the Karling anthologies. Although the various sources offer conflicting details about this nebulous figure, they all agree that it was he who bestowed the Karling treasures on Gyarawa Namkha Chökyi Gyatso.

The Abbot of Menmo

In Jamgön Kongtrül's definitive anthology of Tibet's most famous treasure revealers, the *Garland of Precious Lapis Lazuli* [*Rin-chen baiḍurya'i phreng-ba*], he emphasizes that the *Self-Liberated Wisdom of the Peaceful and Wrathful Deities* and attendant rituals were propagated widely by one Gyatsün Namkha Chökyi Gyatso.[19] Kongtrül's opinion seems to have been shared among the historians of Karma Lingpa's tradition, for it is often written that Gyarawa was the first to establish a lineage of transmission for the Karling treasure and that from him it spread throughout all the regions of Tibet, including Ü, Tsang, Kham, Kongpo, Nyel, and Dakpo.[20] Gyarawa was indeed the first to systematize the Karling teachings and to institutionalize its liturgy. His pioneering achievements resulted in the creation of a coherent and standardized set of ritual practices that could be easily distributed to other monastic institutions. Karma Lingpa's treasure was widely disseminated in this form, and Gyarawa came to be seen as its premier architect. Most of the information we have about his life is found in his own history of the Karling transmissions, the *Garland of Jewels*, and in the short lineage biography by his student Gedün Gyeltsen, the *Series of the Authentic Lineage Teachers*, the details of which are also repeated in the *Religious History* of Guru Tashi.

In the paragraphs that follow I turn to the details of Gyarawa's life and conclude with a few remarks on his role as institutionalizer of the liturgical tradition associated with Karma Lingpa. It should be remembered throughout the discussion that Gyarawa's institutionalization of the treasure cycle of the *Peaceful and Wrathful Deities* was only a partial stage in the development of this tradition. To be sure, Gyarawa's efforts were instrumental in promoting the widespread circulation of this otherwise inconsequential treasure. But his specific line of transmission was not the only one that was handed down in Tibet. As I shall soon show, there was another Karling tradition that passed through an alternative line; namely, the transmission of the *Great Liberation upon Hearing in the Bardo* and the apparently related *Four Initiations: Self-Liberation of Whatever Is Encountered*.

Namkha Chökyi Gyatso was born in the iron male dog year 1430 in lower Kongpo into the Gyarawa family belonging to the Dru clan.[21] The descendants of this clan may have hailed originally from the district of Drugu located near Derge.[22] Gyarawa's father was named Namkha of Tshemyul and his mother Dewa Pema. Following the untimely death of his parents when he was just five years old in 1435, he was placed in the care of his paternal uncle, referred to simply as the lama Chödrup. This lama held the family monastic throne of Menmo,[23] which, judging from the paucity of references in the historical sources appears to have been quite small and relatively insignificant.[24] His earliest years appear to have been a time of unprecedented learning, for he is said to have been able to read and write by the age of six. In 1442, at the age of twelve, in the presence of Drungchö Dorje Tokden (alias Drung Chödenpa)[25] he took layman's vows (Skt., *upāsaka*) and asked his uncle for teachings on a text with the generic title *Lamp That Dispels the Darkness* [*Mun-sel sgron-me*]. The precise identity of Drung Chödenpa is a question worth considering. For this purpose we must delve briefly into the history of two Nyingmapa monasteries that have not received much attention; namely, Dakpo Tsele and its daugher house, Kongpo Thangdrok.

The ancient monastery of Dakpo Tsele, known as Tsele Nyingma, "Old Tsele," was established sometime in the fourteenth century by Kunkhyen Chöku Özer.[26] He was a student of Sedengpa Sangye Pel and his nephew, Guṇaphala, both themselves disciples of Nyendön Dorje Yeshe of the Menlung tradition.[27] Kunkhyen Chöku Özer's main pupil was Gyara Longchenpa of Barkham in eastern Tibet.[28] Over time, Tsele Nyingma fell into decay. During the first decades of the sixteenth century a monk named Rikzin Chenpo Sönam Namgyel, with the support of Dakpo Kurap Depa, refurbished the institution and established a new monastery, appropriately called Tsele Sarpa, "New Tsele."[29] After him, two of Sönam Namgyel's sons came in succession to occupy the abbatial throne: Pel Orgyen Tenzin (1523–1560) and Je Karma Thutop Namgyel (1543–1589), respectively.[30]

In 1564 the Overlord (*dpon-chen*) of Dakpo, Samphel Döndrup, offered the monastery of Thangdrok to Tshungme Tenzin Dorje (1533–1605), who was at that time an important lama at Tsele Sarpa.[31] In the following year Tshungme Tenzin Dorje officially reestablished the bipartisan institution of Thangdrok as a "pure monastery" (*gtsang-dgon*) of unmarried monks.[32] Kongpo Thangdrok remained under the jurisdiction of the abbots of Tsele Sarpa.[33] Connections between Dakpo Tsele and Thangdrok were longstanding even before the time of Tshungme Tenzin Dorje. An early link can be found in the person of Drung Chödenpa.

The original Thangdrok monastery had been established in the fourteenth century by an unnamed student of Chöje Samten Pel, who is claimed to have been the reincarnation of Phadampa Sangye (d. 1117).[34] The monastery was eventually destroyed by fire, and the task of restoring its community was taken up by one Drungpa Lodrö Senge, the younger brother of a certain Chöje Gongchenpa Gyarawa. Drungpa Lodrö Senge assumed the role of abbot of Thangdrok and attracted many students of both the Nyingma and Sarma (primarily Kagyu) persuasions—an ecumenicalism for which Thangdrok soon became famous.[35] After Drungpa Lodrö Senge's death, his premier student Zhelop Rinpoche Chödenpa became abbot and for a long while was renowned as Drungpa Dorje. Not long thereafter, when the monastery had begun to fall into decline, Drungpa Dorje, better known as Drung Chödenpa, moved to Tsele Nyingma monastery in Dakpo.[36] I believe it was this individual who in 1442 bestowed the layman's vows on Gyarawa Namkha Chökyi Gyatso. Gyarawa, then, must have been in close contact with some of the residents of Thangdrok. He had received religious vows either at that institution or at Dakpo Tsele. This detail is just one of many threads connecting Karma Lingpa's successors to Dakpo Tsele and Kongpo Thangdrok.

The background story, however, is not complete. Before I continue, I must also mention a certain Gönpo Dorje, known from the lists of lineage-holders of the *Liberation upon Hearing*. In those lists this figure is indicated as having received the teaching transmissions directly from Karma Lingpa's son, Nyida Chöje. From the anonymous *History of the Treasures* we learn that Nyida Chöje traveled to Kongpo and while in retreat at some unspecified mountain hermitage met a lama named Gönpo Dorje. Nyida Chöje determined through oneiromancy that this solitary holy man was meant to be the appointed third-generation disciple fit to receive the transmission that he had previously inherited from his grandfather, Nyida Sangye.[37] So who was this Gönpo Dorje of Kongpo?

I am aware of only one figure from roughly the same time period with the name Gönpo Dorje, although I hesitate to bring him up because the meagerness of the sources prevents any substantial resolution. I can only offer a few fragments and an uncertain logic that pieces them together in the hope that my picture can be corrected in the future. The Gönpo Dorje I am referring to may have been known more widely as Chödenpa, the younger brother of Menlungpa Shakya Ö (alias Mikyö Dorje, b. 1239) and abbot of an obscure monastery that bore his name.[38] If we accept the birthdate given for Mikyö Dorje, then Chödenpa appears to have lived much earlier than any of the persons that might be of interest us here, including Karma Lingpa himself. However, he might still be worth noting for his close connection to the lineage of Menlung. Chödenpa's eldest brother, Menlungpa, had a number of disciples from Dakpo, and particularly one by the name of Dakdön Wangchuk Dorje (alias Sangye Gonglawa), whose later successors included the teachers of Kunkhyen Chöku Özer, founder of the monastery of Tsele Nyingma. This Dakpo Tsele connection is intriguing, for, as I will show in the following chapters, certain key affiliates of Dakpo Tsele and its sister branch of Thangdrok in Kongpo became pivotal players in the diffusion of both the *Liberation upon Hearing* and the *Four Initiations: Self-Liberation of Whatever Is Encountered*. Can this mean that Chödenpa Gönpo Dorje, Kongpo Gönpo Dorje, and Drung Chödenpa of Menlung may all be one and the same person? At this stage it would be difficult to respond affirmatively to this question, since the dates seem to conflict. However, the Gönpo Dorje that we are searching for may still have been tied in some way to the Menlungpa line, which is expressly linked to the monasteries of Chöden, Dakpo Tsele, and the closely affiliated Kongpo Thangdrok. In this light, I should draw attention to the fact that another of Nyida Chöje's students, Gyarawa's chief mentor Nyida Özer, was also associated with one of these institutions; namely, the monastery of Thangdrok. I should return now to the life of Gyarawa.

In 1443 in the presence of Dampa Ngarisa,[39] Gyarawa asked for the vows of novitiate (Skt., *śramaṇera*). Three years later, when he was only sixteen, he requested the cycle of Dzokchen teachings from the siddha Namgyel Zangpo.[40] Two years later, in 1448, he received from one Namkha Shenyen the main teachings of the *Kālacakra-tantra* (Wheel of Time Tantra), the *Embodiment of the Lama's Realization* [*Bla-ma dgongs-'dus*],[41] and the *All-Knowing* [*Kun-rig*].[42] In 1451, at the age of twenty, presumably following the death of his uncle, he became the throne-holder of Menmo monastery, taking charge of both the religious and secular affairs of that institution. Some time later, he went on pilgrimage to the sacred sites at both Tsari and Lhasa. Apparently while in central Tibet he requested to be fully ordained as a Buddhist monk in the presence of Chöje Tsangchenpa. It was this lama who gave him the name Namkha Chökyi Gyatso.

Could Gyarawa's ordination lama have been Chöje Tsangpa of Khyungtshang monastery? This lama had also been a teacher of the treasure revealer Chokden Gönpo (also Dongak Lingpa, 1497–1521) of Lhodrak. There is evidence that suggests a personal connection between Chokden Gönpo and Gyarawa. We read in the former's autobiography that he, Chokden Gönpo, received instructions called *Direct Introduction to the Bardo* [*Bar-do ngo-sprod*] and *Offering the Transference* ['*Pho-ba 'debs-pa*] from an elderly man named Akhu Gyatsün, who was dying of leprosy.[43] Beyond the obvious references to death and bardo teachings, this detail should strike us immediately. In other contexts, we find the title Gyatsün, "monk of the Gya (clan)," as a specific name for Gyarawa. Gyarawa even refers to himself as Gyatsün at the end of his *Garland of Jewels*.[44] So we must ask if the elderly Akhu Gyatsün in Chokden Gönpo's story was actually Gyarawa. There are additional indications of a relationship. We might note that Chokden Gönpo's father, Sumdar Gyelpo, belonged to the Gya clan. Furthermore, both Gyarawa and Chokden Gönpo shared an affiliation with the monastery of Dakpo Tsele and received the layman's vows from a Chöje Tsangpa or Tsangchenpa.[45] We know that in Chokden Gönpo's case this Chöje Tsangpa was tied to Khyungtshang monastery. Hence it is not too great a stretch to suggest that Gyarawa's ordination lama was the same individual.

The location of Menmo monastery, as well as the locations of other monasteries mentioned in connection with Gyarawa, is a problem that merits some consideration if we are to begin to construct an account of Gyarawa's early history. The fifth Dalai Lama explicitly attests to the latter's close affiliation to Menmo by referring to him as "Gyatsün from Menmo" [*sman-mo-ba rgya-btsun*].[46] For what it is worth, the label "Menmowa" (*sman-mo-ba*) in this title is also found in an inscription listing the patrons of a particular set of wall paintings in the Kubum stupa in Gyantse (built in 1440), on which appears the phrase "[those patrons], the brothers from Menmo in Gyangkhar" (*rgyang-'khar sman-mo-ba spun*).[47] There is a Gyangkhar district located in the region of Tshona (known also as Mönyul) in southern Tibet.[48] But this sort of evidence is insufficient and does not permit us to decide whether this Gyangkhar Menmo is the same as the Menmo cited in Gyarawa's biography. In the end we are no closer to solving the problem of locating this important family institution.

Summarizing what we know thus far, we can place Gyarawa in Kongpo during his formative years, from approximately 1430 to 1435, at which time after the death of his parents he moved to his uncle's monastery of Menmo, where he resided until he was twenty-one in 1452. Some time in the following years, after ascending the monastic throne of Menmo, he traveled on pilgrimage to Lhasa, where he appears to have received the name Namkha Chökyi Gyatso. From Lhasa he must have journeyed back to his birthplace of Kongpo, where, as I will show, he met his root lama, Nyida Özer.

Returning now to the account of Gyarawa's life described in his own biography, he relates that it was at the monastery of a certain Kangme Gyeltsen (probably from lower Kongpo)[49] that he first met the lama Nyida Özer, who had been formerly invited by the head lamas and patrons to visit Kangme Gyeltsen's son. The identity of both Kangme Gyeltsen and his affiliated monastery is a mystery. Perhaps one clue may lie in the colophons of two of Nyida Özer's own works, where it is written that his texts were authored at the behest of the lama Namkha at the monastery of Thangdrok in Kongpo.[50] This is a clear reference to Gyarawa and to the site of the famous daughter house of Dakpo Tsele monastery. It is likely, therefore, that Nyida Özer had been either a resident or extended visitor of Thangdrok monastery sometime in the middle years of the fifteenth century. So we must then ask: could Kangme Gyeltsen and his son also have been at Thangdrok, and if so what exactly would their positions have been? These questions are not easy to answer, but clearly the connections between Nyida Özer, Gyarawa, and the monasteries of Kongpo Thangdrok and Dakpo Tsele are curious indeed and require more thorough investigation.[51]

After returning home from his pilgrimage, a trip that seems to have included a visit to Kongpo Thangdrok monastery and a meeting with Nyida Özer, Gyarawa invited a lama named Sönam Gyeltsen to visit Menmo. As is expected of traveling lamas in Tibet, Sönam Gyeltsen performed rituals and bestowed initiations on Gyarawa and his monastic community. It is interesting to speculate about a possible link between Sönam Gyeltsen and Kangme Gyeltsen, whose son's invitation of Nyida Özer was the occasion of Gyarawa's first meeting with his root teacher. Remember that Gyarawa had received teachings from Nyida Özer at Thangdrok monastery. So for the sake of argument, let us assume the monastery of Kangme Gyeltsen's son was actually Kongpo Thangdrok. Who might Kangme Gyeltsen have been? Again, recall that the monastery of Dakpo Tsele Sarpa had been instituted by Rikzin Chenpo Sönam Namgyel (a name occasionally written as Sönam Gyeltsen) and it was one of his sons who helped to refurbish the old monastery of Thangdrok in Kongpo. We might want to conclude, then, that the lama Sönam Gyeltsen who visited Menmo monastery was none other than Rikzin Chenpo Sönam Namgyel of Dakpo Tsele fame. Furthermore, we might suggest that all three lamas, Sönam Namgyel, Sönam Gyeltsen, and Kangme Gyeltsen, may have been one and the same person. Nevertheless, as enticing a scenario as this may be, the dates of the individuals in question do not quite match up with those of Nyida Özer or Gyarawa. The trail seems to have run cold, and the mysteries continue.

At any rate, Gyarawa claims to have received a great number of religious texts and instructions from Nyida Özer, including initiations and "readings" (lung) of the One Hundred Thousand Tantras of the Ancients [Rnying-ma rgyud-'bum].[52] The fact that Nyida Özer was in possession of some version of this significant corpus of Nyingma scriptures in the middle of the fifteenth century deserves special comment, particularly in light of the evidence that places Nyida Özer at this time in Kongpo at Thangdrok monastery. The One Hundred Thousand Tantras of the Ancients exists in several different versions, none of which are in exact agreement as to the number of texts included or the order of their arrangement. In essence, each of these editions of the collection reflect the individual diversity of a specific history of transmission. These local histories have only recently begun to be documented with some success by scholars in the field.[53] It is not my purpose to reproduce their work in this chapter, but I should point out one intriguing piece of evidence. Franz-Karl Ehrhard has uncovered valuable information regarding the provisional editions (rags-rim) of this collection that date as far back as the fourteenth century.[54] Ehrhard refers us to the biography of Terdak Lingpa, where it is written that for the preparation of Terdak Lingpa's own seventeenth-century edition of the *One Hundred Thousand Tantras* he relied on four earlier versions, the so-called mother-prints (*ma-dpe*) that had been gathered from Ukpalung, Tsangrong, Darling (Dargye Chöling), and Thangdrok.[55] It is likely that the Kongpo Thangdrok edition referred to here by Terdak Lingpa was the very same version of the collection that was bestowed on Gyarawa by his teacher Nyida Özer.

In addition to the *One Hundred Thousand Tantras of the Ancients*, Gyarawa received from Nyida Özer the entire cycle of initiations, oral transmissions, and instructions from Karma Lingpa's *Self-Liberated Wisdom of the Peaceful and Wrathful Deities*, including the smaller cycle of the *Great Liberation upon Hearing in the Bardo*. Nyida Özer admonished him to spread the treasure to anyone he thought was suitable to receive it. By following the lama's advice, the *Peaceful and Wrathful Deities*, in Gyarawa's own words, "shone as bright as the sun" and "came to be of great benefit to all living beings."

Gyarawa's other teachers included such luminaries as the sixth Karmapa Thongwa Dönden (1416–1453), the treasure revealer Ratna Lingpa, Trhimkhang Lotsawa (alias Sönam Gyatso, 1424–1482), the Drigungpa brothers Rinchen Chögyel (1446–1484) and Wang Chökyi Gyelpo (1448–1504), and the second Drukchen Gyelwang Chöje, Kunga Peljor (1428–1476), who was the abbot of Daklha Gampo monastery. He is also said to have received teachings from Sakyapa Pelden Zangpo and one Trhophu Lotsawa, who may have been in fact Gö Lotsawa Zhönu Pel (1392–1481), author of the famed *Blue Annals* [*Deb-ther sngon-po*].[56]

At some point during his mature years, Gyarawa laid the foundations of as many as six or seven monasteries, including one by the name of Pel Chökhor Tse. In his final years, we are told, he rested in solitary retreat at a mountain hermitage, where he claims to have mastered the various stages of tantric practice. On Sunday July 19, 1499,[57] at the monastery of Pel Rinchen Ling, Gyarawa completed as his final testament (*kha-chems*) the *Garland of Jewels*, the first recorded history of the transmissions of Karma Lingpa's *Peaceful and Wrathful Deities*. He dedicated this work to the "young lions of future generations" and reassured them that by practicing the teachings contained in this treasure collection "they may at the very least take comfort in the fact that they will not be anxious and distraught when the moment of death arrives," since his own lama, Nyida Özer, had assured him that "it was impossible for any sentient being to transmigrate to the lower realms if he listens many times to these teachings." Finally, in the colophon we read:

> At the repeated urging of my spiritual friend, the lama Chögyel from Dokham,[58] and for the sake of [increasing] the faith in those inferior-minded people like myself, I, Gyatsün Namkha Chökyi Gyatso, compiled this account of some of the stages in the transmission of this treasure doctrine in the earth sheep year on the tenth day at the beginning of the seventh month at Pel Rinchen Ling, which is on the right side of the golden Lohita river at the bottom of the snowy foothills to the right of Tamnyong [Tamnyok] Gyadrong. The text was copied down by my scribe Sönam Gyatso, the humble monk from Lhogyü. Having

presented this history with virtue, I pray that all sentient beings be quickly liberated from the great oceans of suffering in samsara and the [three] lower realms
and obtain the expansive awakening of complete omniscience [i.e., buddha-
hood]. Sarva-mangalaṃ [May all be auspicious]![59]

The monastery of Pel Rinchen Ling (also Da Rinchen Ling) is mentioned in
the colophons of two other works composed by Gyarawa.[60] Although its location is described in detail, the relevant place names have yet to be properly
identified.[61] The real key seems to lie in the names "Lohita," "Tamnyong
(Tamnyok)," and "Gyadrong." Wylie reports that the Tsangpo (Brahmaputra)
River is traditionally called Rohita in southeastern Tibet at the point where it
runs into India.[62] This exact location, however, is not clearly indicated on the
available maps of the region. Nevertheless, I should mention a few possible
localities. Lohit is the name of a river in the eastern district of Dzayul. This
river, which is formed by the convergence of the Gangri Karpo Chu from the
west and the Zangchu from the east, flows south through lower Dzayul into
Arunachal Pradesh (India) and continues on through eastern Assam. Although
there is a strong likelihood that this Lohit is the river mentioned by Gyarawa,
the name Lohita might instead refer more generally to the southern course of
the Tsangpo. The point where the Tsangpo river actually runs southward into
India is located west of Dzayul in the hidden valley of Pemakö, but there is
no indication that the river is called Lohita in this area. Gyarawa mentions
the right side (g.yas-zur) of this river. Generally, the right side of a river is
determined by someone facing downstream, so in the Pemakö valley the right
of the Tsangpo would point us in the direction of lower Kongpo, the birthplace
of Gyarawa. But then how do we place the name "Tamnyong" (Tamnyok)?
Jamyang Khyentse indicates that the Lohita River flows from the southern
Tibetan region of Nyel.[63] Presuming that the Lohita does flow southward
from Nyel, the right side of this river would point us in the direction of
Lhodrak in the lower Tsangpo valley of southern Tibet. The "Tam" in the
name "Tamnyong" (Tamnyok) might then be an abbreviation for "Tamshul"
(in modern-day Tshome). The identity of the suffix "-nyong(-nyok)," however, remains to be settled. It might just simply be the proper name of a large
town, a "gyadrong" (rgya-grong), in the river valley of Tamshul. Such a suggestion would at least be consistent with the wording in Gyarawa's colophon.
If my speculations on these obscure location names are correct, Gyarawa may
be placed toward the end of his life in the southernmost reaches of Tibet.

   Although we seem to be able to locate Gyarawa in the vicinities of Kongpo,
Pemakö, and Lhogyü, we still do not know much about where he was active
in his mature years, from roughly 1451, when he ascended the throne of Menmo
monastery, to 1499, when he composed his history of the Karling transmissions. Gyarawa's later activities are not specified in the available records,
though, as I will show in chapter 9, it is clear that he had late ties to important
members of Kathok monastery in eastern Tibet. Further biographical details,
therefore, must be sifted out from fragmented references scattered throughout various colophons at the end of works attributed to him.

In addition to the monastery of Pel Rinchen Ling, the names of two other monasteries (both of which I have discussed briefly earlier) are mentioned in the concluding statements of several of Gyarawa's works; namely, the monasteries of Menmo (listed as Menmo Tashi) and Pel Chökhor Tse. I noted that the former institution was previously administered by Gyarawa's paternal uncle, the lama Chödrup, and that it later became Gyarawa's seat in 1451. The monastery of Pel Chökhor Tse was one of six or seven institutions founded by Gyarawa himself. Perhaps Pel Rinchen Ling was also one of these institutions. On the basis of the order of events related in his own biography, we can use these three monasteries as chronological markers in tracing the progress of his literary achievements. Since his formative years were spent at Menmo monastery, the works associated with this institution are probably the earliest examples of his writing. Likewise, those texts written at Chökhor Tse may contain his more mature and developed ideas, while those completed at Pel Rinchen Ling might represent his most refined work. It is certainly fitting that he composed his biography and history of the Karling transmission at Pel Rinchen Ling in the prime of his years, when generally romantic sentiments about one's own past become especially compelling.

A close examination of Gyarawa's works not only allows us to construct a possible literary chronology—for both his own texts and those that he inherited from his teacher Nyida Özer—but also provides us with a means by which we can properly assess his contributions to the ongoing development of Karma Lingpa's tradition. Gyarawa is explicit identified as the author and/or redactor of at least twenty-five Karling texts, which are all scattered throughout the many recensions of the Karling anthology. These works encompass a variety of topics. With only two exceptions (e.g., a history of the treasure's transmission and a memorandum on its register certificate (them-byang zin-bris),[64] Gyarawa's works relate specifically to the performance of ritual. The ritual works include texts for the entire sequence of acts prescribed for the Karling funeral rites, including confession and expiation (bskang-bshags), death ransoms ('chi-bslu, glud), fire offerings (sbyin-sreg), personal direct introductions (ngo-sprod), liberation-upon-hearing instructions (thos-grol), dharma protectors (bka'-srung, chos-skyong), a fourfold illustrated cycle of ritual diagrams (dpe'u-ris-skor), and even a commentary on a dramatic morality play for ceremonial dance ('chams). With this extensive set of liturgical directives and instructional guidelines, we find clear evidence establishing Gyarawa as the decisive figure in the formation of a specialized ritual program based in part on the teachings of his predecessor, Nyida Özer, and altogether derived from the fourteenth-century revelations of Karma Lingpa. As the tradition's pioneering systematizer, he did not so much invent the Karling liturgy—the textual records indicate that an early ritual system was already in place—as impose a coherent and well-organized structure on a complex of preexisting ideas. In so doing he transformed the shape of the whole tradition and created a systematic program that could be easily disseminated from one monastic community to another. This was all made possible not only by an apparent keen scholarly and practical expertise but also by the strength and security of his institutional support. I have shown that Gyarawa was the first lineage-holder of Karma Lingpa's treasure tradition to have held an official ecclesiastical position—and of the highest rank no less— within an established monastic center. He appears, moreover, to have thrived in this environment, founding as many as six or seven additional monasteries within his lifetime. The significance of these facts should not be underestimated. The evidence leaves us in no doubt that Gyarawa exercised a profound influence on the institutionalization of this tradition, which prior to his efforts appears to have largely embodied a simple but ill-supported assortment of beliefs and practices devoted to the dead and dying, and that he succeeded in securing its official sponsorship. Insofar as it was the monasteries in Tibet that largely controlled the rituals and prayers for the benefit of the dead, we cannot exclude the possibility that he also transformed this preexisting tradition into a means of establishing and maintaining prestige and power for his own monastic institutions. By incorporating these practices into an already well-developed system of revenue involving, for example, payments for rites performed at the request of individuals or groups from the lay community, Gyarawa may have been able to "sell" other monasteries on the Karling liturgy's social, religious, and economic cachet. Consequently, its distribution among the neighboring monasteries was guaranteed, and its further spread throughout other parts of Tibet was not far in coming. Throughout the history of the Tibetan treasure tradition in general, the gaining of widespread approval and the securing of a stable institutional base were crucial elements in the preservation and transmission of specific treasure doctrines and practices. Gyarawa was apparently successful in achieving these aims in his handling of the *Self-Liberated Wisdom of the Peaceful and Wrathful Deities*.

A quick glance at the names and affiliations of those students to whom Gyarawa transmitted the Karling teachings reveals just how wide his influence extended. In the traditions of both Kathok and Payul, which later became two of the most important Nyingmapa institutions in eastern Tibet, the lineage of the Karling transmission is traced through Gyarawa to four disciples: Kathokpa Namkha Senge (b. 1443), Ado Könchok Gyeltsen, Khedrup Lhawang Tshenjen, and Gyama Mingyurwa (1497–1568).[65] The eastern Tibetan Nedo tradition founded by Karma Chakme (1613–1678) identifies in its lineage Gyarawa's student Tülku Thukje Özer.[66] The lineage that is traced through Zurchen Chöying Rangdröl to the fifth Dalai Lama mentions a certain student of Gyarawa named Guru Kunga Lhündrup. The Mindroling tradition traces the lineage through Gyarawa to Rikzin Sönam Özer and Namkha Lekpa.[67] Finally, in Bhutan, the Bhutanese Kathok tradition established by Sönam Gyeltsen (1466–1540) traces the Karling transmission back to a lama named Yeshe Lodrö and Rongdön Chenpo Namkha Dorje.[68] I will explore these multiple lines of transmission in the next section.

In the final analysis, we can be certain that Gyarawa Namkha Chökyi Gyatso played a leading and active role in the systematization and diffusion of Karma Lingpa's treasure revelations. As principal leader in the early efforts to spread the newly codified Karling system in Tibet, particularly in the south and southeastern territories, Gyarawa can be linked directly to the foundation of at least five distinct lineage traditions of the *Peaceful and Wrathful Deities*. His success in securely establishing these teachings is confirmed by the historians of the tradition and by the frequency with which his name appears in the transmission lists included in the various recensions of the Karling treasure cycle. The five traditions that he established comprise practically every significant lineage of the Karling transmissions in Tibet and surrounding regions.

The main lines of development of the liturgical corpus of the *Peaceful and Wrathful Deities*, including the texts accompanying the rites of the *Liberation upon Hearing* liturgy, can be traced in the individual histories of the traditions that employed its rituals. As I have shown, the task of identifying the beginning stages in this process, however, is not simple, given our fragmented knowledge of the events of the lives of its earliest promoters. The whereabouts of their activities and the relationships they established are all equally crucial to our understanding the complicated history of this influential cycle of texts and rituals. Many important questions remain. How did this tradition succeed? How did Karma Lingpa's teachings come to be so widely diffused throughout the vast reaches of Tibet? And, more generally, how and why did the rituals for the dead and dying recorded in these texts attract so many diverse followers? What was the process that allowed for the liturgy of the *Peaceful and Wrathful Deities*, and the *Liberation upon Hearing* in particular, to be incorporated as an almost generic ritual in the standard funeral practices of Tibet?

This second part of my study has attempted to address some of these basic issues by highlighting a few of the key events in the initial diffusion of the Karling transmissions. On the question of the appeal of this tradition, and to summarize what I have covered thus far, I want to add that the rituals of the *Peaceful and Wrathful Deities* and the *Liberation upon Hearing* gave expression to many of the cultural attitudes toward death and dying that flowed throughout Tibet and around its borders during the many centuries leading up to the time of Gyarawa. These rituals preserved the ancient Tibetan belief in the vulnerability of the soul (*bla*) and faith in the ritual efficacy of guiding its safe passage (*lam-bstan*) in the realms beyond death. The rituals adapted the old Indo-Buddhist evocations of the long process of the bardo and incorporation into a new existence. They maintained the Buddhist tantric emphasis on ritual purification of the dead and of the living, and drew on technical practices that were directed toward preparation for death and afterlife. Finally, they combined in the mundane forms of prayer and simple performative gestures the popular desire for divine intervention and freedom from fear with the more refined expressions of altruistic concern for the future welfare of the departed. When all of these diverse impulses were blended together in a ritual structure, the result was a balanced and compelling Tibetan Buddhist response to death and dying.

In the final analysis, we still cannot ignore the fundamental importance of the support for these rituals from the monastic institution, bringing with it the support of pious laity in the form of patronage. The further significance of the monastic center in the popularizing and spread of the Karling texts and rituals is verified in the ecclesiastical histories and biographical accounts of subsequent generations of followers. In the next several chapters that follow I will attempt to construct a more elaborate picture of this broad tradition by examining in close detail each of the major teaching-lineages that preserved and actively propagated both the *Peaceful and Wrathful Deities* and the *Liberation upon Hearing*.

III

TRADITIONS IN TRANSFORMATION

9

Traditions in Eastern Tibet

Gyarawa Namkha Chökyi Gyatso's codification of the *Self-Liberated Wisdom of the Peaceful and Wrathful Deities* and his pioneering efforts toward institutionalizing its liturgy appear to have been solidified by the latter half of the fifteenth century. In the following discussion I will examine Gyarawa's legacy, while emphasizing also the closely affiliated but distinctive tradition of the *Great Liberation upon Hearing in the Bardo*. I will explore in close detail each of the major traditions of both textual collections by focusing on their most prominent players. In the end I hope to establish a foundation of evidence for uncovering how and why the Karling liturgy became so widely influential in Tibet and surrounding regions from the fifteenth century onward. Particularly with regard to the diffusion of the *Liberation upon Hearing*, I will show that this literary cycle came to be preserved and maintained by a single lineage that was transmitted through the hierarchs of the Dakpo Tsele and Kongpo Thangdrok monasteries, and shortly thereafter through the Pema Lingpa (abbreviated as Peling) incarnations at Lhalung monastery in southern Tibet. In the seventeenth century, this tradition reached the great treasure revealers Terdak Lingpa and Rikzin Nyima Drakpa. By the late eighteenth century, the texts of this tradition had been preserved in a blockprint edition prepared at Dzokchen monastery by the third Dzokchenpa Ngedön Tenzin Zangpo (1759–1792). The influence of these monumental religious figures and the power of their institutional affiliations developing over several centuries certainly helped to popularize the Karling ritual and literary traditions throughout a widely diverse range of localities.

As I recognized in chapter 8, establishing Gyarawa's later activities and the places where he may have been most active is essential to our understanding the earliest phases in the development of these teachings and practices. Although we seem to be able to locate Gyarawa in the vicinity of Kongpo, Pemakö, and Lhogyü, we still do not know much about where he was active

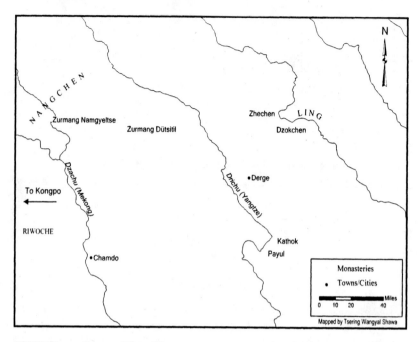

FIGURE 9.1. Eastern Tibet, Kham.

in his mature years. We also have no knowledge of how long Gyarawa lived, although it is certain that he completed his historical work, the *Garland of Jewels*, in the summer of 1499 as a final testament to his spiritual friend the lama Chögyel from Dokham.[1] At the conclusion of this work he humbly refers to himself as an old man (*rgas-po*), but of course, we cannot know with any certainty how old he may have been or whether he may have died shortly thereafter. We do know that the students he left behind spread the newly redacted Karling texts throughout the southern districts of Ü, in parts of Tsang in the west, to the east in Kham (see fig. 9.1), and even across the southern border into Bhutan. I will presume that in these areas from the late fifteenth century onward the teachings and practices contained in the cycle of the *Peaceful and Wrathful Deities* were incorporated into the local ritual customs. Some of those liturgical customs must have already been well established while still others may only have been in the process of solidification. A brief survey of the major historical features of this period from the time of Gyarawa until the standardization of Karma Lingpa's treasure revelations in the eighteenth century reveals some significant factors influencing the later spread of this tradition in Tibet.

In contrast to the somewhat unified but shortlived political and cultural renaissance of the previous century (ending in 1368 with the collapse of the Yüan Dynasty), the history of the fifteenth through seventeenth centuries in Tibet is a picture marred by schisms and mergers among competing religious and academic establishments. These conflicting and competitive communities struggled for patronage of the political elite (generally some representative faction of the Chinese Ming, and later Manchu, government) and fought hard for religious identity and legitimation.[2] Reminiscent of the aftermath of the so-called "Dark Age" in Tibet (mid–ninth to late tenth century), political anarchy, family feuds, rivalries between provinces, and the absence of central authority contributed to the rise of new religious communities, as scattered and disparate teaching-lineages began consolidating around powerful political and ecomonic centers, each vying for a piece of a proverbial pie. Some of the more remote hotspots would in the seventeenth century become the sites of great monastic complexes in areas to the east that had previously been ignored by the main political spotlight, which in the decades before then had been focused primarily on the monumental and antagonistic relations in central and western Tibet between the Gelukpa in Ü, the Karmapa in Tsang, and their competing Mongol protectors.[3]

The seventeenth century witnessed a sudden and explosive blossoming of the Nyingmapa order. With the demise of the Karmapa hegemony in Tsang around 1642, the Gelukpa sect in Lhasa rose to prominence, and the Nyingma followers in the surrounding region initially enjoyed the support of that sect's most prominent leader in the person of the fifth Dalai Lama. In this era, two of the greatest Nyingma monasteries were established just south of the Geluk government in central Tibet, Dorje Drak in 1632 and Mindroling in 1676.[4] In the nomadic area between Ü and Kham, the Dzokchen monastery (later to become the largest monastery in Nyingma history) was founded in 1685.[5] Thirty years earlier, in Kham proper, the ancient monastery of Kathok (first established in 1159) had been refurbished in 1656 (see fig. 9.2).[6] Soon afterward, the closely affiliated monastery of Payul had been founded in 1665.[7] Nearly all of these major monastic institutions, and a few more that I will discuss later, preserved and propagated a distinctive textual lineage of Karma Lingpa's *Peaceful and Wrathful Deities* and followed a specific associated Karling liturgical program. In most cases it was originally from Gyarawa that these different lines of transmission first emanated. In the chapters that follow I will consider each of these teaching-lineages in light of their own history and attempt to trace the Karling literature through these varying layers of tradition. In this way, I hope to uncover some of the principal factors behind the success of Gyarawa's codification following his death in the early decades of the sixteenth century. I begin with one of the oldest monastic institutions of the Nyingmapa tradition.

The Kathok Lineages

The earliest documented evidence, outside the Karling histories themselves, of the transmission of teachings from the *Peaceful and Wrathful Deities* appears in the autobiography of Kathokpa Sönam Gyeltsen, founder of the

FIGURE 9.2. Kathok Monastery, Kham. (Photograph by Andrew Quintman)

Lhomön or Mönluk Kathok tradition in Bhutan.[8] Sönam Gyeltsen mentions that when he was eighteen (in 1485), after traveling to the western district of Rongyul, he received the complete initiations (*dbang*), "readings" (*lung*), guiding instructions (*khrid*), direct introduction (*ngo-sprod*), and associated practices (*lag-len*) of Karma Lingpa's *Liberation upon Hearing* from a certain Rongdön Chenpo Namkha Dorje.[9] This exchange is corroborated in the accession list (*thob-yig*) of Chokle Namgyel, the first Zhapdrung Sungtrül of Bhutan, where the names Yeshe Lodrö[10] and Namkha Dorje appear first in the lineal succession of the *Peaceful and Wrathful Deities* passing from Gyarawa, listed here as Gyatsün Namkha Chökyi Gyatso.[11] In this series, Yeshe Lodrö is indicated as having bestowed the Karling teachings on Namkha Dorje, identified as a "great teacher from Rong" (*rong-ston chen-po*), from whom Sönam Gyeltsen, in turn, received the *Liberation upon Hearing*.[12] It appears then that the precise location of Rong or Rongyul is crucial to our story, since this may be one of the earliest areas in Tibet where Gyarawa's freshly codified liturgical system was first disseminated. The fact that this was specifically a *Liberation upon Hearing* transmission is also of particular interest. I believe the name Rongyul refers to the valley in Tsang (approximately 50 kilometers northeast of Gyantse) known by its river, the Rongchu, which flows north into the Tsangpo at Rinpung. This is an area famous for its rulers, the Rinpung princes, who came into power during the reign of the Phakmo Drü leader Gongma Drakpa Gyeltsen (1374–1440) and ruled until the mid–sixteenth century.[13] The Rinpung princes were patrons of the Zhamarpa subsect of the Karma Kagyu order.

Kathokpa Sönam Gyeltsen

As his title indicates, Sönam Gyeltsen was from Kathok monastery in eastern Tibet. Born in Nyakrong, he spent his formative years at this great Nyingma institution. He studied primarily with Chenyenpa Drodokpa Namkha Pel,[14] author of the *Silver Mirror* [*Dngul-dkar me-long*]—said to be a commentary on the *Great Tantra of the Secret Nucleus* [*Gsang-ba'i snying-po*]—and with Nyakrong Zhakla Yeshebum, master of the threefold *Sutra, Tantra, Mind Series* [*Mdo-rgyud-sems*] (that is, Anuyoga, Mahāyoga, and Atiyoga) who late in life restored the sacred sites of Zur Ukpalung and Sangak Ling in the district of Zhikatse.[15] At some point in his later years, Sönam Gyeltsen traveled to Lhasa and Samye and exchanged teachings with Ngari Panchen Pema Wangyel (1487–1542),[16] from whom he received, among other doctrines, the transmission of the *Peaceful and Wrathful Deities of Magical Emanation* [*'Gyu-sprul zhi-khro*]. From Lhasa he journeyed further south across the border to Paro Taktshang in western Bhutan, where he established the monastery of Orgyen Tsemo.[17]

We may never know fully the actual events surrounding Sönam Gyeltsen's meeting with Namkha Dorje and the early transmission of the Karling teachings in the Rong area of Tsang, but what I can suggest is that both the *Liberation upon Hearing* and the *Peaceful and Wrathful Deities* did pass through that particular region very early in the history of their diffusion. Furthermore, we can be assured that with Sönam Gyeltsen in the late fifteenth or early sixteenth century the *Liberation upon Hearing* was carried over for the first time into Bhutan (and probably Sikkim as well). In addition, it seems that the first institution in that region to foster the liturgy of the *Peaceful and Wrathful Deities* was that of Orgyen Tsemo monastery, following the Kathok-affiliated tradition of the Lhomön, or Mönluk, founded by Sönam Gyeltsen and his son, Namdröl Yeshe Zangpo. This tradition, according to Aris, was divided into two main branches, one in Shar and the other more prominent one in Paro.[18] We can only imagine what role the Karling liturgy played in these Bhutanese communities, since the Kathok tradition unfortunately did not survive the Drukpa Kagyu theocracy established in the middle years of the seventeenth century. At that time the two Kathok branches were absorbed into the new state, along with, I would suppose, some of their more accessible teachings and religious customs.[19] Perhaps the widespread appeal in Bhutan of the *Liberation upon Hearing* in more recent centuries can in part be traced back to this monumental event of political and religious assimilation.[20]

Gyarawa's strong connections to the Kathok mother monastery in Kham are beyond question. Although we lack sufficient evidence to suggest that he ever visited this institution, he defintely cultivated close contacts with several of the monastery's more prominent leaders and teachers of his day. For example, Gyarawa is mentioned several times by name in Jamyang Gyeltsen's recent history of Kathok monastery, where it is reported that Namkha Senge (b. 1431 or 1443), the first teacher in the lineage of Drung, and Ado Könchok Gyeltsen, a leading scholar of Kathok in that period, received directly from

Gyarawa the complete initiations of Karma Lingpa's *Peaceful and Wrathful Deities*.[21] This exchange inaugurated two of the five major Karling lineages traced back to Gyarawa and preserved in the Kathok tradition. In addition to the Bhutanese transmission of Sönam Gyeltsen, there is also the line passing from the fifth Drung Lhawang Dorje, through Pangdön Karma Guru (alias Jangdak Tashi Topgyel) to Takla Pema Gyeltsen, and from him to Takla Pemamati (or Pemalodrö, 1591–1642), and, finally, the transmission spreading from Gyama Mingyurwa Letrho Lingpa through Drigungpa Rinchen Phüntshok and again to Takla Pema Gyeltsen (see table 9.1). Three of these transmission lineages have been given specific names by the tradition itself: (1) the Hepa Tradition (*he[-pa]-lugs*), referring to the teaching lineage that eventually reached Lhazo Hepa Chöjung through Ado Könchok Gyeltsen;[22] (2) the Takla Tradition (*stag-bla-lugs*), referring to the lineage of Takla Pema Gyeltsen and Takla Pemamati from Drung Lhawang Dorje;[23] and (3) the Mön (Bhutan) Tradition (*mon-lugs*), referring, as I have noted, to the lineage originating from Kathokpa Sönam Gyeltsen.

During the late fifteenth and early sixteenth century, the specific collection of the *Peaceful and Wrathful Deities* handed down at the various Kathok-affiliated institutions probably included a number of supplemental texts prepared by the respective representatives of each of the traditions just named. In the unfortunate absence of an actual set of manuscripts dating from this early period, we can only presume, on the basis of comparative analysis of the existing collections, that the basic structure of the earliest Kathok recension of the *Peaceful and Wrathful Deities* must have consisted of the core works discussed in chapter 7, including most prominently the *Religious Liturgy of the Self-Liberation of Karmic Latencies*, the *Triad of Bardo Prayers*, and some form of the *Guiding Instructions on the Six Bardos*. In addition, we can be relatively certain that the extensive liturgical works of Gyarawa detailing his systematized ritual program were also included. Brief commentaries and liturgical digests from the pens of the leaders of the various Kathok traditions during this period must have been added as well, although we can identify only a few examples of such works in current recensions.[24]

This section will attempt briefly to document the ways the individual Kathok transmissions in Tibet were constituted by focusing on the affiliated persons and circumstances responsible for the propagation of the Karling teachings. I begin with what may have been the earliest transmission involving persons connected to the Kathok monastery in Tibet. This is a tradition that is not explicitly identified in the histories, so I have chosen to label it the Drung Tradition (*drung-lugs*) for reasons that will be made clear later.

The Drung Tradition of Kathok

Four periods have been recognized in the history of Kathokpa's abbatial administration: (1) the period of the thirteen deputies or Gyeltshap (*rgyal-tshab*), presumably identical with the thirteen lamas or Larap (*bla-rabs*); (2) the period of the chief administrators or Drung; (3) the period of restoration when the

TABLE 9.1. Kathok Lineages.

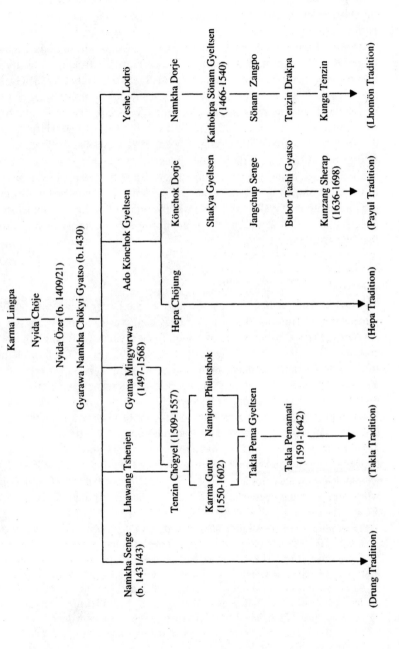

monastery was refurbished by Dudül Dorje (1615–1672) and Longsel Nyingpo (1625–1692); and (4) the period of the religious ministers or Chenyenpa ('chad-nyan-pa), following the end of the seventeenth century and during the era of the thirteen members of the lineage of Mok (rmog).[25] The second and third periods are the most relevant for my consideration here.

Helmut Eimer and Pema Tsering have spoken of a reform in the organization of Kathok monastery sometime in the early fifteenth century shortly after the term of office of the thirteenth and final Gyeltshap, Bubor Yeshe Gyeltsen (1395–1458).[26] The position of "leader-in-residence" (gdan-sa-pa) had been reorganized, and the responsibilities of the Gyeltshap, who to this point had been functioning as abbot (lit., "great scholar," mkhan-chen), shifted over to the chief administrator, the Drung. The suggestion has been offered that this reform might have been due to the changing role of the Drung in religious affairs.[27] Soon, alongside the Drung, a new office was also added that seems to have developed out of the lineage of scholars (mkhan-po) traditionally affiliated with the Gyeltshap.[28] This was the office of "religious minister," the Chenyenpa, which would in later years become increasingly more powerful than the Drung itself.[29]

Drung Namkha Senge

The first in the new line of monastic leaders, the Drung, was Namkha Senge (alias Tsöndrü Bumpa),[30] whom prophecy said was to be born in a pig year (1431 or 1443). He was a student of Bubor Yeshe Gyeltsen and Jangsem Chöje[31] and served as the chief deputy (rgyal-tshab drung) of Lapdön Namkha Rinchen.[32] The latter at that time had been acting as servant (bran) to Bubor Yeshe Gyeltsen.[33] In addition, Namkha Senge was recognized by the treasure revealer Ratna Lingpa as one of his own chief doctrine-masters (chos-bdag).[34] Most important, Namkha Senge was a student of Gyarawa Namkha Chökyi Gyatso, from whom he received the transmission of the Peaceful and Wrathful Deities, including the Guiding Instructions on the Six Bardos. The connection between Gyarawa and Namkha Senge is attested to not only in the Kathok histories but also in the colophon of Nyida Özer's Great Bliss of the Lower Orifice, where this exchange between teacher and student is explicitly cited:

> These guru instructions entitled Experiential Guiding Instructions on the "Self-Liberation of Desire: Great Bliss of the Lower Orifice" were composed during degenerate times by the learned beggar [ku-sā-li] named Suryacandraraśmi [Nyida Özer] at the behest of his mudra [consort]. The writing was begun on an auspicious day of the pig month [eighth month] in the monkey year at Thangdrok monastery in Kongyul. May its virtues help all beings attain quickly the great bliss of the three bodies. Scholars asked that it be written in order to discern flaws [skyon] and repeated contradictory connections ['gal-'brel zlos]. In the presence of the Venerable Suryacandra, who was supremely realized through intrinsic great bliss, this text was requested by [Gyarawa] Namkha Chökyi Gyatso. He, in turn, bestowed it upon Kathokpa Namkha Senge, and from him I requested it.[35]

Leaving aside for the moment the significant reference in this statement to Kongpo Thangdrok monastery, the colophon provides some helpful information about one of the earliest Kathok transmissions of Karma Lingpa's textual tradition. The author, a student of Namkha Senge, does not give his name but instead refers to himself in the first person. Consequently, we can only guess his identity. One obvious candidate would have been Namkha Senge's nephew, Dorje Lodrö, the second in line for the office of Drung.[36] With him as acting resident-chief (*gdan-sa-pa drung*), probably in the first decades of the sixteenth century, the assistant position of Chenyenpa, or religious minister, was established. This office was later filled by another of Namkha Senge's nephews, Azi Sönambum from Nyakrong.[37] Unfortunately, we have no further information about this particular transmission line. We must presume, therefore, that this line was passed down from Namkha Senge to the next two successors to the Drung office, Gönpo Dorje and Lhawang Dorje. We should keep in mind that the managing office of Kathok at this time had just recovered from changes brought on by certain unspecified reforms, and perhaps consequently the duration of any given position in the monastery's governing body may not have been long-term. It is also possible that the chief officer of Drung was meant to serve as monastic leader for only a few years. This short term of office is corroborated by the fact that the main protagonists appear to have been contemporaries. In any case, the important point to stress here is that the first succession of the Drung of Kathok included some of the earliest holders of Karma Lingpa's tradition in eastern Tibet, and as such this lineage of teachers may have played a decisive role in its later diffusion.

Chenyenpa Ado Könchok Gyeltsen

During the term of office of the fourth Drung Gönpo Dorje as abbot (*gdan-sa-pa*) and Drodokpa Namkha Pel as the first official Chenyenpa, a scholar-monk by the name of Ado Könchok Gyeltsen was in residence at Kathok.[38] He studied under both Jangsem Chöje and Drodokpa Namkha Pel, as well as Kunga Nyima Zangpo, the chief disciple of Tibet's great engineer Thangtong Gyelpo (1361–1464).[39] According to the history of Kathok, he received from Kunga Nyima Zangpo the complete instructions on the Dzokchen treasure *Unimpeded Intention of Samantabhadra* [*Kun-tu-bzang-po'i dgongs-pa zang[s]-thal*], after which he had a vision of Padmasambhava.[40] Later, he offered manuscript copies (*phyag-dpe*) of this scripture to the ascetic Jangchup Senge, who was living in the Jangseng caves near Kathok.[41] When Lhawang Dorje, the fifth in the line of Drung, took the office of abbot, Ado Könchok Gyeltsen was promoted and became the second Chenyenpa of Kathok. He traveled extensively throughout Ü and Tsang, where it appears he first met Gyarawa.[42] From Gyarawa, Ado Könchok Gyeltsen received the complete initiations of the *Peaceful and Wrathful Deities*, which, in turn, he then presented to Lhazo Hepa Chöjung, who would later become the fourth Chenyenpa.[43] This particular lineage of the Karling transmission came to be known as the "Hepa

Tradition of the Peaceful and Wrathful Deities" [*zhi-khro he-lugs*]. As I will show, it was this tradition that was transmitted through the Payul lineages of Kunzang Sherap (1636–1698).[44]

Rongpo Könchok Dorje

Ado Könchok Gyeltsen's chief student was Rongpo Könchok Dorje, to whom he taught the general instructions on Mahāmudra and Dzokchen, and especially those of the *Unimpeded Intention of Samantabhadra*. The cycle of the *Peaceful and Wrathful Deities* is not mentioned by name in this context, although we can assume that this collection was included among the teachings that Rongpo Könchok Dorje received from his teacher. He practiced at Kathok for a long period of time before he traveled to Rongyul, where he remained in strict retreat until the end of his life.[45] Although we have little explicit evidence to support the claim that this teacher from Rong and the teacher of Kathokpa Sönam Gyeltsen, Rongdön Chenpo Namkha Dorje, were one and the same person, it seems more than coincidence that Gyarawa's grand-disciple, Rongpo Könchok Dorje, was stationed in Rongyul at what appears to be the same time that Rongdön Namkha Dorje, also in Rongyul, was transmitting the *Liberation upon Hearing* teachings to Kathokpa Sönam Gyeltsen. In the end, even if these two Rong teachers were in fact separate individuals, it is still evident that Karma Lingpa's treasure tradition was available in the Rongyul territory of Tsang quite early in the history of its diffusion.

Drung Lhawang Dorje and Drung Gönpo Dorje

Sometime in the late fifteenth or early sixteenth century, when Ado Könchok Gyeltsen was Chenyenpa of Kathok, the fifth holder of the office of Drung was Lhawang Dorje.[46] Although the history books tell us nothing about the life of this ecclesiastic leader and teacher, there is reason to speculate that he is the same individual referred to in various Karling lineages as Lhawang Tshenjen and as Lhawang Namgyel. The former name appears in the lineage supplications (*brgyud-pa'i gsol-'debs*) found in three of the four recensions of the *Peaceful and Wrathful Deities* affiliated with the Kathok tradition.[47] In those lists, a certain Lhawang Tshenjen is indicated as having received the Karling teachings directly from Gyarawa, and then to have transmitted them to one Tenzin Chökyi Gyelpo (listed also as Kadak Tingzin Chögyel). As I shall argue, the latter individual was probably Drigung Rinchen Phüntshok.

The name Lhawang Namgyel (also Lhewangpo) is found in the lineage series connected with Karma Lingpa's obscure *Four Initiations: Self-Liberation of Whatever Is Encountered*. Curiously, it is this lineage series that is also associated almost exclusively with the transmissions in Tibet of the *Liberation upon Hearing*. In this line, Lhawang Namgyel's teacher is indicated as being one Gönpo Dorje, a student of Karma Lingpa's son, Nyida Chöje. Is it just mere coincidence that Gönpo Dorje was also the name of the fourth Drung of Kathok, and that the next in line for that office was a person named Lhawang, who was a direct associate of Gyarawa's student Ado Könchok Gyeltsen? Questions of contemporaneity and proximity must be taken into consideration before we make too hasty an identification, but it is indeed tempting to imagine that the Gönpo Dorje and the Lhawang Namgyel/Lhawang Tshenjen mentioned in this particular Karling lineage were actually the two successive Drung leaders of Kathok during the late fifteenth and early sixteenth century. Still, in terms of the transmission line of the *Four Initiations*, and also that of the apparently related *Liberation upon Hearing*, we must contend with the apparent anachronism of the fourth Drung receiving teachings from the much earlier figure of Nyida Chöje as it is recorded in some lineage documents. Recall again that the fifth Drung officer of Kathok, Lhawang Dorje, was not only a contemporary but also a working associate of Ado Könchok Gyeltsen. In truth, the general dates of these two figures do not accord easily with the presumably earlier dates of Nyida Chöje. That said, I return to the specific Kathok lineage emanating from Drung Lhawang Dorje, the so-called Takla tradition.

The Takla Tradition of Kathok

According to some of the Kathok lineage supplications, a certain Lhawang Tshenjen, whom I shall identify as Lhawang Dorje, the fifth Drung of Kathok, bestowed the *Peaceful and Wrathful Deities* on Tenzin Chökyi Gyelpo, who, in turn, presented it to Karma Guru, the last of the princely lineage of Jang Ngamring and a leading master of the Northern Treasure or Jangter (*byang-gter*) tradition of Rikzin Gödemjen.[48] Who was this teacher Tenzin Chökyi Gyelpo? Our lack of information on the life of Drung Lhawang Dorje requires that we search elsewhere for clues in the biography of Karma Guru.[49] Here we learn that Karma Guru was a close student of Rinchen Phüntshok Chökyi Gyelpo, the sixth abbot of the Drigung Kagyu monastery in northern Ü.[50]

Drigung Rinchen Phüntshok

Drigung Rinchen Phüntshok is listed in the fifth Dalai Lama's *Transmission Record*, where his name appears in the list of lineage-holders of the *Profound Instructions on the Rainbow Body Transference*, otherwise known as *Planting the Stalk*, a treasure revealed by Karma Lingpa's father, Nyida Sangye.[51] As noted in chapter 6, this treasure of Nyida Sangye lies at the center of a famous Drigungpa festival called the "Great Transference" (*'pho-ba chen-mo*), which incidentally was first established by Rinchen Phüntshok.[52] Further Drigung-Karling affiliations are revealed in an alternative Kathok lineage from Dujom Rinpoche's *Accession Record of the Precious Anthology of Treasures* [*Rin-chen gter-mdzod-kyi thob-yig*], in which one Gyelwang Rinchen Phüntshok appears as the student of Gyama Mingyurwa.[53] As it turns out, both Gyama Mingyurwa and Drigung Rinchen Phüntshok were each student and teacher to the other.[54] In Dujom Rinpoche's lineage list, Gyama

Mingyurwa is indicated as having received the Karling transmission directly from Gyarawa. Drigung Rinchen Phüntshok, in turn, received these Karling teachings from Gyama Mingyurwa and later bestowed them on his student Karma Guru. We can be confident then that the Tenzin Chökyi Gyelpo just mentioned as the Karling teacher of Karma Guru must have been Drigung Rinchen Phüntshok Chökyi Gyelpo. This teacher became a pivotal figure in the transmission of the teachings of both Nyida Sangye and Karma Lingpa during the middle years of the sixteenth century.

Karma Guru Jangdak Tashi Topgyel

Karma Guru (known also as Jangdak Tashi Topgyel) was born in upper Yeru in Ü-Tsang as the son of Namkha Rinchen, a descendant of the kings of Minyak.[55] He studied with a number of leading Tibetan masters, such as Ngari Lekden Dorje (1512–1625), the treasure revealer Sherap Özer, Pema Karpo (1527–1592), Dzokchen Sönam Wangpo, and, of course, Drigung Rinchen Phüntshok. Karma Guru was a major figure in the transmission of Dzokchen teachings, especially those of the *Heart-essence of the Ḍākinīs [Mkha'-'gro-snying-thig]*.[56] His own work evidently left a lasting impression on the fifth Dalai Lama.[57] But he is perhaps best known as the author of a short work about Tibetan treasures entitled *Supplications and Synopsis of the Biographies of One Hundred Treasure Revealers [Gter-brgya'i rnam-thar don-bdus gsol-'debs]*.[58] This work later served as the inspiration for two of the major historical sources I have relied on in this study; namely, Karma Migyur Wangyel's *Religious History of the Treasure Revealers [Lo-rgyus gter-bton chos-'byung]* and the fifth Dalai Lama's large section on the treasures in his *Transmission Record*.[59]

Takla Pema Gyeltsen

As noted earlier, some transmission records indicate that Karma Guru received the *Peaceful and Wrathful Deities* from Drigung Rinchen Phüntshok, although we do not know where or when this transmission may have taken place. We are certain, however, that Karma Guru transmitted these teachings to Takla Pema Gyeltsen, student of both the treasure revealer Zhikpo Lingpa (1524–1583) and Sokdokpa Lodrö Gyeltsen (1552–1624). At the request of Chenyenpa Bubor Tashi Gyatso and through the efforts of Zhikpo Lingpa, Takla Pema Gyeltsen was sent to Kathok monastery.[60] It was there that he met Takla Pemamati, on whom he bestowed the Karling transmission.[61] The title *Takla* (meaning "lama from Tak") in the names of these two important teachers subsequently became the name of their teaching-lineage. It should be noted that Takla Pemamati is said to have received not only this particular Karling transmission but also that of the Hepa tradition initiated by Ado Könchok Gyeltsen. Hence in the person of this important Kathok master the two streams of the Hepa and Takla traditions converged.

Takla Pemamati

Takla Pemamati is said to have composed a commentary on Karma Lingpa's *Peaceful and Wrathful Deities* and a guidebook (*khrid-yig*) on the topic of the six bardos from that cycle.[62] These texts have not yet been located. Several extant recensions of the Karling collection, however, do contain works authored by him, although none of them can be identified as the texts just mentioned. In the existing collections, we find six of Takla Pemamati's works:

1. *Lineage Supplications called "Self-Liberation of the True Meaning"* [*Brgyud-pa'i gsol-'debs nges-don rang-grol*]. This text was written at the behest of a student named Orgyen Lodrö at Kulha Karpo hermitage (in Lhorong)[63]

2. *Heap of Messages of Salutation and Blessing to the Lineage Lamas* [*Bla-ma rgyud-pa'i phyag-'tshal byin-rlabs phrin-phung*][64]

3. *Self-Liberation of Life in Connection with (Requests for) Expiation to the Series of Lineage Lamas* [*Bla-ma brgyud-rim-gyi bskang-ba 'brel tshe rang-grol*][65]

4. *Epitome of the Self-Generation of Peaceful and Wrathful Deities from "The Self-Liberated Wisdom"* [*Zhi-khro'i bdag-bskyed mdor-bsdus dgongs-pa rang-grol*][66]

5. *Explanatory Supplement to "The Garland of Principal Practice Manuals Gathering the Peaceful and Wrathful Deities" to be Used at the Time of the Threefold Offering of Medicine, Rakta, and Torma* [*Zhi-khro'i las-byang rtsar-phreng-gi sman-rag-gtor gsum-gyi skabs-su kha-'phang lhan-thabs*][67]

6. *Self-Liberation of Suffering Which Has Been Fully Compiled from "The Self-Liberation of the Six Classes of Beings, Guiding the Deceased to a Higher State"* [*Tshe-'das gnas-'dren 'gro-drug rang-grol las nye-bar bsdus-pa sdug-bsngal rang-grol*][68]

We see from this list that Takla Pemamati must have perceived a need for clarifying certain rituals in the form of digests and short guidebooks, for he had composed at least two small works on the performance of the rites of the *Peaceful and Wrathful Deities* and a short anthology of liturgical teachings for the guidance of the dead. The latter work is perhaps one of the earliest commentaries on such rituals in the history of the Karling tradition. The three lineage prayers that he had written also indicate his interest in communicating the historical validity of his specific tradition. We can assume that by the middle of the seventeenth century the tradition of the *Peaceful and Wrathful Deities* preserved at Kathok, particularly by followers of the Takla lineage, consisted not only of these supplemental manuals of Takla Pemamati but also the standard *Triad of Bardo Prayers* of Karma Lingpa, the basic sādhanas of the *Peaceful and Wrathful Deities*, and the liturgical works of Gyarawa. Clearly, Takla Pemamati was a crucial figure in the preservation and revision of the Karling liturgy at Kathok during this period. By introducing and incorporating his own texts to better accommodate the local needs of his community, Takla Pemamati was carrying on a longstanding tradition of ritual adaptation inaugurated almost a full century earlier by Gyarawa, the great systematizer of Karma Lingpa's funeral liturgy.

I should point out the names of those teachers and students with whom Takla Pemamati came into close contact, since almost all of them had some influence on the diffusion of Karma Lingpa's teachings in Tibet. Among his teachers I must mention the third Peling Sungtrül Tshültrhim Dorje (1598–1669), Zurchen Chöying Rangdröl, and Tsele Natsok Rangdröl. For my present interests, one of his most notable pupils apart from Tshültrhim Dorje and Tsele Natsok Rangdröl—with both of whom he shared a mutual teacher-student relationship—was a young Kunzang Sherap, the first abbot of the Payul monastery in Kham.[69] Each of these figures stands prominent in a number of distinct Karling transmission lineages to be discussed hereafter, but we have no direct evidence suggesting their connections to the Karling tradition transmitted through Takla Pemamati. I must stress, however, that contacts and exchanges between teachers and students were actually quite fluid in Tibet, given the complexity of the interrelationships between the various traditions. In other words, the transmission of the Karling teachings, and most teachings in general for that matter, were passed along lines moving in multiple directions, rather than strictly along a vertical axis defined by sectarian affiliation. Indeed, it is this very dynamic, in conjunction with a flexible textual structure, that over the centuries has allowed for the widespread diffusion of the *Peaceful and Wrathful Deities* throughout Tibet and surrounding regions. I will now survey another example of this network of tradition in eastern Tibet.

The Payul Transmissions and the Nedo Tradition of Karma Chakme

Two divergent teaching-lineages of the Karling literary and ritual tradition converged to form the Payul tradition of Kunzang Sherap. These two lineages are known as the Hepa Tradition, which as I have shown passed through the Kathok disciples of Ado Könchok Gyeltsen, and the Karma Kagyu affiliated Nedo Tradition (*gnas-mdo-lugs*), which was first established by Karma Chakme (1613–1678) in the mid-seventeenth century.[70] Kunzang Sherap received the Hepa transmission from Trhülzhik Serlo Tenpa Gyeltsen (also Tönpa Gyeltsen) of Muksang, who was a student of Gyelthangpa Tönpa Senge.[71] The Nedo transmission, on the other hand, was passed directly to Kunzang Sherap by Karma Chakme, a figure closely linked in his early life to the Zurmang monastery in Nangchen—seat of the successive incarnations of Drungpa Rinpoche Kunga Gyeltsen.[72] In the following section I will review the details surrounding the origin of this unique and important composite tradition of Karma Lingpa's *Peaceful and Wrathful Deities*.

Kunzang Sherap

Kunzang Sherap was born in Akhyok, which is said to be located in Bubor in the region of Payul.[73] Among Kunzang Sherap's earliest and most influential teachers were Drungpa Rinpoche Chönyi Gyatso of Zurmang and

Trhülzhik Serlo Tenpa Gyeltsen, both of whom were students of Kathokpa Könchok Senge.[74] Kunzang Sherap studied for five years with Drungpa Rinpoche Chönyi Gyatso and received from him instructions on the practices of Mahāmudra.[75] From both this master and Trhülzhik Serlo Tenpa Gyeltsen, Kunzang Sherap received Dzokchen teachings of the oral transmission (bka'-ma) and treasure (gter-ma) lineages. Presumably, it was around this time, when still a young boy, that he briefly met Takla Pemamati.[76] Although there is no explicit indication that he received the transmission of the Peaceful and Wrathful Deities during their meetings, he is said to have eventually received other Takla transmissions from Gyarong Sokmo Rinchen Dorje[77] and from Takla Pemamati's own disciple, Könchok Tashi.[78]

The first recorded person to transmit the Peaceful and Wrathful Deities to Kunzang Sherap was Trhülzhik Serlo Tenpa Gyeltsen at his monastery in Muksang.[79] The latter had received this transmission from his peer Adrowa Namkha Dorje, a fellow student of Gyelthangpa Tönpa Senge.[80] The specific details of the exchange between Trhülzhik Serlo Tenpa Gyeltsen and Kunzang Sherap are not elucidated, although we do know that Tenpa Gyeltsen held the Kathok lineage of Ado Könchok Gyeltsen's most important teachings; namely, those related to the Unimpeded Intention of Samantabhadra.[81] Thus it is certain that the particular Karling tradition that he passed to Kunzang Sherap was that of the Hepa tradition, and indeed this is attested to in the transmission records preserved at Payul (see table 9.2).[82] It was this Hepa transmission that Kunzang Sherap brought with him from Muksang when he assumed the abbatial seat of Payul monastery in 1665.

In that year the king of Derge, Jampa Phüntshok (d. 1667), with the help of the Sakya abbot Sangye Tenpa of Lhündrup Teng monastery, had sponsored the construction of a monastic complex in Payul at an auspicious location known as Namgyeltse.[83] The site had been chosen on the basis of positive geomantic calculations (sa-dpyad).[84] According to the diviners (tho-btsun), this place was to be called Payul Namgyel Jangchup Ling. Trhülzhik Serlo Tenpa Gyeltsen had subsequently been invited from Muksang to be the new monastery's first abbot, but he had graciously declined, claiming to be too old and unfit for the job.[85] As an alternative, he recommended Kunzang Sherap, who was then traveling in Muksang with the young treasure revealer Mingyur Dorje (1645–1667), promoter of the popular Celestial Doctrine [Gnam-chos] treasures.[86] After conferring with Trhülzhik Serlo Tenpa Gyeltsen and Mingyur Dorje, Kunzang Sherap accepted the appointment and arrived at Payul shortly thereafter. At the monastery he established the requisite rules and regulations as well as the standard Buddhist exoteric and esoteric ecclessiastical disciplines.[87] Consequently, he is renowned as the founder of the monastic tradition of Payul.

Not long after assuming his role as abbot, Kunzang Sherap traveled again to the retreat center of Nedo in the region of Ngomyul,[88] where he had earlier received the vows of novitiate (Skt., śramaṇera) from his teacher, Karma Chakme.[89] Once there, he requested to be fully ordained as a Buddhist monk. He was then presented with a number of significant treasure transmissions, which included some of the revelations of Rikzin Gödemjen, Ratna Lingpa,

TABLE 9.2. Payul Lineages.

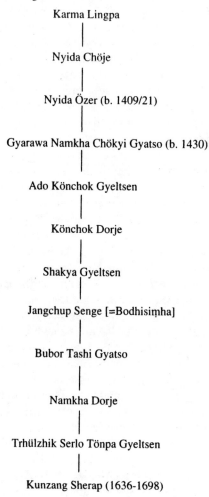

Karma Lingpa

Nyida Chöje

Nyida Özer (b. 1409/21)

Gyarawa Namkha Chökyi Gyatso (b. 1430)

Ado Könchok Gyeltsen

Könchok Dorje

Shakya Gyeltsen

Jangchup Senge [=Bodhisimha]

Bubor Tashi Gyatso

Namkha Dorje

Trhülzhik Serlo Tönpa Gyeltsen

Kunzang Sherap (1636-1698)

Pema Lingpa, Jatsön Nyingpo, and Karma Lingpa.[90] In particular with respect to the latter, Karma Chakme transmitted to Kunzang Sherap the generation- and completion-phase sādhanas of the *Peaceful and Wrathful Deities*.[91]

We do not know the actual content of the Karling transmissions presented to Kunzang Sherap, but presumably these would have included the core texts of Karma Lingpa, Nyida Özer, and Gyarawa, with the addition of supplemental works composed by Karma Chakme himself. It is also possible, given Karma Chakme's close connection to Zurmang monastery, that he would have been in possession of that tradition's special *Liberation upon Hearing* transmissions reaching back to the nebulous lama Gönpo Dorje of Kongpo. This would have meant that Kunzang Sherap received from Karma Chakme not only the major works of the *Peaceful and Wrathful Deities* but also the distinctive texts of the *Liberation upon Hearing*, including perhaps the famous *Reminder of the Bardo of Reality-Itself* and the *Direct Introduction to the Bardo of Becoming*. Whatever the case, the exchange between these two individuals represented a convergence of at least two traditions of Karma Lingpa's treasure, the Nedo and Hepa traditions. Once passed to Kunzang Sherap, this combined transmission was maintained by the principal lineage-holders of Payul monastery. Outside the confines of Payul, however, there were two isolated Nedo transmissions that passed only through the chief disciples of Karma Chakme.

Karma Chakme

Karma Chakme was born in 1613 in the region of Ngomyul as the son of the siddha Pema Wangdrak, master of Anuyoga. Like Karma Lingpa before him, he had been prophesied as being an incarnation of the eighth-century translator Choro Lu'i Gyeltsen.[92] As a young boy, known then as Wangdrak Sung, his father taught him the threefold rites of the Nyingmapa tradition, the rituals of recitation (*bsnyen*), accomplishment (*sgrub*), and service (*las*).[93] In addition, his father also bestowed on him certain long-life practices (*tshe-sgrub*) from the treasure revelations of Ratna Lingpa.[94] At nineteen, in the presence of the fourth Drungpa Rinpoche Kunga Namgyel of the Zurmang monastery, he took layman's vows (Skt., *upāsaka*) and received the name Karma Samdrup.[95] The same year he traveled to Tshurphu monastery, seat of the Karmapa incarnations, and took the vows of novitiate under the sixth Zhamarpa Chökyi Wangchuk (1584–1635). Soon afterward he received full ordination and the name Karma Chakme.[96]

At some point, possibly just before his death, Pema Wangdrak presented his son Karma Chakme with the complete cycle of teachings of the *Peaceful and Wrathful Deities*. We do not know the circumstances surrounding this transmission. According to the available lineage lists, Pema Wangdrak had received these teachings from one Garwang Kunga Tenzin, who in turn had received them from Rikzin Kunga Drakpa. Unfortunately, since the identities of these earlier figures have yet to be established, the history of Pema Wangdrak's lineage remains shrouded in mystery. One suggestion that seems plausible, however, is that these individuals were all closely linked to the Kamtshang or Karma Kagyu–affiliated Zurmang tradition, which had been established sometime in the fifteenth century by Ma Setokden of the Minyak clan—the very same clan from which Karma Guru had also descended.[97] In this light, it may turn out that the earliest figures associated with the Karling tradition inherited by Pema Wangdrak might actually have been important disciples of Ma Setokden, such as one Özer Zangpo, who founded the monastery of Chusöl in lower Den(khok).[98] Özer Zangpo may have been the student of Gyarawa who is listed in some sources as Thukje Özer. Whatever the case, it is clear that a Zurmang line can be traced back to a very early stage in the history of the Karling transmissions, particularly the lineages associated with the *Liberation upon Hearing* (see table 9.3).[99] Karma Chakme's connection at such a young age to Zurmang through its supreme abbot, the fourth

TABLE 9.3. Zurmang Lineage.

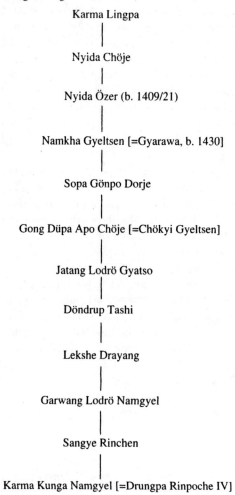

Karma Lingpa

|

Nyida Chöje

|

Nyida Özer (b. 1409/21)

|

Namkha Gyeltsen [=Gyarawa, b. 1430]

|

Sopa Gönpo Dorje

|

Gong Düpa Apo Chöje [=Chökyi Gyeltsen]

|

Jatang Lodrö Gyatso

|

Döndrup Tashi

|

Lekshe Drayang

|

Garwang Lodrö Namgyel

|

Sangye Rinchen

|

Karma Kunga Namgyel [=Drungpa Rinpoche IV]

Drungpa Rinpoche, probably had some influence on his own adaptations of the cycle of Karling teachings.

The presence of these early Zurmang connections in the history of the Karling tradition may provide some justification for the unsubstantiated claim of Chögyam Trungpa, the eleventh Drungpa Rinpoche of Zurmang, that all of Karma Lingpa's students were actually followers of the Kagyu tradition even though Karma Lingpa himself was a Nyingmapa.[100] A similar idea, also without supportive evidence, is found in an article by Antonella Crescenzi and Fabrizio Torricelli, where Karma Lingpa is indicated as having converted in his later life from the Nyingma sect to that of the Kagyupa.[101] The position held by Crescenzi and Torricelli with regard to the conversion of Karma Lingpa is not explicitly supported in the available written sources. There is ample evidence, however, of strong Karma Kagyu associations among many of the most active promoters of Karma Lingpa's textual tradition. Leading figures in both the Pawo and Zhamarpa subsects of the Karma Kagyu, for example, played important roles as teachers of some of the key Karling lineage holders,[102] and as patrons supported some of the tradition's most significant monastic institutions.[103]

By the end of Karma Chakme's career, he had contributed at least seven major literary works pertaining to the teachings of Karma Lingpa. One such work—a commentary on a section of the *Guidebook to the Six Bardos* entitled *Book Yielding an Immediate Direct Introduction to "The Self-Liberated Vision: Guidebook to the Bardo of Reality-Itself"* [*Bar-do khrid-yig chos-nyid bar-do'i khrid-yig mthong-ba rang-grol-gyi ngo-sprod car-phog khyer-ba deb-zhig*]—was included by Jamgön Kongtrül as a central text in the Karling section of his *Precious Anthology of Treasures*.[104] This is the only text we find in that section devoted to the essential topic of the bardo of reality-itself (*chos-nyid bar-do*)—a peculiarity that could be reasonably explained by the fact that Karma Chakme's Nedo tradition appears to have been the primary tradition inherited by Jamgön Kongtrül.[105]

Among Karma Chakme's other more notable works included in the relevant Karling collections, I should mention his redactions and original commentaries on the liturgical practices of the so-called guidance (*gnas-'dren*) and "dredging the depths of hell" (*na-rag dong-sprugs*) rituals. As I showed in chapter 7, the guidance ceremony, designed to guide the deceased to a favorable destiny, stands out as being especially significant in the funeral liturgy of the *Peaceful and Wrathful Deities*. Two works of this sort attributed to Karma Chakme are available in the various recensions of the Karling cycle:

1. *Memorandum on "The Self-Liberation of the Six Classes of Beings, Guiding the Deceased to a Higher State: An Auxiliary Practice of 'The Self-Liberation of Broken Vows through Expiation and Confession in Hell'"* [*Na-rag bskang-bshags nyams-chag rang-grol-gyi cha-lag tshe-'das 'gro-drug rang-grol-gyi zin-bris*]. This work was requested by one Önpo Gyeltsen and composed in the wood snake year 1665.[106]

2. *Iron-Hook of Compassion: Epitome of "Guiding the Deceased to a Higher State"* [*Tshe-'das gnas-'dren bsdus-pa thugs-rje'i lcags-kyu*]. This text appears to be a redaction of an earlier work no longer extant entitled *Self-Liberation of the Six Classes of Beings, Guiding the Deceased to a Higher State* [*Tshe-'das gnas-'dren 'gro-drug rang-grol*].[107]

Much like the guidance practices, the dredging-the-depths liturgy is closely linked to the broader category of ritual referred to as "confession and expiation" (*bskang-bshags*). Ostensibly, the overall goal of the rite of dredging the depths is to first acknowledge and then atone for all of one's faults and broken vows and to then attempt to erase the transgressions of others who may be unable to do so themselves, such as those innumerable beings suffering in the three lower realms. The process is likened to pulling something up from its root (*rtsa-ba nas 'don-pa*) or, more colorfully, churning and dredging the very depths of hell.[108] The dredging-the-depths works of Karma Chakme may

TABLE 9.4. Nedo Lineages.

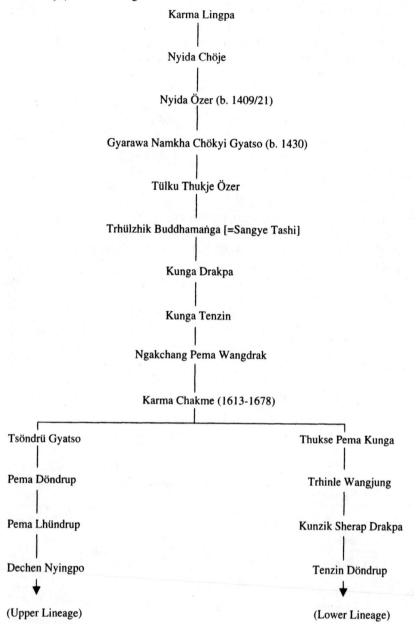

Karma Lingpa

|

Nyida Chöje

|

Nyida Özer (b. 1409/21)

|

Gyarawa Namkha Chökyi Gyatso (b. 1430)

|

Tülku Thukje Özer

|

Trhülzhik Buddhamaṅga [=Sangye Tashi]

|

Kunga Drakpa

|

Kunga Tenzin

|

Ngakchang Pema Wangdrak

|

Karma Chakme (1613-1678)

Tsöndrü Gyatso	Thukse Pema Kunga
Pema Döndrup	Trhinle Wangjung
Pema Lhündrup	Kunzik Sherap Drakpa
Dechen Nyingpo	Tenzin Döndrup
(Upper Lineage)	(Lower Lineage)

represent his most original contributions to the literary tradition of the *Peaceful and Wrathful Deities*, the significance of which is confirmed by the fact that the distinctive Karling tradition associated with him is known alternatively as the "Dredging-the-Depths Tradition" (*dong-sprugs-lugs*).[109] The two extant works of this system written by Karma Chakme are:

1. *Connecting Links in the Ritual of the Tradition of Karma Lingpa's "Dredging the Depths of Hell"* [*Karma-gling-pa'i na-rag dong-sprugs lugs-kyi mtshams-sbyor*][110]
2. *Selection from the Memorandum on the Ritual of Dredging the Depths of Hell of the Exalted Mind of the Peaceful and Wrathful Deities* [*Zhi-khro thugs-kyi na-rak don-sprugs cho-ga'i zin-bris las khol-du phyung-ba*][111]

Karma Chakme's textual contributions and addenda to Gyarawa's liturgy express a greater emphasis on the restoration of broken vows and the atonement of sins. It appears from the existing textual evidence that his contributions to the tradition were made effective through a series of ritual actions intended to purify the sins of the departed, and thereby end the postmortem sufferings caused by past transgressions. The disciple lineage of these and other related Karling transmissions belonging to Karma Chakme's Nedo tradition were passed through two main channels, the "lower lineage" (*smad-brgyud*) of Thukse Pema Kunga and the "upper lineage" (*stod-brgyud*) of Tsöndrü Gyatso (see table 9.4). Appropriately, both traditions were eventually transmitted to Jamgön Kongtrül and propagated by the leaders of the ecumenical Rime movement in eastern Tibet during the late nineteenth and early twentieth century.[112]

10

Traditions in Central
and Southern Tibet

The Fifth Dalai Lama's Inheritance

The historical preoccupation of the Tibetan religious schools with "spiritual genealogy," to use a phrase of Franz-Karl Ehrhard,[1] is most clearly represented in the genre of transmission records (*gsan-yig*, lit., "record of [teachings] heard") or accession lists (*thob-yig*, lit., "record of [teachings] obtained"). These texts generally contain lists of the titles of written texts, verbal instructions, and ritual initiations obtained by an individual during his or her lifetime. In addition, they frequently record the entire line of disciples to whom the rites and teachings had previously been transmitted, and thus they provide essential information for scholars interested in textual and biographical history. Such genealogical records are also quite useful for tracing the transmission of religious disciplines and doctrines in Tibet. One of the most substantial works of this genre is the *Transmission Record* of the fifth Dalai Lama. For my present considerations, this massive work is noteworthy for two reasons. First, the text gives an extensive list of titles and names of compositors for works belonging to the cycle of the *Peaceful and Wrathful Deities*.[2] This list of titles is important because it indicates what texts existed and were available in Tibet during the time of the fifth Dalai Lama's writing of his record; that is, between the years 1665 and 1670. Furthermore, the list also allows us to establish some of the works authored by Karma Lingpa himself by sorting out those works penned by others whose names are not identified in the colophons. Second, the fifth Dalai Lama's *Transmission Record* delimits a more or less complete succession of teachers involved in the transmission of yet another tradition of the *Peaceful and Wrathful Deities* in central and southern Tibet (see fig. 10.1).[3] In the following section I will review briefly this specific Karling lineal tradition inherited by the fifth Dalai Lama.

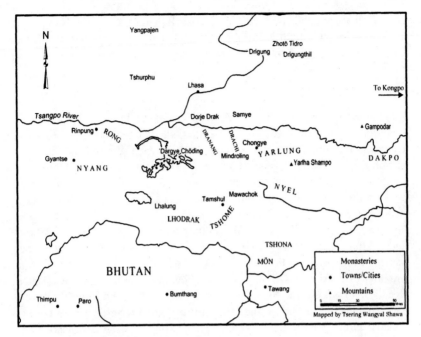

FIGURE 10.1. Central and southern Tibet.

Ösel Longyang

The fifth Dalai Lama's Karling inheritance comprised the convergence of two separate teaching-lineages originating from Karma Lingpa's grand-disciple, Nyida Özer. The first lineage was passed from that teacher to a certain lama named Sangye Drime, who has not yet been identified. Sangye Drime then transmitted the teachings to one Tashi Zangpo, who in turn passed them to Ösel Longyang. This latter figure is known from a lineage described in Guru Tashi's *Religious History* in reference to the Nyingthik system of Longchenpa.[4] Here we learn that Ösel Longyang was born at Kyepuk in Gyemen/Gyelmen (near Chongye in southern Tibet?) as the son of Namkha Dorje, abbot of Dung monastery.[5] He studied with a number of famous masters of the fifteenth century, such as Thangtong Gyelpo, Pema Lingpa, and Dzokchen Kunga Tashi (alias Tashi Zangpo?), but his two most important teachers were his father, Namkha Dorje, and the second Drukpa Gyelwang Je Kunga Peljor, who it may be recalled was also a teacher of Gyarawa. Ösel Longyang later founded the retreat centers of Zangtsho and Ösel Ling, where he established a tradition of meditation combining both systems of Mahāmudrā and Dzokchen.[6] He died at the age of eighty, leaving behind a teaching legacy that spread throughout Ü, Tsang, Dakpo, and Kongpo. Among Ösel Longyang's many students, two deserve special mention: Dzokchen Sönam Rinchen and Nangselwa Tashi Gyatso. The former, I will soon show, played an active role in the transmission of the *Liberation upon*

Hearing that eventually reached Tsele Natsok Rangdröl. The latter, Nangselwa Tashi Gyatso, held both Karling transmissions that reached the fifth Dalai Lama sometime in the middle of the seventeenth century.

Kunga Lhündrup

The second Karling transmission flowing into the tradition of the fifth Dalai Lama passed first through Nyida Özer to Gyarawa and then to one named Kunga Lhündrup. This name appears in many transmission lists, but the person's precise identity is not at all clear. In the search for clues, I must first return to the Kathok transmissions discussed in chapter 9 and focus on an obscure lineage emanating from Gyarawa and listed in Dujom Rinpoche's *Accession Record of the Precious Anthology of Treasures*. In that source, Gyarawa is indicated as having transmitted the complete Karling initiations and reading-transmissions to Gyama Mingyurwa (known also by two other names, Kunga Gyeltsen Pelzangpo and Letrho Lingpa),[7] already familiar from my brief discussion of Drigung Rinchen Phüntshok in the previous chapter. Recall that both Gyama Mingyurwa and Drigung Rinchen Phüntshok were each student and teacher to the other. Born in the fire serpent year 1497 in Gyama, north of Lhasa near Drigung,[8] Gyama Mingyurwa took monastic vows with the fourth Zhamarpa Chenga Chödrakpa (1453–1524) and received the name Kunga Gyeltsen.[9] He was later appointed abbot (*gdan-sa*) of Nyide monastery and took over the duties of the religious institute (*chos-sde*) of Lhündrup, which had been formerly administered by the lama Sordrangpa Zhönu Tshewang.[10] Toward the end of his life, he also became the abbot of Nenang and Yangpajen, the two main monastic strongholds of the Zhamarpa sect in central Tibet.[11]

From Drupchen Kunzang Dorje, a disciple of Gyelse Dawa Drakpa, Gyama Mingyurwa received many Dzokchen transmissions, such as the *Fourfold Heart-essence* [*Snying-thig ya-bzhi*].[12] Among many contemporaries with whom he exchanged various teachings, the most notable were Dzokchen Sönam Rinchen, Tülku Natsok Rangdröl, and, of course, Drigung Rinchen Phüntshok. Dzokchen Sönam Rinchen, in particular, became an influential teacher at Tsele Sarpa monastery in Dakpo after having been invited to teach there by its founder, Rikzin Chenpo Sönam Namgyel.[13] At some point Sönam Namgyel had also invited Gyama Mingyurwa.[14] Note that this is yet another thread linking the successors of Karma Lingpa's treasure tradition to Tsele monastery in Dakpo.

The transmission lineages of the *Liberation upon Hearing* and the apparently related *Four Initiations: Self-Liberation of Whatever Is Encountered* flow exclusively through either Dzokchen Sönam Rinchen or Tülku Natsok Rangdröl. Both transmissions come from a single teacher, referred to simply as Kunga Lhündrup.[15] In the fifth Dalai Lama's *Transmission Record*, the second transmission line listed for the *Peaceful and Wrathful Deities* gives the name Kunga Lhündrup as a student of Gyarawa. The Kunga Lhündrup of this series is indicated as having transmitted the *Peaceful and Wrathful Dei-*

ties to Nangselwa Tashi Gyatso. From Nangselwa Tashi Gyatso the teachings were passed to Kunga Tshechok, and then to Ngawang Yeshe Drupa. The very same lineage is listed in Guru Tashi's *Religious History,* in a short biographical section devoted to Gyama Mingyurwa.[16] Here we see clearly that Gyama Mingyurwa transmitted teachings, including his own treasures, to both Nangselwa Tashi Gyatso and Drigung Rinchen Phüntshok. In light of this evidence, and considering also that Gyama Mingyurwa was known to have received a Karling transmission directly from Gyarawa, I am inclined to believe that the Kunga Lhündrup found listed in the fifth Dalai Lama's teaching-lineage was actually Gyama Mingyurwa (the name Kunga Lhündrup representing an alternative form of the alias Kunga Gyeltsen Pelzangpo). I will have reason to return to this identity question when I examine the *Liberation upon Hearing* transmissions of Terdak Lingpa and Rikzin Nyima Drakpa.

To summarize thus far, the fifth Dalai Lama received two distinct Karling transmissions, one passing from Tashi Zangpo to Ösel Longyang and another from Gyarawa to Kunga Lhündrup (a.k.a. Gyama Mingyurwa Kunga Gyeltsen Pelzangpo). Both streams converged in the person of Nangselwa Tashi Gyatso. This individual passed the teachings to Nangselwa Kunga Tshechok, who in turn transmitted them to Ngawang Yeshe Drupa. It was this master who bestowed the *Peaceful and Wrathful Deities* on Zurchen Chöying Rangdröl, from whom it was then passed to the fifth Dalai Lama (see table 10.1).[17]

Zurchen Chöying Rangdröl

Zurchen Chöying Rangdröl was born in 1604 into the great House of Zur, one of Tibet's most renowned families, as the son of Zhönu Döndrup.[18] At nine, he met Rikzin Ngagi Wangpo (1580–1639), son of Karma Guru and hierarch of Dorje Drak monastery, who prophesied that he would accomplish much benefit in transmitting the old scriptures of the Nyingmapa.[19] When still a young man, sometime around 1615, he went before Ngawang Yeshe Drupa and received the complete initiations, reading-transmission, and experiential instructions for Karma Lingpa's *Peaceful and Wrathful Deities.* During this ceremony, he was given the secret name (*gsang-mtshan*) Zurchen Chöying Rangdröl.[20] At some point later in life, he met Takla Pemamati when the latter was traveling through Lhasa. Each bestowed teachings on the other. From Takla Pemamati he received the *Embodiment of the Lama's Realization,* as well as doctrines and practices pertaining to the *Eight Pronouncements* [*Bka'-brgyad*]. In exchange, Zurchen Chöying Rangdröl presented the Kathokpa lama with Longchenpa's *Dispelling the Darkness in the Ten Directions* [*Phyogs-bcu mun-sel*], a commentary on the *Great Tantra of the Secret Nucleus.*[21] We have no evidence that these transmission exchanges included Karma Lingpa's cycle of treasures, although by this time both Zurchen Chöying Rangdröl and Takla Pemamati had established themselves as leading promoters of the Karling tradition. We do know, however, that around the time Takla Pemamati was visiting Lhasa, the fifth Dalai Lama accepted Zurchen Chöying Rangdröl as his Nyingmapa teacher.[22] We can only presume that soon thereafter the fifth Dalai Lama received the com-

TABLE 10.1. Lineages of the Fifth Dalai Lama.

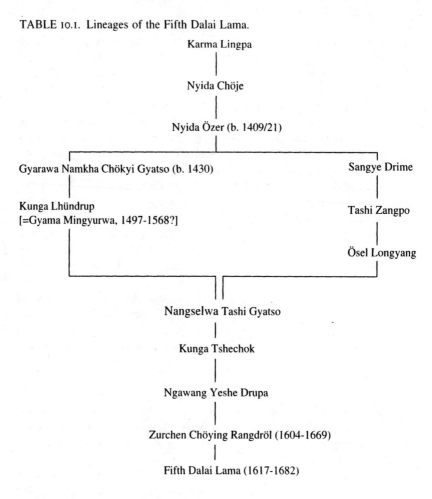

posite Karling transmission held by his Nyingma guru. As far as I can discern from the available sources, this specific Karling transmission remained in the possession of the fifth Dalai Lama and was not spread any further. The fifth Dalai Lama, however, did become a preceptor of two important lineage-holders of the *Peaceful and Wrathful Deities* (namely, the fourth Peling Thukse Tenzin Gyurme Dorje [b. 1641] of Lhalung and Terdak Lingpa of Mindroling), although he does not appear to have been the source of their respective Karling traditions. It is to the tradition of Mindroling that I now turn.

Mindroling and the King of Treasure Revealers

The monastery of Mindroling (see fig. 10.2), the most important Nyingmapa institution in central Tibet during the late seventeenth and early eighteenth centuries, was first established in the fire dragon year 1676 by Terdak Lingpa (alias Pema Garwang Gyurme Dorje).[23] This pivotal figure, renowned as the

FIGURE 10.2. Mindroling Monastery, central Tibet. (Courtesy of Tibetan and Himalayan Digital Library, www.thdl.org)

"King of Treasure Revealers" (*gter-ston chos-kyi-rgyal-po*), was an extraordinarily influential teacher and prolific author whose legacy practically defined the age in which he lived—a period of cultural renaissance and creative expansion of the Nyingmapa throughout central and eastern Tibet. At its height, Mindroling boasted three hundred monks and three lama households (*bla-brang*).[24] The success of this ecclessiastical institution was due in part to the powerful connections Terdak Lingpa and his eminent lineage of descendants cultivated with the political leaders of central Tibet, and particularly the fifth Dalai Lama, who shared a close master-cum-disciple relationship with him. The religious works of Terdak Lingpa came to be known collectively as the "Southern Treasures" (*lho-gter*) and were the essential body of instruction followed at Mindroling. Like the fifth Dalai Lama, Terdak Lingpa also left behind an exhaustive record of all the books, manuscripts, and ritual initiations he had obtained during his illustrious life. His *Transmission Record* is as essential for information on the scriptural and biographical history of Tibetan religion as is the fifth Dalai Lama's work. Similarly, in Terdak Lingpa's *Transmission Record*, an extensive list of titles and names of authors is provided for works belonging to the *Self-Liberated Wisdom of the Peaceful and Wrathful Deities*.[25] A succession of teachers involved in that cycle's transmission is also given.[26] In this lineage section, we find that the specific Mindroling tradition of the *Peaceful and Wrathful Deities* was formed by the convergence of three distinct lines of transmission, two of which emanated from Gyarawa and a third from Gönpo Dorje of Kongpo, whose identity I discussed in chapter 8. I will examine briefly these three strands of the composite lineal tradition of Mindroling.

Puṇya Shri (Sönam Pel)

The first lineage, the principal one, begins with the obscure figure Sönam Özer.[27] From Gyarawa the Karling transmission is said to have been passed through this Sönam Özer to Puṇya Shri (Sönam Pel). The identities of these two individuals have not yet been established, although both names occur with some frequency in a number of Mindroling genealogies.[28] Puṇya Shri also appears in a lineage listed at the end of a manuscript version of the *Liberation upon Hearing* preserved in the Waddell Collection of the British Library:

> [Karma Lingpa] gave the command-authorization [of this teaching] to his son Chöje Lingpa [i.e., Nyida Chöje] in accordance with prophecy. He in turn gave the oral transmission to Guru Sūryacandra [i.e., Nyida Özer], who then presented it to Puṇya Shri. He in turn gave it to Rikzin Jangchup Lingpa, who then gave it to Natsok Rangdröl. From him it went to Tenzin Drakpa, who in turn gave it to Pema Trhinle, and nowadays from him the lineage continues without interruption through the second Kunkhyen Tshültrhim Dorje.[29]

The last name listed in this colophon refers actually to the third, not the second, Peling Sungtrül Tshültrhim Dorje. On the basis of this identification, the manuscript probably dates to around the middle of the seventeenth century, just before the time of Terdak Lingpa (see fig. 10.3). In this list, Puṇya Shri is indicated as having received the transmission directly from Nyida Özer, who we know was also the teacher of Gyarawa. The relationship between Puṇya Shri and Nyida Özer is also attested to in a section of the fifth Dalai Lama's *Transmission Record* on the lineage of *Planting the Stalk*, a treasure text on transference (*'pho-ba*) that, it may be recalled, was discovered by Karma Lingpa's father, Nyida Sangye.[30] Further details regarding the identity of this person are not specified, although it does appear Puṇya Shri was a student of Nyida Özer. Perhaps, given his placement in the lineage and the notable similarities between the names, the Sönam Özer listed in Terdak Lingpa's *Transmission Record* may actually have been Nyida Özer. What is certain, however, is that Puṇya Shri transmitted the teachings of Nyida Sangye and Karma Lingpa to the treasure revealer Jangchup Lingpa Sönam Chökyong.

Jangchup Lingpa and Tülku Natsok Rangdröl

Not much is known about the life of Jangchup Lingpa Sönam Chökyong, other than the fact that he was born in Lhodrak Tamshul and became a disciple of Pema Lingpa and abbot of the monastery that bore his name, Chak Jangchup Ling.[31] He was the teacher of Tülku Natsok Rangdröl, on whom he bestowed the complete transmission of the *Peaceful and Wrathful Deities*.[32] Tülku Natsok Rangdröl was born in Lhodrak Menthang and was recognized as the immedi-

FIGURE 10.3. Manuscript pages of the Waddell/Lhalung edition of the *Great Liberation upon Hearing in the Bardo*, c. late seventeenth century. (Reproduced by permission of The British Library, Oriental and India Office Collections)

ate reincarnation of the treasure revealer Ratna Lingpa.[33] At fifteen, he was ordained at the monastery of Lhalung Lhündrup, which at that time was controlled by the Karmapa.[34] Among his many teachers, in addition to Jangchup Lingpa and Pema Lingpa, he studied with Gyama Mingyurwa, Dzokchen Kunga Tashi, and Mentsewa Matidhvāja (Lodrö Gyeltsen). It was from the latter that Tülku Natsok Rangdröl also received a second transmission of the *Peaceful and Wrathful Deities*. This transmission stream became the second line that fed into the particular Karling tradition fostered at Mindroling.[35]

In the wood sheep year 1535, when Tülku Natsok Rangdröl was forty-two years old, he consecrated the mountain hermitage (*ri-khrod*) of Dargye Chöding (also written as Chöling) in the valley of Dranang, which later came to be identified retroactively as the ancestral seat of Mindroling. Most notable among Tülku Natsok Rangdröl's successors at Dargye Chöding were his "heart-son" or Thukse (*thugs-sras*) Kunga Drakpa and the second Peling

Sungtrül Tenzin Drakpa (1536–1597). He transmitted the *Peaceful and Wrathful Deities* to both students.[36] The fact that, at this time, Tülku Natsok Rangdröl held three distinct teaching-lineages of Karma Lingpa's treasure cycle meant most likely that Dargye Chöding was a major center of practice for its liturgy during the latter half of the sixteenth century. Moreover, Tülku Natsok Rangdröl's bestowal of these teachings on the second Peling Sungtrül Tenzin Drakpa sometime between the years 1549 and 1555 made him also a key link in the introduction of the Karling tradition to his old home of Lhalung monastery in Lhodrak. This was the future residence of the great compilers of the *One Hundred Thousand Tantras of the Ancients*, Gongra Lochen Zhenphen Dorje (1594–1654) and the third Peling Sungtrül Tshültrhim Dorje. I will have reason to return to these pivotal figures later in this chapter. Here, however, I should stress the importance of the relationship that had been established in the sixteenth century between the monasteries of Dargye Chöding in central Tibet and Lhodrak Lhalung. In the generations following that period, this association would have significant consequences in terms of the further dissemination of the Karling tradition, and of the *Liberation upon Hearing* literature in particular, beyond the borders of Tibet.

Dongak Tenzin and Trhinle Lhündrup

Sometime after Tülku Natsok Rangdröl's death in 1570, his two main students, Thukse Kunga Drakpa and Peling Sungtrül Tenzin Drakpa, together transmitted the Karling teachings to Dongak Tenzin (1576–1628/48) of the Nyö (*gnyos/smyos*) clan.[37] Dongak Tenzin was the first recognized reincarnation of Tülku Natsok Rangdröl and childhood student of the fifth Zhamarpa Könchok Yenlakwang (1525–1583).[38] His activities relevant to the preservation of the *Peaceful and Wrathful Deities* are not exactly known, although it is certain that he transmitted this treasure cycle to his son, Trhinle Lhündrup (1611–1662). Trhinle Lhündrup was born at the monastery of Chak Jangchup Ling and spent his early years at Lhodrak Lhalung under the direction of the third Pawo Tsuklak Gyatso (1567–1633). He later studied with Gongra Lochen Zhenphen Dorje, Peling Sungtrül Tshültrhim Dorje, and Zurchen Chöying Rangdröl.[39] His chief disciples were his sons Terdak Lingpa and Lochen Dharma Shri (Chögyel Tenzin, 1654–1718), to whom he granted the entirety of the Karling transmissions that he inherited from his own father, Dongak Tenzin.[40]

Terdak Lingpa and Lochen Dharma Shri

By the end of the seventeenth century, Mindroling had superceded its older mother institution, Dargye Chöding, as the principal center of Nyingma activities in the lower regions of the Dranang and Drachi valleys of central Tibet. The monastery's founder, Terdak Lingpa, with the help of his younger brother, Lochen Dharma Shri, established a vibrant and successful community of scholar-monks, artisans, and meditators, all of whom fostered the scriptural traditions of the Nyingmapa, and in particular the Southern Treasures of

Terdak Lingpa himself. Terdak Lingpa and his benefactors were prolific producers of important religious manuscripts, including editions of both the Tibetan *Kanjur* (in gold and silver) and the *One Hundred Thousand Tantras of the Ancients*.[41] The latter collection, compiled at Mindroling from original manuscripts gathered from Zur Ukpalung, Kongpo Thangdrok, Tsangrong, and Dargye Chöding, was completed in 1685–86 in twenty-three volumes and came to serve as a major source-edition for the famous Derge redaction of 1794–1798.[42] Terdak Lingpa and his brother are thus seen as chief custodians of the major literary traditions that were preserved and promoted by the Nyingmapa of that period. Their recensional efforts had a direct bearing on the history of not only the *Kanjur* and the *One Hundred Thousand Tantras* as authoritative collections but also on the many lineages of teaching that had over time converged and taken shape at Mindroling and surrounding areas of central Tibet.

It is in this light that we must view the particular tradition of the *Peaceful and Wrathful Deities* preserved by Terdak Lingpa and his successors. Their tradition is best exemplified by a few minor texts scattered throughout the various extant recensions of the Karling treasure cycle and by two complete editions that appear to be based originally on traditions followed at Mindroling.[43] One of these editions contains textual interpolations by Lochen Dharma Shri, although this is not indicated explicitly in the actual volume itself.[44] Lochen Dharma Shri's name does appear, however, in the colophon of a single text found in the middle of that collection. This work, entitled *Ritual Thoroughly Purifying Transgressions and Obscurations* [*Choga sdig-sgrib rnam-par sbyong-ba*], appears to have been based on a smaller liturgical work of Terdak Lingpa and enhanced by his brother in the wood female bird year 1705 at the behest of one lama Namdröl Zangpo of Gonjo.[45] In the entire corpus of the available literature associated with the Karling treasure revelations, this text stands as one of three works explicitly linked to Terdak Lingpa and his tradition. The two other works are the brief *Vajraknot Prayer* [*Smon-lam rdo-rje'i rgya-mdud*],[46] attributed to Terdak Lingpa (listed as Rikzin Gyurme Dorje), and the *Self-liberation of Samsara and Nirvana entitled "The Brahma Sound Melody Recitation"* [*'Dzab-bzlas tshangspa'i sgra-dbyangs 'khor-'das rang-grol*], which was completed by one Bentrang Betenpa and derived in part from practices established by the "old-timers" (*rnying-rgan*) Terdak Lingpa, and so forth.[47]

The fundamental texts on which the Mindroling tradition of the *Peaceful and Wrathful Deities* was derived surely contained core material in common with the other Karling traditions, including most likely the prayers and instructions on the six types of bardo, the affiliated ritual techniques of the Karling peaceful and wrathful mandala, and the liturgical manuals of Gyarawa. In addition to the texts prepared by Terdak Lingpa himself, Lochen Dharma Shri, and their immediate descendants, there must also have been earlier texts and practices known only within the teaching-lineages of their predecesors. Of particular interest in this regard is the transmission of the *Liberation upon Hearing* that was handed down through Tülku Natsok Rangdröl at Dargye

Chöding and through the second Peling Sungtrül at Lhodrak Lhalung. Judging from the contents of the Waddell manuscript mentioned earlier, the content of this special *Liberation upon Hearing* transmission would probably have included the *Reminder of the Bardo of Reality-Itself* and the *Direct Introduction to the Bardo of Becoming*, the two works that together have become famous in translation as the *Tibetan Book of the Dead*.

To summarize thus far, the textual and liturgical tradition of the *Peaceful and Wrathful Deities* at Mindroling originated from the convergence of three distinct transmissions received through Tülku Natsok Rangdröl of Dargye Chöding monastery (see table 10.2). The tradition was first promoted by his two main successors, Thukse Kunga Drakpa and the second Peling Sungtrül Tenzin Drakpa, and eventually passed through the descendants of his immediate reincarnation, Dongak Tenzin. Dongak Tenzin's eldest grandson, Terdak Lingpa, continued the lineage and established its practice at Mindroling, the monastery that he founded. This institution became a principal center for the bestowal of the requisite Karling initiations and instructions on religious pilgrims from all regions of Tibet and surrounding areas, including Kham and northwestern Nepal. As an illustration, we should refer to a passage in the biography of the Dolpo lama Sönam Wangchuk (1660–1731), abbot of Yetsher and Thakar monasteries. Sönam Wangchuk is said to have traveled to Mindroling sometime around 1687 (shortly after a terrible outbreak of smallpox) and requested from some unspecified high-ranking lama there the initiations for the *Peaceful and Wrathful Deities*.[48] Given the specific date, we can only presume that the master of ceremonies must have been Terdak Lingpa himself, or perhaps Lochen Dharma Shri.

After the tragic assassinations in 1718 of both Lochen Dharma Shri and Terdak Lingpa's second eldest son, Pema Gyurme Gyatso (1686–1718), at the hands of the Dzungar Mongols,[49] the Mindroling tradition was carried on through the third son, Rinchen Namgyel (1694–1758). It was, however, Pema Gyurme Gyatso who, shortly before his death, transmitted the *Peaceful and Wrathful Deities* to Orgyen Tenzin (1701–1728), the adopted child of Terdak Lingpa and son of the infamous sorcerer from Kham, Rikzin Nyima Drakpa.[50] In the person of this child, Orgyen Tenzin, were combined two major lineal traditions, one emanating from Terdak Lingpa of Mindroling and another from Rikzin Nyima Drakpa of the monastery of Takmogang in eastern Tibet. I should point out that the transmission line of Rikzin Nyima Drakpa's tradition had earlier passed also through Tülku Natsok Rangdröl. This line represented the third lineage that converged with two others to form the full-fledged Mindroling tradition of the *Peaceful and Wrathful Deities*. I will show that this third lineage, the one associated with Rikzin Nyima Drakpa, came from a single transmission received through several diverse personalities, including Rikzin Chenpo Sönam Namgyel of Dakpo Tsele, Dzokchen Sönam Rinchen, Tsele Natsok Rangdröl of Kongpo Thangdrok, and the Peling incarnations of Lhodrak Lhalung. It is this particular lineage that is mentioned exclusively in connection with the obscure Karling cycle *Four Initiations: Self-Liberation of Whatever Is Encountered*.[51] But, most impor-

TABLE 10.2. Dargye Chöding/Mindroling Lineages.

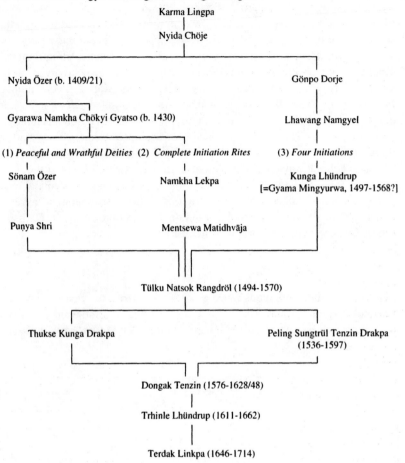

tant, it appears to be the principal transmission lineage in Tibet of the *Liberation upon Hearing*. In the following section I will focus on this distinctive tradition and, reaching further back in time, attempt to document the ways that the scriptural transmission of the *Four Initiations* and the *Liberation upon Hearing* might have been constituted after the period of Karma Lingpa's son, Nyida Chöje.

The Cycle of the *Four Initiations*

The area of the earliest spread of the *Self-Liberated Wisdom of the Peaceful and Wrathful Deities* and the *Great Liberation upon Hearing in the Bardo* was those parts of Tibet where Karma Lingpa's son, Nyida Chöje, had been active in his own lifetime and where his immediate successors were settled. That area covered roughly the southeastern districts of Dakpo, Longpo, and

Kongpo (see fig. 10.4). From there the tradition spread further south from the Dranang valley to the region of Lhodrak. It was here, at the monastery of Lhalung, that two separate Karling transmissions were received through the successive Sungtrül incarnations of Pema Lingpa. The first of these transmissions passed through Tülku Natsok Rangdröl to the second Peling Sungtrül Tenzin Drakpa. Although both figures were probably also involved in the second transmission, specifically associated with the Karling cycle entitled *Four Initiations: Self-Liberation of Whatever Is Encountered*, its main line did not pass through them but rather through Rikzin Chenpo Sönam Namgyel of Dakpo Tsele.[52] The cycle was eventually transmitted through Tsele Natsok Rangdröl of Thangdrok to the third Peling Sungtrül Tshültrhim Dorje of Lhalung. I should say clearly at the outset that this main lineage of the *Four Initiations* and the lineage of the *Liberation upon Hearing* are identical. The pedigrees can get rather confusing, so in this section I will attempt to sketch a basic picture of the history of this tradition's earliest protaganists. To do so, I must first return to the story of Nyida Chöje.

Lama Gönpo Dorje

According to the anonymous *History of the Treasures*, the first person after Karma Lingpa to promote the *Four Initiations* was his father, the treasure revealer Nyida Sangye.[53] This enigmatic figure is said to have bestowed the

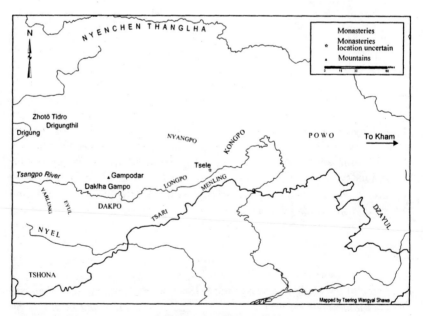

FIGURE 10.4. Southeastern Tibet showing the districts of Dakpo, Longpo, and Kongpo.

Four Initiations on his grandson, Nyida Chöje,[54] with the injunction that it should be transmitted only to the sole person authorized by prophecy.[55] Remember that in some sources it is recorded that after Karma Lingpa's death Nyida Sangye and Nyida Chöje divided up his books and possessions and found several manuscripts detailing the cycle of initiation rites of the *Liberation upon Hearing*.[56] Nyida Sangye and Nyida Chöje were the first promulgators of these teachings. It is conceivable, then, that the cycle of initiation rites found by them was actually the *Four Initiations*. But whatever the case, it is certain that the *Four Initiations* and the *Liberation upon Hearing* are both closely related cycles.

Once Nyida Chöje received the transmission, he traveled to Kongpo in order to locate his appointed student. In Kongpo he is alleged to have gone into retreat at an unspecified mountain hermitage, where at some point he met the lama Gönpo Dorje. Nyida Chöje determined through oneiromancy that this lama was the disciple prophecied to receive the *Four Initiations*. The exchange was thus completed. Previously in chapter 9 I entertained for a brief moment the idea that this Gönpo Dorje may have been the fourth Drung officer of Kathok monastery, but in the end decided that since their dates appear to be anachronistic I could not be certain about this identification. It is unlikely that Nyida Chöje was active in the latter half of the fifteenth century during the term of office of the fourth Drung. If so he would have had to have been a contemporary of Gyarawa, and this is certainly not corroborated in any of the available sources. At this stage, we really do not know who this Gönpo Dorje of Kongpo is.

Gönpo Dorje bestowed the *Four Initiations* (and also presumably the *Liberation upon Hearing*) on one Rikzin Lhawang Namgyel, who in turn presented it to Kunga Lhündrup, whom I have identified on several occasions as Gyama Mingyurwa. This important master, in turn, transmitted the teachings to both Tülku Natsok Rangdröl and Rikzin Chenpo Sönam Namgyel.[57] From Tülku Natsok Rangdröl, the *Four Initiations* was passed through his successors at Dargye Chöding and eventually reached Terdak Lingpa of Mindroling. The transmission of the *Four Initiations* that came from Rikzin Chenpo Sönam Namgyel, on the other hand, was passed through Dzokchen Sönam Rinchen to Jakhyung Ngawang Pema and then to Dzokchen Sönam Wangpo. Both Jakhyung Ngawang Pema and Dzokchen Sönam Wangpo were active in Kongpo during the latter half of the sixteenth century. Dzokchen Sönam Wangpo was the chief mentor of Tsele Natsok Rangdröl, to whom he granted the entirety of the cycle of the *Peaceful and Wrathful Deities*, including the *Four Initiations* and the *Liberation upon Hearing*.[58] I call this particular lineal tradition the Tsele Transmission because it was transmitted by a number of teachers affiliated with Tsele monastery in Dakpo. In the early decades of the seventeenth century, the Tsele tradition of the Karling treasure was conjoined with the tradition of Tülku Natsok Rangdröl and was subsequently maintained by the Peling incarnations at Lhalung monastery in Lhodrak (see fig. 10.5).

FIGURE 10.5. Lhalung Monastery, Lhodrak. (Photograph by Andrew Quintman)

The Tsele/Lhalung Transmissions

Tsele Natsok Rangdröl and Gongra Lochen Zhenphen Dorje

Tsele Natsok Rangdröl (alias Pema Lekdrup)[59] was born in 1608 at the border between Kongpo and Dakpo. He was recognized as the immediate reincarnation of Tshungme Tenzin Dorje, refurbisher of the monastery of Kongpo Thangdrok.[60] At this monastery Tsele Natsok Rangdröl, at the age of six and against his parents' wishes, underwent the tonsure ceremony (*gtsug-phud phul-ba*) at the feet of the third Pawo Tsuklak Gyatso.[61] At that time he was given the name Karma Rikzin Nampar Gyelwa. He was ordained shortly thereafter at Lhodrak Lhalung, Pawo Tsuklak Gyatso's monastery. Between 1615 and 1618, Tsele Natsok Rangdröl studied under Dzokchen Sönam Wangpo and received a number of Dzokchen Nyingthik transmissions, including the *Peaceful and Wrathful Deities*. He later met Takla Pemamati and his entourage while they were passing through Kongpo on their way to central Tibet.[62] Tsele Natsok Rangdröl and Takla Pemamati each bestowed teachings on the other. There is no evidence that the *Peaceful and Wrathful Deities* was among their exchanges.

Tsele Natsok Rangdröl eventually traveled to Gongra Lhündrup Chöding in Tsangrong and met the Sikkimese scholar Gongra Lochen Zhenphen Dorje, student of Sokdokpa Lodrö Gyeltsen and the sixth Zhamarpa Garwang Chökyi Wangchuk.[63] Gongra Lochen Zhenphen Dorje is best known for his efforts in compiling three sets of manuscripts of the *One Hundred Thousand Tantras of the Ancients*, each prepared on separate occasions and for different purposes.[64] The first set of copies remained at Lhündrup Ding in Gongra, the second was sent to a monastery in Kham (possibly Kathok), and the third was sent to Kongpo, presumably to the monastery of Thangdrok as an offering to Tsele Natsok Rangdröl.[65] Gongra Lochen Zhenphen Dorje and Tsele Natsok Rangdröl shared a close mutual teacher-student relationship. Shortly after Tsele Natsok Rangdröl's ordination at Lhalung, he went into retreat at a forest hermitage. For eighteen months, day and night, he studied at this hermitage with Gongra Lochen Zhenphen Dorje.[66] In Tsele Natsok Rangdröl's autobiography, he reminisces that it was during this period that he first presented the Karling transmission to his teacher.[67] Later, Gongra Lochen Zhenphen Dorje passed these teachings on to the third Peling Sungtrül Tshültrhim Dorje, with whom he shared a close disciple-cum-master relationship.

Peling Sungtrül Tshültrhim Dorje

Like Gongra Lochen Zhenphen Dorje, Peling Sungtrül Tshültrhim Dorje was a pivotal figure in the transmission of the *One Hundred Thousand Tantras of the Ancients*. In fact, it was he who first gave Gongra Lochen Zhenphen Dorje the "reading" (*lung*) of this large set of scriptures.[68] Peling Sungtrül Tshültrhim Dorje had been previously granted the transmission of the *One Hundred Thousand Tantras* at Lhündrup Phodrang, the family seat of Ratna Lingpa.[69] This so-called Ratna transmission was eventually received and fostered by both the fifth Dalai Lama and Terdak Lingpa.[70] Peling Sungtrül Tshültrhim Dorje and Gongra Lochen Zhenphen Dorje were responsible for preparing and redacting new complete sets of the *One Hundred Thousand Tantras*, and presumably a number of other fundamental religious works of the Nyingma tradition. Through their efforts the Nyingmapas of that period witnessed the unprecedented proliferation of manuscript copies of some of their most sacred literature. The redactional efforts of these two outstanding scholars were remarkable not only because their work represented a conscious attempt to bring together in complete form numerous individual texts scattered locally throughout Tibet but also because they were intent on distributing such works once compiled to all major centers of learning and practice. The result was the beginning of a widespread diffusion of Nyingma literature just prior to the great age of printing that began in earnest in the eighteenth century.

Much of Tibetan sacred literature in the eighteenth century, and even later into the nineteenth, came essentially in the form of anthologies. These anthologies were not always intended or written as such by either author or scribe. Single works written or copied earlier at one monastery might be attached decades later to a separate series of texts at another institution several hundred miles away. One of the goals of stitching together texts from different periods and locations was to compile complete volumes of works relevant to the traditions and activities of particular local centers. In the case of the monumental *One Hundred Thousand Tantras*, this gathering of texts represented less the tradition of a single monastery and more the definitive teachings of a conglomerate tradition, namely that of the Nyingmapa. On the other hand, smaller anthologized collections like the treasure cycle of Karma Lingpa tended to be patched together in a variety of forms, each reflecting a different lineage of transmission or the idiosyncratic interpretations of local lamas. These manuscript anthologies would later serve as primary versions for woodblock redactions printed for wider distribution. It was the anthologizing pioneers like Peling Sungtrül Tshültrhim Dorje and Gongra Lochen Zhenphen Dorje who contributed to the success of such foundational compilations, both large and small. The efforts of Peling Sungtrül Tshültrhim Dorje and Gongra Lochen Zhenphen Dorje with regard to the preparation of the *One Hundred Thousand Tantras* must have been repeated, though certainly on a much smaller scale, in the preservation of the *Liberation upon Hearing*. In this way, the Karling tradition fostered at Dakpo Tsele and Kongpo Thangdrok, which this duo inherited from Tsele Natsok Rangdröl, was transplanted to Lhodrak Lhalung, where it may then have been more fully edited and freshly calligraphed.

We do not know at this stage the precise content of the early Tsele/Lhalung redaction of the *Liberation upon Hearing*. But if we accept that the old manuscript edition preserved in the Waddell Collection of the British Library referred to earlier might represent a version of the Tsele/Lhalung transmission (with some connection to the Dargye Chöding/Mindroling line), then we could suggest that the redaction originally contained the following texts:

1. *Reminder of the Bardo of Reality-Itself*
2. *Root Verses on the Six Bardos*
3. *Religious Liturgy of the Self-Liberation of Karmic Latencies*
4. *Self-Liberated Vision: A Prayer to the Five Pure Lands*[71]
5. *Direct Introduction to the Bardo of Becoming*
6. *Prayer Requesting Assistance from the Buddhas and Bodhisattvas of the Ten Directions*[72]

With only slight variation in sequence, the arrangement of this set of texts resembles the core set of the *Liberation upon Hearing* that I discussed in chapter 7. We can see that the aforementioned edition contains the requisite bardo prayers and the fundamental peaceful and wrathful sādhana *Religious Liturgy of the Self-Liberation of Karmic Latencies*. In addition, it also includes perhaps the earliest witnesses of the famous *Reminder of the Bardo of Reality-Itself* and *Direct Introduction to the Bardo of Becoming*. These two works, in particular, are found in only a small minority of existing Karling collections, and those collections are associated almost exclusively with the transmission lineage received through the Tsele/Lhalung line. The third Peling Sungtrül Tshültrhim Dorje seems to have been the figure who was most instrumental in editing and compiling these texts. From him, the Tsele/Lhalung transmission was passed to the fourth Peling Thukse Tenzin Gyurme Dorje, who in turn transmitted it to one Rikzin Orgyen Chögyel, identified as a "bone" relative of Pema Lingpa (*pad-gling gdung-brgyud*).[73]

The Peling Thukse incarnation line, based also at Lhalung monastery, descended from Pema Lingpa's son, Dawa Gyeltsen (b. 1499), who was one of Peling Sungtrül Tenzin Drakpa's early teachers at Bumthang in Bhutan.[74]

TABLE 10.3. The Tsele/Lhalung Lineage.

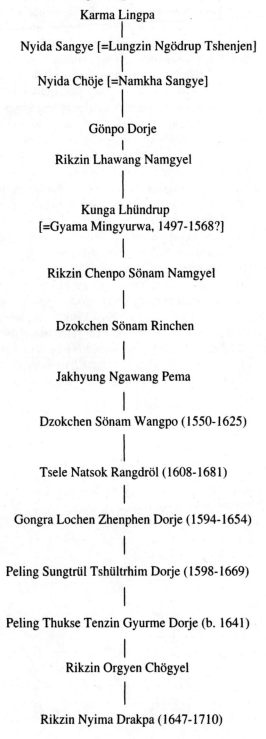

Karma Lingpa
|
Nyida Sangye [=Lungzin Ngödrup Tshenjen]
|
Nyida Chöje [=Namkha Sangye]
|
Gönpo Dorje
|
Rikzin Lhawang Namgyel
|
Kunga Lhündrup
[=Gyama Mingyurwa, 1497-1568?]
|
Rikzin Chenpo Sönam Namgyel
|
Dzokchen Sönam Rinchen
|
Jakhyung Ngawang Pema
|
Dzokchen Sönam Wangpo (1550-1625)
|
Tsele Natsok Rangdröl (1608-1681)
|
Gongra Lochen Zhenphen Dorje (1594-1654)
|
Peling Sungtrül Tshültrhim Dorje (1598-1669)
|
Peling Thukse Tenzin Gyurme Dorje (b. 1641)
|
Rikzin Orgyen Chögyel
|
Rikzin Nyima Drakpa (1647-1710)

Dawa Gyeltsen's own son was Pema Trhinle, who in 1613 founded the important Bhutanese Nyingma monastery of Gangteng Sangak Chöling in Shar.[75] Pema Trhinle is listed in the colophon of the Waddell manuscript previously quoted. Here he is indicated as having received the transmission from the second Peling Sungtrül Tenzin Drakpa. Pema Trhinle later passed it on to the third Peling Sungtrül Tshültrhim Dorje, the last name in the lineal series given in the colophon. The Waddell manuscript, therefore, must have been prepared in the last half of the seventeenth century by either Peling Sungtrül Tshültrhim Dorje himself or one of his immediate disciples. The evidence indicates clearly that this transmission of the *Liberation upon Hearing* was received through a number of important successors of Pema Lingpa's lineage, including his grandson Pema Trhinle. The latter represents a link between the second and third Peling Sungtrül incarnations connecting the Karling transmission lineage of Dargye Chöding/Mindroling with the transmission lineage of Tsele/ Lhalung. Bear in mind also that both lines had earlier passed through Tülku Natsok Rangdröl, Pema Lingpa's student. All these connections lead me to believe that our nebulous "bone" relative of Pema Lingpa, Rikzin Orgyen Chögyel, must have been a descendant (perhaps a son or nephew) of Pema Trhinle. Whatever the case, Rikzin Orgyen Chögyel appears to have been the first holder of the lineage to bestow the Tsele/Lhalung transmission on the controversial treasure revealer Rikzin Nyima Drakpa (see table 10.3). It was Rikzin Nyima Drakpa who was responsible for establishing the standard textual arrangement of the *Liberation upon Hearing* in the form that we now know today as *The Tibetan Book of the Dead*. The story of this intriguing figure and of the creation of this Tibetan classic is the subject of the next chapter.

IV

TEXT AND CONSOLIDATION

Rikzin Nyima Drakpa, Sorcerer from Kham

I mentioned briefly in the preceding chapter that the arrangement of the texts of the *Great Liberation upon Hearing in the Bardo*, in the form that is most accessible to us today, was the work of a controversial treasure revealer from Kham named Rikzin Nyima Drakpa. The various western-language translations of the *Liberation upon Hearing*, immortalized as the *Tibetan Book of the Dead*, were and continue to be based on Nyima Drakpa's standard redaction. Hence this rather unfamiliar figure is of great significance to our understanding the Tibetan history of the *Liberation upon Hearing* from the late seventeenth century onward. In this chapter, therefore, I will focus on the life and work of Rikzin Nyima Drakpa and inquire into how his compilation of the Karling texts came to be the standard arrangement for almost all subsequent editions of the cycle within and beyond the borders of Tibet.

Rumors and Scandals

Regrettably, not much is available about Rikzin Nyima Drakpa in either Tibetan or western-language sources, apart from a rather extensive biographical account of his activities in Guru Tashi's *Religious History*[1] and a few brief references to him in several western academic works.[2] Such meager representation in the Tibetan literature is undoubtedly a consequence in part of sectarian rivalries. I believe it is justifiable, therefore, to provide here a summary of the significant events of Nyima Drakpa's biography as described in Guru Tashi's monumental history.[3] It is my hope that in the near future this picture might be better enhanced by new discoveries of Nyima Drakpa's own works.[4] With the exception of his small two-volume *Hayagrīva, Subjugator of the Arrogant* [*Rta-mgrin dregs-pa zil-gnon*] with attendant practices,[5] no other work by Nyima Drakpa has surfaced until very recently. Nonetheless, it is more than clear that Nyima Drakpa was an active revealer of treasures and a prolific author. So then why are his life and work not easily accessible? The answer is simple, although the details are rather vague and indefinite.

Among certain Tibetan Buddhist circles there is an oral tradition that speaks quietly of a private scandal involving this little-known mystic from eastern Tibet. According to rumor, Nyima Drakpa is alleged to have utilized his extraordinary powers of "black magic" (*mngon-spyod*) to provoke the untimely death of the tenth Karmapa Chöying Dorje (1605–1674). Religious mania (*smyon-pa*) and vengeful arrogance are offered as possible reasons behind this ruthless act of murder. But why exactly was Nyima Drakpa the one blamed for the crime? How did he earn such a terrible reputation when the fact is that during most of his life he seems to have been a beloved miracle-worker? By some accounts, Nyima Drakpa was actually in great demand for his spiritual prowess and control over the hosts of demons plaguing Tibetans and their world. He appears then to have been a rather fierce yet benevolent guardian of Buddhism and perhaps a tragically misunderstood religious savant. More important, in addition to his influential role as guru and exorcist to many of Tibet's chief aristocrats of the day, he also played a leading and active role in the promulgation and standardization of the *Liberation upon Hearing*. In this chapter I will survey the life of Rikzin Nyima Drakpa in an effort to unveil the final stages in the making of the *Liberation upon Hearing*, a process that culminated ultimately in the western creation of *The Tibetan Book of the Dead*. Over the course of this examination, we also begin to discern what may have contributed to the complicated reputation of this most influential redactor of the Karling literature.

We know that in Nyima Drakpa's later years he had become a subject of much anger, jealousy, and even fear among some of his contemporaries. Guru Tashi, who is generally quite sympathetic to Nyima Drakpa, describes an unfortunate episode involving the Karma Kagyu–affiliated treasure revealer Yonge Mingyur Dorje (b. 1628) and some government officials near where Nyima Drakpa was repairing a stupa in Kham.[6] According to the account, Yonge Mingyur Dorje had wanted to meet this treasure revealer from Kham but was stopped short by the officials. These men began hassling Yonge Mingyur Dorje and eventually attacked him physically. For reasons not made clear, Yonge Mingyur Dorje blamed Nyima Drakpa for the irreverent and violent treatment he had suffered at the hands of the government officials. Enraged, he went around shouting, "Nyima Drakpa is a demon!" and set out to ruin the treasure revealer's reputation. Apparently Yonge Mingyur Dorje was successful, for Guru Tashi goes on to report that as a result others with sectarian bias started repeating defaming rumors about him.

In spite of, or perhaps because of, the lavish support given to Nyima Drakpa during his lifetime, in the years following Yonge Mingyur Dorje's conflict with the government officials, his successors and those that shared close ties with the Karmapa continued to maintain the story of Nyima Drakpa's complicity in the affair. Needless to say, these people harbored ill feelings toward him that sowed very deep roots. These negative impressions reached their culmination in the nineteenth century in the person of Jamgön Kongtrül. We may recall that it was this influential scholar who helped define and shape the ecumenical, or nonpartisan (ris-med), movement that swept eastern Tibet during the latter half of the nineteenth century. Despite Jamgön Kongtrül's openly ecumenical stance, however, he did choose sides on the sensitive matter of Rikzin Nyima Drakpa. Consequently, when compiling his *Precious Anthology of Treasures*—that monumental collection of initiations and liturgical directives of almost all treasure traditions available in Tibet at the time— Jamgön Kongtrül intentionally excluded Nyima Drakpa's treasure revelations, presumably out of respect for the Karmapas.[7] His willful exclusion of these texts in favor of other less significant, and even "heretical" (read, Bonpo), works became a hot topic of controversy led by an outspoken Nyingmapa teacher named Tenzin Drakpa. It is not necessary to explore these controversies, since scholars have already investigated them thoroughly.[8] What does bear repeated emphasis, however, is that the scarcity of the works of Nyima Drakpa and the relative paucity of information regarding his life can be linked directly to Jamgön Kongtrül's decision to erase this treasure revealer from history. If it were not for Nyima Drakpa's unsavory reputation and alleged violent activities, then certainly we would know more about this sorcerer from Kham. Perhaps, then, we would also be in a better position to uncover the facts behind the scandals that seemed to pursue him in his later years.

Rikzin Nyima Drakpa was a persistent and devoted journeyman throughout his life, traveling through much of Tibet, Bhutan, Nepal, and India and even into western China. In his many travels, he was often witness to the tumultuous religiopolitical events taking place in those territories during that seminal period. He was, moreover, personally involved with several key players in the political dramas of his day. In Lhasa, he became the teacher of Desi Sangye Gyatso (1653–1705) and the young sixth Dalai Lama, Tshangyang Gyatso (1683–1706). In Kham, he enjoyed the patronage of the royal families of Ling, Lhari, and particularly Derge, where he was especially favored by the Derge king Sangye Tenpa, and later by his successor Chögyel Tenpa Tshering (1678–1738).[9]

In a word, Rikzin Nyima Drakpa was a powerful religious presence in seventeenth-century Tibet. Not only was he a chief protagonist in spreading the teachings of his own mentor, Dzokchen Pema Rikzin (1625–1697), but he was also unfailing in his efforts to preserve and transmit the works of other major religious leaders of the time such as the great treasure revealer Dudül Dorje at Kathok,[10] the treasure revealer Garwang Dorje (1640–1685) of Ngari,[11] and Terdak Lingpa at Mindroling. Furthermore, he was said to have held the special authorization to teach a number of important treasure cycles, including most notably Karma Lingpa's *Self-Liberated Wisdom of the Peaceful and Wrathful Deities*. Guru Tashi portrays Nyima Drakpa as a rather charismatic religious leader, connected with many of Tibet's highest-ranking officials and cherished by legions of faithful followers. This sympathetic portrait of Nyima Drakpa is what I shall highlight here.

Previous Lives

Rikzin Nyima Drakpa was born in the fire female pig year 1647 in the village of Chakbel in the region of Nangchen to a family from the clan of Drakarpo that belonged to the nephew-lineage of the siddha Jame Pholungpa. His father was known as Jame Önpo Karma Namgyel and his mother as Laza Sönamtsho. His birth had been previously forecast in a number of recorded prophecies, such as that found in Orgyen Lingpa's *Testament of Padmasambhava* [*Padma bka'-thang*]:

> To men his clothing will appear incongruous,
> even his sacred teachings will be disconsonant.
> There will be traces left behind of the designs written at Gegye [Jema Ling].[12]
> The treasures of the threefold Sinmo Dzong in Kham
> will not remain there, but signs will appear indicating that they are to be
>   discovered.
> [The revealer of these treasures] will have the name Khampa Nyima Drakpa.[13]

This brief prophecy has been interpreted variously as foretelling the arrival of two treasure revealers by the name of Nyima Drakpa.[14] The first, Khamtö Dakpo Tertön Nyima Drakpa, or as I shall call him, Nyima Drakpa the Elder, lived during the thirteenth century and was believed to have been the incarnation of Lhalung Pelgi Dorje, the infamous monk-assassin of the ninth-century Tibetan emperor Lang Darma.[15] From the hidden valley (*sbas-yul*) of the threefold fortress of Sin Dzong (also Sing Dzong)—that is, Sinpo, Sinmo, and Dorje—Nyima Drakpa the Elder extracted the treasures of the *Play of Yamarāja-Guhyacandra* [*Gshin-rje zla-gsang rol-pa*], the *Karma-Yama with Monkey-fur* [*Las-gshin sprel-slag-can*], and the seven-part cycle of *Fierce Mantras* [*Drag-sngags*]. Curiously, Jamgön Kongtrül locates the fortress of Sin Dzong behind Gampodar Mountain in Dakpo.[16] The identification is not incidental. Remember that Gampodar is the same mountain site where Karma Lingpa excavated the treasure cycles of the *Peaceful and Wrathful Deities* and the *Liberation upon Hearing*. Like Karma Lingpa, Nyima Drakpa the Elder did not live for very long, and sources for his biography are rather scarce. Unfortunately, it seems that most of the Sin Dzong treasures had been lost by the time Jamgön Kongtrül set out to compile the *Precious Anthology of Treasures*.

Although it is true that Nyima Drakpa the Younger also extracted treasure from a place called Sin(mo) Dzong, the two discoverers are clearly distinct individuals separated by several centuries. Still, the similarities between them should not go unnoticed. I find it intriguing, for example, that both figures are reputed to have been fierce practitioners in possession of magical teachings associated with the wrathful forms of Yama or Shinje, Lord of the Dead.

Murderous aggression is also said to be among the hallmarks of their personalities. Moreover, the fact that both are linked in some way to the treasure
revealer Karma Lingpa suggests that some unifying theme of mythic propor-
tion might be lurking behind the sinister details of all three of their lives. If
such a connection exists, it is at present shrouded from view. But then again,
perhaps we are just dealing with a Tibetan stereotype that portrays certain
revealers of treasure as ferocious and demonic sorcerers, particularly those
handling scriptures tainted by the taboos of death. To be sure, an examination of the successive lives of these visionaries would give us a clearer picture, albeit mainly symbolic or impressionistic, of how these personalities were
actually viewed by later generations. With this in mind, I continue the story
of Nyima Drakpa the Younger.

The former embodiments of Rikzin Nyima Drakpa are listed in Guru
Tashi from Nyima Drakpa's own text entitled *Garland of Lives of Lu'i
Wangpo* [*Klu'i-dbang-po'i skye-phreng*].[17] As the title makes clear, Nyima
Drakpa believed that he was fundamentally an incarnation of the translator
Choro Lu'i Gyeltsen. It may be recalled that this eighth-century figure had
also been identified as the previous embodiment of both Karma Lingpa and
Karma Chakme. It would be unnecessary to reproduce all of Nyima Drakpa's
former lives, but I should mention some of the more noteworthy. For example, Nyima Drakpa is said to have previously taken birth in Dakpo as
the consort of Karma Lingpa.[18] This is our first explicit indication that Nyima
Drakpa possessed some intimate connection to the Karling tradition. Bear
in mind that a treasure revealer is generally expected to engage in certain
sexual activities with a female consort and that his union with this consort
is designed to generate and reawaken the original moment in which Padmasambhava had concealed the treasure in the mind of the treasure revealer's
past incarnation; in this case, Choro Lu'i Gyeltsen. Recall also that in some
of our biographies of Karma Lingpa the female partner who had been especially appointed for him by prophecy did not work out, since the auspicious
connections linking them together had been fouled up (*'phyugs-pa*).[19] Consequently, Karma Lingpa was forced to choose another woman, who it so
happens bore him a son. The relationship is said to have aroused gossip
among the people of Dakpo. Which woman, then, was Nyima Drakpa supposed to have embodied? The appointed consort or the unauthorized one?
In both scenarios, the women are problematic. The appointed consort that
never properly matched up with Karma Lingpa was trouble because although
she was destined to be his special partner, she and the treasure revealer could
not, for whatever reason, make it work. Broken auspices are rarely viewed
as productive in Tibet. The other woman was even more detrimental, since
her unauthorized status became the cause of Karma Lingpa's untimely demise. But, in the end, she gave birth to a son, presumably Nyida Chöje, who
carried on his father's legacy and helped to spread his teachings. So it may
be more reasonable to think of Nyima Drakpa as being formerly the "mother"
of Nyida Chöje, even though this would mean that in his past life he had
been less than amiable and had provoked the death of his partner Karma

Lingpa; yet somehow would that not seem oddly appropriate, given his tarnished future reputation?

In another source, the title of which is not specified, Guru Tashi relates that when Nyima Drakpa was residing at Khamshak in Sin Dzong he received a prophecy and sang a song about his previous lives. In this song Nyima Drakpa says clearly that he had taken birth as the obscure siddha Nakpo Thokphen, "Black Thunderbolt-Hurler," who was conceived in the region of Gyatön. Much like the legend of Garap Dorje referred to in chapter 5, Nakpo Thokphen was born without an ordinary father. In a dream, his mother was "blessed" by Vajrapāṇi. When she gave birth to a child soon thereafter, she was dumbstruck and threw the boy in a ravine. He was then nursed by vultures. After awhile, his mother began to see signs indicating that she had made a terrible mistake. She promptly retrieved her son and together they ran off to the predominantly Bonpo district of Khyungpo. There the boy requested from a lama named Khyung Gampo the initiations and instructions of Vajrapāṇi.[20] The child then had a vision and met personally with this deity. Since Vajrapāṇi is understood to be inextricably linked to the rise to prominence of Vajrayāna Buddhism, Nyima Drakpa's vision of this deity is symbolically significant.[21] His vision serves to authenticate his religious power by highlighting his intimate connection to the most fundamental of Buddhist tantric deities. The blessings he received from Vajrapāṇi gave him power over all ferocious gods and demons. A few illustrations are given.

In the region of Shokdu Chu, there is said to be a certain tree where such gods and demons were known to reside. Fearlessly, Nakpo Thokphen cut this tree down and concealed inside its trunk three drums that had been made by the Karma Ḍākinīs. These would later be retrieved by Nyima Drakpa during one of his many treasure excavations. In another episode, Nakpo Thokphen is called Nakpo Gung Phurwa, "Black Sky-Flyer," because he often soared through the sky wearing a black cloak. At Sok Langa Marpo, a group of cannibal demons (srin-po), all of them brothers, had nested in the area and had begun feasting on human victims. A mother and her daughter pleaded with Nakpo Gung Phurwa to help them. On the back of a vulture he flew to the peak of Drak Langa Marpo and instantly killed (lit., "raised the status," gnas-spar) the demon brothers. His valiant actions saved the life-force (srog) of many beings. Afterwards he took the daughter as his consort. From Dorje Nying Dzong, one of the three fortresses of Sin Dzong, he discovered the Pilgrimage Guide to Singmo Dzong [Sring-mo-rdzong-gi gnas-yig], and from the palace of Yumtsho he found hundreds of cattle and livestock, which he used in his pastoral work. When he had plowed the fields at Chakri Kha (also Chari and Chakru) he angered the local spirits, who in retaliation hurled thunderbolts at him. Without much effort he was able to catch the thunderbolts between the tips of his fingers and throw them back at the demons. The rocky mountain homes of these ferocious spirits were thus destroyed. Thereafter, he became known as Nakpo Thokphen, because he had tamed demons with thunderbolts and wrathful magic.

In a third episode it is related that a certain demon named Sokbom Dawa failed to offer alms to Nakpo Thokphen. Offended, the siddha literally cut out Sokbom Dawa's land from the earth and moved it elsewhere. Guru Tashi proclaims that in his day there was still an impression in the ground where this took place.[22] Again, Nakpo Thokphen was also called Nakpo Trhakyuk, "Black Blood-Vomiter," because he often vomited blood when he performed miracles or "liberated" (*bsgral*) hostile demons.[23] His descendants are said to have resided at the siddha's three main seats, the monasteries of Nemtshar Pangjin/Pangjip and Baden and Ka'ok Ngak Drong. In another source, Ka'ok Ngak is said to be the name of a community of Nyima Drakpa's followers at Chari (Chakru, Chakri Kha).[24] These disciples were renowned sorcerers popularly referred to as "exorcists under the *ka*" (ka-'og sngags-pa). Allegedly, the title alludes to the configuration of the mountains that encircled the village at Chari, a shape that resembled the first letter of the Tibetan alphabet (*ka*).[25]

What, we may ask, do these strange and colorful stories tell us about the historical figure of Nyima Drakpa? There are two answers that seem appropriate. First, the tales of the siddha Nakpo Thokphen in all his various guises may have served as a compelling way to illustrate, as well as to justify, certain prominent features of Nyima Drakpa's complex personality. From these legends, we learn that Nakpo Thokphen was of semidivine origin and had been raised partially by vultures, wild birds of prey noted for their savagery. His first encounter with a religious figure took place in Khyungpo, a famous Bonpo stronghold and home of the famed siddha Khyungpo Neljor. He, therefore, might have had early Bonpo associations, and possibly an early yogic training. As a siddha, through divine encounters with Vajrapāṇi, he developed special powers that gave him the ability to control and subjugate demons, which he was often called on to do. He was active in the hidden valley of Sin Dzong as an exorcist and revealer of treasure. His wrath was obstinate and vengeful but oddly compassionate. In the end, Nakpo Thokphen was shown to be a benevolent miracle-worker and a leader of monks. As I will show, all these traits without exception were also attributed to the figure of Nyima Drakpa. Second, these stories reflect the strong spiritual connection that existed between Nyima Drakpa, Chari, and the three hidden fortresses of Sinmo Dzong. The discovery by Nakpo Thokphen of the *Pilgrimage Guide to Singmo Dzong* served to foreshadow, and even validate, Nyima Drakpa's own efforts to open a pilgrimage path at Sin Dzong in 1704. So, in general, these stories about Nyima Drakpa's former rebirths might have been intended to introduce a certain credibility to his powerful historical persona.

Among some of the other notable reincarnations that clearly say something of his character, I should mention the names of Kathokpa Maṇi Rinchen of Bubor Gang,[26] Ngadak Kunga Lhündrup, the eleventh patriarch of the family of Nyangrel,[27] the great scholar Bodong Chokle Namgyel (1375–1451),[28] and Drigung Pholungpa Karma Samdrup of Barkham, master of the *Black Wrathful Goddess* [*Khros-ma nag-mo*]. This last figure immediately preceded Nyima Drakpa and belonged to the clan of his ancestry. All we are told about him is that he completed one hundred million recitations of the *Black Wrathful Goddess* by himself without assistance[29] and that he became expert in the practice of the "transference-transmission" (*'pho-lung*), which earned him his name. It would appear that Pholungpa Karma Samdrup was active in the area of Cham (probably Chamda near Driru), where it seems he once miraculously revived a dead deer by calling her consciousness back into her corpse. Later, at Nabün Dzong he left his footprint in stone. With Pholungpa Karma Samdrup the list of Nyima Drakpa's previous births is complete.

Many Meetings

In the Nangchen region where Rikzin Nyima Drakpa was born there was a famous tantric practitioner named Trhülzhik Chenpo, disciple of Pholungpa Karma Samdrup. According to the story, this tantrika Trhülzhik Chenpo perceived something special about the infant Nyima Drakpa and asked him point blank: "O dear son who are you? What do you have to say for yourself?" The boy responded: "I am Pholungpa Karma Samdrup!" at which point, Trhülzhik Chenpo recognized the little boy as his teacher's reincarnation.[30] The young Nyima Drakpa then proceeded to extract the treasure *Like a Wrathful Stone Dagger* [*Rdo'i-khro phur-'dra-ba*], which he presented to his father, Jame Önpo Karma Namgyel.

Nyima Drakpa's father and grandfather were faithful adherents of the Drukpa Kagyu tradition, and so at the proper age he was sent to his uncle's Kagyu monastery. There he received the refuge vows and the name Karma Trhinle. From a lama named Chibukpa Karma Jangchup he received the *Maṇi Kambum*, the *Biography of Jetsün Milarepa* [*Rje-btsun mi-la'i rnam-thar*], and the "reading" (*lung*) of the *Queen's Precepts* [*Sdom-btsun-ma*]. He also received a second name, Karma Mipham Trhinle Gyatso. His uncle taught him Butön's *Religious History* and the ritual cycles of the Drukpa Kagyu tradition. He then returned home to his father.

At a very young age, Nyima Drakpa had begun to have visions of Padmasambhava and developed an early interest in the Nyingmapa school. While at his uncle's monastery he was disheartened to find that the name of this great saint was rarely uttered and that his activities were never discussed. After his return home, Nyima Drakpa complained to his father and pleaded to be allowed to study with a Nyingma teacher. His father and older brother recommended the name of a lama in Nangchen and suggested that he go and visit with him. This teacher was Dzokchen Pema Rikzin, a nephew of Payul Kunzang Sherap, discussed in chapter 9. Pema Rikzin had recently been invited to the area by the king of Nangchen. At that time the king had also invited Karma Chakme. Nyima Drakpa met both lamas and received teachings from them, but it was Pema Rikzin who really impressed him most. It is even claimed that Nyima Drakpa knew at that very moment that this teacher had been his chief mentor in all his previous lives (*tshe-rabs-kyi bla-ma*) and that he would again become such a central figure in his present life.

Not long after, Nyima Drakpa met the treasure revealer Dudül Dorje of Derge when the latter was visiting Sharyi Phuk. Pema Rikzin asked Dudül Dorje whether Nyima Drakpa was actually the reincarnation of Pholungpa Karma Samdrup. The elder treasure revealer responded without hesitation that the young boy was unmistakably the rebirth of this great siddha. Dudül Dorje even acknowledged, moreover, that Nyima Drakpa was the doctrine-master (*chos-bdag*) of his own *Dagger* [*Phur-ba*] treasures. He requested that the young boy come visit him again after three or fours years when he had properly matured. In the company of Dudül Dorje, Nyima Drakpa underwent the tonsure ceremony and received his first Nyingmapa name, Orgyen Rikzin Namgyel. From Pema Rikzin he then received layman's vows and a second name, Orgyen Rikzin Gyatso. Then, in 1664, at the age of sixteen, Nyima Drakpa accompanied his teacher to Lhasa. The trip was the first of several key visits to central Tibet.

It was fortuitous that Nyima Drakpa met these three important lamas early in life, especially the great treasure revealer Dudül Dorje. This was a lama of impressive stature in eastern Tibet during the second half of the seventeenth century. He was well connected to all the major Nyingmapa monasteries in that region and had cultivated close ties with the rulers of Derge and Ling. In Derge his most influential patron was Jampa Phüntshok, a direct descendant of Derge's ruling family.[31] With the support of such high-ranking patrons, Dudül Dorje was able to carry out a number of important projects like the renovation of Kathok monastery and the construction of his own religious center in Derge.[32] It is significant that Dudül Dorje took such a liking to Nyima Drakpa. The connections they cultivated early on probably opened doors for the young treasure revealer in later years, especially in Ling and Derge, where he would come to wield considerable influence at the royal courts and with Jampa Phüntshok's principal successors at the family monastery of Lhündrup Teng.

For five years beginning in 1664, Nyima Drakpa traveled throughout much of central Tibet establishing connections with a number of important lamas. At Samye in 1665, he met the third Peling Sungtrül Tshültrhim Dorje, who had been visiting the area. This great lama bestowed on Nyima Drakpa, among other instructions, the *Longevity Practices* [*Tshe-sgrub*] of Pema Lingpa. We cannot be sure at this stage whether Peling Sungtrül Tshültrhim Dorje also granted his young student initiation into the cycle of the *Peaceful and Wrathful Deities*. Again we must bear in mind that it was the successors of Pema Lingpa's tradition at Lhodrak Lhalung that held the exclusive transmission of the *Liberation upon Hearing* and that Peling Sungtrül Tshültrhim Dorje was responsible for earlier calligraphing a manuscript edition of that special collection. Nyima Drakpa received this *Liberation upon Hearing* from Orgyen Rikzin Chögyel, a descendant of Pema Lingpa. Was it the case that Nyima Drakpa received this transmission at Lhalung sometime after his meeting with Peling Sungtrül Tshültrhim Dorje in Lhasa? We may never know the answer, but we do know that it was actually at Samye monastery in central Tibet, rather than Lhalung in Lhodrak, where Nyima Drakpa compiled his *Supplications to the [Karling] Lineage* [*Brgyud-pa'i gsol-'debs*] for the transmission he received from Orgyen Rikzin Chögyel.[33] Unfortunately, the texts do not specify exactly when or under what circumstances this occurred.

During these years, Rikzin Nyima Drakpa studied with the great teachers of central and southern Tibet, including Zhapdrung Pema Trhinle (1641–1717) of Dorje Drak monastery, from whom he received teachings from the Jangter or Northern Treasures tradition. Nyima Drakpa also visited some of the major religious institutions of that region, such as Mawachok, Guru Lhakhang, Kharchu Dujom Ling, and Chongye Pelri Thekchen Ling. At these sites he received the principal teachings of such luminaries as Nyangrel Nyima Özer (1136–1204), Guru Chöwang (1212–1270), Longchenpa, Orgyen Lingpa, and Sangye Lingpa (1340–1396). Finally, in 1668, Nyima Drakpa met up again with his root lama, Dzokchen Pema Rikzin, and together they traveled to Tsari on pilgrimage. Here, in the isolated hidden valley of Zaplam Dorje Rawa, Pema Rikzin entered strict retreat for three years. Nyima Drakpa joined him and began his yogic training. Often he would have to leave Tsari in search of provisions. It was during these times that he first began giving religious instruction in exchange for valuable goods and worldly commodities. From the retreat site, he would travel to Dakpo and Kongpo and receive huge and expensive offerings from the pious locals. This is our first indication of Nyima Drakpa's charismatic ability to arouse the faith of the masses and to charm them into heaping lavish gifts on himself and his followers. It would appear that he often had a difficult time maintaining his humility in the face of such bountiful adulation. As I will show, Nyima Drakpa's pride became a point of conflict between himself and his teacher Pema Rikzin.

In 1669, Nyima Drakpa had his second vision of Padmasambhava and received a treasure prophecy from him. While circumambulating Zhingkyong Ghayadara's Lake of Purple Blood (*dmar-nag-rakta*), he saw smoke rising from a boulder on the shore of the lake. He approached the smouldering rock and pushed a staff through it. In Tibet, piercing stones with sticks is an image traditionally associated with the subjugation of demons. From the stone he extracted his first certificate of prophecy (*kha-byang*), containing a list of hiding places, and three yellow manuscript scrolls (*gser shog-dril*).[34] His excitement was such that Pema Rikzin was forced to reprimand him. Over the next several years Nyima Drakpa had many more experiences of this extraordinary sort. His special status as a treasure revealer and fighter of demons was now quite apparent.

From approximately 1671 to 1674, Nyima Drakpa remained in retreat at Pelgi Khamshak Dorje Nying Dzong, one of the three fortresses of Sinmo Dzong. There he is said to have had a third vision of Padmasambhava and to have encountered a host of dangerous nonhuman spirits, which he was able to subdue through his yogic powers. These demons became his slaves, subservient to his every wish. Soon thereafter he received word from Pema Rikzin requesting that he come to Tsang.

On his journey west, Nyima Drakpa stopped again at Samye. The monastery had been severely damaged by fire, and a restoration project had been launched. To help fund the effort, Nyima Drakpa offered all the wealth of materials he had gathered from devotees along the way. Then in Lhasa he made offerings to the fifth Dalai Lama. We must assume that this was the beginning of Nyima Drakpa's favor and support among some of the preeminent leaders of Lhasa. He would eventually meet the young sixth Dalai Lama and develop a sort of patron-priest (mchod-yon) relationship, albeit somewhat strained, with the acting regent Desi Sangye Gyatso.

Nyima arrived in Tsang by way of Namtsho, a popular pilgrimage site (favored especially by Bonpos and Nyingmapas) north of the Nyenchen Thanglha mountain range.[35] He reunited with Pema Rikzin at the monastery of Dregön Sar in Dreyul (near Gongra and Dekyi Ling). There, from Drepa Jamyang Chögyel Dorje of Sikkim (1602–1677) and his son Nyida Longsel, he received Dzokchen instruction and the treasures of Tenyi Lingpa (1480–1535).[36] Later, during Nyima Drakpa's second visit to Dreyul, Jamyang Chögyel Dorje offered him the entire monastery of Dregön Sar as dedication for his introducing them to the treasure doctrines of Garwang Dorje, with whom Nyima Drakpa would share a close personal connection.[37]

In 1675, Nyima Drakpa and Pema Rikzin went on pilgrimage to Mount Kailash, where Nyima Drakpa performed several miracles. From Kailash, the two traveled further west to Ngari. It was here that Nyima Drakpa first met the treasure revealer Garwang Dorje. The latter presented his own treasure texts to Nyima Drakpa and admonished that he wait one year before opening their seal. In the meantime, Nyima Drakpa traveled on pilgrimage to Nepal and visited the sacred places at Swayambunath and the Kathmandu valley.

Upon his return to Ngari, he exchanged teachings with Guru Shakya Dudül, Gyel Thangpa Ngawang Zilnön Dorje, and Garwang Dorje. It is not specified whether the *Liberation upon Hearing* was among the teachings that Nyima Drakpa presented to these teachers, but it is clear that by this point he had become recognized as one of the chief holders of the Karling transmission. This fact is corroborated by Guru Tashi in his description of a significant episode that took place sometime around 1676 involving Nyima Drakpa and Garwang Dorje. According to the story, Garwang Dorje granted Nyima Drakpa the detailed initiations, readings, and sādhanas of three of his own treasure cycles, the *Mirror of the Enlightened Mind of Vajrasattva [Rdor-sems thugs-kyi me-long]*,[38] the *Unsurpassable Innermost Oral Lineage of Padmasambhava [Padma'i snyan-brgyud yang-gsang bla-med]*,[39] and the *Great Compassionate One, the Heart-essence of the Three Roots [Thugs-rje chen-po rtsa-gsum snying-thig]*.[40] During this transmission, Garwang Dorje recounted a recent dream about Nyima Drakpa:

> When you were coming here I had a pure vision that I discovered two thunderbolt-daggers [gnam-lcags phur-pa] and a skull-cup [kapāla] filled with wine. When I drank half of the wine I saw inside the skull-cup the blazing splendor of the five families of blood-drinking deities. This means that you have achieved the great power of the fierce mantras [drag-sngags].[41] You particularly hold the special authorized transmission of the *Self-Liberated Wisdom of the Peaceful and Wrathful Deities*, and so [with these teachings] you must work for the benefit of all beings. Moreover, from this point on your previous aspiration to

benefit the beings of the six regions of Dokham has come together and so you are specially authorized to bring benefit to them, as well. Consequently, I have great hope in you, so use your generated *bodhicitta* for the benefit of beings. From among my own treasure teachings, you are the chief doctrine-master of the *Oral Lineage of Padmasambhava*.[42]

After this, Garwang Dorje enthroned Nyima Drakpa as a "vajra king" (*rdo-rje gyal-po*), a tantric master, and granted him many offerings. He invited Nyima Drakpa to visit him again and promised that at that time he would give him the "inside scoop" (*nang-gtsang-gi gsung nang-ma*), as it were, presumably in regards to Garwang Dorje's own teachings. The brief account of the meeting between these two lamas tells us that Nyima Drakpa was perceived by Garwang Dorje and by his contemporaries as an accomplished exorcist, a master of "fierce mantras." Moreover, the dream itself provides us with another key indication of Nyima Drakpa's close connection to the treasures of Karma Lingpa. I already noted that Nyima Drakpa was believed to have previously taken birth in Dakpo as Karma Lingpa's consort. Garwang Dorje obviously felt that Nyima Drakpa was particularly qualified to transmit Karma Lingpa's *Peaceful and Wrathful Deities*. Nyima Drakpa must have already received these teachings and begun transmitting them to others. I would suggest that he had probably received the Karling transmission while he was traveling through Lhodrak around 1665, about a decade prior to his first meeting with Garwang Dorje. In the years leading up to this meeting, Nyima Drakpa must have bestowed the Karling initiations and instructions on many of the lamas he encountered during his extensive travels throughout Ü and Tsang. By the time he met again with Garwang Dorje, Nyima Drakpa had established himself as a principal holder of the Karling transmission. Indeed, this must certainly be the reason behind Garwang Dorje's pronouncement of Nyima Drakpa's special connection to the *Peaceful and Wrathful Deities*. I will show that his legacy in this regard has continued even down to the present.

The "Book of the Dead"

Nyima Drakpa remained quite active in Tsang and Ngari for several years. In 1676, he traveled to the region of Mangyul north of Mustang. From a temple called Jamdrin he discovered the *Great Compassionate One, Dispelling the Darkness of Ignorance* [*Thugs-rje chen-po ma-rig mun-sel*]. This treasure contained an extremely short piece entitled *Liberation upon Hearing, the Self-Liberation of Feeling* [*Thos-grol tshor-ba rang-grol*]. The text is extant in Nyima Drakpa's redaction of the *Liberation upon Hearing*, where it is usually appended to the end of the *Bardo Prayer That Protects from Fear*.[43] It may be recalled that this bardo prayer belongs to a set of three or four Karling prayers that are uniformly grouped together and incorporated into almost every edition of the cycles of the *Peaceful and Wrathful Deities* and the *Liberation upon Hearing*. Many of the verses of these prayers, including those of the *Bardo Prayer That Protects from Fear*, are also found embedded in the body of a few of the more elaborate Karling works, such the *Religious Liturgy of the Self-Liberation of Karmic Latencies* and the *Reminder of the Bardo of Reality-Itself*. I argued in chapter 7 that these bardo prayers actually constitute the essence of the teachings of the *Liberation upon Hearing* and that the more expansive bardo texts of the cycle were probably derived originally from them. The collective aim of these prayers was, and still is, to provide assistance to the deceased who is believed to be suffering from fear and anxiety in the bardo between lives. Appropriately, Nyima Drakpa's brief appendix to the *Bardo Prayer That Protects from Fear*, his *Liberation upon Hearing, the Self-Liberation of Feeling*, contains a mantra ostensibly given by Padmasambhava that needs only to be heard in order to secure a favorable rebirth.[44] The apparent intention on Nyima Drakpa's part in attaching this additional piece to the Karling prayer must have been to help fulfill the customary and well-established goal of ensuring for the dead a safe and successful journey upward.

According to its colophon, Nyima Drakpa transcribed the yellow scrolls for the *Liberation upon Hearing, the Self-Liberation of Feeling* (and presumably the entire *Dispelling the Darkness of Ignorance* cycle itself) in the sixth month of the iron monkey year 1680 at Padmasambhava's Black Cave at Sinmo Dzong.[45] From Guru Tashi we learn that this was the Black Cave of Chakru.[46] It was here that Nyima Drakpa entered into strict retreat for three years beginning in 1678. At the end of that period, he is said to have excavated three cycles of treasure and several multiplying buddha relics (*sangs-rgyas 'phel-gdung*).[47] In later years, he instituted the liturgies of two of these three Sin Dzong treasures as central practices at monasteries in Minyak and Derge. At Rikhu monastery in Minyak, he initiated the practice of the *Great Compassionate One, Dispelling the Darkness of Ignorance* and personally taught the monks how to perform the proper dances, chants, and ritual procedures. In Derge, he and king Tenpa Tshering instituted the liturgy of the *Profound Instructions on Wrathful Varāhī* [*Zab-khrid phag-mo khros-ma*] at Nyima Drakpa's main monastery of Takmogang.[48]

I mention these details in order to make two important points. First, I want to stress that clearly Nyima Drakpa's own treasure cycles were practiced in many parts of Tibet, particularly in Kham, and were even influential enough to be incorporated as liturgical centerpieces at major ecclesiastical institutions. This runs counter to what we might expect if we accepted at face value the implications raised by the conspicuous absence of Nyima Drakpa's work in such authoritative sources as the *Precious Anthology of Treasures*. I already suggested some of the reasons behind this inadequate representation. Second, Nyima Drakpa was actively composing and transcribing original doctrinal and liturgical works between the years 1678 and 1680. It is conceivable that at this time he was also editing religious works that he had received from other lamas while traveling throughout Tibet. In particular, during this period he possibly began collating the texts of the *Liberation upon Hearing*. At some point he appended to this his own *Liberation upon Hearing, the Self-Liberation of Feeling*, which he had first transcribed in 1680. The question, however, is when precisely all this was accomplished. Although he had probably begun to redact the Karling collection sometime between 1678 and 1680, he may not have finalized its arrangement until much later, possibly toward the end of his life. According to Guru Tashi, in the few years before his death Nyima Drakpa had settled down at his monastery at Takmogang and begun to compile textbooks on the practice of tantric meditation and the performance of rituals.[49]

We know the actual content and textual sequence of Nyima Drakpa's *Liberation upon Hearing* from modern facsimiles of several xylograph prints. It is regrettable that at this stage a manuscript or blockprint of Nyima Drakpa's original redaction has not yet been discovered. We thus cannot make the necessary critical comparisons between the earliest and more recent versions of this textual tradition. On the basis of the uniformity of the later facsimile editions, however, we can reasonably establish that his *Liberation upon Hearing* consisted essentially of the core set of texts discussed in chapter 7, including the requisite bardo prayers, the famous *Reminder of the Bardo of Reality-Itself* and the *Direct Introduction to the Bardo of Becoming*, as well as the fundamental peaceful and wrathful sādhana *Self-Liberation of Karmic Latencies*. The most distinctive feature of Nyima Drakpa's redaction is organizational. In each of its representative editions the fundamental works are placed invariably in the following order.[50]

1. *Reminder of the Bardo of Reality-Itself*
2. *Manifestation of the Bardo of Wrathful Deities*
3. *Prayer Requesting the Buddhas and Bodhisattvas for Assistance*
4. *Root Verses on the Six Bardos*
5. *Prayer for Deliverance from the Perilous Straits of the Bardo*
6. *Direct Introduction to the Bardo of Becoming*

This particular textual sequence is distinctive when compared to the few other available editions of the *Liberation upon Hearing*, including even the closely related manuscript edition preserved in the Waddell Collection of the British Library. This suggests that the foregoing arrangement is unique to the tradition associated with Nyima Drakpa. We can discern a certain conceptual logic in his arrangement. The materials are ordered in continuous sequence to lead from the ceremonies accompanying the moment of dying to those for the journey in the bardo after death and then to those for guidance into the next rebirth. In accordance with the customary doctrines of the Dzokchen tradition, these Karling texts describe the final moment of the dying process as marked by the sudden and dramatic appearance of the fundamental radiance of reality-itself (*chos-nyid*). To those who fail to recognize this luminosity at death, visions begin to emerge of a mandala of forty-two peaceful deities (text 1). On the fourteenth day, this peaceful mandala dissolves into the mandala of fifty-eight wrathful deities (text 2). The deceased awakens to these visions confused and frightened. Prayers are recited as humble petitions for comfort and security (text 3), for remembering important religious instruction (text 4), and for guidance through the perilous pathways of the bardo realm (text 5). After the visions of deities have subsided, the deceased acquires a mental body (*yid-kyi lus*) complete with all five senses and begins the descent to a new birth (text 6).

To the core texts just listed, Nyima Drakpa's *Liberation upon Hearing* adds the following titles, arranged exactly in the following order.

7. *Self-Liberation of the Body: Liberation upon Wearing*
8. *Bardo Prayer That Protects from Fear*
   (Appended: *Liberation upon Hearing, the Self-Liberation of Feeling*)
9. *Self-Liberated Omens and Signs of Death*
10. *Direct Introduction to Awareness: Self-Liberation through Naked Vision*
11. *Self-Liberation of the Bardo of Becoming: Instructions on "The Presentation of the Natural Form of Virtue and Vice in the Bardo of Becoming"*
12. *Supplement to "The Presentation of the Natural Form of Virtue and Vice in the Bardo of Becoming"*
13. *Supplications to the Lineage*
14. *Death Ransom, Self-Liberation of Fear*
15. *Self-Liberation of Speech: Confession to the Expanse of the Peaceful and Wrathful Deities*
16. *Liberation upon Wearing, Pure Wish-Fulfilling Jewel*
17. *Religious Liturgy of the Self-Liberation of Karmic Latencies*

Here we find emphasis on the purification of the sins of the departed through ritual actions and prayers devised to follow the deceased through the extended process of purification in the bardo and incorporation into a new existence. Specifically, the texts include cleansing mantras to be worn on the body (texts 7 and 16), a prayer for protection against fear (text 8), omens of impending doom and death ransoms (texts 9 and 14), a philosophical introduction to the nature of awareness (text 10), stories of postmortem judgment (texts 11 and 12), a lineage supplication (text 13), and the sādhanas of the *Peaceful and Wrathful Deities* (texts 15 and 17). The entire volume thus presents a clearly organized and complete program for the performance of the Karling funeral liturgy. This collection must surely reflect the particular perspective of its compiler. Ostensibly, Nyima Drakpa carefully prepared this specific sequence of texts in accordance with the perceived requirements and interests of his patrons and religious community. What precisely those needs and interests might have been is, unfortunately, a question that for now must remain unanswered.

Subjugating Demons

Sometime after 1682, Nyima Drakpa traveled south toward India. Guru Tashi remarks that at that time there was trouble in the region of Mön (on the border of Bhutan) between followers of the Gelukpa in Lhasa and the Drukpa Kagyu in Bhutan.[51] Consequently, Nyima Drakpa encountered some difficulty crossing through that area, but apparently through charm and graciousness he was able to finagle his way into India. There he was able to extract various treasures.[52] It is not clear how long he remained in India, but it is possible that around that time he also went to Bhutan before traveling again through Mön.

Nyima Drakpa's visit to Bhutan is not mentioned in Guru Tashi's account, although from other sources we know he spent some time in the eastern district of Tashigang. In the biography of the Bhutanese monk Se'ula Jamgön Ngawang Gyeltsen (1647–1732), we learn that while living in Derge as a kind of official ambassador (between 1688 and 1695), Ngawang Gyeltsen met briefly with Nyima Drakpa.[53] This Bhutanese monk had earlier observed at Phodrang Numda the rituals of the *Great Compassionate One, Dispelling the Darkness of Ignorance* from Nyima Drakpa's fifteen-volume collection of treasures.[54] At their meeting, we are told that Nyima Drakpa had once traveled to Tashigang in Shar and developed great faith in the Zhapdrung Ngawang Namgyel (1594–c.1651), although he was never able to meet him in person.[55] During his sojourns, Nyima Drakpa appears to have exerted some influence in both the eastern districts of Bhutan and in the Tawang region of Mön. Guru Tashi notes that he was rather active in these areas and had earned the respect of several prominent Bhutanese lamas.[56]

During the third month of 1684, Nyima Drakpa traveled back up through southern Ü and headed straight for the upper Drachi valley. Responding to a vision he had previously had in Nepal, Nyima Drakpa was intent on meeting with the illustrious treasure revealer Terdak Lingpa. When he arrived at the monastery of Mindroling (consecrated only about a decade before in 1676) he found that the monks were building the foundations for the lama's household (*bla-brang*).[57] It is alleged that Terdak Lingpa was quite delighted to see Nyima Drakpa, perhaps because he had brought with him "various earth, stones, and wood from the holy places around India, particularly a branch of the Bodhi Tree about the size of a forearm and covered with many leaves."[58] All of this Nyima Drakpa offered to Terdak Lingpa, who then recognized him as the secret doctrine-master of his own treasure cycle *Lord of the Dead, Destroyer of Vicious Demons* [*Gshin-rje dregs-pa 'joms-byed*].[59] Nyima Drakpa apparently accomplished its practices perfectly in secret. Later, it is said, he performed its rituals as "last rites" when he was near death, and only then announced publicly that he was practicing Terdak Lingpa's *Lord of the Dead* teaching. The secrecy that both lamas agreed to keep between themselves is reflected in their biographies. Guru Tashi notes that neither one said clearly the name of the other in each of the respective accounts of their meeting. The reason for such strict secrecy is not elucidated. I find it particularly intriguing that Terdak Lingpa did not acknowledge Nyima Drakpa's name when he described their first encounter; he simply called him "the Khampa pilgrim" (*khams-pa gnas-skor-ba*).[60] The central role that Terdak Lingpa would eventually play in the life of Nyima Drakpa's son, Orgyen Tenzin speaks volumes about how Terdak Lingpa truly viewed their relationship. This is a topic I will address shortly.

In 1687, Nyima Drakpa met with Pema Rikzin at Rudam Kyitrham near Derge. Acknowledging his disciple's talent for discovering concealed treasures through visionary means, Pema Rikzin asked his student to survey the area for any hidden objects. Nyima Drakpa remarked that the site was formerly a Bonpo holy place, but a Buddhist site was located just south of there.

At that instant, he had a vision of Padmasambhava and of some Bonpo Vidyādharas, and then a Bon treasure appeared magically in his hand. Pema Rikzin was not pleased. He ordered Nyima Drakpa to put back the Bon text and reconceal it as a "double treasure" (ldab-gter), admonishing him not to pick and choose between Buddhist and Bonpo doctrines.[61] Then, with the Derge king Sangye Tenpa acting as beneficiary, Pema Rikzin established the retreat center of Samten Chöling at this Buddhist holy place below the Bonpo site in the valley of Rudam. This retreat center became more widely known as Dzokchen monastery.[62] Afterward Pema Rikzin requested that Nyima Drakpa occupy the abbatial seat of this newly consecrated institution, but Nyima Drakpa graciously declined, citing passages from his own treasure prophecies that required that he travel constantly. Pema Rikzin gave him his blessing and advised him to obey the commandments of the treasure. It then appears Nyima Drakpa left his teacher and traveled north to the region of Ling.

I should pause here briefly to mention that after Nyima Drakpa's death Dzokchen monastery would become the main seat of his successive incarnations, the so-called Nyidrak Choktrül or Nyitrül line. The transmission of his teachings has continued at this institution down to the present in Tibet and even at the reestablished monastery in southern India.[63] Dzokchen monastery also became perhaps the first institution in Tibet to commission the preparation of a set of blocks for the printing of Nyima Drakpa's Liberation upon Hearing.

Sometime around 1690, Nyima Drakpa went to Langthang in Ling and stayed for awhile at a mountain hermitage. The leaders of that area had apparently developed great faith in him, for we are told that the chieftain of Ling, Dorje Gönpo, offered him the old monastery of Rigül and requested that he also consecrate a new religious center. Nyima Drakpa then built the mountain hermitage of Rezhek Zhechen. It is not clear whether this was the original site of what would become Zhechen monastery, which was formally established in 1735 by Gyurme Kunzang Namgyel (1710–1769).[64] Zhechen was a famous repository of woodblocks for the texts of the Peaceful and Wrathful Deities.[65] It is noteworthy that the Zhechen redaction of the Karling cycle contains relevant liturgical works written by Pema Rikzin and a text said to belong to the Four Initiations: Self-Liberation of Whatever Is Encountered. The first Zhechen Rapjampa, Tenpe Gyeltsen (1654–1709), was one of Pema Rikzin's principal students, and the second Zhechen hierarch was born into a family affiliated with the Dzokchen monastery. It is not inconceivable, therefore, that Nyima Drakpa would have had some influence on the development of the Zhechen tradition. It should be recalled that the cycle of the Four Initiations is known only to have been handed down through a single transmission line—identical to that associated with the Liberation upon Hearing— that eventually reached Nyima Drakpa. Thus the likelihood is quite strong that many of the texts and rituals of the Karling tradition were introduced into the liturgical program at Zhechen monastery by Nyima Drakpa himself or by one of his immediate successors from Dzokchen.[66]

In 1693, Sangye Tenpa invited Nyima Drakpa back to Derge. There he consecrated the religious center of Takmogang, which became his main seat.[67]

Nyima Drakpa offered Sangye Tenpa many priceless gifts, including various treasure objects, yellow scrolls, an image of Vimalamitra, the *Great Hūm-Dagger* (*Phur-pa hūṃ-chen*), the *Medicine Sūtra* [*Sman-mdo*], and an original manuscript and ink-pen (*phyag-smyug*) once owned by the eighth-century translator Lu'i Wangpo, which Nyima Drakpa had discovered as treasure. It would appear from all of this that the Derge ruler was particularly sympathetic to Nyima Drakpa. He also looked to him as a remarkable miracle-worker. As an illustration of their special connection, and of the treasure revealer's extraordinary powers, Guru Tashi tells the story of a Derge woman possessed by demons who had herself become a "living demon" (*gson-'dre*).[68] She had wandered off alone and lost her way. Upon her return, the demons would provoke her, particularly at night, to scream out "I am Orgyen Rinpoche!" or "I am Ling Gesar!" and she would then magically appear in their guise. Eventually, the woman started offering predictions and the local people developed faith in what she had to say. Sangye Tenpa had heard rumors about this female soothsayer and asked several lamas about her authenticity. Disappointed with their answers, he spoke with Pema Rikzin, who claimed that she had been cited in the treasure prophecy of Dudül Dorje and that Nyima Drakpa was the only one who could subdue her demons. Sangye Tenpa then invited Nyima Drakpa to his palace at Jangmeling and asked if he would destroy these demons who had come in human form. The treasure revealer promptly assumed the form of a wrathful deity and, with blazing samādhi (intense meditative concentration), exorcised (*bskrad-pa*) the evil spirits, sending them to a higher plane (*gnas-spar*). But Sangye Tenpa was not convinced that he had done the right thing, since there were so many people who still had faith in this woman. He sent a letter of request to Dudül Dorje and asked for divination. The old treasure revealer responded that demons are deceptive and, in human form, they appear normal to those who cannot see through the illusion. In reality, this woman had wanted to destroy the religious and secular rule of the Derge king. This demon needed to be eliminated, and vanquished she was.

In the end, Nyima Drakpa was lavishly compensated for his efforts by the Derge ruler. Needless to say, these two great figures shared a special bond. Perhaps it was this profitable connection that lay at the root of the inter–treasure revealer feuds, referred to at the beginning of this chapter, between Nyima Drakpa and Yonge Mingyur Dorje that resulted in the repudiation of the former by the Karmapa sect. We learn that this bitter rivalry extended also to the treasure revealer Takshampa Nüden Dorje (b. 1655), whose teaching-lineage was transmitted also through the Karmapa hierarchs.[69] As Dan Martin has suggested, all three were in positions to benefit from the patronage of the royal house of Derge.[70] To be sure there must be more to this contentious tale, but unfortunately all the facts have not yet surfaced.

Pema Rikzin died in 1697. Nyima Drakpa made all the necessary arrangements for the funeral services, made offerings to his teacher's corpse, and performed daily prostrations until his forehead began to bleed (*dbu-dpral nas sku-mtshal 'byung*). At the time, Pema Rikzin's "heart-son" (*thugs-sras*), the first Zhechen Rapjampa Tenpe Gyeltsen, was traveling to Lhokhok in the

Khardo valley near Riwoche, so Nyima Drakpa was given the responsibility of taking care of his teacher's affairs. The headmaster (*dpon-slob*) of Dzokchen monastery, Namkha Ösel, asked Nyima Drakpa repeatedly to take over Pema Rikzin's seat, but the treasure revealer responded that he had already declined the invitation before when his teacher had earlier made the same request. Sometime later he went back to Takmogang and built a thirty-three-storied stupa in honor of his teacher.[71]

At some point during his travels through Minyak and Lithang, Nyima Drakpa ended up in Sok Zamkhar (Zamtsha, Dzamthang?), where he met two emissaries of the Lhasa government (*gzhung sa-chen*), Kachu Ngawang Pelgön and Zhönu Lodrö.[72] Apparently they had already been informed about Nyima Drakpa, either with regard to his earlier efforts to assist in the renovation of Samye or perhaps to his supposed connection through prophecy with the Dalai Lama. To tell this story, however, I must return to one of Nyima Drakpa's earlier visits to central Tibet sometime around 1682. At that time, he had just recently come out of retreat at Sinmo Dzong. Drawing on both prophecy and his own favorable experiences in Lhasa about a decade prior, he realized that there were auspicious connections between himself and the fifth Dalai Lama (here referred to as *gong-sa*, "sovereign") and that the latter was intended to be his chief doctrine-master. However, there would be great obstacles on their path. On several occasions during this period Nyima Drakpa had wanted to speak with the Dalai Lama, but he was not able to break through the bureaucratic barriers blocking him from the highest ranks of the government. Consequently, the auspices between them degenerated. Of course, Nyima Drakpa had no way of knowing at that time that the fifth Dalai Lama was already dead. He died in 1682, but his regent, Desi Sangye Gyatso, concealed this fact and pretended for fifteen years that the Dalai Lama was living in strict retreat.[73] It is no mystery why Nyima Drakpa was never permitted an audience with his prophesied disciple.

Nyima Drakpa was clearly troubled by these constraints. He had asked some other Nyingmapa lamas in the area to go to Lhasa in his place and to speak on his behalf, but they too were unsuccessful. In this context, Guru Tashi quotes a cryptic passage from the fifth Dalai Lama's own secret prophecies (*gsang-lung*):

> Even though the sun shines on the peak of the eastern mountain,
> if obscured by white clouds it does not appear.[74]

The message was clear. Nyima Drakpa and the fifth Dalai Lama were not destined to meet, despite forecasts to the contrary. Two other prophetic verses suggest, moreover, that there were to be some false and even dangerous friends along the way, wolves in sheep's clothing, as it were: "The snake's sharp poisoned tongue [when] stretched out is two-pronged."[75] And again:

> The sheep and wolf sit together,
> but the shepherd sees no reason to separate them.[76]

Guru Tashi informs us that Nyima Drakpa had actually put his trust in the wrong people. Out of jealousy, we are told, those Nyingmapa go-betweens delivered a distorted message, and so the doors to the offices of the Dalai Lama were closed to him. But almost a decade later, certain lines of contact would be reopened again.

At Sok Zamkhar, Nyima Drakpa was venerated by the two government representatives, with whom he discussed his previous attempts to make contact with the ruler of Lhasa (*gzhung-sa*). In particular, he explained to them that prophecy had indicated that an auspicious patron-priest relation was to prevail between himself and Tibet's leader (*gzhung-sa*), but because the latter was such a highranking official both were unable to fulfill the promise. The Lhasa emissaries agreed to pursue the matter with the proper authorities. They seem to have been successful, for shortly thereafter Desi Sangye Gyatso sent an order to Nyima Drakpa that he should come quickly to Lhasa.

In Lhasa, Nyima Drakpa made prostrations and offerings to Desi Sangye Gyatso and to the young sixth Dalai Lama Tshangyang Gyatso, who had only recently been enthroned in 1697.[77] No mention is made of the concealment of the fifth Dalai Lama's death. In accord with Desi Sangye Gyatso's wishes and despite broken auspices, Nyima Drakpa accepted this "protector of the land" (*sa-skyong*) as his student and bestowed his teachings on him.[78] Guru Tashi indicates that despite a positive reception there was some uneasy tension between this patron and priest. For reasons not clearly specified, Desi Sangye Gyatso scolded Nyima Drakpa about his late arrival to Lhasa. As I understand this fragmented account, perhaps Nyima Drakpa was supposed to have come to the capital city much earlier in order to help restore various holy places (as he had done previously at Samye), but because of his failure to network his way into the inner sanctum of the Lhasa government, he was unable to establish contacts with either the Dalai Lama or his acting regent. To be fair, these were indeed some troubled times in Lhasa. Consequently, neither of the two leaders realized that Nyima Drakpa had actually made several unsuccessful attempts to reach them. From their perspective, then, he must have appeared indolent and unreliable. This was not the first time Nyima Drakpa provoked negative feelings in those around him. Certainly, there must have been some layer of truth in the biased portrayals of him as arrogant and boastful. Nonetheless, I think it is telling that someone as politically significant as Desi Sangye Gyatso would have actively sought him out as a teacher. If for a moment we try to imagine the political chaos that was ensuing during those years in central Tibet, then my point is all the more striking. It is not unreasonable that Nyima Drakpa would have actively taken advantage of this sort of political clout to better promote his own ideas. Indeed his fame and success among some of the most prominent leaders in central and eastern Tibet was arguably the result of a potent combination of some key religious and political factors. Doubtless the initial impetus for the widespread appeal of the *Liberation upon Hearing* can be traced to this well-connected sorcerer from Kham.

Before the Mongolian warlord Lhazang Khan assumed full political control of Lhasa, Nyima Drakpa had already fled south to Lhogyü to avoid possible persecution by the Khoshot leader and his Manchu supporters.[79] As the story goes, the patron-priest relationship he had previously shared with the Lhasa government grew cold, for obvious reasons. The profitable relations he had cultivated with the former Tibetan administration had not carried over to the new Mongol regime. We can assume that he was not fully aware of the tumultuous circumstances that led to the government takeover in Lhasa, for he initially made attempts to meet with Tibet's new ruler (presumably Lhazang Khan). As would be expected, he was not successful. Discouraged, and maybe even a bit fearful, he fled to Lhogyü, to some area near the sacred site of Guru Dorje Gyelpo. It was there in the south that Nyima Drakpa began his efforts to refurbish some of the sacred sites in that region. After awhile he received auspicious signs through divination and so he sent a certain Dortshang Trhinle Dorje to Lhasa with a formal letter of request. The response from the new ruler was apparently positive, and he was granted the permission to continue his restoration work. Eventually he worked his way back toward the eastern regions between Powo and Dome, where he is alleged to have renovated and constructed more than fifty stūpas. In 1703 he established the retreat center of Chakru (Char) Ösel at Sin Dzong, which earned him the moniker Char Nyima Drakpa. At the behest of one Gyatön Lozang Lekpa, he also founded the monastery of Dekyi Ling. The next year he opened the pilgrimage path at Sin Dzong Ne, which is said to have been as distinctive as that of the Rongkor at Tsari.[80]

During this period, Nyima Drakpa's reputation seems to have taken a turn for the worse. It is at this point in the narrative that Guru Tashi describes briefly the antagonistic encounters with Yonge Mingyur Dorje and Takshampa Nüden Dorje and his group. In addition, Guru Tashi relates an episode reflecting the sort of mob hysteria that the fearsome Nyima Drakpa was apparently capable of instigating. While the treasure revealer was restoring a certain holy place in the Tamda valley of eastern Tibet, some of the people in the area began to assume, for unspecified reasons, that Nyima Drakpa was practicing black magic (*mthu-gtad*). Outraged, the villagers razed the temple he had just built and from the rubble extracted a *linga*, a type of effigy used in certain rituals of destruction.[81] This device the angry mob then flaunted at the king as proof of Nyima Drakpa's ongoing nefarious activities. To the people's dismay, the king spoke out in support of the treasure revealer and denounced those who had destroyed his auspicious building.

Should we accuse these villagers of planting evidence? In this tale we do find grounds for suggesting that Nyima Drakpa had begun to irk some of those around him to the point that they began indicting him of some very serious offenses. Although we should remain open to the possibility that there might have been some truth to these rumors, it seems a bit extreme to assert that Nyima Drakpa was acting solely as a malicious sorcerer. Instead I am inclined to believe that there was something slightly less exotic about their antagonism; a sort of contagious hostility that appears to have reached a feverish level only toward the end of his life and continued long after his death. A second observation may provide the necessary clue. The king of the Tamda valley region championed the treasure revealer even against apparent mass condemnation. Such unqualified and enthusiastic support from high-ranking leaders and aristocrats seems to have been one of the hallmarks of Nyima Drakpa's career. Clearly, the esteem in which he was held by the aristocracy of his day was largely due to his perceived magical power and skill at subjugating evil forces. In a world driven by religious commerce between potent priests and wealthy donors threatened at all times by destructive demons, it is no mystery why this formidable treasure revealer would be despised and discredited by some who would view him as rival. In this light, it also seems to me that Nyima Drakpa's reputation as a subduer of demons and other evil manifestations of the dead must have surely contributed to his charisma as the unparalleled master of the *Liberation upon Hearing*.

Nyima Drakpa went back to Derge and renewed his connections with the ruling family. By this point, Derge had come under the control of Chögyel Tenpa Tshering, the fortieth king of Derge and concurrently the fifth abbot of the Sakya monastery of Lhündrup Teng.[82] Tenpa Tshering made offerings to the treasure revealer, and in return Nyima Drakpa bestowed his own teachings on him. A story is told that at that time there was a war in Lithang between a certain Sokpo Gomang Chöje and Derge. Nyima Drakpa invoked a great wrathful deity with a fearsome retinue and commanded that they attack the enemy forces. Shortly thereafter Derge emerged victorious. The people claimed that the battle was won through the combined powers of Nyima Drakpa's magic and his divine loyal protectors. Consequently, the treasure revealer was touted as a religious hero, and everyone developed great faith in his abilities, although Tenpa Tshering was still a bit skeptical. He asked Nyima Drakpa to prove to him that his powers were genuine. The treasure revealer then proceeded to recount his many war stories celebrating his success in subjugating innumerable demons over the years. Tenpa Tshering is said to have been promptly convinced of the treasure revealer's prowess. Then Nyima Drakpa performed a ceremony for the king and granted a prophecy that he would remain a prosperous and successful ruler throughout his life. Afterward, he returned to his former seat at Takmogang.

From 1706 onward, Nyima Drakpa remained at his monastery where he concentrated on teaching and granting initiations to his students. There he gave transmissions of his own treasure teachings freely to those disciples prophesied to be masters of his teachings. During this time, he also composed many textbooks on the generation and completion stages of tantric meditation. In addition, he wrote down a variety of liturgical instructions on how to accomplish initiations, visualize mandalas, construct rituals, and so forth. It seems reasonable that in this period Nyima Drakpa may also have compiled and edited the writings of other authors that he had wanted to include in the library at Takmogang. These books would have been intended to reflect the individual character and customs of that institution. Among these works I would imagine the *Liberation upon Hearing* was one that stood prominent, since Nyima Drakpa was reputed to have been one of its special conservators. The question remains, however, whether he had commissioned the production of blocks for its printing. We do know that only within a few decades after Nyima Drakpa's death one blockprint of his *Liberation upon Hearing* was prepared at Dzokchen monastery, but we still have no information about the format of the original on which this print was based.

In the final analysis, I have shown that Nyima Drakpa was not only a leading protagonist in the diffusion of the famed *Liberation upon Hearing* but also a prosperous and successful religious celebrity. His personal involvement with many of the influential leaders of central and eastern Tibet during the latter half of the seventeenth century afforded him direct access to elite levels of society, where he was rewarded lavishly for his skill as exorcist and magician. As revealed in later legend, however, Nyima Drakpa's mastery of such arts did not always merit praise. In later years he was occasionally persecuted by the people around him, and attempts were made to discredit his reputation; subsequent generations even went so far as to exclude him from the historical record. Although the sources are mute on this point, it would appear that a possible reason for clashes between him and some of his contemporaries was not so much a rejection of his magical facility as to the degree of influence he exerted in the social arena. To be sure, his favored status among certain aristocratic patrons and the wealth and prestige he had garnered as a result of his perceived ability to destroy demons and liberate the dead, as well as his apparent aggressive self-assurance, angered and challenged those who stood to benefit from the very same benefactors. Ironically, it was his magic, attractive to so many people during his lifetime, that later opponents would proclaim was the cause of his scandalous fall from grace. But in true conformity with Tibetan hagiography, his supporters would counter by depicting Nyima Drakpa as nothing less than a saint locked in combat with enemies who had become through woeful ignorance the real embodiments of evil. In this regard, Guru Tashi defends Nyima Drakpa, suggesting that those who protest too insistently against him may actually themselves be the problem.[83]

It also seems possible that as master of Karma Lingpa's *Peaceful and Wrathful Deities*, and of the *Liberation upon Hearing* in particular, Nyima Drakpa might have adapted and manipulated this cycle of treasure teachings to better suit his own personal ambitions. As noted in chapter 4, Tibetan funeral rituals always require the performance of exorcisms. In Tibet, demons and death are intimately linked. Those who are skilled in dealing with one are by necessity skilled in dealing with the other. Nyima Drakpa's power over demons must certainly have contributed to his charisma as master of the dead. This would have surely helped also in promoting the authority of his own teachings, and particularly of his own interpretations of the rituals accompanying the *Liberation upon Hearing*, over and against those of the more prestigious treasure revealers whose practices had been well established with stronger political affiliations (e.g., Terdak Lingpa with his ally the fifth Dalai Lama, or Takshampa Nüden Dorje and the Karmapa). Nyima Drakpa's charismatic power would have helped to ensure the popularity of his *Liberation upon Hearing* within those communities that had been introduced to it. This may also give us another perspective on the nature of his troubled relations with other competing religious leaders. Whatever the case, after Nyima Drakpa's death, his

Liberation upon Hearing certainly grew to be enormously popular and came to achieve widespread distribution throughout Tibet and surrounding countries. What may have been some of the factors that made this possible?

Two Streams Converge

Nyima Drakpa is said to have sired three sons, but the only one who survived childhood was Orgyen Tenzin Drakpa (alias Guru Sönam Tenzin), who himself only lived for twenty-seven years.[84] This son became the second abbot of Takmogang and an essential link between the so-called Char Nyidrak tradition, affiliated with Nyima Drakpa, and that of Mindroling, affiliated with Terdak Lingpa. Orgyen Tenzin's role as mediator between the two traditions, however, would not be fulfilled until after his father's death in 1710. According to Guru Tashi, just before Nyima Drakpa died he made several requests for his funeral and left instructions on how to handle the affairs of his surviving son. First he asked that his corpse be preserved intact and that a golden mausoleum be constructed to house his remains. Second, in his final testament he requested that the famed leader of Mindroling, Terdak Lingpa, be invited to assist in the preparation and performance of the funeral services, and, most important, to help raise his young boy, Orgyen Tenzin. Nyima Drakpa's disciples promised to fulfill these final requests.

In the iron male tiger year 1710 Rikzin Nyima Drakpa passed away.[85] Several of his students traveled promptly to the monastery of Mindroling and made offerings of dedication to Terdak Lingpa. They told him what Nyima Drakpa had requested in his final statements, and the "king of treasure revealers" responded:

> Although it may have appeared that we were not very good friends, in truth we were. [Nyima Drakpa] was the secret doctrine-master of the cycle of the *Lord of the Dead [Destroyer of Vicious Demons]*. He perfected its practice and kept it secret. Consequently, our lives continued and our religious activies were greatly enhanced and indeed we even became healers of the [Buddha's] teaching. Now, he has died and that is not good. But I will do whatever needs to be done for his son [*rgyal-sras*].[86]

Terdak Lingpa then announced that the two separate teaching-lineages of Char Nyidrak and Mindroling would from this point on be viewed as one lineage, a single tradition. Afterward arrangements were made to send Nyima Drakpa's son to central Tibet. We must not ignore Terdak Lingpa's admission that he and Nyima Drakpa were close comrades despite perceived animosity. Again we find reference to a secret bond shared between them, but still we cannot explain why they felt it necessary to conceal their friendship. In terms of the secrecy of the practice of the *Lord of the Dead, Destroyer of Vicious Demons*, Terdak Lingpa does give some hint as to why he may have felt indebted to Nyima Drakpa. As I noted earlier in chapter 5, treasure revelations were frequently kept secret for a variety of reasons, although the basic motivation was probably nothing more than to regulate the proliferation and dispersal of these sorts of teachings. In addition, there always seems to have been a certain mistrust of the whole process involved in discovering hidden treasures. In this light, emphasis on secrecy can thus be seen as a means to avoid undue criticism. Whatever the case, the point that should be stressed here is that failure to adhere to the code of secrecy, once stipulated, was believed to result in either the diminishment of the treasure's effective power or, worse yet, endangerment of the life of its discoverer. So, when Terdak Lingpa announced that Nyima Drakpa was true to his word and succeeded in keeping the *Lord of the Dead* practice secret for so long, he was in a sense saying that he owed Nyima Drakpa his very life. This is one of the ways history can justify Terdak Lingpa's adoption of Nyima Drakpa's son, Orgyen Tenzin, and the merger of two different transmission lines.

We should be clear that the convergence of these two traditions did not entirely originate in the person of Orgyen Tenzin. Remember that the Mindroling tradition of Karma Lingpa's *Peaceful and Wrathful Deities* was actually formed by the conjunction of three distinct transmission lines, two of which emanated from Gyarawa Namkha Chökyi Gyatso and a third from Gönpo Dorje of Kongpo. Gönpo Dorje transmitted the single lineage of the cycle of the *Four Initiations* and, it would appear, of the *Liberation upon Hearing* as well. It was this single transmission line that through separate channels eventually reached both Terdak Lingpa and Nyima Drakpa. We see this common source reflected clearly in the transmission lists included in some modern Bhutanese editions of the *Liberation upon Hearing*[87] and in Terdak Lingpa's own *Transmission Record*. I can argue, therefore, that by the end of the seventeenth century the textual tradition of the *Liberation upon Hearing* in Tibet was held and maintained exclusively by the Mindroling and Char Nyidrak traditions—the latter preserved most effectively by Nyima Drakpa's successors at Dzokchen monastery in Kham. By this I do not wish to suggest that the two textual lineages were in no way distinct. Although they share a common lineal ancestry, their different textual histories, degrees of editorial revision, varying content, and so forth meant that the respective textual collections would be somewhat idiosyncratic.[88] In the end, we can say with little doubt that the *Liberation upon Hearing* as we know it today was produced in Tibet by the crossfertilization of certain old textual transmissions belonging originally to the Tsele/Lhalung line and later maintained at Mindroling and Dzokchen.

This specific hybridization is perhaps best illustrated by the example of Nyima Drakpa's son. Guru Tashi reveals that Orgyen Tenzin, who was given the name Orgyen Gyurme Tenphel Gyatso by Terdak Lingpa, his refuge lama, actually received the Karling initiations not from his own father but from Terdak Lingpa's second-oldest son, the second Minling Trhichen Pema Gyurme Gyatso.[89] In addition, from Terdak Lingpa's younger brother, Lochen Dharma Shri, Orgyen Tenzin was granted the "book-authorization" (*pod-lung*) of the *Peaceful and Wrathful Deities*, which presumably meant that he was given copies of the texts. Orgyen Tenzin would later transmit these teachings to Nyima Drakpa's first incarnation, the third abbot of Takmogang Pema Thekchok Tenpe Gyeltsen (1712–1774).[90] In 1755, this lama bestowed the Karling transmission on the third Dzokchenpa Ngedön Tenzin Zangpo, who would later take up the task of arranging the texts and preparing the blocks for what may have been the first printed edition of the *Liberation upon Hearing*. In the last chapter, I will survey what we presently know about the history of the different blockprints and modern facsimiles of the *Liberation upon Hearing* and close with a few final thoughts.

12 🍂

Conclusion: Manuscripts and Printed Texts

In the late eighteenth century, Nyima Drakpa's arrangement of the *Great Liberation upon Hearing in the Bardo* was preserved, perhaps for the very first time, in a blockprint edition prepared at Dzokchen monastery by the third Dzokchenpa Ngedön Tenzin Zangpo.[1] It was this edition that provided the basis in Bhutan for the Bumthang redaction (B2) published in 1952 in memory of the second king of Bhutan, Jikme Wangchuk (1926–1952).[2] Presumably, the Dzokchen blockprint also formed the basis of an earlier Bhutanese edition prepared in Paro in 1943 through the efforts of one Norbu Zangpo, then the Bhutanese Lochak (*lo-phyag*) to the Lhasa government.[3] This Paro redaction, reprinted in various forms (B1, B1a, B4, DH), has since become the most widely available edition of the *Liberation upon Hearing* outside Tibet.

At present the history of the Karling tradition in Bhutan remains obscure, and we do not yet know the specific circumstances involved in the introduction of the Dzokchen blockprint to the printing houses in Bumthang and Paro. The traditions of Dzokchen monastery never seem to have been established in any particular institution in Bhutan.[4] We must assume, then, that the favorable contacts in the previous century between Nyima Drakpa and some of Bhutan's political leaders, such as the ambassador Se'ula Jamgön Ngawang Gyeltsen, must have been at least part of the reason Nyima Drakpa's *Liberation upon Hearing* was accepted in that country. But can we extend this reasoning to explain how Nyima Drakpa's redaction came to be the most commonly represented edition of the *Liberation upon Hearing* in other parts of the Himalayan region, including northern India, Nepal, and Sikkim, and is now preserved also in the west in libraries in London, Berlin, and the United States? We cannot be sure. Perhaps it was simply Nyima Drakpa's power and influence in Tibet that helped to popularize his textual traditions throughout

205

widely diverse localities. A more compelling answer, if there is one, will have to await the appearance of more detailed records, or new insights from the sources already consulted. What we can say for certain, however, is that Nyima Drakpa's *Liberation upon Hearing* was truly the *editio princeps* of the first western-language translation of *The Tibetan Book of the Dead* published in 1927. At the very least this fact stands as certain evidence of the enduring influence of Nyima Drakpa's legacy.

Editions of the *Liberation Upon Hearing*

Since no attempt has been made so far by Tibetanists to collect and collate the editions of the *Liberation upon Hearing*, the textual history of the different print and manuscript versions has remained largely unknown. In this section, then, I will survey the collections that either are presently extant or are known to have existed at some point.[5] The purpose of this survey is to provide a succint overview of some of the main points of the history of the texts themselves. It is my hope that such an overview will help to encourage a more balanced and contextualized approach to the study of the *Liberation upon Hearing* in the future; an approach in which the focus is as much on the role of historical development as it has been on doctrinal content. Except for the first entry listed, the editions are arranged in roughly chronological order, determined by date/period of production or publication, or in certain cases by date of acquisition. In the descriptions that follow, special note should be taken of the many editions of Nyima Drakpa's redaction.

Dawa Samdup/Evans-Wentz Editions

The first western-language translation of the *Liberation upon Hearing*, *The Tibetan Book of the Dead*, by Kazi Dawa Samdup and Walter Y. Evans-Wentz was based on four separate Tibetan editions:[6]

1a. *Darjeeling Edition.* An illuminated manuscript arranged as one work in two parts with thirteen folia of prayers. According to Evans-Wentz, this text was from Darjeeling and in the possession of a young Zhamarpa lama who claimed that it had been passed down through his family for several generations. The Zhamarpa connection here is particularly significant, since we now know that a number of followers of this Karma Kagyu subsect were among the most active promoters of Karma Lingpa's textual tradition. As I have shown, moreover, the pivotal monasteries of Dakpo Tsele and Kongpo Thangdrok shared close alliances with the hierarchs of this tradition.

1b. *Van Manen Edition.* A blockprint arranged as two separate texts, without the usual prayers as an appendix, belonging to Johan van Manen. Evans-Wentz indicates that this and the Darjeeling manuscript are identical. The present location of this particular van Manen print is unfortunately not known, but several incomplete versions of the *Liberation upon Hearing* can be found in the Johan van Manen collection housed in the Library of the Kern Institute, Leiden.[7] The relationship between this incomplete set of prints and the print referred to by Evans-Wentz is not clear. Henk Blezer has suggested, however, that some of the Leiden prints appear to be older versions of the reprint collection currently published in Dharamsala, India (DH).[8] This Dharamsala collection is actually a photographic reproduction of a print from Bhutanese blocks prepared at Paro in 1943 (BI, BIa, B4). The year 1943 was also the year of van Manen's death, which means the Leiden prints probably date earlier than the Paro edition and its Dharamsala reprint. The Leiden prints at the Kern Institute, therefore, might include the van Manen texts that were used by Dawa Samdup and Evans-Wentz. Nevertheless, both sets of van Manen prints were clearly derived from the same source as the Paro edition; that source is, of course, the textual tradition of Rikzin Nyima Drakpa.

IC. *Gyantse/Tengyeling Edition.* A blockprint comprising seventeen individual texts, the titles of which are listed in a note by Evans-Wentz.[9] This edition was purchased in Gyantse in 1919 by Major W. L. Campbell, who was then the British political officer in Sikkim. The blocks from which this print was struck were preserved at the monastery of Tengyeling in Lhasa, once affiliated with Samye but now abandoned.[10] Some prints from the same blocks are kept at the British Library.[11] From Evans-Wentz's list of titles and in light of information provided in the colophon of one of its texts, the *Supplications to the Lineage* (BL 3282), we can be sure the Tengyeling print represents Nyima Drakpa's edition. The colophon reads: "This series of supplications was composed by the incarnate treasure revealer Rikzin Nyima Drakpa at Dudül Ngakpa Ling. May it long abide as inexhaustible as the flow of [the river] Ganges."[12]

Dudül Ngakpa Ling is a tantric chapel attached to the southern Aryapalo temple at Samye monastery. It is likely, therefore, that since Tengyeling had also been affiliated with Samye, the Karling blocks housed at Tengyeling may have been derived from Nyima Drakpa's textual preparations at Dudül Ngakpa Ling. Perhaps even the carving of the Tengyeling blocks had been commissioned originally by Nyima Drakpa himself. We should be aware, however, that the Tengyeling printery also stored print blocks produced and transported from many different locations.[13] Thus the blocks for Nyima Drakpa's redaction might actually have been produced earlier at another institution before being moved to Tengyeling.[14] This Tengyeling edition was possibly used as the basis for the Paro prints.

Id. *Unidentified Edition.* A manuscript belonging to Kazi Dawa Samdup. No information provided.

Waddell/Lhalung Edition

An incomplete manuscript collection of the *Liberation upon Hearing* purchased by the British Museum from Lieutenant Colonel L. Austine Waddell as early as 1898.[15] As I argued in chapter 10, information in a colophon of this collection suggests that the manuscript was probably prepared in the last half of the seventeenth century by the third Peling Sungtrül Tshültrhim Dorje or by one of his immediate disciples. The collection most certainly represents a redaction of the Karling transmission handed down at Lhalung monastery in Lhodrak.[16] It was this textual tradition that was received by both Nyima Drakpa and Terdak Lingpa, each through separate channels.

Waddell/Lhasa Edition

During the Younghusband campaign of 1904, a vast amount of original Tibetan manuscripts and blockprints were collected for the British Museum and the India Office Library under the supervision of Waddell. Among these materials was included a small manuscript collection of the *Liberation upon Hearing*, which is now preserved in the Lhasa collection of the India Office of the British Library (BL OR Tib I 228)[17] (see fig. 12.1). Dieter Back presumed a very early date for this manuscript edition of the *Liberation upon Hearing* and used it as his base text to critically compare other variant editions.[18] Internal evidence, however, suggests that the texts were compiled in the nineteenth century with a probable connection to the tradition of the great Rime treasure revealer Chokgyur Dechen Lingpa (1829–1870).[19]

FIGURE 12.1. Manuscript pages of the Lhasa edition of the *Great Liberation upon Hearing in the Bardo*, nineteenth century. (Reproduced by permission of The British Library, Oriental and India Office Collections)

Waddell/Berlin Edition

The Waddell holdings at the British Library only cover one part of Waddell's collection. Another significant selection of his Tibetan texts was acquired by the former Prussian state library in Berlin, the Staatsbibliothek Preussischer Kulturbesitz.[20] This collection includes a blockprint of the *Liberation upon Hearing* whose content bears a striking resemblance to the Paro and Lahul-Spiti (T3) editions.[21] This similarity suggests that the Berlin prints, like those of Paro and Lahul-Spiti, were derived from Nyima Drakpa's textual tradition.

Genden Phüntshok Ling Edition

A publication list (*par-tho*) for the printing house of the Jonangpa-affiliated Genden Phüntshok Ling was prepared in 1874 by Zhalu Ribuk Tülku Losel Tenkyong (b. 1804).[22] Two Karling print blocks are found in that list, the *Complete Liberation upon Hearing* [*Thos-grol yongs-rdzogs*] and the *Self-Liberation of Karmic Latencies* [*Bag-chags rang-grol*].[23] We do not know the provenance of these texts, but the blocks must date from before the first half of the seventeenth century before the monastery was converted by the Gelukpa. It is conceivable that the texts represent the Lhalung tradition of Peling Sungtrül Tshültrhim Dorje, who is known to have been a student of Jonangpa Tāranātha (1575–1634).[24]

Potala Edition

A rather extensive collection of Karling manuscripts is held in the Potala Library in Lhasa.[25] Unfortunately, the texts are kept under official seal, and permission to access the holdings is difficult, if not impossible, to obtain. Thus we do not yet know the provenance of this Karling collection. Nevertheless, we can assume that at least some of the texts represent the special Karling transmissions received by the fifth Dalai Lama.[26]

Prague Edition

Josef Kolmaś has provided brief details on a fragmented and incomplete manuscript collection of some *Liberation upon Hearing* texts extant in the Library of the Oriental Institute, Prague.[27] However, not enough information is available to determine their provenance.

Lahul-Spiti Edition

The only *Liberation upon Hearing* collection that is explicitly identified in the bibliographical record as having been edited by Rikzin Nyima Drakpa himself is the blockprint edition preserved at Khangsar Dzong in Garzha, Lahul-Spiti (T3). This print was prepared in the nineteenth or early twentieth century from blocks whose origins remain unclear at this point. The important fact, however, is that the content and textual sequence of this edition is essentially identical to the Paro edition and facsimiles, which lends further support to the claim that both the Lahul-Spiti and Paro print sets represent the arrangement of Nyima Drakpa's *Liberation upon Hearing*.

Paro Edition

The printing blocks of the Paro edition were carved in 1943 through the efforts of Lochak Norbu Zangpo and preserved at the Kyechu Lhakhang.[28] My feeling is that this popular blockprint collection was based on the Tengyeling edition, which itself was probably based on an earlier edition prepared by either the third Dzokchenpa Ngedön Tenzin Zangpo or the first Nyitrül (Nyidrak Choktrül) Pema Thekchok Tenpe Gyeltsen. The facsimile reprints from these Paro blocks (BI, BIa, and DH) are now the most widely available versions of the *Liberation upon Hearing* outside Tibet, in India, Nepal, and Bhutan.

Bumthang Edition

The blockprint edition from Bumthang (B2) is explicitly said to be based on an edition of the *Liberation upon Hearing* that was originally arranged for publication by Ngedön Tenzin Zangpo at Dzokchen monastery. The Bhutanese blocks themselves were prepared in the water male dragon year 1952, commemorating the death of king Jikme Wangchuk, and subsequently preserved at the royal palace of Tashi Chöling. This Bumthang edition reflects Nyima Drakpa's textual tradition.

Gangtok Edition

The blockprint edition from Gangtok, Sikkim (SI), was arranged at the behest of one Kunzang Gyatso and printed under the auspices of the Dolung Chipön.[29] This Gangtok arrangement served as the basis for the Kalsang Lhündrup manuscript.

Kalsang Lhündrup Edition

A modern calligraphed manuscript edition first published by Kalsang Lhündrup (KS) in 1969. Both this and the Gangtok blockprint edition of the *Liberation upon Hearing* are derived from an identical Karling source, the syncretic Zhechen transmissions of Dilgo Khyentse Tashi Peljor (1910–1991). The two editions are thus closely tied also to the Karling traditions followed at the Mindroling and Dzokchen monasteries.

Closing Reflections

Looking back over this study, I sense more sharply than ever the difficulty of giving clear and unambiguous answers to the riddles posed by my sources. I have had to accept that many of the statements I have made about the history of Karma Lingpa's *Self-Liberated Wisdom of the Peaceful and Wrathful Deities* and the *Great Liberation upon Hearing in the Bardo* may not necessarily correspond to the past as such, to what "really happened." That past is available to me only through fragments and traces left behind in texts, and those texts were determined in large measure by their own unique function and purpose within very specific contexts often contrary to my own. Thus, among all the statements that could be made about these texts, the conclusions that I offer, although derived from a carefully selected and balanced review of the available data, may be nothing more than my own picture of the past: an educated impression of a perceived unity of "facts" that could be said to be neither entirely true nor entirely false. To be sure, the integrity of my impressions can be guaranteed only by the questions posed and the evidence I choose to highlight. That being said, I hope that more complete evidence will eventually come to light about this literature and that the story presented here might inspire scholars in the future to ask different questions, to clear up some of the doubts, or perhaps even to reject my picture altogether. In light of this, I believe a few concluding remarks and suggestions for further research are in order.

When I was conducting field research for this project among several Tibetan exile communities in India, I asked many lamas and monks about the *Peaceful and Wrathful Deities* and especially the *Liberation upon Hearing*. Invariably, I was told how frightening the bardo could be and about the importance of studying the bardo doctrines. But when I would ask again specifically about the textual tradition of the *Liberation upon Hearing* itself, I often met with blank expressions. A few monks, however, told me about the first time they actually read the text, which was almost always at a very young age.[30] Interestingly, and for reasons still unknown to me, in those cases the *Liberation upon Hearing* had served as a sort of primer for learning the Tibetan language. Other monks promised to show me their own personal copies of the "Liberation upon Hearing." When I finally had the chance to see these copies, I was disappointed to learn that none of the texts had any connection whatsoever to Karma Lingpa's *Liberation upon Hearing*; they were copies of prayers or short texts written by some local lama from the monk's home village. Frustrated I asked myself what did all this mean? It was clear first of all that the Tibetan phrase *bardo thödröl* (*bar-do thos-grol*), "liberation upon hearing in the bardo," meant something entirely different to me than it did to the Tibetans I met in India. For most of them the title referred generally to any doctrine that had the bardo as its main focus, and particularly any doctrine intended to assuage the fear and anxiety of those destined to travel in the bardo. For a few others, the title evoked childhood memories of learning to read for the first time or of the guiding advice of beloved teachers back home. But for me *Liberation upon Hearing* meant a particular body of literature vaguely fixed in time and place, a hidden treasure believed to have been discovered in the fourteenth century by a treasure revealer named Karma Lingpa and rediscovered in the early twentieth century by Walter Y. Evans-

Wentz. For me, the *Liberation upon Hearing* was *The Tibetan Book of the Dead*, plain and simple.

I have since determined that in Tibet and neighboring communities the *Liberation upon Hearing* must have undergone what I playfully call the "kleenex effect." In other words, the *Liberation upon Hearing* started out in Tibetan history with a distinctive identity, a brand name so to speak, but over time and with repeated and widespread use that brand name turned into a generic label for all similar products. The title *Liberation upon Hearing* thus became a floating referent for a sort of public domain type of doctrine. Consequently, Tibetans nowadays tend to think of it as a generic but no less effective teaching on dying and the bardo. As such, for many Tibetans the *Liberation upon Hearing* has no real history in the sense of being tied to a specific compositor and historical tradition.

Oddly enough, a similar impression has emerged and persisted in Europe and America, where *The Tibetan Book of the Dead* has been typically perceived in abstraction as ancient scripture conveying a universal wisdom. This view, like the perspective of contemporary Tibetans, has tended toward an implicit denial of the relevance of the text's history. I cannot help noticing that even in academic studies on *The Tibetan Book of the Dead* few attempts have been made to explore new layers of the primary sources. The authors of both popular and scholarly books on this subject have been satisfied to interpret the texts along similar lines, consistently ignoring the particulars of the formation and distribution of these texts in time and place. Questions of the meaning and significance of *The Tibetan Book of the Dead* must be answered by evidence from its history. It was for the purpose of recovering that history that I undertook this project.

I have shown that the Karling treasure tradition originated in Dakpo sometime in the fourteenth century, was institutionalized in Kongpo in the last decades of the fifteenth century, and was subsequently disseminated throughout Tibet, particularly in the southern districts around Lhodrak and in the eastern region of Kham. The tradition was transmitted in two basic streams. The first was passed between multiple teaching-lineages leading from the lama Nyida Özer of Longpo, and the second came through a single lineage emanating from the lama Gönpo Dorje of Kongpo. Nyida Özer's transmission seems to have consisted mainly of the cycle of the *Peaceful and Wrathful Deities*, including advanced instructions on the six bardos (namely, the cycle of the *Guiding Instructions on the Six Bardos* and the *Great Bliss of the Lower Orifice*). The alternate transmission of Gönpo Dorje, on the other hand, consisted essentially of the *Four Initiations: Self-Liberation of Whatever Is Encountered*. His lineage, moreover, appears to have had some special hold on the *Liberation upon Hearing* transmissions.

Between the fifteenth and early sixteenth centuries, the *Liberation upon Hearing* was received principally through the hierarchs of the Dakpo Tsele and Kongpo Thangdrok monasteries in southeastern Tibet. The particular character of the *Liberation upon Hearing*, distinct from the principal texts of the larger *Peaceful and Wrathful Deities*, was perhaps initially formulated at these two ecumenical institutions. Eventually the transmission was passed to Tülku Natsok Rangdröl at Dargye Chöding monastery, which in that period was the main center for the practice of Dzokchen in central Tibet. The cycle was then transmitted through the Peling Sungtrül and Peling Thukse incarnations at Lhalung monastery in Lhodrak. Historical evidence suggests that the Karling tradition maintained at this important southern establishment held the primary, if not exclusive, transmission of the *Liberation upon Hearing* in Tibet throughout the sixteenth and early seventeenth centuries. This might explain why we do not find some of the most definitive texts of the *Liberation upon Hearing* (e.g., the *Reminder of the Bardo of Reality-Itself* and the *Direct Introduction to the Bardo of Becoming*) in any of the textual collections preserved at Kathok, Payul, or other eastern Tibetan institutions. In this regard, however, we should not ignore the fragmented evidence of an earlier and alternative eastern Tibetan tradition fostered at Zurmang monastery, or also a possible teaching-lineage in the Rong district of Tsang as early as 1485.

The strong Lhodrak Lhalung affiliation meant that the *Liberation upon Hearing* tradition must have been known also in eastern Bhutan at that particular stage in its history. As Michael Aris has pointed out, the monasteries of both territories were in constant contact until recent times. In Tibet, this so-called Tsele/Lhalung transmission was passed in two streams through the Peling incarnations residing in Lhodrak. The first was transmitted through the successors of Tülku Natsok Rangdröl, including most notably Terdak Lingpa and his immediate family at Mindroling in central Tibet. The second line was passed through Rikzin Nyima Drakpa and his lineal descendants at the monasteries of Takmogang and Dzokchen in Kham. Both streams converged in the person of Orgyen Tenzin, Nyima Drakpa's son. But it was Nyima Drakpa himself who, at the beginning of the eighteenth century, first standardized the *Liberation upon Hearing* collection. It was his redaction that was used, quite unintentionally, as the basis for the first western-language translation by Kazi Dawa Samdup in 1919. As we well know, this translation was christened by its editor, Walter Y. Evans-Wentz, with the title *The Tibetan Book of the Dead* and published in 1927.

I set out in this book to explore the origin and circulation of the treasure literature of Karma Lingpa. In so doing, I wanted to avoid some of the pitfalls of earlier studies by focusing my attention on historical context, on the details of lineage and institutional history. I was convinced that a systematic examination of such details ought to be the first task in reconstructing the larger picture. I was not interested, therefore, in generalizing too broadly about the array of ideas and practices pertaining to death and the dead found among Tibetan communities throughout history. Rather I was interested in the history of a particular body of Tibetan literature widely associated with death, dying, and the dead. In the bewildering diversity of manuscripts and blockprints of the Karling tradition, I saw clear indications of development over time and a history that could only begin to be exposed after a meticulous sorting of data and piecing together of fragmented and often conflicting details. Careful and patient attention to the diverging contents of the numerous literary collections, to the scattered and all too frequently deceptive references in the individual texts themselves, and to the patterns of relations exposed in the seemingly endless list of personal names of teachers and their disciples revealed the hazy contours of a dynamic and complicated history that has not been articulated until now. I hope this study has succeeded in providing a vantage point from which to begin to clarify some of the mysteries of this story.

Some readers may feel that the specificity of this study eclipses the more general questions of the religious and social meanings of death and funeral ritual in Tibet. My attention to such broader questions was restricted largely by the limitations of the sources consulted. In tracing the diverse movements of the Karling textual tradition through time and space, I relied primarily on several types of archival and historical records and the ritual books themselves. Tibetan archival documents like the transmission records (*gsan-yig*), lineage lists (*brgyud-rim*), and catalogues (*dkar-chag*), although quite valuable in many respects, frequently provide only the bare minimum of information pertaining to the social and cultural details of text and transmission. Likewise, the ritual books, since they were largely produced for and by monks or lamas already familiar with the accompanying rituals, usually give only the essential components of the formal ritual service. Absent are any references to the peripheral social activities involved in the performance itself. The ritual books thus illuminate only obliquely the liturgical life of the monastic community and rarely if ever shed light on the attitudes and behavior of Tibetan society at large. What still needs to be creatively explored, then, are the ways that the beliefs and practices surrounding death in premodern Tibet were integral to daily life both within and outside the monastery.

Again, in reviewing the range of materials covered in the course of writing this story, I am struck by just how much investigation is still required to understand the true depth of social context in which the books and rituals of the Karling tradition were embedded and through which they were made meaningful. In addition to the suggestions just made, a critical study is much needed of Tibetan books more generally, with special focus on the social and historical circumstances involved in their production and circulation. Texts are always produced with specific audiences in mind, and thus they never exist in isolation from their social and political environments. Invariably, throughout Tibetan history, the production and transmission of literary works has necessitated the close collaboration between compositor and institution. Therefore, we are also in great need of a thorough history of patronage in Tibet, and of relations between the monasteries and local laity vis-à-vis the history of books. In this case in particular, we stand to benefit from a more in-depth examination of the monasteries of Dakpo Tsele, Kongpo Thangdrok, and Lhodrak Lhalung for the light that may be shed on relations between the ecclesiastical and secular leaders of Dakpo, Kongpo, and Lhodrak and between the Nyingmapa and Kagyupa orders in those provinces in the fifteenth through seventeenth centuries. More precisely, in the case of Tsele and Thangdrok we might even uncover the events that led to the formation and eventual decline of these two notoriously ecumenical institutions, and learn also about the precise role the *Liberation upon Hearing* played in the liturgical lives of the local population.

As for the later history of the *Liberation upon Hearing* from the eighteenth century onward, a thorough study of the Khampa tradition, particularly in Derge and its general vicinity, promises to contribute much to our knowledge about the Karling tradition in eastern Tibet. The social and political history of the monasteries of this region is a rich topic that has been relatively neglected in the scholarly literature. There is much need for research on the monastic communities and liturgical customs of, for example, Kathok monastery, which is arguably the oldest and most widely influential Nyingmapa institution in Kham. The later Dzokchen monastery also deserves more focused attention. In this regard, I can only hope that more evidence soon comes to light about Rikzin Nyima Drakpa, who, as I have shown, was certainly an influential and powerful presence in the late seventeenth century not only in Kham but also throughout much of Tibet and Bhutan. Nyima Drakpa's hostile reputation, alleged violent activities, and posthumous and deliberate exclusion from history are subjects that are certainly worth further investigation. In the end, no matter what the focus, questions of historical context must always prevail.

Notes

1. Introduction

1. Biographical information on Walter Y. Evans-Wentz can be found in Winkler 1982.

2. Evans-Wentz and Dawa Samdup [1927] 2000, p. 68.

3. A brief biography of Kazi Dawa Samdup is provided in Fields 1992, pp. 285–287. This lama had produced his own *Tibetan-English Dictionary* in 1919 and had worked previously as translator for a number of notable personalities, including Alexandra David-Neel (1868–1969), Sir Charles Bell (1870–1945), Sir John Woodroffe (alias Arthur Avalon), and Major W. L. Campbell.

4. Tucci [1949] 1972; Fremantle and Trungpa 1975; Dargyay 1991 (first published in German, 1977); Kara 1986; Thurman 1994; Prats 1996; Hodge and Boord 1999. Gyurme Dorje has also announced a new translation forthcoming from Penguin Books (e-mail communication, May 1999).

5. Lauf 1977; Lati Rinbochay and Hopkins 1979; Back 1979, 1987; Lama Lodrö 1982; Kunsang 1987; J. Reynolds 1989; Chökyi Nyima Rinpoche 1991; Sogyal Rinpoche 1992; Trungpa 1992; Tenga Rinpoche 1996; Blezer 1997; Gyatrul Rinpoche and Wallace 1998; Fremantle 2001.

6. Mori, Hayashi, and McLean 1994.

7. van Itallie 1998.

8. Gorn 1983.

9. In this regard, Dargyay 1991 had already noted that "c'est le mérite incontestable d'Evans-Wentz d'avoir rendu le Bardo Thödol plus célèbre en Occident qu'il ne l'était en Orient" (p. 42).

10. Lopez 1998, p. 47. I do not wish to suggest, however, that the proliferation of multiple commentarial voices was confined solely to Europe and America. Tibetans themselves have long possessed great skill in creative elaboration and imaginative invention in matters of textual interpretation. Lopez's position on this issue has been the subject of some criticism. See especially Germano 2001.

11. Evans-Wentz and Dawa Samdup [1927] 2000 was the one responsible for christening the texts of the *Bar-do thos-grol* with the title *The Tibetan Book of the Dead*. He did this deliberately in order to convey "to the English reader the true character of the book as a whole" (p. 2 n.1). Evidently, he had chosen this particular title in hopes that it might be better recognized by a wider audience already captivated by the *Egyptian Book of the Dead*, which had been published much earlier, in 1897. See Budge 1985.

12. Evans-Wentz and Dawa Samdup [1927] 2000: "This, he thought, would not only help to justify his translation, but, moreover, would accord with the wishes of his later *guru* with respect to all translations into a European tongue of works expository of the esoteric lore of the Great Perfectionist School into which that *guru* had initiated him" (p. 1, n. 1). That "guru" of Dawa Samdup was a certain Bhutanese lama named Slob-dpon Mtshams-pa-nor-bu, and the Great Perfectionist School to which he ascribed is, of course, the Rdzogs-chen tradition. I have not yet identified this Mtshams-pa-nor-bu, but I will have much to say about his school and its relationship to *The Tibetan Book of the Dead* in chapter 3.

13. The vast majority of scholars who have written on the topic of *The Tibetan Book of the Dead*—although occasionally working from the original source materials—have tended to base their interpretations on long-outdated and uncritical secondary opinion. Evans-Wentz's book, and the successive generations of commentaries and new translations that it inspired, has remained the standard point of reference for most experts. Why does this popular literature continue to be accepted so uncritically as a valid and authoritative source on the topic? Surely the fact that there have been far too few critical studies of the *Bar-do thos-grol* and related matter must be at least part of the answer.

14. See Brauen and Kvaerne 1978a, p. 10.

15. Consider, for example, the following declaration, so emblematic of this presupposition as to appear generic: "There is a mechanism in the purified individual which expands the consciousness to share an ever-present ocean of truth and wisdom infinitely beyond the limitations of a single brain and senses. In ancient times this was the prime means of knowledge, and provided mankind with an unexcelled wisdom. The divine inspirations of the great sages and religious geniuses of the past have been recorded in sacred scriptures like the present work." Michael Lord, introduction to Evans-Wentz and Dawa Samdup [1927] 1973).

16. Bishop 1993, p. 73.

17. Lopez 1998, p. 72.

18. For further discussion see the essays collected in Lopez 1988. This twofold Buddhist hermeneutical trope can be traced to India as far back as the *Saṃdhinirmocana-sūtra*. Snellgrove 1987, pp. 94–95; Williams 1989, pp. 78–80.

19. Evans-Wentz and Dawa Samdup [1927] 2000, p. 34.

20. Blavatsky was perhaps an exception to this general rule, for apparently she was opposed to Darwin, whom she playfully labeled her "baboon." Washington 1995, p. 45. But even she, it appears, could not escape the appeal of the evolutionary model. See discussion in Lopez 1998, pp. 49–52. Actually, much of Evans-Wentz's evolutionary focus rested on the authority of the anthropologist Edward Burnett Tylor. Evans-Wentz and Dawa Samdup [1927] 2000, pp. 59–60. It was Tylor's intention to demonstrate the continuity of human culture by proving the theory that civilization was the result of a gradual process of growth, adaptation, and evolution, from an original primitive state to one of increased complexity, such as that witnessed in the societies of modern Europe. This theory of the progress of human development also had a profound effect on the work of the infamous James Frazer.

21. Evans-Wentz and Dawa Samdup [1927] 2000, pp. 42–43.

22. Evans-Wentz and Dawa Samdup [1927] 2000, p. 59.

23. Evans-Wentz and Dawa Samdup [1927] 2000, pp. 54–55.

24. This was typical of the view of Victorian scholars regarding the history of Buddhism in India, and particularly of Tantrism, which was seen as the final stage in the utter degeneration of "original Buddhism." The work of L. Austine Waddell (1854–1938) serves as a fine example of such a viewpoint. See Waddell [1895] 1972.

25. More detailed criticisms of Evans-Wentz can be found in Reynolds 1989, pp. 71–115; Bishop 1993, pp. 53–76; Lopez 1998, pp. 46–57, 63–71, 2000.

26. Thurman 1994.

27. Thurman 1994, p. 51.

28. Thurman 1994, p. 33.

29. Thurman 1994, p. 81.

30. Jung's commentary originally appeared in the 1938 Swiss edition of *The Tibetan Book of the Dead*, *Das Tibetanische Totenbuch* (Zurich: Rascher Verlag).

31. Evans-Wentz and Dawa Samdup [1927] 2000, p. xxxvii.

32. For an insightful critique of Jung's interpretations of Asian thought, see Gómez 1995.

33. Evans-Wentz and Dawa Samdup [1927] 2000, p. xlix.

34. Govinda [1969] 1989.

35. Evans-Wentz and Dawa Samdup [1927] 2000, p. lix.

36. Evans-Wentz and Dawa Samdup [1927] 2000, p. lix.

37. Fremantle and Trungpa 1975, p. 1.

38. Fremantle and Trungpa 1975, p. 2.

39. Fremantle (2001) has recently attempted to provide a more contextualized interpretation of the main concepts behind *The Tibetan Book of the Dead*, but still few details are offered about the history of those concepts or of the Tibetan book itself.

40. Evans-Wentz and Dawa Samdup [1927] 2000, p. 35. This quest for common origins was the hallmark of the early twentieth century comparative mythologists led chiefly by Georges Dumézil. Basic to Dumézil's approach was a fundamental proposition that similarities between linguistic, mythic, and sociocultural data point to common origin. Myths, religious narratives, and so forth, were thus best interpreted in terms of the extent to which they reflected common ideologies. This stance has been criticized for its lack of historical sensitivity. Some critics have cautioned that efforts to reconstruct through comparative evaluation common prototypes or proto-patterns without paying close attention to specific localized contexts lead ultimately to generalist and universalizing conclusions. See Dumézil 1973; Lincoln 1981b; Littleton 1982; also the critique of Dumézil in Puhvel 1987.

41. Lopez 1998, p.

42. Evans-Wentz and Dawa Samdup [1927] 2000, p. lix.

43. Leary, Metzner, and Alpert 1964.

44. Dargyay 1991. Dargyay's translation, first published in German in 1977, was prepared in collaboration with Geshe Lobsang Dargyay and includes a preface by Lama Govinda. For what it is worth, Dargyay evokes the "trope of the esoteric meaning" in her introduction: "Cette nouvelle traduction présentée ici devrait permettre d'avoir en mains un texte lisible et compréhensible, transmettant le sens implicite du texte original, s'écartant le moins possible du mot tibétain" (p. 42).

45. J. Reynolds 1989. This is a translation of Karma-gling-pa, *Rig-pa ngo-sprod gcer-mthong rang-grol*, which is included in several Tibetan editions of the *Bar-do thos-grol*. Reynolds's book includes a forward by Namkhai Norbu.

46. Prats 1996.

47. Gyatrul Rinpoche and Wallace 1998. This is a translation of the *Bar-do drug-gi khrid-yig* (often abbreviated *Bar-do khrid-yig*) and several other texts belonging to the larger Kar-gling literary cycle. Wallace's translation is accompanied by the oral commentary of Gyatrul Rinpoche.

48. Evans-Wentz and Dawa Samdup [1927] 2000, p. lxiii.

49. Bishop 1993, p. 73.

50. Tucci [1949] 1972.

51. Back 1979.

52. Back 1987.

53. Blezer 1997.

54. Tucci [1949] 1972, p. 77.

55. Back 1987, pp. 5–19.

56. Blezer 1997, pp. 67–93.

57. Martin 1998a, p. 106.

58. Tanselle 1992, p. 16.

59. Situated roughly in the western direction of Jālandhara (Za-hor), Kashmir (Kha-che), and Gilgit (Bru-sha).

60. Uray noted that this mountain was the sacred site of an ancient cult centered on the deity Dwags-lha Sgam-po, who is known from Dunhuang sources as the god of Dags-shul. See Uray 1988, p. 1506. Elsewhere we read that the mountain was variously referred to by the names Sgam-po Dpal-ri, Sgam-po-gangs, and Dag-lha Sgam-bu. Its chief deity was said to have been the ruler of all the *sa-bdag*, the "earth-masters" of Dwags-po. See Nebesky-Wojkowitz 1956, pp. 221–223, 229.

61. The Sgam-po-gdar treasure site is said to have "resembled a dancing servant deity" (*lha-bran gar-byed-pa 'dra-ba*). There has been question as to whether this phrase refers to the name of the excavation site itself or simply to its description. According to the suggestion made by Geshe Phema Tsering (Bonn) to Dieter Back, the expression refers to two different size mountains, Sgam-po-gdar being the smaller of the two. In this regard, *lha-phran* is taken to mean "the smaller one of a divine pair." See Back 1987, p.10 n. 26.

62. On the myth of Gri-gum-btsan-po in the Dunhuang documents, see Macdonald and Imaeda 1978–79, pp. 21–31; Bacot, Thomas and Toussaint 1940, pp. 123–124; Haarh 1969, pp. 402–403; Gibson 1991, pp. 118–123; and, in later Tibetan Buddhist records, see especially GLRB, pp. 55–57; Sorensen 1994, pp. 141–144; Sakyapa Sonam Gyaltsen 1996, pp. 82–83.

63. Tucci 1950.

64. Haarh 1969, p. 18.

65. A thorough history of reading practices and of the use of texts in Tibet is an important desideratum. See comments in Kapstein 2000, pp. 78 and 237 n. 75.

66. For a marvelous study of such uses of scripture in China, see Teiser 1994.

67. Snellgrove & Richardson 1986, p. 139 and 160; Harrison 1996, p. 81. For reflections on the history of printing in central Tibet see Jackson 1983, 1989b, and 1990; Kuijp 1993, and Schaeffer 1999. On the beginnings of xylography in China, see Drège 1986.

68. Skilling 1991, p. 138, commenting on the proliferation of printed editions of the *Bka'-'gyur* and *Bstan-'gyur* during this period. See also Mayer 1996, pp. 233–235 on the first xylographic print of the *Rnying-ma rgyud-'bum* (Sde-dge edition) in the late eighteenth century.

69. Included in the Pelliot and Stein collections. See Lalou 1939–61; Macdonald and Imaeda 1978–79; Savitsky 1984.

70. In Europe, I should mention the Tibetan manuscript collections of the British Library (Denwood 1976; Pagel 1997), the Russian Academy of Sciences in St. Petersburg (Schmidt and Böhtlingk 1847; Pagel 1997), the Library of the Oriental Institute of Prague (Kolmaś 1969), and the Staatsbibliothek Preussischer Kulturbesitz in Berlin (Schuh 1981, 1985). Some of the more noteworthy Tibetan manuscript collections in Asia are held at the Library of the Cultural Palace of Nationalities in Beijing (Nakane 1999, p. 45) and in India at the Library of Tibetan Works and Archives (J. Shastri 1983; L. Shastri 1990, 1995).

71. The United States Library of Congress (LC) collection of Tibetan literature, instituted under the directive of Public Law 480 (PL 480), is certainly the largest repository of Tibetan language books in the western hemisphere. The immense value of the PL 480 collection is beyond dispute, but it does have its limitations; for example, the collection comprises only those Tibetan language materials printed in India since 1964. Some of these reproductions, however, do include copies of early manuscripts that had been preserved in the libraries of Tibet, as well as impressions made from woodblocks dating back to the eighteenth century. For a general discussion of the PL 480 program, see Schoening 1988; also Smith 2001, pp. xi–xii.

72. Many of the Bka'-brgyud monasteries in the Dwags-po region were forcibly converted over to Dge-lugs-pa institutions in the seventeenth century, such as the monastery of Dwags-po Bshad-grub-gling, which had previously been the seat of the Zhwa-dmar-pa. By the end of the seventeenth century that institution had become the main settlement of the Dge-lugs-pa monks of Dwags-po Grwa-tshang. See Nornang 1990; Dorje 1996, pp. 285–286.

73. Skorupski 1982; Boord 1993.

74. Wylie 1965, esp. p. 238 and 241.

75. Snellgrove 1987, pp. 453–454.

76. LGNB. A transcription and translation of this work is included in Cuevas 2000, pp. 378–407.

77. On the meaning of these categories, see particularly Vostrikov 1970, pp. 139–145; Gyatso 1993, pp. 110–126; Kuijp 1996, pp. 46–47; Martin 1997, p. 13. For specific details of sources consulted, refer to the discussion in chapter 5.

78. Only a handful of scholars actually have recognized the utility of these texts, see particularly Tucci 1949, pp. 95, 124–125; Vostrikov 1970, pp. 199–202; Savitsky 1970; Ehrhard 1993; Kuijp 1995; Martin 1997, p. 16; Gyatso 1998, p. 104.

79. DLSY and TLSY, respectively. Other gsan-yig of note are those of Gnyos-ston Dpal-ldan-bzang-po (1447–1507), Blo-bzang-'phrin-las (b. 1642), Zhabs-drung Gsung-sprul I Phyogs-las-rnam-rgyal (1708–1736, ZDTY), Khams-sprul VI Bstan-pa'i-nyi-ma (1849–1907), and Bdud-'joms-'jigs-bral-ye-shes-rdo-rje (1904–1987, DJTY).

80. On gdan-rabs, see Vostrikov 1970, pp. 88–92; Martin 1997, p. 14.

81. On autobiography in Tibet, see the recent work of Gyatso 1997 and 1998.

82. TSNG.

83. TLNT.

84. GKCB, pp. 820–860.

85. On dkar-chag, see E. Smith 1970; Martin 1996a.

86. Chandra 1981.

87. On the structure and content of Tibetan colophons and their potential value for textual historians, see Cabezon 2001.

2. Beginnings

1. The term is short for *srid-pa'i bar-ma-do* and equivalent to the Sanskrit *antarābhava*.

2. Dunhuang was a settlement on the trade routes through Central Asia controlled by the Tibetans in the seventh and eighth centuries. Samuel 1993, p. 442. Much of what scholars know of the ancient Tibetan kingdom has depended to a great extent on the manuscripts recovered from this site and preserved in both the Bibliothèque Nationale, Paris (Pelliot Collection) and the British Library, London (Stein Collection). Materials for the study of these important texts can be found in Lalou 1939–61; Bacot, Thomas, and Toussaint 1940; Macdonald and Imaeda 1978–79.

3. Karmay 1998, p. 290; also Macdonald 1971, p. 218.

4. Snellgrove 1987 has insisted that "the activities of *bon* and *gshen* as functionaries of early Tibetan religion is one thing; a constituted Bon religion is another". (p. 403 n. 47).

5. The distinction between Buddhism and Bon has been a topic of some controversy among scholars. The interpretation of Bon that has been largely accepted in academic circles was first formulated in Snellgrove 1967b and 1987. An opposing opinion is supported in Karmay 1998, esp. pp. 157–168; see also the response to Karmay's argument in Stein 1988b.

6. Karmay 1991 has defined the *bla* as "a support upon which the physiological and intellectual aspects of life rest. It is thus considered the most important of the three physiological principles, which also include 'respiratory breath' (*dbugs*) and 'vital force' (*srog*). 'Vital force' is as essential as the *bla*, but 'respiratory breath' is perishable and therefore temporary in comparison with the *bla*. As life principle the *bla* pervades all parts of the body, but it depends upon 'respiratory breath' and cannot function without it. The *bla* is also regarded as one of the three intellectual principles together with 'thought' (*yid*) and 'mind' (*sems*)."(p. 311).

7. On Bon-po funeral materials from Dunhuang, see especially Lalou 1949, 1952; Stein 1970; Chu Junjie 1991.

8. Haarh 1969, p. 327.

9. Haarh 1969, p. 14.

10. Haarh 1969, p. 14; Tucci 1949, 1950.

11. Karmay has argued that the terms of at least two of these traditions, the *Gragspa bon-lugs* and *Gsang-ba chos-lugs* "were Buddhist creations which do not have any intrinsic meaning as far as these historical traditions are concerned." Karmay 1998, p. 294.

12. Haarh 1969, p. 17; also Blondeau 1990; Karmay 1998, pp. 240–244.

13. Haarh 1969, pp. 413–414.

14. Karmay 1998 notes similarities between the Bon-po version of the origin of the first king and that found in certain Dunhuang manuscripts, namely Pelliot Tibetain mss. 1038 and 1236. From this he argues that the *Grags-pa bon-lugs* is "not entirely a fabrication dating from after the tenth century". (p. 259); see also Tucci 1949, p. 733; Haarh 1969, pp. 212–217; Gibson 1991, p. 107.

15. Gibson 1991, p. 107.

16. Haarh 1969, pp. 17–18, 168–230.

17. This also appears to be the prevailing view among scholars after Haarh. See, for example, Kirkland 1982; Gibson 1991, pp. 113–116; Samuel 1993, p. 441; Smith 1996, pp. 39–41.

18. For a relatively complete list, see Sorensen 1994, p. 141 n.372.

19. Macdonald and Imaeda 1978–1979, pp. 21–31; Bacot, Thomas, and Toussaint 1940–1946, pp. 123–124; Haarh 1969, pp. 402–403; Gibson 1991, pp. 118–123.

20. The myth is found in GLRB, pp. 55–57; translation in Sorensen 1994, pp. 141–144; Sakyapa Sonam Gyaltsen 1996, pp. 82–83.

21. Macdonald has argued that Long-ngam was historically the name of a prince of Myang-ro. See Macdonald 1971, p. 197; also Richardson 1998, p. 125.

22. Stein 1972 writes: "the name applied to this rope, *dmu*, was also used both for the sky, i.e., heaven, and for the king's maternal family (whose home it was)" (p. 48); see also Norbu 1995, pp. 75–76; Karmay 1998, p. 252.

23. Located in the south-central district of 'Phyong-rgyas, 'Phying-yul, or simply 'Phying-ba, was the ancient seat of the Yar-lung kings and the principal center of imperial power prior to the establishment of Lhasa.

24. Gibson 1991 (see also Haarh 1969, p. 343) writes: "The deity lDe-bla-guṅ-rgyal undoubtedly belongs to an ancient stratum, and his function is somehow connected with the idea of bla, the life-power" (p. 122 n. 42). On the meaning of *sku-bla* in this context, see Gibson 1991, pp. 77–82; also Karmay 1998, pp. 441–447.

25. Richardson 1991 suggests that this site was probably not as far west as Kailash, but rather closer to Kong-po in the Nyang-chu valley. (p. 125). It is interesting to note certain similarities in the early Tibetan notion of Mount Ti-se and that of the Chinese Mount T'ai-shan. In the cosmology of pre-Buddhist China, the upwardly mobile "soul," called *hun*, returned at death to Mount T'ai. The capital of Mount T'ai, Liang-fu, was the traditional site where imperial sacrifices were performed to the supreme deity of the earth, named Ti chu, the Lord of Earth. By some obscure circumstance, Ti chu became known as Ti-hsia chu, the Lord of the Underworld, and later transformed into the familiar T'ai-shan fu-chün, the Lord of Mount T'ai. With its close connections to the rite of sacrifice, which involved the establishment of an effective link between the living and the dead, Mount T'ai was guaranteed a central position in later Chinese conceptions of the afterlife. See Yü 1987, pp. 389–390. Teiser 1994 notes that Ta'i-shan "was recognized as the seat of the administration of the dead even before the Han dynasty" (p. 176) and was later conflated with the Buddhist concept of hell (*naraka*).

26. The *klu* is akin to the *nāga* in Indian mythology.

27. Haarh 1969, p. 344.

28. Gibson 1991, p. 124.

29. On the history of the concept of *glud* and its attendant rituals, see Karmay 1998, pp. 339–379; also Nebesky-Wojkowitz 1956, pp. 359–361, 507–511; Ramble 1982; Mumford 1989, pp. 149–157; Norbu 1995, pp. 77–86.

30. Tucci 1988, p. 246.

31. Haarh 1969, p. 309.

32. Haarh 1969, p. 314.

33. Alternatively, as I noted briefly in chapter 1, the Gri-gum legend has been viewed by Haarh as a myth preserving a collective memory of a monumental conflict between indigenous Tibetan clans already settled in Yar-lung (the so-called Bird Dynasty, *Bya-khri*) and foreign groups or tribes following strikingly different customs in Kong-po (*Nya-khri*), with the eventual outcome of the latter's defeat of the former. Haarh 1969, p. 18.

34. GLRB, pp. 57–58; Sorensen 1994, pp. 144–147; Sakyapa Sonam Gyaltsen 1996, pp. 85–86.

35. On the Bon-po funeral priests, also called "priests of existence" (*srid-gshen*), see Snellgrove 1967a, pp. 116–123; Norbu 1995, pp. 87–102.

36. A possible description of these rites may be found in several Dunhuang manuscripts, particularly PT 1042 and PT 239/II studied in Lalou 1949 and 1952; also Stein
1970, also in the passage referred to above, examined by Haarh 1969, p. 344. In the
latter piece, the mother of the ransomed girl makes the following request to Ngar-le-
skyes: "I want nothing but this: that in all future when a *bTsan-po*, who has with-
drawn as a ruler, dies, the topknot of the hair should be bound like a braid (*'phren-
mo*), the surface (of the body) should be annointed with vermilion (*mtshal*), the body
should be lacerated and scratched, incision should be made into the corpse of *bTsan-
po*, and it should be taken away from men that it may decay. Food should be eaten
and drunk. Will you do like that, or will you not do like that?" (*de blu na ji 'dod ces
ma la dris na / ma na re gzhan myi 'dod / nam nam zha zhar / btsan po rje dbyal zhig
nongs na / thor to 'phreng mo ni bcings / ngo la mtshal gyis byugs / lus la ni bzhags
/ btsan po'i spur la ni 'tshog / myi la 'phrog phom / zas la ni za 'thun / de ltar bya
'am myi bya zhas mchi nas*). Haarh 1969, p. 405. The removal of the corpse from
society so that it may decompose in isolation prior to the final rites is common in
societies that employ the practice of "double burial". For the classic anthropological
interpretation of such customs, see Hertz 1960, pp. 27–86. For an example of how
this model might be applied in the context of Tibetan Buddhist ritual, see Ramble
1982.

37. Karmay 1998, p. 315.

38. See Lessing 1951; Karmay 1998, pp. 310–338.

39. Karmay 1998, p. 337.

40. To my knowledge there is no evidence at this stage to support the claim that
an equivalent ritual existed in Buddhist India. Despite numerous references to the
notion of *antarābhava* in Buddhist Sanskrit literature, I have yet to locate any mention of an actual *antarābhava* liturgy per se. On early Buddhist funeral rites in India,
see particularly Schopen 1997. In China, on the other hand, we do find *antarābhava*
(Ch., *chung-yu*) rituals as early as the tenth century, see Teiser 1994. Questions of
the probable historical links between the Chinese and Tibetan rites have yet to be
addressed and are important topics for future research.

41. Reproduced in Macdonald and Imaeda 1978–79, p. 22, plates 168–175.

42. Lalou 1949 and 1952; Stein 1970; Macdonald 1971, pp. 373–376; now also
Kapstein 2000, pp. 7–8

43. PT 37, fols. 8a–17a. Macdonald 1971, p. 373 n. 613; Macdonald and Imaeda
1978–79, p. 37, plates 27–32.

44. Macdonald and Imaeda 1978–79, plate 171, fol. 19.4.

45. Macdonald and Imaeda 1978–79, plate 168, fol. 1.1.

46. Macdonald 1971, p. 373.

47. Macdonald 1971, pp. 373–374.

48. Imaeda 1981, p. 83.

49. Kvaerne 1985, p. 8.

50. Haarh 1969, p. 316.

51. Tucci 1958; Stein 1961; Ruegg 1989; Martin 1997, p. 23; Kapstein 2000, pp. 23–
30, 32–49, 71–75, 212 n. 11; Wangdu and Diemberger 2000.

52. Date suggested by Per Sorenson in his preface to Wangdu and Diemberger
2000, p. xiv.

53. Sorenson argues strongly that, given its content and phraseology, the *Zad-
gtad lo-rgyus* section of the *Dba'-bzhed* must be dated to the ninth century; see
Wangdu and Diemberger 2000, p. xv.

54. Wangdu and Diemberger 2000, pp. 92–105.

55. Wangdu and Diemberger 2000, p. 37-38.

56. Following Stein, Kapstein 2000 suggests the term *tshe* bears no relation to the Tibetan term for "lifespan" but translates the Chinese *zhāi* as "fast of abstinence", and the idiomatic *dazhāi* as "to perform rituals to deliver souls in purgatory" (p. 39).

57. Wangdu and Diemberger 2000, p. 35. On Jinchen Gongzhu, see Kapstein 2000, pp. 26-30.

58. Wangdu and Diemberger 2000, p. 39. An insightful analysis of this story is found in Kapstein 2000, pp. 38-50.

59. The fallen kingdoms mentioned include Zing-po, Zhang-zhung, 'A-zha, Mchims Dwags-po, and Snubs. See Wangdu and Diemberger 2000, pp. 102-103.

60. See Skorupski 1983.

61. Wangdu and Diemberger 2000, p. 105. On the early history of Buddha Vairocana in Tibet, see Richardson 1998, pp. 177-181; Kapstein 2000, pp. 60-65.

62. Wangdu and Diemberger 2000, p. 101.

63. The Chinese T'ang records and certain Dunhuang documents suggest that the Tibetans of pre-Buddhist times may have practiced human sacrifice. See Snellgrove and Richardson 1986, p. 93; Chu Junjie 1991, pp. 145-149.

64. Samuel 1994, p. 704.

65. The passage appears in *Srid-pa bar-do'i ngo-sprod*, quoted here from version B1a, fol. 166.2-4: *mtho ris kyi snang bar shar ba'i tshe : shul du nye ba gson po rnams kyis gshin po'i don du bsngos nas : sems can mang pos srog bcad de mchod sbyin byas pas : khyod ma dag pa'i snang ba shar te : zhe sdang drag po skyes nas : des mtshams sbyor byas nas dmyal bar skye bar 'gyur bas : shul du las ci byas nas 'dug kyang khyod rang zhe sdang ma skye bar byams pa sgom shig.* See also the discussion in Mumford 1989, pp. 80-92, 195, and 197.

66. Imaeda 1981, p. 84.

67. See brief discussion in Kapstein 2000, pp. 7-10.

68. *bde-skyid phun-gsum tshogs-pa'i lha-yul dam-par 'gro-ba'i lam.*

69. The mantra of Durgatipariśodhana: *nama sarva durgade pariśodani rajaya tathagataya arihadi samyag sambudaya dadyatha oṃ śodani sarvapapaviśodhani śudde viśudde sarva karma avarana viśudde svahā.* Compare to Skorupski 1983, p. 126 (5b.10-13): *sarvadurgatipariśodanarājanāmatathāgatahṛdayaṃ niścārayām āsa / OṂ śodhane śodhane sarvapāpaviśodani śuddhe viśuddhe sarvakarmāvara[n]aviśuddhe SVĀHĀ.* ("As soon as he [Vajrasattva] uttered this formula, the evil destinies of all living beings were checked, every approach into hell, animal life and tormented spirits was eliminated, severe sufferings were removed and many living beings became happy," p. 7.)

70. This has already been noted by Imaeda in his excellent study of the nine versions of the Dunhuang work *Skye-shi'i lo-rgyus* See Imaeda 1981, pp. 77-78.

71. Snellgrove 1987, p. 183.

72. Tsepak Rigzin 1986, p. 8; Skorupski 1983; Tucci 1988, p. 197.

73. For details, consult Skorupski 1983, pp. 81-87 and 319-323.

74. B1a, fols. 166.2-169.5.

75. B1a, fols. 167.5-168.5: *yang khyod kyi don du gshin po'i cho ga kang ka ni 'don pa dang : ngan song sbyong ba la sogs pa [168] khyod kyi don du byas kyang : de ma dag pa dang : g.yeng ba la sogs pa byas pa dang : dam tshig dang sdom pa mi gtsang ba dang : bag med pa'i spyod pa de khyod kyi mngon shes phya mos mthong nas 'ong gi : de la khyod ma dad pa dang : log lta skyes pa dang : 'jigs shing skrag nas las nag po la sogs pa dang : chos spyod dang cho ga ma dag pa rnams kyang shes nas 'ong gi : der khyod kyi bsam pa : kye ma 'di rnams kyis bdag bslus so : nges*

par bslus so snyam nas shin tu yi mug ste : mi dga' ba chen po dang bcas te : dag snang mos gus ma skyes kyi steng du : log lta dang ma dad pa skyes nas 'ong bas : des mtshams sbyor byas nas nges par ngan song du 'gro bas.

76. Evans-Wentz and Dawa Samdup [1927] 2000, p. 171 n.1.

77. Thurman 1994, p. 178.

78. On the Tibetan history of "sky burial" in general and speculations about possible Persian origins of the practice, see Martin 1996b.

79. The *dhāraṇī* of Akṣobhya is often recited before eating meat as expiation for the sin of butchery. I wish to thank Matthew Kapstein for these clarifications (e-mail correspondence, November 21, 2002).

3. Transitions

1. Later Tibetan schema would identify this fourth stage, the Indo-Buddhist intermediate state proper, by the literal expression "bardo of becoming" (*srid-pa'i bar-ma-do*).

2. Cuevas 1996.

3. Kritzer 1993, 1997, 1998a, 1998b, 1999a, 1999b.; see also Dietz 1994 and Blezer 1997, pp. 6–13.

4. The schools that rejected the *antarābhava* are usually listed as the Theravāda, Vibhajyavāda, Mahāsāṅghika, and Mahīśāsaka. Some of the schools that accepted the theory were the Sarvāstivāda, Saṃmitīya, Pūrvaśaila, and Dārṣṭāntika. See Bareau 1955, pp. 283, 291; Wayman 1974, p. 227.

5. Sangharakshita 1985, pp. 81–83; Hirakawa 1990, pp. 90–91, 109–110

6. Shwe Zan Aung and Davids [1915] 1979, pp. 212–213; Blezer 1997 (appendix 2, Work-Editions), pp. 19–20.

7. Tucci 1988, p. 111; Snellgrove 1987, p. 431.

8. Vasubandhu's points have been explored in some detail in La Vallée Poussin 1988 and Dietz 1994.

9. Dietz 1994, p. 157; see also La Vallée Poussin 1988, p. 383.

10. On this being in the context of the *antarābhava*, see Wijesekera 1945; Cuevas 1996. For an informative discussion of non-Buddhist parallels to *antarābhava*, see Kritzer 1999a.

11. Among the five *anāgāmin*, the reference here is to the *antarāparinirvāyin*, the one who obtains nirvāṇa in the intermediate state.

12. Dietz 1994, p. 158; La Vallée Poussin 1988, p. 386.

13. Dietz 1994, p. 159; La Vallée Poussin 1988, p. 392.

14. La Vallée Poussin 1988, p. 393.

15. Cuevas 1996, pp. 283–284.

16. Kritzer 1999b.

17. On the stages of development of the embryo, see Norbu 1987; Kritzer 1998b.

18. Kritzer 1997, p. 90–91.

19. See Sangharakshita 1985, pp. 91–92.

20. The Chinese translation was by Saṅghadeva and Buddhasmṛti in 383. See Sangharakshita 1985, p. 91; Nakamura 1987, p. 105 n. 19. Kritzer 1999a suggests that the *Vibhāṣā* exposition of *antarābhava*, and hence that of Vasubandhu as well, may have relied on the detailed accounts of the intermediate state in the *Yogācārabhūmi*.

21. See Kritzer 1997, pp. 15–28 (87–74).

22. Kritzer 1999b.

23. Kritzer 1999b, p. 13 (89).

24. Tib., '*Phags-pa tshe-dang ldan-pa dga'-bo la mngal-du 'jug-pa bstan-pa zhes-bya-ba theg-pa chen-po'i mdo.*

25. Full title, *Āyuṣmannandagarbhāvakrāntinirdeśa-sūtra.* The Chinese translation was completed in 542–43 and the Tibetan in the eleventh or twelfth century. See Li-kouang 1949; Nakamura 1987, p. 175. The translators traditionally associated with the text are given as Śāntākaragupta, Abhayākaragupta, Śākyarakṣita, Vidyākaraśānti, Subhūticandra, Aḍitacandra, and in Tibet Pa-tshab Tshul-khrims-rgyal-mtshan.

26. On the Abhidharma position of the *Garbhāvakrāntinirdeśa-sūtra*, see Kritzer 1998a, p. 12.

27. Kritzer 1998a, pp. 4–7 (12–9).

28. Kritzer 1998a, p. 4 (12); Kritzer 1999b, p. 4.

29. Kritzer 1999b, p. 4.

30. Norbu 1987.

31. See for instance Tsong-kha-pa's (1357–1419) discussion of bardo in ZBNA; trans. Mullin 1996, pp. 184–198. Also of note is the remarkably clear and orthodox Dge-lugs-pa presentation found in ZHKS; trans. Lati Rinbochay and Hopkins 1979.

32. Li-kouang 1949, pp. 52–53; Blezer 1997, p. 11. This text also includes details about the conditions in which the liminal beings died, their state of mind in *antarābhava*, and so forth.

33. Arthur Waley in Conze 1954, p. 283.

34. BRDS, vol. 8, fol. 663; trans. Kunsang 1987, p. 69.

35. These stages are described in some detail in Lati Rinbochay and Hopkins 1979; Gyatso 1982; Cozort 1986.

36. On the siddha traditions in India, see Dasgupta 1976; Sanderson 1985, 1988; White 1996. On the development of the tradition in Tibet, see Dowman 1985; Snellgrove 1987, pp. 117–303; Samuel 1993, pp. 406–435.

37. This threefold scheme was not new. The Sarvāstivādins and related schools, including the Sautrāntikas and Mahāyāna Yogācārins, posited the existence of an intermediate state in the context of a threefold dynamic: death (*maraṇa*), transition (*antarābhava*), and rebirth (*upapattibhava*). As I will show, this triune arrangement was reinterpreted in some circles to refer to two separate types of *antarābhava* such that death was then discussed as a bardo of dying ('*chi-kha'i bar-do*) and rebirth as a bardo of becoming (*srid-pa'i bar-do*).

38. Widely known from the nineteenth-century comprehensive Tibetan anthology of 'Jam-mgon Kong-sprul Blo-gros-mtha'-yas, the *Gdams-ngag mdzod* (DMDZ).

39. For a brief summary of the different traditions, see Kapstein 1996.

40. Kapstein 1996, p. 276.

41. On this period in Tibetan religious history, see GJGT, fols. 169–173; GKCB, esp. pp. 939–996; Dudjom 1991, pp. 524–527.

42. Kapstein 1996, pp. 276–277.

43. YGLG, vol. 2, fol. 548.

44. *Mnga'-bdag nyang-ral-pa-can-gyi bar-do gnad-kyi gdam-ngag.*

45. *Chos-drug-gi bar-du[o] lugs mi-'dra-ba gsum.*

46. *Pha-brgyud-kyi gdam-ngag paṇḍita-mngon-shes-can.*

47. *Btsun-mo-can-gyi bar-do'i gdam-ngag.*

48. *Jo-mo lha-rje-ma*: (a) *bar-do snyan-rgyud*, (b) *bar-do mkha'-spyod*, (c) *bar-do mngon-sum-ma.*

49. *Shangs-po ri-bo-che-pa'i bar-do'i gdam-ngag.*

50. *Zhang rin-po-che'i bar-do'i dmar-khrid.*

51. *Dbyar-ston dbu-ma-pa'i bar-do nad-sel bdud-rtsi thegs-pa.*

52. For example, the *lam-'bras* tradition of Jo-mo Lha-rje-ma.

53. Torricelli and Ācharya Sangye T. Naga 1995, p. 69 n. 32; Dowman 1985, pp. 179–185. According to Rdo-rje-mdzes-'od, Tilopa received bardo instructions not from Lavapa directly but from his pupil Rol-pa'i-rdo-rje. See Khenpo Könchog Gyaltsen 1990, p. 44. This would be more in line with Dowman's dating of Lavapa to the mid to late ninth century.

54. Torricelli and Ācharya Sangye T. Naga 1995, p. 69 n. 30. The great number of female teachers one runs across in these biographical materials, especially in connection with bardo transmissions, is striking. The influence of female siddhas during this early period deserves more thorough attention. On the religious roles of women in tantra generally, see Klein 1985, 1995; Shaw 1994; Campbell 1996; Gyatso 1998, pp. 243–264.

55. Specifically the *Śrī-Ḍākārṇavamahāyoginī-tantra* (Tib., *Bde-mchog mkha'i-'gro rgya-mtsho'i-rgyud*). See Roerich 1949, pp. 388, 390, and 497.

56. *Chos-drug-gi man-ngag shes-bya-ba*. In TOH no. 2330. The colophon identifies Nāropa and Mar-pa Chos-kyi-blo-gros as translators in Kashmir. The anonymous text that immediately follows the *Ṣaḍdharmopadeśa* in TOH no. 2331 (also in DMDZ, vol. 5, fols. 68–89), the *Ājñāsamyakpramāṇa-nāma-ḍākinyupadeśa* (Tib., *Bka'-yang dag-pa'i tshad-ma zhes-bya-ba mkha'-'gro-ma'i mang-ngag*), has traditionally been attributed to Tilopa. However, Torricelli and Ācharya Sangye T. Naga 1995, p. 31, has suggested that the text (at least the version in DMDZ) "can be ascribed to the authorship of Nāropa" or "to a tradition very close to that *mahāsiddha*." I tend to agree with this conclusion, on the basis of comparative examination of the topics addressed in both versions of the text. In the DMDZ version, we encounter references to three individual bardo states: (1) *skye-shi bar-do*, (2) *rmi-lam bar-do*, and (3) *'chi-ka dus-kyi bar-do*. These three states are correlated to the yoga of apprehending the clear light at death, of purifying the dream state, and of blocking the next birth (described originally as related techniques, but not as individual states), with each in turn corresponding to the attainment of one of three buddha bodies (*tri-kāya*). The scheme is well correlated not only to components of the four *bhava-s* doctrine but also to Naropa's threefold classification of the bardo. The passages that describe this system (including also the colophon identifying Nāropa and Mar-pa as translators) are completely absent in TOH, no. 2331. It seems to me then that this more elaborate discussion is an interpretive gloss on the earlier verses—apparently authored by Tilopa himself—dealing with the techniques for blocking rebirth (*srid-pa khegs-pa*) and that the "author" of that gloss would probably have been Nāropa (or maybe even Mar-pa). My thanks to Henk Blezer for pointing me in the direction of the DMDZ version of this text and for helping me refine my thoughts on the issue of its possible authorship.

57. *Rnal 'byor 'chi ba'i dus kyi tshe / dbang po rnams dang 'byung ba sdus / zla nyi rlung rnams snying gar 'dus / rnal 'byor ting nge 'dzin sna tshogs 'char / rnam shes phyi rol yul song na / rmi lam yul bzhin sna tshogs snang / bdun bdun dus tshe 'chi snang dang / de nas skye bar 'gyur ba nyid / de tshe lha yi rnal 'byor sgom / yang na de nyid ngang la gzhag / de rjes skye la phyogs pa'i tshe / mnga' bdag lha yi rnal 'byor gyis / snang srid lha yi rnal 'byor sgom / des ni bar do khegs par 'gyur / sukhasiddhi'i upadeśa'o.*

58. *Snyan-rgyud rdo-rje'i tshig-rkang*. Variant Sanskrit title, *Karṇa-tantra-vajragāthā*. In TT, no. 4632 (also in TOH, no. 2338): *bar do ngo sprod yang dag zab don bstan / skye shi rmi lam srid pa bar do gcod / ltar med ltas pas / mthong med mthong ba'i mchog / rang rig / gsal / stong / mi rtog / sgrib g.yogs bral / bde chen chos dbyings ye shes rnam par dag / rang bzhin dbyer med sku gsum rang*

shar ltos / ma rtogs lus ldan bar do rnam gsum la / bskyed rim / sgyu lus / 'od gsal chos skur bsre / sa chu me rlung 'byung ba rim kyis thim / brgya cu 'gag nas snang ba gsum 'das te / dkar dmar sems gsum chu skye nang du 'dzom / 'od gsal ngos zin ma bu dbyer med 'dres.

59. According to Yang-dgon-pa, Nāropa's development of a dream bardo was inspired by a quote from the *Rdo-rje 'chang-gi rgyud* (Skt., *Vajradhāra-tantra*), which reads: "just as a dream is illusory, so is the bardo existence" (*ji ltar sgyu ma rmi lam dang / ji ltar bar do'i srid yin pa*). YGLG, vol. 2, fol. 547.3–4.

60. Khyung-po Rnal-'byor's triune bardo system is described in BDNS. For brief comments, see Kapstein 2000, p. 9. See NPBD for Zhang Rin-po-che's bardo system. On the life and work of Zhang, see Martin 1992.

61. Khyung-po Rnal-'byor is alleged to have received in visions the bardo tradition of Sukhasiddhī, Tilopa's female mentor, and directly in person the transmission of Nāropa's consort Niguma. See Kapstein 1980, 1991.

62. See BDZH.

63. See PHMO. I am indebted to Dan Martin for this reference.

64. Roerich 1949, p. 226; Khenpo Könchog Gyaltsen 1990, p. 208.

65. According to legend, Ma-cig Zhwa-ma had sought the help of Dam-pa Sangs-rgyas for a seemingly incurable venereal disease that she had contracted as a result of practicing with so many different male yogis. It was her relationship with Dam-pa Sangs-rgyas that may have caused Roerich to confuse Ma-cig Zhwa-ma for Ma-cig Lab-sgron-ma. See Roerich 1949, pp. 220–226; Lo Bue 1994; Edou 1996, p. 111; also Diemberger and Hazod 1994.

66. See ZBNA; trans. Mullin 1996.

67. See YANG; trans. Lati Rinbochay and Hopkins 1979.

68. For a general overview of this system, see Sweet 1996.

69. BDGR, pp. 62–105; GKCB, p. 966; LRCB, pp. 352–365.

70. Mullin 1997, p. 14.

71. See Wayman 1980; Nakamura 1987, pp. 332–334.

72. Roerich 1949, p. 361.

73. Boord and Losang Norbu Tsonawa 1996, pp. 63–64.

74. Boord and Losang Norbu Tsonawa 1996, pp. 46–54; also K. Gyatso 1994, p. 49.

75. On whom see LRCB, pp. 68–69; Roerich 1949, pp. 414–416.

76. See BDLC and MLAM.

77. In DMDZ, fol. 206, the larger text from which the *Bar-do blos-chod* is drawn, a transmission lineage is presented in the following order: Mar-pa, Mtshur Dbang-nge, Stod-lung 'Ga'-ras, Slob-dpon Nyi-ma-lung-ba, Bde-gshegs Rin-po-che. The actual author of this text may therefore have been Bde-gshegs Rin-po-che, but this is not certain.

78. Hopkins 1996 (p. 177) suggests generally that the Tibetan structure of the doxographical categories basis, path, and fruit may have been based on specific features of the Mādhyamika, particularly the coordinated sets of the two truths (conventional and ultimate), the two practices (method and wisdom), and the two bodies of a buddha (form and truth).

79. DMDZ, vol. 8, fol. 227.

80. "Signs" (*mtshan*) in this context refers to meditation props such as mental or painted images, objects, and other such aids to visualization.

81. MLAM, fol. 48.

82. Blezer 1997, writes: "the Tibetan translation of *antarābhava: bar mo do'i srid pa* probably provided the term *bar ma do* or *bar do* as an equivalent for what in the

Abhidharmakośabhāṣya was referred to as *bhava*, whereas in the translation of *antarābhava*, *bhava* was translated by *srid pa* and not by *bar mo do*. This clearly indicates that in Tibetan traditions all *bhava-s* were styled after one *bhava* that according to their perception represented the central or original one, the blueprint of the concept of an intermediate state, the *antarābhava*, *bar ma do'i srid pa*, or in short *bar ma do*, hence, *bar ma do* or *bar do* and not *srid pa*" (p. 29 n. 124).

83. This is clearly indicated in Hirakawa 1973–78, p. 29. Alternative equivalents include *srid-pa bar-ma*, *srid-pa'i bar-ma*, and *bar-ma*.

84. It is not clear whether the phrase *snang-mun srid-pa'i bar-do* might be better translated as "bardo of becoming, illumination and darkness" in reference to the standard dyad of awareness (*rig-pa*) and ignorance (*ma-rig-pa*).

85. Mi-la-ras-pa's student Ras-chung Rdo-rje-grags was possibly the author of the *Bar-do lam-khyer 'khor-'das rgyun-gcod-kyi gdams-ngag*, a bardo text inspired by these path of blending (*bsre-ba lam*) teachings. See MKGR, fols. 129–142.

86. MLGB, pp. 489–517; trans. Chang 1962, pp. 333–356.

87. See MLGB, p. 516; Chang 1962, p. 354; also Roerich 1949, p. 435. Brief biographical sketches for Guru Bodhirāja (Ngam-rdzong-ras-pa) and 'Od-kyi-mtha'-can (Zhi-ba-'od) can be found in LRCB, pp. 151–152 and pp. 166–167, respectively.

88. Six bardos are listed in MLGB, p. 509: (1) *snang-mun srid-pa'i bar-do*, (2) *da-res 'khor-'das bar-do*, (3) *rang-bzhin lam-gyi bar-do*, (4) *rmi-lam gnyid-kyi bar-do*, (5) *tha-ma srid-pa'i bar-do*, and (6) *skye-gnas brgyud-pa'i bar-do*.

89. Mullin 1996, pp. 34, 112, 1997, pp. 21 and 156 n. 6.

90. For example, consider the *Bar-do 'phrang-sgrol-gyi smon-lam*, perhaps one of the earliest basic prayers of the *Bar-do thos-grol* cycle. See in chapter 7.

91. GRLP and BDRL.

92. *Thos-grol bar-do 'phrang-grol chen-po* in BPCT.

93. *'Byung-'jig 'byung-thim-gyi smon-lam bar-do'i 'phrang-sgrol* in ZKGK, fols. 757–779.

94. LZBP; trans. Lopez 1997a also YANG.

95. Nebesky-Wojkowitz 1956, pp. 167–168. On the deity Tsi'u-dmar-po, see Ladrang Kalsang 1996, pp. 114–116; Pommaret 1998b, pp. 83–85.

96. On the *bar-do 'phrang-lam* in pilgrimage literature, see especially GANG, p. 55; ZHAB, p. 500; BYNG, pp. 29–31; Stein 1988, p. 11, n. 34; Dowman 1997, p. 127, 195; Huber 1999, p. 233 n. 28. My thanks to Toni Huber for kindly pointing me to these references.

97. Mi-la-ras-pa's text plays a prominent role in Rtse-le Sna-tshogs-rang-grol's seventeenth-century *Bar-do spyi'i-don thams-cad rnam-par gsal-bar byed-pa dran-pa'i me-long* (BRDS), where it is frequently juxtaposed to the *Bar-do thos-grol chen-mo*. Apparently for this author both texts were paradigmatic of their respective traditions, the *Bar-do 'phrang-sgrol* for the Bka'-brgyud-pa and the *Bar-do thos-grol* for the Rnying-ma-pa.

98. *Rang-bzhin gnas-pa'i bar-do*, YGLG, vol. 2, fols. 564.3–567.6.

99. *Rnam-smin skye-shi'i bar-do*, YGLG, vol. 2, fols. 567.6–587.5.

100. *Ting-nge-'dzin bsam-gtan-gyi bar-do*, YGLG, vol. 2, fols. 587.5–594.5.

101. *Bag-chags rmi-lam-gyi bar-do*, YGLG, vol. 2, fols. 594.5–600.2.

102. *Lugs-zlog 'chi-ka'i bar-do*, YGLG, vol. 2, fols. 600.2–617.5.

103. *Lugs-'byung srid-pa'i bar-do*, YGLG, vol. 2, fols. 617.5–643.2.

104. On the life of Yang-dgon-pa, see LRCB, pp. 700–715; Roerich 1949, pp. 688–691.

105. GBNG; Kapstein 1992, pp. 90–91, and 2000, pp. 145–146; Sorensen 1994, pp. 585–588.

106. The six bardo states are identified as follows: (1) *rang-bzhin gnas-pas bar-ma-do*, (2) *skye-shi'i bar-ma-do*, (3) *shes-pa snga-phyi'i bar-ma-do*, (4) *rmi-lam-gyi bar-ma-do*, (5) *'chi-kha'i bar-ma-do*, and (6) *srid-pa'i bar-ma-do*.

107. Sorensen (1994) places the "recovery" of the *Gab-pa mngon-byung* in 1150–60, despite the fact that the text is generally attributed to Śākya-bzang-po (Zur-Pakṣi Śākya-'od) who flourished in the thirteenth century.

108. On this nebulous period, see Wylie 1964a; Snellgrove 1987, pp. 463–470. Martin 1996c examines evidence for the existence of alternative groups or popular religious movements in the eleventh and twelfth century that may have roots going back to this period.

109. See especially Karmay 1988a; Ehrhard 1990; Germano 1994, forthcoming.

110. See NGB (Mtshams-brag), vol. 1, fols. 2–262; also Dargyay 1985, 1992; Reynolds 1996, pp. 236–248; Karmay 1998, pp. 69–75. This is the same monk Vairocana who is encountered in the *Dba'-bzhed* discussed in chapter 2.

111. See Karmay 1998, pp. 71–73.

112. Germano 1994, p. 272.

113. The Snying-thig system of Rdzogs-chen is explored in some detail in Germano (1994, forthcoming). My descriptive account of its cosmogony is based fundamentally on David Germano's research. I wish to thank David for sharing his work with me and for many years of fruitful conversation on this and related subjects.

114. On the life of Dga'-rab-rdo-rje, see particularly GKCB, pp. 111–117; Dudjom Rinpoche 1991, pp. 490–494; Reynolds 1996, pp. 177–189.

115. Germano forthcoming.

116. The relevant works are too numerous to mention, but I can provide a list of some standard divisions. Threefold bardo: (1) *rang-bzhin bar-do*, (2) *rmi-lam bar-do*, (3) *srid-pa bar-do*. Fourfold bardo: (1) *rang-bzhin bar-do*, (2) *ting-nge-'dzin-gyi bar-do*, (3) *chos-nyid bar-do*, (4) *srid-pa'i bar-do*. Fivefold bardo: (1) *rang-bzhin bar-do*, (2) *ting-nge-'dzin-gyi bar-do*, (3) *rmi-lam bar-do*, (4) *skye-shi bar-do*, (5) *srid-pa'i bar-do*. Sixfold bardo: (1) *rang-bzhin bar-do*, (2) *ting-nge-'dzin-gyi bar-do*, (3) *rmi-lam bar-do*, (4) *skye-shi bar-do*, (5) *chos-nyid bar-do*, (6) *srid-pa'i bar-do*.

117. It is not my intention to argue that alternative Rdzogs-chen bardo expositions possibly predating the earliest texts of the *Rgyud-bcu-bdun* cannot be identified. Instead, what I mean to say is simply that the tantras of the *Rgyud-bcu-bdun* contain the clearest presentation of a completely integrated bardo system in accord with the then emergent fundamental Rdzogs-chen theories. Two examples of relevant Rdzogs-chen texts that immediately come to mind as possibly earlier than the *Rgyud-bcu-bdun* are the *Rin-po-che srid-pa bar-do rang-snang-ba'i rgyud* (alternative title *Rdo-rje sems-dpa'i rgyud*), found in NGB (Mtshams-brag), vol. 4, fols. 609–632.6; NGB (Gting-skyes), vol. 4, fols. 416–434; VGB, vol. 3, fols. 387–411 (listed as *Rin-po-che srid-pa bar-ma-do snang-ba'i rgyud*); and the *Rdzogs-pa chen-po bar-do gsang-ba'i rgyud*, found in NGB (Mtshams-brag), vol. 4, fols. 526.5–531.6; VGB, vol. 4, fols. 68.3–72.4.

118. In NGB (Mtshams-brag), vol. 12, fols. 491–559; NGB (Gting-skyes), vol. 9, fols. 386–435. Portions of this tantra have been translated in Orofino 1990, pp. 31–59.

119. *Rang-bzhin gnas-pa'i bar-do*, NGB (Gting-skyes), vol. 9, fols. 394.6–416.1.

120. *'Chi-kha-ma'i bar-ma-do*, NGB (Gting-skyes), vol. 9, fols. 416.1–425.5.

121. *Chos-nyid bar-do*, NGB (Gting-skyes), vol. 9, fols. 425.5–431.6.

122. *Srid-pa bar-do*, NGB (Gting-skyes), vol. 9, fols. 431.6–435.1.

123. NGB (Gting-skyes), vol. 9, fols. 417–419.

124. NGB (Gting-skyes), vol. 9, fols. 419–420.

125. NGB (Gting-skyes), vol. 9, fols. 423–424.

126. The sleep experience had already been incorporated earlier into the expanding bardo doctrine. Consider, for example, Nāropa's bardo of dreams (*rmi-lam bardo*) referred to in the previous section.

127. These are usually (1) Vairocana, (2) Akṣobhya, (3) Ratnasambhava, (4) Amitābha, (5) Amoghasiddha.

128. NGB, fol. 222: *yang snang ba de dag sku'i rnam par rang shar te / sku de dag kyang mi che ba / mi chung ba / cha mnyam pa / rgyan dang / kha dog dang / bzhugs tshul dang / gdan khri dang / phyag rgya dang bcas te / sku de dag kyang lnga lnga'i gzugs kyis khyab pa / lnga tshan re re la 'od kyi mu khyud dang bcas pa / yab kyi cha 'dzin pa'i rigs dang / yum gyi cha 'dzin pa'i rigs dang / sems dpa' dang / sems ma dang / dkyil 'khor thams cad gcig la rdzogs par gnas so.* It is significant that this same passage occurs with only slight variation in the *Chos-nyid bar-do gsal-'debs* of the *Bar-do thos-grol,* translated here from version Bla, fol. 63.1–4: "O son of good family, these bodies are neither large nor small, but well proportioned each with its own ornaments, colors, postures, thrones, and gestures. These pure bodies embrace as five couples, each one encircled by a halo of five lights. The [bodhi]sattvas, who possess the implements of father and mother, and all [five] mandalas appear all at once. Recognize them, because they are your [own] personal deities!" *[kye rigs kyi bu : sku de dag kyang mi che ba : mi chung ba cha mnyam pa: rgyan kha dog bzhugs tshul dang : gdan khri rang rang gyi phyag rgya dang bcas te : sku de dag kyang lnga lnga 'i zung gis khyab pa : lnga tshan re re la 'od lnga 'i tshom bus mu khyud dang bcas pa : yab kyi cha 'dzin pa 'i rigs kyi sems dpa' dang : yum gyi cha 'dzin pa 'i rigs kyi sems ma dang : dkyil 'khor thams cad gcig la rdzogs par 'char du 'ong bas : de khyod kyi yi dam kyi lha yin bas ngo shes par gyis shig].*

129. Blezer 1997, 1998. In my opinion, Blezer's comments in this regard are weakened both by his choice of source material, the bulk of which postdates the fourteenth century, and by an inadequate examination of the conceptual background of the sources in question, namely the Snying-thig system of Rdzogs-chen.

130. See NGB (Mtsham-brag), vol. 14, no. 3, fols. 152–218. A Sanskrit edition is not extant. The text has been edited and translated in Dorje 1987.

131. Dorje 1987, pp. 50–56.

132. The standard set of five is generally listed as: (1) the primordial wisdom of the expanse of reality (*chos-dbyings-kyi ye-shes*), (2) the mirrorlike primordial wisdom (*me-long-gi ye-shes*), (3) the primordial wisdom of discernment (*so-sor rtog-pa'i ye-shes*), (4) the primordial wisdom of sameness (*mnyam-nyid-kyi ye-shes*), and (5) the primordial wisdom of accomplishment (*bya-ba grub-pa'i ye-shes*).

133. *Zhi-khro bka'-'dus.* In RCTD, vol. 23.

134. *Zhi-khro dgongs-pa rang-grol.* See bibliography for references. Blezer 1997, (pp. 128–129) demonstrates that the Kar-gling *Zhi-khro* is not identical to the mandala of the *Gsang-ba'i snying-po,* although it is probably derived from it.

135. *Grol-thig zhi-khro.* In RCTD, vols. 4 and 11.

136. *Zhi-khro nges-don snying-po* (ZKND).

137. Germano 1994, p. 274.

138. Germano 1997.

139. On the rediscovery of the works of Klong-chen-pa by the *gter-ston* 'Jigs-med-gling-pa (1730–1798), see Goodman 1992; Gyatso 1998.

140. GKCB, p. 225.

141. GKCB, pp. 238–239.

4. Death to Disposal

1. Brauen 1978 and Brauen and Kvaerne 1978c; Brauen and Kvaerne 1982; Kvaerne 1985, 1997a; Ramble 1982; Mumford 1989; THUP; trans. Sangay 1984.

2. Wylie 1965, p. 232.

3. Tucci 1950; Haarh 1969, pp. 327–397.

4. Wylie 1965, p. 234.

5. Wylie 1965, p. 232. In areas where firewood was not easily available, the custom of "sky burial" seems to have predominated. See arguments in Martin 1996b, esp. pp. 360–365.

6. THUP, p. 21.

7. Wylie 1965, p. 233; THUP, p. 21; also Bell [1928] 1994, p. 289. The connection between water and death of an unusual sort bears crosscultural comparison with the medieval European notion of water as a liminal space between the living and the dead. See Barber 1988, pp. 147–153; Schmitt 1998, p. 184.

8. Bell [1928] 1994, p. 295. Details of the techniques used by Tibetans in mummifying the saintly dead can be found in Govinda 1970, p. 119.

9. Martin 1996c. One might argue that as a form of sky burial, the rite of vulture disposal represents, on some sublevel of Tibet's historical consciousness, a means of restoring a link between heaven and earth, a link that is reported to have been severed by an ancient and gullible king. See the short section on Gri-gum-btsan-po in chapter 2.

10. Mumford 1989, p. 198.

11. Bell [1928] 1994, pp. 138–139; Wylie 1964b.

12. THUP, p. 7; also Brauen and Kvaerne 1982, pp. 321–322; Ramble 1982, p. 335; Mumford 1989, pp. 198–204.

13. Mumford 1989, p. 198.

14. Mumford 1989, p. 111.

15. THUP, p. 10.

16. Ramble 1982, p. 335.

17. THUP, p. 11.

18. Ramble 1982, p. 336.

19. Ramble 1982, p. 337.

20. THUP, p. 18.

21. THUP, p. 19.

22. Ramble 1982, p. 341.

23. THUP, p. 3.

24. On Tibetan exorcism rites, see Ortner 1978, pp. 91–127; Mumford 1989, pp. 149–164, 204–205.

25. See B1a, fols. 189.5–191.1: *de rnams kyis gang zag dbang po rab 'bring tha ma yang mi grol mi srid do : de ci'i phyir zhe na : bar do'i rnam shes de la zag bcas kyi mngon shes yod pas : bdag gi ji smras khos* [190] *thos pa dang cig : 'on long yin yang : de'i dus su dbang po tshangs bas ci smras go ba dang gnyis : 'jigs skrag gis*

rtag tu bdas nas ci drag na snam pa'i dran pa yengs med du yod pas bdag gis ci smras nyan nas 'ong pa dang gsum : rnam shes rten med pas mdun pa gar gtad du thal gyis slebs te kha lo bsgyur du sla ba dang bzhi : dran pa dgu 'gyur gyis gsal bas lkug pa yin kyang de'i dus su las kyi dbang gis rigs pa gsal du song nas : ci bslab pa thams cad sgom shes pa'i yon tan dang gnas le lta bu'i yon tan yod pa'i phyir ro : des na gshin po'i cho ga byas pas phan yon yod pa'i rgyu mtshan yang de ltar yin no : de bsan zhag bzhi bcu zhe dgu'i bar : bar [191] *do thos grol chen mo 'di klog par nan tan bya ba shin tu nas gal che'o.* A similar reasoning is found in B1a, fols. 208.4–209.4, but with more emphasis on the compassion and grace of the deities.

26. *Sangs-rgyas dang byang-chub sems-dpa' rnams-la ra-mda' sbran-pa'i smon-lam,* B1a, fol. 126.2–5: *gcig por grogs med par 'gro dgos ba'i dus la babs na thugs rje can rnams che ge mo skyabs med pa 'di la skyabs mdzod cig : mgon mdzod cig : dpung gnyen mdzod cig : bar do'i mun nag chen po las skyobs shig : las kyi rlung dmar chen po las bzlog cig : gshin rje'i 'jigs skrag chen po las skyobs shig : bar do'i 'phrang ring po las sgrol cig.*

27. Ramble 1982, p. 339.

28. Lauf 1977, p. 76.

29. Evans-Wentz and Dawa Samdup [1927] 2000, 1960, p. 20.

30. Brauen and Kvaerne 1978a, pp. 12–13.

31. The deceased's success in locating a favorable destiny can also be negatively affected by the family's wealth, or lack thereof. See Mumford 1989, pp. 203–204.

32. Ramble 1982, p. 340.

33. In the more abbreviated versions of this ceremony the *byang-bu* rite takes place only three days after death. See Kvaerne 1997a, p. 494.

34. Lauf 1977, pp. 127–128.

35. Ramble 1982, p. 341.

36. On death rituals for children, see Blondeau 1997.

37. THUP, p. 22.

5. Prophecies of the Lotus Guru

1. See LGNB. The text was composed in 1499.

2. See OGTL. Not much is known about the life of Chos-rje Dge-'dun-rgyal-mtshan other than what we find reported in his own text. There we learn that he was born in the fire male tiger year 1446 at a place called So-rgyal into the Sbas family of the Sna clan. His father was named Sngo-'dos and his mother, Ye-shes-sgron-ma. His principal student was one Saṃgharatna (Dge-'dun-nor-bu), who in turn was the master of a certain Ratnabhadra (Nor-bu-bzang-po). He may have been the same Chos-rje Dge-'dun-rgyal-mtshan who acted as master of ceremonies during the ordination of 'Khon-ston Dpal-'byor-lhun-grub (1561–1637), teacher of Zur-chen Chos-dbyings-rang-grol. See GKCB, p. 299.

3. The colophon says that the text was written by Dge-'dun-rgyal-mtshan in a forest hermitage during the first half of the last month of autumn in the year of the pig. See OGTL, fol. 26: *drin chen saṃga'i mtshan can gyis : thugs dgongs rdzogs phyir dge 'dun rgyal mtshan gyis : phag lo ston zla tha chung yar ngo la chanda nags kyi khrod du bris ba'o.*

4. See GKCB, esp. pp. 457–460 and 480–481.

5. See TMLG, fols. 65a.5–66b.8. It has been suggested that the author of this work was Sha-gzugs-pa Ngag-dbang-bkra-shis-rnam-rgyal, disciple of Rdo-rje-brag

Rig-'dzin Ngag-gi-dbang-po (1580–1639). The manuscript, therefore, has been dated to around the seventeenth century. Recently, the authorship of the text has been a source of some confusion. So far the latest official word on the matter has been offered by Dan Martin as an unpublished addendum (entry no. 638) to Martin 1997 (in reference to p. 93, no. 180). He writes: "[TMLG] should be identified with a title found on a photocopy in the possession of E. Gene Smith, *Zab Rgyas Gter-ma 'i Lo-rgyus Gter-ston Chos-'byung Nor-bu'i 'Phreng-ba,* made from a ms. in 99 (?) folios. The title of this work, as found in the colophon [fol. 96v.81] is: *Gter-ston Rgya-mtsho'i Rnam-thar Nor-bu'i 'Phreng-ba.* Gter-ston Bdud-'dul-rdo-rje (1615–72) is mentioned on fol. 91v.4 and Gter-ston Padma-rig-'dzin-rtsal (1625–97) is mentioned on fol. 90v.3, and further study ought to narrow down the date of this work still further. The fact that these gter-stons of such late date are included here would preclude identifying the present gter-ston history with that of Sha-gzugs-pa, which after all should have a very different title" (e-mail correspondence of January 19, 1999).

Upon closer investigation, however, I believe there is sufficient textual evidence to suggest again that Sha-gzugs-pa, or someone very close to him, was in fact the author of this history. But since I have not uncovered much about Sha-gzugs-pa's life I cannot be certain at this stage. As noted, Sha-gzugs-pa is said to have been a student of Ngag-gi-dbang-po. He must then have been closely tied to the Byang-gter tradition. Such a connection is clearly reflected in the manuscript, where we find a strong emphasis on the major Byang-gter associates including Ngag-gi-dbang-po himself (see TMLG, fol. 90r.2–5). A few lines later, there is explicit reference to the Byang-gter community of E-wam-lcog and 'Phrang-po Rdo-rje-brag (TMLG, fol. 90r.3–4). Interestingly, on line 4, the author tells us that "nowadays the reincarnation of Ngag-dbang Rig'dzin-rdo-rje is known as the Rdo-rje-brag incarnation" *(sras ngag dbang rig su 'dzin rdo rje'i sku 'i skye sprul ni / da lta rdo rje brag sprul pa'i sku zhes).* The first reincarnation of Ngag-gi-dbang-po was Padma-'phrin-las (1641–1717), who at the age of eleven (in 1651) was invited by the fifth Dalai Lama to the monastery of Rdo-rje-brag. Given that the author of this text makes reference to the Rdo-rje-brag incarnation of Ngag-gi-dbang-po, but does not mention Padma'phrin-las by name, the history was probably written sometime before 1651 (the year Padma-'phrin-las was officially recognized) but no earlier than 1639 (the date of Ngag-gi-dbang-po's death). This could explain why we see references in the body of the text to certain prominent seventeenth-century figures, such as the tenth Karma-pa Chos-dbyings-rdo-rje (1605–74) (TMLG, fol. 91r.6), Rtse-le Padma-legs-sgrub (alias Rtse-le Sna-tshogs-rang-grol) (TMLG, fol. 91v.1), Stag-bla Padma-mati (1591–1637) (TMLG, fol. 91v.1), and so forth. Now, the question is the reference to Sha-gzugs-pa's history in Sog-bzlog-pa from 1605–06 (Martin 1997, p. 93, no. 180). We should note that the title of the manuscript under scrutiny is different from the title(s) mentioned in Sog-bzlog-pa, i.e., *Gter-ma'i lo-rgyus dpag-bsam rab-rgyas* (or *Chos-'byung phan-bde dpag-bsam rab-tu rgyas-pa'i 'dod-'jo).* Curiously, the first title is indeed the same title listed under Sha-gzugs-pa's name in the library catalogue of the Potala palace (see PLKC, p. 480). I do not believe, however, that our text could have been written as early as 1605, even if we were to allow for later emendations. Hence, it appears the question of authorship still remains unsettled.

6. See GTCB, fols. 182.6–185.3. Reprinted in BDTT, vol. 3, part 1, pp. 523–524.
7. See NBDS, fols. 139.3–6 and 228.4–231.
8. See RCBP, vol. 1, fols. 524.6–525.6 and 537.3–538.2.
9. See GJGT, vol. 1, fols. 588.3–589.4.
10. LTKG.

11. Consider, for example, the trials and tribulations of Padma-gling-pa (1450–1521) described in Aris 1988a. For a defense of the *gter-ma* tradition, see Dudjom Rinpoche 1991, vol. 1, pp. 927–928. On false *gter-ma* revelations, see Thondup 1986, pp. 154–156. A detailed defense of the *Bar-do thos-grol*, in particular, can be found in THGL.

12. I borrow these expressions from Schopen 1997, p. 3. In the use of the term *historical*, I have in mind basic assumptions on which historical research as a professional discipline has developed in Europe and North America. See, for example, the scholarship surveyed in Iggers 1997.

13. On the early history of the *gter-ma* discoveries, see Dargyay 1979; Dudjom Rinpoche 1991; Thondup 1986; Kapstein 1989; and Germano 1994. A modern example of *gter-ma* discovery is discussed in Germano 1998.

14. For insightful discussions of the *gter-ma* tradition in general, see Gyatso 1986, 1993, 1994, 1996, 1998.

15. See discussion in Gyatso 1993. On the relationship between canonicity and authenticity in Tibet, especially in light of the issue of ongoing revelation in the Rnying-ma-pa tradition, see Mayer 1996; Germano forthcoming. To be sure, the clearest distinction between the Rnying-ma-pa and the Gsar-ma-pa schools is the degree to which each accepted ongoing revelation as valid.

16. This threefold process follows the traditional mode described for the transmission of the ancient tantras compiled in the *Rnying-ma'i rgyud-'bum*. See Dudjom Rinpoche 1991, pp. 447–456.

17. LGNB, fols. 28–31. In this mode of transmission, no direct teaching actually takes place, since the enlightened mind of the teacher is one and the same with the minds of his disciples.

18. LGNB, fols. 32–35.

19. LGNB, fols. 35–36.

20. LGNB, fols. 36–37.

21. Gyatso 1998, p. 154.

22. Gyatso 1998, p. 155.

23. Understood in terms of the renunciation of ten nonvirtues (*mi-dge-ba bcu*): (1) murder (*srog-gcod-pa*), (2) theft (*ma-byin-par len-pa*), (3) sexual misconduct (*'dod-pas log-par g.yem-pa*), (4) falsehood (*rdzun-du smra-ba*), (5) slander (*phra-ma*), (6) senseless chatter (*ngag-bkyal-ba*), (7) verbal abuse (*tshig-rtsub-mo*), (8) covetousness (*brnab-sems*), (9) vindictiveness (*gnod-sems*), and (10) holding wrong views (*log-lta*).

24. LTKG, fols. 523–524: *e ma ho : 'di ltar rgyal po'i thugs dgongs rdzogs byas nas : bod khams bde zhing skyid pa 'di nyid ni : lo pan skyes mchog rnams kyis* [524] *byin rlabs dang : bod kyis dge bcu spyad pa'i byin rlabs yin te : nam zhig 'di yang mi rtag 'gyur zhing 'gro : spyir ni 'dus byas thams cad mi rtag cing : ring por mi thogs 'jig pa'i chos can yin : khyad par bod kyi bde skyid lha 'dra 'di : mi rtag 'gyur ba nam kha'i 'ja' tshon 'dra : de ltar slob dpon padma 'byung gnas gyis : phi ma ci 'byung da lta sems la stos.*

25. LTKG, fol. 524.

26. One of the earliest temples in the Yar-lung valley built by Srong-btsan-sgam-po. See Vitali 1990, p. 13; Dorje 1996, pp. 255–257.

27. LTKG, fol. 525: *gson cig lo pan rgyal blon bod 'bangs rnams : chos khrims mi rtag sde dpon thams cad 'tsho rlag byed : rgyal khrims 'jig rtags rje la 'bangs mi nyan : blon po khrims med rje la kha log byed : 'gro la phan pa'i sangs rgyas bsgrub mkhan med : yon tan 'bras bus bsod nams su la 'byung : lha sa khra 'brug bsam yas*

'o re brgyal : gtsug lag khang du lud dang sha chang bsog : phyir yang dgon mchog gsum po mi ro bzhin du dor : sgos ni drin can pha ma dam sri bzhin du brdung : rje yi bzhengs pa'i chos 'khor kun kyang gog : phyogs kyi mi rnams sems can sdug tu 'jug : skabs gcig bod yul du chos med pa yang 'byung : rje med 'bangs med pa yang lo mang du 'byung : skabs gcig bod hor gyi 'jigs pa yang 'byung : long spyod chung zhing 'byor pa zhag du 'gro : kye ma thub pa'i dam chos bstan pa 'di : dam nyams bdud kyi rim par 'jigs pa 'byung.

28. LTKG, fol. 526: *'dul ba'i bstan pa nyams pa'i snga ltas su : klu mo gangs bzang bu mo 'od zer ldan : bdud kyi sprul pa bud med snying la 'jug : log pa'i blo gsal nyon mongs lnga la brtson : phra ma lkog zas bud med rnams kyi zhim lto byed : bud med pho rgyab smad tshong byed pa 'ong : phyi bdar sal sil zur mig byed cing skyes pa 'di : dge slong rnams la snying sdug shar po 'ong : chos pa rnams kyang chags pa bcad do zer : bud med brten cing bu chung gso ba 'byung : chos pa 'di 'dra zer zhing sdig pa gsog : mi rnams chos la dad pa med pa 'byung : chos skor zhugs nas khengs grags 'tshol ba 'byung : snying rje chung zhing khrims la mi gnas shing : log spyod byed cing dmag las byed pa 'byung : de ltar byas pas nag phyogs bdud rigs dga' : dkar phyogs pham nas bstan pa nyams pa 'byung.*

29. The reference may be to a text found in a vast majority of Kar-gling collections entitled *Sku-gsum bla-ma'i rnal-'byor-gyi gsol-'debs dug-gsum ma-spangs rang-grol.* See B1a, fols. 3–7; B2, fols. 14b.4–15b.2; B3, fols. 1–2; B5; CH, fols. 457–460; DH, fols. 1–5; GK, fols. 49–52; KS, fols. 1–3; NE; PY, fols. 29–31; S1, fols. 1–5; S3; T5; T6, fols. 37–40; T7, vol. 2, fols. 273–276; T8, vol. 1, fols. 29–33; ZH, fols. 23–25. Translation in Thurman 1994, pp. 99–104, and Gyatrul Rinpoche and Wallace 1998, pp. 305–307.

30. LGNB, fols. 37–38.

31. LGNB, fol. 38: *thos pa tsam gyis ngan song gi skye sgo gcod pa / go ba tsam gyis bde chen gyi sa la bshegs pa / don yid la byed pa rnams ni lhun gyis grub pa'i rig 'dzin phyir mi ldog pa'i sa la gshegs par byed pa.*

32. Tib., *res 'ga' ngam nag glan pa lta bu la / res 'ga' gtad med byis pa'i rnam pa can.* The expression "aimless child" (*gtad-med byis-pa*) carries the sense of living openly without fixating on predetermined goals. This is a description that is frequently applied to wandering yogis and other such religious visionaries.

33. TMLG, fol. 66a: *zab chos zhi khro dgongs pa rang grol 'di / spel bar 'phang pas rin chen gter du sba e ma / 'di nyid 'don pa'i skal ldan rigs kyi bu / mdog dkar gzugs mdzes smra 'don khro bo'i dbyibs / res 'ga' ngam nag glan pa lta bu la / res 'ga' gtad med byis pa'i rnam pa can / ma dang mkha' 'gro 'du ba'i rigs kyi bu / dad pa stobs che shes rab dbang po rno / mi sems mi 'dzin dpa' bo'i tshul 'dzin pa / 'brug sprul lo pa dpal gyi ming can 'byung / de nyid lo tstsha klu'i rgyal mtshan yin / 'di dang 'phrad kyis chos la zong ma byed / mthong thos 'brel pas 'khor ba mtha' can yin.* Cf. also LTKG, fol. 533; GKCB, p. 457.

34. Tib., *ring zhing ldem bag dal bus khyung [g]shog bgros.* My guess is that this is an archaic idiomatic expression meaning graceful and sagacious.

35. LTKG, fols. 527–528: *mdog dkar dri zhim spyan gyi dbang po mdzas : shangs kyi dbyibs mtho cung zad zhal 'dzum pa : ring zhing ldem bag dal bus khyung [g]shog bgros : byi ba'i lo pa 'gro ba'i skyabs gcig po : byang sems yin rtags brla g.yas rme bas mdzas : bzang po'am ni dpal gyi ming can gcig : nyang kong phyogs sam khams kyis phyogs nas 'ong : sangs rgyas stong gi bstan pa ma rdzogs bar : 'gro 'dren karma'i [528] bstan pa rdzogs mi 'gyur : 'di la bdud byed bde ba can du skye : skad cig cha shas 'di yi zhal mthong bas : skye ba bdun gyis las sgrib nges par dag : thugs rje chen po'i sprul pa byang chub sems : nges par 'byung rjes bod 'bangs skyobs par nges : 'di nyid gang du gnas kyang long spyod 'du : bdud gyi bar cad glo bur ye*

'brog 'byung : '*khor gyi nang nas bar chad brtsams byed pa :* dam nyams lcags phag nag po grib zon gyis.

36. LGNB, fols. 39–40: *e ma chos rnams kun gyi mthar thug pa / yang gsang bla med kun gyi snying po mchog / sdug bsngal bde ba chen por grol ba'i thabs / da lta mngon par sangs rgyas rang thob yin / dus gsum rgyal ba'i dgongs pa snying po'i don / bcud bsdus mar gyi snying po yang zhun 'di / bdag 'dra o rgyan padma 'byung gnas gyis / phyi rabs 'gro ba rnams kyi don du bkod / su la ma spel rin chen gter du sbas / ma 'ongs snyigs ma dus kyi tha ma la / lnga bcu khar la dus kyi tha ma'i dus / de dus 'di 'dra'i* [40] *gdams pa med pa kun / ngan song gnas su 'gro bar the tshom med / de phyir snyigs ma'i sems can la phan phyir / yi ger btab nas sgam po'i ri la sbas / de dus snying gi bu mchog skal ldan gcig / pha la grub thob nyi zla'i ming can 'byung / karma gling pa zhes bya snying stobs can / brla g.yas sme ba ye shes spyan drangs mtshan / 'brug sbrul lo pa las kyis dpa' po'i rigs / skal ldan skye bu de dang 'di 'phrad shog.* Cf. also OGTL, fols. 22–23; GKCB, p. 457.

37. OGTL, fol. 23.

38. The sources are not consistent with regard to the total number of years required for these teachings to be held under seal. In several cases, the number six is given rather than seven. See TMLG, fol. 65b; GKCB, p. 459; NBDS, fol. 231.

39. OGTL, fol. 24.

40. See Thondup 1986, pp. 161–162.

41. Gyatso 1998, p. 169.

42. LGNB, fol. 42. The '*Og-sgo bde-chen* belongs to the completion stage "path of means" (*thabs-lam*) genre of yogic literature, and as such describes techniques of sexual yoga aimed at generating the four types of bliss. In the Kar-gling tradition these texts are usually affiliated with the teachings of Nyi-zla-'od-zer. See chapter 7.

43. OGTL, fol. 24.

44. OGTL, fols. 24–25.

45. LGNB, fol. 42.

6. A Tale of Fathers and Sons

1. GKCB, p. 480.

2. TMLG, fol. 66a: *yos kyi lo pa dngos grub ming can cig / mig ni che zhing dpral ba'i dbyibs mtho ba / shes rab btson 'grus dad dang snying rus can / las can rtags su lto bar rme bas mdzes / de nyid dbang gis bla ma'i rnam thar skyong.* See also LTKG, fol. 535.

3. GKCB, p. 480.

4. A version of the *Gdams-zab 'pho-ba 'ja'-gzugs-ma* can be found in RCTD, vol. 32, pp. 547–599. The expression '*pho-ba 'jag-zug-ma,* meaning "planting the stalk," refers to the practice of placing a blade of grass in the hole that forms at the crown of the head induced by the successful practice of transference. This *gter-ma* of Nyi-zla-sangs-rgyas lies at the center of the pilgrimage festivities of the famous '*Bri-gung 'Pho-ba chen-mo* celebration first established by Rin-chen-phun-tshogs (1509–1557) and later instituted by the brothers Dkon-mchog-rin-chen (1590–1654) and Rig-'dzin-chos-grags (1595–1659). See Kapstein 1998, p. 180 n. 23. As I will show in part III, the 'Bri-gung hierarch Rin-chen-phun-tshogs was a leading figure in the transmission of the Kar-gling *Zhi-khro.*

5. Huber 1999, p. 51, discusses the symbolic and ritual significance of mandala lakes in relation to the sacred mountains of Tibet.

6. GKCB, p. 480.

7. In the *Blue Annals*, we find reference to another *gter-ma* recovered from this Black Mandala Lake, which is said to be located behind Sgam-po monastery. Evidently, this treasure had been concealed by Sgam-po-pa himself and was extracted by his own disciple Dung-tsho-ras-pa between the years 1315 and 1316. The precise content of this *gter-ma* is not specified. See Roerich 1949, pp. 718–719.

8. GKCB, p. 480; NBDS, fol. 139. On the possible identity of this mythic figure, Gtsug-na Rin-chen is mentioned by name in a list of deities from a Bon-po manuscript entitled *Bon-po'i lha-bsangs*. See Nebesky-Wojkowitz 1956, p. 324. In addition, a *klu* by the name of Gtsug-na is said to be the father of 'Gog-bza', mother of the famous Gesar of Gling. See Karmay 1998, p. 489.

9. This is the most important mandala lake of Dag-pa shel-ri, the Pure Crystal Mountain. See Huber 1999, pp. 28–29, 51–52, and 61–71.

10. GKCB, p. 480.

11. On whom see LRCB, pp. 302–303. He was said to have founded in Kong-po the monastery of Dga'-ldan-ma-mo. GKCB, p. 961.

12. See DLSY , vol. 3, fol. 429.1–3. The names Nyi-zla-sangs-rgyas and Mkha'-spyod-dbang-po appear together in a series in the transmission lineage for Padma-las-'brel-rtsal's *Sgab-'dre'i 'khor-lo dang bcas-pa phyag-len dam-'khrid*. Note also the names Nyi-zla-chos-rje and Nyi-ma-zla-ba. The former is, of course, the son of Karma-gling-pa and the grandson of Nyi-zla-sangs-rgyas; the latter is the teacher of Rgya-ra-ba Nam-mkha'-chos-kyi-rgya-mtsho. The complete lineage is listed as follows: Gter-ston Rin-chen-tshul-rdor [i.e., Padma-las-'brel-rtsal, b.1228]; Grub-chen Legs-ldan-pa [i.e., Shwa-ban Rgyal-sras Legs-pa, 1290–1366]; Mtshungs-med Rang-byung-rdo-rje [i.e., Karma-pa III, 1284–1339]; Mkhas-grub Nor-bu-bzang-po; Sprul-sku Mkha'-spyod-dbang-po [i.e., Zhwa-dmar-pa II, 1350–1405]; Chos-rje Nyi-zla-sangs-rgyas; De-dbon Nyi-zla-chos-rje; Bla-ma Nyi-ma-zla-ba [i.e., Nyi-zla-'od-zer, b.1409/1421]; Drin-can Kumāratha [i.e., Kumārādza ?]; Drin-can; Yadyavajra; Lha-sras Rnam-sprul 'Bri-gung-pa Rin-chen-phun-tshogs; Ras-chung Rnam-sprul Bkra-shis-rgya-mtsho; G.yu-sgra'i sprul-pa Kun-dga'-tshe-mchog.

13. NBDS, fol. 139.

14. GKCB, pp. 480–481.

15. In the fifth Dalai Lama's *Gsan-yig*, two transmissions are listed for Nyi-zla-sangs-rgyas's *'pho-ba* treasure: one that had been transmitted in writing (*'Pho-ba 'jag-tshugs-ma'i nyams-'khrid yi-ge'i lung*) and another that had not (*'Pho-ba 'jag-tshugs-ma shin-tu zab-pa'i nyams-'khrid yi-ger ma-'khod*). Presumably, the transmission that was eventually written down was the one Nyi-zla-sangs-rgyas discovered at Black Mandala Lake. The unwritten scripture is said to have been transmitted directly from Padmasambhava in a pure vision (*dag-snang*). See DLSY, vol. 3, fols. 175.3–176.4; TLSY, fol. 390.

16. GKCB, p. 480–481: *bla ma sku gsum dang / padma zhi khro'i skor bton pa yin zer ba 'dug kyang nges pa mi snang ste padma zhi khro ni karma [481] gling pa'i gter chos yin no.*

17. GKCB, p. 481: *'on kyang gter ston 'di'i sras gter ston karma gling pa yin pas / de'i gter 'don pa'i grogs kyang mdzad cing / chos brgyud kyang yab 'di las kyang 'phel bar snang ngo.*

18. According to all available sources, Nyi-zla-sangs-rgyas supposedly lived for at least 120 years! See LGNB, fol. 41; OGTL, fol. 22; TMLG, fol. 66b; GKCB, p. 481; NBDS, fol. 139; RCBP, fol. 525; BDTT, p. 441.

19. LGNB, fol. 40; TMLG, fol. 65a; GTCB, fol. 182; GKCB, p. 457; NBDS, fol. 228; RCBP, fol. 537; GJGT, fol. 588; BDTT, p. 523. According to a prophecy re-

ported in Rgya-ra-ba's *Nor-bu'i phreng-ba* (LGNB, fol. 40.3), Karma-gling-pa was to be born in either the dragon or snake year (*'brug-sbrul-lo*). Guru Bkra-shis reports that Karma-gling-pa was born sometime during the sixth *rab-byung*, which corresponds to the period 1327–87. See GKCB, p. 597; also the discussion in Back 1987, p. 18. Within that cycle the dragon and snake match the years 1328–29, 1352–53, 1364–65, and 1376–77. The dates 1356–1405 offered without reference to a source in Reynolds 1989, p. 3, and later repeated in both Samuel 1993, p. 503, and Prats 1996, p. 14, are therefore not probably correct.

20. Unfortunately, this work is not presently extant. Reference in TMLG, fol. 65a; GTCB, fol. 182; NBDS fols. 228–229; BDTT, vol. 3, p. 523.

21. GKCB, p. 457; also B3, fol. 62.

22. GKCB, p. 457–458.

23. T7, vol. 2, fols. 303–432; Gyatrul Rinpoche and Wallace 1998, pp. 83–273.

24. T7, vol. 2, fol. 432.1–2: *grub thob karma gling pas sgam po gdar gyi ri bo nas bton pa'o / gcig brgyud du byas nas / guru nyi zla 'od zer la zab chos 'di'i bdag por bka' babs pa'o.* Karma-gling-pa is also the implied author of the *Bar-do drug-khrid* in the various *Gsan-yig* of the fifth Dalai Lama, of Gter-bdag-gling-pa, of Phyogs-las-rnam-rgyal, and of Bdud-'joms Rin-po-che. See DLSY, fol. 89.1; TLSY, fol. 389.2; ZDTY, fols. 510.5–511.2; DJTY, fol. 175.5, respectively.

25. Additional evidence supporting Nyi-zla-'od-zer's role as custodian and redactor of the *Bar-do drug-khrid* teachings comes to us in the form of a short introductory text that he wrote for his student Nam-mkha'-chos-kyi-rgya-mtsho, the *Nyams-khrid dgongs-pa rang-grol-gyi sa-bcad lde-mig rang-grol.* See T7, vol. 2, fols. 255–265. This work lays out the entire content of the *Bar-do-drug-gi khrid-yig* in a simple outline format arranged topically beginning with the preliminary practices (*sngon-'gro*) and followed by a succession of details for each of the six bardo periods. The language of the text is so closely identical to that of the larger work on which it is based that the framework of the *Bar-do khrid-yig* can almost be reconstructed verbatim from the outline—a fact that suggests the consistent hand of a single author, or at least intimate knowledge of a preexisting written document.

26. See B1, fols. 171–188; B1a, fols. 499–533; B4; DH, fols. 403–437. Translation in Tucci [1949] 1972, pp. 189–205. A supplement to this work by Rgya-ra-ba is still extant, the *Srid-pa bar-do'i dge-sdig rang-gzugs bstan-pa'i lhan-thabs* [i.e., *Srid-pa bar-do'i ngo-sprod-kyi lhan-thabs dbyangs-snyan lha'i gaṇdhe*]. Included in B1, fols. 189–196; B1a, fols. 535–549; B4; DH, fols. 439–453; T3; T7, vol. 3, fols. 163–173.

27. See 'Cham-dpon Nag-'phel, *'Brug-gzhung 'cham-gyi bshad-pa* and *Lho-tsang dang nags-mo'i ljongs-kyi 'cham-yig kun-gsal me-long.* This was also suggested to me by Lawrence Epstein (personal communication, July 1998) and was later reaffirmed independently by both Françoise Pommaret and Gyurme Dorje (e-mail communications, September 11, 1998, and May 13, 1999, respectively).

28. Pommaret 1989, p. 117.

29. Gyurme Dorje, e-mail communication, September 11, 1998.

30. Also, the incipit of the *Brgya-phyag sdig-sgrib rang-grol* states clearly that it belongs to the *Bar-do thos-grol* of the *Padma zhi-khro.* See, for example, B1a, fol. 500.3–4. Is it possible that this text and the *Srid-pa bar-do'i dge-sdig rang-gzugs bstan-pa'i gdams-pa srid-pa bar-do rang-grol* are the only surviving works from Karma-gling-pa's *Thugs-rje chen-po padma zhi-khro*? On that question, we should also consider the evidence for the existence of another manuscript identified as belonging to the *Padma zhi-khro.* In the *dkar-chag* of an unpublished Kar-gling *Thos-grol* collection preserved

in the library of Ri-bo-che Rje-drung Byams-pa-'byung-gnas of Padma-bkod (RB), there is indication that the version of the famous *Chos-nyid bar-do gsal-'debs* included there actually forms part of the larger *Padma zhi-khro* collection. The evidence comes from the full title given in that index, *Thugs-rje chen-po padma zhi-khro'i nyams-khrid yang-snying lam-khyer las chos-nyid bar-do'i gsal-'debs thos-grol chen-mo.* I wish to thank Gene Smith for kindly sharing his notes on this rare collection. We might furthermore consider the rediscovered treasure (*yang-gter*) known by the similar title *Bla-rdzogs thugs-gsum thugs-rje chen-po padma zhi-khro* in RCTD, vol. 34, pp. 235–432. The original text is said to have been revealed by a certain Nyi-ma-seng-ge and later recovered by 'Jam-dbyangs Mkhyen-rtse'i-dbang-po (1820–1892). Gyurme Dorje claims that Nyi-ma-seng-ge was a descendant of Karma-gling-pa, but I have seen no evidence in support of this identification. See Dorje 1987, p.170 n.186.

31. Thondup 1986, p. 82; Gyatso 1998, p. 256.

32. Gyatso 1998, p. 256.

33. Thondup 1986, p. 83.

34. GKCB, p. 458.

35. LGNB, fol. 40; TMLG, fol. 65a; NBDS, fol. 229; RCBP, fol. 537; GJGT, fol. 589.

36. LGNB, fol. 40; TMLG, fol. 65a; NBDS, fol. 229.

37. Mumford (1989) provides interesting ethnographic detail about the link between gossip and untimely death. In his particular case study from Nepal, he writes about the importance of the timeliness of death and the consequences of an unlucky one. Untimely death instigates malicious talk (*mi-kha*), which is believed to harm the deceased's family and to force the soul (*bla*) to wander (p. 199).

38. GKCB, p. 458.

39. Gyatso 1986, p. 17.

40. There is yet another tale about the untimely death of Karma-gling-pa involving his female partner. This brief episode, which I have not found in any Tibetan source, is reported by Chris Butters in Tshewang et al. 1995: "[Karma Lingpa] was writing out the full text of a Terma when his bamboo pen needed sharpening. (To sharpen a pen for such tasks, one needs a very special knife). He called outside for any of his disciples, but none of them were there to attend on him. Then his wife, seeing him, laughed disrespectfully and threw an old kitchen knife to him. It hit him and cut him deeply on the thigh. The result of this bad auspice was that the text of Karma Lingpa could not be completed, and it is incomplete to this day; the Terton died shortly afterwards" (p. 11).

41. LGNB, fol. 40; OGTL, fol. 25; TMLG, fol. 65a; NBDS, fol. 229.

42. OGTL, fol. 25.

43. OGTL, fol. 25: *shog ser bu dang bcas pa slob ma dam tshig can gcig la bcol ba dang : khyod kyi nga'i bu chung bsam pa ma tshar gyis bar du nyar ra legs por gyis : dus phyis kho rang la gtod dang kho la slob ma brgyud pa gsum pa nyi zla'i ming can 'ong ba la gtad dgos pa yin gsungs.*

44. LGNB, fol. 41; TMLG, fol. 65a; NBDS, fol. 229; GKCB, p. 458.

45. LGNB, fol. 41; GKCB, p. 458.

46. LTKG, fol. 528.3.

47. TMLG, fol. 65b.

48. See GTCB, fol. 183; GKCB, p. 458; NBDS, fol. 229; BDTT, p. 523.

49. TMLG, fol. 65b; NBDS, fol. 229.

50. TMLG, fol. 65b.

51. TMLG, fol. 65a; GTCB, fol. 183; NBDS, fol. 229; BDTT, p. 523.

52. GTCB, fol. 182; repeated in BDTT, p. 523 and referred to in GKCB, p. 458.

53. The error is repeated in Gu-ru Bkra-shis, and later in Mkhas-btsun-bzang-po's *Biographical Dictionary* (BDTT), but of course both of them are simply quoting Karma-mi-'gyur-dbang-rgyal's earlier account in GTCB.

54. TMLG, fol. 65b: *bdag gi nad 'di gso ba la 'jig rten gyi sman phal gyis mi gsos pas / grong 'jug byas ba'i phyir bdag gis ri rab kyi byang phyogs nas / shi gsos kyi sman blangs nas zhag gsum la sleb ste 'ongs / de bar yab kyis spur la bsrung bsdom gyis shig gsungs nas grongs ngo.* See also GTCB, fol. 183; GKCB, p. 458; NBDS, fol. 229; BDTT, p. 523.

55. GKCB, p. 458. Charles Ramble informs us that among certain tribes along the Tibetan-Nepalese border it was commonly held that a poisoner's lineage dies out within one or two generations. See Ramble 1997, p. 157.

56. Aris 1988a, p. 69.

57. Chan 1994, p. 653. Note also Karmay's interesting discussion of these three regions in relation to the early myths of Gnya'-khri-btsan-po and the death of Gri-gum-btsan-po. Karmay 1998, pp. 211–227.

58. Chan 1994, p. 653.

59. Chan 1994, p. 653; Karmay 1998, p. 216–217; Ramble 1997, pp. 144–146, 156–158.

60. These being the (1) *Bar-do drug-gi rtsa-tshig* (see B1, fols. 60–62; B1a, fols. 129–133; B2, fols. 95a.3–96a.2; B4; B5; DH, fols. 179–183; GK, fols. 233.4–236.3; KS, fols. 113.6–115.1; NE; PY, fols. 341.2–343–6; RB; S1, fols. 218.4–221.4; T3; T4, fols. 50b.2–53a.3; T5; T6, fols. 403.6–407.1; T8, vol. 2, fols. 387–389; and ZH. Translation in Evans-Wentz and Dawa Samdup [1927] 2000, pp. 199–202; Fremantle and Trungpa 1975, pp. 100–102; Thurman 1994, pp. 108–111; Gyatrul Rinpoche and Wallace 1998, pp. 286–291); (2) the *Bar-do 'phrang-sgrol-gyi smon-lam* (see B1, fols. 63–66; B1a, fols. 135–141; B2, fols. 96a.2–97a.4; B4; B5; DH, fols. 185–191; GK, fols. 236.3–239.4; KS, fols. 115.2–117.2; PY, fols. 343.6–346.4; RB; S1, fols. 221.4–224.5; T3, T4; fols. 53a.3–58a.2; T5; T6, fols. 407.1–411.2; T7, vol. 3; T8, vol. 2, fols. 389–393; and ZH. Translation in Evans-Wentz and Dawa Samdup [1927] 2000, pp. 202–205; Fremantle and Trungpa 1975, pp. 98–99; Thurman 1994, pp. 115–116; and, Gyatrul Rinpoche and Wallace 1998, pp. 277–286; and (3) the *Bar-do'i smon-lam 'jigs-skyobs-ma* (see B1, fols. 126–128; B1a, fols. 261–266; B2, fols. 94a.1–95a.2; B4; B5; DH, fols. 313–319; GK, fols. 239.5–242; KS, fols. 117.3–119; NE; PY, fols. 346.4–350; S1, fols. 224.5–228; T3; T4, fols. 58a.2–61a.3; T5; T6, fols. 411.2–416; T7, vol. 3; T8, vol. 2, fols. 393–395; and ZH. Translation in Evans-Wentz and Dawa Samdup [1927] 2000, pp. 205–208; Fremantle and Trungpa 1975, pp. 103–105; Thurman 1994, pp. 112–114; and, Gyatrul Rinpoche and Wallace 1998, pp. 291–295).

61. Generally, the four initiations (*dbang-bzhi*) of Supreme Yoga Tantra (*anuttarayoga-tantra*) consist of the common vase initiation (*thun-mong-pa bum-dbang*) and the three higher initiations (*thun-min mchog-dbang gong-ma gsum*); that is, (1) the secret initiation (*gsang-dbang*), (2) the initiation of discriminating pristine wisdom (*shes-rab ye-shes-kyi dbang*), and (3) the initiation of word and meaning (*tshig-don-gyi dbang*). For details consult the lengthy discussion in Snellgrove 1987, pp. 213–277. More specifically in the Kar-gling tradition, as presented by Nyi-zla-'od-zer, the four initiations are listed as (1) the vase initiation (*bum-dbang*), (2) the secret initiation (*gsang-dbang*), (3) the pristine initiation (*ye-shes-dbang*), and (4) the indivisible innate initiation (*dbyer-med lhan-skyes dbang*). See, for example, *Gsangs-sngags rdo-rje theg-pa'i chos-spyod thun-bzhi'i rnal-'byor sems-nyid rang-grol*, T8, vol. 1, fols. 18.4–19.4. The precise manner in which the four initiations relate to the

bardo practices is a topic that requires a more thorough treatment. It must suffice to comment here that these initiations are founded on a distinctively Rdzogs-chen soteriology, which is aimed at the recovery of a primordial state of realization (*ye-shes*) through recognition of the intrinsic purity of reality (*chos-nyid*). As noted in chapter 3, freeing oneself (*rang-grol*) from the bondage of conditioned existence can be achieved in this life in dependence on the techniques of breakthrough (*khregs-chod*) and direct transcendence (*thod-rgal*), or naturally during the experiences of dying and postmortem transition. The four initiations provide a preliminary introduction to the realization of these methods.

62. TMLG, fol. 66b. 'Jam-mgon Kong-sprul writes that a certain Dngos-grub-rgya-mtsho (identified as Nyi-zla-sangs-rgyas in the TMLG) had been the first to receive this transmission. See B3, fol. 63.

63. See DLSY, vol. 4, fols. 90–91; RCKC, fols. 69–70; B1, fols. 1–6; B2, fols. 15–16; B4; CH; DH; T3.

64. DLSY, vol. 4, fol. 90.6–91.1: *deng sang brgyud yig phal cher la gter ston gyis sras la gnang ba 'dra zhig 'dug kyang / gter ston sku tshe thung bas gnang long ma* [91] *byung / yab kyis dgung lo brgya lo brgya nyi shu gzhugs pas des gnang ba yin / gter ston dam sel gyis gshegs zer ba'i sil can de nas brgyud pa ni min no.*

65. TMLG, fol. 66b; GTCB, fol. 185.

7. The Gampodar Treasures

1. In some of the later histories a third work was also said to be included, the *Mgon-po sde-brgyad*.

2. GKCB, pp. 457–458: *'on kyang bar do* [458] *drug khrid sogs ni zhi khro gnyis thun mong yin la dbang dang gdams zab gzhan rnams chig brgyud mdzad.*

3. See chapter 6, note 30.

4. GTCB, fol. 184; GKCB, p. 458; BDTT, p. 524.

5. For details on the importance of certificates (*byang*) in the treasure tradition, see Gyatso nd. On the traditional preparations for the discovery of treasure literature, see Thondup 1986, pp. 137–141.

6. DLSY, vol. 4, fols. 86.3–91.3.

7. Gter-bdag-gling-pa (TLSY, fol. 389) lists the following categories: (1) *lo-rgyus*, (2) *dbang-sgrub*, (3) *rdzogs-rim*, (4) *ngo-sprod*, (5) *thabs-lam*, and (6) *bstan-srung*. Phyogs-las-rnam-rgyal (ZDTY, fol. 510.1) gives (1) *bskyed-rim* (2) *rdzogs-rim*, (3) *khrid*, (4) *ngo-sprod*. Bdud-'joms Rin-po-che (DJTY, fol. 175.6) divides the collection into seven categories: (1) *lo-rgyus*, (2) *dbang*, (3) *bskyed-rim*, (4) *rdzogs-rim*, (5) *ngo-sprod*, (6) *thabs-lam*, and (7) *bstan-srung*.

8. RCKC, vol. 1.

9. The relevant sources are too numerous to mention, but a sampling of some of the more important secondary references can be listed as follows: On the category history, see Tucci 1947; Vostrikov 1970; Hoffman 1970; Satô 1993; Kuijp 1996; Martin 1997. To date, the most extensive study on ritual is still Beyer 1978. This source offers reliable information on several of the subcategories listed earlier; see especially pp. 64–226 (*sgrub-thabs*), 264–275 (*sbyin-sreg*), 340–345 (*gtor-ma*), 399–403 (*dbang*), 432–458 (*bsnyen-pa*). On death ritual and cremation, see Ramble 1982; Kvaerne 1985; Mumford 1989, pp. 195–224. Religious protectors are discussed in Nebesky-Wojkowitz 1956, pp. 343–454. And a brief description of catalogues, or table of contents, can be found in Martin 1996a.

10. An exception is Back 1987, p. 18.

11. In many Tibetan *gter-ma* traditions, the forecast statements are found usually within the cycle itself in the so-called *kha-byang*, "prophecy certificate", or they may be located in more comprehensive works such as the *Padma bka'-thang* of O-rgyan-gling-pa (1323–c.1360). Unfortunately, in the case of the Kar-gling collections, a *kha-byang* has not been located. Also a prophecy for Karma-gling-pa does not appear anywhere in O-rgyan-gling-pa's text. Consequently, we must piece one together through quoted passages in other sources.

12. Bentor 1996, p. 290.

13. Contained in B1, fols. 263–283; B1a, fols. 267–317; B2, fols. 123b.3–134b.6; B4; CH, fols. 25–74; DH, fols. 7–57; GK, fols. 195–227; KS, fols. 147–169; NE; PY, fols. 305–338; RB; S1, fols. 173–211; S3; T2; T3; T4, fols. 5a.1–47a.2; T5; T6, fols. 363–397, T7, vol. 1, fols. 169–197.6; T8, vol. 2, fols. 353–386; ZH, fols. 357–388; trans. Thurman 1994, pp. 205–225.

14. Only two of the three works appear to be extant: the *Zhi-khro 'dus-pa'i las-byang rtsar-phreng tshor-ba rang-grol* (in CH, fols. 85–238; GK, fols. 75–144, 453–491; NE; PY, fols. 61–150, 351–356; T5; T6, fols. 61–177; T7, vol. 1, fols. 233–325; T8, vol. 1, fols. 59–161; and ZH, fols. 33–130); and the *Las-byang chung-ba tshor-ba rang-grol snying-po* (in B3, fols. 3–23; CH, fols. 239–284; GK, fols. 243–265, 509–517; NE; PY, fols. 417–440, 451–461; S3; T5; T6, fols. 179–204, 353–361; T7, vol. 1, fols. 327–353; T8, vol. 2, fols. 5–38; and ZH, fols. 135–161). The former was probably redacted in the mid–fifteenth century by Nyi-zla-'od-zer.

15. This text can be categorized both as *sgrub-thabs* and as *bskang-bshags*. It is contained in B1, fols. 215–238; B1a, fols. 349–395; B2, fols. 31b.5–43b.3; B4; B5; CH, fols. 371–422; DH, fols. 491–537; GK, fols. 383–422; KS, fols. 168.11–192; NE; PY, fols. 265–303; RB; S1, fols. 282–324; S3; T3; T5; T6, fols. 254–293; T7, vol. 1, fols. 397–429; T8, vol. 1, fols. 291–328; ZH, fols. 297–332.

16. See, for example, the brief references in Back 1987, p. 9 and Blezer 1997, pp. 34 n. 155, 65.

17. DLSY, fol. 88.

18. See, for instance, the *Na-rag bskang-bshags nyams-chag rang-grol-gyi cha-lag tshe-'das 'gro-drug rang-grol-gyi zin-bris*, a liturgical supplement by Karma-chags-med (1613–1678) composed in 1665. See GK, fols. 849–939. This same text, with the alternate title *Gnas-'dren 'gro-drug rang-grol khrigs-su bkod-pa*, is included also in PY, fols. 585–685; T5; and T8, vol. 1, fols. 391–471.

19. Blezer 1997, p. 59.

20. It may be possible, however, to reconstruct part of the text on the basis of passages quoted in the exegetical literature. Perhaps the short work entitled *Tshe-'das gnas-'dren bsdus-pa* contains elements of an earlier version, but since the text was later redacted by Karma-chags-med it is probably more representative of the seventeenth century than it is of the fourteenth. See PY, fols. 553–583; S3; and T5. A similar title, *Tshe-'das gnas-'dren rigs-drug rang-grol*, is listed in the *Gsan-yig* of the fifth Dalai Lama (DLSY, fol. 88.4). Unfortunately, without the text in hand it is not possible to determine whether or not this a reference to the same work.

21. See the running commentary by Vajravarman in Skorupski 1983, pp. 81–87, n. 16–33.

22. See B1a, fols. 319–348; B2, fols. 22b.4–30b.2; B5; CH, fols. 329–360; DH, fols. 563–592; GK, fols. 343–369; KS, fols. 131–146; NE; PY, fols. 229–252; RB; S1, fols. 254–281; S3; T5; T6, fols. 227–252.3; T7, vol. 1, fols. 369–390; T8, vol. 2, fols. 39–62; ZH, fols. 267–289; trans. Tucci [1949] 1972, pp. 187–205.

23. The earliest being two fifteenth-century works attributed to Rgya-ra-ba: (1) *Bskang-bshags nyams-chags rang-grol-gyi thugs-dam bskang-ba'i rim-pa* (in CH, fols. 461–512; GK, fols. 499–501, 551–594; NE; PY, fols. 487–514, 525–540; S3; T5; T6, fols. 295–332; T7, vol. 1, fols. 431–465; T8, vol. 1, fols. 329–376; and ZH, fols. 227–263), and (2) *Bskang-bshags nyams-chags rang-grol-gyi sngon-'gro lhan-thabs* (see GK, fols. 53–72, and T7, vol. 1, fols. 217–232).

24. Colophon: *zhes pa rnal 'byor mched lcam du yod kun : gcer bur phyungs te rkyang phyag gus pas 'tshal : ngag gis tshig dbyangs snyan pos bstod byas nas : yid kyis dus gsum bsags pa'i sdig sgrib rnams : gnong 'gyod tshul gyis brga phyag gus bar 'tshal : zhi khro'i lha phyag brgya dang bcur longs pa'i : sgrib sbyongs khyang 'phags sdig sgrib rang grol 'di : na rag bskang bshags la sogs gang byed kyang : 'di bzhin byas pa'i bsod nams tshad las 'das : de phyir brgya phyag 'di la rab tu 'bad : zhi khro dam pa rigs brgya'i brgya phyag sdig sgrib rang grol zhes bya ba : 'khor ba ma stongs bar du ma rdzogs so : bar do thos grol gyi cha lag : na rag bskang bshags kyi cha rkyen : zhi khro las byang gsum gyi don 'dus : shin tu zab par bstan pa 'di ni : kun la spel zhing dus gsum ma chag par brtson par gyis shig.* See B1a, fols. 346.3–347.3; B5; CH, fols. 359.5–360.4; DH, fols. 590.3–591.3; GK, fol. 368.3–6; KS, pp. 145.19–146.10; NE; PY, fols. 251.6–252.4; S1, fols. 280.5–281.6; S3; T5; T6, fols. 251.5–252.3; T7, vol. 1, fol. 390.1–5; T8, vol. 2, fols. 61.6–62.5; ZH, fols. 288.4–289.4.

25. LGNB, fol. 38.

26. B1a, fols. 89.5–90.2: *thos grol chen mo 'di ni ma bsgom par [90] sangs rgyas pa'i chos thos pa tsam gyis grol ba thob pa'i chos : sdig po che gsang lam la 'khrid pa'i chos : skad cig gcig gis bye brag phyed pa'i chos : skad cig gcig gis rdzogs sangs rgyas pa'i chos zab mo yin te : 'dis sleb pa'i sems can ngan song du song ba mi srid do.*

27. T7, vol. 2, fols. 303–432; trans. Gyatrul Rinpoche and Wallace 1998, pp. 83–273.

28. Instructions for *khregs-chod* meditation are contained largely in book 3 of the *Rdzogs-rim bar-do drug-gi khrid-yig*, while the techniques of *thod-rgal* are the subject of book 5. For general descriptions of these practices, see Germano 1994, pp. 286–296.

29. T7, vol. 2, fol. 432.1–2: *grub thob karma gling pas sgam po gdar gyi ri bo nas bton pa'o / gcig brgyud du byas nas / guru nyi zla 'od zer la zab chos 'di'i bdag por bka' babs pa'o.*

30. In T7, vol. 2, fols. 255–265.

31. TLSY, fol. 390.2–4.

32. See ZDTY, fol. 511.4 and DJTY, fols. 179.6–180.1.

33. *Srid-pa bar-do'i ngo-sprod*, B1a, fol. 165.1–4: *kyai rigs kyi bu : de ltar sgom ma shes na : sangs rgyas dang : chos dang : dge 'dun dang : thugs rje chen po rnams dran par gyis la gsol ba thob cig : 'jigs skrag gi snang ba thams cad thugs rje chen po'am : khyod rang gi yi dam du sgoms shig : mi yul du dbang gang zhus pa'i mtshan dang : bal ma dran par gyis la gshin rje chos kyi rgyal po la ma zhed cig.*

34. B1, fols. 57–59; B1a, fols. 123–127; B2, fols. 43b.3–44b.1; B4; B5; DH, fols. 173–177; GK, fols. 229–233; KS, fols. 111–113.5; NE; PY, fols. 338.4–341.2; RB; S1, fols. 213–218.4; T3; T4, fols. 47a.5–50.1; T5; T6, fols. 399–403; T7, vol. 1, fols. 197.6–200; T7, vol. 3, fols. 315–327; and ZH, fols. 389–400; trans. Evans-Wentz and Dawa Samdup [1927] 2000, pp. 197–198; Fremantle and Trungpa 1975, pp. 96–97; Thurman 1994, pp. 105–107; Gyatrul Rinpoche and Wallace 1998, pp. 296–297.

35. Evans-Wentz and Dawa Samdup [1927] 2000, pp. 136 n. 1, 192 n. 4; Tenga Rinpoche 1996, p. 11.

36. See B1, fols. 102–125; B1a, fols. 213–260; B2, fols. 105b.4–117b.5; B4; DH, fols. 263–311; T3; and T7, vol. 3, fols. 255–286.

37. The four joys are: (1) joy (*sga'-ba*), (2) supreme joy (*mchog-dga'*), (3) transcendent joy (*dga'-bral-gyi dga'-ba*), and (4) coemergent joy (*lhan-cig skyes-pa'i dga'-ba*). For discussion, see Gyatso 1982, pp. 66–99.

38. Generally, the third initiation is called "secret initiation" (*gsang-dbang*), involving sexual yoga and the ritual exchange of sexual fluids. In the Kar-gling tradition, as presented by the lama Nyi-zla-'od-zer, this particular initiation is called "pristine wisdom initiation" (*ye-shes dbang*) and is said to culminate in the purification of mental defilements (*yid-sgrib dag*). See Gsangs-sngags rdo-rje theg-pa'i chos-spyod thun-bzhi'i rnal-'byor sems-nyid rang-grol, in T8, vol. 1, fols. 18.4–19.4.

39. T7, vol. 2, fols. 426.6–427.1: *der yang ngos ma zin na srid pa bar dor : pho mo chags pa spyod pa mthong ma zag lhan cig skye pa'i dga' ba'i ye shes dbang gsum bde ba'i ye shes ngos zin nas : mngal sgo khegs nas nges par bar dor grol te.*

40. T7, vol. 3, fols. 329–419.

41. T7, vol. 3, fols. 439–481.

42. The protective deities are discussed at length in Nebesky-Wojkowitz 1956; see also Heller 1990; Ladrang Kalsang 1996; Pommaret 1996; Blondeau 1998.

43. See Samuel 1993, pp. 167–170; Dowman 1997, pp. 18–31.

44. See Blondeau 1971, 1987.

45. See CH, fols. 513–526; GK, fols. 609–618; NE; PY, fols. 541–551; T5; T6, fols. 332–345; T7, vol. 3, fols. 491–498; T8, vol. 1, fols. 379–388; and ZH, fols. 215–223.

46. Nebesky-Wojkowitz 1956, p. 33.

47. Nebesky-Wojkowitz 1956, pp. 31–33.

48. Nebesky-Wojkowitz 1956, p. 92

49. Nebesky-Wojkowitz 1956, pp. 259–263.

50. Nebesky-Wojkowitz 1956, pp. 154–159, 181–198.

51. Nebesky-Wojkowitz 1956, p. 92.

52. Nebesky-Wojkowitz 1956, pp. 318–340.

53. Gyatso 1991, p. 100.

54. Gyatso 1993, p. 109.

55. Gyatso 1991, p. 100.

56. The Tibetan text can be found in B1, fols. 156–170; B1a, fols. 367–426; B4, no. 11; DH, fols. 373–402; T3, no. 10; T7, vol. 2, fols. 479–488. As for the main secondary literature, see Evans-Wentz [1954] 2000, pp. 202–240; Back 1987; Reynolds 1989; Ehrhard 1990, esp. pp. 122–125, n. 140, 143, and 146; Thurman 1994, pp. 227–242. On the so-called *rig-pa gcer-mthong* tradition of Bon Rdzogs-chen, see Achard 1998. It is peculiar that Achard makes no reference to the Buddhist *gter-ma* of the same name.

57. See Back 1987, esp. pp. 9, 19–30; Reynolds 1989, pp. x, xii, and 1; Thurman 1994, p. 227.

58. Gyatso 1991, p. 101. Emphasis added.

59. See in chapter 12.

60. I should mention, for example, Karma-chags-med's *Tshe-'das gnas-'dren bsdus-pa*, in PY, fols. 553–583; S3, no. 8; T5, no. 34, and 'Jam-mgon Kong-sprul's popular *Nyams-chags sdig-sgrib thams-cad bshags-pa'i rgyal-po na-rag dong-sprug(s)*, in CH, fols. 423–450; NE, no. 9; ZH, fols. 333–355.

61. This text is frequently appended to the *Chos-nyid bar-do gsal-'debs*, sometimes without a break in the text and sometimes as a separate book. It is usually found in one form or another in all editions that contain the *Chos-nyid bar-do gsal-'debs*.

See B1, fols. 36–56, B1a, fols. 81–121, B2, fols. 62b.5–74a.4, B4, no. 3, DH, fols. 131–171, KS, pp. 43.7–69, S1, no. 3, T3, no. 2, T7, vol. 3, fols. 87.4–113.3.

62. Consider, for example, Rgya-ra-ba's *Bskang-bshags nyams-chags rang-grol-gyi sngon-'gro lhan-thabs* and *Bskang-bshags nyams-chags rang-grol-gyi thugs-dam bskang-ba'i rim-pa* (see note 23); the *Skong-bshags nyams-chag rang-grol-gyi dbang-bskur gnas-spar 'gro-drug rang-grol* (T7, vol. 1, fols. 127–160); or, the *Bskang-bshags nyams-chags rang-grol-gyi cha-lag tshe-'das gnas-'dren 'gro-drug rang-grol* (CH, fols. 527–536; GK, fols. 733–837; NE; T5; T7, vol. 2, fols. 1–52; T8, vol. 2, fols. 69–169; ZH, fols. 401–459).

63. Khenpo Namdrol, personal communication, August 24, 1997.

64. See Evans-Wentz and Dawa Samdup [1927] 2000, p. 193 n.1.

65. According to Khenpo Namdrol, the *Chos-spyod bag-chags rang-grol* is the main text of the Kar-gling liturgy and represents the actual "book of the dead" (*gshin-yig*) employed during the elaborate *zhi-khro* funeral rites (personal communication, August 15, 1997). This view was also confirmed by the Ven. Nyichang Rinpoche Tuptan Chodak Gyatso, head lama of the Rdzogs-chen monastery in Tokyo. According to Nyichang Rinpoche, in the Rdzogs-chen tradition the text is the sole liturgical text recited every day for the first seven days of the funeral service (personal communication, July 29, 1998).

66. This title is not found among the texts of the various Kar-gling *Zhi-khro* collections consulted thus far. Perhaps it is linked to the *mthong-ba rang-grol* series that appears to be affiliated with the *Rig-pa ngo-sprod gcer-mthong rang-grol*. See, for example, *Dkyil-'khor rnam-dag mthong-ba rang-grol*, see DJTY, fol. 176.4; Nyi-zla-'od-zer's *Chos-nyid bar-do'i khrid-yig mthong-ba rang-grol*, T7, vol. 2, fols. 401–417; the five works attributed to Rgya-ra-ba: (1) *Ngo-sprod mthong-ba rang-grol-gyi mar-me ngo-sprod-kyi lhan-thabs*, T7, vol. 3, fols. 37–40; (2) *Ngo-sprod mthong-ba rang-grol-gyi gzhi'i 'od-gsal ngo-sprod-kyis lhan-thabs*, T7, vol. 3, fols. 29–36; (3) *Chos-nyid bar-do thod-rgal-gyi ngo-sprod mthong-bas rang-grol;* see DLSY, vol. 4, fol. 89.6, TLSY, fol. 390.2–3, and ZDTY, fol. 511.2; (4) *Bar-do'i thos-grol-gyi ngo-sprod mthong-ba rang-grol-gyi lag-len-gyi zin-bris*, see DJTY, fols. 179.6–180.1; (5) *Shel-rdo ngo-sprod mthong-ba rang-grol;* see DLSY, vol. 4, fol. 89.6, and contained in T7, vol. 3, fols. 21–28; and Karma-chags-med's *Chos-nyid bar-do'i khrid-yig mthong-ba rang-grol-gyi ngo-sprod car-phog khyer-ba deb-zhig*, B3, fols. 147–187.

67. See T2. For what it is worth, the *Chos-spyod bag-chags rang-grol* also appears as a separate work, together with the *Thos-grol* itself, in Zhwa-lu ri-sbug sprul-sku Blo-gsal bstan-skyong's (b.1804) publication list (*par-tho*) for the famous Phun-tshogs-gling printing house in Gtsang. The library collection dates from around the late sixteenth or early seventeenth century. See Chandra 1981, vol. 1, p. 31, nos. 632–633. Curiously, the only version of the Kar-gling *Zhi-khro* in which the *Chos-spyod bag-chags rang-grol* is not included is the version collected in the *Rin-chen gter-mdzod*, see text B3. In its place is included another principal sādhana known as the *Las-byang chung-ba tshor-ba rang-grol snying-po*, one of three such texts comprising the *Zhi-khro'i las-byang tshor-ba rang-grol gsum*. See B3, fols. 3–23.

8. The Third Generation

1. Thondup 1986, p. 226 n. 102.
2. Thondup 1986, pp. 162–163.
3. TMLG, fol. 65a.

4. The five sciences are: (1) spiritual philosophy (*nang-gi rig-pa*); (2) dialectics and logic (*gtan-tshigs-kyi rig-pa*); (3) grammar (*sgra'i rig-pa*); (4) medicine (*gso-ba'i rig-pa*); (5) arts and crafts (*bzo-gnas-kyi rig-pa*).

5. LGNB, fol. 41; TMLG, fol. 65b; GKCB, p. 459.

6. LGNB, fol. 41 reads ten rather than seventeen.

7. Several sources give the name Long-po Rtsi-dkar. Long-po was the site of numerous *gter-ma* discoveries attributed to the Rnying-ma visionary Sangs-rgyas-gling-pa (1340–1396), who kept close ties with the Karma Bka'-brgyud tradition. See Dorje 1996, p. 294.

8. LGNB, fol. 42; TMLG, fol. 65b; GKCB, p. 459.

9. The author of the *Gter-ma'i lo-rgyus* (TMLG) only briefly mentions the name of Nyi-zla-'od-zer but discusses at great length an alternative "third-generation disciple," an obscure lama from Kong-po named Mgon-po-rdo-rje. If we accept that there may have been two third-generation disciples, then Nyi-zla-chos-rje may have first traveled to Long-po to present the *Zhi-khro dgongs-pa rang-grol* to Nyi-zla-'od-zer, and then later gone on to Kong-po to give Mgon-po-rdo-rje the authorized transmission of the *Dbang-bzhi 'phrad-tshad rang-grol*. See TMLG, fols. 66a–66b, and the discussion hereafter.

10. LGNB, fol. 42: *khyed lung bstan nas zin / brgyud pa gsum pa yin / ngas chos 'di rlung gi phyogs tsam yang su la bstan pa med / brgyud pa gsum gyi bar du gcig brgyud gces / brgyud pa gsum nas 'gro don rgya chen 'byung gsungs pa yod khyed kyang lo drug gi bar du su la'ang ma bstan / khyed rang nyams su longs / lo drug song nas gzhan la ston pa dang 'gro don rgya chen 'ong / karma gling pa'i 'gro don byang phyogs rgyas / zhes gsungs pas / byang phyogs su bstan pa dar rgyas su 'ong ba'i lung bstan yod.* See also TBZB, fol. 6; TMLG, fol. 65b; GKCB, p. 459; NBDS, fol. 231.

11. LGNB, fol. 42: *zab chos 'di'i 'og sgo bde chen kyi skor ni / lo bcu'i bar du su la ma bstan / de nas ston dang bar chad las grol ba yin gsungs.* See also GKCB, p. 459. I have already noted that the *'Og-sgo bde-chen* is probably a generic title referring to the two "path of means" (*thabs-lam*) texts that are extant in Bdud-'joms Rin-po-che's definitive arrangement of the Kar-gling *Zhi-khro* (T7)—one of these works is in fact attributed to Nyi-zla-'od-zer; this being the *'Og-sgo bde-chen 'dod-chags rang-grol-gyis nyams-khrid gud-du bkol-ba don-bsdus zab-khrid bde-ba rang-grol.* There is also an anonymously authored work that could have been penned by Nyi-zla-'od-zer—the *'Og-sgo bde-ba chen-po'i khrid 'dod-chags rang-grol.* Both texts are found in T7, vol. 3, fols. 439–481 and 329–419, respectively

12. LGNB, fols. 42–43; GKCB, p. 459. Rlang-chen Dpal-gyi-seng-ge was one of Padmasambhava's twenty-five chief disciples. Dge-'dun-rgyal-mtshan gives completely different information, claiming that Nyi-zla-'od-zer was born into the Sdong lineage within the family of Glod. The birthdate given earlier—female-ox (*mo-glang*)—is taken from this source. See OGTL, fol. 25.

13. It is clearly written in the *Gter-ma'i lo-rgyus* that Nyi-zla-'od-zer was the reincarnation of Vajramati. See TMLG, fol. 66a. However, both Rgya-ra-ba and Guru Bkra-shis do not seem to agree. Instead, they claim that Nyi-zla-'od-zer was only prophesied *in the work of* Vajramati. See LGNB, fol. 43, GKCB, p. 459. For a brief biographical sketch of the *gter-ston* Vajramati, see GKCB, p. 490; Bradburn et al. 1995, p. 155.

14. Again Dge-'dun-rgyal-mtshan gives a different name for the father, Lha-rje-phyag-rdor. Rgya-ra-ba and Guru Bkra-shis do not name his mother.

15. OGTL, fol. 25.

16. LGNB, fol. 43. Usually, this is the appellation used for the Sa-skya historian Grags-pa-rgyal-mtshan (1146–1216), but here it may refer to the Phag-mo-gru leader Gong-ma Grags-pa-rgyal-mtshan (1374–1440), who was active in the Rong-yul region of Gtsang in western Tibet.

17. GKCB, p. 459.

18. GKCB, p. 459.

19. RCBP, fol. 538.

20. LGNB, fol. 47; TMLG, fol. 66a; GKCB, p. 460; NBDS, fol. 231; RCBP, fol. 538; GJGT, fol. 589.

21. Rgya-ra-ba is identified by 'Jam-mgon Kong-sprul as the reincarnation of Lha-lcam Gang-'bum, who was perhaps the daughter of Khri-srong-lde'u-btsan. See B3, fol. 63.1.

22. Das [1902] 1988 p. 246, mentions a village in this area named Gru-gu Rgya-ra.

23. Given as Sman-mo Bkra-shis-mgon in Rgya-ra-ba's *Dbyangs-snyan lha'i gandhe*, a supplement to the *Brgya-phyag sdig-sgrib rang-grol*. See, for example, B1a, fol. 546.3.

24. A place called Sman-mo is mentioned in the *Blue Annals* as the site where one Rgya-dar-seng-ge received teachings from Zhang Dga'-ldan-pa, a disciple of the Zhi-byed-pa Rma Chos-kyi-shes-rab (b. 1055). See Roerich 1949, p. 875.

25. GKCB, p. 459.

26. Full name given as Byang-mkhar-po G.yu-shul-ba Kun-mkhyen Chos-sku-'od-zer.

27. GKCB, p. 727.

28. Bar-khams-pa Rgya-ra Klong-chen-pa should not be confused with Rgya-ra-ba Nam-mkha'-chos-kyi-rgya-mtsho as in Martin 1997, p. 58, no. 90. Here the name Nam-mkha'-chos-kyi-rgya-mtsho is mentioned in the context of a controversial fourteenth-century history entitled *Chos-'byung rin-po-che 'i gter-mdzod thub-bstan gsal-bar byed-pa'i nyi-'od*. According to Martin's notes, there are two separate authors associated with the title of this work, Klong-chen-pa (1308–1363) and a certain Rgyal-sras Thugs-mchog-rtsal. Following Bsod-nams-don-grub, Martin proposes that the latter was actually Rgya-ra Klong-chen Nam-mkha'-chos-kyi-rgyal-mtshan (alias Nam-mkha'-chos-kyi-rgya-mtsho), who he then mistakenly conflates with the Kah-thog-pa lama, Kha-ba-dkar-po Nam-mkha'-chos-kyi-rgya-mtsho (on whom see GLKT, pp. 72–3) and with Rgya-ra-ba Nam-mkha'-chos-kyi-rgya-mtsho, holder of the Kar-gling treasure lineage. None of the previously suggested authors, however, can be identified as this latter figure. At this juncture, I am not concerned to argue that Rgya-ra-ba could not have written the *Chos-'byung rin-po-che'i gter-mdzod thub-bstan gsal-bar byed-pa'i nyi-'od*—that problem has yet to be explored—but I will say that it is highly unlikely that either Rgyal-sras Thugs-mchog-rtsal or Rgya-ra Klong-chen could be the fifteenth-century Rgya-ra-ba who systematized Karma-gling-pa's funerary teachings. First, Rgyal-sras Thugs-mchog-rtsal is not a name that is found in any of the available historical and biographical sources that document the transmission of the Kar-gling treasure revelations. If this name Thugs-mchog-rtsal referred to Rgya-ra-ba then we would see both names overlap in other contexts. It is noteworthy, for instance, that a historian as thorough as the fifth Dalai Lama would not have equated the two in his voluminous *Gsan-yig*, assuming of course that he had information on the identity of this Thugs-mchog-rtsal, and indeed he does seem to have had some opinion on the matter (see Martin 1997, p. 59; also Karmay 1988a, p. 33 n. 45). As for the second named author, Rgya-ra Klong-chen, he does share the

names of both Rgya-ra-ba and Klong-chen-pa, and is tied through his teacher to the institution of Dwags-po Rtse-le, but he appears to have been neither one of these two figures. A reference to Rgya-ra Klong-chen-pa is found in GKCB (p. 728), where we learn that he was the principal student of Kun-mkhyen Chos-sku-'od-zer, founder of the old Rtse-le Rnying-ma monastery. This particular Rgya-ra, renowned as the second Klong-chen-pa, was best known for polemical religious writings and not for liturgical redactions of the treasure texts of Karma-gling-pa, which he evidently had nothing to do with. For what it is worth, Rgya-ra Klong-chen's successor, the third Klong-chen-pa, was known also by the name Sha-gzugs-pa Ngag-dbang-bkra-shis-rnam-rgyal, who is the alleged author of TMLG.

29. See GKCB, p. 424. When the old Rtse-le monastery had begun to fall apart, it was transformed into an institution of married monks. At the beginning of the sixteenth century, Bsod-nams-rnam-rgyal—disciple of the eighth Karma-pa Mi-bskyod-rdo-rje (1507–1554) and the second Dpa-bo Gtsug-lag-phreng-ba (1503–1563)—instituted reforms and tried to reestablish the monastery as "pure" (*gtsang-dgon*), that is, celibate. But since Bsod-nams-rnam-rgyal had been recognized as an incarnation of Guru Chos-dbang, a married lama, he was obliged to follow the model of his predecessor. Rtse-le Gsar-pa thus remained a monastery of married monks. See TSLG, fols. 316–320.

30. On the abbatial succession of Dwags-po Rtse-le and Kong-po Thang-'brog monasteries, see TSLG and TSNG, esp. fols. 10–17. Summary treatment can be found in GKCB, pp. 727–28, 745–59.

31. TSLG, fol. 337. Thang-'brog had earlier been a celibate *grwa-tshang* attached to Rtse-le monastery called Smin-grol-bskyed-rdzogs-gling. Mtshungs-med Bstan-'dzin-rdo-rje was the lama at this institution. The *grwa-tshang* was moved to Kong-po to the old site of Thang-'brog 'Od-gsal-rtse sometime between 1560 and 1564 by Mthu-stobs-rnam-rgyal after the death of his brother Dpal O-rgyan-bstan-'dzin. See the brief summary in GKCB, p. 745.

32. TSLG, fol. 339. This was in the wood fire sheep year 1565. Bstan-'dzin-rdo-rje would go on to establish the monasteries of Gtsang-po Mgo-dgu (in 1577) and Long-po Bde-chen (in 1579). Samuel 1993, p. 131, gives some hint as to why a religious institution might shift its celibate status in either direction, citing evidence from modern case studies in Nepal. In the examples among the Sherpas, the building of a new monastery, or even perhaps the renovation of an older established center of celibate monks (as we see in the case of Kong-po Thang-'brog) seemed to be inspired either by some recent economic boom or by the founding of a new center in a nearby village. In the example from Limi in far western Nepal, the shift from a "pure monastery" to one inhabited by married religious specialists was made largely for practical interests, specifically to maintain the monastery and keep it in operation.

33. After Bstan-'dzin-rdo-rje's death, his reincarnation was discovered in the person of Rtse-le Sna-tshogs-rang-grol (Padma-legs-grub, 1608–1680), on whom see chapter 10.

34. TSLG, fol. 337.

35. TSLG, fol. 338.

36. TSLG, fol. 339.

37. TMLG, fol. 66a

38. GKCB, pp. 296, 667. Guru Bkra-shis speculates that the monastery of Chos-ldan-pa must have been an important and active Rnying-ma-pa center since he had seen many fragments of the *Rgyud 'bum* preserved at its ruins.

39. Listed also as Dam-pa-yang Ngo-bo-ris-po.

40. Rnam-rgyal-bzang-po is listed as the author of a treatise included among the texts of the Kar-gling transmissions entitled *Dam-chos rdzogs-pa-chen-po ngo-sprod-kyi skor las kham-pa'i mi-mo la-brten-nas rnam-shes 'byung-'jug gnas-gsum ngo-sprod*. See references in DLSY, vol. 4, fol. 89.5; TLSY, fol. 390.2; also DJTY, fol. 179.4; ZDTY, fol. 511.3. A version of this work is extant in T7, vol. 2, fols. 443–467.

41. A *gter-ma* of Sangs-rgyas-gling-pa (1340–1396), who was born in Kong-po, on whom see GKCB, pp. 430–437.

42. The *Kun-rig* contains funeral practices particularly favored by the Sa-skya-pa and in some ways akin to the rites of the *Bar-do thos-grol* for the Rnying-ma-pa. The literature is drawn from the Yoga-tantra cycle of the *Sarvadurgatipariśodhana-tantra* and is centered on the Buddha Vairocana. See the brief discussion in chapter 2.

43. See CHGP, fols. 95.5–97.5. Mchog-ldan-mgon-po is discussed briefly in Ehrhard 1997c, pp. 338–341, 349 n. 9.

44. See LGNB, fol. 48b. The Tibetan *rgya-btsun* is an abbreviation of *rgya-yi btsun-pa*, "venerable monk of the Rgya [clan]". It does not mean "Chinese monk," as translated in Gyatrul Rinpoche and Wallace 1998, p. 74.

45. See GKCB, pp. 422, 460.

46. DLSY, vol. 4, fol. 91.2–3.

47. This inscription is located in the twelfth chapel on the third floor. In full it reads: *zhing khams rnams kyi dgos kyi sbyin bdag kyang rgyang 'khar [mkhar] sman mo ba spun / bya phrug spun / gos pa zo ba / chos rgyal nye 'khor rnams kyis gus pas bgyis*. See Tucci 1989, part 2, pp. 60, 201.

48. Tucci 1989, part 1, p. 36, mistakenly locates Rgyang-mkhar in Lha-rtse in far western Tibet.

49. LGNB, fol. 43. As a place name, *rkang* is an alternative form of *kong*. Thus, Rkang-smad would probably be Kong-smad, lower Kong-po.

50. T7, vol. 3, fols. 480–481; T7, vol. 2, fol. 265.

51. The riddles cannot be fully resolved until we have a broader and more detailed picture of the history of the personalities involved. In this regard it would certainly help if we could locate and consult the biography of Nyi-zla-'od-zer mentioned in LGNB, fol. 43.

52. Title given as *Gsang-sngags rgyud-'bum* in LGNB, fol. 45.

53. See, for example, Ehrhard 1997c; Mayer 1996; van Schaik 2000. Of special note is the Samantabhadra Collection, a truly innovative web-based *Rnying-ma rgyud-'bum* cataloguing project initiated by David Germano and based at the Institute for Advanced Technology in the Humanities at the University of Virginia. The Samantabhadra Collection is one of several collaborative electronic projects currently being developed at the Tibetan and Himalayan Digital Library (www.thdl.org).

54. See Ehrhard 1997c.

55. See TLNT, vol. 1, fol. 290.6. Ehrhard 1997a omits the reference to Dar-gling (Dar-rgyas-chos-gling), the ancestral seat of Smin-grol-gling monastery.

56. I am grateful to Gene Smith for his help in identifying some of the abbreviated names listed in this text.

57. The date is calculated according to the Old Phugs-pa calendrical system that was in use roughly between 1447 and 1695. See Schuh 1973; Dudjom Rinpoche 1991, p. 400.

58. The names of a few possible candidates for this Lama Chos-rgyal are worth mentioning. I am thinking specifically of either one of the 'Bri-gung-pa brothers, Rin-chen-chos-rgyal (1446–1484) or Dbang-chos-kyi-rgyal-po (1448–1504), or even per-

haps Dgongs-'dus-pa Chos-kyi-rgyal-mtshan, the holder of a special *Bar-do thos-grol* transmission that I identify as the "Zur-mang transmission."

59. LGNB, fol. 48b: *de ltar brgyud pa'i rim pa zur tsam 'di / mdo khams kyi bshes gnyen dam pa bla ma chos rgyal gyis yang yang bskul nas / rang 'dra blo dman rnams yid ches pa'i phyir / sa lug lo zla ba bdun pa'i yar tshes bcu la / gdam myong rgya grong gi g.yas zur gangs phu'i 'dab / chu bo gser ldan lo hi ta'i g.yas phyogs / dpal rin chen gling du rgya btsun nam mkha' chos kyi rgya mtshos bkod pa / yi ge pa ni lho rgyud kyi ban chung bsod nams rgya mtsho bris pa'o / dge ba yis mtshon nas sems can thams cad 'khor ba dang ngan song gi sdug bsngal gyi rgya mtsho chen po la myur du grol nas / rnam mkhyen rdzogs pa'i sangs rgyas thob pa'i rgyu ru smon / sarvamangala.*

60. That is, *Bka'-srung dam-can sde-bdun chos-skyong kun-'dus-kyi mdangs-bskang gdug-pa rang-grol* (in GK, fol. 71.6–72, T7, vol. 1, fol. 232) and *Bskyed-rim sngon-'gro lhan-thabs* (in PY, fol. 59.2–3; T5; T6, fol. 60.2–3; and T8, vol. 1, fol. 56.4–5).

61. The *'Dzam-gling rgyas-bshad* makes reference to a monastery along the Gtsang-po called Rin-chen-gling, founded by Dpal-chos-kyi-grags-pa near the monastery of 'Ol-kha-byams-pa-gling in the southern district of Zangs-ri. See Wylie 1962, pp. 92, 172 n. 530; also Dorje 1996, pp. 282–284. This places us in the general vicinity of Dwags-po to the east, Lhasa to the far northwest, and Gnyal to the far south.

62. Wylie 1962, p. 118 n. 38; Das 1902, p. 1222.

63. See JAM, vol. 3, fols. 124–146, esp. fols. 129–130: (no. 9): *kā ma rū pa ni 'dod pa'i gzugs te / gnyal gyi lho thod na grong khyer chen po gcig yod / de'i phyogs na sgrub gnas rdo'i lingga chos 'byung mi gang tsam gyis mtho ba zhig yod /* [130] *phyogs de nas chu bo lo hi ta yang 'bab bo.* I am grateful to Dan Martin for this reference and for helping me think through some of the geographical obscurities presented here in Rgya-ra-ba's colophon.

64. The *them-byang* is usually a text received by the revealer before the full discovery of the actual *gter-ma*. The *them-byang* for Karma-gling-pa's treasure, extant only in the form of notes written by Rgya-ra-ba, recounts the myth of origin of the *Zhi-khro* teachings and places them in the broad context of the whole of Buddhist doctrine, outlined according to the familiar system of the nine vehicles (*theg-pa-dgu*) of the Rnying-ma and Bon traditions. See T7, vol. 1, fols. 1–6.

65. B5, fols. 1–2; DJTY, fols. 181–184; GK; PY, fols. 33–38; GLKT, pp. 66, 77, 83–84.

66. DJTY, fols. 181–184; RCKC, fols. 69–70; T5; T8,vol. 2, fols. 1–3.

67. B2, fols. 15–16; CH; DJTY, fols. 181–184; TLSY, fols. 390–391.

68. ZDTY, fols. 507–513.

9. Traditions in Eastern Tibet

1. LGNB, fol. 48.

2. By the late fourteenth century, for example, the Rnying-ma-pa (as well as the Bon-po) had begun to be embroiled in what would become an almost never-ending defense against polemical attacks by some of the other Buddhist orders in Tibet. Among the names of some of the more famous defenders of the Rnying-ma-pa are 'Gos Lo-tsā-ba Gzhon-nu-dpal (1392–1481), Mnga'-ris-paṇ-chen Padma-dbang-rgyal (1487–1542), and Sog-zlog-pa Blo-gros-rgyal-mtshan (1552–1624). See E. Smith 2001, p. 16. On Bon-po polemics see Martin 1991a. An intriguing collec-

tion of polemical writings by Dkar-brgyud Bstan-'dzin-nor-bu (1859–1959)—the last active representative of Brag-dkar Rta-so monastery in southwestern Tibet—on the authenticity of the *Bar-do thos-grol* has been recently published in THGL. Here we find Bstan-'dzin-nor-bu responding to the criticisms of one Rab-'byams-pa-chen-po Thub-bstan, an outspoken Dge-lugs-pa scholar from the monastery of Sera-smad. This work deserves a careful study for the light it promises to shed on Dge-lugs and Rnying-ma polemics over the *Bar-do thos-grol* teachings and other Rdzogs-chen related doctrines.

3. For a general overview of this period, see Shakabpa 1984, pp. 91–139; Snellgrove and Richardson 1986, pp. 183–217; Samuel 1993, pp. 499–533; Smith 1996, pp. 105–123.

4. GKCB, pp. 697–715.

5. GKCB, pp. 750–759, 765–817.

6. GLKT; GKCB, pp. 750–759; Eimer and Tsering 1979, 1981, 1986. Richardson 1998 informs us that Kah-thog "takes its name from a hill, on the slopes of which the monastery lies, bearing near its summit marks resembling the letter *kah*" (p. 382). See figure 9.2.

7. GKCB, pp. 759–765; Tsering Lama 1988.

8. See SHAR; also Aris 1979, pp. 153–154. Kah-thog-pa Bsod-nams-rgyal-mtshan was also very active in Sikkim.

9. SHAR, fol. 57.4–6. The *Bar-do thos-grol* is mentioned again by name in several other passages (see fols. 134, 137, 148, and 174), as well as the titles *Zhi-khro dgongs-pa rang-grol* and *Srid-pa bar-do'i ngo-sprod* (fol. 160). I have thus far found no information on the identity of Nam-mkha'-rdo-rje, although it is conceivable that he could have been the father of 'Od-gsal-klong-yangs, a renowned figure in the lineage of the *Snying-thig* system of Klong-chen-pa (1308–1363) and an early link in the transmission of one of the two Kar-gling *Zhi-khro* traditions that reached the fifth Dalai Lama. See GKCB, p. 214–240, esp. p. 225; DLSY, fol. 91.

In consideration of other possibilities, there also exists in this period one Zhang-ston Nam-mkha'-rdo-rje, a student of Sangs-rgyas-rin-chen (1350–1431), from whom the former received the Anuyoga transmission. From Sangs-rgyas-rin-chen this transmission line was spread as follows: Zhang-ston Nam-mkha'-rdo-rje, Sha-mi Rdo-rje-rgyal mtshan, Rig-'dzin G.yu-'brug-rdo-rje, Sog-bzlog-pa Blo-gros-rgyal-mtshan (1552–1624). See Bradburn et al. 1995, p. 177.

For what it is worth, a Kun-mkhyen Rong-ston-chen-po from Shar Rgyal-mo-rong is briefly discussed in GKCB, p. 948, although it is not likely that the two are related. This is Rong-ston Shes-bya-kun-rig (alias Śākya-rgyal-mtshan, 1367–1449), founder of 'Phan-po Na-lendra monastery. On this important Sa-skya-pa scholastic, see Jackson 1988, 1989a, pp. 6–8. Curiously, a manuscript arrangement does in fact exist of the Kar-gling *Zhi-khro* from 'Phan-po Na-lendra. See T6. I have found no information, however, about the details of this specific Kar-gling tradition.

10. This may be Gzhag-bla Ye-shes-'bum from Nyag-rong, a student of Mkhas-grub Ye-shes-rgyal-mtshan (1395–1458) and a contemporary of Kha-ba-dkar-po Nam-mkha'-chos-kyi-rgya-mtsho. See GLKT, pp. 60, 72–73.

11. ZDTY, fols. 512–513. Here the succession of names is given as follows: Karma-gling-pa, Skyes-mchog Nyi-zla-chos-rje, Lama Nyi-zla-'od-zer, Rgya-btsun Nam-mkha'-chos-kyi-rgya-mtsho, Lama Ye-shes-blo-gros, Nam-mkha'-rdo-rje, Kah-thog-pa Bsod-nams-rgyal-mtshan, Mkhas-grub Bsod-nams-bzang-po [i.e., Rnam-grol-ye-shes-bzang-po, the son of Bsod-nams-rgyal-mtshan], Bstan-'dzin-grags-pa-rgyal-mtshan, Chos-rje Kun-dga'-bstan-'dzin, Chos-rje Susarvamantra,

Bslab-gsum-'dzin-pa Grags-pa-rgya-mtsho, Dpal Jñānasiddhi [i.e., Ye-shes-dngos-grub], Phyogs-las-rnam-rgyal.

12. Ye-shes-blo-gros, however, may not have given the Kar-gling *Zhi-khro* to Nam-mkha'-rdo-rje as indeed the line of transmission appears to suggest, but rather both may have received the transmission from Rgya-ra-ba directly. The period in which Rgya-ra-ba flourished (c. 1451–1499) and the early contact between Nam-mkha'-rdo-rje and Kaḥ-thog-pa Bsod-nams-rgyal-mtshan in 1485 leads me to believe that Ye-shes-blo-gros and Nam-mkha'-rdo-rje were of similar age and may have each received the Kar-gling transmission simultaneously, or at least within a short period of time of each other. It is common for lineage lists to place two simultaneous transmissions in hierarchical succession, making it appear as if the individual on top presented the teaching directly to the individual below. In some cases a footnote (*mchan*) is sometimes added after the second name alerting the reader to this fact.

13. See Shakabpa 1984, pp. 86–90.

14. GLKT, p. 72.

15. GLKT, p. 73. 'Ug-pa-lung, in the village of Gsang-sngags-gling, was the seat of the Zur clan and principal center of the Rnying-ma scriptural tradition (*bka'-ma*) during and after the alleged persecution and suppression of Buddhism by the emperor Glang-dar-ma. See Roerich 1949, pp. 110–124; Dudjom Rinpoche 1991, pp. 617–649.

16. Dudjom Rinpoche 1991, pp. 805–808; Bradburn et al. 1995, pp. 207–208.

17. GLKT, p. 74. Aris 1979, p. 153, mistakenly attributes the founding of this monastery to Bsod-nams-rgyal-mtshan's teacher, Bzhag-bla Ye-shes-'bum, for whom he also gives the erroneous dates of 1245–1311.

18. According to Aris 1979, p. 153, the main institutions of the Shar tradition were Spyi-rdzong at Lud-mtsho-ri, and Ba-ling and Theg-chen-sgang in Mkho-thang. The Spa-gro branch was attached to Dol-po Sha-la-brag, Mkha'-'gro-spyi-'dus, Btsan-stong-chos-sding, and Byi-dgon-gong-ma.

19. Aris 1979, p. 154.

20. In this regard, we should note that the great majority of extant xylograph prints of the *Bar-do thos-grol* were originally produced from blocks housed at various printeries throughout Bhutan, including those of Spa-gro-rdzong and Bum-thang Thar-pa-gling. See B1, B1a, B2, B3, B4, B5, and DH. These Bhutanese versions, however, are not affiliated with any of the Kaḥ-thog lineages in Bhutan.

21. GLKT, p. 77, 83–84; Eimer and Tsering 1979, p. 476.

22. GLKT, p. 77, 84; GK, fol. 2.

23. GK, fol. 2.

24. See, for example, the contents of GK.

25. Eimer and Tsering 1979, p. 462. For biographical details, see GLKT, pp. 15–94.

26. Eimer and Tsering 1979, p. 463 and 476; also GKCB, p. 751.

27. Eimer and Tsering 1979, p. 463.

28. GLKT, p. 55–65.

29. Eimer and Tsering 1979, p. 476; GLKT, pp. 69–85; GKCB, p. 751.

30. This contradicts the view of Eimer and Tsering 1979, p. 476, who identify Lab-ston Nam-mkha'-rin-chen as holder of this first position. Both 'Jam-dbyangs-rgyal-mtshan and Guru Bkra-shis agree, however, that Nam-mkha'-seng-ge was the first Drung-rabs. See GLKT, p. 66, and GKCB, p. 751, respectively.

31. GLKT, p. 63.

32. GLKT, p. 62.

33. GLKT, p. 66; GKCB, p. 751.

34. History records a number of notable connections between Ratna-gling-pa and the holders of Karma-gling-pa's tradition. Besides Rgya-ra-ba and Nam-mkha'-seng-ge, another of Ratna-gling-pa's disciples associated with the Kar-gling tradition was one Dgongs-'dus-pa Chos-kyi-rgyal-mtshan, from whom the Zur-mang lineage of the Kar-gling *Zhi-khro* is said to have emanated. See B3, fol. 63. We should note with some interest, moreover, that Sprul-sku Sna-tshogs-rang-grol, the great ancestral patriarch of Smin-grol-gling, was believed to have been Ratna-gling-pa's immediate reincarnation.

35. T7, vol. 3, fols. 480–481: *zab lam rdzogs rim nyams khrid bde ba rang grol zhes bya ba / guru'i gdams pa mudra nyid kyis bskul ba'i don du snyigs ma'i ku sa li suryacandrarasmi'i ming can gyis kong yul lta bar thang 'brog dgon pa tu sprel lo phag gi zla ba'i dus bzang la 'di brtsam pa'i dge bas 'gro kun sku gsum bde ba chen po myur du thob bar gyur cig / 'gal 'brel zlos skyon ma brtogs lu col bris / 'di la mkhas rnams bjod pa mdzad par zhu / bde chen lhan skyes kyis nyams rtogs phul phyin pa'i rje btsun suryacandra'i drung du nam mkha' chos kyi rgya mtshos zhus de la kah thog pa nam mkha' seng ges zhus / de la bdag gis zhus so.*

36. GLKT, p. 67.

37. GLKT, p. 70–71.

38. Eimer and Tsering 1979, p. 476; also GLKT, p. 67, 76; GKCB, p. 751.

39. GLKT, p. 76. On the achievements and legacy of Thang-ston-rgyal-po, see Gyatso 1981, 1991.

40. GLKT, p. 76. The *Kun-tu-bzang-po'i dgongs-pa zang(s)-thal* was revealed in 1366 by Rig-'dzin Rgod-ldem-can (1337–1409) and contains a number of texts dealing with *zhi-khro* mandalas and *bar-do* practices, e.g., *Rdzogs-pa chen-po chos-nyid mngon-sum zhi-khro lhun-grub-kyi phrin-las, Zhi-khro rab-'byams-kyi bsnyen-sgrub-kyi dmigs-rim grub-mchog zhal-lung bzang-po, Rigs-drug 'khor-ba gnas-'dren, Bar-do lnga'i ngo-sprod, Bar-do lnga'i snyan-brgyud thams-cad-kyi phyi-mo, Bar-do 'od-gsal sgron-ma'i dbu,* and *Bar-do rang-gi snang-ba thams-cad nges-par bstan-pa'i rgyud.* A thorough discussion of this *gter-ma* cycle by Peter Schwieger is contained in Schuh 1985. The texts themselves are found scattered throughout the *Rin-chen gter-mdzod* and also in separate volumes.

41. The identity of this ascetic has not yet been determined, but it is possible that he may have been the famed Byang-chub-seng-ge of Nyag-rong, a *'das-log* (i.e., a person who has died and returned to life) alleged to have had close ties to Kah-thog monastery. The *'das-log* Byang-chub-seng-ge was renowned for establishing a devotional practice for the veneration of Avalokiteśvara that employed the use of votary flags called *jo-dar.* A version of his visionary experiences of hell is recorded in BYCS.

42. We know also that he spent time in Kong-po and in north-central Tibet at Rwa-sgreng. See GLKT, p. 77.

43. GLKT, p. 77.

44. Tsering Lama Jampal Zangpo 1988, p. 30. Oddly enough, however, the direct transmission of these teachings from Dkon-mchog-rgyal-mtshan to He-pa-chos-'byung is not indicated in the lineage lists found in the Dpal-yul recensions of the Kar-gling *Zhi-khro* cycle. Instead, the standard names of Dkon-mchog-rgyal-mtshan's Kah-thog lineage are given in the following order: Rong-po Dkon-mchog-rdo-rje, Hor-po Śākya-rgyal-mtshan, Byang-chub-seng-ge, Bu-'bor Bkra-shis-rgya-mtsho. See GK and PY, fols. 33–38. This transmission line represents also the main lineage of the *Dgongs-pa zang(s)-thal,* with which A-rdo Dkon-mchog-rgyal-mtshan had become especially associated. See GLKT, pp. 77–79; also Eimer and Tsering 1979, p. 477.

45. GLKT, p. 77.

46. GLKT, p. 67; GKCB, p. 751.

47. See B5, fols. 1b-2b; DJTY, fols. 181–184; GK.

48. See, for example, DJTY, fol. 182.

49. On the life of Karma-guru, see GKCB, pp. 556–562; ZCGT, pp. 267, 272; GLKT, p. 79; Bradburn et al. 1995, pp. 224–225. On the clan of Byang Ngam-rings, one of Tibet's original thirteen myriarchs (*khri-dpon*), see Tucci 1949, pp. 631–632.

50. GKCB, p. 557. On the life of 'Bri-gung Rin-chen-phun-tshogs, see BDGR, pp. 185–201; Sperling 1992, pp. 741–750; Bradburn et al. 1995, pp. 216–217.

51. DLSY, vol. 3, fols. 175.3–176.4. Also in the same work (fol. 429.1–3) we find a series of names in the lineage of Padma-las-'brel-rtsal's *Sgab-'dre'i 'khor-lo dang bcas-pa phyag-len dam-'khrid* that include the three earliest lineage-holders of Karma-gling-pa's *gter-ma*. The lineage is arranged in the following order: Gter-ston Rin-chen-tshul-rdor [i.e., Padma-las-'brel-rtsal, b. 1228], Grub-chen Legs-ldan-pa [i.e., Shwa-ban Rgyal-sras Legs-pa, 1290–1366], Mtshungs-med Rang-byung-rdo-rje [i.e., Karma-pa III, 1284–1339], Mkhas-grub Nor-bu-bzang-po, Sprul-sku Mkha'-spyod-dbang-po [i.e., Zhwa-dmar-pa II, 1350–1405], *Chos-rje Nyi-zla-sangs-rgyas, De-dbon Nyi-zla-chos-rje, Lama Nyi-ma-zla-ba* [i.e., Nyi-zla-'od-zer, b.1409/1421], Drin-can Kumāratha [i.e., Kumārādza ?], Drin-can Yadyavajra, Lha-sras Rnam-sprul 'Bri-gung-pa Rin-chen-phun-tshogs (1509–1557), Ras-chung Rnam-sprul Bkra-shis-rgya-mtsho, G.yu-sgra'i sprul-pa Kun-dga'-tshe-mchog.

52. The festival was later instituted by the brothers Dkon-mchog-rin-chen (1590–1654) and Rig-'dzin-chos-grags (1595–1659). See Kapstein 1998, p. 180 n. 23.

53. DJTY, fol. 184.

54. BDGR, pp. 189, 201; GKCB, pp. 238–239, 463; ZCGT, p. 181; Bradburn et al. 1995, p. 210.

55. GKCB, p. 556–562.

56. Thondup 1996, pp. 32, 37.

57. See Karmay 1988b.

58. See RCTD, vol. 2, fols. 1–31.

59. See comment in Martin 1997, p. 110, no. 229.

60. GKCB, p. 763–764; Tsering Lama Jampal Zangpo 1988, p. 28.

61. GLKT, pp. 83–84; B5, fol. 2b; DJTY, fols. 183–184.

62. GLKT, p. 84.

63. B5; GK, fols. 27–32.

64. GK, fols. 327–335; PY, fols. 219–228; T5; T8, vol. 1, fols. 283–290.

65. GK, fols. 533–543.

66. B3, fols. 27–29.

67. GK, fols. 147–157.

68. GK, fols. 971–1010.

69. Tsering Lama Jampal Zangpo 1988, p. 55.

70. Tsering Lama Jampal Zangpo 1988, p. 30.

71. GLKT, pp. 79–80.

72. T5; T8, vol. 2, fols. 1–3; Tsering Lama Jampal Zangpo 1988, pp. 30, 60. According to the colophon of T5, this Gnas-mdo/Dpal-yul lineage list is said to have been originally composed by Bu-'bor Bkra-shis-rgya-mtsho, third 'Chad-nyan-pa of Kaḥ-thog and teacher of He-pa-chos-'byung.

73. GKCB, p. 759; Tsering Lama Jampal Zangpo 1988, p. 54. Bu-'bor-sgang is located in the Li-thang district, see Dorje 1996, p. 496.

74. GKCB, p. 752. Dkon-mchog-seng-ge was a student of Rgyal-thang-pa Ston-pa-seng-ge. See GLKT, pp. 80, 83.

75. GKCB, p. 760; Tsering Lama Jampal Zangpo 1988, p. 55.

76. GKCB, p. 760; Tsering Lama Jampal Zangpo 1988, p. 55.

77. Rgya-rong-pa Rin-chen-rdo-rje was a student of Bu-'bor Bkra-shis-rgya-mtsho; see GLKT, p. 79. On Sog-rdzong in Rgya-rong, see Dorje 1996, p. 454–455.

78. Tsering Lama Jampal Zangpo 1988, p. 56.

79. The precise location of Rmug-(b)sang is not specified in the available sources. It is apparently near the region of Dpal-yul, perhaps northwest of that area. See Tsering Lama 1988, p. 54; Dorje 1996, p. 516. It was also in this region that Kun-bzang-shes-rab received the *Gnam-chos* transmission directly from its discoverer, the *gter-ston* Mi-'gyur-rdo-rje (1645–1667); see GKCB, p. 628; Tsering Lama Jampal Zangpo, p. 62; Bradburn et al. 1995, p. 269.

80. A-gro-ba Nam-mkha'-rdo-rje is indicated as having received the Kar-gling transmission from Bu-'bor Bkra-shis-rgya-mtsho; see PY, fols. 33–38; also GLKT, p. 80.

81. Tsering Lama Jampal Zangpo 1988, p. 57.

82. GK; PY, fols. 33–38; Tsering Lama Jampal Zangpo 1988, p. 30.

83. On Byams-pa-phun-tshogs, Sangs-rgyas-bstan-pa, and the abbatial succession of Sde-dge Lung-grub-steng monastery, see Kolmaš 1968, 1988.

84. GKCB, p. 761.

85. GKCB, p. 761; Tsering Lama Jampal Zangpo 1988, p. 59.

86. On whom see GKCB, pp. 624–629; Bradburn et al. 1995, pp. 268–269.

87. Tsering Lama Jampal Zangpo 1988, p. 60.

88. GKCB, pp. 629 and 760. Most likely, Ngom-yul refers to the Ngom-chu valley north of Chab-mdo near the lower reaches of 'Bri-zla Zal-mo-sgang. See Tsering Lama Jampal Zangpo 1988, p. 35; Dorje 1996, p. 470.

89. GKCB, p. 760; Tsering Lama Jampal Zangpo 1988, p. 58.

90. GKCB, p. 761; Tsering Lama Jampal Zangpo 1988, p. 60.

91. Tsering Lama Jampal Zangpo 1988, p. 60.

92. Tsering Lama Jampal Zangpo 1988, p. 36; Bradburn et al. 1995, p. 248. In speaking with various Rnying-ma-pa lamas in India, I found, much to my frustration, that these two figures—Karma-gling-pa and Karma-chags-med—were often conflated with one another, so that when Karma-gling-pa's name was mentioned Karma-chags-med was thought to be the referent, and vice versa. Needless to say, this created a few problems when discussing either one of them individually.

93. GKCB, p. 629; Dudjom Rinpoche 1991, vol. 2, pp. 114–115.

94. Tsering Lama Jampal Zangpo 1988, p. 36.

95. GKCB, p. 629; Tsering Lama Jampal Zangpo 1988, p. 38. It is conceivable that Drung-pa Rin-po-che Kun-dga'-rnam-rgyal may also have bestowed the distinctive Zur-mang transmission of the *Bar-do thos-grol* upon Karma-chags-med at this time. As ample evidence in the biographical sources indicates, it was not uncommon for students to receive the Kar-gling transmissions at a young age or at the time of monastic ordination.

96. Incidentally, it was on the occasion of the sixth Zhwa-dmar-pa's death that Karma-chags-med first offered in dedication one of his fingers as a burning "butter-lamp," giving rise to the popular legend of his intense and unfailing devotion. The story is recounted in GKCB, pp. 629–630; Tsering Lama Jampal Zangpo 1988, p. 39.

97. Brief biographical details about Rma-se-rtogs-ldan can be found in LRCB, p. 305. On Zur-mang, see Roerich 1949, pp. 510–512; Trungpa 1971, chs. 2–3.

98. Roerich 1949, p. 511.

99. According to 'Jam-mgon Kong-sprul, B3, fol. 63, the Zur-mang tradition of the Kar-gling transmission originated from one Dgongs-'dus-pa Chos-kyi-rgyal-mtshan, a student of Ratna-gling-pa. From him the lineage was passed to Bya-btang

Blo-gros-rgya-mtsho and eventually reached the fourth Drung-pa Kun-dga'-rnam-rgyal. According to the lineage included in S3, Dgongs-'dus-pa (alias A-po-chos-rje) had received the transmission from the nebulous lama Mgon-po-rdo-rje.

100. Fremantle and Trungpa 1975, p. ix.

101. Crescenzi and Torricelli 1997, p. 73.

102. I might cite, for instance, the student-teacher relations of Nyi-zla-sangs-rgyas and the second Zhwa-dmar-pa Mkha'-spyod-dbang-po, Rgya-ma Mi-'gyur-ba and the fourth Zhwa-dmar-pa Spyan-snga Chos-grags-pa, Mdo-sngags-bstan-'dzin and the fifth Zhwa-dmar-pa Dkon-mchog-yan-lag-'bangs, Gong-ra Lo-chen and the sixth Zhwa-dmar-pa Gar-dbang-chos-kyi-dbang-phyug, and finally Rtse-le Sna-tshogs-rang-grol and the third Dpa'-bo Gtsug-lag-rgya-mtsho.

103. The monasteries of Dwags-po Rtse-le and Kong-po Thang-'brog immediately come to mind. Both institutions were supported financially by the second Dpa'-bo Gtsug-lag-'phreng-ba, with close ties also to the fourth Zhwa-dmar-pa Spyan-snga Chos-grags-pa and the eighth Karma-pa Mi-bskyod-rdo-rje.

104. B3, fols. 147–187.

105. RCKC, fols. 69–70; DJTY, fols. 181–184.

106. Also known as *Gnas-'dren 'gro-drug rang-grol khrigs-su bkod-pa*. See GK, fols. 849–939; PY, fols. 585–685; T5; T8, vol. 1, fols. 391–471.

107. Also known as *Tshe-'das gnas-'dren bsdus-pa*. See PY, fols. 553–583; S3; T5.

108. The earliest texts of this type known to me are the two works belonging to the *Bka'-brgyad* revelations of Guru Chos-dbang (1212–1270)—the *Bka'-brgyad drag-po rang-byung rang-shar las byung-ba'i zhi-khro na-rag skong-bshags-kyi cho-ga* and the *'Khor-ba dong-sprug*. See RCTD, vol. 23, nos. 24–27, and vol. 66, no. 28, respectively. It is not clear whether the latter text is actually Guru Chos-dbang's *'Khor-ba dong-sprug*. Since the nineteenth century, however, the work most commonly used for this *dong-sprugs* practice is 'Jam-mgon Kong-sprul's *Nyams-chag sdig-sgrib thams-cad bshags-pa'i rgyal-po na-rag dong-sprugs*, which is based on the afore-mentioned texts of Guru Chos-dbang. See CPYR, pp. 371–387. A partial translation is found in Dowman 1994, pp. 53–61.

109. Tsering Lama Jampal Zangpo 1988, p. 30.

110. GK, fols. 297–304.

111. GK, fols. 371–382.

112. On the Ris-med movement, Smith 2001, pp. 235–272; also Blondeau 1985, pp. 153–157; Karmay 1988a, pp. 35–37.

10. Traditions in Central and Southern Tibet

1. Ehrhard 1993, p. 80.

2. DLSY, vol. 4, fols. 86.6–90.5.

3. DLSY, vol. 4, fols. 90.5–91.3.

4. GKCB, pp. 214–240, esp. p. 225.

5. This Nam-mkha'-rdo-rje may also have been the teacher of Kaḥ-thog-pa Bsod-nams-rgya-mtsho. On the township of Rgyal-sman, see Dorje 1996, p. 270.

6. GKCB, p. 225.

7. DJTY, fol. 184. There have been four treasure revealers known by the name Las-'phro-gling-pa: (1) Sngag-'chang Las-'phro-gling-pa of Do-la, disciple of Rdo-

rje-gling-pa (1346–1405) (see GKCB, p. 460–461; Bradburn et al. 1995, pp. 191–192); (2) 'Gro-'dul Las-'phro-gling-pa of Gnyal, disciple of Padma-gling-pa (see GKCB, p. 461–463; Bradburn et al. 1995, pp. 192–193); (3) Mi-'gyur Las-'phro-gling-pa of Rgya-ma (see GKCB, pp. 238–239, 463; ZCGT, pp. 181–182; Bradburn et al. 1995, p. 210); and (4) Gar-dbang Las-'phro-gling-pa of E-yul, a sixteenth-century mystic belonging to the "nephew-lineage" (dbon-brgyud) of Ratna-gling-pa (see GKCB, p. 464; Bradburn et al. 1995, pp. 226–227).

8. Rgya-ma was the birthplace of Emperor Srong-btsan-sgam-po and one of the thirteen original myriarchies, ruling provinces.

9. GKCB, p. 238; ZCGT, p. 181.

10. GKCB, p. 238–239; ZCGT, p. 181. These institutions are unidentified.

11. Gnas-nang was founded in 1333 by the first Zhwa-dmar-pa Rtogs-ldan Grags-pa-seng-ge and became the seat of the successive incarnations of the first Dpa'-bo-gtsug-lag Chos-dbang-lhun-grub (1440–1503). Yangs-pa-can was founded in 1490 on the advice of the fourth Zhwa-dmar-pa and was the main residence of the subsequent Zhwa-dmar incarnations. See GKCB, pp. 961–962; Dorje 1996, pp. 193–199.

12. GKCB, p. 239; ZCGT, pp. 178–181.

13. TSLG, fols. 317.

14. TSLG, fol. 317. Rgya-ma Mi-'gyur-ba is listed here as the gter-ston Las-'phro-gling-pa.

15. More precisely, Grup-chen Kun-dga'-lhun-grub or Mkhas-grub Kun-dga'-lhun-grub. See B1; B2, fol. 15–16; B4; DH; T3;

16. GKCB, p. 463.

17. GKCB, p. 300.

18. On the Zur, see GKCB, pp. 250–321; Dudjom Rinpoche 1991, pp. 617–649; Tsering 1978.

19. GKCB, p. 300; ZCGT, p. 242.

20. GKCB, p. 300; ZCGT, p. 242.

21. GKCB, p. 302. On the Phyogs-bcu mun-sel, see Dorje 1987.

22. GKCB, p. 302.

23. TLNT, fol. 157.

24. Smith 2001, p. 18.

25. TLSY, fols. 388.7–390.6.

26. TLSY, fols. 390.6–391.4.

27. Given his placement in the lineage, it is possible that Bsod-nams-'od-zer is actually Nyi-zla-'od-zer.

28. See B2, fols. 15–16; CH; DJTY, fols. 181–184; T7.

29. Zab-chos zhi-khro dgongs-pa rang-grol las srid-pa bar-do'i ngo-sprod gsal-'debs chen-mo, BL OR-5355.13, fol. 47b, volume foliation 180b.1–4: des [karma gling pa] sras chos rje gling pa la bka' gtad : lung bstan: des gu ru surya tsanda ra mi la bka babs so : des punye shri la : des rigs 'dzin byang chub gling pa la : des sna tshogs rang grol la : des bstan 'dzin grags pa la : des padma phrin las la : de nas da lta kun mkhyen gnyis pa tshul khrims rdo rje'i bar du brgyud pa'i zar ma chad pa'o. I am grateful to Burkhard Quessel for providing images of this text. See fig. 10.3.

30. DLSY, vol. 4, fols. 90–91.

31. GKCB, p. 653. During the time of the fifth Dalai Lama, the monks of Chag Byang-chub-gling were responsible for playing the role of the ging in the famous glud-'gong ceremony. See Nebesky-Wojkowitz 1956, p. 509.

32. B2, fols. 15–16; CH; DJTY, fols. 181–184; T7; TLSY, fol. 390.

33. BDTT, vol. 3, p. 723; GKCB, p. 697; ZCGT, p. 182. This figure should not be confused with either Rgod-tshang-ras-pa Sna-tshogs-rang-grol, author of the biography of Gtsang-smyon He-ru-ka (1452–1507), or Rtse-le Sna-tshogs-rang-grol (1608–1680), first incarnation of Mtshungs-med Bstan-'dzin-rdo-rje (1533–1605).

34. This Rnying-ma monastery became the principal seat of the Gsung-sprul and Thugs-sras incarnations of *gter-ston* Padma-gling-pa. In its later history, Lha-lung became closely affiliated with the Dge-lugs-pa order after it had been taken over by the fifth Dalai Lama. See GKCB, pp. 653–664; also Aris 1988a, pp. 69–71; Richardson 1998, p. 323–324.

35. TLSY, fol. 391.

36. Sprul-sku Sna-tshogs-rang-grol had invited Bstan-'dzin-grags-pa to Tibet in 1549. After remaining for six years at Dar-rgyas-chos-sding, he left for Lho-brag in 1555. See PGKR, fol. 558.

37. The Gnyos/Smyos is the ancestral clan of Padma-gling-pa, renowned for its long lineage of tantric priests. See Aris 1988b; Martin 1997, pp. 68, no. 114, 197–198, no. 516.

38. TLSY, fol. 390.

39. GKCB, p. 702.

40. According to TLNT, vol. 2, fols. 43–44, 'Phrin-las-lhun-grub bestowed the Kar-gling transmission upon his son Gter-bdag-gling-pa in 1655 at Byang-chub-gling.

41. GKCB, p. 705; Mayer 1996, pp. 228–229; Ehrhard 1997c, p. 253.

42. TLNT, vol. 1, fol. 290.4–6; see also Mayer 1996, pp. 229, 235.

43. See B2 and B5. These two collections are not derived, however, from witnesses preserved at Smin-grol-gling but rather represent later reproductions from print blocks housed at two monasteries in Bhutan. The Smin-grol-gling connections are still apparent nonetheless. Edition B2, for example, was originally arranged for publication in the late eighteenth century by the third Rdzogs-chen-pa Nges-don-bstan-'dzin-bzang-po (1759–1792), who had received the Kar-gling *Zhi-khro* transmission from Padma-theg-mchog Bstan-pa'i-rgyal-mtshan (1712–1774), a disciple of Gter-bdag-gling-pa's son, the third Smin-gling-khri-chen Rin-chen-rnam-rgyal (1694–1758). See B2, fols. 15–16.

44. This information is provided in the catalogue description of edition B5.

45. B5, text 3; See also B3, fols. 275.5–276.2. Go-'jo is the name of a large Sa-skya estate in eastern Tibet.

46. ZH, fols. 511–512.

47. See NE; T6, fols. 218.2–3; T8, vol. 1, fols. 211.5–6.

48. Snellgrove 1967a, p. 258.

49. On the Dzungar massacres, see Petech 1972, pp. 29–30; Shakabpa 1984, pp. 134–139; Smith 1996, pp. 123–126.

50. GKCB, pp. 859–860, 866. It is certainly conceivable that O-rgyan-bstan-'dzin was the lama Mkhan-chen Oḍḍiyāna, who is identified in some histories of Smin-grol-gling as the son of Rin-chen-rnam-rgyal. See, for example, GKCB, pp. 713–14; Dudjom Rinpoche 1991, pp. 733–734; Bradburn et al. 1995, pp. 309–310.

51. TLSY, fol. 391; see also B1; B2, fols. 15–16; B4; DH; T3; T6; TMLG, fols. 66a-b; NBDS, fol. 231.

52. The transmission line for the *Dbang-bzhi 'phrad-tshad rang-grol* that actually passed through Sprul-sku Sna-tshogs-rang-grol was the one that eventually reached Gter-bdag-gling-pa at Smin-grol-gling. See table 10.2.

53. TMLG, fol. 66a. According to this text, Nyi-zla-sangs-rgyas must also have gone by the name Lung-zin Dngos-grub-rgyal-po. GKCB, p. 460, gives the name Dngos-grub-rgya-tsho but does not identify him as Nyi-zla-sang-rgyas.

54. See TMLG, fol. 66a, where the alias Nam-mkha'-sangs-rgyas is given for Nyi-zla-chos-rje. GKCB, p. 460, seems to confuse this alias for the name Nam-mkha'-chos-kyi-rgya-mtsho.

55. TMLG, fol. 66b.

56. See the discussion in chapter 7.

57. B1; B2, fols. 15–16; B4; DH; T3; T6; TLSY, fol. 391.

58. TSNG, fol. 34.3.

59. Other aliases include Kong-po Rgod-tshang-pa and Kong-po Thang-'brog Sprul-sku.

60. TSLG, fols. 332–363; GKCB, pp. 745–746.

61. TSNG, fol. 31; GKCB, p. 746.

62. TSNG, fol. 48; GKCB, p. 746. Remember that it was also during this trip that Stag-bla Padma-mati first met Zur-chen Chos-dbyings-rang-grol. See chapter 9.

63. ZCGT, pp. 274–275; Dudjom Rinpoche 1991, pp. 723–724.

64. BDTT, vol. 4, p. 360; Dudjom Rinpoche 1991, pp. 723–724.

65. Mayer 1996, p. 228.

66. GKCB, p. 746.

67. TSNG, fol. 133.

68. GKCB, p. 655.

69. Ehrhard 1997c, p. 256 n. 8.

70. Mayer 1996, p. 227, citing Ehrhard.

71. Tib., *Zhing-khams lnga'i smon-lam thong-bar rang-grol.*

72. Tib., *Phyogs-bcu'i sangs-rgyas dang byang-chub sems-dpa' ram-'da' sgron-pa'i smon-lam.*

73. GKCB, p. 858.

74. PGKR, fol. 559.

75. PGKR, fol. 562; Aris 1979, p. 164.

11. Rikzin Nyima Drakpa

1. See GKCB, pp. 820–860. Guru Bkra-shis was closely affiliated with Rig-'dzin Nyi-ma-grags-pa's tradition. He was a student of Nyi-ma-grags-pa's first reincarnation, Nyi-sprul I Padma-theg-mchog Bstan-pa'i-rgyal-mtshan (1712–1774) and composed his *Chos-'byung* at Nyi-ma-grags-pa's main monastic seat at Stag-mo-sgang. He also appears to have been a direct descendant of one of Nyi-ma-grags-pa's chief patrons, Sangs-rgyas-bstan-pa, the third abbot of Lhun-grub-steng and "dharma king" (*chos-rgyal*) of Sde-dge (see GKCB, p. 847). It was Sangs-rgyas-bstan-pa who commissioned the establishment of Stag-mo-sgang.

2. Prats 1982, p. 73 n. 14; Blondeau 1988, p. 60 n. 24; Martin 1991b, pp. 174–178; see also Back 1987, p. 11. Back is the only scholar of the *Bar-do thos-grol* literature to have mentioned Rig-'dzin Nyi-ma-grags-pa by name. However, Back fails here to acknowledge Nyi-ma-grags-pa's proper position in the transmission lineage.

3. Unless otherwise noted, the details of the life of Rig-'dzin Nyi-ma-grags-pa presented here are based on information recorded in GKCB. I wish to thank Khenpo Nyima Dondup for his gracious assistance and advice during early preparations of this material.

4. A list of fifty-nine titles of Nyi-ma-grags-pa's writings can be found in the catalogue of Rnying-ma-pa works deposited in the Potala library (see PLKC, pp. 165–167), but these are not readily available. According to information provided by Franz-Karl Ehrhard, a large manuscript anthology of Nyi-ma-grags-pa's works in thirteen volumes has been recently photographed on microfilm by the Nepal-German Manu-script Preservation Project (personal communication, August 1999). I am sure future research on Nyi-ma-grags-pa and his legacy will benefit from a thorough study of the contents of this potentially valuable collection.

5. See RZND. Volume 1 of this collection contains the main liturgical texts for the practice of *Rta-mgrin dregs-pa zil-gnon*, which was excavated in 1682 from the Flaming Cave (*me-'bar-phug*) of Nag-shod. Volume 2 includes short related works on various smoke purification rituals (*bsangs-brngan*). See GKCB, p. 841.

6. GKCB, p. 851. On Yongs-dge Mi-'gyur-rdo-rje, see BDTT, vol. 8, part 2, pp. 419–426; Bradburn et al. 1995, pp. 256–257.

7. 'Jam-mgon Kong-sprul had close ties with the Dpal-spungs Karma-pa, with whom he had taken a second ordination as a Buddhist monk. Supposedly, the lamas of Dpal-spungs refused to recognize his Rnying-ma-pa vows. See Smith 2001, pp. 247–248.

8. See Blondeau 1985, pp. 111–158; Martin 1991b, pp. 173–181.

9. Kolmaš 1968, p. 37, 1988, p. 130. It was Chos-rgyal Bstan-pa-tshe-ring who almost singlehandedly launched the political power of Derge's ruling house by ex-panding its territory and establishing official contacts with the Manchu rulers of China.

10. On the life of Bdud-'dul-rdo-rje, see BDTT, vol. 3, part 1, pp. 815–820; GKCB, pp. 566–570; Bradburn et al. 1995, pp. 250–251.

11. On the life of Gar-dbang-rdo-rje, see GBNT; also GKCB, pp. 580–581; Bradburn et al. 1995, pp. 265–266.

12. A temple near Bsam-yas built by 'Brong-za, princess of Khri-srong-lde-btsan. See Das [1902] 1988, p. 270; Sorensen 1994, pp. 375–403.

13. PMKT, p. 568: *mi la lus chas ya ma zung du 'ong : bstan pa'i chos kyang ya ma zung du 'gro : dge rgyas bris pa'i ri mo shul rjes 'ong : khams kyi srin mo rdzong gsum gter ka 'di : mi bzhag 'don pa'i rtags der bstan nas byung : khams pa nyi ma grags kyi ming can 'byung.* See also GKCB, pp, 399 and 826; RCBP, fol. 410; Prats 1982, pp. 71, 105.

14. GKCB, p. 399.

15. RCBP, fol. 411.

16. According to 'Jam-mgon Kong-sprul, this area of Dwags-po is located in Khams-stod or upper Khams (see RCBP, fol. 411). Wylie 1962, pp. xxvii, 98, 177 n. 578, suggests that Khams-stod refers roughly to the region of Spo-bo, which is of course east of Dwags-po and west of Khams. But Guru Bkra-shis places Srin-rdzong in Cham, which might be near 'Bri-ru and Sog-rdzong, rather than Spo-bo.

17. The *Klu'i-dbang-po'i skye-phreng* is apparently the abbreviated version of Nyi-ma-grags-pa's autobiography. It is alternately titled **Rnam-thar zhal-gsung-ma bdus*. The extensive version is called **Rnam-thar zhal-gsung-ma rgyas*. To my knowl-edge neither work is presently extant.

18. GKCB, p. 823.

19. See the discussion in chapter 6.

20. For what it is worth, the Khyung lineage, famous for its long line of Buddhist and Bon-po siddhas, was the family from which 'Jam-mgon Kong-sprul's birth-father claimed descent. See Smith 2001, pp. 247, 332 n. 840. One of the most prominent early figures of this clan was of course Khyung-po Rnal-'byor.

21. See discussion of Vajrapāṇi in Snellgrove 1987, pp. 134–141.

22. GKCB, p. 824.

23. A certain Rtogs-ldan Khrag-skyugs, abbot of Nag-phu, is mentioned briefly in LRCB, p. 293, but it is not clear whether the two are related.

24. Prats 1982, p. 74. Smith 1979 suggests that Char-ri (Chags-ru, Chags-ri) is located in 'Dzin-pa near Sde-dge.

25. Incidentally, this is similar to how Kaḥ-thog monastery got its name as well.

26. On whom see GLKT, pp. 41–42.

27. GKCB, p. 652.

28. On whom see Diemberger et al 1997; Smith 2001, pp. 179–208. Bo-dong was apparently a rather arrogant and combative scholar. See comments in Mullin 1996, pp. 104–105.

29. Tib., *ljags thog-nas songs* (lit., "with his own tongue"). In Tibet it was quite common to arrange to have people "sit-in" for one's program of recitation in order to more quickly and easily accomplish the requisite number of repetitions.

30. GKCB, p. 828.

31. See Kolmaś 1968, pp. 33–34.

32. GLKT, pp. 86–88; GKCB, pp. 566–570.

33. BI, fols. 201.5–202.2; DH, fols. 465.5–466.2. The precise location at Bsam-yas where Nyi-ma-grags-pa composed this work is listed as Bdud-'dul-sngags-pa-gling, a tantric chapel southeast of the southern Aryapalo temple. This chapel is dedicated to the worship of Hayagrīva.

34. On yellow scrolls, see discussion in chapter 6.

35. There is an interesting Kar-gling connection with Gnam-mtsho lake. According to Bellezza 1997, pp. 159, 161, 161–162, the "geomantic heart" of Gnam-mtsho is an island known as Srin-mo-do (also Sri-mo-do, Se-mo-do, and Nang-do) situated at the northwestern tip of the lake. Referring to the third Kaḥ-thog Si-tu Chos-kyi-rgya-mtsho's pilgrimage guide to that area, Bellezza mentions a legend about Karma-gling-pa and a black stone that contained "a white clockwise hand spiral." Karma-gling-pa is alleged to have received this stone from some unnamed person at the Dga'-ba-tshal cemetery at Srin-mo-do. Bellezza slightly embellishes the Tibetan passage, which reads literally: "In north Gnam-mtsho at Bya-dur [Bya-do] the siddha Karma-gling-pa extracted treasure from a sky-stone, [including] a small pearl conch that spiraled to the right" (*grub thob karma gling pas byang gnam mtsho'i bya dur nam mkha' do nas gter bzhes pa mu tig dung g.yas 'khyil chung*, SITU, fol. 492.1–2). The precious right-turning conch shell is one of eight traditional auspicious symbols (*bkra-shis rtags-brgyad*) and evokes the fame of the Buddha's teaching. No further details are provided about Karma-gling-pa's discovery at Gnam-tsho.

36. On whom see GKCB, pp. 425–427; Bradburn et al. 1995, pp. 200–201.

37. In fact, Nyi-zla-klong-gsal's own son and chief disciple, Kun-mkhyen Chos-dbang-rdo-rje-'dzin-pa, was later recognized as the reincarnation of Gar-dbang-rdo-rje. See Bradburn et al. 1995, p. 266.

38. This text is extant in a separate volume, see RDJS. Here it may be worth mentioning the comment in Boord 1993, p. 32, that at Rdo-rje-brag monastery "during the third month, five days are devoted after the first half-moon to the *Zhi khro* cycle of Karma gling-pa and at the end of the month the *maṇḍala* of Gar-dbang rdor-sems is constructed in accordance with the text *Thugs kyi me long*." I presume that the title *Thugs-kyi me-long* is a reference to the *Rdor-sems thugs-kyi me-long* of Gar-dbang-rdo-rje and that the Kar-gling tradition observed at Rdo-rje-brag was the one received through Rig-'dzin Nyi-ma-grags-pa. It would seem to be more than just

coincidence that Gar-dbang-rdo-rje's *Thugs-kyi me-long* and Karma-gling-pa's *Zhi-khro* cycle would have been joined together in the same month of the monastery's ritual calendar. In this regard, it is noteworthy that the edition of the *Rdor-sems thugs-kyi me-long* found in the Potala library supposedly includes Gar-dbang-rdo-rje's own *khrid-yig* on the *Bar-do thos-grol* entitled *Bar-do thos-pa rang-grol-gyi khrid-yig 'jigs-skyob chen-mo*. See PLKC, p. 69 no. 12.

39. RCTD, vol. 12, pp. 363–380, 385–434.

40. RCTD, vol. 38, pp. 1–52 (nos. 1–3).

41. Generally speaking, wrathful mantras are employed as tools of exorcism to dispel demons (*bdud-bzlog*). See Beyer 1978, pp. 231–245.

42. GKCB, pp. 837–838: *de skabs gter chen de nyid kyis khyod 'dir phebs dus mtshan lam du gnam lcags kyi phur pa gnyis rnyed pa dang / chang ka pā la gang 'dug pa la hub gcig brgyab pa phyed la song tshe / ka pā la'i nang khrag 'thung rigs lnga gzi brjid lam lam 'dug pa sogs kyi dag snang byung bas / khyod drag sngags kyi nus pa chen po thon pa zhig yin pa gda' / khyad par du zhi khro dgongs pa rang grol gyi 'gro don bka' babs khyod la yod pas 'gro don la rem gsungs pa dang [p.838] da ltar gyi mi thog 'di la mdo khams sgang drug gi 'gro ba la smon lam gyis mtshams sbyor 'gro don gyi bka' babs khyod la yod pas nga khyod la re che bas 'gro don la sems bskyed rgya ma chung zhig ces dang / nga'i gter kha 'di rnams kyi nang nas padma'i snyan brgyud kyi rtsa ba'i chos bdag khyod yin gsungs.*

43. See B1, fols. 128–130; B2, fols. 134b.6–135b.2; B4; DH, fols. 319–321; T3.

44. The mantra: *oṃ ā : hūṃ hrī : oṃ maṇi pad me hūṃ : oṃ vairocana hūṃ : akṣobhya : ratnasaṃbhava : amidheva : amoghasiddhi hūṃ : padma ha mahā amoghapaśa : saha āṃ samaya hri am cara cara hūṃ : namo bhagavat ārya avalokeśvaraya : bhodhisatvaya : mahāsatvaya : mahākarunikaya : siddhimaṇṭaya āni svāhā.*

45. See, for example, B2, fol. 135b.2: *bdag khams pa nyi ma grags pas mang yul byams sprin gyi gtsug lag khang nas gdan drangs shing : khams sring mo rdzong gi phug nag o rgyan sgrub gnas su shogs ser las lcags spre hor zla drug par zhal bzhus pa'o.*

46. GKCB, p. 839. This was also a sacred site of one Grub-chen Nag-po-rdo-rje.

47. These were the *Zab-khrid phag-mo khros-ma*, the *Phur-pa hūṃ-chen sgra-sgrogs ma-bu*, and the *Nor-bdag rnam-sras*. It is indicated that Nyi-ma-grags-pa was not able to recover all the teachings of the *Nor-bdag rnam-sras* because his consort was impure, and as an even more dramatic sign of corrupted auspices, it was also rumored that the particular site where this treasure had been discovered was later blown apart by lightning.

48. After Nyi-ma-grags-pa's death the practice of the *Zab-khrid phag-mo khros-ma* was not continued at Stag-mo-sgang because the succeeding abbots were supposedly confused about how to perform it properly. See GKCB, p. 849.

49. GKCB, p. 856.

50. The list of texts presented here is based on the sequence found in edition T3, which is explicitly identified as Nyi-ma-grags-pa's adaptation.

51. According to John Ardussi, Bhutan and Tibet were technically at peace at this time, since a treaty was signed in 1679. However, there was still a great deal of friction along the borders (e-mail communication, February 1999); also Ardussi 1997, pp. 17–20. Shakabpa mentions that the eastern and western borders into Bhutan were closed around 1676. See Shakabpa 1984, p. 122. On the Dge-lugs-pa invasions of Bhutan in the seventeenth century, see Aris 1979, pp. 219–227.

52. Such as the *Lha-mo sngags-srung-ma* and two lead statues of Jo-bo Mi-bskyod-rdo-rje and Chos-sku Mi-bskyod-rdo-rje. The former statue was perhaps a

replica of the famous Buddha image brought from Nepal by Khri-btsun, the Nepalese wife of Emperor Srong-brtsan-sgam-po. See Tucci 1962, Richardson 1998, pp. 207–215.

53. See *Sku-bzhi'i dbang-phyug rje-btsun ngag-dbang rgyal-mtshan-gyi rnam-par thar-pa thams-cad mkhyen-pa'i rol-mo*, fols. 89b-91b. I am grateful to John Ardussi for kindly providing a copy of the relevant sections of this biography and for sharing with me some of his research on Ngag-dbang-rgyal-mtshan's travels in eastern Tibet.

54. *Sku-bzhi'i dbang-phyug*, fol. 90b. The recently discovered manuscript collection preserved in Nepal consists of thirteen volumes.

55. This is not at all surprising since the Zhabs-drung had died much earlier under mysterious circumstances. His death had been kept a state secret for more than fifty years. During that time the official word was that this popular religious leader was in secret retreat absorbed in deep meditation. For details, see Aris 1979, pp. 233–254.

56. A certain lama Rin-chen-rdo-rje was alleged to have offered him the monastery of Mon-gzigs Tshang-rong, perhaps at Rtsang-sgang in eastern Bhutan, but he graciously declined the offer. At Sha-'ug (Stag-sgo) in the Rta-dbang district of Shar-mon (this was an area much disputed by the governments of Bhutan and Tibet, see Aris 1988, pp. 118–122), he received a clear prophecy indicating that he was to extract the *Dpal mgon-po-ma-ning*. He was, however, unable to obtain the necessary objects, and, moreover, he did not think the teaching was that important. The agitated political atmosphere of this region at the time probably contributed to the difficulties Nyi-ma-grags-pa experienced. By the last decades of the seventeenth century, just about the time Nyi-ma-grags-pa was traveling through Mon-yul, the Rta-dbang district had become a Dge-lugs-pa stronghold, officially annexed in 1680. See Aris 1979, p. 259, 1988a pp. 118–119.

57. See TLNT, vol. 1, fol. 266.

58. GKCB, p. 842, quoting TLNT, vol. 1, fol. 266.5.

59. This cycle can be found in RCTD, vol. 27.

60. TLNT, vol. 1, fol. 266.5; GKCB, p. 842.

61. GKCB, p. 845; Martin 1991b, p. 177. Guru Bkra-shis goes on to say that this sacred site had also once been a place where Padmasambhava and his retinue produced special medicines. Later, Rje-dbon 'Gyur-med-padma-kun-grol-rnam-rgyal (1706–1773) obtained this medicine and discovered many mortar stones (*rdo-gzhong*) at that location. On the life of Rje-dbon Rin-po-che, see GKCB, pp. 793–800.

62. Full name Rdzogs-chen O-rgyan-bsam-gtan-gling. A brief history of this monastery with its abbatial lineage (*gdan-rabs*) is given in GKCB, pp. 765–817.

63. Khenpo Nyima Dondup, personal communication, August 1998.

64. On the history of Zhe-chen monastery and its succession of abbots, see GKCB, pp. 913–922.

65. Dorje 1996, p. 526. Prints from some of these blocks have been gathered and reproduced recently in Delhi under the title *Kar-gling zhi-khro'i 'don-cha*. See ZH.

66. On the other hand, we cannot discount the enormous influence of Smin-grol-gling on Zhechen's liturgical cycles. The two monasteries shared a very close affiliation.

67. Full name, Stag-mo-sgang Bskal-bzang-phun-tshogs-gling.

68. On this type of demon, see Tucci 1988, p. 187.

69. On whom see GKCB, pp. 574–575; Bradburn et al. 1995, pp. 275–276.

70. Martin 1991, pp. 176–177.

71. After Padma-rig-'dzin's death, Nyi-ma-grags-pa is said to have met his teacher's wisdom-body (*chos-sku*) many times in visions and in dreams. In one such vision at Rtsi-lu-gu-rab, he is alleged to have received a teaching entitled *Rgyal-mtshan rtse-mo*.

72. At the monastery at Li-thang there was an epidemic of some sort, and Nyi-ma-grags-pa was asked to exorcise the demon responsible for the disease" (*nad-kyi bdag-po*). His success resulted in his receiving special favor among the leading lamas of that institution. Housed at the monastery were woodblocks of the complete Buddhist *Bka'-'gyur*. This was the famous 'Jang-sa-tham redaction believed to have been produced in the years 1609–14 in 110 volumes and to have served as the basis for the Co-ne edition of 1721–31. See Imaeda 1982–84; Samten Jampa 1987; Harrison 1996, pp. 81–82. Nyi-ma-grags-pa offered everything he owned in order to pay the expenses of having three copies prepared from these blocks, which he then brought back with him to the temple at Stag-mo-sgang.

73. Shakabpa 1984, pp. 125–128; Smith 1996, pp. 117–121. Compare also the secrecy of the Zhabs-drung's death in Bhutan at roughly the same time period; see Aris 1979, pp. 201–254.

74. GKCB, p. 841: *shar ri rtser nyi ma shar na yang / sprin dkar pos bsgribs nas gsal ma 'gyur.*

75. GKCB, p. 841: *sprul lce gnyis brkyangs pa'i dug lce rno.*

76. GKCB, p. 841: *lug spyang kir bag phebs sdod pa la / da rdzi bos nyan sel ci rang byed.*

77. See Shakabpa 1984, pp. 125–39; Aris 1988a pp. 149–153. The sixth Dalai Lama was notoriously unfit for the job as leader of the Tibetan government. He is alleged to have been a rather capricious and impassioned young man and is best renowned as an accomplished poet and romantic lyricist. For translations and analysis of the sixth Dalai Lama's poems, see especially Houston 1982; Sorensen 1990.

78. Nyi-ma-grags-pa presented the initiations and readings of the *Rta-mgrin dregs-pa zil-gnon* and the *Lha-chen*. The Sde-srid would later offer him in return the monasteries of Rta-rna and Yi-phug in Nang-chen, and in the region of Nem-tsha, Spang-lcib[-lcin?]-dgon, and Ba-dan-dgon—the ancient monastic seats of Nag-po-thog-'phen. However, because of some turbulent circumstances, Nyi-ma was only able to accept the monastery of Rta-rna-dgon.

79. Lha-bzang Khan and his Tibetan allies actively sought out and punished the supporters of Sde-srid Sangs-rgyas-rgya-mtsho, so there is no mystery why lamas such as Nyi-ma-grag-pa would have not wanted to remain in Lhasa during this period.

80. The Tsa-ri Rong-skor is discussed at length in Huber 1999, ch. 8.

81. On the use of *linga* in Tibetan ritual, see Nebesky-Wojkowitz 1956, p. 360; Stein 1957; Tucci 1988, pp. 185–187; Beyer 1978, pp. 310–312; Norbu 1995, pp. 98–102.

82. Kolmaś 1988, p. 130.

83. GKCB, p. 852: *ha cang bdud du nan gyis bsgrubs na bsgrub bya sgrub byed go log pa'i skyon 'byung ba'ang srid de.*

84. O-rgyan-bstan-'dzin was believed to have been the reincarnation of the *gter-ston* Bzang-po-rdo-rje of Dwags-po, a student of both Rtse-le Sna-tshogs-rang-grol and 'Ja'-tshon-snying-po. See GKCB, p. 865.

85. Tib., *lcags-pho-stag dbo-zla'i nya*. This coresponds to the western date Wednesday, March 15, 1710, according to the New Phug-pa calendrical system, which became official in 1696 and is the one currently in use today. See Dudjom Rinpoche 1991, vol. 1, p. 400.

86. GKCB, p. 859: *nged rang gnyis ltar snang mthun 'jug mi mdzad pa ltar yod kyang / don du nged rang ni gshin rje'i skor gyi gsang pa'i chos bdag khong pa yin te khong gis nyams bzhes dang gsang rgya mthar phyin mdzad pa des nged rang gnyis char gyi sku tshe dang 'phrin las la phan pa che zhing bstan pa'i gsos su'ang gyur mod / da cha khong pa zhi bar gshegs pa ma legs / 'on kyang rgyal sras la bdag rkyen gang drag 'di nas phul chog pa byed ces.*

87. For example, see B5.

88. Compare, for example, the content and textual sequence of KS, representing Gter-bdag-gling-pa's tradition, and T3.

89. GKCB, p. 866.

90. Alternative name Rig-'dzin Bstan-skyong-rgya-mtsho, on whom see GKCB, pp. 871–886.

12. Conclusion

1. See the colophon of edition B2: *zab chos zhi khro dgongs pa rang grol las bar do'i ngo sprod thos grol chen mo la / mthad 'os su gyur nga'i mdo rgyud dang chos spyod sogs byin rlabs zab gnad che ba cu ma'i kha bskang gis brgyan ste bklag chog tu bgyis pa 'di ni / thos grol par du bzhengs pa po rnams kyi bskul ngor śākya'i dge slong nges don bstan 'dzin bzang pos bsam gtan chos gling gi dge gnas su bkod pa'i dge bas mkha' khyab kyi 'gro ba thams cad gdod ma'i mgon po kun tu bzang po'i go 'phangs myur du thob pa'i rgyur gyur cig.* A brief account of the life of Rdzogs-chen-pa Nges-don-bstan-'dzin-bzang-po can be found in GKCB, pp. 800–808.

2. On King 'Jigs-med-dbang-phyug, see Aris 1994, pp. 115–143.

3. The title *lo-phyag* refers to the custom in Bhutan of dispatching a regular diplomatic representative to the Tibetan government in Lhasa as a mission of tribute. The establishment of the *lo-phyag* was initiated by Pho-lha-nas Bsod-nams-stobs-rgyas (1689–1747) in 1730 after the Tibetan invasion of Bhutan. According to Shakabpa (1984, p. 145), the tradition continued until 1950. See also Bell [1928] 1994, p. 126; Aris 1979, p. 259. Nor-bu-bzang-po was probably the last of such Bhutanese diplomats. It was Gene Smith's impression that he was a student of Bdud-'joms Rin-po-che (1904–1987) and that he had some connection with the house of Lha-rgya-ri in Tibet, perhaps through his son who married into this family (personal communication, June 1998).

4. Aris 1979, p. 154.

5. For a more complete index and catalogue of all extant editions of the Kar-gling Zhi-khro cycle, including both the *Zhi-khro dgongs-pa rang-grol* and the *Bar-do thos-grol chen-mo*, see Cuevas 2000, pp. 416–501.

6. Evans-Wentz and Dawa Samdup [1927] 2000 pp. 68–73.

7. See Cuevas 2000, pp. 429–430. The relevant texts are listed at the Kern Institute as Inv. No. 2740/H12 (17 titles); Inv. No. 2740/H19 (4 titles); and Inv. No. 2740/H187 (15 titles). References kindly provided by Henk Blezer.

8. Personal communication, March 1999.

9. Evans-Wentz and Dawa Samdup [1927] 2000, pp. 71–72 n.1. The phonetic English titles given by Evans-Wentz correspond to the following Tibetan titles (arranged in the order listed): (1) *Chos-nyid bar-do'i gsal-'debs thos-grol chen-mo*; (2) *Khro-bo'i bar-do 'char-tshul bstan-pa*; (3) *Sangs-rgyas dang byang-chub sems-dpa' rnams-la ra-mda' sbran-pa'i smon-lam*; (4) *Bar-do'i rtsa-tshig*; (5) *Bar-do 'phrang-sgrol-gyi smon-lam*; (6) *Bar-do thos-grol chen-mo las srid-pa bar-do'i ngo-sprod*;

(7) *Btags-grol phung-po rang-grol*; (8) *Bar-do'i smon-lam 'jigs-skyobs-ma*; (9) *'Chi-ltas mtshan-ma rang-grol*; (10) *Rig-pa ngo-sprod gcer-mthong rang-grol*; (11) *Srid-pa bar-do'i dge-sdig rang-gzugs bstan-pa'i gdams-pa srid-pa bar-do rang-grol*; (12) *Srid-pa bar-do'i dge-sdig rang-gzugs bstan-pa'i lhan-thabs*; (13) *Brgyud-pa'i gsol-'debs*; (14) *'Chi-bslu 'jigs-pa rang-grol*; (15) *Zhi-khro'i klong-bshags brjod-pa rang-grol*; (16) *Btags-grol yid-bzhin nor-mchog*; (17) *Chos-spyod bag-chags rang-grol*.

10. Bstan-rgyas-gling monastery was the seat of the successive De-mo Qutuqtu, from whom were chosen some of the regents to the Dalai Lamas. On the troubled history of this monastery, see Bell [1931] 1994, pp. 162–164; Shakabpa 1984, p. 241; Goldstein 1989, pp. 63–64. Waddell [1985] 1972, pp. 515–539, describes a ceremonial dance that was performed regularly at Bstan-rgyas-gling. This was the *Stag-(mgrin-)dmar 'chams*, devoted to the deity Hayagrīva. According to descriptions, it would appear that this drama closely resembles the popular Bhutanese dance of the judgment of the dead, called *rakṣa-mang-'chams*, or *rakṣa-mar-'chams*. It maybe recalled that this dance is said to have been based on Karma-gling-pa's *Srid-pa bar-do'i dge-sdig rang-gzugs bstan-pa'i gdams-pa srid-pa bar-do rang-grol*.

11. See BL OR 19999 ns. 248–264. Unless otherwise noted, all references to the Tibetan holdings at the British Library (BL) are based on information kindly supplied by Burkhard Quessel.

12. See BL OR 19999 n. 260, fols 6a5–6b2: *gsol 'debs kyi rim pa 'di sprul pa'i gter ston rigs 'dzin nyi ma grags pas bdud 'dul sngags pa gling du sbyar ba 'di yang zad mi shes pa gang gā'i rgyun ltar yun ring gnas par gyur cig // sarvamaṅgalaṃ.* This is the same colophon that we find in B1, B4, DH, and T3.

13. Smith 1970, p. 3 n. 16.

14. According to the inventory in KCPT, fol. 236.6, the Bstan-rgyas-gling *Bar-do thos-grol* consisted of 275 separate xylographic blocks.

15. Corresponding to ms. BL OR 5355.1, BL OR 5355 10–13, BL OR 5355 15, respectively (158 folia total).

16. Reference to what appears to be another Lha-lung edition is cited in Back 1987, p. 105, a photocopy of a blockprint (SGA) belonging to Lama Sherab Gyaltsen Amipa of the Tibetan Institute in Rikon, Switzerland. According to the colophon of its fifth text, the *Chos-spyod bag-chags rang-grol*, this blockprint collection was published at Lha-lung and preserved at the monastery of Bsam-gtan-gling (in Skyid-grong?): *grub thob kar ma gling pas gter nas gdan drangs po'i / sngags ban khams gsum yongs grol gyi lha lung chos kyi sde ru par du bskrun / par 'di sho rong 'ja' sa'i khrid bsam gtan gling dgon du bzhugs.*

17. BL OR Tib I 228 is ms. K25 no. 438 in Denwood 1976.

18. See Back 1987, pp. 6–7.

19. The closing sections of two of the collection's manuscripts (BL OR Tib I 228, no. 2, fol. 18r.1–5 and BL OR Tib I 228, no. 4, fol. 11r.3–5, respectively) refer to the names Rgyal-sras Sde-chen-kling[-gling]-pa [i.e., Mchog-gyur-gling-pa], Nor-bu-dar-rgyas [alternate name of Mchog-gyur-gling-pa?], and Jo-bo Tshe-dbang-dar-rgyas [i.e., Mkhyen-brtse'i-dbang-po?]. My thanks to Burkhard Quessel for kindly sending me digital images of these manuscript folia.

20. Schuh 1981, p. xxv.

21. For example, compare the colophon of Wad B Wadd 87a (*Rdzogs-chen dgongs-pa rang-grol la khro-bos bar-do'i bsal-'debs*) to that of the *Khro-bo'i bar-do 'char-tshul bstan-pa* found in B1, B1a, B4, DH, and T3.

22. According to Gene Smith this important printing house was closed around 1700 and only reopened in 1870 (personal correspondence, July 1998).

23. Chandra 1981, vol. I, p. 31, nos. 632–633.

24. Incidentally, Nyi-ma-grags-pa spent considerable time in Rgyang-yul, which is near the Dga'-ldan Phun-tshogs-gling printery.

25. See PLKC, pp. 127–130.

26. Evidence for this can be drawn from a comparative analysis of the texts listed in both the *gsan-yig* of the fifth Dalai Lama and the Polala catalogue.

27. See Kolmaś 1969, pp. 49–50, nos. 34–36.

28. The famous temple of Bskyed-chu lha-khang (Skyer-chu) is believed to have been built in the seventh century by the emperor Srong-btsan-sgam-po. See Pommaret 1998a, pp. 119–121.

29. See S1, fol. 51a.6; also KS, pp. 4–5.

30. Ample historical evidence exists in the biographical literature indicating that it was standard for students to receive the Kar-gling *Zhi-khro* transmissions at a young age or at the time of their monastic ordination. From this study alone, I might cite as examples Kaḥ-thog-pa Bsod-nams-rgyal-mtshan, Zur-chen Chos-dbyings-rang-grol, Gter-bdag-gling-pa, and O-rgyan-bstan-'dzin.

Bibliography

Tibetan References

The following is a list of Tibetan editions of the *Self-Liberated Wisdom of the Peaceful and Wrathful Deities* and the *Great Liberation upon Hearing in the Bardo*. The sources are arranged in alphabetical order according to the abbreviations used in the notes.

B1   *Zab-chos zhi-khro dgongs-pa rang-grol las thos-grol chen-mo'i skor.* Paro, Bhutan, 1976. I(Bhu)-Tib-82; 76–905033. JVM no. 2740/H12, 19, and 187. Printed from blocks carved in 1943 through the efforts of Nor-bu-bzang-po, Bhutanese Lo-phyag to the Lhasa government, and preserved at Bskyed-chu-lha-khang in Spa-gro, Bhutan. Text produced from blocks identical to those used in printing B1a, B4, and DH. 18 titles, 283 folios.

B1a   *Zab-chos zhi-khro dgongs-pa rang-grol las bar-do thos-grol chen-mo.* Delhi, 1993. JVM no. 2740/H12, 19, and 187. Reproduced from a print from the Spa-gro-rdzong blocks by Konchhog Lhadrepa. Text produced from blocks identical to those used in printing B1, B4, and DH. 17 titles, 280 folios.

B2   *Zab-chos zhi-khro dgongs-pa rang-grol las bar-do'i gsal-'debs thos-grol chen-mo bklag-chog-tu bkod-pa 'khrul-snang rang-grol.* 1976. I(Bhu)-Tib-118; 77–902202. Printed from blocks preserved at Bum-thang Bkra-shis-chos-gling-pho-brang. Originally arranged for publication by Nges-don-bstan-'dzin-bzang-po (Rdzogs-chen III, 1759–1792). 17 titles, 177 folios.

B3   "Zab-chos zhi-khro dgongs-pa rang-grol." In Kong-sprul-blo-gros-mtha'-yas, *Rin-chen gter-mdzod.* Paro, Bhutan: Ngodrup and Sherab Drimay, 1976. Vol. 4, fols. 1–281. I(Bhu)-Tib-124; 77–900739. Stod-lung Mtshur-phu redaction, with supplemental texts from the Dpal-spungs redaction and other manuscripts. 10 titles, 94 folios.

B4   *Zab-chos zhi-khro dgongs-pa rang-grol las thos-grol chen-mo'i skor.* Paro, Bhutan, 1977. I(Bhu)-Tib-149; 79–902879. Printed from blocks carved in 1943 through the efforts of Lo-phyag Nor-bu-bzang-po. A collection of texts for use in the practice initiated by H.H. Bdud-'joms Rin-po-che (1904–1987) and his followers. Text produced from blocks identical to those used in printing B1, B1a, and DH. 18 titles, 282 folios, 563 pages.

B5   *Zab-chos zhi-khro dgongs-pa rang-grol chos-skor.* Thimphu, Bhutan, 1978.
      I(Bhu)-Tib-165; 79–903061. Printed from blocks preserved at Bum-thang
      Thar-pa-gling monastery in Bhutan. Interpretations by Smin-gling Lo-chen
      Dharma-śrī (1654–1718). 7 titles, 101 folios, 201 pages.

BL   Tibetan manuscripts and blockprints held in the India Office of the British
      Library. Catalogue numbers listed for the library's own shelfmarks in the rare
      mss. department (OR). References supplied by Burkhard Quessel, curator of
      the Tibetan Collections. OR Tib I 228 ms [=Denwood 438 (MS K 25)] (4
      titles, 96 folios); OR Tib CC 61 ms [=Denwood 520] (7 folios); OR 13813 ms
      (9 folios); OR 5355.1, 10–13, 15 ms (6 titles, 158 folios); OR 19999d.21.1 ms
      (26 folios); OR 19999d.23 bp (35 folios); OR 19999d.110 bp (4 folios); OR
      19999n.248–264 bp (Bstan-rgyas-gling) [=CM?] (17 titles); OR 15190.1–8 ms
      (8 titles, 405 folios); OR 19999z.11.1–12 bp (Bstan-rgyas-gling) [=CM?] (16
      titles, 260+ folios).

CH   *Kar-gling zhi-khro.* Ch'eng-tu: Si-khron mi-rigs dpe-khang-gis bskrun-nas
      bkram, 1992. Ch-Tib 123; 93–927830. 21 titles, 387 folios.

CM   (*Zab-chos zhi-khro dgongs-pa rang-grol*). Blockprint from Rgyal-rtse pur-
      chased in 1919 by Major W. L. Campbell. List of contents printed in Evans-
      Wentz and Dawa Sandup [1927] 2000, p. 7¹n.1. [=BL OR 19999n.248–264
      bp; BL OR 19999z.11.1–12 bp ?]. 17 titles.

DH   *Zab-chos zhi-khro dgongs-pa rang-grol las bar-do thos-grol-gyi skor.*
      Dharamsala, Kangra H.P., India: Tibetan Cultural Printing Press, 1994.
      Printed from blocks carved in 1943 through the efforts of Lo-phyag Nor-
      bu-bzang-po. Commercial ed. Text produced from blocks identical to those
      used in printing B1, B1a, and B4. 19 titles, 296 folios.

GK   *Sga-rje khams-gzhung dgon-pa'i phyag-bzhes grub-thob karma-gling-pa'i*
      gter-byon zhi-khro dgongs-pa rang-grol-gyi chos-sde. Dharamsala, Kangra
      H.P., India: Library of Tibetan Works and Archives, 1988. I-Tib-3056. Com-
      piled by Khams-sprul 'Jam-dbyangs-don-grub. 86 titles, 537 folios.

JVM   Johan van Manen Collection housed in the Library of the Kern Institute,
      Leiden. References provided by Henk Blezer. Inv. no. 2740/H12 [=B1, B4,
      DH] (17 titles); inv. no. 2740/H19 (4 titles); inv. no. 2740/H187. 15 titles.

KS   *Bar-do'i thos-grol: The Tibetan Book of the Dead by the Great Acharya Shri*
      Sing-ha. Varanasi, India: E. Kalsang Lhundup, Buddhist Temple, 1969. Hand-
      written print based on a blockprint edition arranged by Dil-mgo Mkhyen-
      rtse Bkra-shis-dpal-'byor (1910–1991) and preserved at the Jo-khang-ri-khrod
      of Dben-dgon monastery in Gangtok. 14 titles, 122 pages.

NE   *Zhi-khro dgongs-pa rang-grol.* Solu, Nepal, 1970. N-Tib-1159; 74–919674.
      Printed from blocks preserved at Dgon-steng Bshad-sgrub-chos-gling mon-
      astery in Solu. 30 titles, 260 folios.

PY   *Dpal-yul phyag-srol kar-gling zhi-khro.* Delhi: Konchhog Lhadrepa, [1986?;
      reprint 1997?]. Reproduced from a rare manuscript from Dpal-yul Monas-
      tery. 51 titles, 432 folios, 863 pages.

RB   *Thos-grol dkar-chags dga'-bas 'dzum-bton ces-bya-ba.* Included in an un-
      published manuscript of the *Zhi-khro dgongs-pa rang-grol* in the possession
      of Ri-bo-che Rje-drung Byams-pa-'byung-gnas of Padma-bkod. Typescript
      of E. Gene Smith. 12 titles, 254 folios.

S1   *Zhi-khro dgongs-pa rang-grol.* Gangtok, Sikkim, 1972. I(Sik)-Tib-132; 72–
      906841. Printed from blocks preserved at the Jo-khang-ri-khrod of Dben-dgon
      monastery in Gangtok. Text arranged by Dil-mgo Mkhyen-rtse Bkra-shis-

dpal-'byor (1910–1991) at the behest of one Kun-bzang-rgya-mtsho and printed under the auspices of the Do-lung Spyi-dpon [in Sikkim?]. 14 titles, 187 folios.

S2   *Badzra gu-ru'i phan-yon dang 'bru-'grel.* Gangtok, Sikkim, 1972. I(Sik)-Tib-192; 72–906583. Printed from blocks preserved at the Jo-khang-ri-khrod of Dben-dgon monastery in Gangtok. 10 folios, 19 pages.

S3   *Zhi-khro dgongs-pa rang-grol.* Gangtok, Sikkim, 1972. I(Sik)-Tib-209; 73–907041. Printed from blocks preserved at 'Ba'-nyag House in Gangtok. 10 titles, 121 folios, 241 pages.

SGA   *(Bar-do thos-grol).* Photocopy of a blockprint belonging to Lama Sherab Gyaltsen Amipa of the Tibetan Institute in Rikon, Switzerland. The print blocks appear to have been prepared at Lha-lung and preserved at the monastery of Bsam-gtan-gling in Skyid-grong. List of contents printed in Back 1987, p. 105. 9 texts, 136 folios.

T1   *Sprul-sku karma-gling-pa'i gter-byang badzra gu-ru'i phan-yon dang 'bru-grel.* Ka-sbug (Ka-lon-spungs): Phun-gling gsung-rab rnams-gso rgyun-spel dpar-khang, 1962. I-Tib-74; sa 68–020980. Printed from blocks carved by Khams-sprul VIII Don-brgyud-nyi-ma. 5 folios.

T2   *Zab-chos zhi-khro dgongs-pa rang-grol chos-spyod.* Yuru, Ladakh, 1969. I-Tib-582; 79–906375. Printed from blocks preserved at Gnyang-drung monastery. 33 folios, 65 pages.

T3   *Zhi-khro dgongs-pa rang-grol.* Kelang, 1969. I-Tib-601; 75–907154. Printed from blocks preserved in the Khang-gsar fortress (Gemur temple) in Gar-zhwa in Lahul-Spiti [?]. Edited and supplemented by Rig-'dzin Nyi-ma-grags-pa (1647–1710). 17 titles, 228 folios, 456 pages.

T4   *Gti-mug gnyid-skrogs and Other Liturgical Texts from the Zab-chos zhi-khro dgongs-pa rang-grol.* Kelang, 1969. I-Tib-608; 72–913510. Printed from blocks preserved at the Rta-yul temple in Gar-zhwa, Lahul-Spiti [?].6 titles, 61 folios, 121 pages.

T5   *Zhi-khro dgongs-pa rang-grol.* Sahāranapura, India: Barakā Presa, c. 1969. I-Tib-613; 76–927219. Commercial ed. 36 titles, 450 folios.

T6   *Zhi-khro dgongs-pa rang-grol.* New Delhi: Ngawang Topgay, 1972. I-Tib-887; 72–901751. Reprint, New Delhi, 1994. Arranged according to the tradition followed at Nalanda monastery in 'Phan-po. Commercial ed. 23 titles, 256 folios.

T7   *Zhi-khro dgongs-pa rang-grol-gyi chos-skor.* 3 vols. Delhi: Sherab Lama, 1975–76. I-Tib-1440; 75–903780. Reproduced from a manuscript collection found in the library of Bdud-'joms Rin-po-che (1904–1987). Authoritative ed. 66 titles in 3 vols., 764 folios.

T8   *Zhi-khro dgongs-pa rang-grol.* 2 vols. Kalimpong, Sikkim: Mani Dorji, 1979. I-Tib-1990; 79–905078. Reprinted in 1 vol. as *Kar-gling zhi-khro.* New Delhi, c. 1994. The tradition followed among the Rnying-ma-pa of eastern Bhutan. 38 titles in 2 vols., 468 folios.

WadB   *Bar-do thos-grol chen-mo.* Manuscripts and blockprints collected in 1904 under the supervision of Lieutenant Colonel. L. A. Waddell and preserved at the Staatsbibliothek Preussischer Kulturbesitz Berlin. Catalogue numbers and titles listed in Schuh 1981. Wadd 84 bp (14 titles, 161 folios); Wadd 87 ms (3 titles, 146 folios).

ZH   *Kar-gling zhi-khro'i 'don-cha.* Delhi, 1994. Reproduced from a print made from xylographs carved at Zhe-chen monastery in eastern Tibet. Arranged according to the teaching lineage of Mkhas-grub 'Gyur-med-mthu-stobs-rnam-rgyal (1710–1769). 29 titles, 279 folios, 557 pages.

The following is a general list of Tibetan sources, with abbreviations in alphabetical order.

BDGR   Bstan-'dzin-padma'i-rgyal-mtshan, Che-tshang Sprul-sku IV. *'Bri-gung gdan-rabs gser-phreng* [i.e., *Nges-don bstan-pa'i snying-po mgon-po 'bri-gung-pa chen-po'i gdan-rabs chos-kyi byung-tshul gser-gyi phreng-ba*]. Lhasa: Bod-ljongs bod-yig dpe-rnying dpe-skrun-khang, 1989.

BDLC   Mtshur-ston Dbang-nge (Dbang-gi-rdo-rje). *Bar-do blos-chod-kyi man-ngag* of *Rje-btsun lho-brag-pa'i khyad-par-gyi gdams-pa snyan-gyi shog-dril bzhi'i lo-rgyus gzhung lhan-thabs dang bcas-pa*. In DMDZ, vol. 8, fols. 226–233.

BDNS   Khyung-po Rnal-'byor. *Bar-do rnam-gsum-gyi zhal-gdams*. In *Śangs-pa Bka'-brgyud-pa Texts: A Collection of Rare Manuscripts of Doctrinal, Ritual, and Biographical Works of Scholars of the Śangs-pa Bka'-brgyud-pa Tradition from the Monastery of Gsang-sngags-cho-gling in Kinnaur.* Sumra, H.P., India: Urgyan Dorje, 1977, vol. 1, fols. 263–286. I-Tib-1734; 77–906849.

BDRL   Ratna-gling-pa. *Bar-do 'phrang-sgrol-gyis gsol-'debs pho-nya myur-mgyogs*. In *Selected Works of Ratna gling pa*. Tezu, A.P., India: Tibetan Nyingmapa Monastery, 1973, vol. 1, fols. 661–667. I-Tib-1041; 73–901830.

BDTT   Khetsun Sangpo [Mkhas-btsun-bzang-po]. *Biographical Dictionary of Tibet and Tibetan Buddhism.* Dharamsala: Library of Tibetan Works and Archives, 1973. I-Tib-1119; 73–904404.

BDZH   Sgam-po-pa Bsod-nams-rin-chen. *Bar-do'i dmar-khrid-kyi zhal-gdams.* In (1) *Collected Works [Gsuṅ 'bum] of Sgam-po-pa Bsod-nams-rin-chen.* Delhi: Khasdub Gyatsho Shashin, 1975, vol. 2, fols. 53.5–58.5. I-Tib-1478; 75–905460); and (2) *Collected Works [Gsuṅ-'bum] of Sgam-po-pa Bsod-nams-rin-chen.* Darjeeling, West Bengal: Kargyud Sungrab Nyamso Khang, [1982], vol.2, fols. 198.6–207.2. I-Tib-2250; 82–902155.

BPCT   *Bonpo Popular Canonical Texts.* Dolanji H.P., India: Tibetan Bonpo Monastic Center, 1974. I-Tib-1240; 74–900987.

BRCB   Kun-mkhyen Padma-dkar-po, 'Brug-chen IV. *'Brug-pa chos-'byung* [i.e., *Chos-'byung bstan-pa'i padma rgyas-pa'i nyin-byed*]. Gangs-can Rig-mdzod series no. 19. Lhasa: Bod-ljongs bod-yig dpe-rnying dpe-skrun-khang, 1992.

BRDS   Rtse-le Sna-tshogs-rang-grol. *Bar-do spyi'i-don thams-cad rnam-par gsal-bar byed-pa dran-pa'i me-long.* (1) Solu, Nepal, 1983. N-Tib-4294; 84–901065; in (2) *The Complete Works of Rtse-le Rgod-tshang-pa Padma-legs-grub* (Gangtok, Sikkim: Mgon-po-tshe-brtan, Palace Monastery, 1979, vol. 8, fols. 569–689. I-Tib-1982; 79–904985; and (3) *The Collected Works [Gsung 'bum] of Rtse-le Sna-tshogs-rang-grol* (New Delhi: Sanje Dorji, 1974, vol. 2, fols. 139–233. I-Tib-1274; 74–901176.

BYCS   Byang-chub-seng-ge. *The Visions of Hell of Byang-chub-senge* [i.e., *Spyan-ras-gzigs-kyi sprul-pa 'das-log byang-chub-senge'i dmyal-snang shar-ba las dge-sdig-gi shan-dbye dang gshin-rje chos-kyi rgyal-po'i 'phrin-yig rgyas-pa*]. Thimphu, Bhutan: Kunsang Topgay, 1976. I(Bhu)-Tib-136.

BYNG   *Byang-bya-dur (Gnas-ri byang-bya-dur dkar-chag).* Chengdu, China: Si-khron zhing-chen zung-chu-rdzong shar-dung-ri shes-rig dpar-khang, 1993.

CHGP   Mchog-ldan-mgon-po. *Sprul-sku rig-'dzin mchog-ldan-mgon-po'i rnam-thar mgur-'bum dad-ldan spro-ba bskyed-byed.* Paro, Bhutan: Ugyen Tempai Gyaltsen, 1979. I(Bhu)-Tib-268; 80–902345.

CPYR   Anonymous. *Chos-spyod-kyi rim-pa ne-bar mkho-ba.* Sarnath, Varanasi U.P., India: Central Institute of Higher Tibetan Studies, 1996–97.

DJTY   Bdud-'joms 'Jigs-bral-ye-shes-rdo-rje. *Rin-chen gter-mdzod-kyi thob-yig.* Dal-hor, India 1968. I-Tib-1148; 70–904325.

DLSY   Ngag-dbang-blo-bzang-rgya-mtsho, Dalai Lama V. *Gsan-yig of the Fifth Dalai Lama. Gsan-yig gaṅgā'i chu-rgyun* [i.e., *Zab-pa dang rgya-che-ba'i dam-pa'i chos-kyi thob-yig gaṅgā'i chu-rgyun las glegs-bam gsum-pa*]. 4 vols. Delhi: Nechung and Lhakhar, 1970: vol. 4, fols. 86.3–91.3. I-Tib-739; 78–918067.

DMDZ   'Jam-mgon Kong-sprul Blo-gros-mtha'-yas. *Gdams-ṅag mdzod.* Delhi: N. Lungtok and N. Gyaltsen, 1971–72. 12 vols. Reproduced from a xylographic print from the Dpal-spungs blocks. I-Tib-763; 76–921818.

DZSN   Rtse-le Sna-tshogs-rang-grol. *Rje-btsun dam-pa rdzogs-chen-pa bsod-nams dbang-po'i rnam-thar mdor-bsdus.* In *The Complete Works of Rtse-le Rgod-tshang-pa Padma-legs-grub,* vol. 1, fols. 385–405. Gangtok, Sikkim: Mgon-po-tshe-brtan, Palace Monastery, 1979. I-Tib-1982; 79–904985.

GANG   Gangs-ri-ba Chos-dbyings-rdo-rje. *Gangs-mtsho gnas-gsum-gyi lo-rgyus skal-ldan shing-rta.* Beijing: Bod-ljongs-nang-bstan, 1990.

GBNG   *Thugs-rje chen-po bar-do mun-sel-gyi sgron-me'i gdams-pa.* In *Gab-pa mngon-byung: A Collection of Ma-ni bka'-'bum Texts.* Thobgyal, H.P., India: Tibetan Bonpo Monastic Centre, 1973, fols. 260–284. I-Tib-1058; 73–903023.

GBNT   Gar-dbang-rdo-rje, Mnga'-ris Gter-ston, *Rig-'dzin chen-po Gar-dbang-rdo-rje'i rnam-thar phyi-nang-gsang gsum-sogs.* Dalhousie, H.P., India: Damchoe Sangpo, 1984. I-Tib-2574.

GJGT   Bdud-'joms 'Jigs-bral-ye-shes-rdo-rje. *Gang-ljong rgyal-bstan yongs-rdzogs-kyi phyi-ma snga-'gyur rdo-rje theg-pa'i bstan-pa rin-po-che ji-ltar byung-ba'i tshul-dag cing gsal-bar brjod-pa lha-dbang gyul-las rgyud-ba'i rnga-bo-che'i sgra-dbyangs.* In *Collected Works,* vol. 1, no. 2. I-Tib-1905; 79–901972.

GKCB   Guru Bkra-shis Ngag-dbang-blo-gros. *Gu-bkra'i chos-'byung* [i.e., *Bstan-pa'i snying-po gsang-chen snga-'gyur nges-don zab-mo'i chos-kyi byung-ba gsal-bar byed-pa'i legs-bshad mkhas-pa dga'-byed ngo-mtshar gtam-gyi rol-mtsho*]. Beijing: Krung-go'i bod-kyi shes-rig dpe-skrun-khang, 1990.

GLKT   Jam-dbyangs-rgyal-mtshan, Mkhan-chen. *Rgyal-ba kaḥ-thog-pa'i lo-rgyus mdor-bsdus* [i.e., *Gsang-chen bstan-pa'i chu-'go rgyal-ba kaḥ-thog-pa'i lo-rgyus mdor-bsdus rjod-pa 'chi-med lha'i rnga-sgra ngo-mtshar rna-ba'i dga'-ston*]. Chengdu China: Si-khron mi-rigs dpe-skrun-khang, 1996.

GLRB   Bla-ma Bsod-nams-rgyal-mtshan. *Rgyal-rabs gsal-ba'i me-long.* Lhasa: Bod-ljongs mi-rigs dpe-skrun-khang, 1981.

GRLP   Ratna-gling-pa. *Guru ratna-gling-pa'i rmi-lam rang-snang 'khrul-grol bar-do gnad-kyi 'phrang-grol zhes-bya-ba mdzod-khang skabs-dgu-pa.* In *Selected Works of Ratna gling pa.* Tezu, A.P., India: Tibetan Nyingmapa Monastery, 1973, vol. 1, pp. 545–557. I-Tib-1041; 73–901830.

GTCB   Karma-mi-'gyur-dbang-gi-rgyal-po. *Gter-bton brgya-rtsa'i mtshan-sdom gsol-'debs chos-rgyal bkra-shis stobs-rgyal-gyi mdzod-pa las de'i-'brel-pa lo-rgyus gter-bton chos-'byung.* I-Tib-1902; 79–903886.

JAM   'Jam-dbyangs-mkhyen-brtse'i-dbang-po. *The Collected Works (Gsung-'bum) of the Great 'Jam-dbyangs-mkhyen-brtse' i-dbang-po.* 24 vols. Gangtok, Sikkim: Gonpo Tseten, 1977. I-Tib-1708; 77-905324.

KCPT   *Gangs-can-gyi ljongs-su bka' dang bstan-bcos sogs-kyi glegs-bam spar-gzhi ji-ltar yod-pa rnams nas dkar-chag spar-thor phyogs-tsam du bkod-pa phan-bde'i pad-tshal 'byed-pa'i nyin-byed.* In *Three Karchacks,* edited by Ngawang Gelek Demo. Gedan Sungrab Minyam Gyunphel series 13. New Delhi: 1970, fols. 169–243. I-Tib-720; 70–917195.

LGNB   Rgya-ra-ba Nam-mkha'-chos-kyi-rgya-mtsho. *Zab-chos zhi-khro dgongs-pa rang-grol-gyi brgyud-pa'i lo-rgyus mdor-bsdus nor-bu'i phreng-ba.* In T7, vol. 1, fols. 27–48b.

LRCB   Ri-bo-che Dpon-tshang (Rta-tshag Tshe-dbang-rgyal). *Lho-rong chos-'byung thub-bstan gsal-byed* [i.e., *Dam-pa'i chos-kyi byung-ba'i legs-bshad lho-rong chos-'byung ngam rta-tshag chos-'byung zhes rtsom-pa'i yul ming-du chags-pa'i ngo-mtshar-zhing dkon-pa'i dpe khyad-par-can*]. Gangs-can Rig-mdzod series no. 26. Lhasa: Bod-ljongs bod-yig dpe-rnying dpe-skrun-khang, 1994.

LTKG   *Zab-chos zhi-khro dgongs-pa rang-grol dang thugs-rje chen-po padma zhi-khro las lung-bstan bka'-rgya.* In T7, vol. 1, fols. 521–536 [incomplete].

LZBP   Blo-bzang-chos-kyi-rgyal-mtshan. *Bar-do 'phrang-sgrol.* I(Sik)-Tib-39; 71–909698.

MKGR   Kun-mkhyen Padma-dkar-po, 'Brug-chen IV, ed. *Mkha'-'gro snyan-brgyud-kyi yig-rnying.* Darjeeling, West Bengal: Kargyud Sungrab Nyamso Khang, 1982. I-Tib-2249; 82–902170.

MLAM   Mi-la-ras-pa. *Lam blo-nas gcod-pa bar-do ngo-sprod-kyi gdams-ngag zab-mo.* In (1) MKGR, vol. 2, fols. 99–128; and (2) *Rare Dkar-brgyud-pa Texts from the Library of Ri-bo-che Rje-drung of Padma-bkod.* Tezu, A.P., India: Tibetan Nyingmapa Monastery, 1974, fols. 47–76. I-Tib-1293; 74–901474.

MLGB   Gtsang-smyon He-ru-ka Sangs-rgyas-rgyal-mtshan. *Mi-la'i mgur-'bum.* Dharamsala: Sherig Parkhang, 1990. I-Tib-2436; 83–907128.

NBDS   Kun-bzang-nges-don-klong-yangs. *Bod-du byung-ba'i gsang-sngags snga-'gyur-gyi bstan-'dzin skyes-mchog rim-byon-gyi rnam-thar nor-bu'i do-shal.* I-Tib-1633.

NGB   *Rnying-ma rgyud-'bum.* (1) Mtshams-brag ed. in 46 vols., Thimphu, Bhutan 1982. I(Bhu)-Tib-313; 82–902165; (2) Gting-skyes ed. in 36 vols., Thimphu, Bhutan 1973. I(Bhu)-Tib-9; 73–903590.

NPBD   Zhang G.yu-brag-pa Brtson-'grus-grags-pa. *Na-ro-pa'i bar-do'i gdam-ngag la bar-do rnam-pa-gsum.* In *bKa'-'bum (Collected Works).* Nepalese National Archives microfilm collection, L448/2–L450/4, vol. 4, fols. 181–186.

OGTL   Chos-rje Dge-'dun-rgyal-mtshan. *O-rgyan rin-po-che'i gter-ston lung-bstan dang khung-btsun-pa bla-ma brgyud-pa'i rim-pa rnams.* In T7, vol. 1, fols. 21–26.

PGKR   Kun-bzang-bde-chen-rdo-rje, Lha-lung Gsung-sprul VIII. *Pad-gling 'khrungs-rabs-kyi rtogs-brjod nyung-gsal dad-pa'i me-tog.* In *Rediscovered Teachings of the Great Padma-gling-pa,* vol. 14, fols. 511–600. Thimphu, Bhutan: Kunsang Tobgay, 1975–76. I(Bhu)-Tib-27; 75–903254.

PHMO   Phag-mo-gru-pa Rdo-rje-rgyal-po. *Phag-mo gru-pa rdo-rje rgyal-po bka'-'bum,* vol. 3, fols. 209–211. Incipit: *Slob-dpon chen po la ba-pa'i bar-do rnam-pa gsum.* A golden manuscript prepared under the patronage of 'Bri-gung Kun-dga'-rin-chen in the possession of Dan Martin.

PLKC   Dom-po-pa Thub-bstan-rgyal-mtshan. *Rnying-ma'i gsung-'bum dkar-chag.* Lhasa: Bod-ljongs gsar-dpe dpe-skrun-khang, 1992.

PMKT   O-rgyan-gling-pa. *Padma bka'-thang-yig* [i.e., *O-rgyan guru padma-'byung-gnas-kyi skyes-rabs rnam-par thar-pa rgyas-par bkod-pa padma bka'i-thang-yig*]. Chengdu, China: Si-khron mi-rigs dpe skrun-khang, 1993.

RCBP   'Jam-mgon Kong-sprul. *Zab-mo'i gter dang gter-ston grub-thob ji-ltar byon-pa'i lo-rgyus mdor-bsdus bkod-pa rin-chen baiḍurya'i phreng-ba.* In RCTD, vol. 1, fols. 291–759.

RCKC   'Jam-mgon Kong-sprul. *Rin-chen gter-mdzod-gyi dkar-chag.* In RCTD, vol. 2, fols. 49–617.

RCTD   'Jam-mgon Kong-sprul. *Rin-chen gter-mdzod.* I(Bhu)-Tib-124; 77–900739.

RDJS   Gar-dbang-rdo-rje, Mnga'-ris Gter-ston. *Rdo-rje sems-dpa' thugs-kyi me-long.* Dalhousie, H.P, India: Damchoe Sangpo, 1984. I-Tib-2573; 85–901462.

RZND   Rig-'dzin Nyi-ma-grags-pa. *The Collected Rediscovered Teachings of Rig-'dzin Nyi-ma-grags-pa with Rituals of the Char Nyi-grags Tradition.* 2 vols. Bir, H.P. India: Pema Lodoe, 1979. I-Tib-2066; 80–900308.

SHAR   Kaḥ-thog-pa Bsod-nams-rgyal-mtshan. *Śar kaḥ-thog-pa bsod-nams-rgyal-mtshan dpal-bzang-po'i rnam-par thar-pa dri-med yid-bzhin nor-bu'i phreng-ba.* Gangtok, Sikkim, 1979. I-Tib-2068; 80–900328.

SITU   Kaḥ-thog Si-tu Chos-kyi-rgya-mtsho. *Gangs-ljongs dbus-gtsang gnas-bskor lam-yig nor-bu zla-shel-gyi se-mo-do.* Tashijong, Palampur, India, 1972. I-Tib-875; 72–901801.

TBZB   Rgya-ra-ba Nam-mkha'-chos-kyi-rgya-mtsho. *Zab-chos zhi-khro dgongs-pa rang-grol-gyi them-byang zin-bris.* In T7, vol. 1, fols. 1–6.

THGL   Dkar-brgyud Bstan-'dzin-nor-bu. *Thos-grol dgag-len.* In *The Collected Works of Dkar-brgyud Bstan-'dzin-nor-bu.* Smanrtsis shesrig Spendzod 142. Leh, Ladakh: D.L. Tashigang, 1996, fols. 315–414.

THUP   Thupten Sangay [Thub-bstan-sangs-rgyas]. *Bod-mi'i 'das-mchod.* Dharamsala: Library of Tibetan Works and Archives, 1974.

TLNT   Gter-bdag-gling-pa. *Gter-chen chos-kyi rgyal-po'i rnam-thar dad-pa'i shing-rta.* In *The Life of Gter-bdag-gliṅ-pa 'Gyur-med-rdo-rje of Smin-grol-gliṅ.* 2 vols. Paro, Bhutan: Lama Ngodrub and Sherab Drimey, 1982. I(Bhu)-Tib-320; 82–902941, vol. 1, fols. 1–355.

TLSY   Gter-bdag-gling-pa. *Gsan-yig of Gter-bdag-gling-pa 'Gyur-med-rdo-rje of Smin-grol-gling* [i.e., *Zab-pa dang rgya-che-ba'i dam-pa'i chos-kyi thob-yig rin-chen byung-gnas*]. Delhi: Sanje Dorje, 1974. I-Tib-1243; 74–900490.

TMLG   Anonymous [Sha-gzugs-pa Ngag-dbang-bkra-shis-rnam-rgyal?]. *Gter-ma'i lo-rgyus gter-ston chos-'byung nor-bu'i 'phreng-ba.* Photocopy of manuscript provided by E. Gene Smith and the Himalayan and Inner Asian Resource Center, New York.

TOH   Ui Hakuju, Munetada Suzuki, Yenshō Kanakura, Tōkan Tada, eds. *A Complete Catalogue of the Tibetan Buddhist Canons (Bkaḥ- 'gyur and Bstan-ḥgyur).* Sendai, Japan: Tōhoku Imperial University, 1934.

TSLG   Rtse-le Sna-tshogs-rang-grol. *Rtse-le gong-'og grwa-tshang-dgon gsum-po rnams-kyi bstan-pa ji-ltar btsugs-pa'i lo-rgyus.* In *The Complete Works of Rtse-le Rgod-tshang-pa Padma-legs-grub*, vol. 1, fols. 313–383. Gangtok, Sikkim: Mgon-po-tshe-brtan, Palace Monastery, 1979. I-Tib-1982; 79–904985.

TSNG   Rtse-le Sna-tshogs-rang-grol. *Snyigs-dus-kyi bla-ma'i gzugs-brnyan 'dzin-pas rang-gi mtshan-nyid ji-lta-bar brjod-pa drang-po'i sa-bon (rnam-thar).*

In (1) *The Complete Works of Rtse-le Rgod-tshang-pa Padma-legs-grub*, vol. 1, fols. 1–200. Gangtok, Sikkim: Mgon-po-tshe-brtan, Palace Monastery, 1979. I-Tib-1982; 79–904985; and (2) *The Collected Works [Gsung 'bum] of Rtse-le Sna-tshogs-rang-grol*, vol. 1, fols. 1–166. New Delhi, 1974. I-Tib-1274; 74–901176.

TT   Suzuki, Daisetz T., ed. *The Tibetan Tripiṭaka: Peking Edition*. Tokyo-Kyoto: Tibetan Tripitaka Research Institute, 1957–58.

VGB   *Vairo-rgyud-'bum*. Edited by Tashi Y. Tashigangpa. *The Rgyud-'bum of Vairocana*. Leh, Ladakh: S.W. Tashigangpa, 1971.

YANG   Dbyangs-can-dga'-ba'i-blo-gros. *Bar-do 'i 'phrang-sgrol-gyi gsol-'debs 'jigs-sgrol dba'-po zhes-bya-ba'i 'grel-pa gdams-ngag gsal-ba'i sgron-me*. In *Collected Works of A-kya Yongs-'dzin*, vol. 1, fols. 336–64. New Delhi: Lama Guru Deva, 1971. ITib-836; 74-926906.

YGLG   Yang-dgon-pa-rgyal-mtshan (Lha-gdong-pa). *The Collected Works of Yang-dgon-pa rgyal-mtshan-dpal*. Thimphu, Bhutan: Kunsang Topgey, 1976.

ZBNA   Tsong-kha-pa Blo-bzang-grags-pa. *Zab-lam nā-ro'i chos-drug-gi sgo-nas 'khrid-pa'i rim-pa yid-ches gsum-ldan*. In (1) *The Collected Works [Gsuṅ 'bum] of The Incomparable Lord Tsoṅ-kha-pa Blo-bzaṅ-grags-pa*. Delhi, 1978, vol. 9, fols. 84.5–98.5. I-Tib-1809; and (2) *The Collected Works [Gsuṅ 'bum] of Rje Tsoṅ-kha-pa Blo-bzaṅ-grags-pa*. Delhi: Ngawang Gelek Demo, 1979, vol. 13, no. 9, fols. 489.3–503.6. I-Tib-1481; 75–905462.

ZCGT   Zhe-chen Rgyal-tshab Padma-rnam-rgyal. *Zhe-chen rgyal-tshab chos-'byung* [i.e., *Snga-'gyur rdo-rje theg-pa gtso-bor gyur-pa'i sgrub-brgyud shing-rta brgyad-kyi byung-ba brjod-pa'i gtam mdor-bsdus legs-bshad padma dkar-po'i rdzing-bu*]. Chengdu: Si-khron mi-rigs dpe-skrun-khang, 1994.

ZDTY   Phyogs-las-rnam-rgyal, Zhabs-drung Gsung-sprul I. *Zab-rgyas chos-kyi thob-yig dbyangs-can mgrin-rgyan*. Thimphu, Bhutan: Druk Sherig Press, 1984. I(Bhu)-Tib-390; 85-902180.

ZHAB   Zhabs-dkar-ba Tshogs-drug-rang-grol. *Snyigs-dus 'gro-ba yongs-kyi skyabs-mgon zhabs-dkar rdo-rje-'chang chen-po'i rnam-par thar-pa rgyas-par bshad-pa skal-bzang gdul-bya thar-'dod rnams-kyi re-ba skong-ba'i yid-bzhin-gyi nor-bu bsam-'phel dbang-gi rgyal-po*. Xining, China, 1985.

ZHKS   Dbyangs-can-dga'-ba'i-blo-gros. *Gzhi 'i-sku-gsum-gyi rnam-gzhag rab-gsal sgron-me*. In *Collected Works of A-kya Yongs-'dzin*, vol. 1, fols. 302–35. New Delhi: Lama Guru Deva, 1971. I-Tib-836; 74-926906.

ZHRL   *Dbang-ldan zhu-yi ring-lugs-kyi zhi-khro'i sgrub-skor*. Dolanji: Tibetan Bonpo Monastic Center, 1975. I-Tib-1420; 75–903251.

ZKGK   *Zhi-khro sgrub-skor glegs-bam-gyi dbu'i-rdul-len thar-lam 'dren-byed*. Delhi: 1968. I-Tib-761; 76–924678.

ZKND   'Ja-tshon-snying-po. *Zhi-khro nges-don snying-po*. In *Rig-'dzin 'ja'-tshon snying-po'i gter-chos*. Bylakuppe, India, c.1997.

Western Language References

Achard, Jean-Luc. 1998. "Bon zhig khyung nag and the *Rig pa gcer mthong* Tradition of rDzogs chen." *Tibet Journal* 23.4: 28–57.

Ahmad, Zahiruddin. 1970. *Sino-Tibetan Relations in the Seventeenth Century*. Serie Orientale Roma 50. Rome: Istituto Italiano per il Medio ed Estremo Oriente.

————. 1995. *A History of Tibet by the Fifth Dalai Lama of Tibet*. Bloomington: Indiana University Research Institute for Inner Asian Studies.

Ardussi, John A. 1997. "The Rapprochement between Bhutan and Tibet under the Enlightened Rule of Sde-srid XIII Shes-rab-dbang-phyug (R.1744–1763)." In *Tibetan Studies: Proceedings of the Seventh Seminar of the International Association for Tibetan Studies, Graz 1995*, Helmut Krasser, Michael Torsten Much, Ernst Steinkellner, and Helmut Tauscher, eds. Vienna: Verlag der Österreichischen Akademie der Wissenschaften, pp. 17–27.

Aris, Michael. 1979. *Bhutan: The Early History of a Himalayan Kingdom*. Warminster, England: Aris and Phillips.

————. 1988a. *Hidden Treasures and Secret Lives*. Shimla: Indian Institute of Advanced Study.

————. 1988b. "New Light on an Old Clan of Bhutan: The Smyos-rabs of Bla-ma Gsaṅ-sṅags." In *Tibetan Studies: Proceedings of the Fourth Seminar of the International Association for Tibetan Studies, Schloss Hohenkammer–Munich 1985*, Helga Uebach and Jampa L. Panglung, eds. Munich: Kommission für Zentralasiatische Studien Bayerische Akademie der Wissenschaften, pp. 15–24.

————. 1994. *The Raven Crown: The Origins of Buddhist Monarchy in Bhutan*. London: Serindia.

————. 1997. "Himalayan Encounters." In *Les habitants du toit du monde. Études recueillies en hommage à Alexander W. Macdonald*, Samten G. Karmay and Philippe Sagant, eds. Nanterre: Societé d'Ethnologie, pp. 179–188.

Back, Dieter M. 1979. *Eine buddhistische Jenseitsreise: Das sogenannte "Totenbuch der Tibeter" aus philologischer Sicht*. Wiesbaden: Otto Harrassowitz.

————. 1987. *Rig pa ṅo sprod gcer mthoṅ raṅ grol: Die Erkenntnislehre des Bar do thos grol*. Freiburger Beiträge zur Indologie, 18. Wiesbaden: Otto Harrassowitz.

Bacot, Jacques, F. W. Thomas, and Ch. Toussaint. 1940. *Documents de Touen-houang relatifs à l'histoire du Tibet*. Paris: Librairie Orientaliste Paul Geuthner.

Barber, Paul. 1988. *Vampires, Burial, and Death: Folklore and Reality*. New Haven: Yale University Press.

Bareau, André. 1955. *Les Sectes bouddhiques de Petit Véhicule*. Saigon: École française d'Extrême-Orient.

Batchelor, Stephen. 1987. *The Tibet Guide*. London: Wisdom.

Bell, Sir Charles. [1928] 1994. *The People of Tibet*. Reprint, New Delhi: Motilal Banarsidass.

————. [1931] 1994. *Religion of Tibet*. Reprint, New Delhi: Motilal Banarsidass.

Bellezza, John Vincent. 1997. *Divine Dyads: Ancient Civilization in Tibet*. Dharamsala: Library of Tibetan Works and Archives.

Benavides, Gustavo. 1995. "Giuseppe Tucci, or Buddhology in the Age of Fascism." In *Curators of the Buddha: The Study of Buddhism under Colonialism*, Donald S. Lopez, ed. Chicago: University of Chicago Press, pp. 161–196.

Bentor, Yael. 1996. "Literature on Consecration (*Rab gnas*)." In *Tibetan Literature: Studies in Genre*, José Ignacio Cabezon and Roger R. Jackson, eds. Ithaca, N.Y.: Snow Lion, pp. 290–311.

Beyer, Stephan. 1978. *The Cult of Tārā: Magic and Ritual in Tibet*. Berkeley: University of California Press.

Bishop, Peter. 1993. *Dreams of Power: Tibetan Buddhism and the Western Imagination*. London: Athlone Press.

Blezer, Henk. 1997. *Kar gliṅ Źi khro: A Tantric Buddhist Concept*. Leiden: Research School CNWS.

————. 1998a. "A Preliminary Report on Investigations into *(Bon nyid)* *'Od gsal-* and *Zhi khro bar do* in Earlier *(Zhang zhung) sNyan rgyud-* Literature." Paper presented at the Eighth Seminar of the International Association for Tibetan Studies, Bloomington, Indiana.

————. 1998b. "Some Further Reflections on *Kar gling Zhi khro*: A Study of Sources Referred to in Dan Martin's Review of Kar gling Zhi khro: A Tantric Buddhist Concept." *Tibet Journal*, 23.4: 134–143.

————. 1999. "The *'Bon' dBal mo Nyer bdun(/brgyad)* and the *Buddhist dBang phyug ma Nyer brgyad*, a Brief Comparison." Paper presented at the symposium "New Horizons in Bon Cultural Studies," Osaka, Japan.

————. 2001. "Karma gling pa: Treasure Finder or Creative Editor?" In *Reading Asia: New Research in Asian Studies*, Frans Hüsken and Dick van der Meij, eds. Richmond, England: Curzon, pp. 292–338.

Blondeau, Anne-Marie. 1971. "Le Lha-'dre bKa'-than." In *Etudes tibétaines dédiées à la mémoire de Marcelle Lalou*. Paris: Adrien-Maisonneuve, pp. 29–126.

————. 1980. "Analysis of the Biographies of Padmasambhava According to Tibetan Tradition: Classification of Sources." In *Tibetan Studies in Honour of Hugh Richardson*, Michael Aris and Aung San Suu Kyi, eds. Warminster, England: Aris and Phillips, pp. 45–52.

————. 1985. "Mkhyen-brce'i dban-po: La biographie de Padmasambhava selon la tradition du Bsgrags-pa Bon, et ses sources." In *Orientalia Iosephi Tucci Memoriae Dicata*, G. Gnoli and L. Lanciotti, eds. Rome: Istituto Italiano per il Medio ed Estremo Oriente, vol. I, pp. III–158.

————. 1987. "Une polémique sur l'authenticité des *Bka'-than* au 17e siècle." In *Silver on Lapis: Tibetan Literary Culture and History*, Christopher I. Beckwith, ed. Bloomington, Ind.: Tibet Society, pp. 125–160.

————. 1988. "La controverse soulevée par l'inclusion de rituel bon-po dans le *Rin-chen gter-mjod*. Note préliminaire." In *Tibetan Studies: Proceedings of the Fourth Seminar of the International Association for Tibetan Studies, Schloss Hohenkammer–Munich 1985*, Helga Uebach and Jampa L. Panglung, eds. Munich: Kommission für Zentralasiatische Studien Bayerische Akademie der Wissenschaften, pp. 55–67.

————. 1990. "Identification de la tradition appelée *bsGrags-pa Bon-lugs.*" In *Indo-Tibetan Studies: Papers in Honour and Appreciation of Professor David L. Snellgrove's Contribution to Indo-Tibetan Studies*, Tadeusz Skorupski, ed. Buddhica Britannica Series Continua 2. Tring, England: Institute of Buddhist Studies, pp. 37–54.

————. 1994. "Bya-rung kha-shor, légende fondatrice du bouddhisme tibétain." In *Tibetan Studies: Proceedings of the Sixth Seminar of the International Association for Tibetan Studies Fagernes 1992*, Per Kvaerne, ed. Oslo: Institute for Comparative Research in Human Culture, vol. I, pp. 31–48.

————. 1997. "Que notre enfant revienne! Un rituel méconnu pour les enfants morts en bas-âge." In *Les habitants du toit du monde. Études recueillies en hommage à Alexander W. Macdonald*, Samten G. Karmay and Philippe Sagant, eds. Nanterre: Societé d'Ethnologie, pp. 193–220.

————, ed. 1998. *Tibetan Mountain Deities, Their Cults and Representations: Proceedings of the Seventh Seminar of the International Association for Tibetan Studies, Graz 1995*. Vienna: Verlag der Österreichischen Akademie der Wissenschaften.

Blondeau, Anne-Marie, and Ernst Steinkellner, eds. 1996. *Reflections of the Mountain: Essays on the History and Social Meaning of the Mountain Cult in Tibet and the Himalaya.* Vienna: Verlag der Österreichischen Akademie der Wissenschaften

Boord, Martin J. 1993. *The Cult of the Deity Vajrakīla: According to the Texts of the Northern Treasures Tradition of Tibet (Byang-gter phur-ba).* Buddhica Britannica Series Continua 4. Tring, England: Institute of Buddhist Studies.

Boord, Martin J., and Losang Norbu Tsonawa. 1996. *Overview of Buddhist Tantra: General Presentation of the Classes of Tantra, Captivating the Minds of the Fortunate Ones by Panchen Sonam Dragpa.* Dharamsala: Library of Tibetan Works and Archives.

Bradburn, Leslie, et al. 1995. *Masters of the Nyingma Lineage.* Crystal Mirror Series 11. Berkeley, Calif.: Dharma.

Brauen, Martin. 1978. "A Bon-po Death Ceremony." In *Tibetan Studies*, Martin Brauen and Per Kvaerne, eds. Zurich: Völkerkundemuseum der Universität Zürich, pp. 53–63.

Brauen, Martin, and Per Kvaerne. 1978a. "A Tibetan Death Ceremony." *Temenos* 14: 9–24.

———. 1982. "Death Customs in Ladakh." 1982. *Kailash* 9.4: 319–332.

Brauen, Martin, and Per Kvaerne, eds. 1978b. *Tibetan Studies.* Zurich: Völkerkundemuseum der Universität Zürich.

Budge, E. A. Wallis. 1985. *The Ancient Egyptian Book of the Dead.* Translated by R. O. Faulkner. New York: Macmillan.

Cabezon, José Ignacio. 2001. "Authorship and Literary Production in Classical Buddhist Tibet." In *Changing Minds: Contributions to the Study of Buddhism and Tibet in Honor of Jeffrey Hopkins*, Guy Newland, ed. Ithaca, N.Y.: Snow Lion, pp. 233–263.

Cabezon, José Ignacio, and Roger R. Jackson, eds. 1996. *Tibetan Literature: Studies in Genre.* Ithaca, N.Y.: Snow Lion.

Campbell, June. 1996. *Traveller in Space: In Search of Female Identity in Tibetan Buddhism.* New York: Braziller.

Carter, Thomas Francis. 1955. *The Invention of Printing in China and Its Spread Westward.* Rev. by L. Carrington Goodrich. 2nd ed. New York: Roland Press.

Chan, Victor. 1994. *Tibet Handbook: A Pilgrimage Guide.* Chico, Calif.: Moon.

Chandra, Lokesh, ed. 1981. *Materials for a History of Tibetan Literature.* 3 vols. New Delhi: Sharada Rani, 1963; reprint, Kyoto, Japan: Rinsen Book.

Chang, Garma C. C. 1962. *The Hundred Thousand Songs of Milarepa.* Boston: Shambhala.

———. 1963. *Six Yogas of Naropa and Teachings on Mahamudra.* New York: Snow Lion.

Chökyi Nyima Rinpoche. 1991. *The Bardo Guidebook.* Translated by Erik Pema Kunsang. Hong Kong: Rangjung Yeshe.

Chu Junjie. 1991. "A Study of Bon-po Funeral Ritual in Ancient Tibet: Deciphering the Pelliot Tibetan Mss 1042." In *Theses on Tibetology in China*, Hu Tan, ed. Beijing: China Tibetology, pp. 91–157.

Conze, Edward, ed. 1954. *Buddhist Texts through the Ages.* Oxford: Oxford University Press.

———, ed. 1968. "The Meditation on Death." In *Thirty Years of Buddhist Studies: Selected Essays*, Edward Conze, ed. Columbia: University of South Carolina Press, pp. 87–104.

————. 1974. "The Intermediary World." *Eastern Buddhist* 7.2: 22–31.

Cornu, Philippe. 1997. *Tibetan Astrology*. Translated by Hamish Gregor. Boston: Shambhala.

Cozort, Daniel. 1986. *Highest Yoga Tantra*. New York: Snow Lion.

Crescenzi, Antonella, and Fabrizio Torricelli. 1997. "Tibetan Literature on Dreams: Materials for a Bibliography.". *Tibet Journal* 22.1: 58–82.

Cuevas, Bryan J. 1996. "Predecessors and Prototypes: Toward a Conceptual History of the Buddhist Antarābhava." *Numen* 43.3: 263–302.

————. 1997. *The Tibetan Book of the Dead: Literature and Artwork on Prayer, Ritual, and Meditation from the Religious Traditions of Tibet, India, and Nepal.* Charlottesville: University of Virginia.

————. 2000. "The Hidden Treasures of Sgam-po-gdar Mountain: A History of the *Zhi-khro* Revelations of Karma-gling-pa and the Making of the *Tibetan Book of the Dead.*" Ph.D. diss., University of Virginia, Charlottesville.

————. Forthcoming. "A Textual Survey of the *gter-ma* of Karma-gling-pa: *Zab-chos zhi-khro dgongs-pa rang-grol* and *Bar-do thos-grol chen-mo.*" In *Tibetan Studies: Proceedings of the Eighth Seminar of the International Association for Tibetan Studies,* Elliot Sperling, ed. Bloomington: Indiana University Press.

Dargyay, Eva K. 1978. "Probleme einer neubearbeitung des Bar-do Thos-grol." In *Tibetan Studies,* Martin Brauen and Per Kvaerne, ed. Zürich: Völkerkunde-museum der Universität Zürich, pp. 91–101.

————. 1979. *The Rise of Esoteric Buddhism in Tibet.* New Delhi: Motilal Banarsidass.

————. 1985. "A Rñiṅ-ma Text: The *Kun-byed rgyal-po'i mdo.*" In *Soundings in Tibetan Civilization: Proceedings of the 1982 Seminar of the International Association for Tibetan Studies Held at Columbia University,* Barbara Nimri Aziz and Matthew Kapstein, eds. New Delhi: Manohar, pp. 283–293.

————. 1991. *Bardo-Thödol: Le Livre tibétain des Morts.* Translated by Valdo Secretan. Paris: Dervy.

————. 1992. *The Sovereign All-Creating Mind.* New York: Motherly Buddha.

Das, Sarat Chandra. [1902] 1988. *A Tibetan-English Dictionary.* Reprint, Kyoto: Rinsen Book Company.

Dasgupta, Shashibhushan. 1976. *Obscure Religious Cults.* 3rd edition. Calcutta: Firma K.L. Mukhopadhyay.

David-Neel, Alexandra. 1977a. "Le cycle littéraire du Bardo Thös Tol." In *Textes Tibétains Inédits.* Paris: Pygmalion, pp. 128–144.

————. 1977b. "Phowa." In *Textes Tibétains Inédits.* Paris: Pygmalion, pp. 145–150.

————. 1997. *Immortality and Reincarnation: Wisdom from the Forbidden Journey.* Translated by Jon Graham. Rochester, Vt.: Inner Traditions.

Denwood, Phillip. 1976. *Catalogue of Tibetan Manuscripts and Block-Prints outside the Stein Collection in the India Office Library.*

Diemberger, Hildegard, and Guntram Hazod. 1994. "Machig Zhama's Recovery. Traces of Ancient History and Myth in the South Tibetan Landscape of Kharta and Phadrug." *Tibet Journal* 19.4: 23–45.

Diemberger, Hildegard, Pasang Wangdu, Marlies Kornfeld, and Christian Jahoda. 1997. *Feast of Miracles: The Life and the Tradition of Bodong Chole Namgyal (1375/6–1451 A.D.) according to the Tibetan Texts "Feast of Miracles" and "The Lamp Illuminating the History of Bodong."* Porong Pema Chöding Editions. Clusone, Italy.

Dietz, Siglinde. 1994. "The Chapter on *Nirmatta* (*sprul pa*) and *Antarābhava* (*bar ma do'i srid pa*) in the Abhidharmaśāstra *Kāranaprajñāpti* (*rgyu gdags pa*)." In

Tibetan Studies: Proceedings of the Sixth Seminar of the International Association for Tibetan Studies, FAGERNES 1992, Per Kvaerne, ed. Oslo: Institute for Comparative Research in Human Culture, vol. 1, pp. 154–167.

Dorje, Gyurme. 1987. "The *Guhyagarbhatattvaviniścayamahātantra* and its Fourteenth Century Tibetan Commentary: *Phyogs bcu mun sel*." Ph.D. diss., University of London.

———. 1996. *Tibet Handbook with Bhutan*. Bath, England: Footprint Handbooks.

Douglas, Nik, and Meryl White. 1976. *Karmapa: The Black Hat Lama of Tibet*. London: Luzac.

Dowman, Keith. 1985. *Masters of Mahamudra: Songs and Histories of the Eighty-Four Buddhist Siddhas*. Albany: State University of New York Press.

———. 1988. *Power Places of Central Tibet*. London: Routledge and Kegan Paul.

———. 1994. *The Flight of the Garuda*. Boston: Wisdom.

———. 1997. *The Sacred Life of Tibet*. London: Thorsons.

Drège, Jean-Pierre. 1986. "Le livre manuscrit et les débuts de la xylographie." In *Le livre et l'imprimerie en Extrême-Orient et en Asie du sud*, Jean-Pierre Drège, Mitchiko Ishigami-Iagolnitzer, and Monique Cohen, eds. Bordeaux: Société des Bibliophiles de Guyenne, pp. 19–39.

Dudjom Rinpoche, Jigdrel Yeshe Dorje. 1991. *The Nyingma School of Tibetan Buddhism*. Translated by Gyurme Dorje and Matthew Kapstein. 2 vols. Boston: Wisdom.

Dumézil, Georges. 1973. *Gods of the Ancient Northmen*. Edited by Einar Haugen. Berkeley: University of California Press.

Edou, Jérôme. 1996. *Machig Labdrön and the Foundations of Chöd*. Ithaca, N.Y.: Snow Lion Publications.

Ehrhard, Franz-Karl. 1990. *"Flügelschläge des Garuḍa": Literar- und Ideengeschichtliche Bemerkungen zu einer Liedersammlung des rDzogs-chen*. Stuttgart: Franz Steiner.

———. 1993. "Two Documents on Tibetan Ritual Literature and Spiritual Genealogy." *Journal of the Nepal Research Centre* 9: 87–93.

———. 1997a. "'The Lands Are Like a Wiped Golden Basin': The Sixth Zhva-dmar-pa's Journey to Nepal." In *Les habitants du toit du monde. Études recueillies en hommage à Alexander W. Macdonald*, Samten G. Karmay and Philippe Sagant, eds. Nanterre: Societé d'Ethnologie, pp. 125–138.

———. 1997b. "A 'Hidden Land' in the Tibetan-Nepalese Borderlands." In *Mandala and Landscape*, Alexander W. Macdonald, ed. New Delhi: D.K. Printworld, pp. 335–364.

———. 1997c. "Recently Discovered Manuscripts of the *Rnying ma rgyud 'bum* from Nepal." In *Tibetan Studies: Proceedings of the Seventh Seminar of the International Association for Tibetan Studies, Graz 1995*, Helmut Krasser, Michael Torsten Much, Ernst Steinkellner, and Helmut Tauscher, eds. Vienna: Verlag der Österreichischen Akademie der Wissenschaften, pp. 253–267.

———. 1999. "Early Xylographs of Buddhist Classics from Mang-yul Gung-thang (Fifteenth/Sixteenth Century)." Paper presented at the Twelfth Conference of the International Association of Buddhist Studies, Lausanne, Switzerland.

Eimer, Helmut, and Pema Tsering. 1979. "Äebte und Lehrer von Kaḥ thog: Eine erste Übersicht zur Geschichte eines Rñiṅ ma pa-Klosters in Derge/Khams." *Zentralasiatische Studien* 13: 457–509.

———. 1981. "A List of Abbots of Kaḥ-thog Monastery according to Handwritten Notes by the Late Katok Ontul." *Journal of the Tibet Society* 1: 11–14.

————. 1986. "Eine Liste der geretteten Druckplatten aus dem Kloster Kah thog in Derge/Khams." In Helmut Eimer, ed., *Vicitrakusumāñjali, Volume Presented to Richard Othon Meisezahl on the Occasion of his Eightieth Birthday.* Series no. 11. Bonn: Indica et Tibetica Verlag, pp. 61–70.

Eimer, Helmut. 1997a. "A Source for the First Narthang Kanjur: Two Early Sa skya pa Catalogues of the Tantras." In *Transmission of the Tibetan Buddhist Canon: Proceedings of the Seventh Seminar of the International Association for Tibetan Studies, Graz 1995*, Helmut Eimer, ed. Vienna: Verlag der Österreichischen Akademie der Wissenschaften, pp. 11–78.

————. ed., 1997b. *Transmission of the Tibetan Buddhist Canon: Proceedings of the Seventh Seminar of the International Association for Tibetan Studies, Graz 1995* Helmut Einer, ed. Vienna: Verlag der Österreichischen Akademie der Wissenschaften.

Epstein, Lawrence. 1982. "On the History and Psychology of the 'Das-Log." *Tibet Journal*, 7.4: 20–85.

————. 1990. "A Comparative View of Tibetan and Western Near-Death Experiences." In *Reflections on Tibetan Culture: Essays in Memory of Turrell V. Wylie*, Lawrence Epstein and Richard F. Sherbourne, eds. Lewiston, N.Y.: Edwin Mellen Press, pp. 315–328.

Evans-Wentz, W. Y., and Kazi Dawa Samdup. [1927] 1973. *The Tibetan Book of the Dead.* Reprint, New York: Causeway Books.

————. [1927] 2000. *The Tibetan Book of the Dead.* Reprint, Oxford: Oxford University Press.

Evans-Wentz, W. [1954] 2000. *The Tibetan Book of the Great Liberation.* Reprint, Oxford: Oxford University Press.

————. [1958] 2000. *Tibetan Yoga and Secret Doctrines.* Reprint, Oxford: Oxford University Press.

Ferrari, Alfonsa. 1958. *Mk'yen Brtse's Guide to the Holy Places of Central Tibet.* Luciano Petech, ed. Rome: Istituto Italiano per il Medio ed Estremo Oriente.

Fields, Rick. 1992. *How the Swans Came to the Lake: A Narrative History of Buddhism in America.* Boston: Shambhala.

Filibeck, Elena de Rossi. 1994. "A Manuscript on the Stag lung pa Genealogy." In *Tibetan Studies: Proceedings of the Sixth Seminar of the International Association for Tibetan Studies Fagernes 1992*, Per Kvaerne, ed. Oslo: Institute for Comparative Research in Human Culture, vol. 1, pp. 237–240.

Filliozat, Jean. 1971. "Le complexe d'oedipe dans un tantra bouddhique." In *Etudes tibétaines dédiées à la mémoire de Marcelle Lalou.* Paris: Librarie D'Amerique at d'Orient, pp. 142–148.

Foster, Barbara M. 1998. *The Secret History of Alexandra David-Neel.* Woodstock, N.Y.: Overlook Press.

Fremantle, Francesca. 2001. *Luminous Emptiness: Understanding the Tibetan Book of the Dead.* Boston: Shambhala.

Fremantle, Francesca, and Chögyam Trungpa. 1975. *The Tibetan Book of the Dead: The Great Liberation through Hearing in the Bardo.* Boston: Shambhala.

Gabain, Annemarie von. 1972. "The Purgatory of the Buddhist Uighurs: Book Illustrations from Turfan." In *Mahayanist Art after A.D. 900*, William Watson, ed. Colloquies on Art and Archaelogy in Asia, no. 2. London: University of London, School of Oriental and African Studies pp. 25–35.

Germano, David. 1994. "Architecture and Absence in the Secret Tantric History of the Great Perfection (*rdzogs chen*)." *Journal of the International Association of Buddhist Studies* 17.2: 203–335.

———. 1997. "Dying, Death, and Other Opportunities." In *Religions of Tibet in Practice*, Donald S. Lopez, Jr., ed. Princeton, N.J.: Princeton University Press, pp. 458–493.

———. 1998. "Re-membering the Dismembered Body of Tibet: Contemporary Tibetan Visionary Movements in the People's Republic of China.". In *Buddhism in Contemporary Tibet: Religious Revival and Cultural Identity*, Melvyn C. Goldstein and Matthew T. Kapstein, eds. Berkeley: University of California Press, pp. 53–94.

———. 2001. "Encountering Tibet: The Ethics, Soteriology, and Creativity of Cross-cultural Interpretation." *Journal of the American Academy of Religion* 69.1: 165–182.

———. Forthcoming. *Mysticism and Rhetoric in the Great Perfection: The Transformation of Buddhist Tantra in Ancient Tibet*.

Gethin, Rupert. 1994. "*Bhavaṅga* and Rebirth According to the Abhidharma." In *The Buddhist Forum*, vol. 3, 1991–93 (Papers in Honour and Appreciation of Professor David Seyfort Ruegg's Contribu-tion to Indological, Buddhist and Tibetan Studies), Tadeusz Skorupski and Ulrich Pagel, eds. London: University of London, School of Oriental and African Studies, pp. 11–35.

Gibson, Todd. 1991. "From *bstanpo* to *bstan*: The Demonization of the Tibetan Sacral Kingship." Ph.D. diss., University of Indiana, Bloomington.

———. 1997. "Notes on the History of the Shamanic in Tibet and Inner Asia." *Numen* 44.1: 39–59.

Goldstein, Melvyn C. 1989. *A History of Modern Tibet, 1913–1951: The Demise of the Lamaist State*. Berkeley: University of California Press.

Goldstein, Melvyn C., and Matthew T. Kapstein, eds. 1998. *Buddhism in Contemporary Tibet: Religious Revival and Cultural Identity*. Berkeley: University of California Press.

Gómez, Luis O. 1995. "Oriental Wisdom and the Cure of Souls: Jung and the Indian East." In *Curators of the Buddha: The Study of Buddhism under Colonialism*, Donald S. Lopez, ed. Chicago: University of Chicago Press, pp. 197–250.

Goodman, Steven D. 1992. "Rig-'dzin 'Jigs-med gling-pa and the kLong-Chen sNying-Thig." In *Tibetan Buddhism: Reason and Revelation*, Ronald M. Davidson and Steven D. Goodman, ed. Albany: State University of New York Press, pp. 133–146.

Gorn, Steven. 1983. *The Tibetan Book of the Dead: Music for a Play by Jean-Claude van Itallie from Translations of Tibetan Texts*. New York: Dramatists Play Service.

Govinda, Lama Anagarika.[1969] 1989. *Foundations of Tibetan Mysticism*. Reprint, York Beach, Maine: Samuel Weiser.

———. 1970. *The Way of the White Clouds*. Boston: Shambhala.

Greetham, D.C. 1994. *Textual Scholarship: An Introduction*. New York: Garland.

Grof, Stanislav. 1994. *Books of the Dead: Manuals for Living and Dying*. London: Thames and Hudson.

Guenther, Herbert V. 1963. *The Life and Teaching of Nāropa*. Boston: Shambhala.

Gyatrul Rinpoche and B. Alan Wallace. 1998. *Natural Liberation: Padmasambhava's Teachings on the Six Bardos*. Boston: Wisdom.

Gyatso, Geshe Kelsang. 1982. *Clear Light of Bliss: Mahamudra in Vajrayana Buddhism*. London: Wisdom.

———. 1994. *Tantric Grounds and Paths*. London: Tharpa.

Gyatso, Janet. 1986. "Signs, Memory and History: A Tantric Buddhist Theory of Scriptural Transmission." *Journal of the International Association of Buddhist Studies* 9.2: 7–35.

———. 1991. "Genre, Authorship and Transmission in Visionary Buddhism: The Literary Traditions of Thang-stong-rgyal-po." In *Tibetan Buddhism: Reason and Revelation*, Ronald M. Davidson and Steven D. Goodman, eds. Albany: State University of New York Press, pp. 95–106.

———. 1993. "The Logic of Legitimation in the Tibetan Treasure Tradition." *History of Religions* 33.1: 97–134.

———. 1994. "Guru Chos-dbang's *Gter 'byung chen mo*: An Early Survey of the Treasure Tradition and Its Strategies in Discussing Bon Treasure." In *Tibetan Studies: Proceedings of the Sixth Seminar of the International Association of Tibetan Studies, Fagernes 1992*, Per Kvaerne, ed. Oslo: Institute for Comparative Research in Human Culture, pp. 275–287.

———. 1996. "Drawn from the Tibetan Treasury: The *gTer ma* Literature." In *Tibetan Literature: Studies in Genre*, José Ignacio Cabezon and Roger R. Jackson, eds. Ithaca, N.Y.: Snow Lion, pp. 147–169.

———. 1997. "Counting Crows' Teeth: Tibetans and Their Diary-Writing Practices." In *Les habitants du toit du monde. Études recueillies en hommage à Alexander W. Macdonald*, Samten G. Karmay and Philippe Sagant, eds. Nanterre: Societé d'Ethnologie, pp. 159–177.

———. 1998. *Apparitions of the Self: The Secret Autobiographies of a Tibetan Visionary*. Princeton, N.J.: Princeton University Press.

———. N.d. "The Relic Text as Prophecy: The Semantic Drift of *Byang-bu* and Its Appropriation in the Treasure Tradition." Manuscript.

Haarh, Erik. 1969. *The Yar-luṅ Dynasty*. Copenhagen: Gad's Forlag.

Harrison, Paul. 1994. "In Search of the Source of the Tibetan Bka' 'gyur: A Reconnaissance Report." In *Tibetan Studies: Proceedings of the Sixth Seminar of the International Association for Tibetan Studies, FAGERNES 1992*, Per Kvaerne, ed. Oslo: Institute for Comparative Research in Human Culture, vol. 1, pp. 295–317.

———. 1996. "A Brief History of the Tibetan bKa' 'gyur." In *Tibetan Literature: Studies in Genre*, José Ignacio Cabezon and Roger R. Jackson, eds. Ithaca, N.Y.: Snow Lion, pp. 70–94.

Harrison, Paul, and Helmut Eimer. 1997. "Kanjur and Tanjur Sigla: A Proposal for Standardisation." In *Transmission of the Tibetan Buddhist Canon: Proceedings of the Seventh Seminar of the International Association for Tibetan Studies, Graz 1995*, Helmut Eimer, ed. Vienna: Verlag der Österreichischen Akademie der Wissenschaften, pp. xi–xiv.

Hayashi, Keijin. 1999. "Historical Development of the Notion 'Intermediate Being' (*antarābhava*) in Dharmakīrtian School." Paper presented at the Twelfth Conference of the International Association of Buddhist Studies, Lausanne, Switzerland. August.

Hazod, Guntram. 1998. "bKra shis 'od 'bar. On the History of the Religious Protector of the Bo dong pa." In *Tibetan Mountain Deities, Their Cults and Representations: Proceedings of the Seventh Seminar of the International Association for Tibetan Studies, Graz 1995*, Anne-Marie Blondeau, ed. Vienna: Verlag der Österreichischen Akademie der Wissenschaften, pp. 57–78.

Hecker, H. 1950. "Das Tibetanische Totenbuch." *Die Einsicht*, pp. 13–15.

Helffer, Mireille. 1992. "An Overview of Western Work on Ritual Music of Tibetan Buddhism (1960–1990)." In *European Studies in Ethnomusicology: Historical Developments and Recent Trends*, M.P. Baumann, A. Simon, and U. Wegner, eds. Intercultural Studies 4. Wilhelmshaven, Germany: Florian Noetzel Verlag, pp. 87–101.

———. 1993. "Tibetan Monasteries in the Valley of Kathmandu and Their Role in the Preservation of Musical Traditions: The Case of the Monastery of Zhechen." In *Nepal, Past and Present*, G. Toffin, ed. Paris: CNRS Editions, pp. 205–214.

———. 1997. "Traditions Musicales des Rnying-ma-pa." In *Tibetan Studies: Proceedings of the Seventh Seminar of the International Association for Tibetan Studies, Graz 1995*, Helmut Krasser, Michael Torsten Much, Ernst Steinkellner, and Helmut Tauscher, eds. Vienna: Verlag der Österreichischen Akademie der Wissenschaften, pp. 369–383.

Heller, Amy. 1990. "Remarques préliminaires sur les divintés protectrices *srung ma dmar nag*." In *Tibet civilisation et société*, F. Meyer, ed. Paris: Fondation Singer-Polignac, pp. 19–27.

Hertz, Robert. 1960. *Death and the Right Hand*. Translated by R. and C. Needham. New York: Free Press.

Hirakawa, Akira. 1973–78. *Index to the Abhidharmakośabhāsya = Abidatsuma kusharon sakuin*. Shohan. Tokyo: Daizo Shuppan.

———. 1990. *A History of Indian Buddhism: From Śākyamuni to Early Mahāyāna*. Translated and edited by Paul Groner. Honolulu: University of Hawaii Press.

Hodge, Stephen, and Martin Boord. 1999. *The Illustrated Tibetan Book of the Dead*. New York: Godsfield Press.

Hoffman, Helmut. 1970. "Tibetan Historiography and the Approach of the Tibetans to History." *Journal of Asian History* 4.2: 169–177.

———. 1990. "Early and Medieval Tibet." In *The Cambridge History of Early Inner Asia*, Dennis Sinor, ed. Cambridge: Cambridge University Press, pp. 371–399.

Hopkins, Jeffrey. 1996. "The Tibetan Genre of Doxography: Structuring a Worldview." In *Tibetan Literature: Studies in Genre*, José Ignacio Cabezon and Roger R. Jackson, eds. Ithaca, N.Y.: Snow Lion Publications, pp. 170–186.

Houston, G. W. 1982. *Wings of the White Crane: Poems of Tshangs dbyangs rgya mtsho*. Delhi: Motilal Banarsidass.

Huber, Toni. 1999. *The Cult of Pure Crystal Mountain: Popular Pilgrimage and Visionary Landscape in Southeast Tibet*. New York: Oxford University Press.

Iggers, Georg G. 1997. *Historiography in the Twentieth Century: From Scientific Objectivity to the Postmodern Challenge*. London: Wesleyan University Press.

Imaeda, Yoshiro. 1981. *Histoire du cycle de la naissance et de la mort: étude d'un texts tibétaine de Touen-houang*. Geneva: Librarie Droz.

———. 1982–84. *Catalogue du Kanjur tibétain de l'édition de 'Jang sa-tham*. Première partie, Edition en fac-similé avec introduction. Seconde partie, Texte en translittération. Bibliographia Philologica Buddhica. Series Maior 2. Tokyo: IIBS.

Jackson, David. 1983. "Notes on Two Early Printed Editions of Sa-skya-pa Works." *Tibet Journal* 8: 5–24.

———. 1988. *Rong-ston on the Prajñāpāramitā Philosophy of the Abhisamayālaṃkāra: His Sub-commentary on Haribhadra's 'Sphuṭārthā,' A Facsimile Reproduction of the Earliest Known Blockprint Edition, from an Exemplar Preserved in the Tibet House Library, New Delhi*. Biblia Tibetica Series, vol. 2. Edited in collaboration with S. Onoda. Kyoto: Nagata Bunshodo.

————. 1989a. *The Early Abbots of 'Phan-po Na-lendra: The Vicissitudes of a Great Tibetan Monastery in the Fifteenth Century*. Vienna: Für Tibetische und Buddhistische Studien Universität Wien.

————. 1989b. "More on the Old Dga' ldan and Gong dkar ba Xylographic Editions." *Studies in Central and East Asian Religions* 2: 1–18.

————. 1990. "The Earliest Printings of Tsong-kha-pa's Works: The Old Dga'-ldan Editions." In *Reflections on Tibetan Culture: Essays in Memory of Turrell V. Wylie*, Lawrence Epstein and Richard F. Sherbourne, ed. Lewiston, N.Y.: Edwin Mellen Press, pp. 107–116.

Jisheng, Xie. 1996. "The Universe Structure of Three Realms and the Development of Tibetan Shamanism's Concept about the Soul." In *Theses on Tibetology in China*, Liao Zugui Zhang Zuji, comp. Beijing: China Tibetology.

Kaneko, Eiichi. 1982. *Ko-Tantora Zenshā Kaidai Mokuroku*. Tokyo: Kokusho Kankokai.

Kapstein, Matthew. 1980. "The Shangs-pa bKa'-brgyud: An Unknown Tradition of Tibetan Buddhism." In *Tibetan Studies in Honour of Hugh Richardson*, Micheal Aris and Aung San Suu Kyi, eds. Warminster, England: Aris and Phillips, pp. 138–144.

————. 1989. "The Purificatory Gem and Its Cleansing: A Late Tibetan Polemical Discussion of Apocryphal Texts." *History of Religions* 28.3: 217–244.

————. 1991. "The Illusion of Spiritual Progress: Remarks on Indo-Tibetan Buddhist Soteriology." In *Paths to Liberation*, Robert Buswell and Robert Gimello, eds. Honolulu: University of Hawaii Press, pp. 193–224.

————. 1992. "Remarks on the *Maṇi-bka'-'bum* and the Cult of Avalokiteśvara in Tibet." In *Tibetan Buddhism: Reason and Revelation*, Ronald M. Davidson and Steven D. Goodman, eds. Albany, N.Y.: State University of New York, pp. 79–93.

————. 1996. "*gDams ngag*: Tibetan Technologies of the Self." In *Tibetan Literature: Studies in Genre*, José Ignacio Cabezon and Roger R. Jackson, eds. Ithaca, N.Y.: Snow Lion, pp. 275–289.

————. 1998. "A Pilgrimage of Rebirth Reborn: The 1992 Celebration of the Drigung Powa Chenmo." In *Buddhism in Contemporary Tibet: Religious Revival and Cultural Identity*, Melvyn C. Goldstein and Matthew T. Kapstein, eds. Berkeley: University of California Press, pp. 95–119.

————. 2000. *The Tibetan Assimilation of Buddhism: Conversion, Contestation, and Memory*. New York: Oxford University Press.

Kara, György. 1986. *A Köztes Lét Könyvei: tibeti tanácsok halandóknak és születendöknek*. Budapest: Európa Könyvkiadó.

Karmay, Samten G. 1972. *The Treasury of Good Sayings: A Tibetan History of Bon*. London: Oxford University Press.

————. 1977. *A Catalogue of Bonpo Publications*. Tokyo: Tokyo Bunko.

————. 1988a. *The Great Perfection*. London: E. J. Brill.

————. 1988b. *Secret Visions of the Fifth Dalai Lama: The Gold Manuscript in the Fournier Collection*. London: Serindia.

————. 1998. *The Arrow and the Spindle: Studies in History, Myths, Rituals and Beliefs in Tibet*. Kathmandu: Mandala Book Point.

Karmay, Samten G., and Philippe Sagant, eds. 1997. *Les habitants du toit du monde. Études recueillies en hommage à Alexander W. Macdonald*. Nanterre: Societé d'Ethnologie.

Kessler, Peter. 1982. *Laufende Arbeiten zu einem Ethnohistorischen Atlas Tibets (EAT). Lieferung* 47.1: *Das historische Königreich MI-LI.* Rikon, Switzerland: Tibet-Instituts.

———. 1983. *Laufende Arbeiten zu einem Ethnohistorischen Atlas Tibets (EAT). Lieferung* 40.1: *Das his-torische Königreich LING und DERGE.* Rikon, Switzerland: Tibet-Instituts.

———. 1984. *Laufende Arbeiten zu einem Ethnohistorischen Atlas Tibets (EAT). Lieferung* 41.1: *Die his-torische Landschaft TEHOR unter besonderer Berücksichtigung der frühen Geschichte Südosttibets (Khams).* Rikon, Switzerland: Tibet-Instituts.

Khenpo Könchog Gyaltsen. 1990. *The Great Kagyu Masters: The Golden Lineage Treasury.* Victoria Huckenpahler, ed. Ithaca, N.Y.: Snow Lion.

Kirkland, J. Russell. 1982. "The Spirit of the Mountain: Myth and State in Pre-Buddhist Tibet." *History of Religions* 21: 257–271.

Klein, Anne. 1985. "Primordial Purity and Everyday Life: Exalted Female Symbols and the Women of Tibet." In *Immaculate and Powerful,* C. W. Atkinson, C. H. Budhanan, and M. R. Miles, eds. Boston: Beacon Press.

———. 1995. *Meeting the Great Bliss Queen: Buddhists, Feminists, and the Art of the Self.* Boston: Beacon Press.

Kolmaś, Josef. 1968. *A Genealogy of the Kings of Derge: Sde-dge'i Rgyal-rabs.* Prague: Oriental Institute in Academia, Publishing House of the Czechoslovak Academy of Sciences.

———. 1969. *Catalogue of Tibetan Manuscripts and Blockprints in the Library of the Oriental Institute, Prague.* Prague: Oriental Institute in Academia, Publishing House of the Czechoslovak Academy of Sciences.

———. 1971. *Prague Collection of Tibetan Prints from Derge: A Facsimile Reproduction of 5,615 Book-Titles Printed at the Dgon-chen and Dpal-spungs Monasteries of Derge in Eastern Tibet.* 2 vols. Wiesbaden: Otto Harrassowitz.

———. 1988. "Dezhung Rinpoche's Summary and Continuation of the *Sde-dge'i Rgyal-rabs.*" *Acta Orientalia* (Hungary), 42.1: 119–152.

Kritzer, Robert. 1993. "Vasubandhu on *saṃskārapratyayaṃ vijñānam.*" *Journal of the International Association of Buddhist Studies* 16.1: 24–55.

———. 1997. "Antarābhava in the Vibhāsā." *Nôtom Damu Joshi Daigaku Kirisutokyô Bunka Kenkyūjo Kiyô [Maranata]* 3.5: 69–91.

———. 1998a. "*Garbhāvakrāntisūtra*: A Comparison of the Contents of Two Versions." *Nôtom Damu Joshi Daigaku Kirisutokyô Bunka Kenkyūjo Kiyô [Maranata]* 3.6: 3–12.

———. 1998b. "Semen, Blood, and the Intermediate Existence." *Journal of Indian and Buddhist Studies* 46.2: 1025–1031.

———. 1999a. "An *Ātman* by Any Other Name: Two Non-Buddhist Parallels to *antarābhava.*" Manuscript.

———. 1999b. "The Four Ways of Entering the Womb (*garbhāvakrānti*)." Manuscript.

———. 1999c. "*Rūpa* in the *antarābhava.*" Paper presented at the Twelfth Conference of the International Association of Buddhist Studies, Lausanne, Switzerland. August.

———. 2000. "Rūpa and the Antarābhava." Journal *of Indian Philosophy* 29: 235–272.

Kuijp, Leonard W. J. van der. 1985. "Some Recently Recovered Sa-skya-pa Texts: A Preliminary Report." *Journal of the Nepal Research Centre* 7: 87–94.

————. 1993. "Two Mongol Xylographs (*Hor Par Ma*) of the Tibetan Text of Sa Skya Paṇḍita's Work on Buddhist Logic and Epistemology." *Journal of the International Association of Buddhist Studies* 16.2: 279–298.

————. 1995. "Fourteenth-Century Tibetan Cultural History 6: The Transmission of Indian Buddhist Pramāṇavāda according to Early Tibetan Gsan-yig." *Asiatische Studien* 49.4: 919–941.

————. 1996. "Tibetan Historiography.". In *Tibetan Literature: Studies in Genre*, José Ignacio Cabezon and Roger R. Jackson, eds. Ithaca, N.Y.: Snow Lion, pp. 39–56.

Kunsang, Erik Pema. 1987. *The Mirror of Mindfulness: The Cycle of the Four Bardos*. Boston: Shambhala.

————. 1993. *The Lotus-Born: The Life Story of Padmasambhava*. Boston: Shambhala.

Kvaerne, Per. 1985. *Tibet Bon Religion: A Death Ritual of the Tibetan Bonpos*. Leiden: E. J. Brill.

————. 1990. "A Preliminary Study of the Bonpo Deity Khro-bo Gtso-mchog Mkha'-'gying." In *Reflections on Tibetan Culture: Essays in Memory of Turrell V. Wylie*, Lawrence Epstein and Richard F. Sherbourne, ed. Lewiston, N.Y.: Edwin Mellen Press, pp. 117–125.

————. 1994. "The Bon Religion of Tibet: A Survey of Research." In *The Buddhist Forum*, vol. 3, 1991–93 (Papers in Honour and Appreciation of Professor David Seyfort Ruegg's Contribution to Indological, Buddhist and Tibetan Studies), Tadeusz Skorupski and Ulrich Pagel, eds. London: University of London, School of Oriental and African Studies, pp. 131–141.

————. 1996. *The Bon Religion of Tibet*. Boston: Shambhala.

————. 1997a. "Cards for the Dead." In *Religions of Tibet in Practice*, Donald S. Lopez, ed. Princeton, N.J.: Princeton University Press, pp. 494–498.

————. 1997b. "The Succession of Lamas at the Monastery of sNang-zhig in the rNga-ba District of Amdo." In *Les habitants du toit du monde: Études recueillies en hommage à Alexander W. Macdonald*, Samten G. Karmay and Philippe Sagant, eds. Nanterre: Societé d'Ethnologie, pp. 155–157.

Ladrang Kalsang. 1996. *The Guardian Deities of Tibet*. Dharamsala: Little Lhasa.

Lalou, Marcelle. 1939–61. *Inventaire des manuscrits tibétains de Touen-houang conservés à la Bibliothèque Nationale* (Fonds Pelliot tibétains). 3 vols. Paris.

————. 1949. "Les chemins du mort dans les croyances de Haute Asie." *Revue de l'Histoire des Religions* 135.1: 42–48.

————. 1952. "Rituel Bon-po des funérailles Royales." *Journal Asiatique* 240.3: 339–361.

Lama Lodrö. 1982. *Bardo Teachings: The Way of Death and Rebirth*. Ithaca, N.Y.: Snow Lion.

Lati Rinbochay and Jeffrey Hopkins. 1979. *Death, Intermediate State and Rebirth*. New York: Snow Lion.

Lauf, Detlef Ingo. 1970. "Initiationsrituale des tibetischen Totenbuch." *Asiatische Studien* 24: 10–24.

————. 1977. *Secret Doctrines of the Tibetan Books of the Dead*. Translated by Graham Parkes. Boston: Shambhala.

La Vallée Poussin, Louis de. 1988. *Abhidharmakośabhāṣyam*. Translated by Leo M. Pruden. 5 vols. Berkeley, Calif.: Asian Humanities Press.

————. 1926. "Death and Disposal of the Dead (Buddhism)." *Encyclopedia of Religion and Ethics* 4: 446–449.

Leary, Timothy, Ralph Metzner, and Richard Alpert. 1964. *The Psychedelic Experience: A Manual Based on the Tibetan Book of the Dead.* New Hyde Park, N.Y.: University Books.

Lessing, Ferdinand D. 1951. "Calling the Soul: A Lamaist Ritual." *Semitic and Oriental Studies* 11: 263–284.

Li-kouang, Lin. 1949. *L'aide-mémoire de la vraie loi (Saddharma-smṛtyupastāna-sūtra).* Musée Guimet Bibliothèque d-études 54. Paris: Librairie d'amérique et d'orient Adrien-Masisonneuve.

Lincoln, Bruce. 1981a. "The Lord of the Dead." *History of Religions* 20.3: 224–241.

———. 1981b. *Priests, Warriors, and Cattle: A Study in the Ecology of Religions.* Berkeley: University of California Press.

Littleton, C. Scott. 1982. *The New Comparative Mythology: An Anthropological Assessment of the Theories of George Dumézil.* Berkeley: University of California Press.

Lo Bue, Erberto F. 1994. "A Case of Mistaken Identity: Ma-gcig Labs-sgron and Ma-gcig Zha-ma.". In *Tibetan Studies: Proceedings of the Sixth Seminar of the International Association for Tibetan Studies Fagernes 1992*, Per Kvaerne, ed. Oslo: Institute for Comparative Research in Human Culture, vol. 1, pp. 481–490.

———. 1997. "The Role of Newar Scholars in Transmitting the Indian Buddhist Heritage to Tibet (c.750–c. 1200)." In *Les habitants du toit du monde: Études recueillies en hommage à Alexander W. Macdonald*, Samten G. Karmay and Philippe Sagant, eds. Nanterre: Societé d'Ethnologie, pp. 629–658.

Lopez, Donald S., ed. 1988. *Buddhist Hermeneutics.* Kuroda Institute Studies in East Asian Buddhism 6. Honolulu: University of Hawaii Press.

———, ed. 1995. *Curators of the Buddha: The Study of Buddhism under Colonialism.* Chicago: University of Chicago Press.

———. 1996. *Elaborations on Emptiness: Uses of the Heart Sūtra.* Princeton, N.J.: Princeton University Press.

———. 1997a. "A Prayer for Deliverance from Rebirth." In *Religions of Tibet in Practice*, Donald S. Lopez, ed. Princeton, N.J.: Princeton University Press, pp. 442–457.

———. ed. 1997b. *Religions of Tibet in Practice.* Princeton, N.J.: Princeton University Press.

———. 1998. *Prisoners of Shangri-La: Tibetan Buddhism and the West.* Chicago: University of Chicago Press.

———. 2000. "Afterword: The Long Life of The Tibetan Book of the Dead." In Evans-Wentz and Dawa Sandup [1927] 2000, pp. 243–253.

Macdonald, Alexander W. 1967. *Matériaux pour l'étude de la littérature populaire tibétaine, I. Édition et traduction de deux manuscrits tibétains des 'Histoires du cadavre.'* 2 vols. Annales du Musée Guimet, Bibliothéque d'études, no. 72. Paris: Presses Universitaires de France.

———. 1975. *Essays on the Ethnology of Nepal and South Asia.* Kathmandu: Ratna Pustak Bhandar.

Macdonald, Ariane. 1971. "Une lecture des Pelliot tibétain 1286, 1287, 1038, 1047 et 1290. Essai sur la formation et l'emploi des mythes politiques dans la religion royale de Sroṅ-bcan sgam-po." In *Etudes tibétaines dédiée à la mémoire de Marcelle Lalou.* Paris: A. Maisonneuve, pp. 190–391.

Macdonald, Spanien, and Yoshiro Imaeda. 1978–79. *Choix de documents tibétains conservés à la Bibliothèque nationale.* 2 vols. Paris: Bibliothèque nationale.

Martin, Dan. 1982. "The Teachers of Mi-la-ras-pa." *Journal of the Tibet Society* 2.
———. 1987. "Illusion Web: Locating the Guhyagarbha Tantra in Buddhist Intellectual History." In *Silver on Lapis: Tibetan Literary Culture and History*, Christopher I. Beckwith, ed. Bloomington, Ind.: Tibet Society, pp. 175–220.
———. 1991a. "A Brief Political History of Tibet By Gu-ru Bka-shis." In *Tibetan History and Language: Studies Dedicated to Uray Géza on His Seventieth Birthday*, E. Steinkellner, ed. Vienna: Arbeitkreis für Tibetische und Buddhistische Studien Universität Wien, pp. 329–351.
———. 1991b. "The Emergence of Bon and the Tibetan Polemical Tradition." Ph.D. diss., University of Indiana, Bloomington.
———. 1992. "A Twelfth-Century Tibetan Classic of Mahāmudrā, *The Path of Ultimate Profundity: The Great Seal Instructions of Zhang.*" *Journal of the International Association of Buddhist Studies* 15.2: 243–319.
———. 1994a. *Mandala Cosmogony: Human Body Good Thought and the Revelation of the Secret Mother Tantras of Bon.* Asiatische Forschungen Band 124. Wiesbaden: Harrassowitz Verlag.
———. 1994b. "Pearls from Bones: Relics, Chortens, Tertons and the Signs of Saintly Death in Tibet." *Numen* 41: 273–324.
———. 1994c. "Tibet at the Center: A Historical Study of Some Tibetan Geographical Conceptions Based on Two Types of Country-Lists Found in Bon Histories." In *Tibetan Studies: Proceedings of the Sixth Seminar of the International Association for Tibetan Studies, Fagernes 1992*, Per Kvaerne, ed. Oslo: Institute for Comparative Research in Human Culture, vol. 1, pp. 517–532.
———. 1996a. "Tables of Contents (dKar chag)." In *Tibetan Literature: Studies in Genre*, José Ignacio Cabezon and Roger R. Jackson. Ithaca, N.Y.: Snow Lion, pp. 500–514.
———. 1996b. "On the Cultural Ecology of Sky Burial on the Himalayan Plateau." *East and West* 46.3–4: 353–370.
———. 1996c. "The Star King and the Four Children of Pehar: Popular Religious Movements of Eleventh- to Twelfth-Century Tibet." *Acta Orientalia Academiae Scientiarum Hungaricae* 49 (1–2): 171–195.
———. 1996d. "Unearthing Bon Treasures: A Study of Tibetan Sources on the Earlier Years in the Life of gShen-chen kLu-dga.'" *Journal of the American Oriental Society* 116.4: 619–644.
———. 1997. *Tibetan Histories: A Bibliography of Tibetan-Language Historical Works.* London: Serindia.
———. 1998a. Review of *Kar gliṅ Źi khro: A Tantric Buddhist Concept*, by Henk Blezer. *Tibet Journal* 23.3: 106–114.
———. 1998b. Review of *Drung, De'u and Bönn: Narrations, Symbolic Languages, and the Bön Tradition in Ancient Tibet*, by Namkhai Norbu. *Tibet Journal* 23.4: 108–119.
Mayer, Robert. 1990. "Tibetan Phur-pas and Indian Kīlas." *Tibet Journal* 15.1: 3–41.
———. 1991. "Observations on the Tibetan Phur-pa and the Indian Kīla." In *The Buddhist Forum*, vol. 2. London: University of London, School of Oriental and African Studies.
———. 1994. "Scriptural Revelation in India and Tibet: Indian Precursors of the gTer-ma Tradition." In *Tibetan Studies: Proceedings of the Sixth Seminar of the International Association for Tibetan Studies, FAGERNES 1992*, Per Kvaerne, ed. Oslo: Institute for Comparative Research in Human Culture, pp. 533–543.

———. 1996. *A Scripture of the Ancient Tantra Collection: The Phur-pa bcu-gnyis.* Oxford: Kiscadale.

———. 1997. "Were the gSar-ma-pa Polemicists Justified in Rejecting Some rNying-ma-pa Tantras?" In *Tibetan Studies: Proceedings of the Seventh Seminar of the International Association for Tibetan Studies, Graz 1995,* Helmut Krasser, Michael Torsten Much, Ernst Steinkellner, and Helmut Tauscher, eds. Vienna: Verlag der Österreichischen Akademie der Wissenschaften, vol. 2, pp. 619–632.

Michael, Franz. 1982. *Rule by Incarnation: Tibetan Buddhism and Its Role in Society and State.* Boulder, Colo.: Westview Press.

Mori, Hiroaki, Yukari Hayashi, and Barrie Angus McLean, dirs. 1994. *The Tibetan Book of the Dead: The Great Liberation after Death.* Narration by Leonard Cohen. 2 videocassettes. Santa Monica, Calif.: Direct Cinema.

Mullin, Glenn H. 1978. Review of *Secret Doctrines of the Tibetan Books of the Dead,* by Detlef Ingo Lauf, translated by Graham Parks. *Tibet Journal* 3.1: 52–57.

———. 1986. *Death and Dying: The Tibetan Tradition.* Boston: Arkana Paperbacks.

———. 1996. *Tsongkhapa's Six Yogas of Naropa.* Ithaca, N.Y.: Snow Lion.

———. 1997. *Readings on the Six Yogas of Naropa.* Ithaca, N.Y.: Snow Lion.

Mumford, Stan Royal. 1989. *Himalayan Dialogue: Tibetan Lamas and Gurung Shamans in Nepal.* Madison: University of Wisconsin Press.

Nakamura, Hajime. 1987. *Indian Buddhism: A Survey with Bibliographical Notes.* Delhi: Motilal Banarsidass.

Nakane, Chie. 1999. "New Trends in Tibetan Studies: Towards an Elucidation of Tibetan Society." *Acta Asiatica* 76: 40–80.

Nanamoli, Bhikkhu, and Bhikkhu Bodhi. 1995. *The Middle Length Discourses of the Buddha: A New Translation of the Majjhima Nikāya.* Boston: Wisdom.

Nebesky-Wojkowitz, Réne de. 1956. *Oracles and Demons of Tibet.* The Hague: Mouton.

Norbu, Namkhai. 1995. *Drung, Deu and Bön: Narrations, Symbolic Languages, and the Bön Tradition in Ancient Tibet.* Translated from Tibetan into Italian, edited, and annotated by Adriano Clemente. Translated into English from Italian by Andrew Lukianowicz. Dharamsala: Library of Tibetan Works and Archives.

Norbu, Thupten Jigme. 1987. "The Development of the Human Embryo According to Tibetan Medicine: The Treatise Written for Alexander Csoma de Körös by Sangs-rgyas Phun-tshogs." In *Silver on Lapis: Tibetan Literary Culture and History,* Christopher I. Beckwith, ed. Bloomington, Ind.: Tibet Society, pp. 57–62.

Nornang, Ngawang L. 1990. "Monastic Organization and Economy at Dwags-po Bshad-grub-gling." In *Reflections on Tibetan Culture: Essays in Memory of Turrell V. Wylie,* Lawrence Epstein and Richard F. Sherbourne, eds. Lewiston, N.Y.: Edwin Mellen Press, pp. 249–268.

Orofino, Giacomella. 1990. *Sacred Tibetan Teachings on Death and Liberation.* Great Britain: Prism Press.

———. 1999. "Notes on the Early Phases of Indo-Tibetan Buddhism." Paper presented at the Twelfth Conference of the International Association of Buddhist Studies, Lausanne, Switzerland. August.

Ortner, Sherry B. 1978. *Sherpas through Their Rituals.* Cambridge: Cambridge University Press.

Pagel, Ulrich. 1997. "The British Library Tibetica: A Historical Survey." In *Tibetan Studies: Proceedings of the Seventh Seminar of the International Association for Tibetan Studies, Graz 1995,* Helmut Krasser, Michael Torsten Much, Ernst

Steinkellner, and Helmut Tauscher, eds. Vienna: Verlag der Österreichischen Akademie der Wissenschaften, pp. 725–732.

Paltul Jampal Lodoe (Dpal-sprul 'Jam-dpal-blo-gros). 1965. *Record of Nyingma Monasteries in Tibet* [Tibetan title: *Bod-na bzhugs-pa'i rnying-ma'i dgon-deb*]. Dalhousie: Paltul Jampal Lodoe. I-Tib-61.

Panglung, Jampa L. 1985. "On the Origin of the Tsha-gsur Ceremony." In *Soundings in Tibetan Civilization: Proceedings of the 1982 Seminar of the International Association for Tibetan Studies Held at Columbia University*, Barbara Nimri Aziz and Matthew Kapstein, eds. New Delhi: Manohar, pp. 268–271.

Parry, Jonathan. 1994. *Death in Banaras*. Cambridge: Cambridge University Press.

Pathak, Suniti Kumar. 1997. "Prolegomenon for a History of Tibetan Literature." In *Tibetan Studies: Proceedings of the Seventh Seminar of the International Association for Tibetan Studies, Graz 1995*, Helmut Krasser, Michael Torsten Much, Ernst Steinkellner, and Helmut Tauscher, eds. Vienna: Verlag der Österreichischen Akademie der Wissenschaften, vol. 2, pp. 751–759.

Patrul Rinpoche. 1994. *The Words of My Perfect Teacher*. Translated by the Padmakara Translation Group. New York: HarperCollins.

Petech, Luciano. 1972. *China and Tibet in the Early Eighteenth Century*. Leiden: E. J. Brill.

———. 1988. *Selected Papers on Asian History*. Rome: Istituto Italiano per il Medio ed Estremo Oriente.

———. 1990. *Central Tibet and the Mongols: The Yüan-Sa-Skya Period of Tibetan History*. Rome: Istituto Italiano per il Medio ed Estremo Oriente.

Pommaret, Françoise. 1989. *Les Revenants de l'au-delà dans le monde tibétain: Sources littéraires et tradition vivante*. Paris: Editions du Centre National de la Recherche Scientifique.

———. 1996. "On Local and Mountain Deities in Bhutan." In *Reflections of the Mountain: Essays on the History and Social Meaning of the Mountain Cult in Tibet and the Himalaya*, Anne-Marie Blondeau and Ernst Steinkellner, eds. Vienna: Verlag der Österreichischen Akademie der Wissenschaften, pp. 39–56.

———. 1997. "Returning from Hell." In *Religions of Tibet in Practice*, Donald S. Lopez, ed. Princeton, N.J.: Princeton University Press, pp. 499–510.

———. 1998a. *Bhutan*. 3rd edition. Translated by Elisabeth B. Booz. Chicago: Passport Books.

———. 1998b. "'Maîtres des trésors' (*gter bdag*): Divinités locales et médiums au Bhoutan." In *Tibetan Mountain Deities, Their Cults and Representations: Proceedings of the Seventh Seminar of the International Association for Tibetan Studies, Graz 1995*, Anne-Marie Blondeau, ed. Vienna: Verlag der Österreichischen Akademie der Wissenschaften, pp. 79–97.

Poucha, Pavel. 1952. "Das tibetanische Totenbuch im Rahmen der eschatologischen Literatur." *Archiv Orientální* 20: 136–162.

———. 1974. "Une version mongole—texte bilingue—du Livre des morts tibétain." *Études mongoles* 5: 97–106.

Prats, Ramon. 1980. "Some Preliminary Considerations Arising from a Biographical Study of the Early gTer-ston." In *Tibetan Studies in Honour of Hugh Richardson*, Michael Aris and Aung San Suu Kyi, eds. Warminster, England: Aris and Phillips, pp. 256–260.

———. 1982. *Contributo allo studio biografico dei primi gter-ston*. Naples: Istituto Universitario Orientale.

———. 1996. *El libro de los muertos tibetano*. Madrid: Edicianes Siruela.

————. 1997. "Towards a Comprehensive Classification of rNying-ma Literature." In *Tibetan Studies: Proceedings of the Seventh Seminar of the International Association for Tibetan Studies, Graz 1995*, Helmut Krasser, Michael Torsten Much, Ernst Steinkellner, and Helmut Tauscher, eds. Vienna: Verlag der Österreichischen Akademie der Wissenschaften, vol. 2, pp. 789–801.

Pruden, Leo M. 1988. "The Abhidharma: The Origins, Growth and Development of a Literary Tradition." In Louis de La Vallée Poussin, *Abhidharmakośabhāṣyam*, translated by Leo M. Pruden. 5 vols. Berkeley, Calif.: Asian Humanities Press, pp. xxx–lxii.

Puhvel, Jaan. 1987. *Comparative Mythology*. Baltimore: Johns Hopkins University Press.

Ramble, Charles. 1982. "Status and Death: Mortuary Rites and Attitudes to the Body in a Tibetan Village." *Kailash* 9.4: 333–360.

————. 1996. "Patterns of Places." In *Reflections of the Mountain: Essays on the History and Social Meaning of the Mountain Cult in Tibet and the Himalaya*, Anne-Marie Blondeau and Ernst Steinkellner, eds. Vienna: Verlag der Österreichischen Akademie der Wissenschaften, pp. 141–153.

————. 1997. "The Creation of the Bon Mountain of Kongpo." In *Mandala and Landscape*, Alexander W. Macdonald, ed. New Delhi: D. K. Printworld, pp. 133–232.

Reynolds, John Myrdhin. 1989. *Self-Liberation through Seeing with Naked Awareness*. Barrytown, N.Y.: Station Hill Press.

————. 1996. *The Golden Letters*. Ithaca, N.Y.: Snow Lion.

Ricca, Franco, and Erberto Lo Bue. 1993. *The Great Stupa of Gyantse: A Complete Tibetan Pantheon of the Fifteenth Century*. London: Serindia.

Richardson, Hugh. 1998. *High Peaks, Pure Earth: Collected Writings on Tibetan History and Culture*. London: Serindia.

Robinet, Isabelle. 1955. *The Zhi mä Funeral Ceremony of the Na-khi of Southwest China; described and translated from Na-khi manuscripts*. Vol. 9. Vienna: Studia Instituti Anthropos.

Roerich, George. 1949. *The Blue Annals*. Reprint, New Delhi: Motilal Banarsidass, 1979.

Rose, Leo E. 1990. "Modern Sikkim in an Historical Perspective." In *Reflections on Tibetan Culture: Essays in Memory of Turrell V. Wylie*, Lawrence Epstein and Richard F. Sherbourne, eds. Lewiston, N.Y.: Edwin Mellen Press, pp. 59–74.

Ruegg, David Seyfort. 1989. *Buddha-Nature, Mind, and the Problem of Gradualism in a Comparative Perspective: On the Transmission and Reception of Buddhism in India and Tibet*. London: University of London, School of Oriental and African Studies.

Sadakata, Akira. 1997. *Buddhist Cosmology: Philosophy and Origins*. Translated by Gaynor Sekimori. Tokyo: Kosei.

Sakyapa Sonam Gyaltsen. 1996. *The Clear Mirror: A Traditional Account of Tibet's Golden Age*. Translated by McComas Taylor and Lama Choedak Yuthok. Ithaca, N.Y.: Snow Lion.

Samten Jampa. 1987. "Notes on the Lithang Edition of the Tibetan bKa'-'gyur." Translated by Jeremy Russell. *Tibet Journal* 12.3: 17–40.

————. 1994. "Notes on the Bka'-'gyur of O-rgyan-gling, the Family Temple of the Sixth Dalai Lama (1683–1706)." In *Tibetan Studies: Proceedings of the Sixth Seminar of the International Association for Tibetan Studies, FAGERNES 1992*, Per Kvaerne, ed. Oslo: Institute for Comparative Research in Human Culture, vol. 1, pp. 393–402.

Samuel, Geoffrey. 1993. *Civilized Shamans: Buddhism in Tibetan Societies.* Washington, D.C.: Smithsonian Institution Press.

————. 1994. "Tibet and the Southeast Asian Highlands: Rethinking the Intellectual Context of Tibetan Studies." In *Tibetan Studies: Proceedings of the Sixth Seminar of the International Association for Tibetan Studies, FAGERNES 1992,* Per Kvaerne, ed. Oslo: Institute for Comparative Research in Human Culture, vol. 2, pp. 696–710.

————. 1997a. "Some Reflections on the Vajrayāna and its Shamanic Origins." In *Les habitants du toit du monde. Études recueillies en hommage à Alexander W. Macdonald,* Samten G. Karmay and Philippe Sagant, eds. Nanterre: Societé d'Ethnologie, pp. 325–342.

————. 1997b. "The Vajrayāna in the Context of Himalayan Folk Religion." In *Tibetan Studies: Proceedings of the Seventh Seminar of the International Association for Tibetan Studies, Graz 1995,* Helmut Krasser, Michael Torsten Much, Ernst Steinkellner, and Helmut Tauscher, eds. Vienna: Verlag der Österreichischen Akademie der Wissenschaften, vol. 2, pp. 843–850.

Sanderson, Alexis. 1985. "Purity and Power among the Brahmins of Kashmir." In *The Category of the Person: Anthropology, Philosophy, History,* Michael Carrithers, Steven Collins, and Steven Lukes, eds. Cambridge: Cambridge University Press, pp. 191–216.

————. 1988. "Śaivism and the Tantric Tradition." In *The World's Religions,* S. Sutherland, ed. London: Routledge and Kegan Paul, pp. 660–704.

Sangay, Thupten. 1984. "Tibetan Ritual for the Dead." Translated by Gavin Kilty. *Tibetan Medicine* 7: 30–40.

Sangharakshita. 1985. *The Eternal Legacy: An Introduction to the Canonical Literature of Buddhism.* London: Tharpa.

Satô, Hisashi. 1993. "The Origins and Development of the Study of Tibetan History in Japan.". *Acta Asiatica* 64: 81–120.

Savitsky, L.S. 1970. "Zapisi dostignutogo i zapisi proslusannogo i ih znacenie dlja izucenija istorii i literatury Tibeta" (Thob-yig and Gsan-yig and Their Importance for the Study of the History and Literature of Tibet). In *Istorija, kul'tura, jazyki narodov Vostoka,* Jurij A. Petrosjan, ed. Moscow, pp. 46–50.

Savitsky, L.S., and Louis Legeti, eds. 1984. "Tunhuang Tibetan Manuscripts in the Collection of the Leningrad Institute of Oriental Studies." In *Tibetan and Buddhist Studies Commemorating the Two Hundredth Anniversary of the Birth of A. Csoma de Koros* 2. Budapest: Académiai Kiadó.

Schaeffer, Kurtis R. 1999. "Printing the Words of the Master. Tibetan Editorial Practice in the *Collected Works* of 'Jam dbyangs bzhad pa'i rdo rje I (1648–1721)." *Acta Orientalia* 60: 159–177.

Schmidt, I. J., and O Böhtlingk. 1847. "Verzeichnis der tibetischen Handschriften und Holzdrucke im Asiatischen Museum der kaiserlichen Akademie der Wissenschaften, St. Petersburg." Reprinted from *Bulletin de la classe historico-philologique de l'académie impériale des sciences de St. Petersbourg* [Izvestija imperatorskloj Akademii Nauk] 4: 82–126.

Schmitt, Jean-Claude. 1998. *Ghosts in the Middle Ages: The Living and the Dead in Medieval Society.* Translated by Teresa Lavender Fagan. Chicago: University of Chicago Press, 1998.

Schoening, Jeffrey D. 1988. "A Bibliography of Tibetan Historical Works at the University of Washington," In *Tibetan Studies: Proceedings of the Fourth Seminar of the International Association for Tibetan Studies, Schloss Hohenkammer–Munich*

1985, Helga Uebach and Jampa L. Panglung, eds. Munich: Kommission für Zentralasiatische Studien Bayerische Akademie der Wissenschaften, pp. 421–426.

Schopen, Gregory. 1991. "An Old Inscription from Amarāvatā and the Cult of the Local Monastic Dead in Indian Buddhist Monasteries." *Journal of the International Association of Buddhist Studies* 14.2: 281–329.

————. 1992. "On Avoiding Ghosts and Social Censure: Monastic Funerals in the *Mūlasarvāstivāda-vinaya*." *Journal of Indian Philosophy* 20: 1–39.

————. 1994. "*Stūpa* and *Tīrtha*: Tibetan Mortuary Practices and an Unrecognized Form of Burial Ad Sanctos at Buddhist Sites in India." In *The Buddhist Forum*, vol. 3, 1991–93 (Papers in Honour and Appreciation of Professor David Seyfort Ruegg's contribution to Indological, Buddhist, and Tibetan Studies), Tadeusz Skorupski and Ulrich Pagel, eds. London: University of London, School of Oriental and African Studies, pp. 273–293.

————. 1994. "Ritual Rights and Bones of Contention: More on Monastic Funerals and Relics in the *Mūlasarvāstivāda-vinaya*." *Journal of Indian Philosophy* 22: 31–80.

————. 1997. *Bones, Stones, and Buddhist Monks: Collected Papers on the Archaeology, Epigraphy, and Texts of Monastic Buddhism in India*. Honolulu: University of Hawaii Press.

Schuh, Dieter. 1973. *Untersuchungen zur geschichte der tibetischen kalenderrechnung*. Wiesbaden: Franz Steiner Verlag GMBH.

————. 1981. *Tibetische Handschriften und Blockdrucke*. Teil 8 *(Sammlung Waddell der Staatsbibliothek Preussischer Kulturbesitz Berlin)*. Wiesbaden: Franz Steiner Verlag GMBH.

————, ed. 1985. *Tibetische Handschriften und Blockdrucke*. Teil 9 *(Die Werksammlungen Kun-tu bzaṅ-po'i dgoṅs-pa zaṅ-thal, Ka-dag raṅ-byuṅ raṅ-śar und mKha'- 'gro gsaṇ-ba ye-śes-kyi rgyud)*. Beschrieben von Peter Schwieger. Stuttgart: Franz Steiner Verlag Wiesbaden GMBH.

Schwieger, Peter. 1988. "The Biographies of the Grand Lamas of Dagyab (Brag-g.yab) as a Contribution to the History of East Tibet." In *Tibetan Studies: Proceedings of the Fourth Seminar of the International Association for Tibetan Studies, Schloss Hohenkammer–Munich 1985*, Helga Uebach and Jampa L. Panglung, eds. Munich: Kommission für Zentralasiatische Studien Bayerische Akademie der Wissenschaften, pp. 435–438.

————. 1989. *Die ersten dGe-lugs-pa-Hierarchen von Brag-g.yab (1572–1692)*. Bonn: VGH Wissenschaftsverlag.

————. 1997. "A Note on the History of the Cult of Padmasambhava on the Tenth Day of the Month." In *Tibetan Studies: Proceedings of the Seventh Seminar of the International Association for Tibetan Studies, Graz 1995*, Helmut Krasser, Michael Torsten Much, Ernst Steinkellner, and Helmut Tauscher, eds. Viennan: Verlag der Österreichischen Akademie der Wissenschaften, vol. 2, pp. 851–855.

Shakabpa, Tsepon W. D. 1984. *Tibet: A Political History*. New York: Potala.

Shardza Tashi Gyaltsen. 1993. *Heart Drops of Dharmakaya: Dzogchen Practice of the Bön Tradition*. Commentary by Lopon Tenzin Namdak. Ithaca, N.Y.: Snow Lion.

Shastri, Jampa Samten. 1983. *Catalogue of the Library of Tibetan Works and Archives (Manuscript Section)*. Vol. 1. *Historical Works*. Dharamsala: Library of Tibetan Works and Archives.

Shastri, Lobsang. 1990. *Catalogue of the Library of Tibetan Works and Archives (Manuscript Section)*. Vol. 2. *Historical Works*. Dharamsala: Library of Tibetan Works and Archives.

————. 1995. *Catalogue of the Library of Tibetan Works and Archives (Manuscript Section)*, Vol. 4: *Tibetan Medicine and Astrology*. Dharamsala: Library of Tibetan Works and Archives.

Shaw, Miranda. 1994. *Passionate Enlightenment: Women in Tantric Buddhism*. Princeton: Princeton University Press.

Shoren, Ihara, and Yamaguchi Zuiho, eds. 1992. *Tibetan Studies: Proceedings of the Fifth Seminar of the International Association for Tibetan Studies (Narita 1989)*. 2 vols. Narita: Naritasan Shinshojji.

Shwe Zan Aung and Caroline A. F. Rhys Davids. [1915] 1979. *Points of Controversy, or, Subjects of Discourse: Being a Translation of the Kathā-vatthu from the Abhidhammapiṭaka*. Pali Text Society, no. 5. Reprint, London: Routledge and Kegan Paul.

Sinor, Dennis, ed. 1990. *The Cambridge History of Early Inner Asia*. Cambridge: Cambridge University Press.

Skilling, Peter. 1991. "A Brief Guide to the Golden Tanjur." *Journal of the Siam Society* 79.2: 138–146.

————. 1997. "From bKa' bstan bcos to bKa' 'gyur and bsTan 'gyur." In *Transmission of the Tibetan Buddhist Canon: Proceedings of the Seventh Seminar of the International Association for Tibetan Studies, Graz 1995*, Helmut Eimer, ed. Vienna: Verlag der Österreichischen Akademie der Wissenschaften, pp. 87–111.

Skorupski, Tadeusz. 1982. "The Cremation Ceremony According to the *Byang-gTer* Tradition." *Kailash* 9.4: 361–376.

————. 1983. *The Sarvadurgatipariśodhana Tantra: Elimination of All Evil Rebirths*. Delhi: Motilal Banarsidass.

————. 1994. "A Prayer for Rebirth in the Sukhāvatī". In *The Buddhist Forum*, vol. 3 1991–1993 (Papers in Honour and Appreciation of Professor David Seyfort Ruegg's Contribution to Indological, Buddhist, and Tibetan Studies), Tadeusz Skorupski and Ulrich Pagel, ed. London: University of London, School of Oriental and African Studies, pp. 375–409.

Smith, E. Gene. 1970. Introduction to *Three Karchacks*, Ngawang Gelek Demo, ed. Gedan Sungrab Minyam Gyunphel Series 13. New Delhi, pp. 1–6.

————. 1972. Introduction to *bLa ma dgongs 'dus: A Cycle of Precious Teachings and Practices of the Nyingmapa Tradition Rediscovered from its Place of Concealment by gTer-chen Sangs-rgyas-gling-pa*, Sonam Topgay Kazi, ed. Ngagyur Nyingmay Sungrab 44. Gangtok, Sikkim: Sonam T. Kazi.

————. 1979. Preface to *The Collected Rediscovered Teachings of Rig-'dzin Nyi-ma-grags-pa with Rituals of the Char Nyi-grags Tradition*. 2 vols. Bir, H.P., India: Pema Lodoe. I-Tib-2066; 80–900308.

————. 2001. *Among Tibetan Texts: History and Literature of the Himalayan Plateau*. Boston: Wisdom.

Smith, Warren W. 1996. *Tibetan Nation: A History of Tibetan Nationalism and Sino-Tibetan Relations*. Boulder, Colo.: Westview Press.

Snellgrove, David. 1957. *Buddhist Himalaya*. Oxford: Bruno Cassirer.

————. 1959. *The Hevajra Tantra: A Critical Study*. 2 vols. London: Oxford University Press.

————. 1967a. *Four Lamas of Dolpo*. Reprint, Nepal: Himalayan Book Seller. 1992.

————. 1967b. *The Nine Ways of Bon*. London: Oxford University Press.

————. 1987. *Indo-Tibetan Buddhism: Indian Buddhists and Their Successors*. 2 vols. Boston: Shambhala.

Snellgrove, David, and Hugh Richardson. 1986. *A Cultural History of Tibet.* Boston: Shambhala.

Sogyal Rinpoche. 1992. *The Tibetan Book of Living and Dying.* San Francisco: HarperCollins.

Sorensen, Henrik H. 1996. Review of *The Scripture on the Ten Kings and the Making of Purgatory in Medieval Chinese Buddhism,* by Stephen F. Teiser. *Studies in Central and East Asian Religions* 9: 114–121.

Sorensen, Per K. 1986. *A Fourteenth-Century Tibetan Historical Work—rGyal-rabs gsal-ba'i me-long: Author, Date and Sources, A Case Study.* Copenhagen: Akademisk Forlag.

————. 1990. *Divinity Secularized. An Inquiry into the Nature and Form of the Songs Ascribed to the Sixth Dalai Lama.* Vienna: Arbeitkreis für Tibetische und Buddhistische Studien Universität Wien.

————. 1994. *Tibetan Buddhist Historiography—The Mirror Illuminating the Royal Genealogies: An Annotated Translation of the Fourteenth Century Tibetan Chronicle: rGyal-rabs gsal-ba'i me-long.* Wiesbaden: Harrassowitz Verlag.

Sperling, Elliot. 1992. "Notes on References to 'Bri-gung-pa: Mongol Contact in the Late Sixteenth and Early Seventeenth Centuries." In *Tibetan Studies: Proceedings of the Fifth Seminar of the International Association for Tibetan Studies (Narita 1989),* Ihara Shoren and Yamaguchi Zuiho, eds. Narita: Naritasan Shinshojji, vol. 2, pp. 741–750.

Stein, Rolf A. 1957. "Le *Liṅga* des danses masquées lamaïques et la théorie des âmes." *Sino-Indian Studies (Liebenthal Festschrft)* 5 .3–4: 200–234.

————. 1959. *Recherches sur l'Epopée et le Barde du Tibet.* Bibliothèque de l'Institut des hautes Études Chinoises 13. Paris: Presses Universitaires de France.

————. 1961. *Une chronique ancienne de bSam-yas: sBa'-bźed.* Paris: Presses Universitaires de France.

————. 1970. "Un document ancien relatif aux rites funéraires des Bon-po tibétains." *Journal Asiatique* 257: 155–185.

————. 1971. "Du recit au rituel dans les manuscrits tibetains de Touen- Houang." In *Etudes tibétaines dédiées à la mémoire de Marcelle Lalou.* Paris: Librarie D'Amerique at d'Orient, pp. 479–547.

————. 1972. *Tibetan Civilization.* Translated by J. E. Stapleton Driver. Stanford, Calif.: Stanford University Press.

————. 1988a. *Grottes-matrices et lieux saints de la déesse en Asie orientale.* Paris: École Française d'Extrême-Orient.

————. 1988b. "La religion indigène et les *bon-po* dans les manuscrits de Touen- Houang." *Tibetica Antiqua* V. *Bulletin d'École Française d'Extrême-Orient* 77: 27–56.

Stoddard, Heather. 1997. "The Nine Brothers of the White High. On the 'Re-membering' of History and the Creation of Gods." In *Les habitants du toit du monde. Études recueillies en hommage à Alexander W. Macdonald,* Samten G. Karmay and Philippe Sagant, eds. Nanterre: Societé d'Ethnologie, pp. 75–109.

Sweet, Michael J. 1996. "Mental Purification *(Blo sbyong):* A Native Tibetan Genre of Religious Literature." In *Tibetan Literature: Studies in Genre,* José Ignacio Cabezon and Roger R. Jackson, eds. Ithaca, N.Y.: Snow Lion Publications, pp. 244–260.

Tanselle, G. Thomas. 1992. *A Rationale of Textual Criticism.* Philadelphia: University of Pennsylvania Press.

Teichman, Eric. 1921. *Travels of a Consular Officer in North-west China*. Cambridge: Cambridge University Press.

Teiser, Stephen F. 1993. "The Growth of Purgatory." In *Religion and Society in T'ang and Sung China*, Patricia Buckley Ebrey and Peter N. Gregory, eds. Honolulu: University of Hawaii Press, pp. 115–145.

———. 1994. *The Scripture on the Ten Kings and the Making of Purgatory in Medieval Chinese Buddhism*. Honolulu: University of Hawaii Press.

Tenga Rinpoche. 1996. *Transition and Liberation: Explanations of Meditation in the Bardo*. Translated into German by Susanne Schefczyk. English translation by Alex Wilding. Osterby, Denmark: Khampa Buchverlag.

Thinley, Karma. 1980. *The History of the Sixteen Karmapas of Tibet*. Edited with an essay by David Stott. Boulder, Colo.: Prajñā Press.

Thondup, Tulku. 1986. *Hidden Teachings of Tibet: An Explanation of the Terma Tradition of the Nyingma School of Buddhism*. London: Wisdom.

———. 1987. *Buddhist Civilization in Tibet*. New York: Routledge and Kegan Paul.

———. 1996. *Masters of Meditation and Miracles: The Longchen Nyingthig Lineage of Tibetan Buddhism*. Boston: Shambhala.

Thurman, Robert. 1994. *The Tibetan Book of the Dead: Liberation through Understanding in the Between*. New York: Bantam Books.

Torricelli, Fabrizio. 1996. "A Tanjur Text on gTum-mo: Tôhoku No. 2332-I." *Tibet Journal* 21.1: 30–46.

Torricelli, Fabrizio, and Āchārya Sangye T. Naga, trans. 1995. *The Life of the Mahāsiddha Tilopa by Mar-pa Chos-kyi bLo-gros*. Dharamsala: Library of Tibetan Works and Archives.

Trungpa, Chögyam. 1971. *Born in Tibet*. New York: Penguin Books.

———. 1992. *Transcending Madness: The Experience of the Six Bardos*. Boston: Shambhala.

Tsepak Rigzin. 1986. *Tibetan-English Dictionary of Buddhist Terminology*. Dharamsala: Library of Tibetan Works and Archives.

Tsering Lama Jampal Zangpo. 1988. *A Garland of Immortal Wish-Fulfilling Trees: The Palyul Tradition of Nyingmapa*. Translated by Sangye Khandro. New York: Snow Lion.

Tsering, Pema. 1978. "*rÑiṅ ma pa* Lamas am Yüan-Kaiserhof." In *Proceedings of the Csoma de Köros Memorial Symposium Held at Matrafüred, Hungary, 24–30 September 1976*, Louis Ligeti, ed. Budapest: Akadémiai Kiadó, pp. 511–540.

Tshewang, Padma, Khenpo Phuntsok Tashi, Chris Butters, and Sigmund K. Saetreng. 1995. *The Treasure Revealer of Bhutan: Pemalingpa, the Terma Tradition and Its Critics*. Bibliotheca Himalayica Series 3, vol. 8. Kathmandu: EMR.

Tucci, Giuseppe. 1932–41. *Indo-Tibetica*. 4 vols. Rome: Istituto Italiano per il Medio ed Estremo Oriente.

———. 1947. "The Validity of Tibetan Historical Tradition." In *India Antiqua: A Volume of Oriental Studies Presented by His Friends and Pupils to Jean Philippe Vogel, C.I.E., on the occasion of the Fiftieth Anniversary of His Doctorate*. Leiden: E. J. Brill, pp. 309–322.

———. 1949. *Tibetan Painted Scrolls*. 3 vols. Rome: La Libreria Dello Stato.

———. [1949] 1972. *Il libro tibetano dei morti (Bardo Tödöl)*. Reprint, Torino, Italy: Unione Tipografico-Editrice.

———. 1950. *The Tombs of the Tibetan Kings*. Rome: Istituto Italiano per il Medio ed Estremo Oriente.

———. 1958. *Minor Buddhist Texts*, Part 2: *First Bhāvanākrama of Kamalaśīla*.

Sanskrit and Tibetan Texts with Introduction and English Summary. Serie Orientale Roma 9, 2. Rome: Istituto Italiano peril Medio ed Estremo Orienteo.

——. 1962. "The Wives of Sroṇ btsan sgam po." *Oriens Extremus* 9: 121–130.

——. 1971. *Deb ther dmar po gsar ma: Tibetan Chronicles by bSod nams grags pa*, vol. 1. Serie Orientale Roma 24. Rome: Istituto Italiano per il Medio ed Estremo Oriente.

——. 1988. *The Religions of Tibet.* Translated by Geoffrey Samuel. Berkeley: University of California Press.

——. 1989. *Gyantse and Its Monasteries.* 3 vols. Reprint of *Indo-Tibetica 4.* New Delhi: Aditya Prakashan.

Uray, Géza. 1988. "Ñag.ñi.dags.po: A Note on the Historical Geography of Ancient Tibet." In *Orientalia Iosephi Tucci Memoriae Dicata*, G. Gnoli and L. Lanciotti, eds. Rome: Istituto Italiano per il Medio ed Estremo Oriente, vol. 3, pp. 1503–1510.

van Itallie, Jean-Claude. 1998. *The Tibetan Book of the Dead for Reading Aloud.* Berkeley, Calif.: North Atlantic Books.

van Schaik, Sam. 2000. "A Catalogue of the First Volume of the Waddell Manuscript *rNying ma rgyud 'bum.*" *Tibet Journal* 25.1: 27–50.

van Tuyl, Charles D. 1975. "The Tshe riṅ ma Account: An Old Document Incorporated into the Mi la ras pa'i mgur 'bum?" *Zentralasiatische Studien* 9: 23–36.

Vitali, Roberto. 1990. *Early Temples of Central Tibet.* London: Serindia.

——. 1996. *The Kingdoms of Gu.ge Pu.hrang According to mNga'.ris rgyal.rabs by Gu.ge mkhan.chen Ngag.dbang grags.pa.* Dharamsala: Tho-ling gtsug-lag-khang lo-gcig-stong 'khro-ba'i rjes-dran-mdzad sgo'i go-sgrig tshogs-chung.

——. 1998. Review of *Tibetan Histories: A Bibliography of Tibetan-Language Historical Works*, by Dan Martin. *Tibet Journal* 23.4: 120–128.

Vostrikov, A. I. 1970. *Tibetan Historical Literature.* Translated by Harish Chandra Gupta. Calcutta: Indian Studies, Past and Present.

Waddell, L. Austine. [1895] 1972. *Tibetan Buddhism with Its Mystic Cults, Symbolism and Mythology.* Reprint, New York: Dover.

Walshe, Maurice. 1995. *The Long Discourses of the Buddha: A Translation of the Dīgha Nikāya.* Boston: Wisdom.

Wangdu, Pasang, and Hildegard Diemberger. 2000. *dBa'-bzhed: The Royal Narrative Concerning the Bringing of the Buddha's Doctrine to Tibet.* Vienna: Verlag der Österreichischen Akademie der Wissenschaften.

Washington, Peter. 1995. *Madame Blavatsky's Baboon: A History of the Mystics, Mediums, and Misfits Who Brought Spiritualism to America.* New York: Shocken Books.

Wayman, Alex. 1974. "The Intermediate-State Dispute in Buddhism." In *Buddhist Studies in Honour of I. B. Horner*, L. Cousins, ed. Dordrecht, Holland: D. Reidel, pp. 227–239.

——. 1980. *Yoga of Guhyasamājatanta: The Arcane Lore of Forty Verses.* New York: Samuel Weiser.

White, David Gordon. 1996. *The Alchemical Body: Siddha Traditions in Medieval India.* Chicago: University of Chicago Press.

Wijesekera, O. H. 1945. "Vedic Gandharva and Pali Gandhabba." *University of Ceylon Review* 3.1: 73–107.

Williams, Paul. 1989. *Mahāyāna Buddhism: The Doctrinal Foundations.* London: Routledge.

Winkler, Ken. 1982. *Pilgrim of the Clear Light: The Biography of Dr. Walter Y. Evans-Wentz.* Berkeley, Calif.: Dawnfire Books.

Woodroffe, Sir John. 1919. *Shrichakrasambhara Tantra*. In *Tantrik Texts*, vol. 7. London: Luzac.

Wylie, Turrell. 1959. "A Standard System of Tibetan Transcription." *Harvard Journal of Asiatic Studies* 22: 261–267.

———. 1962. *The Geography of Tibet According to the 'Dzam-gling-rgyas-bshad*. Rome: Istituto Italiano per il Medio ed Estremo Oriente.

———. 1964a. "Mar-pa's Tower: Notes on Local Hegemons in Tibet." *History of Religions* 3.2: 278–291.

———. 1964b. "Ro-langs: The Tibetan Zombie." *History of Religions* 4.1: 69–80.

———. 1965. "Mortuary Customs at Sa-Skya, Tibet." *Harvard Journal of Asiatic Studies* 25: 229–242.

———. 1978. "Reincarnation: A Political Innovation in Tibetan Buddhism." In *Proceedings of the Csoma de Kőrös Memorial Symposium Held at Matrafüred, Hungary, 24–30 September 1976*, Louis Ligeti, ed. Budapest: Akadémiai Kiadó.

Yamabe, Nobuyoshi. 1996. ""On the School Affiliation of An Shigao: Sarvāstivāda and Yogācāra." Unpublished paper given at the international workshop entitled "The Works of An Shigao," Leiden, December 19–20.

Yamaguchi, Zuiho. 1984. "Methods of Chronological Calculations in Tibetan Historical Sources." In *Tibetan and Buddhist Studies*, vol. 2, L. Ligeti, ed. Budapest: Akadémiai Kiadó, pp. 405–434.

Younghusband, Colonel Francis. 1910. *India and Tibet*. London: J. Murray.

Yü, Ying-shih. 1987. "O Soul, Come Back!' A Study in the Changing Conceptions of the Soul and Afterlife in Pre-Buddhist China." *Harvard Journal of Asiatic Studies* 47.2: 363–395.

Zieme, Peter, and Gyorgy Kara. 1979. *Ein Uigurisches Totenbuch*. Wiesbaden: Otto Harrassowitz.

List of Tibetan Spellings

Proper Names

Ado Könchok Gyeltsen,
    *A-rdo Dkon-mchog-
    rgyal-mtshan*
Adrowa Namkha Dorje,
    *A-gro-ba Nam-mkha'-rdo-
    rje*
Akhu Gyatsün, *A-khu Rgya-
    btsun*
Akya Yongzin, *A-kya
    Yongs-'dzin*
Azi Sönambum, *A-gzi
    Bsod-nams-'bums*
Bentrang Betenpa, *Ban-
    sprang 'Bad-bstan-pa*
Bodong Chokle Namgyel,
    *Bo-dong Phyogs-las-
    rnam-rgyal*
Bubor Tashi Gyatso,
    *Bu-'bor Bkra-shis-rgya-
    mtsho*
Bubor Yeshe Gyeltsen,
    *Bu-'bor Ye-shes-rgyal-
    mtshan*
Butön, *Bu-ston*
Cenga Chödrakpa,
    *Spyan-snga Chos-
    grags-pa*
Chak Jangchup Lingpa,
    *Chag Byang-chub-
    gling-pa*
Chenyenpa Drodokpa
    Namkha Pel, *'Chad-
    nyan-pa Sgro-mdog-pa
    Nam-mkha'-dpal*

Chibukpa Karma Jangchup,
    *Spyi-bug-pa Karma-
    byang-chub*
Chödenpa, *Chos-ldan-pa*
Chögyel Tenpa Tshering,
    *Chos-rgyal Bstan-pa-
    tshe-ring*
Chögyel Tenzin, *Chos-
    rgyal-bstan-'dzin*
Chöje Gedün Gyeltsen,
    *Chos-rje Dge-'dun-rgyal-
    mtshan*
Chöje Gongchenpa
    Gyarawa, *Chos-rje Gong-
    chen-pa*
Chöje Lingpa, *Chos-rje-
    gling-pa*
Chöje Samten Pel, *Chos-rje
    Bsam-gtan-dpal*
Chöje Tsangchenpa, *Chos-
    rje Gtsang-chen-pa*
Chöje Tsangpa, *Chos-rje
    Gtsang-pa*
Chokden Gönpo, *Mchog-
    ldan-mgon-po*
Chokgyur Dechen Lingpa,
    *Mchog-gyur Bde-chen-
    gling-pa*
Chokle Namgyel, *Phyogs-
    las-rnam-rgyal*
Chökyi Wangchuk, *Chos-
    kyi-dbang-'phyugs*
Chönyi Gyatso, *Chos-nyid-
    rgya-mtsho*
Choro Lu'i Gyeltsen, *Cog-
    ro Klu'i-rgyal-mtshan*

Chöying Dorje, *Chos-
    dbyings-rdo-rje*
Chöying Rangdröl, *Chos-
    dbyings-rang-grol*
Dakdön Wangchuk Dorje,
    *Dwags-ston Dbang-
    phyug-rdo-rje*
Dakpo Kurap Depa, *Dwags-
    po Sku-rab sde-pa*
Dampa Ngarisa, *Dam-pa
    Mnga'-ris-sa*
Dampa Rangdröl Yeshe
    Gyeltsen, *Dam-pa-rang-
    grol Ye-shes-rgyal-
    mtshan*
Dampayang Ngoworipo,
    *Dam-pa-yang Ngo-bo-
    ris-po*
Dawa Drakpa, *Zla-ba-
    grags-pa*
Dawa Gyeltsen, *Zla-ba-
    rgyal-mtshan*
Dela Gungyel, *Lde-bla-
    gung-rgyal*
Desi Sangye Gyatso, *Sde-
    srid Sangs-rgyas-rgya-
    mtsho*
Dewa Pema, *Bde-ba-pad-ma*
Dharma Shri, *Dharma-śrī*
Dilgo Khyentse Tashi
    Peljor, *Dil-mgo Mkhyen-
    rtse Bkra-shis-dpal-
    'byor*
Dolung Chipön, *Do-lung
    Spyi-dpon*
Dong, *Sdong, Ldong*

Dongak Lingpa Chokden
Gönpo, *Mdo-sngags-gling-pa Mchog-ldan-mgon-po*
Dongak Tenzin, *Mdo-sngags-bstan-'dzin*
Dorje Gönpo, *Rdo-rje-mgon-po*
Dorje Lodrö, *Rdo-rje-blo-gros*
Dortshang Trhinle Dorje, *Dor-tshang 'Phrin-las-rdo-rje*
Drakarpo, *Dbra-dkar-po*
Drakpa Özer, *Grags-pa-'od-zer*
Drepa Jamyang Chögyel Dorje, *Bres-pa 'Jam-dbyang-chos-rgyal-rdo-rje*
Drigum Tsenpo, *Gri-gum-btsan-po*
Drigung, Drigungpa, *'Bri-gung, 'Bri-gung-pa*
Drigungpa Rinchen Phüntshok, *'Bri-gung-pa Rin-chen-phun-tshogs*
Drigung Pholungpa Karma Samdrup, *'Bri-gung 'Pho-lung-pa Karma-bsam-grub*
Drodokpa Namkha Pel, *Sgro-mdog-pa Nam-mkha'-dpal*
Drodül Letrho Lingpa, *'Gro-'dul Las-'phro-gling-pa*
Dru, *Gru*
Drukchen Gyelwang Chöje, *'Brug-chen Rgyal-dbang-chos-rje*
Drukpa Kagyu, *'Brug-pa Bka'-brgyud*
Drukpa Gyelwang Je, *'Brug-pa Rgyal-dbang-rje*
Drung Chödenpa, *Drung Chos-ldan-pa*
Drungchö Dorje Tokden, *Drung-chos Rdo-rje-rtogs-ldan*
Drung Lhawang Dorje, *Drung Lha-dbang-rdo-rje*
Drungpa Lodrö Senge, *Drung-pa Blo-gros-seng-ge*
Drungpa Rinpoche Chönyi Gyatso, *Drung-pa Rin-po-che Chos-nyid-rgya-mtsho*
Drungpa Rinpoche Kunga Gyeltsen, *Drung-pa Rin-*

po-che Kun-dga'-rgyal-mtshan
Drupchen Kunzang Dorje, *Grub-chen Kun-bzang-rdo-rje*
Dudül Dorje, *Bdud-'dul-rdo-rje*
Dujom Rinpoche, *Bdud-'joms Rin-po-che*
Dzangibu Rulakye, *'Dzang-gi-bu Ru-la-skyes*
Dzokchen Kunga Tashi, *Rdzogs-chen Kun-dga'-bkra-shis*
Dzokchen Ngedön Tenzin Zangpo, *Rdzogs-chen Nges-don-bstan-'dzin-bzang-po*
Dzokchen Pema Rikzin, *Rdzogs-chen Padma-rig-'dzin*
Dzokchen Sönam Rinchen, *Rdzogs-chen Bsod-nams-rin-chen*
Dzokchen Sönam Wangpo, *Rdzogs-chen Bsod-nams-dbang-po*
Gampopa, *Sgam-po-pa*
Gampopa Sönam Rinchen, *Sgam-po-pa Bsod-nams-rin-chen*
Gangzang Bumo Özer, *Gangs-bzang Bu-mo-'od-zer*
Garap Dorje, *Dga'-rab-rdo-rje*
Garwang Chökyi Wangchuk, *Gar-dbang-chos-kyi-dbang-phyug*
Garwang Dorje, *Gar-dbang-rdo-rje*
Garwang Kunga Tenzin, *Gar-dbang Kun-dga'-bstan-'dzin*
Gedün Gyeltsen, *Dge-'dun-rgyal-mtshan*
Gesar, *Ge-sar*
Gödemjen, *Rgod-ldem-can*
Gö Lotsawa Zhönu Pel, *'Gos-lo-tsā-ba Gzhon-nu-dpal*
Götshangpa, *Rgod-tshang-pa*
Gongma Drakpa Gyeltsen, *Gong-ma Grags-pa-rgyal-mtshan*
Gongra Lochen Zhenphen Dorje, *Gong-ra Lo-chen Gzhan-phan-rdo-rje*
Gönpo Dorje, *Mgon-po-rdo-rje*

Guru Chöwang, *Guru Chos-dbang*
Guru Dorje Gyelpo, *Guru Rdo-rje-rgyal-po*
Guru Shakya Dudül, *Guru Śākya-bdud-'dul*
Guru Sönam Tenzin, *Guru Bsod-nams-bstan-'dzin*
Guru Tashi, *Guru Bkra-shis*
Gyama Mingyurwa Letrho Lingpa, *Rgya-ma Mi-'gyur-ba Las-'phro-gling-pa*
Gyara Longchenpa, *Rgya-ra Klong-chen-pa*
Gyarawa, *Rgya-ra-ba*
Gyarong Sokmo Rinchen Dorje, *Rgya-rong Sog-mo Rin-chen-rdo-rje*
Gyatön Lozang Lekpa, *Rgya-ston Blo-bzang-legs-pa*
Gyatsün, *Rgya-btsun*
Gyelse Dawa Drakpa, *Rgyal-sras Zla-ba-grags-pa*
Gyel Thangpa Ngawang Zilnön Dorje, *Rgyal-thang-pa Ngag-dbang-zil-gnon-rdo-rje*
Gyel Thangpa Tönpa Senge, *Rgyal-thang-pa Ston-pa-seng-ge*
Gyurme Kunzang Namgyel, *'Gyur-med-kun-bzang-rnam-rgyal*
Hepa Chöjung, *He-pa Chos-'byung*
Jakhyung Ngawang Pema, *Bya-khyung Ngag-dbang-padma*
Jame Önpo Karma Namgyel, *Byams-me Dbon-po Karma-rnam-rgyal*
Jame Pholungpa, *Byams-me 'Pho-lung-pa*
Jampa Phüntshok, *Byams-pa-phun-tshogs*
Jamyang Chögyel Dorje, *'Jam-dbyangs-chos-rgyal-rdo-rje*
Jamyang Gyeltsen, *'Jam-dbyangs-rgyal-mtshan*
Jamyang Khyentse, *'Jam-dbyangs-mkhyen-brtse*
Jangchup Lingpa, *Byang-chub-gling-pa*
Jangchup Lingpa Sönam Chökyong, *Byang-chub-gling-pa Bsod-nams-chos-skyong*

Jangchup Senge, *Byang-chub-seng-ge*

Jangdak Rikzin Ngagi Wangpo, *Byang-bdag Rig-'dzin Ngag-gi-dbang-po*

Jangdak Tashi Topgyel, *Byang-bdag Bkra-shis-stobs-rgyal*

Jangsem Chöje, *Byang-sems-chos-rje*

Jatang Namkha Lhündrup, *Bya-btang Nam-mkha'-lhun-grub*

Jatrhi, *Bya-khri*

Jatsön Nyingpo, *'Ja'-tshon-snying-po*

Je Karma Thutop Namgyel, *Rje Karma-mthu-stobs-rnam-rgyal*

Jetsün Drakpa Rinpoche, *Rje-btsun-grags-pa Rin-po-che*

Jetsün Lhodrakpa, *Rje-btsun Lho-grags-pa*

Jikme Lingpa, *'Jigs-med-gling-pa*

Jikme Wangchuk, *'Jigs-med-dbang-phyugs*

Jikten Gönpo, *'Jig-rten-mgon-po*

Jomo Lhajema, *Jo-mo Lha-rje-ma*

Kachu Ngawang Pelgön, *Bka'-bcu Ngag-dbang-dpal-mgon*

Kadak Tingzin Chögyel, *Ka-dag Ting-'dzin-chos-rgyal*

Kagyu, Kagyupa, *Bka'-brgyud, Bka'-brgyud-pa*

Kangme Gyeltsen, *Rkang-med-rgyal-mtshan*

Karling, *Kar-gling*

Karma Chakme, *Karma-chags-med*

Karma Guru, *Karma-guru*

Karma Jangchup, *Karma-byang-chub*

Karma Kagyu, Kagyupa, *Karma Bka'-brgyud, Bka'-brgyud-pa*

Karma Kamtshang, *Karma Kam-tshang*

Karma Lingpa, *Karma-gling-pa*

Karma Mipham Trhinle Gyatso, *Karma Mi-pham-'phrin-las-rgya-mtsho*

Karma Migyur Wangyel, *Karma-mi-'gyur-dbang-rgyal*

Karma Namgyel, *Karma-rnam-rgyal*

Karmapa Chöying Dorje, *Karma-pa Chos-dbyings-rdo-rje*

Karmapa Thongwa Dönden, *Karma-pa Mthong-ba-don-ldan*

Karma Rikzin Nampar Gyelwa, *Karma-rig-'dzin-rnam-par-rgyal-ba*

Karma Samdrup, *Karma-bsam-'grub*

Karma Thutop Namgyel, *Karma-mthu-stobs-rnam-rgyal*

Karma Trhinle, *Karma-'phrin-las*

Kathokpa Könchok Senge, *Kaḥ-thog-pa Dkon-mchog-seng-ge*

Kathokpa Maṇi Rinchen, *Kaḥ-thog-pa Ma-ṇi Rin-chen*

Kathokpa Namkha Senge, *Kaḥ-thog-pa Nam-mkha'-seng-ge*

Khedrup Dongak Tenzin, *Mkhas-grub Mdo-sngags-bstan-'dzin*

Khedrup Kunga Lhündrup, *Mkhas-grub Kun-dga'-lhun-grub*

Khedrup Lhawang Tshenjen, *Mkhas-grub Lha-dbang-mtshan-can*

Khyentse Tashi Peljor, *Mkhyen-rtse Bkra-shis-dpal-'byor*

Khyung Gampo, *Khyung-sgam-po*

Khyungpo Neljor, *Khyung-po Rnal-'byor*

Kodrakpa Sönam Gyeltsen, *Ko-brag-pa Bsod-nams-rgyal-mtshan*

Könchok Dorje, *Dkon-mchog-rdo-rje*

Könchok Gyeltsen, *Dkon-mchog-rgyal-mtshan*

Könchok Senge, *Dkon-mchog-seng-ge*

Könchok Tashi, *Dkon-mchog-bkra-shis*

Könchok Yenlakbang, *Dkon-mchog-yan-lag-'bangs*

Kongpo Götshangpa, *Kong-po Rgod-tshang-pa*

Kongpo Thangdrok Tülku, *Kong-po Thang-'brog Sprul-sku*

Kunga Drakpa, *Kun-dga'-grags-pa*

Kunga Gyeltsen, *Kun-dga'-rgyal-mtshan*

Kunga Gyeltsen Pelzangpo, *Kun-dga'-rgyal-mtshan-dpal-bzang-po*

Kunga Lhündrup, *Kun-dga'-lhun-grub*

Kunga Namgyel, *Kun-dga'-rnam-rgyal*

Kunga Nyima Zangpo, *Kun-dga'-nyi-ma-bzang-po*

Kunga Peljor, *Kun-dga'-dpal-'byor*

Kunga Tashi, *Kun-dga'-bkra-shis*

Kunga Tshechok, *Kun-dga'-tshe-mchog*

Kunkhyen Chöku Özer, *Kun-mkhyen Chos-sku-'od-zer*

Kunrik, *Kun-rig*

Kuntu Zangpo, *Kun-tu-bzang-po*

Kunzang Dorje, *Kun-bzang-rdo-rje*

Kunzang Gyatso, *Kun-bzang-rgya-mtsho*

Kunzang Namgyel, *Kun-bzang-rnam-rgyal*

Kunzang Ngedön Longyang, *Kun-bzang-nges-don-klong-yangs*

Lachen Jampa Phüntshok, *Bla-chen Byams-pa-phun-tshogs*

Lang Darma, *Glang-dar-ma*

Langchen Pelgyi Senge, *Rlang-chen Dpal-gyi-seng-ge*

Lapdön Namkha Rinchen, *Lab-ston Nam-mkha'-rin-chen*

Laza Sönamtsho, *Bla-za Bsod-nams-mtsho*

Lekden Dorje, *Legs-ldan-rdo-rje*

Letrho Lingpa, *Las-'phro-gling-pa*

Lhadongpa, *Lha-gdong-pa*

Lhajema, *Lha-rje-ma*

Lhalung Pelgi Dorje, *Lha-lung Dpal-gyi-rdo-rje*

Lhawang Dorje, *Lha-dbang-rdo-rje*

Lhawang Namgyel, *Lha-dbang-rnam-rgyal*

Lhawang Tshenjen, *Lha-dbang-mtshan-can*
Lhazang Khan, *Lha-bzang Khan*
Lhazo Hepa Chöjung, *Lha-bzo He-pa-chos-'byung*
Lhewangpo, *Lha'i-dbang-po*
Ling Gesar, *Gling Ge-sar*
Lochak Norbu Zangpo, *Lo-phyag Nor-bu-bzang-po*
Lochen Dharma Shri, *Lo-chen Dharma-śrī*
Lodrö Gyeltsen, *Blo-gros-rgyal-mtshan*
Lodrö Senge, *Blo-gros-seng-ge*
Longam Tazi, *Long-ngam-rta-rdzi*
Longchenpa, *Klong-chen-pa*
Longchen Rapjampa, *Klong-chen-rab-'byams-pa*
Longsel Nyingpo, *Klong-gsal-snying-po*
Losel Tenkyong, *Blo-gsal-bstan-skyong*
Lozang Chökyi Gyeltsen, *Blo-bzang-chos-kyi-rgyal-mtshan*
Lozang Lekpa, *Blo-bzang-legs-pa*
Lu'i Wangpo, *Klu'i-dbang-po*
Lungzin Ngödrup Gyelpo, *Lung-zin Dngos-grub-rgyal-po*
Machik Zhama, *Ma-cig Zhwa-ma*
Ma Lotsawa, *Rma Lo-tsā-ba*
Maṇi Rinchen, *Ma-ṇi Rin-chen*
Marpa Chökyi Lodrö, *Mar-pa Chos-kyi-blo-gros*
Ma Setokden, *Rma-se-rtogs-ldan*
Menlungpa Shakya Ö, *Sman-lung-pa Śākya-'od*
Mentsewa Matidhāja, *Sman-rtse-ba Mati-dhāja*
Mikyö Dorje, *Mi-bskyod-rdo-rje*
Milarepa, *Mi-la-ras-pa*
Minling Trhichen Pema Gyurme Gyatso, *Smin-gling Khri-chen Padma-'gyur-med-rgya-mtsho*
Mingyur Dorje, *Mi-'gyur-rdo-rje*
Mingyur Letrho Lingpa, *Mi-'gyur Las-phro-gling-pa*
Minyak, *Mi-nyag*

Mitok Thupa, *Mi-rtog-thub-pa*
Mönluk, *Mon-lugs*
Munetsenpo, *Mu-ne-brtsan-po*
Nakpo Gung Phurwa, *Nag-po-dgung-'phur-ba*
Nakpo Thokphen, *Nag-po-thog-'phen*
Nakpo Trhakyuk, *Nag-po-khrag-skyugs*
Namdröl Yeshe Zangpo, *Rnam-grol-ye-shes-bzang-po*
Namdröl Zangpo, *Rnam-grol-bzang-po*
Namgyel Zangpo, *Rnam-rgyal-bzang-po*
Namkha Chökyi Gyatso, *Nam-mkha'-chos-kyi-rgya-mtsho*
Namkha Dorje, *Nam-mkha'-rdo-rje*
Namkha Lekpa, *Nam-mkha'-legs-pa*
Namkha Ösel, *Nam-mkha'-'od-gsal*
Namkha Pel, *Nam-mkha'-dpal*
Namkha Rinchen, *Nam-mkha'-rin-chen*
Namkha Sangye, *Nam-mkha'-sangs-rgyas*
Namkha Senge, *Nam-mkha'-seng-ge*
Namkha Shenyen, *Nam-mkha'-bshes-gnyen*
Nangselwa Tashi Gyatso, *Snang-gsal-ba Bkra-shis-rgya-mtsho*
Natsok Rangdröl, *Sna-tshogs-rang-grol*
Nedo, Nedoluk, *Gnas-mdo, Gnas-mdo-lugs*
Neljorpa Zhiwa Ö, *Rnal-'byor-pa Zhi-ba-'od*
Ngadak Kunga Lhündrup, *Mnga'-bdag Kun-dga'-lhun-grub*
Ngadak Nyang Relpajen, *Mnga'-bdag Nyang-ral-pa-can*
Ngagi Wangpo, *Ngag-gi-dbang-po*
Ngak Chang Letrho Lingpa, *Sngag-'chang Las-'phro-gling-pa*
Ngamdzong Repa, *Ngam-rdzong-ras-pa*
Ngari Lekden Dorje, *Mnga'-ris Legs-ldan-rdo-rje*

Ngari Panchen Pema Wangyel, *Mnga'-ris Paṇ-chen Padma-dbang-rgyal*
Ngarlekye, *Ngar-las-skye*
Ngawang Gyeltsen, *Ngag-dbang-rgyal-mtshan*
Ngawang Lozang Gyatso, *Ngag-dbang-blo-bzang-rgya-mtsho*
Ngawang Namgyel, *Ngag-dbang-rnam-rgyal*
Ngawang Pelgön, *Ngag-dbang-dpal-mgon*
Ngawang Pema, *Ngag-dbang-padma*
Ngawang Yeshe Drupa, *Ngag-dbang-ye-shes-grub-pa*
Ngedön Tenzin, *Nges-don-bstan-'dzin*
Ngedön Tenzin Zangpo, *Nges-don-bstan-'dzin-bzang-po*
Ngödrup, *Dngos-grub*
Ngödrup Gyelpo, *Dngos-grub-rgyal-po*
Ngönshejen, *Mngon-shes-can*
Norbu Zangpo, *Nor-bu-bzang-po*
Nüden Dorje, *Nus-ldan-rdo-rje*
Nyangrel Nyima Özer, *Nyang-ral Nyi-ma-'od-zer*
Nyatrhi, *Nya-khri*
Nyatrhi Tsenpo, *Gnya'-khri-btsan-po*
Nyakrong Zhakla Yeshebum, *Nyag-rong Bzhag-bla Ye-shes-'bum*
Nyaktrhi Tsenpo, *Nyag-khri-btsan-po*
Nyakyhi, *Nya-khyi*
Nyendön Dorje Yeshe, *Gnyan-ston Rdo-rje-ye-shes*
Nyida Chöje, *Nyi-zla-chos-rje*
Nyida Longsel, *Nyi-zla-klong-gsal*
Nyida Özer, *Nyi-zla-'od-zer*
Nyida Sangye, *Nyi-zla-sangs-rgyas*
Nyima Drakpa, *Nyi-ma-grags-pa*
Nyima Özer, *Nyi-ma-'od-zer*
Nyingma, Nyingmapa, *Rnying-ma, Rnying-ma-pa*

Nyö, *Gnyos, Smyos*
Öde Purgyel, *'O-lde-spu-rgyal*
Ökyi Thajen, *'Od-kyi-mtha'-can*
Önpo Gyeltsen, *Dbon-po-rgyal-mtshan*
Orgyen Chögyel, *O-rgyan-chos-rgyal*
Orgyen Gyurme Tenphel Gyatso, *O-rgyan 'Gyur-med-bstan-'phel-rgya-mtsho*
Orgyen Lingpa, *O-rgyan-gling-pa*
Orgyen Lodrö, *O-rgyan-blo-gros*
Orgyen Rikzin Chögyel, *O-rgyan Rig-'dzin-chos-rgyal*
Orgyen Rikzin Gyatso, *O-rgyan Rig-'dzin-rgya-mtsho*
Orgyen Rikzin Namgyel, *O-rgyan Rig-'dzin-rnam-rgyal*
Orgyen Tenzin, *O-rgyan-bstan-'dzin*
Orgyen Tenzin Drakpa, *O-rgyan Bstan-'dzin-grags-pa*
Ösel Longyang, *'Od-gsal-klong-yangs*
Özer Zangpo, *'Od-zer-bzang-po*
Panchen Lama Lozang Chökyi Gyeltsen, *Paṇ-chen Bla-ma Blo-bzang-chos-kyi-rgyal-mtshan*
Panchen Sönam Drakpa, *Paṇ-chen Bsod-nams-grags-pa*
Pangdön Karma Guru, *Dpang-ston Karma-guru*
Pawo, *Dpa'-bo*
Pawo Tsuklak Gyatso, *Dpa'-bo Gtsug-lag-rgya-mtsho*
Pelgi Dorje, *Dpal-gyi-rdo-rje*
Pel Orgyen Tenzin, *Dpal O-rgyan-bstan-'dzin*
Peling, *Pad-gling*
Peling Sungtrül Tenzin Drakpa, *Pad-gling Gsung-sprul Bstan-'dzin-grags-pa*
Peling Sungtrül Tshültrhim Dorje, *Pad-gling Gsung-sprul Tshul-khrims-rdo-rje*

Peling Thukse Tenzin Gyurme Dorje, *Pad-gling Thugs-sras Bstan-'dzin-'gyur-med-rdo-rje*
Pelpung, *Dpal-spungs*
Pema Garwang Dorje, *Padma-gar-dbang-rdo-rje*
Pema Garwang Gyurme Dorje, *Padma-gar-dbang-'gyur-med-rdo-rje*
Pema Gyeltsen, *Padma-rgyal-mtshan*
Pema Gyurme Gyatso, *Padma-'gyur-med-rgya-mtsho*
Pema Karpo, *Padma-dkar-po*
Pema Lekdrup, *Padma-legs-grub*
Pema Lingpa, *Padma-gling-pa*
Pemalodrö, *Padma-blo-gros*
Pemamati, *Padma-mati*
Pema Rikzin, *Padma-rig-'dzin*
Pema Thekchok Tenpe Gyeltsen, *Padma-theg-mchog Bstan-pa'i-rgyal-mtshan*
Pema Trhinle, *Padma-'phrin-las*
Pema Wangdrak, *Padma-dbang-drag*
Pema Wangyel, *Padma-dbang-rgyal*
Phadampa Sangye, *Pha-dam-pa Sang-rgyas*
Phakmo Drü, Phakmo Drüpa, *Phag-mo-gru, Phag-mo-gru-pa*
Phakmo Drüpa Dorje Gyelpo, *Phag-mo-gru-pa Rdo-rje-rgyal-po*
Pholungpa Karma Samdrup, *'Pho-lung-pa Karma-bsam-grub*
Pönlop Namkha Ösel, *Dpon-slob Nam-mkha'-'od-gsal*
Pude Gungyel, *Spu-de-gung-rgyal*
Pükyibu Ngarlekye, *Spus-kyi-bu Ngar-las-skyes*
Puṇya Shri, *Puṇya-śrī*
Rāgasya Karma Chakme, *Rāgasya Karma-chags-med*
Ratna Lingpa, *Ratna-gling-pa*
Rechung Dorje Drak, *Ras-chung Rdo-rje-grags*

Rikzin Chenpo Sönam Namgyel, *Rig-'dzin-chen-po Bsod-nams-rnam-rgyal*
Rikzin Gödemjen, *Rig-'dzin Rgod-ldem-can*
Rikzin Kunga Drakpa, *Rig-'dzin Kun-dga'-grags-pa*
Rikzin Nyima Drakpa, *Rig-'dzin Nyi-ma-grags-pa*
Rikzin Orgyen Chögyel, *Rig-'dzin O-rgyan-chos-rgyal*
Rikzin Sönam Özer, *Rig-'dzin Bsod-nams-'od-zer*
Rikzin Tenkyong Gyatso, *Rig-'dzin Bstan-skyong-rgya-mtsho*
Rinchen Chögyel, *Rin-chen-chos-rgyal*
Rinchen Namgyel, *Rin-chen-rnam-rgyal*
Rinchen Phüntshok, *Rin-chen-phun-tshogs*
Rinchen Phüntshok Chökyi Gyelpo, *Rin-chen-phun-tshogs-chos-kyi-rgyal-po*
Rongdön Chenpo Namkha Dorje, *Rong-ston-chen-po Nam-mkha'-rdo-rje*
Rongpo Könchok Dorje, *Rong-po Dkon-mchog-rdo-rje*
Rulakye, *Ru-la-skyes*
Sakya, Sakyapa, *Sa-skya, Sa-skya-pa*
Sakyapa Pelden Zangpo, *Sa-skya-pa Dpal-ldan-bzang-po*
Samphel Döndrup, *Bsam-'phel-don-grub*
Sangdak Trhinle Lhündrup, *Gsang-bdag 'Phrin-las-lhun-grub*
Sangye Drime, *Sangs-rgyas-dri-med*
Sangye Gonglawa, *Sangs-rgyas Gong-la-ba*
Sangye Gyatso, *Sangs-rgyas-rgya-mtsho*
Sangye Lingpa, *Sangs-rgyas-gling-pa*
Sangye Mikyö Dorje, *Sangs-rgyas Mi-bskyod-rdo-rje*
Sangye Tenpa, *Sangs-rgyas-bstan-pa*
Sarma, Sarmapa, *Gsar-ma, Gsar-ma-pa*

Sedengpa Sangye Pel, *Se-sdeng-pa Sangs-rgyas-dpal*

Serlo Tenpa Gyeltsen, *Gser-lo Bstan-pa-rgyal-mtshan*

Serlo Tönpa Gyeltsen, *Gser-lo Ston-pa-rgyal-mtshan*

Se'ula Jamgön Ngawang Gyeltsen, *Se'u-la Byams-mgon Ngag-dbang-rgyal-mtshan*

Shakya Dudül, *Śākya-bdud-'dul*

Shakya Ö, *Śākya-'od*

Shakyhi, *Sha-khyi*

Shangpo Riwoche, *Shangs-po Ri-bo-che*

Shatrhi, *Sha-khri*

Shazukpa, *Sha-gzugs-pa*

Sherap Özer, *Shes-rab-'od-zer*

Shinje Chökyi Gyelpo, *Gshin-rje Chos-kyi-rgyal-po*

Sokbom Dawa, *Sog-'bom-mda'-ba*

Sokdokpa Lodrö Gyeltsen, *Sog-bzlog-pa Blo-gros-rgyal-mtshan*

Sönambum, *Bsod-nams-'bums*

Sönam Drakpa, *Bsod-nams-grags-pa*

Sönam Gyatso, *Bsod-nams-rgya-mtsho*

Sönam Gyeltsen, *Bsod-nams-rgyal-mtshan*

Sönam Namgyel, *Bsod-nams-rnam-rgyal*

Sönam Özer, *Bsod-nams-'od-zer*

Sönam Pel, *Bsod-nams-dpal*

Sönam Rinchen, *Bsod-nams-rin-chen*

Sönam Tenzin, *Bsod-nams-bstan-'dzin*

Sönam Wangchuk, *Bsod-nams-dbang-phyug*

Sönam Wangpo, *Bsod-nams-dbang-po*

Songtsen Gampo, *Srong-bstan-sgam-po*

Sordrangpa Zhönu Tshewang, *Sor-'brang-pa Gzhon-nu-tshe-dbang*

Sumdar Gyelpo, *Sum-dar-rgyal-po*

Sungtrül Tshültrhim Dorje, *Gsung-sprul Tshul-khrims-rdo-rje*

Takla, Taklaluk, *Stag-bla, Stag-bla-lugs*

Takla Pema Gyeltsen, *Stag-bla Padma-rgyal-mtshan*

Takla Pemamati, *Stag-bla Padma-mati*

Takshampa Nüden Dorje, *Stag-sham-pa Nus-ldan-rdo-rje*

Tashi Gyatso, *Bkra-shis-rgya-mtsho*

Tashi Peljor, *Bkra-shis-dpal-'byor*

Tashi Tseringma, *Bkra-shis Tshe-ring-ma*

Tashi Zangpo, *Bkra-shis-bzang-po*

Tenpa Gyeltsen, *Bstan-pa-rgyal-mtshan*

Tenpa Tshering, *Bstan-pa-tshe-ring*

Tenpe Gyeltsen, *Bstan-pa'i-rgyal-mtshan*

Tenyi Lingpa, *Bstan-gnyis-gling-pa*

Tenzin Chökyi Gyelpo, *Bstan-'dzin-chos-kyi-rgyal-po*

Tenzin Dorje, *Bstan-'dzin-rdo-rje*

Tenzin Drakpa, *Bstan-'dzin-grags-pa*

Tenzin Gyurme Dorje, *Bstan-'dzin 'Gyur-med-rdo-rje*

Terdak Lingpa, *Gter-bdag-gling-pa*

Thangtong Gyelpo, *Thang-stong-rgyal-po*

Thongwa Dönden, *Mthong-ba-don-ldan*

Thukje Özer, *Thugs-rje-'od-zer*

Tönpa Gyeltsen, *Ston-pa-rgyal-mtshan*

Tönpa Senge, *Ston-pa-seng-ge*

Trhi Detsuktsen, *Khri Lde-gtsug-btsan*

Trhi Dudumtsen, *Khri Bdu-dum-brtsan*

Trhi Songdetsen, *Khri Srong-lde-btsan*

Trhimkhang Lotsawa, *Khrims-khang lo-tsā-ba*

Trhinle Dorje, *'Phrin-las-rdo-rje*

Trhinle Lhündrup, *'Phrin-las-lhun-grub*

Trhitsün, *Khri-btsun*

Trhophu Lotsawa, *Khro-phu-lo-tsā-ba*

Trhülzhik Chenpo, *'Khrul-zhig-chen-po*

Trhülzhik Serlo Tenpa Gyeltsen, *'Khrul-zhig Gser-lo Bstan-pa-rgyal-mtshan*

Tsangnyön Heruka, *Gtsang-smyon He-ru-ka*

Tsele Natsok Rangdröl, *Rtse-le Sna-tshogs-rang-grol*

Tsele Sönam Namgyel, *Rtse-le Bsod-nams-rnam-rgyal*

Tseringma, *Tshe-ring-ma*

Tshangyang Gyatso, *Tshangs-dbyangs-rgya-mtsho*

Tshepong, *Tshe-pong*

Tshültrhim Dorje, *Tshul-khrims-rdo-rje*

Tshungme Tenzin Dorje, *Mtshungs-med Bstan-'dzin-rdo-rje*

Tsi'u Marpo, *Tsi'u-dmar-po*

Tsöndrü Bumpa, *Brtson-'grus-'bum-pa*

Tsöndrü Gyatso, *Brtson-grus-rgya-mtsho*

Tsongkhapa Lozang Drakpa, *Tsong-kha-pa Blo-bzang-grags-pa*

Tsuklak Gyatso, *Gtsug-lag-rgya-mtsho*

Tsukna Rinchen, *Gtsug-na-rin-chen*

Tsünmojen, *Btsun-mo-can*

Tshurdön Wange, *Mtshur-ston Dbang-nge*

Tülku Natsok Rangdröl, *Sprul-sku Sna-tshogs-rang-grol*

Tülku Thukje Özer, *Sprul-sku Thugs-rje-'od-zer*

Wang Chökyi Gyelpo, *Dbang-chos-kyi-rgyal-po*

Wangdrak Sung, *Dbang-drag-gsungs*

Wangi Dorje, *Dbang-gi-rdo-rje*

Yangjen Gawe Lodrö, *Dbyangs-can-dga'-ba'i-blo-gros*

Yangönpa, *Yang-dgon-pa*

Yangyel, *Yang-rgyal*

Yardön Umapa, *Dbyar-ston Dbu-ma-pa*
Yarlha Shampo, *Yar-lha-sham-po*
Yeshebum, *Ye-shes-'bum*
Yeshe Lodrö, *Ye-shes-blo-gros*
Yeshe Tshogyel, *Ye-shes-mtsho-rgyal*
Yonge Mingyur Dorje, *Yongs-dge Mi-'gyur-rdo-rje*
Yungdrung Gyen, *G.yung-drung-rgyan*
Zhakla Yeshebum, *Bzhag-bla Ye-shes-'bum*
Zhalu Ribuk Tülku Losel Tenkyong, *Zhwa-lu Ri-sbug-sprul-sku Blo-gsal-bstan-skyong*
Zhamarpa, *Zhwa-dmar-pa*
Zhamar Garwang Chökyi Wangchuk, *Zhwa-dmar Gar-dbang-chos-kyi-dbang-phyug*
Zhamarpa Cenga Chödrakpa, *Zhwa-dmar-pa Spyan-snga Chos-grags-pa*
Zhamarpa Chökyi Wangchuk, *Zhwa-dmar-pa Chos-kyi-dbang-phyug*
Zhamarpa Khachö Wangpo, *Zhwa-dmar-pa Mkha'-spyod-dbang-po*
Zhamarpa Könchok Yenlakbang, *Zhwa-dmar-pa Dkon-mchog-yan-lag-'bangs*
Zhang Rinpoche, *Zhang Rin-po-che*
Zhang Yudrakpa Tsöndru Drakpa, *Zhang G.yu-brag-pa Brtson-'grus-grags-pa*
Zhapdrung Ngawang Namgyel, *Zhabs-drung Ngag-dbang-rnam-rgya*
Zhapdrung Pema Trhinle, *Zhabs-drung Padma-'phrin-las*
Zhapdrung Sungtrül Chokle Namgyel, *Zhabs-drung Gsung-sprul Phyogs-las-rnam-rgyal*
Zhechen Rapjampa Tenpe Gyeltsen, *Zhe-chen Rab-'byams-pa Bstan-pa'i-rgyal-mtshan*

Zhelop Rinpoche Chödenpa, *Zhal-slob Rin-po-che Chos-ldan-pa*
Zhikpo Lingpa, *Zhig-po-gling-pa*
Zhönu Döndrup, *Gzhon-nu-don-'grub*
Zhönu Lodrö, *Gzhon-nu-blo-gros*
Zurchen Chöying Rangdröl, *Zur-chen Chos-dbyings-rang-grol*

Place Names

Akhyok, *A-'khyog*
Baden, *Ba-dan*
Barkham, *Bar-khams*
Bubor, *Bu-'bor*
Bubor Gang, *Bu-'bor-sgang*
Bumthang, *Bum-thang*
Chakbel, *Phyag-sbal*
Chak Jamchup Ling, *Chags Byang-chub-gling*
Chakri, *Chags-ri*
Chakri Kha, *Chags-ri-kha*
Chakru, *Chags-ru*
Chakru Ösel, *Chags-ru 'Od-gsal*
Cham, *Cham*
Chamda, *Cham-da*
Chari, *Char-ri*
Chingwa, *'Phying-ba*
Chingyul, *'Phying-yul*
Chödenpa, *Chos-ldan-pa*
Chökhor Tse, *Chos-'khor-rtse*
Chongye, *'Phyong-rgyas*
Chongye Pelri Thekchen Ling, *'Phyong-rgyas Dpal-ri Theg-chen-gling*
Chusöl, *Chu-gsol*
Da Rinchen Ling, *Mda'-rin-chen-gling*
Daklha Gampo, *Dwags-lha-sgam-po*
Dakpo, *Dwags-po*
Dargye Chöding/Dargye Chöling, *Dar-rgyas-chos-sding/Dar-rgyas-chos-gling*
Darthang, *Dar-thang*
Dekyi Ling, *Sde-skyid-gling*
Den(khok), *Ldan[-khog]*
Derge, *Sde-dge*
Dokham, *Mdo-khams*
Dola, *Do-la*
Dome, *Mdo-smad*
Dorje, *Rdo-rje*
Dorje Drak, *Rdo-rje-brag*
Dorje Nying Dzong, *Rdo-rje-snying-rdzong*

Drachi, *Grwa-phyi*
Drak Langa Marpo, *Brag Sla-nga-dmar-po*
Drakpo, *Brag-po*
Dranang, *Grwa-nang*
Dregön Sar, *Bres-dgon-gsar*
Dreyul, *'Bras-yul*
Drigung, *'Bri-gung*
Drigungthil, *'Bri-gung-mthil*
Driru, *'Bri-ru*
Drugu Gyara, *Gru-gu Rgya-ra*
Dudül Ngakpa Ling, *Bdud-'dul-sngags-pa-gling*
Dung, *Dung*
Dzayul, *Rdza-yul*
Dzinpa, *'Dzin-pa*
Dzokchen, *Rdzogs-chen*
Dzokchen Orgyen Samten Ling, *Rdzogs-chen O-rgyan-bsam-gtan-gling*
Eyul, *E-yul*
Gampodar, *Sgam-po-gdar*
Gangri Karpo Chu, *Gangs-ri-dkar-po-chu*
Gangteng Sangak Chöling, *Sgang-steng Gsang-sngags-chos-gling*
Gangtok, *Sgang-tog*
Garzha, *Gar-zhwa*
Gegye, *Dge-rgyas [bye-ma-gling]*
Genden Phüntshok Ling, *Dge-ldan-phun-tshogs-gling*
Gongra, *Gong-ra*
Gongra Lhündrup Chöding, *Gong-ra Lhun-grub-chos-sding*
Gonjo, *Go-'jo*
Guge, *Gu-ge*
Guru Dorje Gyelpo, *Guru Rdo-rje-rgyal-po*
Guru Lhakhang, *Guru Lha-khang*
Gyadrong, *Rgya-grong*
Gyama, *Rgya-ma*
Gyangkhar, *Rgyang-'khar*
Gyantse, *Rgyal-rtse*
Gyarong, *Rgya-rong*
Gyarong Sok, *Rgya-rong Sog*
Gyatön, *Rgya-ston*
Gyemen/Gyelmen, *Rgyas-sman/ Rgyal-sman*
Jambaling, *Byams-pa-gling*
Jamdrin, *Byams-sprin*
Jangchup Ling, *Byang-chub-gling*
Jangmeling, *Byang-me-ling*

Jangseng, *Byang-seng*
Kangme, *Rkang-smad*
Ka'ok Ngak Drong, *Ka-'og-sngags-grong*
Kathok, *Kaḥ-thog*
Kathok Dorjeden, *Kaḥ-thog Rdo-rje-gdan*
Kham, *Khams*
Khamshak, *Kham-shag*
Khamtö, *Khams-stod*
Khangsar Dzong, *Khang-gsar-rdzong*
Kharchu Dujom Ling, *Mkhar-chu Bdud-'joms-gling*
Khardo, *Mkhar-mdo*
Kyechu Lhakhang, *Bskyed-chu lha-khang*
Khyerdrup, *Khyer-grub*
Khyungpo, *Khyung-po*
Khyungtshang, *Khyung-tshang*
Kongpo, *Kong-po*
Kubum, *Sku-'bum*
Kulha Karpo, *Sku-lha-dkar-po*
Kyepuk, *Skyed-spug*
Langthang, *Glang-thang*
Lhalung, *Lha-lung*
Lhalung Lhündrup, *Lha-lung Lhun-grub*
Lhari, *Lha-ri*
Lhasa, *Lha-sa*
Lhodrak, *Lho-brag*
Lhogyü, *Lho-rgyud*
Lhokhok, *Lho-khog*
Lhorong, *Lho-rong*
Lhündrup, *Lhun-grub*
Lhündrup Ding, *Lhun-grub-sding*
Lhündrup Phodrang, *Lhun-grub-pho-brang*
Lhüngdrup Teng, *Lung-grub-steng*
Ling, *Gling*
Lingtshang, *Gling-tshang*
Lithang, *Li-thang*
Lohita, *Lo-hi-ta*
Longpo, *Long-po*
Longpo Dechen, *Long-po Bde-chen*
Longpo Tsikar, *Long-po Rtsi-dkar*
Mangyul, *Mang-yul*
Mawachok, *Smra-ba-cog*
Menling, *Sman-gling*
Menmo, *Sman-mo*
Menmo Tashi Gön, *Sman-mo Bkra-shis-mgon*
Menthang, *Man-thang*

Mindroling, *Smin-grol-gling*
Minyak, *Mi-nyag*
Mönyul, *Mon-yul*
Muksang, *Rmug-bsangs*
Mustang, *Mu-stang*
Nabün Dzong, *Na-bun-rdzong*
Namgyel Jangchup Ling, *Nam-rgyal-byang-chub-gling*
Namgyeltse, *Rnam-rgyal-rtse*
Namtsho, *Gnam-mtsho*
Nangchen, *Nang-chen*
Nedo, *Gnas-mdo*
Nemtshar Pangjin/Pangjip, *Nem-tshar Spangs-lcin[-lcib?]*
Nenang, *Gnas-nang*
Ngari, *Mnga'-ris*
Ngomyul, *Ngom-yul*
Nyakrong, *Nyag-rong*
Nyangchu Kyamo, *Nyang-chu-skya-mo*
Nyangpo, *Nyang-po*
Nyel, *Gnyal*
Nyenchen Thanglha, *Gnyan-chen-thang-lha*
Nyide, *Nyi-lde*
Orgyen, *O-rgyan*
Orgyen Mindroling, *O-rgyan Smin-grol-gling*
Orgyen Samten Ling, *O-rgyan-bsam-gtan-gling*
Orgyen Tsemo, *O-rgyan-rtse-mo*
Ösel Ling, *'Od-gsal-gling*
Paro, *Spa-gro*
Paro Taktshang, *Spa-gro Stag-tshang*
Payul, *Dpal-yul*
Pel Chökhor Tse, *Dpal Chos-'khor-rtse*
Pelgi Khamshak, *Dpal-gyi-kham-shag*
Pel Rinchen Ling, *Dpal-rin-chen-gling*
Pemakö, *Padma-bkod*
Phodrang Numda, *Pho-brang Snum-mda'*
Powo, *Spo-bo*
Rezhek Zhechen, *Re-zheg Zhe-chen*
Rigül Gön, *Ri-'gul-dgon*
Rikhugön, *Ri-khud-dgon*
Rinpung, *Rin-spungs*
Riwoche, *Ri-bo-che*
Rong, *Rong*
Rongchu, *Rong-chu*

Rongkor, *Rong-skor*
Rongyul, *Rong-yul*
Rudam, *Ru-dam*
Rudam Kyitrham, *Ru-dam Skyid-khram*
Samten Chöling, *Bsam-gtan-chos-gling*
Samye, *Bsam-yas*
Sangak Ling, *Gsang-sngags-gling*
Shar, *Shar*
Sharyi Phuk, *Shar-yi-phug*
Shokdu Chu, *Shog-rdu-chu*
Sin Dzong, *Srin-rdzong*
Sin Dzong Ne, *Srin-rdzong-gnas*
Singmo Dzong, *Sring-mo-rdzong*
Sinmo, *Srin-mo*
Sinmo Dzong, *Srin-mo-rdzong*
Sinpo, *Srin-po*
Sok Dzamthang, *Sog Dzam-thang*
Sok Langa Marpo, *Sog Sla-nga-dmar-po*
Sok Zamkhar, *Sog Zam-khar*
Sok Zamtsha, *Sog Zam-tsha*
Sokpo Gomang Chöje, *Sog-po Sgo-mang Chos-rje*
Sosaling, *Sosa-gling*
Takgang, *Stag-sgang*
Takmogang, *Stag-mo-sgang*
Takmogang Kelzang Phüntshok Ling, *Stag-mo-sgang Bskal-bzang-phun-tshogs-gling*
Tamda, *Rta-mda*
Tamnyong/Tamnyok Gyadrong, *Gtam-myong/ Gtam-myog Rgya-grong*
Tamshul, *Gtam-shul*
Tana Gön, *Rta-rna-dgon*
Tashi Chöling, *Bkra-shis-chos-gling*
Tashigang, *Bkra-shis-sgang*
Tashi Menmo, *Bkra-shis-sman-mo*
Tawang, *Rta-dbang*
Tengyeling, *Bstan-rgyas-gling*
Thakar, *Mtha'-dkar*
Thangdrok, *Thang-'brog*
Thangdrok Öseltse, *Thang-'brog 'Od-gsal-rtse*
Tise, *Ti-se*
Trhadruk, *Khra-'brug*

Tsang, *Gtsang*
Tsangpo, *Gtsang-po*
Tsangpo Gogu, *Gtsang-po Mgo-dgu*
Tsangrong, *Gtsang-rong*
Tsari, *Tsa-ri*
Tsele, *Rtse-le*
Tsele Gongok, *Rtse-le Gong-'og*
Tshemyul, *Tshem-yul*
Tshome, *Mtsho-smad*
Tshona, *Mtsho-sna*
Tshurphu, *Mtshur-phu*
Tsi'u Marjok Ukhang, *Tsi-'u-dmar-lcog dbug-khang*
Ü, *Dbus*
Ukpalung/Ukpajalung, *'Ug-pa-lung/'Ug-pa-bya-lung*

Yangpajen, *Yangs-pa-can*
Yarlha Shampo, *Yar-lha-sham-po*
Yarlung, *Yar-lung*
Yeru, *G.yas-ru*
Yetsher, *G.yas-mtsher*
Yumtsho, *Yum-mtsho*
Zangchu, *Zangs-chu*
Zangtsho, *Zangs-mtsho*
Zaplam Dorje Rawa, *Zab-lam Rdo-rje'i-ra-ba*
Zhalu, *Zhwa-lu*
Zhechen, *Zhe-chen*
Zhechen Gön, *Zhe-chen-dgon*
Zhikatse, *Gzhis-ka-rtse*

Zhingkyong Ghayadara *Zhing-skyong Gha-ya-rda-ra*
Zhotö Tidro, *Zho-stod Ti-sgro*
Zurmang, *Zur-mang*
Zur Ukpalung, *Zur 'Ug-pa-lung*

General Terms

bardo, *bar-do*
la, *bla*
lama, *bla-ma*
lu, *klu*
terma, *gter-ma*
tertön, *gter-ston*
tülku, *sprul-sku*

Index

Derge, 151, 167, 181, 187, 191, 194–196, 200, 262n.9
Desi Sangye Gyatso, 181, 189, 197–198, 266n.78
desire, as existence realm, 40, 111
destiny, based on wealth, 76, 234n.31
Dewa Pema, 123
dharma protectors, as treasure, 103, 111–113
Dharma Shri. See Lochen Dharma Shri
Dilgo Khyentse Tashi Peljor, 210
direct encounter, as bardo category, 53
direct personal introduction, to texts, 108–109, 114, 118, 130
direct transcendence, 61, 109
disciples, sun-moon, 92, 120–122, 248n.4–n.16
disposal. See burial; funeral rituals
divine laws, 112
dmu, 30, 223n.22
doctrine-masters, 120, 171, 187, 194, 197
Dokham, 128, 251n.58
Dolung Chipön, 210
Dome, 199
Dong (clan), 56
Dongak Lingpa, 125
Dongak Tenzin, 166, 168, 260n.37, 260n.40
Dorje, 182
Dorje Drak, 20, 139, 188, 263n.38
Dorje Gönpo, 195
Dorje Lekpa, 112
Dorje Lodrö, 145
Dorje Nying Dzong, 184, 188
Dortshang Trhinle Dorje, 199
Drachi, 194
Drak Langa Marpo, 184
Drakarpo (clan), 182
Drakpa Özer, 67
Drakpo, 89
drama, as judgement of the dead, 94–95
Dranang, 165, 170
dreams, in bardo, 35, 47–49, 51, 53, 56, 229n.59
dredging-the-depths tradition, 155, 157, 258n.108
Dregön Sar monastery, 189
Drepa Jamyang Chögyel Dorje, 189
Dreyul, 189
Drigum Tsenpo, 17, 30–31, 223n.33
Drigung, 50, 95, 160
Drigung Pholungpa Karma Samdrup, 185, 263n.29
Drigungpa (sect), 147
Drigungpa Rinchen Phüntshok, 95, 128, 142, 145–147, 160–161
Drigungthil. See Drigung
Driru, 186
Drodokpa Namkha Pel, 141, 144
Drodül Letrho Lingpa, 160, 258n.7
Dru (clan), 123
Drukchen Gyelwang Chöje, 128
Drukpa Gyelwang Je Kunga Peljor, 128, 159

Drukpa sect. See Kagyupa (Kagyu)
Drung Chödenpa, 123–124. See also Gönpo Dorje
Drung Lhawang Dorje. See Lhawang Dorje
Drung Namkha Senge, 131, 141, 144–145, 254n.30
Drung tradition, of Kathok, 142–147, 171
Drungchö Dorje Tokden, 123–124
Drungpa Lodrö Senge, 124
Drungpa Rinpoche Chönyi Gyatso, 150–151
Drungpa Rinpoche Kunga Gyeltsen, 150
Drungpa Rinpoche Kunga Namgyel, 153
Drupchen Kunzang Dorje, 160
Dudül Dorje, 144, 181, 187, 196
Dudül Ngakpa Ling, 207
Dujom Rinpoche, 82, 103, 109, 147, 243n.7
Dumézil, Georges, 219n.40
Dung monstery, 159
Dunhuang manuscripts, 28–30, 37, 110, 222n.2, 224n.36
Dzangibu Rulakye, 30
Dzayul, 129
Dzokchen Kunga Tashi, 159
Dzokchen monastery, 137, 139, 148, 159, 195, 205, 210
bardo innovations in, 56–68, 83, 93
Dzokchen Ngedön Tenzin Zangpo, 204–205, 210
Dzokchen Orgyen Samten Ling, 195
Dzokchen Pema Rikzin, 181, 186–189, 194–197, 266n.71
Dzokchen Sönam Rinchen, 159–160, 168, 171
Dzokchen Sönam Wangpo, 66, 148, 171–172
Dzokchen texts, on bardo, 231n.117, 232n.129

earth, in intermediate state interpretations, 43, 69
effigy, framework, of deceased, 71–72, 74, 76
Egyptian Book of the Dead, 218n.11
Elimination of All Evil Rebirths, 21
emanation body, of buddha, 44, 59–60
embodied beings, as bardo category, 52–53
emperors, impact on translations, 17
energy, in bardo, 59–60
enjoyment body, of buddha, 44, 59–60
enlightenment, in bardo, 59–60, 63
esoteric interpretations, 6–7, 17, 219n.44
essence, in bardo, 59
ethnographic data, on bardo, 69, 241n.37
European interpretations, 4, 18, 174, 221n.70
Evans-Wentz, Walter Yeeling, 3, 5, 7, 38, 117, 211, 218n.11–n.14
edition of Liberation upon Hearing, 206–207
evil spirits, protection against, 70, 72–73, 111–113

Tshurphu monastery, 153
Tsi'u Marjok Ukhang, 55
Tsi'u Marpo, 55
Tsöndrü Bumpa. *See* Drung Namkha
Senge
Tsöndrü Gyatso, 157
Tsongkhapa Lozang Drakpa, 50
Tsuklak Gyatso. *See* Pawo Tsuklak Gyatso
Tsukna Rinchen, 92
Tsünmojen, 50
Tucci, Giuseppe, 12–14
Tülku Drakpa Özer, 66
Tülku Natsok Rangdröl, 67, 160, 164–168,
170–171, 176, 213
Tülku Thukje Özer, 131

Ü, 100, 123, 138–139, 145, 159, 190, 194
Ukpalung/Ukpajalung, 128
universal truth, as interpretation basis, 6–8,
212, 218n.15
untimely death, significance of, 96,
241n.37, 241n.40

Vairocana, 35, 37, 58
Vajradhara, 62, 84
Vajramati, 122, 248n.13
Vajrapāṇi, 35, 37, 106, 184–185, 262n.20
Vajrasattva, 84
van Manen edition, of *Liberation upon
Hearing*, 206–207
Vasubandhu, 40–42
Vimilamitra, 46, 84
virtues, of Buddhism, 85, 236n.23
visionary core texts, of Gampodar, 102,
113–119
visions, with bardo, 52–53, 229n.80
visualization, in exorcism, 73
vulnerability, of the soul, 32, 132
vultures, in rituals, 69–72, 184, 233n.9

Waddell editions, of *Liberation upon
Hearing*, 164–165, 174–175, 192
Berlin, 209
Lhalung, 168, 207–208, 268n.16
Lhasa, 208
Wallace, B. Allan, 12, 220n.47
wandering souls
path of related to funeral rituals, 28, 32–
38, 106–107
term for, 87, 237n.32
Wang Chökyi Gyelpo, 128
Wangdrak Sung, 153. *See also* Karma
Chakme
Wangi Dorje. *See* Tshurdön Wange
water burial, 43, 69–70, 233n.7
wealth, deceased's destiny based on, 76,
234n.31
Western interpretations, 4–14, 179,
205
wind, in intermediate state interpretations,
43, 59

wisdom
primordial, in bardo, 45, 59–60, 64,
232n.132
universal, 212
wisdom-mind transmission, of buddhas, 83,
87
witches, 99
womb, intermediate state link to, 41–42, 48,
51, 77, 111
woodblocks
as historical study focus, 21–24, 174
text engraving on, 18–19, 221n.71
wrathful deities. *See also Self-Liberated
Wisdom of the Peaceful and Wrathful
Deities*
in bardo interpretations, 63–65, 75, 196,
200
in Gampodar treasures, 105, 116–118,
246n.61
wrathful mantras, 189–190, 264n.41

xylographs, 18–19, 24, 192, 221n.71,
254n.20

Yama, 182
Yangjen Gawe Lodrö, 50, 55
Yangönpa, 46, 56–57
Yangpajen, 160
Yangyel, 122, 248n.14
Yardön Umapa, 46
Yarlha Shampo, 30
Yarlung, 17, 32, 223n.33
yellow paper, 97, 196
Yeru, 148
Yeshe Lodrö, 131, 140
Yeshe Tshogyel, 85, 96
Yeshebum, 141, 254n.15
Yetsher monastery, 168
yoga
instruction for, 108–109
intermediate states of, 44–45, 47–50, 55–
56, 64, 120
Yonge Mingyur Dorje, 180, 196, 199
youthful body, in bardo, 59
Yumtsho, 184
Yungdrung Gyen, 122, 248n.14

Zahor Yoṣa. *See* Tsünmojen
Zangchu River, 129
Zangtsho, 159
Zaplam Dorje Rawa, 188
Zhakla Yeshebum, 141, 254n.15
Zhalu Ribuk Tülku Losel Tenkyong, 209
Zhamar Garwang Chökyi Wangchuk,
172
Zhamarpa (Zhamar), as sect, 19, 140, 155,
160, 206
Zhamarpa Chenga Chödrakpa, 160
Zhamarpa Chökyi Wangchuk, 153
Zhamarpa Khachö Wangpo, 92
Zhamarpa Könchok Yenlakwang, 166

Printed in the United States
51721LVS00003B/122

9 780195 306521